Advances in Mathematics Education

For further volumes:
www.springer.com/series/8392

Yeping Li • Glenda Lappan

Editors

Mathematics Curriculum in School Education

 Springer

Editors

Yeping Li
Dept. Teaching, Learning & Culture
Texas A&M University
College Station, TX, USA

Glenda Lappan
Michigan State University
East Lansing, MI, USA

ISSN 1869-4918   ISSN 1869-4926 (electronic)
Advances in Mathematics Education
ISBN 978-94-007-7559-6   ISBN 978-94-007-7560-2 (eBook)
DOI 10.1007/978-94-007-7560-2
Springer Dordrecht Heidelberg New York London

Library of Congress Control Number: 2013954441

Printed on acid-free paper

Springer is part of Springer Science+Business Media (www.springer.com)

Series Preface

The eighth volume of the series Advances in Mathematics Education on "Mathematics Curriculum in School Education" edited by Yeping Li and Glenda Lappan commences from one of the most important perspectives on mathematics education in school, namely questions on the curriculum. Curricular structures are decisive for the organization and structure of mathematics education, as they directly influence teaching and learning processes. However, despite this strong influence of the curriculum on education in general and learning-and-teaching processes, extensive empirical research has not been carried out so far. The international comparative studies on mathematics and science education implemented by the IEA already introduced the differentiation of the intended, the implemented and the achieved curriculum in the Second International Study on Mathematics and Science Education (SIMS). However, these distinctions have not led to extensive studies comparing these different kinds of curricula. Studies accompanying the Third International Mathematics and Science Study (TIMSS) brought forward the cultural dependency of the curriculum and pointed out the difficulty in finding a common curricular core for the school subject of mathematics all over the world.

This is one of the foundation points of the present book, in which contributions from Eastern and Western mathematics educators are collected. In this respect, the book represents an extension of an issue of ZDM—The International Journal on Mathematics Education on 'Curriculum Research to Improve Mathematics Teaching and Learning: Practices and Approaches in China and the United States' edited by Yeping Li and Gerald Kulm in 2009, which was restricted to China and the USA. The present book contains a collection of studies on mathematics curriculum from more than ten education systems across the world with additional reflective chapters across various countries.

With this impressive overview on curricular practices all over the world this book will provide an insightful overview on the role and the influence of the mathematics curriculum internationally, which the reader will hopefully find interesting.

Hamburg, Germany
Missoula, USA

Gabriele Kaiser
Bharath Sriraman

Acknowledgements

We want to take this opportunity to thank and acknowledge all of those who have been involved in the process of preparing this book. This has been a wonderful experience. The work on this book has not only brought together long time friends and colleagues, but also created new professional connections and friends. We want to thank all those who were so ready and willing to contribute to the topic that has now been proven to be indispensable to the international mathematics education community.

Indeed, this book wouldn't be possible without the dedicated group of 54 contributors from 14 education systems across the world (Australia, Brazil, Canada, China, Hong Kong, Israel, Japan, Singapore, South Korea, Taiwan, the Netherlands, Turkey, U.K., and the U.S.) and we thank them for their contributions. This group of contributors also worked together as a team to help blind review the chapters. Their collective efforts help ensure this book's quality.

Thanks also go to a group of external reviewers who took the time to help review many chapters of the book. They are Richard A. Askey, Ana Canavarro, Janice Grow-Maienza, Minsung Kwon, Arne Mogensen, and Ji-Won Son. Their reviews and comments helped improve the quality of many chapters. We also want to thank Nikki Butchers for her assistance in proof reading many chapters of the book.

Last but not least, we want to thank our families for their love and continuous support along the way. The book wouldn't have been completed without their support and understanding. We want to let them know again that we are so grateful for their patience and support that make our work possible.

Contents

Part I
Introduction and Perspectives

Mathematics Curriculum in School Education: Advancing Research and Practice from an International Perspective

Yeping Li and Glenda Lappan

Abstract Mathematics curriculum, often a focus in education reforms, has not received extensive research attention until recently. To advance relevant research and practice in mathematics curriculum, this book is designed to survey, synthesize, and extend current research development on mathematics curriculum in different education systems. In this introduction chapter, we highlight the background of this book project, its purposes, and what can be learned from reading this book.

Keywords Curriculum research · Education system · International perspective · Mathematics curriculum · School education · School mathematics

Introduction

School education is organized to provide students with structured learning experiences. Mathematics curriculum, when viewed as an outline of teaching and learning requirements for content and performance, is put in place to structure students' learning experiences in school education (Schmidt et al. 1997). In order to improve students' learning experiences and outcomes, mathematics curriculum and its changes have often been a main focus in large educational reforms in the history of mathematics education in many education systems. Ironically, curriculum has not been a focus in mathematics education research until recent years. For example, the first *Handbook on Mathematics Teaching and Learning* (Grouws 1992) published by the U.S. National Council of Teachers of Mathematics (NCTM) in 1992 does not have a chapter on mathematics curriculum. However, the curriculum issue has attracted more and more attention with the release of NCTM Standards (1989, 2000) and the U.S. National Science Foundation's efforts in promoting and evaluating new

Y. Li (✉)
Texas A&M University, College Station, TX, USA
e-mail: yepingli@tamu.edu

G. Lappan
Michigan State University, East Lansing, MI, USA

Y. Li, G. Lappan (eds.), *Mathematics Curriculum in School Education*,
Advances in Mathematics Education, DOI 10.1007/978-94-007-7560-2_1.
© Springer Science+Business Media Dordrecht 2014

curriculum material development over the years. Consequently, the *Second Handbook on Mathematics Teaching and Learning* (Lester 2007) contains one chapter specifically related to curriculum (see Stein et al. 2007).

Given the importance of mathematics curriculum in school education, it is not surprising that mathematics curriculum and its impact on teaching and learning have received increasingly more research attention both in the United States and internationally (e.g., Leung and Li 2010; Li and Kulm 2009; Schmidt et al. 1997; Senk and Thompson 2003). For example, the Third International Mathematics and Science Studies (TIMSS) examined curriculum materials and specified the process of curriculum transformation as a guideline to conceptualize the relationship between curriculum analysis and students' learning (e.g., Schmidt et al. 1997, 2002). While students' performance was viewed as the achieved curriculum, what is provided in curriculum guidelines was treated as the intended curriculum. The results obtained from TIMSS curriculum studies and relevant others illustrated the unique value of examining mathematics curriculum in school education in an international context (e.g., Schmidt et al. 2002).

Education systems differ in many ways, including the social-cultural context and specific motivations behind curriculum reforms. However, across education systems, curriculum changes are inevitably connected to a range of common factors throughout the process of school education; including policy, curriculum development, school context, teachers' knowledge, classroom instruction, and student learning. The inclusion and connection of multiple contributing factors arising in the process of school education make the improvement of mathematics education through curriculum changes an extremely complex process. Thus a basis of sound research is thus very important for designing and guiding needed curriculum changes. Learning and sharing of mathematics curriculum and its changes in different education systems should provide us with a unique lens to advance curriculum research and practice from an international perspective.

Recent curriculum studies have indeed expanded to explore a range of important topics, including policy issues in school mathematics (e.g., Reys 2006; Usiskin and Willmore 2008), curriculum development and analysis (e.g., Hirsch 2007; Usiskin and Willmore 2008; Valverde et al. 2002), teachers' use of curriculum materials (e.g., Gueudet et al. 2012; Remillard et al. 2009), and curricular impact on students' learning (e.g., Senk and Thompson 2003). Given the increasing number of curriculum studies, it becomes important to survey, synthesize, and extend current research development on mathematics curriculum. The development of this book project reflects this growing research interest in mathematics curriculum on these important topics. This led to the book's structure of an introduction followed by four parts (i.e., Parts II to V) with different, yet connected, focuses on policy, curriculum development and analysis, teachers and teaching, and student learning. Moreover, this book is also designed to connect with recent international studies that have documented curriculum practices in different education systems across the world. In particular, this book was initiated and motivated by the following two further reasons.

First, this book presents an extension of a thematic issue of ZDM on mathematics curriculum ("Curriculum Research to Improve Mathematics Teaching and

Learning: Practices and Approaches in China and the United States" edited by Li and Kulm 2009). As the thematic issue of ZDM focuses on curriculum practices and approaches, relevant studies illustrate curriculum practices in China (e.g., teachers' lesson planning, textbook development) that are interestingly different from many of others in other systems such as in the United States. With limited knowledge available about many aspects of mathematics curriculum across education systems, this book contains a collection of studies on mathematics curriculum from more than ten education systems across the world.

Second, this book also builds upon another previous work on mathematics curriculum and teacher education in East Asia (Leung and Li 2010). In particular, in that work, changes and issues in mathematics curriculum in six selected education systems in East Asia (Chinese Mainland, Hong Kong, Japan, Singapore, South Korea, and Taiwan) were included and discussed. Surprisingly, although these six education systems in the same region share many similarities (e.g., system structures and students' high achievement in mathematics), their mathematics curricula differ in many ways including curriculum development trajectories and what is valued for students to learn. The differences reinforce the notion that curriculum is a system and cultural artifact that cannot be detached from its system and cultural context (Li and Leung 2010). This book thus contains a collection of chapters in Parts II to V with a focus on curriculum research and practice in individual education systems.

Developing and editing this thematic book also builds upon our ongoing work and interests in mathematics curriculum development and research (e.g., the widely distributed middle school standards-based *Connected Mathematics Project* curriculum developed by Lappan et al. 2014a, 2014b; Hirsch et al. 2012; Leung and Li 2010; Li and Kulm 2009). At the same time, we would very much like to let readers know that editing this international volume is our second collaboration as co-editors. Our first collaboration was in 2002, a special issue of the *International Journal of Educational Research* (Li and Lappan 2002). Through editing international volumes, we appreciate the great opportunities of learning from our contributors across the world then and now. We are convinced that taking an international perspective, as this book does, provides a unique lens for international readers to reflect, discuss, and advance curriculum research and practice in different education systems.

What Can Readers Expect to Learn from Reading the Book?

Examining and Understanding Mathematics Curriculum in School Education as Presented in Individual Chapters

This book is structured in six parts. The simplest way of reading the book is to follow the book's structure as outlined with several major topics related to curriculum research and practice. Readers can expect to learn about recent curriculum research, perspectives, and practices on topics ranging from policy to student learning in many different education systems.

The first part provides an introduction and related research perspectives, and is made up of four chapters. This introduction chapter is the first, and includes background and purposes. The second chapter by Hugh Burkhardt provides an overview and discussion about possible issues along the process of designing, developing, and implementing curriculum. Hugh argues that some deep-seated problems at school system level should be addressed for making intended curriculum changes a reality. In the third chapter, Barbara Reys highlights current curriculum changes as happened in a specific educational system (the United States), which are reflected mainly in how curriculum standards are established and students' learning outcomes are assessed. Chapter 4 by Alan Schoenfeld provides an overview and reflection on worldwide curriculum changes across educational systems. The diverse changes in curriculum, as a system and cultural artifact, across selected education systems led Alan to conclude that there is no single worldwide trend in curricula.

For each of Parts II to V, the inclusion of prefaces should provide readers with an overview of and some insights into these parts. In general, the second part contains a collection of five chapters that examine policy issues related to mathematics curriculum that are in operation in different education systems. Specific topics include the process of curriculum decision-making, curriculum changes as imposed by system-wide curriculum standards, curriculum policy, and education changes viewed from a historical perspective. The three follow-up parts contain a similar number of chapters from different education systems but with focuses on "curriculum development and analysis" (Part III with six chapters), "curriculum, teacher, and teaching" (Part IV with six chapters), and "curriculum and student learning" (Part V with five chapters), respectively.

Part VI is the last section for cross-national comparison and commentary. Chapter 27 by Zalman Usiskin provides a summary of the results from several large-scale international studies over the past 48 years, with a focus on U.S. students' mathematics performance. He argues that international comparisons of students' performance cannot be a fair assessment of the achieved curricula of different countries, with many other contributing factors and restrictions in place. Finally, there are two commentary chapters contributed by scholars: one from the East and one from the West. These two chapters help to draw together the research reported in Parts II to V, and to reflect on what we can learn from this international collaborative publication effort and on possible research directions for the future.

Cross-Examining and Reflecting on Mathematics Curriculum in School Education from an International Perspective

Readers can learn more beyond what is provided in individual chapters through reading and reflecting across chapters in the book. As a collection, this book provides diverse perspectives and approaches that are developed and used in more than ten education systems. It is important for readers to take further steps to cross-examine and reflect on issues that are pertinent to their interest. Here we would like to highlight the following four aspects that are important to the broad international readership interested in mathematics education and curriculum studies.

(1) *Identifying and understanding what is important in mathematics for teaching and learning in different education systems*

We know that school mathematics as a subject and school mathematics as a curriculum are two closely related but different concepts. On the one hand, school mathematics as a subject is what every student is expected to learn. It refers to the same body of mathematics knowledge and logic across different system and cultural contexts. For example, "$3 + 2 = 5; 2 \times 5 = 5 \times 2$" are true no matter whether they are taught in Africa, Asia, or the US with the use of different languages or manipulatives. On the other hand, school mathematics as a curriculum is specified and organized differently across education systems (or even within a single education system such as the U.S.; see Reys 2014). There is no single curriculum that works equally well for every student or every system, and the reason is quite straight forward: curriculum is a system and cultural artifact that reflects values, history, students' learning, and cultural contexts embedded in different system contexts (e.g., Kulm and Li 2009; Schoenfeld 2014). The dual nature of school mathematics suggests to us to go beyond possible surface differences in school mathematics to examine and understand what is important in mathematics for teaching and learning, an important topic of research for mathematics educators to cross-examine and understand mathematics curricular contributions to students' learning.

Over the past two decades, students' mathematics performance has been assessed through several large-scale international studies. One popular approach is to identify and specify certain content topics and performance expectations in curriculum that are important across many education systems (e.g., TIMSS). However, what students have learned as reflected in the assessment results can be different from what is expected in the intended curriculum. The issue of identifying and specifying what is important in school mathematics can and should be examined and addressed at different levels: the intended, textbook, implemented, assessed, and achieved curriculum (e.g., Schmidt et al. 1997; Travers and Westbury 1989). Across these levels along the process of curriculum development and implementation, there are often mismatches (Burkhardt 2014). Thus, readers should be aware of the specific curriculum level when trying to identify and understand what is important in mathematics for teaching and learning. For example, chapters in Parts II and III provide examples of what mathematics is identified as important for teaching and learning in the intended curriculum or textbooks. Possible content specifications can be on what mathematics topics are required in school education, when certain content topics are placed at specific grade levels, or how certain mathematics content topics are specified for teaching and learning. Readers can find various specifications both within and across education systems. As an illustration, Zanten and Van den Heuvel-Panhuizen (2014) examined textbooks' presentations of the content topic of subtraction up to 100 that is required very broadly in the Dutch intended curriculum. Their analyses of two Dutch textbook series revealed dramatic differences in their content treatment and the performance expectations of this same content topic. The content specification differences among the Dutch intended curriculum and these two Dutch textbooks suggest not only the complexity of curriculum issues, but also the importance of specifying the curriculum level when identifying and examining mathematics that is required and important for teaching and learning.

Moreover, Dylan Wiliam (2014) reminds us that both our understanding of the nature of mathematics and what mathematics is important for teaching and learning evolve over time, especially with the increased use of technology in mathematics and mathematics education. It is unrealistic to find or define a universal curriculum that works all the time across education systems. Yet it is realistic and desirable to identify or develop world-class mathematics curricula that can help students to achieve their greatest potential.

(2) *Understanding mathematics curriculum and its changes that are valued over time in different education systems*

Readers may quickly notice that mathematics curriculum varies from system to system and over time. Thus, it is not surprising if a worldwide trend in mathematics curriculum is not readily identifiable (Schoenfeld 2014). In fact, such diversity is also evident for several high-achieving education systems in the same region (e.g., Li and Leung 2010; Wong et al. 2014). For example, Japan, Korea and Singapore share some similarities in certain aspects of mathematics curriculum policies, but differ in others (Wong et al. 2014). Also, policy-making in these systems is often influenced by different factors over time, relating to specific values, politics, and history in different education systems.

However, curricular differences across system and cultural contexts do not rule out the great value of learning from each other, but place a strong cautious note for what can be learned from a specific education system. With this understanding in mind, readers should be able to learn more when reading across chapters.

(3) *Identifying and analyzing curriculum practices that are effective*

Efforts to improve students' mathematics performance have led to ever-increased interest in identifying and learning possible best practices, including curriculum. It is undeniable that curriculum plays a key role in guiding and structuring students' learning of mathematics. Questions are often asked about curriculum such as, what mathematics is important for students to learn (as discussed above as the first point), how mathematics content topics can be placed and sequenced for teaching and learning at different grade levels, and how school mathematics can be organized and structured in ways to best facilitate teaching and learning. The diverse approaches practiced in different education systems provide unique opportunities for readers to learn and examine different practices that are effective in specific system contexts. For example, Lee (2014) discusses curriculum development practices in Singapore that have evolved from a deductive approach to a mixed model approach that contains elements of both the deductive and inductive approaches. He illustrates how school-based curriculum innovations contribute to the deductive approach typically used in a centralized education system. Similar changes have also taken place in China, where local education administrations are given more responsibilities in curriculum development and implementation with more textbook choices (Li et al. 2014; Liu and Li 2010).

In contrast to curriculum practices in centralized education systems such as China and Singapore, several decentralized education systems have moved in the opposite direction. For example, common curriculum standards are now developed and implemented in Australia and most states of the US (Anderson 2014; Reys 2014; Stephens 2014; Wu 2014). These seemingly opposite moves in curriculum practices actually suggest a middle-ground approach that is now welcomed and used in both centralized and decentralized education systems.

Readers are also encouraged to go into the details about specific curriculum practices, such as approaches used in textbook development and content presentation (e.g., Cai et al. 2014; Even and Olsher 2014; Li et al. 2014), and teachers' implementation of curriculum (e.g., Huang et al. 2014; Stein et al. 2014; Takahashi 2014). Learning about specific curriculum practices that are effective in certain context should encourage us to think more about what is possible in our own context.

(4) *Identifying and examining effective infrastructure for curriculum development and implementation*

Mathematics curriculum does not simply stay at the policy level as intended, but goes throughout the whole process of school education including textbooks, the implemented, assessed, and achieved curriculum. Curriculum is an essential element that helps make school education into a structured experience for students. Thus, the connections and alignments of different levels of curriculum along the process of school education are very important, but its research is long overdue. As Fey (2014) points out, reforming the intended curriculum is often taken as the simplest and most common strategy for seeking improvement in school education. Yet, such efforts often fail to lead to expected changes. Systematic research is missing to develop and examine effective infrastructure for the entire process of curriculum development and implementation.

Readers can quickly realize that such systematic research would be a massive undertaking. In fact, it is not clear to us whether such research can be productive, given that curriculum is just one contributing factor to the improvement of students' learning. However, we encourage readers to pay close attention to different curriculum practices that are presented in different parts of the book. Although no direct connections are readily available for different curriculum practices discussed in various chapters, it is the overarching idea that should guide readers to explore and identify different practices that might be pieced together for effective curriculum development and implementation. It should be pointed out that this is another reason for how we have structured the book with four distinctive yet closely related curriculum parts.

Significance and Limitations

In summary, this book is positioned to make unique contributions to a growing body of mathematics curriculum studies and provides a platform for mathematics educators all over the world to share and discuss different curriculum practices, both those that were effective and those that were less successful. We would like to emphasize the following points. First, chapters in this book present and discuss system-based curriculum approaches and practices. This helps readers not only to learn and understand curriculum approaches and practices in a specific system and cultural context, but also to reflect on possible advantages and restrictions of different curriculum approaches and practices. Second, the book is organized into chapters with a structure of parts that is consistent with the process of curriculum development and implementation. It is important for readers to read not just individual chapters or parts but also across different chapters and parts. Identifying possible connections among diverse curriculum practices can thus be made possible for considering systematic improvement. Third, this book is not restricted to the mathematics curriculum itself, but includes topics related to mathematics teaching and learning. Such a comprehensive picture allows readers to see the complexity of curriculum issues, and also various possibilities for helping make curriculum changes a success.

Meanwhile, we are also aware of the limitations of this book. The inclusion of different education systems does not imply any specific representations, but rather illustrates diversity. Specific curriculum approaches and practices, as presented and discussed in different chapters, are important sources of knowledge but are not pre-specified. Thus, it is unclear whether specific approaches and practices are representative in selected education systems. Nevertheless, this book takes an important step to promote the sharing and exchange of different curriculum research and practices across education systems. Advancing curriculum research and practice from an international perspective provides us with a unique opportunity that is otherwise not available within an education system.

References

Anderson, J. (2014). Forging new opportunities for problem solving in Australian mathematics classrooms through the first national mathematics curriculum. In Y. Li & G. Lappan (Eds.), *Mathematics curriculum in school education*. Dordrecht: Springer.

Burkhardt, H. (2014). Curriculum design and systemic change. In Y. Li & G. Lappan (Eds.), *Mathematics curriculum in school education*. Dordrecht: Springer.

Cai, J., Nie, B., Moyer, J., & Wang, N. (2014). Teaching mathematics using standards-based and traditional curricula: a case of variable ideas. In Y. Li & G. Lappan (Eds.), *Mathematics curriculum in school education*. Dordrecht: Springer.

Even, R., & Olsher, S. (2014). Teachers as participants in textbook development: the integrated mathematics wiki-book project. In Y. Li & G. Lappan (Eds.), *Mathematics curriculum in school education*. Dordrecht: Springer.

Fey, J. (2014). Preface to part IV. In Y. Li & G. Lappan (Eds.), *Mathematics curriculum in school education*. Dordrecht: Springer.

Grouws, D. (Ed.) (1992). *Handbook of research on mathematics teaching and learning*. New York: Macmillan.

Gueudet, G., Pepin, B., & Trouche, L. (Eds.) (2012). *From text to 'lived resources—mathematics curriculum materials and teacher development*. New York: Springer.

Hirsch, C. R. (Ed.) (2007). *Perspectives on the design and development of school mathematics curricula*. Reston: National Council of Teachers of Mathematics.

Hirsch, C. R., Lappan, G., & Reys, B. (2012). *Curriculum issues in an era of Common Core State Standards for Mathematics*. Reston: National Council of Teachers of Mathematics.

Huang, R., Ozel, Z. E. Y., Li, Y., & Osborne, R. V. (2014). Does classroom instruction stick to textbooks?—a case study of fraction division. In Y. Li & G. Lappan (Eds.), *Mathematics curriculum in school education*. Dordrecht: Springer.

Kulm, G., & Li, Y. (2009). Curriculum research to improve teaching and learning: national and cross-national studies. *ZDM—The International Journal on Mathematics Education, 41*, 709–715.

Lappan, G., Phillips, E. D., Fey, J., & Friel, S. N. (2014a). *Connected mathematics—covering and surrounding*. Boston: Pearson Education.

Lappan, G., Phillips, E. D., Fey, J., & Friel, S. N. (2014b). *Connected mathematics—thinking with mathematical models*. Boston: Pearson Education.

Lee, N. H. (2014). The Singapore mathematics curriculum development—a mixed model approach. In Y. Li & G. Lappan (Eds.), *Mathematics curriculum in school education*. Dordrecht: Springer.

Lester, F. K. Jr. (Ed.) (2007). *Second handbook of research on mathematics teaching and learning*. Charlotte: Information Age.

Leung, F. K. S. & Li, Y. (Eds.) (2010). *Reforms and issues in school mathematics in East Asia—sharing and understanding mathematics education policies and practices*. Rotterdam: Sense.

Li, Y. & Kulm, G. (Eds.) (2009). Curriculum research to improve mathematics teaching and learning. *ZDM—The International Journal on Mathematics Education, 41*, 709–832.

Li, Y. & Lappan, G. (Eds.) (2002). Developing and improving mathematics teachers' competence: practices and approaches across educational systems. *A special issue of the International Journal of Educational Research, 37*(2), 107–232.

Li, Y., & Leung, F. K. S. (2010). Practices and changes in mathematics curriculum and teacher education in selected education systems in East Asia: what can we learn? In F. K. S. Leung & Y. Li (Eds.), *Reforms and issues in school mathematics in East Asia—sharing and understanding mathematics education policies and practices* (pp. 233–244). Rotterdam: Sense.

Li, Y., Zhang, J., & Ma, T. (2014). School mathematics textbook design and development practices in China. In Y. Li & G. Lappan (Eds.), *Mathematics curriculum in school education*. Dordrecht: Springer.

Liu, J., & Li, Y. (2010). Mathematics curriculum reform in the Chinese mainland: changes and challenges. In F. K. S. Leung & Y. Li (Eds.), *Reforms and issues in school mathematics in East Asia* (pp. 9–31). Rotterdam: Sense.

National Council of Teacher of Mathematics (1989). *Curriculum and evaluation standards for school mathematics*. Reston: Author.

National Council of Teacher of Mathematics (2000). *Principles and standards for school mathematics*. Reston: Author.

Remillard, J. T., Herbel-Eisenmann, B. A., & Lloyd, G. M. (Eds.) (2009). *Mathematics teachers at work: connecting curriculum materials and classroom instruction*. New York: Routledge.

Reys, B. J. (Ed.) (2006). *The intended mathematics curriculum as represented in state-level curriculum standards: consensus or confusion?* Charlotte: Information Age.

Reys, B. J. (2014). Mathematics curriculum policies and practices in the U.S.: the common core state standards initiative. In Y. Li & G. Lappan (Eds.), *Mathematics curriculum in school education*. Dordrecht: Springer.

Schmidt, W. H., McKnight, C. E., Valverde, G. A., Houang, R. T., & Wiley, D. E. (1997). *Many visions, many aims (Vol. 1): a cross-national investigation of curricular intentions in school mathematics*. Dordrecht: Kluwer Academic Press.

Schmidt, W. H., McKnight, C. E., Houang, R. T., Wang, H., Wiley, D. E., Cogan, L. S., et al. (2002). *Why schools matter: a cross-national comparison of curriculum and learning*. San Fransisco: Jossey-Bass.

Schoenfeld, A. (2014). Reflections on curricular change. In Y. Li & G. Lappan (Eds.), *Mathematics curriculum in school education*. Dordrecht: Springer.

Senk, S. L., & Thompson, D. R. (2003). *Standards-based school mathematics curricula: what are they? What do students learn?* Mahwah: Lawrence Erlbaum Associates.

Stein, M. K., Remillard, J., & Smith, M. S. (2007). How curriculum influences student learning. In F. K. Lester Jr. (Ed.), *Second handbook of research on mathematics teaching and learning* (pp. 319–369). Charlotte: Information Age.

Stein, M. K., Kaufman, J., & Kisa, M. T. (2014). Mathematics teacher development in the context of district managed curriculum. In Y. Li & G. Lappan (Eds.), *Mathematics curriculum in school education*. Dordrecht: Springer.

Stephens, M. (2014). The Australian curriculum: mathematics—how did it come about? What challenges does it present for teachers and for the teaching of mathematics? In Y. Li & G. Lappan (Eds.), *Mathematics curriculum in school education*. Dordrecht: Springer.

Takahashi, A. (2014). Supporting the effective implementation of a new mathematics curriculum: a case study of school-based lesson study at a Japanese public elementary school. In Y. Li & G. Lappan (Eds.), *Mathematics curriculum in school education*. Dordrecht: Springer.

Travers, K. J., & Westbury, I. (1989). *The IEA study of mathematics I: analysis of mathematics curricula*. Supplement, available from ERIC as ED306111.

Usiskin, Z., & Willmore, E. (Eds.) (2008). *Mathematics curriculum in Pacific Rim countries: China, Japan, Korea, and Singapore*. Charlotte: Information Age.

Valverde, G. A., Bianchi, L. J., Wolfe, R. G., Schmidt, W. H., & Houang, R. T. (2002). *According to the book: using TIMSS to investigate the translation of policy into practice through the world of textbooks*. Dordrecht: Kluwer.

Wiliam, D. (2014). What mathematics do children learn at school? (preface to part V). In Y. Li & G. Lappan (Eds.), *Mathematics curriculum in school education*. Dordrecht: Springer.

Wong, K. Y., Koyama, M., & Lee, K.-H. (2014). Mathematics curriculum policies: a framework with case studies from Japan, Korea, and Singapore. In Y. Li & G. Lappan (Eds.), *Mathematics curriculum in school education*. Dordrecht: Springer.

Wu, H.-H. (2014). Potential impact of the common core mathematics standards on the American curriculum. In Y. Li & G. Lappan (Eds.), *Mathematics curriculum in school education*. Dordrecht: Springer.

Zanten, M., & Van den Heuvel-Panhuizen, M. (2014). Freedom of design: the multiple faces of subtraction in Dutch primary school textbooks. In Y. Li & G. Lappan (Eds.), *Mathematics curriculum in school education*. Dordrecht: Springer.

Curriculum Design and Systemic Change

Hugh Burkhardt

Abstract This chapter describes and comments on the large qualitative differences between curriculum intentions and outcomes, within and across countries. It is not a meta-analysis of research on international comparisons; rather the focus is the relationship between what a government intends to happen in its society's mathematics classrooms and what actually does. Is there a mismatch? In most countries there is. Why? This leads us into the dynamics of school systems, in a steady state and when change is intended—and, finally, to what might be done to bring classroom outcomes closer to policy intentions. Two areas are discussed in more detail: problem solving and modeling, and the roles of computer technology in mathematics classrooms.

Keywords Curriculum change · Curriculum design · Curriculum goals · Curriculum implementation · Pushback · Modeling · Systemic change · Technology

"Curriculum" and Curriculum Change

The term "curriculum" is used with many different meanings. In the US it often means a textbook series, in the UK the set of experiences a child has in school classrooms. Neither of these fits the purposes of this chapter, which is concerned with the interrelations and differences between the variant definitions set out, for example, by the Second International Mathematics Study (Travers and Westbury 1989). I want to distinguish and compare the:

"*intended curriculum*": that described in official documents carrying the status of policy;

H. Burkhardt (✉)
Shell Centre for Mathematical Education, University of Nottingham, Nottingham, NG8 1BB, UK
e-mail: Hugh.Burkhardt@nottingham.ac.uk

H. Burkhardt
University of California, Berkeley, USA

Y. Li, G. Lappan (eds.), *Mathematics Curriculum in School Education*,   13
Advances in Mathematics Education, DOI 10.1007/978-94-007-7560-2_2,
© Springer Science+Business Media Dordrecht 2014

"tested curriculum": the range of performances covered by the official tests, particularly when the results have serious consequences for students' or teachers' future lives;

"implemented curriculum": what is actually taught in most classrooms.

The "achieved curriculum", what most students actually learn, would take us into much too large a field of research. Other chapters address this.

Thus the focus in this paper is on the path from government intentions, usually set out in policy documents, to the actual pattern of teaching and learning activities in classrooms—some typical, some that are unusually innovative.

As always, studying the steady state tells you little about causation. Accordingly, I look at two areas where there has long been general international agreement on the need for change in mathematics curricula: problem solving and modeling, and the roles of computer technology. I have benefited from special issues of the *Zentralblatt für Didaktik der Mathematik*, in which distinguished authors from around the world describe what has happened over recent decades to problem solving and to modeling in their own curricula.[1]

Curriculum Goals in Mathematics

Around the world people seem to have much the same goals for the outcomes of a mathematics education. Students should emerge with a reliable command of a wide range of mathematical skills, a deep understanding of the concepts that underlie them, and an ability to use them, flexibly and effectively, to tackle problems that arise—within mathematics and in life and work beyond the classroom. Students should, as far as possible, find learning and using mathematics interesting and enjoyable.

If all these "goods" were commonly achieved, mathematics education would be just an interesting academic field of study, rather than a centre of social concern and political disputation. Far from that *nirvana*, we are still much closer to the historical picture of school mathematics. 100 years ago, there was good middle class employment for all those who could "do mathematics". Command of the procedures of arithmetic was enough for employment as a clerk or bookkeeper. Command of algebra, a rare accomplishment, gave access to professions like engineering or teaching. But in today's world, those skills are far from enough; arithmetic is largely done with technology, while jobs in finance require higher-level skills involving analysis of data and of risks, using prediction based on models—hence the widely agreed goals summarized in the first paragraph.

In seeking to get closer to these goals different groups have very different priorities—shown, for example, by the "as far as possible" in the sentence on

---

[1]My thanks to Kaye Stacey, Michel Doorman, Berinderjeet Kaur, Akihiko Takahashi and, particularly, Gabriele Kaiser, the editor of ZDM.

student feelings about mathematics. Indeed, one of the striking results from the Third International Mathematics and Science Study (TIMSS) is the *anti-correlation* between attitude and performance: East Asian students appear to combine high-achievement with a dislike of mathematics, stronger in both respects than those in lower-achieving countries.[2] It is fair to say that student enjoyment of mathematics, while seen as desirable, if only for motivation, is rarely given high priority. The next few paragraphs set out attitudes characteristic of various groups that promote their priorities for teaching and learning mathematics, more or less effectively.

"Basic skills people" focus on the importance of students' building fluency and accuracy in standard mathematical procedures, moving over time through the four operations of arithmetic on whole numbers, fractions and decimals to manipulating algebraic expressions. Calculators are for use in other subjects. This group recognizes the ultimate importance and satisfaction of being able to use these skills in solving problems that arise outside the classroom but they are happy to defer this until the procedural skills have been "mastered". For most students this gratification is deferred indefinitely. This curriculum consists of routine exercises, supplemented by routine "word problems". "Basic skills people" cannot understand why students find these problems so difficult.

"Mathematical literacy people" occupy the opposite end of the spectrum of priorities. They see mathematics as primarily a toolkit of concepts and skills that, learned and used properly, can help people understand the world better and make better decisions. They want students to develop their mathematics with close links to real world problems. They believe skills need to be rooted in solid conceptual understanding, so those that are not used every day can be refreshed when needed. They accept the research evidence (see e.g. Brown and Burton 1978) that successful performers do not remember *precisely* the procedures they have been taught but have the understanding to reconstruct and check them. Calculators and computers should be used freely. Understanding should be consolidated through concrete illustrations of the concept in action. This curriculum spends time on the development of modeling skills: formulation of mathematical models of new problem situations, transforming them to give solutions, the interpretation of solutions and of data, and explanation of what has been learnt.

"Technology people" start from the way mathematics is done outside the classroom—with the unquestioning use of computing devices. They believe that mental arithmetic is important for estimation but would only use pencil and paper for sketching diagrams and graphs, for formulating models, and for recording results. They accept the research that shows that concepts can be learned faster and understood more deeply through carefully designed uses of technology. They also believe that this research justifies the return of programming to the math curriculum.

---

[2]This, like every other statement in this chapter, is a trend; it is not true for everyone in each group.

They, too, would focus curriculum on rich problem situations, particularly from the real world.

"*Investigation people*" focus on mathematical reasoning and see the beauty of mathematics itself as the main driver for students to develop conceptual understanding and reasoning skill. They are less concerned with the real world, seeing the inexactitude of modeling as clouding that beauty. Their curriculum is dominated by a rich variety of mathematical microworlds that students are led to explore, discovering properties of and patterns in such systems—from "odd and even numbers" through "the 10 by 10 multiplication table" to non-commuting algebras. Skills are learned as they are needed and fluency built by their repeated use in diverse situations.

There is general acceptance that each of these aspects of learning mathematics should have a place; the balance of the intended curriculum in each school system reflects the tensions among these groups. Those mainly influenced by their own education tend to the first of the positions listed; more sophisticated thinkers about mathematical education tend to the later views.

The curriculum areas that I will discuss are examples where the mismatch between policy intentions and what happens in most classrooms is stark. "Problem solving" and "modeling" are suitable choices because, over many decades, the difference between declared curriculum intentions and the classroom outcomes has been not just large, but qualitative. "Technology" shows a striking double mismatch, both between aspirations and practice and between the real world and mathematics classrooms.

I will not discuss a universal priority area: the development of concepts and skills. Even here, there are mismatches: for example, all intended curricula recognize that conceptual understanding is important while, in contrast, learning procedural skills dominates in many classrooms. These matters are discussed in other chapters.

Problem Solving and Modeling

I have chosen "problem solving" and modeling[3] as the first area to study because for many decades these have been widely accepted goals for curriculum improvement in mathematics across much of the developed world. The need seems unanswerable; yet, observing at random in classrooms in any country, one is unlikely to see students engaged in tackling rich non-routine problems requiring substantial chains of autonomous reasoning by the student. In this section we outline something of the history in this area, looking for plausible explanations of the limited progress that has been made.

---

[3] Modeling, the now-standard term for the use of mathematics in tackling problems from the world outside mathematics, uses the same practices as mathematical problem solving—plus a few more.

What Is Problem Solving?

Why have I put "problem solving" in quotes? Because, even within mathematics curricula, the phrase is used by different people with different meanings. At its most basic level it is commonly used for "word problems" that are intended to be routine exercises presented in the form of a sentence or two; such word exercises normally appear in the curriculum unit where the method of solution is taught. I use "problem solving" in the very different sense, illustrated in Figs. 1 and 2,[4] that is now widely accepted in the international mathematics education community.

This defines a "problem" as a task that is:

Non-routine: A substantial part of the challenge is working out *how* to tackle the task. (If the student is expected to *remember* a well-defined method from prior teaching, the task is routine—an exercise not a problem.)

Mathematically rich: Substantial chains of reasoning, involving more than a few steps, are normally needed to solve a task that is worth calling a problem.

Well-posed: Both the problem context and the kind of solution required are clearly specified. (In an "investigation" the problem context is defined but the student is expected to *pose* questions as well as to answer them; investigations are implicit in the following discussion.)

Reasoning-focused: Answers are not enough; in problem solving students are also expected to *explain* the reasoning that led to their solutions and *why* the result is true.

These properties make a problem *more difficult* than a well-defined exercise on the same mathematical content. So, for a problem to present a challenge that is comparable to a routine exercise it must be *technically* simpler, involving mathematics that was taught in earlier grades and has been well-absorbed by the students. Problem solving depends on building and using *connections* to other contexts and to other parts of mathematics.

Various problem solving approaches to *Boomerangs* are shown in the samples of student work in Fig. 3, two of which show students "inventing" standard graphical and algebraic approaches to linear programming.[5]

From the above it will be clear that what is a problem depends on a student's prior experience. A problem becomes an exercise if the student has seen, or been taught, a solution. Equally, some rich curricula regularly present as problems some tasks

---

[4]These examples were developed by the Shell Centre/Berkeley *Mathematics Assessment Project*, see http://map.mathshell.org.uk/materials/index.php. The "expert tasks" under the "Tasks" tab epitomize problem solving. *Boomerangs*, Figs. 2 and 3, is from a MAP formative assessment lesson-lesson on problem solving.

[5]None of the solutions in Fig. 3 is fully correct and complete—a design choice that makes them a better stimulus for classroom discussion, because the students are put into a *critiquing* "teacher role", which is more proactive than merely *understanding* someone else's solution. The more sophisticated solutions are beyond most students' problem solving at this level, but are there to show the potential of more powerful mathematics.

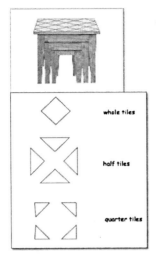

Table tiles

Maria makes square tables, then sticks tiles to the top.

Square tables have sides that are multiples of 10 cm.

Maria uses quarter tiles at the corners and half tiles along edges.

How many tiles of each type are needed for a 40 cm x 40 cm square?

Describe a method for quickly calculating how many tiles of each type are needed for larger, square table tops.

Fig. 1 *Table tiles*—a problem solving task

Boomerangs

Phil and Cath make and sell boomerangs for a school event.
They plan to make them in two sizes: small and large.
Phil will carve them from wood.

The small boomerang takes 2 hours to carve and the large one takes 3 hours. Phil has a total of 24 hours available for carving.

Cath will decorate them. She only has time to decorate 10 boomerangs of either size.

The small boomerang will make $8 for charity.
The large boomerang will make $10 for charity.
They want to make as much money as they can.

•How many small and large boomerangs should they make?
•How much money will they then make?

Fig. 2 *Boomerangs*—a problem solving task

that will become exercises when new techniques are taught in later years. For example, pattern generalization tasks like *Table Tiles* in Fig. 1 become exercises if and when students have learned the "method of differences". Similarly, the *Boomerangs* task in Fig. 2 becomes a straightforward exercise when you have been taught linear programming.

Whole class discussion:
comparing different approaches

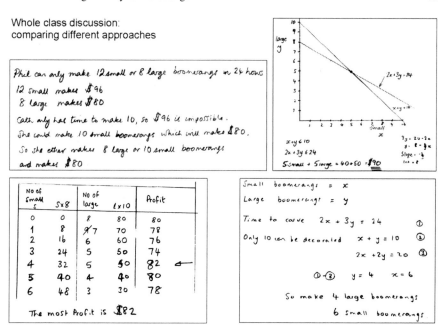

Phil can only make 12 small or 8 large boomerangs in 24 hours

12 small makes $96
8 large makes $80

Cath only has time to make 10, so $96 is impossible.
She could make 10 small boomerangs which will make $80.
So she either makes 8 large or 10 small boomerangs
and makes $80

$x + y \leq 10$
$2x + 3y \leq 24$
5 small + 5 large = 40 + 50 = $90

No of small s	$s \times 8$	No of large	$\ell \times 10$	Profit
0	0	8	80	80
1	8	7	70	78
2	16	6	60	76
3	24	5	50	74
4	32	5	50	82
5	40	4	40	80
6	48	3	30	78

The most Profit is $82

Small boomerangs = x
Large boomerangs = y

Time to carve $2x + 3y = 24$ ①
Only 10 can be decorated $x + y = 10$ ②
$2x + 2y = 20$ ③

①-③ $y = 4$ $x = 6$

So make 4 large boomerangs
6 small boomerangs

Fig. 3 Sample student solutions from the *Boomerangs* lesson

Problem Solving around the World

In 2007 ZDM produced special issues (Törner et al. 2007) in which contributors from around the world described the position of problem solving in their country's curriculum. The pictures presented were broadly similar. Problem solving is recognized as an element that *should* have a substantial place in the mathematics curriculum but, in practice, it plays little or no part in the pattern of learning activities in most classrooms. This subsection gives a flavour of my reading of the articles. These extracts are no substitute for reading these rich pictures of history, research and practice.

For **England**, Alan Bell and I offer a rather gloomy picture of a current situation, largely driven by the 1989 National Curriculum, which the then-government required to be based on "levels" described in terms of detailed content criteria. Because the difficulty of a task depends on many factors, the wish to give students their best chance of achieving a higher "level" led inevitably (see Burkhardt 2009, Sect. 2B) to testing the criteria in their simplest form—as short items on each criterion. Problem solving, still seen as important in principle, disappeared from the high-stakes public examinations and, consequently, from most classrooms.

We noted some hope of improvement through recent changes in the National Curriculum with an emphasis on "key processes" and an explicit recognition that non-routine problems have various sources of difficulty, as listed above. Improved examinations have now appeared in pilot form but performance on the problem solving tasks has been weak—not surprising since teachers have little experience in this area. The 1980s remain the high-point for problem solving and modeling in England,[6] though even then implementation was patchy.

From **Australia**, Clarke, Goos and Morony noted that the collaboration between states has, at various times, produced position statements that represent a form of national curricular consensus, including the view that

> Problem solving is the process of applying previously acquired knowledge in new and unfamiliar situations. Being able to use mathematics to solve problems is a major reason for studying mathematics at school. Students should have adequate practice in developing a variety of problem solving strategies so they have confidence in their use.

And yet

> video studies of grade 8 mathematics classrooms in Australia show little evidence of an active culture of problem solving.

Again the 1980s saw an outstanding development in problem solving through the VCE (Victoria Certificate of Education) school leaving examinations in Mathematics, which produced significant change throughout secondary schools (Clarke and Stephens 1996; Burkhardt 2009).

Current examinations (addressing students at different levels) are innovative and of high quality, containing tasks that probe concepts and skills. The lower level has a strong applications emphasis while all students have access to computer-algebra systems for part of the examination. But the tasks are essentially routine.

From the **Netherlands**, Doorman, Drijvers, Dekker, van den Heuvel-Panhuizen, de Lange, and Wijers present a similar picture.

> As in primary education, problem solving in secondary mathematics education has only a marginal position. In the introduction to this paper, it has already been pointed out that even an application and modeling-oriented curriculum like the one for Mathematics A tends to standardize problem-solving tasks into routine assignments. The national examination does not encourage paying much attention to problem solving skills. Textbooks usually do not address problem solving as a result of examination demands, designing teacher and student proof activities, and the time need for designing problem solving activities.

They report some exceptional textbooks and initiatives outside the mainstream, such as the national "Mathematics A-lympiad: an experimental garden for problem solving" (Freudenthal Institute 2010) which, in many schools, plays a role in the school-based component of national assessment. Many mathematics tasks are set in more realistic contexts than in other countries.

These authors make an important point—that, to stimulate and sustain problem solving in a curriculum, "an important challenge is the design of good problem solving tasks that are original, non-routine and new to the students". This is an ongoing challenge, at least until a population of tasks has been developed that is large enough for teaching them all to be an ineffective strategy (Daro and Burkhardt 2012).

---

[6]Equally, until the 1950s the Geometry examinations for the highest achieving 20 % of 16 year old students included proofs of standard Euclidean theorems, each followed by a non-routine application of the theorem—an example of solving problems with a well-controled "transfer distance".

There are some interesting variations on the global trend sketched above.

From **Hungary**, Julianna Szendrei paints a more encouraging picture, albeit a mixed one. The examination at the end of secondary schools includes a non-routine problem as one of seven tasks. This influences some secondary school teachers to include such problems in the classroom as well. Lower secondary teachers prefer to use routine problems in the classroom. However, the government requires assessments at ages 10, 12 and 14 that contain problem solving as well. Though the results are not public, this motivates teachers to prepare children for problem solving.

Problem solving in the culture of Hungarian teachers also involves an approach to teaching: "not to show routine problems directly but to hide them a little".

> Let us prepare all the three digit numbers using the digits 2, 3, 5. Let us choose one of these numbers randomly. What is the probability of the event that the number will be odd?

Almost all Hungarian teachers know how to teach in this way but only about 10 % of them will do so in their classroom.

This looks rather like the picture from **China**, where Jinfa Cai and Bikai Nie write:

> The purpose of teaching problem solving in the classroom is to develop students' problem solving skills, help them acquire ways of thinking, form habits of persistence, and build their confidence in dealing with unfamiliar situations. Second, problem-solving activities in the classroom are used as an instructional approach that provides a context for students to learn and understand mathematics. In this way, problem solving is valued not only for the purpose of learning mathematics but also as a means to achieve learning goals.

They describe as typical the "teaching with variation" approach, in that the transition from routine problems is supported by gently increasing the transfer distance in various ways, including "... three problem-solving activities: one problem, multiple solutions; multiple problems, one solution; and one problem, multiple changes".[7]

> Situation. A factory is planning to make a billboard. A master worker and his apprentice are employed to do the job. It will take 4 days by the master worker alone to complete the job, but it takes 6 days for the apprentice alone to complete the job. Please create problems based on the situation. Students may add conditions for problems they create.
> Posed problems:
> 1. How many days will it take the two workers to complete the job together?
> 2. If the master joins the work after the apprentice has worked for 1 day, how many additional days will it take the master and the apprentice to complete the job together?
> 3. After the master has worked for 2 days, the apprentice joins the master to complete the job. How many days in total will the master have to work to complete the job?
> 4. If the master has to leave for other business after the two workers have worked together on the job for 1 day, how many additional days will it take the apprentice to complete the remaining part of the job?
> 5. If the apprentice has to leave for other business after the two workers have worked together for 1 day, how many additional days will it take the master to complete the remaining part of the job?

---

[7]The authors add "However, there is little empirical data available to confirm the promise of 'teaching with variation' ".

6. The master and the apprentice are paid 450 Yuans after they completed the job. How much should the master and the apprentice each receive if each worker's payment is determined by the proportion of the job the worker completed?

The picture presented here reflects an approach to teaching concepts and skills that can be found in other countries (see e.g. Swan 2006); it is a long way from the holistic problems exemplified in Figs. 1 and 2.

From **Japan**, Keiko Hino focuses on how ideals are reflected in approaches to lesson structure at a research level, partly reflected in lesson study, but reports on some evidence on its scale of implementation:

> The TIMSS video study identified the lesson patterns as cultural scripts for teaching in Germany, Japan, and the US (Stigler and Hiebert 1999). They identified the Japanese pattern of teaching a lesson as a series of five activities: reviewing the previous lesson; presenting the problem for the day; students working individually or in groups; discussing solution methods; and highlighting and summarizing the major points (p. 79). Here, a distinct feature of the Japanese lesson pattern, compared with the other two countries, was that presenting a problem set the stage for students to work on developing solution procedures. In contrast, in the US and in Germany, students work on problems after the teacher demonstrates how to solve the problem (U.S.) or after the teacher directs students to develop procedures for solving the problem (Germany). This pattern, or the motto of Japanese teaching, has been called "structured problem solving" by Stigler & Hiebert.

School leaving examinations are replaced by entrance examinations, set by different universities, that vary in difficulty. I find no suggestion that they involve non-routine problem solving.

From **Germany** Reiss and Törner describe an active program of curriculum and professional development on problem solving and, particularly, modeling that is "work in progress".

> The situation in Germany now parallels that of the United States some years ago. Stanic and Kilpatrick (1989, p. 1) get to the point when stating: Problems have occupied a central place in the school mathematics curriculum since antiquity, but problem solving has not. Only recently have mathematics educators accepted the idea that the development of problem-solving ability deserves special attention.

Finally, from the **USA**, as well as the implementation challenges, conflict over the *intended* curriculum has been a major factor. In the "math wars" a politically active group from outside mathematics education demand a curriculum focused on students' developing fluent manipulative skills. Alan Schoenfeld summarizes it thus:

> What optimism one might have regarding the re-infusion of problem solving into the US curriculum in meaningful ways must come from taking a long-term perspective.

The recent widespread adoption of Common Core State Standards that emphasize *mathematical practices* featuring reasoning, problem solving and modeling gives some grounds for hope—but, given all the political and institutional barriers, not for holding one's breath.

In reviewing these extracts, it is notable that the countries that give the most optimistic picture of implementation describe a relatively unambitious form of problem solving. The "teaching with variation" problems from China, for example, are rather like the "exercises with a twist that makes you think" that we see in England. Problems like the examples at the beginning of this section, involving more substantial chains of problem solving and reasoning, are still rare.

Problem Solving: The Challenges

Why is this pattern the way it is? What are the factors that impede the implementation of problem solving?

Testing traditions have a role, at least in those countries that have high-stakes tests. These have a strong influence on what is taught and valued in classrooms. Some people feel it is "unfair" to give students non-routine problems in tests, though evidence shows that score distributions for well-engineered tasks are similar to those for exercises. Designing non-routine tasks, year after year, presents a challenge to examination providers that they are happy to avoid; it is much easier to recycle minor variants of standard problems. However, since many countries have no high-stakes tests, this cannot be the main factor in the absence of problem solving.

Equity concerns play a role in most advanced societies. "We must give all kids the best chance to reach high standards". Since 'high standards' are usually seen in terms of the mathematical content covered, this supports the focus on short routine exercises. Further, since this fragmentation obscures the meaning of mathematics, it does not help disadvantaged students whose parents may not pressure them into persisting with, to them, meaningless activities in pursuit of long-term goals.

Difficulty Complex non-routine problems, which must be technically easier, make some people concerned that in problem solving "the math is not up to grade". They want students to be learning more techniques rather than "wasting time on stuff they already know". This issue is sometimes referred to as "acceleration" versus "enrichment".

Teaching challenges Handling non-routine problems in the classroom presents teachers with substantial challenges, both mathematical and pedagogical, that are not met in a traditional curriculum. Concepts and skills can be taught in the standard "XXX" approach: *explanation* by the teacher or the book, a worked *example*, then multiple imitative *exercises*. This teacher-centered approach cannot be used for problem solving, where students must work out their own approach to each problem.

Early materials to support teachers of problem solving simply provided teachers with some interesting problems and general guidance, based on the Polya (1945) "strategies" for problem solving. Schoenfeld (1985) showed that this is not enough; effective problem solvers need more detailed "tactics", elaborating the strategies for specific types of problem. For example, the strategy "Try some simple cases" is more powerful if you know what is "a simple case": perhaps "low n" in pattern generalization problems, but "end games" in game problems. More sophisticated and supportive materials have been developed over succeeding decades. We developed more powerful support for problem solving in "The Blue Box" (*Problems*

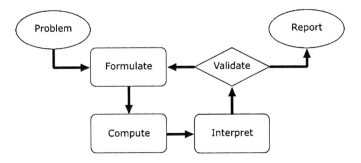

Fig. 4 The modeling process

with Patterns and Numbers, Swan et al. 1984), the first package to integrate examples of *examination tasks* with *teaching materials* and do-it-yourself *professional development materials* for teachers. This approach proved popular and effective. The sophistication of materials to support teachers in facing these challenges has developed over the last 30 years (see, for example, Swan et al. 2011). It is now fair to say that, as a field, we know how to enable typical teachers to handle non-routine problem solving in their classrooms.

System change challenges and how they might be more effectively tackled will be discussed below.

Modeling: the Further Challenges

Modeling justifies a separate coda to this section for three main reasons: it is the activity at the core of the *utility* of mathematics; its history has been rather different from that of pure mathematical problem solving; it is the focus of PISA, the now-dominant measure for international comparisons.

Modeling is problem solving that involves the processes, summarized in Fig. 4, that are involved in taking the world outside mathematics seriously. Real world problems are often messy—you can't address everything. Part of the modeling challenge is to identify the features of the situation that you need to analyze, select the essential relevant variables, and represent the relationships between them with mathematics. Only then will you have a well-posed mathematical problem to solve.[8] The ability to interpret the solution and evaluate the model requires an understanding of the practical situation and the ability to select what data is most relevant, to collect and analyze it.

All countries say that they want students to be able to use their mathematics in everyday life situations; yet the special issues of ZDM on modeling (Kaiser et al.

---

[8]The earlier examples, though they are related to practical problems, have been taken to this "well-posed" stage—the reason to call them problem solving not modeling.

2006) present a kaleidoscopic picture of work in the community of innovators (see also www.ICTMA.net) but little on modeling in typical classrooms. It is not unreasonable to infer that the situation is, at best, no better than for problem solving.

This fits the picture from other sources. For example, in ZDM Henry Pollak and I (Burkhardt and Pollak 2006) report on the history of modeling in England and the US over the last 50 years—from the diverse early explorations that we and others began in the 1960s, through the development of exemplar courses to the present day. We noted some hopeful signs: the growing awareness of the importance of *mathematical literacy* and the growth of PISA. Nonetheless, the impact in typical UK and US classrooms is minimal.

What are the factors, beyond those listed for problem solving, that impede implementation?

The real world is an unwelcome intruder in many mathematics classrooms. "I'm a math teacher, not a teacher of ….".[9] The clean abstraction of mathematics is something that attracted many mathematics teachers, particularly at the higher levels. Teaching mathematics, they say, is demanding enough without the messiness of modeling reality. This attitude also reflects concern about their ability to handle other areas of knowledge, at least with the same authority and control as for mathematics itself. In modeling, there are rarely "right answers". (There are wrong ones!)

Concerns about getting and handling real data which require skills that are new to many mathematics teachers.

The time modeling takes is a cause for concern for teachers facing curricula that are usually already too full. While all problem solving involves a time-scale longer than the few-minute exercises that dominate in many classrooms, it is possible to work through some interesting well-posed problems in 15 minutes or so. Modeling an interesting problem situation with attention to reality usually needs longer than this.

Again, the 1980s was a high point, with successes like *Numeracy through Problem Solving* (Swan et al. 1987-89), which supported students modeling real life problems in group projects.

Why "Technology" Remains Peripheral

Mathematics has long been done with microprocessor-based technology everywhere —except in the mathematics classroom. While a doctor from a century ago would be astonished and bemused in a hospital today, a teacher would be quite at home watching most current mathematics classrooms.

---

[9]This contrasts with the attitude of teachers of English, who welcome the opportunity to link the technical and stylistic aspects of language with the student's world.

In business, accounting, scheduling and stock control, not to mention check-out tills, are all computer-based. In industry, CAD-CAM systems are at the heart of design and manufacturing. Most routine repetitive tasks are done by computer-controlled machines. In research, where it all began, computers are everywhere. Why has school mathematics not changed to reflect this?

In addition to the roles of technology in *doing* mathematics, the last half-century has seen the development of a huge range of educationally powerful software for *learning* mathematics. The early efforts were behaviorist "learning machines", building fluency through simple exercises with instant feedback (and built-in testing). These "integrated learning systems" are still around, but the reinforcement they provide doesn't help those many children whose conceptual understanding is somewhat "dis-integrated". In contrast, the variety of software designed as a *supportive* learning resource is impressive. Perhaps most important for stimulating learning are the "microworlds" that offer domains for investigation by students.

The best known of these, because they cover a large domain, are the Euclidean Geometry programs: Judah Schwartz's *Geometric Supposer*, Jean-Michel Laborde's *Cabri Geometre*, Nick Jackiw's *Geometer's Sketchpad* and their followers. These enable an investigative approach to the learning of Euclidean Geometry in which the students play a much more active role than in the traditional learning of theorems and their proofs.

There are many smaller investigative microworlds that simulate specific situations in mathematics or science. From the late 1970s the British project ITMA, *Investigations on Teaching with Microcomputers as an Aid*, developed a wide range of such software. Rosemary Fraser's *Jane* is a "function machine" that invites conjecture and the weighing of evidence; this work showed that the concept of function as a consistent input-output process is natural for children no older than seven, providing a natural route into algebra through functions. Richard Phillip's *Eureka* is about a man taking a bath. It links a cartoon, a 4-command programming language[10] that controls the bath sequence, and a line graph of the depth of water against time. A research program on teachers use of these and other classics showed their power (Burkhardt et al. 1988). Teachers with little experience of handling non-routine problem solving in their classroom moved quite naturally from the traditional directive roles (manager, explainer, task setter) into the supportive roles that are essential for teaching problem solving (counselor, fellow student, resource). The single computer screen took on some of the traditional roles, hence the "teaching aid" name for this mode of use.

More familiar are computer game modes, some of which have significant mathematics content beyond behaviourist skills training.

The mathematical software tools themselves can be used to promote learning. Spreadsheets and programming languages provide environments that help students explore problems, and learn to design algorithms for modeling the real world, and

---

[10]T ~ tap on/off, P ~ plug in/out, M ~ man in/out, and S ~ sings/stops singing—because it is important to recognize that there are some variables that do not affect the quantity of interest, in this case water level.

for investigations in pure mathematics. As a curriculum element, such activities equip students with tools that will be used in life beyond the classroom.

Why are these powerful tools for doing and for learning mathematics still only used in a small minority of classrooms in most countries?

How effective these learning activities are depends on the teacher and, one would expect, on the textbooks that embody the intended curriculum. This brings us to a big surprise: there are no published mathematics curricula that exploit the potential of technology. Why? At least three powerful forces have contributed to this: cost, equity and, perhaps most important, mismatched timescales.

Timescale mismatch: The timescale of change for computer technology is short, with new devices appearing every few years; in contrast, curriculum changes take a decade or two from initial discussions to widespread implementation.[11]

Cost: When a new technology is introduced, it is expensive.[12] The cost of equipping every child in a class seems prohibitive. As the price comes down, new technologies appear that offer much greater educational possibilities. Each implies a substantial curriculum and professional development program, if teachers are to learn how to exploit its potential.

Equity: Students and school systems give a high priority to fairness, to trying to give all kids the same opportunities. The challenge of equipping all schools in a short time makes it difficult for school systems to require any specific technology as part of the intended curriculum.

And there is always conservatism. While the importance of technology in mathematics is accepted at a rhetorical level, when it comes to deciding on the intended curriculum, politicians are reluctant to abandon traditional goals.[13] Perhaps they find traditional values in education play well with electorates, particularly for mathematics where many parents feel insecure. "Look what it did for me". But is fluency in pencil-and-paper arithmetic still a sensible priority for children, particularly those who struggle? In this sense, the mismatch for technology is different from that for problem solving and modeling in that, even in the intended curriculum, its place is far from clear.

There are signs that the situation may be changing. The basic tablet computer is getting cheaper and offers a stable platform that can offer a very wide range of support for learning and teaching. School systems are talking of "the post-textbook era" and publishers are responding by supporting the development of technology-based curricula.

---

[11]For example, in the 1980s the National Council of Teachers of Mathematics developed "standards", setting out curriculum goals, the National Science Foundation funded the development of curricula and assessment in the 1990s, while substantial impact in classrooms began from 2000 onwards.

[12]The first 4-function calculator I used cost $450 ∼ several thousand dollars in current money.

[13]Against the advice of the mathematics education experts, the British Government insisted on retaining fluent "long division" as an essential skill in the National Curriculum.

On the other hand, the timescale mismatch continues to present problems. Within a few years the focus has moved from laptops to tablets and smartphones. The design opportunities for any of these platforms are immense but they are rather different—and realizing their potential will take many times longer than publishers' deadlines usually allow.

The fundamental challenge remains: to move school mathematics closer to the way math is done in the world outside. Whatever happens next, this will remain an exciting area.

Systemic Change: Failures and Ways Forward

Why does this mismatch persist? Why are the activities in mathematics classrooms still so like those of a century ago? I have listed some of the factors that help to explain. In this section I will argue that the problems lie mainly at school system level, describe some important causes of failure in implementation, and suggest possible ways forward. Key failures include: underestimating the challenge; misalignment and mixed messages; unrealistic pace of change; pressure with inadequate support; inadequate evaluation in depth; and inadequate design and "engineering". A challenging list.

These deep-seated problems, involving as they do multiple constituencies with well-grooved attitudes and modes of working, have no well-established solutions. However, we know enough to set out a path that has real prospects of improving the convergence between intentions and outcomes. In the following, I shall discuss each of them in turn.

Underestimating the Challenge

When countries are concerned about education, there are intense and ongoing debates about *what* should go into the curriculum. There is much less discussion as to *how* to get it to happen. It is assumed that once the decisions have been made and a process of implementation specified, things will work out as intended.[14] Curriculum changes of the kinds discussed in this chapter involve fairly profound changes in the professional practice of many people across a range of constituencies: textbook writers, test designers, professional development leaders and, particularly, teachers. All these need to be not just *motivated* but *enabled* to meet the new challenges. Further, some may feel threatened, producing "pushback", overt or covert, against the change. To have a reasonable chance of realization, a change must have (at least)

---

[14] As the Mathematics Working Group finished its design of the original 1989 National Curriculum in England, I asked a senior civil servant why we should expect it to happen; she replied "But it's the law of the land"!

the consent of teachers, principals, curriculum directors, superintendents, the relevant professions, and the public. Some groups, within or outside the school system, may disapprove of the change and work to undermine it—the US "math wars" being an extreme example.[15]

Misalignment and Mixed Messages

It is important to avoid mixed messages by ensuring close alignment of learning goals, curriculum, teaching materials, professional development support, and assessment. A common problem arises when the curriculum intentions are broad and deep, the textbooks and professional development only partly reflect that, and narrow official tests have consequences for teachers or students. It is not difficult to guess which message is likely to influence teaching most strongly. Yet it is common to ignore the effect of high-stakes tests on the implemented curriculum, seeing them as "just measurement", and to underfund key elements, notably professional development. Progress will depend on enhancing awareness of the central importance of alignment and of the engineering needed to achieve it.

Unrealistic Pace of Change

The design of an implementation program has many aspects that clearly need attention, including all those mentioned above. One that is commonly ignored is the planned pace of change. This is often grotesquely misjudged, again due to a mismatch of timescales. Politicians feel the need to be seen to "solve" problems—and before the next election. As we have seen, the timescales for the design, development and implementation of new curriculum elements, assessments and professional development programs are much longer than this.

There is much to be said for an *ongoing* program of improvements of the kind that is seen as normal in other spheres of public policy: health care and the military, for example. There are many advantages in the incremental introduction of small but significant steps that address major weaknesses in the curriculum. Unlike "big bang" changes, this approach does not fundamentally call in question the established practice of the professionals, be they teachers, principals or the leadership of the school system. Professional development can be focused on the few weeks of challenging new teaching and learning involved. Most teachers find innovation on this scale stimulating and enjoyable; though many will be relieved to get back to the comfort zone of their established practice, they usually welcome the next increment when it comes along, six months or a year later. Most important, a qualitative

---

[15]Paul Black (2008) describes the process of consensus building across communities behind a successful curriculum innovation, Nuffield A-level Physics.

change that is modest in scale can be done well, in contrast with major changes that so often degenerate back into "business as usual". Burkhardt (2009) describes a successful example of this approach: the introduction of new task-types into a high-stakes examination, supported by teaching and professional development materials. The materials came to be known as The Blue Box (Swan et al. 1984) and The Red Box (*The Language of Functions and Graphs*, Swan et al. 1985).[16] They included exemplar test tasks, materials for the three weeks of teaching, and a do-it-yourself professional development package.

Gradual change approaches have been used in various ways. "Replacement units" have been used in California and elsewhere. The introduction of "coursework" into British examinations was of this kind: 25% of the examination score was based on student performances in class. Portfolio assessment was introduced in some US states. It is important to note that these and other successful initiatives have often not survived, often for unconnected reasons arising from systemic changes.

Pressure without Support

Pressure and support need to be balanced if improvement is to happen as intended. That both are important is widely accepted but the amount of each is often determined by financial and political considerations that are not guided by likely cost-effectiveness. Normally pressure costs less than support, so "accountability" systems, largely based on tests, are a favourite tool of policy makers. Conversely, effective support systems normally involve teachers and other professionals regularly working outside the classroom on their professional development.

Professional development support is recognized rhetorically as essential but implementation is almost always inadequate, constrained by politically-determined financial limits. Typically, a few sessions will be specifically funded, or it may simply be left to existing structures to fit new demands into their current programs, themselves usually inadequate. Yet the timescale for becoming an accomplished teacher of problem solving and modeling, or for learning about how to exploit the multiple opportunities that technology affords, is decade-long, with an ongoing need for professional development support.

Regular time for professional development in the teacher's week has financial and logistic implications. The main cost of an education system is the cost of having a teacher in every classroom, which reinforces the simplistic view that other activities are "time off" from a teacher's job. To an administrator an hour a week is 4 % increase in this major cost. Average class size, the complementary variable, is so

---

[16]The Blue and Red Boxes are still widely regarded as classics. In 2008, one of the first "Eddies", the $10,000 prizes for excellence in educational design of the *International Society for Design and Development in Education*, was awarded to Malcolm Swan, its lead designer, for The Red Box. (The other went to an Editor of this book.)

controversial that a small increase to compensate for professional development time is rarely discussed.[17]

In contrast to this attitude, "continuing professional development" for doctors is a requirement of their continuing license to practice, taken into account in financial planning.

Evaluation in Depth

The standards for evaluation of the outcomes of interventions are abysmal. Curriculum materials are reviewed by inspection, only rarely using evidence on their effect on student learning and attitude. Professional development programs are evaluated by the perceptions of those who took part, not on evidence of change in the teachers' classroom practice—presumably the key goal. Studies of effects on student learning often use tests that cover only a subset of the stated learning goals, usually using narrow state tests.

In education, there are no equivalents of consumer magazines like *Consumer Reports* that test products systematically, let alone government bodies like the US *Food and Drug Administration* (*FDA*) or the British *National Institute for Clinical Excellence* (*NICE*) which evaluate medicines. This reflects the limited acceptance that education can be a research-based field. Making it so depends on improving evaluation in both range and depth.

This situation reflects various factors. Studies in depth are expensive, involving observation and analysis of what happens in many classrooms, as well as the learning outcomes.[18] Yet it is only such studies that provide a sound basis for choosing curriculum materials and, even more important, the formative feedback to inform for the next phase of improvement.

Equally, there are not yet enough good instruments for such a program to provide a sound research basis for such judgments. Broad spectrum tests of mathematical concepts, skills and practices, including problem solving, modeling and other forms of mathematical reasoning have been developed, but there is no accepted set that most studies use. For professional development, we need better protocols for classroom observation and analysis.

In the absence of better evaluation tools and methods, studies have fallen back on inadequate measures that are widely accepted for quite different purposes, usually accountability. The evaluation picture for the NSF-funded curricula had to be pieced

---

[17] Japan, where a substantial part of the teacher's week is spent in lesson planning and lesson study, has larger classes. In the US and UK teachers and their unions are profoundly skeptical that the trade-off would be sustained. "They'll cut the PD again after a year without reducing the class sizes". This exemplifies a whole set of other system issues.

[18] I estimate that a thorough formative evaluation of some NSF-funded curricula and some traditional comparators would require funding comparable to the original development program, roughly $100 million.

together (Senk and Thompson 2003) from a large number of separate studies. Together they gave a result that was fairly unambiguous, but not clear enough to command the acceptance it deserved. The results on the widely accepted narrow tests were comparable with those from other curricula, but these tests did not assess the broader performance goals that were the raison d'etre for these curricula. The studies that showed substantial gains on broad spectrum tests did not receive the same attention, probably because they were fewer and the tests were "non-standard".

We need to go beyond this, to look behind the outcomes in depth at the range of what happens throughout the process, in classrooms, and in the associated professional development. We need to know how the outcomes depend on the processes and the variables: students, teachers, school and district environments, and system structures. This information will provide a sound basis for future development.

Design and "Engineering"

Realizing a planned curriculum change is an unsolved problem in most school systems; nonetheless, a lot is known about what to do and what *not* to do. The smooth implementation of a substantial change in the curriculum requires a pathway of change for all the key groups along which they can move. Ideally, all should feel that the change is, in a broad sense, in their interest; this limits pushback to outsiders—often formidable enough. A change program like this requires a well-engineered mixture of pressure and support on each of the groups involved, with the tools and processes that will enable all those involved to succeed. This is clearly a major design and development challenge; it is rarely recognized as such.

In a rational outcome-focused world, pressure and support should be developed with policy, with the goals matched with the resources available. However, this is a constraint that, in education, politicians are so far unwilling to contemplate. As a result of the political sense of urgency, policy decisions on innovation are usually developed with some "consultation" but without either exploratory design or careful development. Viewed strategically like this, it is not surprising that few changes work out as intended.

The last decade has seen the growth of a more organized community of professional designers in mathematics and science education, supported through the *International Society for Design and Development in Education* and its on-line journal *Educational Designer*. However, as we have seen, much more remains to be done to raise standards—above all, policy makers' awareness of the contribution that high-quality engineering can make to realizing their goals.

In Summary

This chapter has argued that we know enough, and have the tools, to enable typical teachers with reasonable support to deliver a mathematics education for their students that is vastly better than most of them get currently. That is good news. Less encouraging is the evidence that the major problems in the way of implementation are at system level, involving the factors just described.

Since design and development at system level is inevitably larger in scale than, for example, classroom studies, progress will require substantial commitment, probably at a political level. History in other fields suggests (Burkhardt 2006; Burkhardt and Schoenfeld 2003) that, while persuasion is important, large scale research funding will follow only from unmistakable examples of successful impact—like antibiotics in medicine or radar and operational research in military science. Breaking out of this "chicken and egg" situation will require the creation, identification and trumpeting of successful examples like some of those mentioned above.

References

Black, P. (2008). Strategic decisions: ambitions, feasibility and context. *Educational Designer, 1*(1). Retrieved from: http://www.educationaldesigner.org/ed/volume1/issue1/article1/index.htm.

Brown, J. S., & Burton, R. B. (1978). Diagnostic models for procedural bugs in basic mathematical skills. *Cognitive Science, 2*, 155–192.

Burkhardt, H. (2006). From design research to large-scale impact: engineering research in education. In J. Van den Akker, K. Gravemeijer, S. McKenney, & N. Nieveen (Eds.), *Educational design research*. London: Routledge.

Burkhardt, H. (2009). On strategic design. *Educational Designer, 1*(3). Retrieved from: http://www.educationaldesigner.org/ed/volume1/issue3/article9.

Burkhardt, H., & Pollak, H. (2006). Modelling in mathematics classrooms: reflections on past developments and the future. *ZDM. Zentralblatt für Didaktik der Mathematik, 38*(2), 178–192.

Burkhardt, H., & Schoenfeld, A. H. (2003). Improving educational research: toward a more useful, more influential, and better-funded enterprise. *Educational Researcher, 32*(9), 3–14.

Burkhardt, H., Fraser, R., Coupland, J., Phillips, R., Pimm, D., & Ridgway, J. (1988). Learning activities & classroom roles with and without the microcomputer. *The Journal of Mathematical Behavior, 6*, 305–338.

Clarke, D. J., & Stephens, W. M. (1996). The ripple effect: the instructional impact of the systemic introduction of performance assessment in mathematics. In M. Birenbaum & F. Dochy (Eds.), *Alternatives in assessment of achievements, learning processes and prior knowledge* (pp. 63–92). Dordrecht: Kluwer.

Daro, P., & Burkhardt, H. (2012). A population of assessment tasks. *Journal of Mathematics Education at Teachers College, 3*. Spring-Summer 2012.

Freudenthal Institute (2010) *Mathematics A-lympiad*. Retrieved from http://www.fisme.science.uu.nl/alympiade/en/welcome.html.

Kaiser, G., Blomhøj, M., & Sriraman, S. (2006). Analyses: Mathematical modelling and applications: empirical and theoretical perspectives. *ZDM. Zentralblatt für Didaktik der Mathematik, 38*(2 & 3).

Polya, G. (1945). *How to solve it*. Princeton: Princeton University Press.

Schoenfeld, A. H. (1985). *Mathematical problem solving*. Orlando: Academic Press.

Senk, S. L. & Thompson, D. R. (Eds.) (2003). *Standards-based school mathematics curricula: what are they? What do students learn?* Mahwah: Erlbaum.

Stanic, G., & Kilpatrick, J. (1989). Historical perspectives on problem solving in the mathematics curriculum. In R. Charles & E. Silver (Eds.), *The teaching and assessing of mathematical problem solving* (pp. 1–22). Reston: National Council of Teachers of Mathematics.

Stigler, J. W., & Hiebert, J. (1999). *The teaching gap*. New York: Free Press.

Swan, M. (2006). *Collaborative learning in mathematics: a challenge to our beliefs and practices*. Leicester: NIACE.

Swan, M., Pitts, J., Fraser, R., Burkhardt, H., & the Shell Centre team (1984). *Problems with patterns and numbers*. Manchester: Joint Matriculation Board and Shell Centre for Mathematical Education, reprinted 2000, Shell Centre Publications, Nottingham, U.K. http://www.mathshell.com/scp/index.htm.

Swan, M., Pitts, J., Fraser, R., Burkhardt, H., & the Shell Centre team (1985). *The language of functions and graphs*. Manchester: Joint Matriculation Board and Shell Centre for Mathematical Education, reprinted 2000, Nottingham, U.K., Shell Centre Publications. http://www.mathshell.com/scp/index.htm.

Swan, M., Binns, B., Gillespie, J., Burkhardt, H., & the Shell Centre team (1987-89). *Numeracy through problem solving: five modules for teaching and assessment: design a board game, produce a quiz show, plan a trip, be a paper engiineer. Be a shrewd chooser*. Harlow: Longman, reprinted 2000, Shell Centre Publications, Nottingham, U.K. URL http://www.mathshell.com/scp/index.htm.

Swan, M., & the Mathematics Assessment Project team (2011). Materials retrieved from http://map.mathshell.org.uk/materials/lessons.php.

Törner, G., Schoenfeld, A. H., & Reiss, K. M. (2007). Problem solving around the world: summing up the state of the art. *ZDM. Zentralblatt für Didaktik der Mathematik*, *39*(5 & 6).

Travers, K. J., & Westbury, I. (1989) *The IEA study of mathematics I: analysis of mathematics curricula*. Supplement, available from ERIC as ED306111.

Mathematics Curriculum Policies and Practices in the U.S.: The Common Core State Standards Initiative

Barbara J. Reys

Abstract In the U.S. three curriculum strategies are being used to improve school mathematics programs and student learning outcomes: (a) the movement to common standards; (b) advances in technology-based instructional resources; and (c) the pressure of accountability measured by end-of-year assessments. Together, these strategies are creating a "perfect storm" for significant changes in mathematics curriculum. Elements of the reform strategy are reviewed and discussed. In addition, an argument is made for systematic monitoring of the initiative in order to learn about its impact and inform future policy decisions.

Keywords Mathematics · Curriculum · Standards · Textbooks · Digital · Assessments

Introduction

Current efforts to improve the K-12 educational system in the U.S. and promote increased student learning in mathematics employ a "standards-based" reform strategy. That is, the reform agenda seeks to "establish clear goals for student achievement through the establishment of standards and related assessments, generate data to improve teaching and learning, create incentives for change through rewards and sanctions, and provide assistance to low-performing schools" (Goertz 2009).

Confrey and Maloney (2011) describe standards and high-stakes assessments as policy-imposed "bookends" of a reform strategy designed to stimulate change (see Fig. 1). In this system, success is defined by the extent to which student scores on annual assessments increase and eventually match or exceed international benchmarks. What happens between the bookends of this system is the hard work of educational leaders and teachers—designing, and implementing instruction that supports student learning of mathematics. Key features of the "internal" work (central column) of a standards-based accountability system are: instructional practices and curriculum

B.J. Reys (✉)
Center for the Study of Mathematics Curriculum, University of Missouri, Columbia, USA
e-mail: ReysB@missouri.edu

Y. Li, G. Lappan (eds.), *Mathematics Curriculum in School Education*,
Advances in Mathematics Education, DOI 10.1007/978-94-007-7560-2_3,
© Springer Science+Business Media Dordrecht 2014

Fig. 1 Standards-based
school reform strategy

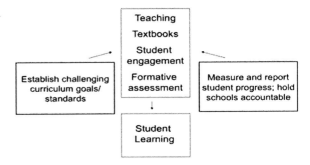

materials that teacher's use to engage students and formative assessments to inform instructional modifications and plan for individual needs. These internal features are highly dependent on the knowledge and skills of teachers and are influenced by the nature and extent of their initial and ongoing professional development as well as by the support provided to teachers within curriculum materials.

In this paper, I provide a summary of how the standards-based reform strategy is currently being structured and implemented in the U.S. In particular, several key curricular tools of the system are highlighted: standards, textbooks, and assessments. Although instructional practices (the processes of teaching) are not directly discussed in this paper, it is not because of lack of importance. Indeed, I acknowledge that teaching is at the heart of any effort to improve student learning. However, current school improvement initiatives in the U.S. are focused primarily on curriculum (initially with curriculum standards) rather than teaching. Therefore, this paper will focus on the influence of standards, textbooks, and assessments and how these curriculum tools function as levers to promote and advance improvement in the U.S. educational system.

The Intended Curriculum: Standards for Mathematics Learning

> Content standards consist of (a) a negotiated settlement among authorized experts concerning the specification of what a person should know or be able to do, (b) with consideration of how that is to be measured and/or documented, and (c) as a means of modulating or effecting change within the system of education and restricting excessive variation. (Confrey 2007, pp. 6–7)

Governance for educational policies in the U.S., including the establishment of curriculum standards (the core content of school mathematics), resides at the local (state or district) level. The level of local authority varies from state-to-state depending on the state's governance structure and constitutional authority. For example, some states such as North Carolina, Texas, and California exert control for aspects of curriculum regulation such as standard setting, textbook review, and assessment of student learning at the state level. Other states such as Nebraska and Colorado defer control for these decisions to the local school district. The U.S. federal government has very limited authority on curriculum decisions, although it has exerted influence through mandates associated with the distribution of particular federal resources.

Curriculum standards for school mathematics were first developed nationally by the National Council of Teachers of Mathematics (NCTM) in the late 1980's (NCTM 1989) and refined over the past two decades (NCTM 2000, 2006), launching a broad and far-reaching curriculum reform initiative in the U.S. From 1989 to 2010 hundreds of state and district level committees, with varying levels of governance authority, worked diligently to apply the suggested NCTM *Standards* to local and state-level curriculum documents. In 2001 the *No Child Left Behind* (NCLB) federal legislation advanced this movement, requiring states to articulate curriculum standards for mathematics learning and to regularly (annually in grades 3–8 and once during high school) assess the extent to which students are learning the mathematics outlined in the standards.

While some states (e.g., Virginia) were monitoring student learning through annual end-of-grade or end-of-course assessments prior to NCLB, most states' accountability systems were less aggressive. For example, Missouri administered assessments at particular points in time along the K-12 continuum (Grade 4, 8 and 10). However, since the passage of NCLB, all states are required to design, administer and report to the public on annual assessments, grades 3–8 and once in high school. In establishing state-level curriculum standards, most states drew heavily from source documents such as the NCTM *Standards* (1989 and 2000). However, nearly all have worked independently, resulting in variation across state-level curriculum standards, and in the format and focus of annual assessments. Therefore, by 2009 the situation could accurately be described as 50 states with 50 different sets of curriculum standards using 50 different assessments to monitor learning outcomes.

An example of the variation across state standards is illustrated in Fig. 2. It provides a summary of the grade at which addition and subtraction of fractions is introduced and when proficiency is expected as outlined in 42 state standards documents in 2006 (Reys 2006). As noted, some state standards introduced computation with fractions (with common fractions such as 1/2) as early as grade 1 while others began instruction on the topic in grade 3 or 4. Some state standards included an expectation of fluently computing (all operations) with fractions by the end of grade 5 and other state standards included this expectation at grade 8. In fact, state standards differed regarding when addition and subtraction of fractions was introduced (ranging from grade 1 to grade 7), the number of years this topic was developed (ranging from 1 to 6 years), and the grade level at which students were expected to be proficient with addition and subtraction of fractions (ranging from grade 4 to grade 7). The variation of learning goals across states lead to several unintended outcomes including: large textbooks that cover many topics, repetition from grade to grade (to accommodate variation in learning goals across state standards), and superficial attention to many topics.

The central goal of NCLB is to ensure that, by 2014, 100 percent of students are proficient in mathematics. High stakes annual assessments developed and administered by each state are the primary gauge as to how the standards-based reform strategy is working. Based on state assessments, student performance in most states

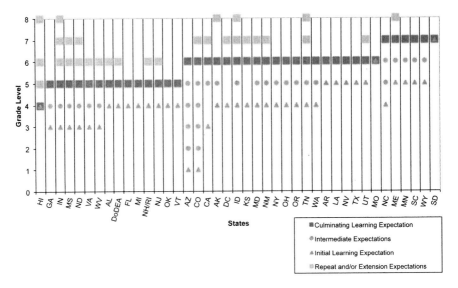

Fig. 2 Summary of grade level at which state level standards (prior to CCSSM) indicated proficiency with additional and subtraction of fractions

(at all grade levels) has risen since the enactment of NCLB in 2002. However, based on a common measure of student performance in mathematics (the National Assessment of Educational Progress or NAEP), administered to a representative sample of students in each state every five years, the evidence does not support state claims of consistent and steady growth. That is, there is not a strong correlation between performance of students on state assessments and performance on NAEP (Bandeira de Mello et al. 2009).

From a policy perspective, NCLB had the desired effect of focusing school reform efforts on advancing student learning, as measured by annual end-of-year assessment instruments. However, since NCLB left the setting of standards and the creation of assessments up to individual states, implementation has varied and the results are difficult to interpret. Implementation of NCLB has also been very costly and called upon resources (monetary and personnel) that few states can afford to sustain.

Research such as that reported in *The Intended Mathematics Curriculum as Represented in State-Level Curriculum Standards: Consensus or Confusion?* (Reys 2006) called attention to the variability of grade level learning goals in mathematics across a variety of topics. It helped promote national discussions about the lack of agreement on what mathematics content should be taught as well as when it should be the focus of instruction.

In March 2009 state governors agreed that collaboration on the development of common learning goals (standards), Grades K-12, in mathematics and English/language arts was necessary to increase the quality and rigor of content standards. The National Governors Association (NGA) and the Council of Chief State School Officers (CCSSO) commissioned a writing group to first describe goals for

Table 1 NCTM Process Standards, Mathematical Proficiency, and CCSSM Standards for Mathematical Practice

NCTM (2000)	Adding It Up (2001)	CCSSM (2010)
Problem solving	Strategic competence	Make sense of problems and persevere in solving them.
Reasoning	Adaptive reasoning	Reason abstractly and quantitatively
Connections	Conceptual understanding	Look for and express regularity in repeated reasoning.
Communication	Procedural fluency	Construct viable arguments and critique the reasoning of others.
Representations	Productive disposition	Look for and make use of structure
		Use appropriate tools strategically
		Attend to precision
		Model with mathematics

college and career readiness and then, using those goals, develop standards for Grades K-12 mathematics and English language arts. The authors of the mathematics standards drew upon a variety of expertise and resources, including: mathematical content experts, cognitive scientists, and mathematics education researchers and practitioners. Standards from countries such as Singapore and Japan, whose students performed well on the Trends in International Mathematics and Science Study (TIMSS), were also reviewed. In addition, the authors studied "learning progressions detailing what is known today about how students' mathematical knowledge, skill, and understanding develop over time" (Common Core State Standards Initiative [CCSSI] 2010, p. 4). Mathematicians also contributed progressions based on mathematical analysis of key topics (e.g., fractions) and these progressions also influenced the standards. In June 2010, 15 months after the governors' meeting, the *Common Core State Standards for Mathematics* (CCSSM) was released (see http://www.corestandards.org/).

CCSSM includes two types of learning goals—standards for mathematical practice and standards for mathematical content. The standards for mathematical practice address eight "habits of mind" that students should develop over the course of K-12 schooling. They include a focus on problem solving and reasoning, a primary goal of mathematics education reform initiatives in the U.S. since the publication of NCTM's *Agenda for Action* (1980). A list of the eight practices is included in Table 1. The table also includes NCTM's process standards and the elements of mathematical proficiency outlined in *Adding It Up* (2001). As noted, the mathematical practices are not completely new to the lexicon of mathematics education and are certainly not independent of one another. Rather, CCSSM reinforces the importance of these overarching mathematical ideas.

The mathematics content of CCSSM is organized by grade (K-8) and by conceptual category in the high school. At each grade, several key ideas are the primary focus. For example, at grade 4, three critical areas are targeted:

(1) Develop an understanding of and fluency in multi-digit multiplication, and an understanding of dividing to find quotients involving multi-digit dividends;
(2) Develop an understanding of fraction equivalence, addition and subtraction of fractions with like denominators, and multiplication of fractions by whole numbers;
(3) Understand that geometric figures can be analyzed and classified based on their properties, such as having parallel sides, perpendicular sides, particular angle measures, and symmetry.

To date, all but a few states (e.g., Alaska, Minnesota, Nebraska, Texas, and Virginia) have adopted the CCSSM. For the first time in the United States, a significant majority of schools, teachers, and students will focus on common and, in Grades K-8, grade-level specific learning goals for mathematics. In addition, states have come together as part of one of two state-led consortia to develop new assessments aligned to CCSSM (see more about the assessment consortia in a later section of this paper).

What began with a federal policy initiative (NCLB) has now moved to state-led collaboration on the two critical "bookends" of the standards-based reform strategy. Common standards coupled with common grade-level assessments aligned with the CCSSM are likely to impact other important elements critical to students' mathematical learning. In particular, this initiative will impact the content and nature of curriculum materials and policies related to course-taking and graduation requirements.

The Written Curriculum: Trends in Mathematics Textbook Development

Historically, mathematics textbooks serve as a tool for translating curriculum standards into practical guidance for teachers. In fact, throughout the past 50 years, textbooks have been a staple in American classrooms. That is, teachers use the textbook (student or teacher edition) daily to plan and deliver lessons. In most schools, each student is provided a mathematics textbook at the beginning of the school year to use in class and at home, conveying to parents the activities that take place in the mathematics classroom. Other than teacher salaries and transportation costs, textbooks represent the next largest share of educational costs in the U.S. For example, in 2009 K-12 school districts spent over 8 billion dollars on textbooks (Association of American Publishers 2010).

Mathematics textbooks have also played a key role as a school improvement strategy. For example, from 1990–98 the National Science Foundation funded several large-scale curriculum development projects to create and test new textbook models (see Senk and Thompson 2003). These materials differed from publisher-generated textbooks in their content and pedagogical focus (see Trafton et al. 2002). Key features of the NSF-funded curriculum materials are summarized in Fig. 3 (Hirsch 2007). Materials such as these, which focus on conceptual understanding and student engagement, differ from traditional American textbooks in that they

- Updated content to include data analysis, probability, and, in the high school curricula, topics from discrete mathematics
- Focus on "big ideas" across grade levels and multiple representations
- Applications that provide a connection between mathematics and the world in which students live and consider interesting
- Connections among ideas across mathematical strands and grade levels
- Incorporation of technological tools, especially calculators
- Attention to issues of equity and access
- Active engagement of students through investigations of important mathematical ideas and solving more-challenging problems
- Focus on depth over coverage to promote deeper understanding of important mathematical ideas
- Support for teachers to become stimulators and guides of inquiry
- Learning opportunities for teachers through extensive teacher guides and professional development opportunities
- Assessment embedded in the curriculum materials and used to guide instruction

Fig. 3 Key features of NSF-funded K-12 mathematics textbooks

are "research-based." That is, they are developed based on a cycle of initial lesson preparation, pilot testing in classrooms, feedback from teachers, and revision before final publication (something not generally done with publisher-generated textbooks).

Regardless of the nature, philosophy or source of funding of textbook materials, authors have been constrained by the lack of national consensus on grade-level learning expectations as well as the concern with getting an adequate market share. That is, in order to address the many diverse standards of states, authors of mathematics textbooks needed to include a wide range of mathematics content in a single textbook to respond to many varied state standards (Seeley 2003). The result was a collection of lessons focused on concepts and skills that "aligned" with the standards of many states but often failed to focus on or develop in-depth mathematical ideas across grades. American mathematics textbooks are generally larger and focus on more topics per grade than textbooks in other countries. In fact, the average page length of a U.S. 4th grade student mathematics textbook is 530 pages compared to 4th grade mathematics textbooks in other countries participating in the TIMSS study which average 170 pages (Schmidt and Valverde 1997; Reys and Reys 2006).

Reviews of textbooks conducted by the American Association for the Advancement of Science and the U.S. Department of Education characterized many publisher-developed middle school mathematics textbooks as "unacceptable" with regard to content emphasis (AAAS 2000). Furthermore, evaluators found that, "many textbooks provide little development in sophistication of mathematical ideas from grades 6 to 8" and "most of the textbooks are inconsistent and often weak in their coverage of conceptual benchmarks in mathematics" (AAAS 2000, p. 1).

Most U.S. mathematics textbooks from Grade 3-high school are non-consumable. That is, they are owned and retained by the school each year so that they can be used by subsequent groups of students for up to 8–10 years before being replaced. In this system, schools typically purchase new textbooks in one discipline (e.g., science, language arts, reading, social studies, and mathematics) each year; thereby distributing the financial cost somewhat evenly from year to year. Textbooks are replaced because they deteriorate physically and/or because content emphasis shifts or new teaching approaches are emphasized. However, there was generally no single time (month or year) when all U.S. schools adopted new mathematics textbooks. This meant that textbook publishers produced materials that were continuously marketable in states with different adoption timelines.

For many U.S. teachers, the textbook (teacher's edition) is the primary resource used to plan daily mathematics instruction (Weiss et al. 2001). It serves as a "scope and sequence"—determining what mathematics content is taught and often in what order. In addition to guiding the content of a course and providing a sequence of major topics, textbooks also play an important role in providing activities and instructional ideas to the teacher on how to engage students in studying topics presented. They serve as a set of lesson plans for the teacher to use in presenting the material, complete with sample problems, diagrams, worked out examples, and homework assignments. The textbook influences what content is taught and the amount of time—usually a reflection of the number of pages—that is devoted to the topic (Chávez 2003). Given the limited amount of preparation in mathematics that most elementary teachers have and the shortage of teachers certified to teach mathematics at the middle and secondary schools, for a large segment of the teaching corps the mathematics textbooks being used in school are the de facto mathematics program. The major role the textbook plays was succinctly reflected by a middle school teacher who referred to the textbook as "the bible in math for my students."

On the other hand, there are many anecdotal reports of teachers who "throw out the textbook" and assemble their own instructional materials based on their experience and beliefs about what is important and what will motivate students (Seeley 2003). To cloud the issue further, Chávez (2003) reports that teachers in the same school or district use the same textbook very differently. In fact, one of the truisms of teaching in the United States is that teachers exercise great autonomy in making decisions about their classroom practice. Therefore, students in the same school or district are likely to experience a different mathematics curriculum, depending on decisions made by the teacher. Teacher variability in the enacted curriculum is acknowledged by Kilpatrick (2003):

> Two classrooms in which the same curriculum is supposedly being "implemented" may look very different; the activities of teacher and students in each room may be quite dissimilar, with different learning opportunities available, different mathematical ideas under consideration, and different outcomes achieved. (p. 473)

In spite of the acknowledged role of textbooks, until recently (cf. Schoenfeld 2002; Senk and Thompson 2003) little research has studied the effects of textbooks on students' learning of mathematics. Kilpatrick (2003) described some of the challenges of researching the impact of textbooks on student learning and called for additional scholarly work in this critical area.

With the adoption of CCSSM by all but a few states, attention is turning to development of textbooks to support teachers' instruction of the CCSSM. Publishers have been eager to respond, some revising existing materials to incorporate the new standards and others creating whole new sets of instructional materials based on the new standards.

Coupled with the emergence of CCSSM is the growing attention to the use of technology as a way to design and deliver instructional materials for students and teachers. On the one hand, some publishers are "digitizing" existing textbooks—that is, creating e-versions (e.g., pdf documents) of textbook lessons and loading them onto a website for access by students and teachers. On the other hand, some individual authors and innovative tech companies are developing internet-based e-textbooks and/or platforms that take full advantage of the power, flexibility and adaptability of the medium to deliver lessons, problems, activities and other classroom material for use by teachers and/or students. For example, *Inkling* (a technology company whose goal it is to "reinvent the way people learn") has developed a platform by which to deliver textbooks. Working initially in the college textbook market, the company's motto is that, "textbooks don't have to be text and they don't have to be books."

Technology, including digital textbooks, has the potential to revolutionize school (and out-of-school) learning experiences for students and teachers. However, that potential has not yet been realized. Chad Dorsey of the Concord Consortium, summarizes the situation in this way,

> Whispers of a technology revolution in teaching and learning are becoming audible… Digital textbooks provide some of the loudest of these rumbles, and the benefits seem clear. Heavy backpacks would be banished forever. Content would be annotated, highlighted, and shared. Interactive aspects would accentuate the text. But these are far from enough … too often we see examples heralded as the education of tomorrow that are simply surface-level implementations that fail to deliver technology's true potential. (http://www.concord.org/publications/newsletter/2011-fall/perspective)

What is currently available to most U.S. teachers are digital versions of traditional textbooks. Originally produced as a hardbound textbook, some of the materials have been digitized (produced in electronic format) so that they can be accessed during or after school. In fact, it is not uncommon to walk into a U.S. mathematics classroom today and not see a textbook at all. Rather, the teacher works from a Smart Board display, drawing from the digital textbook resources and supplementing these resources with other materials found on various internet sites. More recently, the announcement by Apple of a new textbook authoring tool, iBooks2, coupled with collaboration of the largest textbook publishing companies has brought new attention to digital textbooks. Utilizing iBooks2, McGraw-Hill, Pearson, and Houghton Mifflin Harcourt have created a few high school math and science textbooks using the new technology, offering them to consumers for $15 per book (see: http://www.apple.com/education/ibooks-textbooks/publishers.html).

The pressure to focus instruction on what is valued (that is, what is measured on the end-of-year test) has increased the likelihood that teachers will venture outside their school adopted textbook, particularly if they believe that the textbook does not adequately address key topics. Digital textbooks make it easier to do so as the range and amount of supplemental resources available from the publisher and from other internet sites is almost unlimited.

In response to CCSS, several philanthropic groups (e.g., the Gates Foundation) have contributed to teacher use of a variety of instructional resources (rather than a single textbook) by sponsoring projects to create and provide supplementary, internet-based instructional materials (individual lessons or unit of instruction) at no charge. In addition, commercial textbook publishers are offering digital textbook formats to schools and this movement is likely to accelerate to the point that in the not-too-distant future, traditional hard-bound mathematics textbooks will no longer be found in U.S. classrooms. Instead, student laptops or e-tablets will provide access to instructional resources for both teachers and students.

The Assessed Curriculum: Trends in Mathematics Assessment

As noted earlier, standards-based reform uses annual student assessments as the primary means of monitoring student learning outcomes and holding schools accountable for student learning. Specifically, No Child Left Behind ushered in, for the first time in many states, a highly structured state system of annual assessments (at each grade, grades 3–8, and one time in high school). These assessments began in 2002 and continue today under the original framework of NCLB. As with curriculum standards, each state in the U.S. has governance over the assessments used since 2002 to measure student learning within their state. That is, each state has either constructed an assessment based on their own state standards or purchased the services of an assessment developer to design such an assessment system.

Results of the annual state assessments are routinely published locally and statewide for the public to examine. The results are used to gauge school progress and, if necessary, to trigger sanctions. For example, if a school fails to have a sufficient number of students assessed as "proficient" in mathematics for three years in a row, the school must notify parents that students are eligible for additional services (e.g., tutoring) or that they may transfer to another school in the district.

According to NCLB, all students within all schools must be "proficient" in reading and mathematics by 2014. If not, schools whose students do not achieve proficiency suffer increasingly high-stakes sanctions, including closure. As 2014 approaches, it is clear that all schools will not reach the NCLB goal. In fact, given the current law, virtually no schools will reach the goal. The U.S. Congress is currently working to modify the law. In the meantime, the U.S. Department of Education is considering proposals by individual states for "waivers"—that is, permission to opt out of the NCLB requirements. Proposals for waivers must outline what processes a state will put into place instead of the NCLB mandates in order to increase student learning and prepare students for college and career readiness.

As noted, NCLB operates at the federal level, however, until recently, curriculum standards and assessments were created and managed at the state level. That is, prior to the CCSSM initiative, there were 50 different sets of state standards for mathematics and 50 different assessments aligned to these state standards. Additionally, each state set a cut score (determination of passing mark) for the assessments. Given this system, it is virtually impossible to compare student performance across states.

As a follow-up to the state-led development of common standards for mathematics, in 2011 the U.S. Department of Education funded two state consortia to develop assessments aligned with CCSSM. As with the development of common standards, the work is based at the state, rather than federal level. That is, two different consortia of states have been working for the past several years to design assessment systems that will be used within the states, in most cases replacing the existing state developed assessments.

The two state consortia are Partnership for Assessment of Readiness for College and Careers (PARCC) and the SMARTER Balanced Assessment Consortium (SBAC). Both consortia are committed to developing technology-based mathematics assessments for students in grades 3–12 that provide valid, reliable, fair measures of students' progress toward and attainment of the knowledge and skills required for college and career readiness as defined by CCSSM. These assessments will be ready for use in the 2014–15 school year. Each state-led consortia has developed an assessment framework (see: http://www.smarterbalanced.org/wordpress/wp-content/uploads/2011/12/MathContentSpecifications.pdf and http://www.parcconline.org/sites/parcc/files/PARCC%20MCF%20for%20Mathematics_Fall%202011%20Release.pdf) that will guide test development. The SBAC will include summative assessments administered in the last 12 weeks of the school year consisting of a computer adaptive test and a set of performance tasks. In addition, optional interim assessments will be available to school districts to monitor student progress toward the learning goals outlined in CCSSM. The PARCC assessment system includes four components, each computer-delivered: two summative, required assessment components designed to assess student progress in achieving the CCSSM learning goals; and two non-summative, optional assessment components designed to provide information to inform instruction, interventions, and professional development during the school year. In the meantime, states will continue to use current state assessments, reporting on student proficiency annually, as defined by NCLB.

A Research Agenda for Monitoring the Impact of the CCSS Initiative

Given the major policy initiative of CCSSM, it is critical that data be gathered to understand the impact on the system and gauge its success in supporting increased student learning and college/career readiness (Weiss and Heck 2011). With support of the National Science Foundation, Weiss and Heck developed a priority research agenda that includes a set of case studies, investigations of relationships, and status studies to address the following broad questions:

(1) *How is the mathematics education system responding to the introduction of the CCSSM?*

(2) *What happens, and for whom, as a result?*
(3) *How can the CCSSM and future standards be improved?*

The agenda prioritizes research that monitors responses to CCSSM and documents the impact of these responses. Some of the priority questions include:

- *How are curriculum materials changing in response to the CCSSM?*
- *How are teachers interpreting the CCSSM and developing their capacity for implementing them?*
- *To what extent are the CCSSM influencing classroom practice?*
- *How are consortia assessments being developed, and how are they affecting the mathematics education system?*
- *What is the relationship between CCSSM-influenced classroom practice and student outcomes?*

To date, some information regarding state-level actions in response to CCSSM is available. For example, a survey of state education leaders conducted by Kober and Stark (2011) indicates that the transition to *CCSSM* has been slow. In fact, many states indicated "they do not expect to fully implement major changes in assessment, curriculum, teacher evaluation, and teacher certification until 2013 or later, or to institute a requirement for local districts to implement the common standards until that time." (p. 1). Regarding teacher responses to CCSSM, Schmidt (2012) reports that while 80 percent of teachers surveyed indicate that CCSSM is "pretty much the same" as their former curriculum standards, only about half of elementary teachers (60 percent of middle school teachers and 70 percent of high school teachers) feel well prepared to teach the topics in *CCSSM*. Clearly, much work is needed to support the goals of the CCSSM initiative.

Summary

In the U.S. three curriculum-focused strategies are being utilized to improve school mathematics programs: common standards (CCSSM), advances in technology-based instructional resources, and accountability assessments. Together, these strategies are creating a "perfect storm" for significant changes in mathematics curriculum. These changes are intended to advance student learning and enable all students to be college- and career-ready. Whether or not the reform strategy has the desired effect depends on many factors. Perhaps the most important questions are, can and will the U.S. educational system support the transition to CCSSM and CCSSM-aligned assessments with high quality curriculum materials and professional development? Will the CCSSM-aligned assessments provide good measures of student learning? Finally, can the standards-based system be managed so that it can evolve and improve over time?

References

American Association for the Advancement of Science (2000). *Middle grades mathematics textbooks: a benchmarks-based evaluation*. Washington: Author.

Association of American Publishers (2010). Opportunity to learn in high-stakes testing. An AAP white paper developed by Dr. Susan E. Phillips. http://www.aapschool.org/pdf/Opptolearn-Phillipspaper.pdf.

Bandeira de Mello, V., Blankenship, C., & McLaughlin, D. H. (2009). *Mapping state proficiency standards onto NAEP scales: 2005–2007 (NCES 2010-456)*. Washington: National Center for Education Statistics, Institute of Education Sciences, U.S. Department of Education.

Chávez, O. (2003). *From the textbook to the enacted curriculum: textbook use in the middle school mathematics classroom*. University of Missouri-Columbia, Unpublished doctoral dissertation.

Common Core State Standards Initiative (2010). *Common core state standards for mathematics*. Washington: National Governors Association Center for Best Practices and the Council of Chief State School Officers.

Confrey, J., & Maloney, A. (2011). Engineering [for] effectiveness in mathematics education. In *Highly successful STEM schools or programs for K-12 STEM education: a workshop*. Washington: National Academies Board on Science Education and Board on Testing and Assessment.

Confrey, J. (2007). *Tracing the evolution of mathematics content standards in the united states: looking back and projecting forward towards national standards*. Paper presented at the Conference on K-12 Mathematics Curriculum Standards.

Goertz, M. E. (2009). Standards-based reform: lessons from the past, directions for the future. In K. Wong & R. Rothman (Eds.), *Clio at the table: using history to inform and improve education policy* (pp. 201–219). New York: Peter Lang Publishing.

Hirsch, C. R. (2007). Curriculum materials matter. In C. R. Hirsch (Ed.), *Perspectives on the design and development of school mathematics curricula* (pp. 1–5). Reston: National Council of Teachers of Mathematics.

Kilpatrick, J. (2003). What works? In S. Senk & D. Thompson (Eds.), *Standards-oriented school mathematics curricula: what does research say about student outcomes?* (pp. 471–488). Mahwah: Lawrence Erlbaum Associates.

Kober, N., & Stark, D. (2011). *States' progress and challenges in implementing common core state standards*. Washington: Center for Education Policy.

National Council of Teachers of Mathematics (1980). *An agenda for action*. Reston: Author.

National Council of Teachers of Mathematics (1989). *Curriculum and evaluation standards for school mathematics*. Reston: Author.

National Council of Teachers of Mathematics (2000). *Principles and standards for school mathematics*. Reston: Author.

National Council of Teachers of Mathematics (2006). *Curriculum focal points for prekindergarten through grade 8 mathematics*. Reston: Author.

Reys, B. J. (Ed.) (2006). *The intended mathematics curriculum as represented in state-level curriculum standards: consensus or confusion?* Charlotte: Information Age.

Reys, B. J., & Reys, R. E. (2006). The development and publication of elementary mathematics textbooks: let the buyer beware! *Phi Delta Kappan, 87*(5), 377–383.

Schmidt, W. H. (2012). Common core math standards implementation can lead to improved student achievement [PowerPoint slides]. Retrieved from http://www.achieve.org/CCSS-schmidt-research.

Schmidt, W. H., & Valverde, G. (1997). *Policy lessons from TIMSS*. Paper prepared for the National Governors Association.

Schoenfeld, A. H. (2002). Making mathematics work for all children: issues of standards, testing, and equity. *Educational Researcher, 31*(1), 13–25.

Seeley, C. L. (2003). Mathematics textbook adoption in the United States. In G. M. Stanic & J. Kilpatrick (Eds.), *A history of school mathematics* (pp. 957–988). Reston: National Council of Teachers of Mathematics.

Senk, S., & Thompson, D. (2003). *Standards-based school mathematics curricula: what are they? What do students learn?* Mahwah: Lawrence Erlbaum Associates.

Trafton, P., Reys, B. J., & Wasman, D. (2002). Standards-based mathematics instructional materials: a phrase in search of a definition. *Phi Delta Kappan, 83*(3), 259–264.

U. S. Department of Education (2001). *The no child left behind act of 2001.* Washington: Author. http://www.ed.gov/policy/elsec/leg/esea02/index.html. Accessed 21 October 2007.

Weiss, I. R., & Heck, D. (2011). *CCSSM priority research agenda.* Alhambra: Horizon Research, Inc.

Weiss, I. R., Banilower, E. R., McMahon, K. C., & Smith, P. S. (2001). *Report of the 2000 national survey of science and mathematics education.* Chapel Hill: Horizon Research, Inc. Retrieved February 28, 2003 from http://2000survey.horizon-research.com/reports/status.php.

Reflections on Curricular Change

Alan H. Schoenfeld

Abstract Within any national perspective, curricular change may be viewed as evolutionary, with curricula evolving in ways responsive to the surrounding political and intellectual environments. There is, however, less global coherence than any intranational perspective might suggest. Historical and political contexts matter, just as ecological niches do in evolutionary biology. This chapter begins with a meta-level discussion describing the consequential nature of (typically national) values, goals, and cultural context and traditions as shapers of curricula. It then proceeds with a discussion of curricular trends in the United States over the past decades, and thumbnail descriptions of changes in the Netherlands, Great Britain, Germany, France, China, and Japan. A concluding discussion reflects on the diversity of curricular directions worldwide, and suggests some ways in which we can profit from it.

Keywords Curriculum · Curriculum change · High stakes assessment · International trends

I begin with two meta-level issues.

Issue 1: Values and goals—typically, at the national level—are consequential.

If "rich and powerful mathematical understanding" were a straightforward goal, then curricula worldwide would presumably be aiming for it. But, the fact that a nation's rankings on TIMSS and PISA can differ significantly suggests that some national curricula emphasize skills more than mathematical modeling and problem solving (the rough foci of TIMSS and PISA, respectively) and vice-versa. Thus, for example, Russia scored above the United States (and above average) on the TIMSS 8th grade 2007 test, while it scored below the U.S. (and below average) on the PISA 2009 mathematics exams (Mullis et al. 2008; OECD 2010). The differences are not huge (scores on any two mathematics tests will correlate to a significant degree), but they reflect non-trivial differences in curricular emphases in the two nations.

A.H. Schoenfeld (✉)
University of California, Berkeley, CA, USA
e-mail: alans@berkeley.edu

Y. Li, G. Lappan (eds.), *Mathematics Curriculum in School Education,*
Advances in Mathematics Education, DOI 10.1007/978-94-007-7560-2_4,
© Springer Science+Business Media Dordrecht 2014

A nation such as the Netherlands, which emphasizes modeling and applications, would expect to do relatively well on PISA. Nations that do not have such emphases (the U.S. among them) would not expect to do as well.

This should not be surprising. Stigler and Hiebert (1999) indicated that there is much greater pedagogical variability between nations than within nations. The same is the case with regard to curricula, especially in nations where there is essentially one curriculum, specified by a national agency such as a ministry of education. Different nations aim in different directions.

This is consequential with regard to both pedagogy and curricula. In China and Korea, for example, curricular specifications and standards have focused largely if not exclusively on content, and the primary pedagogical "ideal" is a beautifully constructed lecture, which makes the mathematics involved absolutely clear to the students (Li and Huang 2013; Park and Leung 2006). The teacher may check in with students to determine their understanding, but it is the teacher's responsibility to lay out the curriculum content, and the student's responsibility to master what has been presented. In contrast, a significant trend in the U.S. has been to break away from this direction—to provide students with opportunities to engage with mathematical ideas and to develop some of the core mathematics (under the teacher's careful guidance) for themselves. Some American curricula, then, have been evolving to provide such support structures. This differs from curricular practice in some (but not all: cf. Japan) Asian nations. Indeed, the contrast between Japanese and Chinese curricula provides an indication of significantly different trends in those two nations. Many Japanese lessons depend very heavily on the orchestration of student responses to carefully chosen problems, while comparably rich Chinese lessons emphasize the unfolding of the mathematics from the teacher.

In sum, different national premises about the nature of thinking and learning lead to different premises about the most effective forms of instruction, which lead to different forms of curricula. Here is an illustrative anecdote. In my problem solving courses I have students work together in small groups for a significant part of class, before I discuss the work that has emerged and move things forward. One of my students, who comes from Korea, expressed bafflement at the class organization. "Why am I listening to other students," she said, "when you know so much more than we do? Shouldn't you be telling us about the mathematics?"

Issue 2: Cultural context and traditions are consequential.[1]

Curricula are tools, to be used in the hands of teachers. Like any tools, their effectiveness depends on the preparation of those who will be using them. Those who construct curricula make assumptions about the people who will be using them, and construct the curricula accordingly. Thus, a particular curriculum may work well in certain contexts and be problematic in others.

---

[1] What follows contains broad generalities. I am describing trends, in the way that (for example) Stigler and Hiebert (1999) describe trends.

Consider Singaporean curricula. There is no questioning the effectiveness of Singaporean teaching: Singaporean students have consistently scored near the top on both TIMSS and PISA. Singaporean textbooks are models of clarity, and some school districts in the U.S. have tried to adopt them—with mixed success. Why? To put it bluntly, Singaporean texts are designed for Singaporean teachers. Those teachers know the curriculum, and (broadly speaking) they are well versed in the relevant mathematics. Thus, having a "lean" textbook is not an issue: teachers can be trusted to flesh out the examples and make connections between the examples and the underlying mathematical concepts by themselves. In contrast, teachers in the U.S. tend not to have the kinds of backgrounds that would enable them to make good use of the Singaporean texts. Textbooks in the U.S. tend to be "fat" because textbook publishers make the assumption that American teachers require support in implementing curricula. If the publisher expects something to happen in the classroom, then explicit guidance for that event is likely to be presented in the text.

National pedagogical style also makes a huge difference—see, for example, the contrast between the TIMSS videotapes of American and Japanese mathematics classrooms. For many years in the US, "traditional" instruction followed what Lappan and Phillips (2009) called the "show and practice" model of instruction, in which a teacher demonstrates and explains a particular procedure, and students are then given extensive practice at working similar examples. Traditional textbooks in the U.S. were designed to support this approach. Many texts offered a "two page spread" per lesson. The student edition contained worked examples on two facing pages demonstrating the procedures to be learned, and a series of exercises for the students to complete. The teacher's edition contained the student edition as an inset, surrounded by a pre-made lesson plan for the teacher that contained descriptions of the sequence of activities, timing for the lesson, things to highlight, possible assignments, and answers and/or worked-out solutions to the exercises in the inset. Thus, teachers could teach a lesson by opening the text to the day's two-page spread and following the script it embodied. Given the factory model of much mathematics instruction in the U.S.—a typical secondary teacher might be responsible for teaching five or six classes with 30 students each, with three different course preparations—such easy-to-pick-up-and-use texts were in essence a survival tool for many teachers.

This teacher-plus-textbook picture must be seen against the backdrop of teacher preparation and the opportunities for professional development in the US. Typically, a candidate for a teaching license in the U.S. can either obtain certification as an education major during a 4-year baccalaureate career or in a 1-year post-baccalaureate teacher certification program. During the teacher preparation program, the candidate will typically observe and discuss instruction by a "master teacher," and then "take over" the master teacher's classroom instruction for some weeks. This is *the entirety of* the candidate's pedagogical apprenticeship. Once hired, the teacher will tend to have classroom autonomy—but little opportunity to interact with colleagues, either during the workweek or during (rare) "professional development days." (Lortie 1975 likened the insularity of teaching to that of an egg crate, with each separate cell its own private province, insulated from the others.) Within this context, "ready-to-use" curricula make it possible for the teacher to get through the day. Given that extended opportunities to learn on or outside the job are rare in the US, more ambitious curricular goals have to be supported by more ambitious curricula that provide extensive support.

This picture stands in stark contrast to the national norms in Japan. To oversimplify somewhat, the assumption underlying the professional development of teachers in Japan is that even the most talented beginning teachers will require a decade of supported professional growth before they become truly expert teachers. The work setting for teachers in Japan is radically different from the work setting for teachers in the U.S. Working with colleagues is defined as part of one's responsibilities, and the workweek is arranged so that some percentage of one's official work time is spent collaborating with one's colleagues.

The Japanese practice of lesson study (see, e.g., Fernandez and Yoshida 2004) exemplifies the difference. Obvious contrasts between the social contexts represented by lesson study and typical U.S. practice are that (1) teachers in Japan are given time to collaborate on lesson design as part of their defined work, in contrast to the isolation experienced by most U.S. teachers; and (2) the lesson as designed is taught by one member of the lesson study team and observed and refined by the entire team. In particular, that means that *Japanese classrooms are open to knowledgeable visitors as a matter of practice*. This openness provides opportunities for beginning teachers to learn by observation, discussion, and practice—opportunities that are typically not available for teachers in the U.S.

There is more. Typically, lessons in the U.S. are focused on the mathematics, or the mathematical activities, that students are to experience. In the U.S. a good lesson is typically considered to be one that contains an engaging activity or series of activities that highlight the important mathematical content and practices to be learned. At least as represented in the literature (Fernandez and Yoshida 2004; Takahashi 2004), a major focus of lesson study lessons concerns not just the mathematics itself, but *student thinking about the mathematics*. Questions that shape lesson design include, what understandings do students bring to the topic? what choice of examples will best reveal student understandings? how can one build on what is solid, and lead students to see the limitations or errors in what they understand? how can a lesson be sequenced to help students see connections across ideas, and to build deeper understandings? Building and using such lessons calls for mathematical knowledge, every bit as much as the content-oriented lessons in the U.S. But, content knowledge is not enough to make such lessons succeed. Thus, teachers steeped in lesson study approach the lessons with a different mindset than teachers who have not benefitted from that cultural surround. This is one reason that attempts to use lesson study in the U.S. have generally not succeeded. Unless the introduction to lesson study provides mechanisms for U.S. teachers to become comfortable with the "student thinking focus" of lesson study lessons, and the cultural surround provides opportunities for shared think time and development, the skills sets of U.S. teachers are likely to put them in a position where they are not prepared to implement lesson study in the ways Japanese teachers do.

To be clear, I am talking about structural and cultural issues here. The cultural and administrative contexts of education in the U.S. result in most teachers having limited opportunities to develop certain kinds of skills. In some other nations teachers have much greater opportunity to develop those skills. The differences have nothing to do with the inherent capacity of teachers, or how hard they work. A secondary teacher in the U.S. may meet with 6 classes of 30 students during the workday. In addition to planning for the next day's lessons, that teacher will, if he or she spends just one minute per student looking over homework, spend three hours during the evening doing so. Part of the challenge in the U.S. context is that the workday is defined in ways that deny teachers the opportunities to grow professionally that are available to teachers in other nations.

A final contextual factor that must be considered as a component of teacher professionalism is teacher autonomy. The starkest current contrast may be between the U.S. and Finland. In Finland, trust in adequately prepared teachers, school systems willing to take responsibility for educational outcomes, and adequate resources are the key:

> Experience from Finland ... suggests that it is not enough to establish world-class teacher education programs or pay teachers well. Finland has built world-class teacher education programs. And Finland pays its teachers well. But the true Finnish difference may be that teachers in Finland may exercise their professional knowledge and judgment both widely and freely. They control curriculum, student assessment, school improvement, and community involvement. (Sahlberg 2012, p. 4)

Trends in those directions since the 1990s, says Sahlberg, are the main reasons for the stellar performance of the Finnish educational system. By contrast, the U.S. has seen strong trends in precisely the opposite direction. As elaborated below, the "standards" championed by the National Council of Teachers of Mathematics (1989) were intended in the following sense:

> A standard is a statement that can be used to judge the quality of a mathematics curriculum or methods of evaluation. Thus, standards are statements about what is valued. (NCTM 1989, p. 2)

However, the "standards movement," epitomized by the federal "No Child Left Behind" law (U.S. Department of Education; see http://www2.ed.gov/nclb/landing.jhtml) came instead to focus on "accountability"—the idea that students, schools, districts and states *must meet certain standards* or suffer the consequences. Standards became targets for performance, with rewards for meeting or exceeding them, and penalties for failing to do so. Federally enforced policy moved in reverse of the direction taken by Finland: in districts that failed to meet statewide standards (as determined by statewide examinations), teachers and schools were given less and less autonomy. In many schools "teaching to the test" became the norm, essentially negating the very idea of teacher autonomy.

In summary, values, goals and context matter. Different nations (if they operate at the national level; some devolve significant authority to states, provinces, or other such entities) emphasize different aspects of mathematical proficiency in their standards or curricula. The teaching forces in various nations have significantly different levels of preparation before they enter the classroom, comparably different opportunities for professional development or growth, and radically different levels of autonomy in structuring what takes place in their classrooms. A curriculum well suited to one context will be poorly suited for another. There is no "one size fits all" and no one curriculum direction, given the diversity of contexts in which teachers do their work. Attempts to move educational systems in any particular directions will have to be suited to the local educational ecologies—or (see the concluding discussion) conscious efforts will need to be made to alter those local ecologies.

Curricular Stories

Prologue: There Is More than Can Be Summarized in a Chapter

The forces that shape curricular evolution, and the tangled histories that result, are far more complex than can be dealt with in a chapter of this length (Just one example: As (some of) the U.S. was becoming enthralled with the kinds of lessons exemplified in the TIMSS videos of Japanese classrooms, the Japanese ministry of education was backing off from some of the underpinnings of those lessons.) Fine-grained detail is impossible here, but it exists. For a general overview of curriculum change in 15 nations spanning the globe, see Törner et al. (2007). That volume focuses on problem solving, but in that context, national curricular histories are given. In particular, my article (Schoenfeld 2007) provides a more extended discussion of trends in the U.S. up to 2007 than I can give here. I summarize those telegraphically, and then give more detail about events over the past half dozen years.

The United States

I think it is fair to say that for the most part, mathematics education received little attention during the bulk of the 20th century save for times when the nation was in crisis.[2] After World War II broke out, for example, the U. S. Office of Education and the National Council of Teachers of Mathematics (NCTM) jointly characterized the level of mathematical competency that schools needed to provide prior to students' entry into the military (see NCTM 1943). Likewise, the cold war had a significant impact on mathematics education. Following the launch of Sputnik in 1957, science and mathematics education were seen as major national security issues; in response to the Soviet threat, alliances of scientists, mathematicians, and educators produced novel curricula in the sciences and mathematics. In mathematics, the School Mathematics Study Group or SMSG curriculum (see http://www.lib.utexas.edu/taro/utcah/00284/cah-00284.html) exemplified what

---

[2]It was this perception that led to the formation of the Mathematical Sciences Education Board (MSEB) at the National Research Council. MSEB "was established in 1985 to provide "a continuing national overview and assessment capability for mathematics education." (National Research Council 1989, p. ii) The idea was to keep mathematics education from being put back on the "back burner" after the flurry of attention it was getting in the wake of the Japanese "economic miracle" of the 1970s.

came to be known as the "New Math"—which was perceived to have "failed" over the course of the 1960s and was replaced by a decade of "back to basics" instruction in the 1970s.[3]

The next crisis was economic rather than military. The "Japanese economic miracle" of the 1970s threatened to unseat the U.S. as the world's dominant economic power. The iconic response was the production of the report *A Nation at Risk* (National Commission on Excellence in Education 1983), which described the crisis as follows:

> Our Nation is at risk. Our once unchallenged preeminence in commerce, industry, science, and technological innovation is being overtaken by competitors throughout the world ... If an unfriendly foreign power had attempted to impose on America the mediocre educational performance that exists today, we might well have viewed it as an act of war. We have, in effect, been committing an act of unthinking, unilateral educational disarmament. (p. 1)

In addition to the economic crisis, there was evidence of American students' poor mathematical performance on the Second International Mathematics Study (McKnight et al. 1985a, 1985b, 1987). These could be seen as a mandate for change.

Change came. For political reasons (see Schoenfeld 2004, 2007) this change was stimulated not by the government, but from the National Council of Teachers of Mathematics, which undertook the task of creating a nationwide statement of high quality expectations—"standards"—for mathematics curriculum and evaluation. The NCTM's (1989) *Curriculum and evaluation standards for school mathematics*, which was grounded in the research of previous decades, opened up significant new territory. Previous discussions of curriculum desiderata focused on the content—the body of mathematics students should learn. The *Standards* broke new ground, focusing on mathematical processes as well as content. As in previous documents, the *Standards* listed (by grade band) the essentials of number, patterns, measurement, geometry, algebra, and pre-calculus (for college-intending students) that students should learn. But for every grade band, the first four standards concerned essential processes: mathematics as problem solving; as communication; as reasoning, and mathematical connections. Being able to *think mathematically*, as well as knowing certain bodies of mathematics, became part of the goal of a mathematics education. This was revolutionary.[4]

Aware of the fact that commercial publishers would not produce "standards-based" curricula on their own, the National Science Foundation supported the development of curricula aligned with the standards. Fast forward twenty-plus years, and standards-based curricula—which, although varied in style, are all demonstrably different from the "traditional" curricula that predominated in 1989[5]—hold a

---

[3]This is a gross over-simplification. Some of the ideas behind the creation of the New Math, such as attention to mathematical structure and the idea of "hands on" mathematics (parallel to "hands on" activities introduced in all of the alphabet curricula) live on to this day.

[4]And, it was controversial, giving rise to the "math wars." I will not discuss those here; see Schoenfeld (2004, 2007).

[5]Roughly speaking, the "traditional" curricula placed significant attention on conceptual and procedural knowledge, focusing on the bodies of skill that students were intended to master, and their

significant portion of the curriculum market. (Some estimates are that 25 % of the texts sold nationwide are standards-based, but publishers are notoriously secretive about sales figures and various hybrids exist, so it is hard to know what the actual figure might be.) What is not in doubt, however, is the main finding of the research literature: students who studied curricula that offered a balance of concepts, procedures, and problem solving did as well on tests of skills as students who studied from skills-oriented curricula, and far better on tests that called for using concepts and doing problem solving (Senk and Thompson 2003; Schoenfeld 2007). Here we shall simply stipulate that finding, and address two questions:

1. What are some of the main changes that characterize the standards-based curricula?
2. What trends have shaped the evolution of curricula over the past two decades, and what changes may they produce over the decade to come?

1. What are some of the main changes that characterize the standards-based curricula?

The 1989 NCTM *Standards* provided curriculum standards by grade bands (grades K-4, grades 5–8, grades 9–12), rather than by grade. They were also pedagogically agnostic, in that a wide range of pedagogical strategies were consistent with the intentions of the *Standards*. Thus they provided tremendous latitude in interpretation: As long as they were consistent with the broad outlines of the content standards in the *Standards* and paid specific attention to the process standards, curricula could claim to be standards-based. The NSF-supported standards-based curricula reflected a broad range of approaches and foci.[6] These included experiential, hands-on curricula, curricula that focused on applications, and curricula that used large thematic units in order to provide rich "surrounds" for the mathematical content they offered. Once again, I am painting with a very broad brush when I make statements about trends in those curricula. But, there were some clear trends. In what follows I draw very heavily on Lappan and Phillips (2009). Lappan and Phillips describe the history and development of the *Connected Mathematics Project* (*CMP*) curriculum, a widely distributed middle school standards-based curriculum. I also draw on exchanges with Zalman Usiskin and Diane Resek, who, respectively, played pivotal roles in the University of Chicago School Mathematics Project (2009) (which produced the preK-6 series *Everyday Mathematics* and UCSMP texts for middle and high school) and the *Interactive Mathematics Project* curriculum.

Lappan and Phillips describe their goals as follows:

---

conceptual underpinnings. Standards-based curricula placed a greater emphasis on the process standards discussed above: problem solving, communication, reasoning, connections.

[6]This was done in part because it makes good sense to have a range of models when trying something new, and in part in order to avoid putting NSF in the position of advancing a "national curriculum," which would have been extremely dangerous politically (see Schoenfeld 2004, 2007).

All students should be able to reason and communicate proficiently in mathematics. They should have knowledge of and skill in the use of the vocabulary, forms of representation, materials, tools, techniques, and intellectual methods of the discipline of mathematics. This knowledge should include the ability to define and solve problems with reason, insight, inventiveness, and technical proficiency. (Lappan and Phillips 2009, p. 4)

For many educators today, these goals—which are, I believe, shared by all of the standards-based curricula—may seem unexceptional. Of course one wants students to be powerful mathematical thinkers! But from the vantage point of the 1970s and to some degree the 1980s, they represent a major paradigm shift. No longer is the sole focus of the curriculum the specifics of the content that students should learn. That content is part of a student's "mathematical tool kit," with which the student solves problems,[7] reasons, and communicates.

This stance has not only curricular but also pedagogical implications. Standard 1 in NCTM's (1991) *Professional standards for teaching school mathematics*, entitled "Worthwhile Mathematical Tasks," says:

The teacher of mathematics should pose tasks that are based on—

- sound and significant mathematics;
- knowledge of students' understandings, interests, and experiences;
- knowledge of the range of ways that diverse students learn mathematics;

and that

- engage students' intellect;
- develop students' mathematical understandings and skills;
- stimulate students to make connections and develop a coherent framework for mathematical ideas;
- call for problem formulation, problem solving, and mathematical reasoning;
- promote communication about mathematics;
- represent mathematics as an ongoing human activity;
- display sensitivity to, and draw on, students' diverse background experiences and dispositions;
- promote the development of all students' dispositions to do mathematics. (NCTM 1991, p. 25)

Although this is presented as a curricular challenge it is also a fundamental professional development challenge. Having students grapple successfully with "worthwhile mathematical tasks" of the type described above requires a significant shift in classroom activity structures. Crafting environments in which students feel comfortable grappling with tasks that they do not necessarily know how to solve, often in small groups (remember the communication goals!), and providing enough support so that students do not flail but are not simply told "how to do it," is an enormous pedagogical challenge. This challenge is faced by teachers working with any of the

---

[7] All curricula have students solve problems, of course. But for pre-standards curricula, those problems were typically exercises similar to the examples students had been shown how to solve. In the new curricula, "problem solving" came to mean working on problems for which the precise solution methods had not been demonstrated.

standards-based curricula. Consider, for example, what it takes to orchestrate a productive conversation about problem 1.1 from the *Connected Mathematics* text given in Fig. 1.

Lappan and Phillips (2009) describe the challenges of designing tasks, such as Fig. 1, that present enough of the real world context so that the challenges can be meaningful, but do not, in asking students to perform various tasks, provide non-mathematical distractions. Resek (January 10, 2012) notes the degree of support required for differing classrooms—with "warm-ups" being useful for some classrooms to remind students of relevant skills and understandings, while they may be superfluous in others. The challenges of tailoring curricula to student needs should not be underestimated. Nor should the challenges of teacher knowledge. It is one thing to show students how to implement a particular procedure and monitor their execution of it, in "show and practice" mode. It is quite something else to be prepared to respond in the moment to the things students say (some seemingly sensible, some not) in ways that build on and shape their current understandings.

To take a somewhat different perspective on changes in curricula, let me move from goals to beliefs. Volume 40 of the *UCSMP Newsletter*, which introduced the third edition UCSMP materials, provided a recap of "some beliefs underlying the UCSMP Pre-K-12 curriculum." Here I cite three:

3. The scope of school mathematics should expand at all levels, including number and operation, algebra and functions, geometry and measurement, probability and statistics, and discrete mathematics.
4. The classroom should reflect the real world both in the choices of activities and problems and the choices of methods (paper and pencil, calculator, computer).
5. Students learn best when they are actively involved in their learning, and usually need practice and review over time in order to achieve mastery. (*UCSMP Newsletter, 40*, p. 1.)

These, too, reflect general trends in standards-based curricula, and are broadly consistent with the trends in the NCTM Standards documents (1989, 1991, 1995, 2000).

Finally, in terms of curricular criteria (in the U.S.), I note that the NCTM documents (particularly the 1991 NCTM *Professional standards for teaching school mathematics*) placed much greater emphasis on supporting classroom discourse around the relevant mathematics. This too makes significant demands on teachers. But it also makes significant demands on curriculum designers, in that curricula should provide the affordances for such classroom discourse. Thus, for example, one sees the following "criteria for a mathematics task" in the Connected Mathematics Project:

In our work a good task is one that supports some or all of the following:

- The problem has important, useful mathematics embedded in it.
- Investigating the problem should contribute to the conceptual development of important mathematical ideas.
- Work on the problem promotes the skillful use of mathematics.
- The problem has various solutions paths or allows different decisions or positions to be taken and defended.

Problem 1.1 Whole Numbers and Fractions

A. Based on the thermometer at the right for Day 2, which of the
following statements could the principal use to describe the
sixth-graders' progress?

- The sixth-graders have raised $100.
- The sixth-graders have reached $\frac{1}{4}$ of their goal.
- The sixth-graders have reached $\frac{2}{8}$ of their goal.
- The sixth-graders only have $225 left to meet their goal.
- The sixth-graders have completed 50% of their goal.
- At this pace, the sixth-graders should reach their goal in six
  more days.

B. Make up two more statements the principal could use in the
announcement.

C. 1. What are two claims the sixth-graders can make if they collect
$15 on the third day?

2. Draw and shade the thermometer for Day 3.

AC **Homework starts on page 12.**

Fractions like the ones the principal uses
can be written using two whole numbers
separated by a bar. For example, one
half is written $\frac{1}{2}$ and two eighths is
written $\frac{2}{8}$. The number above the bar is
the **numerator,** and the number
below the bar is the **denominator.**

As you work on the problems in this
unit, think about what the numerators
and denominators of your fractions
are telling you about each situation.

Goal
$300

Day 2

6   Bits and Pieces I

Fig. 1 Problem 1.1 from Bits and Pieces II, CMP 2

- The mathematical content of the problem should build on and connect to other important mathematical ideas.
- The problem requires higher-level thinking, reasoning, and problem solving.
- The problem should engage students and encourage classroom discourse.
- The problem creates an opportunity for the teacher to assess what his or her students are learning and where they are experiencing difficulty. (Lappan and Phillips 2009, p. 8)

In sum, standards-based curricula—a significant chunk of the textbook market in the U.S., but not a majority—have moved in very clear directions, consistent with the directions outlined in the various NCTM *Standards* documents. But what of the rest, and what is to come? There we must discuss politics.

2. What trends have shaped the evolution of curricula over the past two decades, and what changes may they produce over the decade to come?

I introduce the issue of politics with a quote from a piece I wrote at the turn of the century.

> In the political arena, "standards" may be evolving from a progressive to a conservative force. The move toward standards catalyzed by the National Council of Teachers of Mathematics was designed to focus on mathematical understanding. However, in the very recent past "standards" have been adopted as rhetorical banners for programs of testing and accountability. Many states have instituted strict testing regimens... These accountability tests tend to focus on the mastery of facts and procedures, since that is what can be tested cheaply and easily... Since the accountability measures are "high stakes," teachers feel compelled to focus on them, with a corresponding de-emphasis on the aspects of mathematics learning (reasoning, representation, problem solving, communication, making connections) that are not tested. (Schoenfeld 2001, p. 274)

This turned out, alas, to be prophetic. In 2001 the U.S. congress passed PL 107-110, the *No Child Left Behind Act*, known as NCLB. Paying homage to a political tradition of states' rights, NCLB said that each State was entitled to establish its own set of standards, and its own tests of those standards. But, to receive federal funding, the state had to produce a plan that would result in 100 % of its students being proficient (as measured by the state test) by 2014. Because of this, Hugh Burkhardt's coinage, WYTIWYG ("What You Test Is What You Get") became increasingly true nationwide. When test scores determine whether a student passes to the next grade, whether a teacher gets a raise or gets fired, whether a principal keeps his or her job, whether a school or school district has its management replaced, then testing drives the curriculum. If the tests do not represent high quality mathematics, then the quality of instruction suffers. It takes a brave teacher to teach for complex problem solving skills when the high stakes assessments focus on more mundane skills.

Consider, for example, the California State Tests. The entire test is multiple choice. Figures 2 and 3 offer two typical items from the Algebra I test.

These problems are trivial—and representative. For the past decade, tasks like this have been shaping instruction in California. That is about to change, and not just in California.

The largest change in the American educational landscape of the past decade is the emergence of the Common Core State Standards in Mathematics (CCSS-M;

Fig. 2 Released item from
the CST

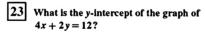

23 What is the y-intercept of the graph of
$4x + 2y = 12$?

A   −4

B   −2

C   6

D   12

CSA00239

Fig. 3 Released item from
the CST

25 Which *best* represents the graph of $y = 2x − 2$?

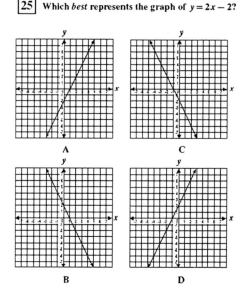

A   C

B   D

see www.corestandards.org/the-standards/mathematics). Because of a strong tradition of states' rights, suggestions of national standards, curricula and/or testing in the U.S. would provoke extremely strong resistance. Thus the successor to NCLB, called the "Race to the Top," set no mandate—but, it offered funding to consortia of states that produced collections of "high standards" and plans to meet them. The National Governors' Association and the Council of Chief State School Officers obtained funding to create a set of "voluntary" standards that were offered to all the states. States had the option to adopt the CCSS-M standards (which were likely to be "pre-approved" by the government), or they could join a consortium to craft their own. Ultimately all but five states (Alaska, Minnesota, Nebraska, Texas, and Virginia) adopted the CCSS-M, making them a de facto set of national standards.

The CCSS-M specify content progressions at the grade level. This may require some rearrangement on the part of curriculum developers who want to be "standards compliant." At least as important, however, is the fact that CCSS-M maintain the previous commitment to classroom activities that engage students *doing* mathematics. In the language of CCSS-M, the desired activities are called *practices*, but the

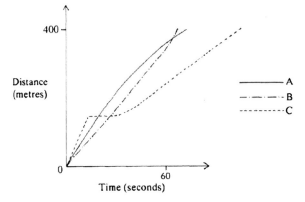

The rough sketch graph shown above describes what happens when 3 athletes A, B, and C enter a 400 metres high hurdles race.

Imagine that you are the race commentator. Describe what is happening as carefully as you can. You do not need to measure anything accurately.

Fig. 4 Hurdles Race

CCSS-M commitment to NCTM's framing of problem solving, reasoning and proof, communication, representation, and connections, as well as the NRC's (2001) concepts of adaptive reasoning, strategic competence, conceptual understanding, procedural fluency, and productive disposition, are made clear.

In short, there is great continuity with the process-oriented view that was a key component of the NCTM Standards volumes and the standards-based curricula. The question is, how much will the emphasis on *practices* matter in classrooms? The answer, assuming WYTIWIG, is that what happens in classrooms will be a function of the assessments that students and teachers face. Here too there is a new landscape.

As part of the Race to the Top, Federal funding supported the development of two assessment consortia, the Smarter Balanced Assessment Consortium (SBAC; see www.smarterbalanced.org/) and the Partnership for Assessment of Readiness for College and Careers (PARCC; see www.parcconline.org/). Roughly half of the states that have adopted the Common Core State Standards have signed up with each of the two assessment consortia, and will be using their assessments. Thus, rather than there being a patchwork of assessments across the nation, there will be (save for the five non-CCSS states) just two.

Both consortia have issued sets of specifications describing their intended assessments. As noted below, there is significant potential for things to change, so nothing that follows should be taken as carved in stone. But if things stay as they are now, things will be very different than they have been—at least in some states.

Consider, for example, the task "Hurdles Race," given in Fig. 4.

Content-wise, Hurdles Race demands a good deal more than the tasks in Figs. 2 and 3. To deal with it successfully, students must interpret distance-time graphs in a real-world context. This includes realizing that "to the left" is faster in the context of a distance-time graph (the racer whose graph crosses the $d = 400$ line to the left has reached that mark in less time). It means interpreting the point where two runners' graphs cross as meaning that, at that point in the race, the two runners are tied. It means recognizing that runner C was ahead at the beginning of the race, and that the horizontal line segment in C's graph indicates that C has stopped moving forward (presumably having tripped over a hurdle).

Moreover, the student must put all of this information together in an explanation that respects the chronology of the graph. This calls for perseverance. It calls for producing a coherent narrative that does justice to a real-world event. This is the kind of task that is likely to appear on the SBAC assessments: see SBAC (2012).[8]

The key to understanding the character of the SBAC summative assessments lies in their reporting structure. Typically, a mathematics test reports one score for a student. In contrast, the SBAC assessments are intended to report four scores, along the following dimensions:

Dimension 1, concepts and procedures: "Students can explain and apply mathematical concepts and interpret and carry out mathematical procedures with precision and fluency."

Dimension 2, problem solving: "Students can solve a range of complex well-posed problems in pure and applied mathematics, making productive use of knowledge and problem solving strategies."

Dimension 3, reasoning: "Students can clearly and precisely construct viable arguments to support their own reasoning and to critique the reasoning of others."

Dimension 4, modeling: "Students can analyze complex, real-world scenarios and can construct and use mathematical models to interpret and solve problems."

Given that the tests will be "high stakes," classroom activities are likely to fall more in line with these dimensions of mathematical activity. Note that this is entirely consistent with the goals for curricula quoted above from Lappan and Phillips (2009), and, more generally with the two volumes of NCTM standards, the CCSS-M (by design), and, in broad-brush terms, the standards-based curricula.

There are similarities and differences for the PARCC draft specifications. Somewhat in parallel, the PARCC summative assessments have three classes of tasks:

Type I: Tasks assessing concepts, skills and procedures;
Type II: Tasks assessing expressing mathematical reasoning;
Type III: Tasks assessing modeling / applications.

However, it is not clear whether PARCC will assign separate scores to student proficiency on tasks of types I, II, and III. PARCC appears to have committed itself to computer-based tests: sample tasks may be found, for example, through the links at http://www.parcconline.org/samples/mathematics/high-school-mathematics. Some of the questions (e.g., the golf balls" modeling task), given the technological medium, look very different from an "essay test" with the same questions and pose different demands.

---

[8] Hugh Burkhardt and I were the lead authors of the SBAC content specifications.

Because of the power of high stakes tests to drive curricula, it is hard to know where instruction in the U.S.—not just curricula—will be heading over the next decade. As I write, SBAC has not fully adopted the specs discussed above or released sample tests. (Sample items have been released.) Ultimately, what does get adopted will in large measure be a political decision. To date, PARCC has released even less information. Moreover, it is not yet clear how well the SBAC and PARCC assessments are aligned with each other. How they will drive curricula, and in what directions, remains to be seen.

Snapshots of other Nations

As noted above, curricular trends vary substantially across the globe, as do the traditions underlying them and the support structures for implementing them. Here I offer either summaries or quotes in response to my requests for information about trends in various nations. See the ZDM special issue *Problem solving around the world—summing up the state of the art* (Törner et al. 2007) for additional detail.

The Netherlands

Paul Drijvers (personal communication, May 21, 2012) reported that trends in Dutch mathematics education are diverse.

On the one hand, we still have investigation tasks in secondary school (e.g., see http://www.fisme.science.uu.nl/alympiade/en/welcome.html and http://www.fisme.science.uu.nl/wisbdag/, the latter only in Dutch). Also, the new 2015 curriculum explicitly mentions problem solving and modeling skills, in the frame of overall "thinking activities." ... Most textbooks for secondary school still make use of many contexts, even if these problem situations are in many cases far from realistic and their use is very limited, and may even have a tendency to just 'dress up' the mathematics.

On the other hand, there is an important back-to-the-basics movement, with a strong focus on arithmetic and algebraic by-hand skills, knowledge on how to carry out rules for simplification, solving equations, and differentiation. From this perspective, the realistic approach is questioned and we see textbook series and national examinations following this trend. The role of technology is criticized as well. The ministry is introducing examinations in arithmetic skills in addition to the mathematics national examinations.

Great Britain

There is a significant amount of detail in Hugh Burkhardt's chapter in this volume, "Curriculum Design and Systemic Change." Burkhardt's jaundiced summary of problem solving (personal communication, May 21, 2012) is that curricular work on problem solving "goes back to 1870, peaks in 1945, with a false dawn in the

1980s, [and was] choked off by the National Curriculum." This is not unlike the history of mathematical modeling, in which there have been a number of exemplary projects (existence proofs) but nothing that has had lasting impact and is deeply embedded in current curricula. More generally, there appears to be a certain level of entropy: the National Curriculum has had various revisions since 1989, with the most recent promised revisions under the Tory government delayed.

Germany

Germany appears to be somewhat in a state of flux, according to information from Guenter Toerner and Kristina Reiss. In some ways, the situation appears to parallel the situation in the U.S. (though with significant allowances for cultural context, teacher support, etc.):

> The state of the education system and its prospects for development have become the subject of increasing debate in Germany since publication of the TIMSS results … In recent months, the Forum Bildung, a working party set up by the German federation and states to elaborate recommendations for educational reform, and the tremendous response to the PISA study … have given this debate an intensity and a range not seen in years. (German Federal Ministry of Education and Research 2004, p. 7)

With sixteen Bundesländer and perhaps 50 different curricula at primary, lower secondary, and upper secondary school (gymnasium), the quest for national standards and coherence has been a challenge; it is difficult to paint a simple picture of current events. Yet, there are trends. Modeling and applications are getting more attention than before. And, perhaps most interestingly, there is a change in language: German standards now emphasize *competencies* rather than *knowledge*. Competencies are defined as "cognitive abilities and skills possessed by or able to be learned by individuals that enable them to solve particular problems, as well as the motivational, volitional and social readiness and capacity to utilise the solutions successfully and responsibly in variable situations" (Weinert 2001, p. 27).

One sees, then, moves toward coherence grounded in a set of standards that emphasize a broader set of competencies than descriptions of content knowledge.

France

The French, as Artigue and Houdement (2007) indicate, have a curricular and didactic history that is at some remove from the traditions of the other nations discussed in this chapter. Problem solving *per se* has never been a major theme in French curricula, although problems themselves play a central role. Artigue and Houdement indicate that the dominant theoretical frames in French didactic research are Brousseau's theory of didactic situations (Brousseau 1997) and Chevallard's anthropological theory of didactics (Chevallard 1992). Both of these theoretical orientations bring unique perspectives to classroom activities in France: Brousseau's by virtue of the core idea that classroom activities can be structured in ways that are inherently mathematical, and that reveal student conceptions to the teacher (see, e.g., Schoenfeld 2012), Chevallard's by way of situating classroom actions within the larger context of school, schooling, and society. These, of course, are developments over the past quarter century; and they have not fully permeated the French school system. In another paper, for example, Artigue (2011) traces the history of the high school teaching of calculus in France as an example of curricular change. That paper documents seven distinct periods of instruction over the course of the 20th century.

China

Chinese mathematics education has its own very strong traditions, which tend to separate curricular development in China from that in other nations. As Cai and Nie (2007) indicate, "research in China has been much more content and experience-based than cognitive and empirical-based." (p. 459) That said, it should be noted that the tradition of honoring and sharing beautifully designed lessons—with journals devoted to such activities—flourishes in China, as a robust complement to the kind of research done in the West.

But, curricula in China are changing rapidly, partly as a function of deliberate study of some practices in the West. Liu and Li (2010) report that, prior to 2001, "mathematics education in China held an important but simplified objective: acquisition of knowledge and skills." (p. 11) From 1996 to 1998 the Chinese undertook the systematic study of curricula in Western nations, and curriculum reform and curriculum standards for all disciplines were released in 2001. There were major changes, these being the first three:

> 1. Curriculum objectives: moving away from over-emphasizing knowledge acquisition to emphasizing the formation of students' positive attitudes toward learning, so that students can learn how to learn and develop positive attitudes in the process of learning basic knowledge and skills.
> 2. Curriculum structure: moving away from over-emphasizing content-based subjects, having too many school subjects and lack of integration. School curriculum needs to be structured with balance, comprehensiveness, and selectivity.
> 3. Curriculum content ... needs to emphasize its connections with students' life and knowledge development in science and technology, pay close attention to students' interests and their experiences, and carefully select those basic knowledge and skills needed for students' life-long learning." (Liu and Li 2010, p. 14)

One can be sure that, although these goals echo those from the west, their instantiation in curricular practice will take root in ways that are unique to Chinese context and history.

Japan

For my final example we return to the somewhat more familiar territory. For many years American mathematics educators have been inspired by aspects both of Japanese curriculum and professional development, e.g., the ideas that one rich problem could be the source of a whole lesson's activities, and that (at least at the elementary level, through lesson study) teacher communities could serve as the ongoing homes for the professional development of the teaching force. As Hino (2007) portrays it, Japanese mathematics educators were strongly influenced by the NCTM's recommendations that "problem solving should be the focus of school instruction," from the 1980s on. Some would argue that the Japanese, with help from their Ministry of Education (which revises the Course of Study every 10 years) were more successful than the U.S. in doing so.

Here too, it would be a mistake to assume stability or unidirectionality. As Koyama (2010) notes in his chronological survey of Japanese curricular trends, there have been some significant changes, even after the adoption of "problem solving" as a major theme. Here is Koyama's survey of the two decades from 1988 to 2007.

- *Integration of Cognitive and Affective Aspects (1988–1997)*
  In 1989 the Courses of Study were revised to integrate cognitive and affective aspects. For example: ... "To help students develop their abilities to consider daily life problems insightfully and logically, and thereby foster their attitudes to appreciate the way of thinking mathematically, and to willingly make use of the above mentioned qualities and abilities in their lives."

- *Latitude through Intensive Selection of Teaching Contents (1998–2007)*
  During these ten years, such problems as 'un-schooling' and 'classroom in crisis' have became quite notable and they were attributed to the excessively stressed life of students. Therefore the Courses of Study were revised and the teaching and learning contents were slimmed down intensively. About 30 % of mathematical content was removed from elementary school and lower secondary school levels. (Koyama 2010, p. 62)

Discussion

I trust that the snapshots above have made one point clear: there is no single worldwide trend in curricula. Curricula are, in deep ways, a function of a nation's history and culture, its governance structures, and the kinds of support given teachers in their professional lives. Moreover, within any one nation, one sees radical shifts over the course of time—often in contradictory directions. This raises two questions: (1) is there such a thing as progress? And (2) what can one do, profitably, with the great diversity of curricular trends that one sees worldwide?

Is there Such a Thing as Progress?

I believe so. When I entered the field as a researcher, the dominant paradigm for classroom research was the process-product paradigm, which was essentially correlational; curricula were similarly evaluated by controlled experiments; we had little or no idea of how to understand a student's 20-minute attempt at problem solving, much less the blooming complexity of the classroom; and, curricula focused on content, with little or no explicit attention to the concepts of mathematical thinking processes or practices. Over the decades since the 1970s, our understanding of learning and teaching has grown dramatically—and, there has been a lovely dialectic between what we understand and the evolution of curricula over that time period. The 1989 NCTM *Curriculum and evaluation standards* were inspired by research, and set the stage for the first wave of standards-based curricula. There is clear evidence (e.g., Senk and Thompson 2003) that they make a difference. The evolution of standards in the U.S., from the 1989 *Standards* to the 2000 volume of *Principles and Standards* to the Common Core State standards, represents increasing sophistication as well as a better understanding of the political surround that envelops curricular practices.

One can hardly be sanguine about the role (or power) of politics; it can be a powerful force both for the benefit of students and to their detriment. But, looking at curricula now in place in the U.S. as opposed to the one I learned from, one sees significant progress. There are many ups and downs, and retrogressions—but on average, curricula are more mathematically rich, as well as being tailored to be accessible to a far larger proportion of the school population. That is in the U.S., but I am reasonably confident that comparable statements (regarding the long view) could be made across much of the globe.

What can one do, profitably, with the great diversity of curricular trends that one sees worldwide?

As I have noted, it is a mistake to think one can simply import good curricula or effective pedagogical practices from one country into another. Singaporean textbooks "work" because Singaporean teachers are well prepared to teach from them, for example. So, what can one do?

Cross-national comparisons are tremendously valuable in helping one to understand one's strengths and one's weaknesses, and also to realize that things don't necessarily have to be the way they are. I grew up, for example, assuming that the "ninth grade algebra, tenth grade geometry, eleventh grade advanced algebra" curriculum was the only way to do things. It was a surprise to discover that the U.S. was a singular point in that regard, and that most of the world offered integrated curricula. And, when I began studying problem solving, I was astounded by the challenges offered by the Russian and Hungarian problem books. It would have been unthinkable at the time to imagine that such problems could be offered to students in the U.S. But, once one realizes that such things can be done, doors are opened. The same goes for structural supports for the professional development for teachers, and organizing the contexts of work in ways that become learning communities for teachers (cf. Japan and Finland).

There is, of course, a substantial amount of cross-national comparative research. But, I think it could be expanded or focused in ways that would be beneficial to all concerned. For one thing, it would be good to be much more explicit about the goals and underpinnings of the exams that are used for cross-national comparisons (TIMSS and PISA). Better yet, it would be good to construct exams that explicitly aim at assessing the wide range of understandings that represent the *union* of mathematical goals for students, and that report out different dimensions of mathematical proficiency. The dimensions of concepts and procedures, problem solving, producing and critiquing reasoning, and mathematical modeling would seem to be a good start in this direction.

Alongside this, the systematic study of how different nations are organized systemically with regard to mathematics education could help all of us learn from one another. Some of this information exists, but not in a way that supports a meaningful and potentially productive compare-and-contrast across nations, or the meaningful adaptation of ideas and artifacts from one culture to another. One could imagine a project in which teams of scholars from nations across the globe put together the following kinds of information about each nation:

- What is the history of curricular change?
- How does curriculum change take place? Who makes decisions, and how are support structures put in place? What are the impediments to change?
- What is the role of research in the process?
- What are the systemic levers (e.g., high stakes testing) for supporting change and how powerful a (positive or negative) role do they play?
- The nature and processes of change: are they stable and evolutionary (as Japan was for many years), unpredictable (as the U.S. has been), or something in between?
- Systemic affordances and constraints—what resources are available; what kinds of changes are plausible, given systemic organization and resources; what kinds of changes would be difficult because of various limiting factors?
- As one major example, consider teaching as a profession:

  - How well are teachers regarded, how well paid are they?
  - What opportunities for learning and professional development do teachers have?
  - How knowledgeable are teachers? How well prepared might they be for implementing problem solving, supporting robust mathematical conversations among students, etc.?
  - What is the career trajectory of teachers? What are the demographics of the teaching force? (For example, in the U.S., 50 % of new teachers leave the profession within 5 years—a higher percentage in urban districts.)

- Case studies of curriculum change: what succeeded, for what reasons (in terms of organization, supports, etc.); what did not succeed, for what reasons?

With such information it might be possible to understand, for example, how Japanese lesson study functions as a form of professional development and what cultural and intellectual support structures are necessary for it to be productive; what kinds of preparation and what kinds of structural supports are necessary for teachers to make effective use of Singaporean curricula; what kinds of teacher preparation, societal incentives, and institutional "surrounds" are needed in order for the kinds of teacher autonomy heralded in Finland to be productive; and so on. Understanding the culturally embedded nature of curricular change in other nations may enable people to think more productively about how to foster effective curriculum change within their own cultural and educational ecologies.

References

Artigue, M. (2011). Les questions de développement curriculaire à travers un exemple: l'enseignement de l'analyse en France au lycée depuis le début du XXème siècle. *Quadrante, XX*(1), 7–29 (Issues of curriculum development through an example: the teaching of analysis in school in France from the early twentieth century).

Artigue, M., & Houdement, C. (2007). Problem solving in France: didactic and curricular perspectives. *ZDM. Zentralblatt für Didaktik der Mathematik, 39*(5–6), 365–382.

Brousseau, G. (1997). *Theory of didactical situations in mathematics (1970–1990)*. Dordrecht: Kluwer.

Burkhardt, G. H. (2013). Curriculum design and systemic change. In Y. Li & G. Lappan (Eds.), *Mathematics curriculum in school education*. Dordrecht: Springer.

Burkhardt, G. H. (May 21, 2012). Personal communication.

Cai, J., & Nie, B. (2007). Problem solving in Chinese mathematics education: research and practice. In G. Törner, A. H. Schoenfeld, & K. Reiss (Eds.), *Problem solving around the world— summing up the state of the art*. Special issue of the *Zentralblatt für Didaktik der Mathematik, 39*(5–6), 459–474.

Chevallard, Y. (1992). Concepts fondamentaux de la didactique. Perspectives apportées par une approche anthropologique (Fundamental concepts of teaching. Perspectives brought by an anthropological approach.). *Recherches en Didactique des Mathématiques, 12*(1), 73–112.

Drijvers, P. (2012). Personal communication.

Fernandez, C., & Yoshida, M. (2004). *Lesson study: a Japanese approach to improving mathematics teaching and learning*. Mahwah: Erlbaum.

Foresman, S. (2001). *California mathematics, grade 6*. Glenview: Scott Foresman.

German Federal Ministry of Education and Research (2004). *The development of national educational standards: an expertise*. Berlin: Federal Ministry of Education and Research.

Hino, K. (2007). Toward the problem-centered classroom: trends in mathematical problem solving in Japan. In G. Törner, A. H. Schoenfeld, & K. Reiss (Eds.), *Problem solving around the world— summing up the state of the art*. Special issue of the *Zentralblatt für Didaktik der Mathematik, 39*(5–6), 503–514.

Koyama, M. (2010). Mathematics curriculum in Japan. In F. K. S. Leung & Y. Li (Eds.), *Reforms and issues in school mathematics in East Asia: pursuing excellence in mathematics curriculum and teacher education* (pp. 59–78). Rotterdam: Sense Publishers.

Lappan, G., & Phillips, E. (2009). Challenges in U.S. mathematics education through a curriculum developer lens. *Educational Designer, 1*(3). Downloaded January 10, 2009, from http://www.educationaldesigner.org/ed/volume1/issue3/article11/.

Li, Y., & Huang, R. (2013). *How Chinese teach mathematics and improve teaching*. New York: Routledge.

Liu, J., & Li, Y. (2010). Mathematics curriculum reform in the Chinese mainland: changes and challenges. In F. K. S. Leung & Y. Li (Eds.), *Reforms and issues in school mathematics in East Asia: pursuing excellence in mathematics curriculum and teacher education* (pp. 9–31). Rotterdam: Sense Publishers.

Lortie, D. C. (1975). *Schoolteacher: a sociological study*. Chicago: University of Chicago Press.

McKnight, C., Travers, K., Crosswhite, J., & Swafford, J. (1985a). Eighth grade mathematics in the secondary schools: a report from the second international mathematics study. *Arithmetic Teacher, 32*(8), 20–26.

McKnight, C., Travers, K., & Dossey, J. (1985b). Twelfth grade mathematics in U.S. high schools: a report from the second international mathematics study. *Mathematics Teacher, 78*(4), 292–300.

McKnight, C., Crosswhite, J., Dossey, J., Kifer, E., Swafford, J., Travers, K., & Cooney, T. (1987). *The underachieving curriculum: assessing U.S. mathematics from an international perspective.* Champaign: Stipes Publishing Company.

Mullis, I. V. S., Martin, M. O., & Foy, P. (with Olson, J. F., Preuschoff, C., Erberber, E., Arora, A., & Galia, J.) (2008). *TIMSS 2007 international mathematics report: findings from IEA's trends in international mathematics and science study at the fourth and eighth grades.* Chestnut Hill: TIMSS & PIRLS International Study Center, Boston College.

National Commission on Excellence in Education (1983). *A nation at risk.* Washington: U.S. Government Printing Office.

National Commission on Excellence in Education (1943). Essential mathematics for minimum army needs. *Mathematics Teacher, 6,* 243–282.

National Council of Teachers of Mathematics (1989). *Curriculum and evaluation standards for school mathematics.* Reston: NCTM.

National Council of Teachers of Mathematics (1991). *Professional standards for teaching school mathematics.* Reston: NCTM.

National Council of Teachers of Mathematics (1995). *Assessment standards for school mathematics.* Reston: NCTM.

National Council of Teachers of Mathematics (2000). *Principles and standards for school mathematics.* Reston: NCTM.

National Research Council (1989). *Everybody counts: a report to the nation on the future of mathematics education.* Washington: National Academy Press.

National Research Council (2001). Adding it up: helping children learn mathematics. J. Kilpatrick, J. Swafford, and B. Findell (Eds.). Mathematics Learning Study Committee, Center for Education, Division of Behavioral and Social Sciences and Education. Washington: National Academy Press.

OECD Programme for International Student Assessment (PISA) (2010). *PISA 2009 results: what students know and can do: student performance in reading, mathematics and science* (Vol. I). Paris: OECD.

Park, K., & Leung, F. (2006). Mathematics lessons in Korea: teaching with systematic variation. In D. Clarke, C. Keitel, & Y. Shimizu (Eds.), *Mathematics classrooms in twelve countries: the insider's perspective* (pp. 247–262). Rotterdam: Sense Publishers.

Resek, D. (January 10, 2012) Personal communication.

Sahlberg, P. (2012). *Finnish lessons: what can the world learn from educational change in Finland?* New York: Teachers College Press.

Schoenfeld, A. H. (2001). Mathematics education in the 20th century. In L. Corno (Ed.), *Education across a century: the centennial volume (100th yearbook of the national society for the study of education)* (pp. 239–278). Chicago: National Society for the Study of Education.

Schoenfeld, A. H. (2004). The math wars. *Educational Policy, 18*(1), 253–286.

Schoenfeld, A. H. (2007). Problem solving in the United States, 1970–2008: research and theory, practice and politics. In G. Törner, A. H. Schoenfeld, & K. Reiss (Eds.), *Problem solving around the world—summing up the state of the art.* Special issue of the *Zentralblatt für Didaktik der Mathematik, 39*(5–6), 537–551.

Schoenfeld, A. H. (2012). Problematizing the didactic triangle. *ZDM—The International Journal of Mathematics Education, 44,* 587–599.

Senk, S. L. & Thompson, D. R. (Eds.) (2003). *Standards-based school mathematics curricula: what are they? What do students learn?* Mahwah: Erlbaum.

Smarter Balanced Assessment Consortium (2012). Content specifications for the summative assessment of the *Common Core State Standards for Mathematics.* Can be downloaded from http://www.smarterbalanced.org/wordpress/wp-content/uploads/2011/12/Math-Content-Specifications.pdf.

Stigler, J., & Hiebert, J. (1999). *The teaching gap.* New York: The Free Press.

Takahashi, A. (2004). Ideas for establishing lesson study communities. *Teaching Children Mathematics, 2004,* 436–443.

Törner, G., Schoenfeld, A. H., & Reiss, K. (Eds.) (2007). *Problem solving around the world—summing up the state of the art.* Special issue of the *Zentralblatt für Didaktik der Mathematik,* *39*(5–6).

University of Chicago School Mathematics Project (2009). *UCSMP newsletter #40.* Chicago: University of Chicago.

Weinert, F. E. (2001). Vergleichende Leistungsmessung in Schulen—eine umstrittene Selbstverständlichkeit. In F. E. Weinert (Ed.), *Leistungsmessungen in Schulen* (pp. 17–31). Weinheim and Basel: Beltz Verlag. (Weinert, F. E. Comparative performance measurement in schools—a controversial matter of course. In F. E. Weinert (Ed.), *Performance measures in schools* (pp. 17–31). Weinheim: Beltz Verlag).

Part II
Curriculum and Policy

Preface

As information sharing has become virtually instantaneous, the policies that drive curriculum and examples of specific curriculum have become available to both developers and policy makers around the world. Writers have access to ideas that can impact current and future editions of curricula and of testing. However, this is a two way street. Policy makers who hold the power to influence the curriculum need the assessments that are created and used to evaluate what students have learned. This raises the question of whether the testing actually gives the field information or establishes the boundaries for what curriculum writers can create to help teachers engage students in the study of mathematics. In the case of the US, the relatively new Common Core State Standards for Mathematics (CCSSM) has instigated revisions of nearly all established curricula across the 50 States. The timeline for the first CCSSM assessments has driven this round of curriculum revision in the US. If the CCSSM remains stable for a few years, it is likely that the development and revision of current curricula will intentionally reflect the CCSSM. However, what is unknown at present is whether the CCSSM will remain stable or will be revised to reflect changes in policy as US Presidents change. From a broader international perspective, one thing is certain: curricula from around the world are likely to have an influence on curriculum writers, regardless of where they reside. The results of this influence can be a significant improvement in the quality of schooling for students regardless of the country in which they reside. The worldwide melting pot for policy and curricula has the potential to raise the level of mathematical understanding and use across the world in significant ways. It is in this spirit that this part of the book provides rich information for us to learn about different policy and perspectives that are developed and used in various educational systems around the world.

In 2008, Charles M. Payne published a book entitled "So Much Reform, So Little Change." The subtitle is "The Persistence of Failure in Urban Schools." In the book he articulated "impediments to program implementation". Here are three of his concerns: inappropriate pace and scale of change (a tendency to try to do too much too quickly), discounting the social and political environment, and a lack of program coherence. For readers who have curriculum development experience, these three ring especially true. Change is hard. Teachers who have established certain routines in their classrooms over time find it difficult to give students the freedom to do more proposing, thinking, solving and articulating results. However, unless the students are charged with and allowed to do the thinking and reasoning, the mathematics developed is unlikely to be accessible to them in new situations. Consequently, change is necessary for improving students' learning of mathematics, not only at the policy level but also throughout the process of curriculum development and implementation. Learning about different policies and perspectives that are developed and used in different educational systems can certainly help us to reflect on our own curriculum policy and practice.

The chapters in this section reflect the state of the curriculum in 9 education systems across the world. A thread through all of the system reports is a focus on the articulation of system policies and the expected impact of the curriculum on student performance. By examining the differences in system policies and how such policies may affect the performance of students in different system contexts, we get a picture of different cultures and different expectations. We also have an opportunity to consider new ideas and ways of engaging students that may have significant impact on their learning.

In Chapter 5, Khoon Yoong Wong, Masataka Koyama, and Kyeong-Hwa Lee describe mathematics curriculum policies in Japan, Korea, and Singapore. The similarities and differences among the policies in these three education systems raise interesting questions for consideration. For example, can a curriculum that is designed for and used in a particular education system be used with the similar expected results in another system? Other than language, what are the obstacles to be overcome for such a transition of curriculum to succeed? Based on a framework proposed in this chapter, the authors emphasize the importance of studying mathematics curriculum policies and suggest further research in this topic area.

Chapter 6, contributed by Hak Ping Tam together with five other scholars, focuses on the Chinese mainland, Hong Kong, and Taiwan. These education systems have had longstanding success in producing students who excel in mathematics, and they share many similarities in terms of system structures and the general process of curriculum development and implementation. Yet, changes in curriculum policy and practices have been frequent from time to time to address different issues in these three education systems. As the interaction among education systems around the teaching and learning of mathematics has escalated, the spread of mathematics materials designed in different education systems around the world has also escalated. This wealth of information has the potential to improve the understanding and use of mathematics across the world. Examining the decisions made in these three systems gives insight into the similarities and differences and the possible results of these differences, and raises questions for other systems to consider.

In Chapter 7, Hung-Hsi Wu discusses the potential impact on curriculum in the US where nearly all of the 50 states have made a commitment to the Common Core State Standards, CCSSM. In such a decentralized education system, CCSSM functions as a leading force in changing curriculum development and practices in most states of the country. Wu specifies the challenges in helping teachers in the curriculum implementation process. The national testing will reflect the CCSSM and will provide a picture of students' facility with mathematics across the US. This kind of information is likely to be a wakeup call for states with underperforming students. In the long run, the CCSSM testing may stimulate greater attention to university teacher education, mathematics education, and to the support of practising teachers.

Chapters 8 and 9 provide curriculum information about Brazil and Australia, but from different perspectives. Chapter 8 focuses on educational directives and public policies related to mathematics education in Brazil, whereas Chapter 9 considers the recent development of the Australian mathematics curriculum and what challenges teachers face in their instantiation of the curriculum into classroom lessons.

Taken together, these chapters give us insight into mathematics education in different systems across the world. They also present us a charge to improve what we are offering to teachers and students in our mathematics programs at all levels. Additionally, the information in these chapters can give test developers and curriculum writers information and a challenge to create tests and curriculum that can support a World-class education for students and their teachers in all systems.

Michigan State University, USA   Glenda Lappan
Texas A&M University, USA   Yeping Li

References

Payne, C. M. (2008). *So much reform, so little change: the persistence of failure in urban schools.* Boston: Harvard Education Press.

Mathematics Curriculum Policies: A Framework with Case Studies from Japan, Korea, and Singapore

Khoon Yoong Wong, Masataka Koyama, and Kyeong-Hwa Lee

Abstract Mathematics curriculum policy (MCP) can be differentiated from mathematics curriculum by the former's focus on the objectives of mathematics education and practices implemented at different systemic levels by different groups of stakeholders to bring about those objectives, whereas the latter covers mostly mathematics curriculum standards, resource materials, and teaching strategies. Not much has been written about MCP in different education systems. In this chapter, we attempt to fill this "gap" by proposing a framework to cover four aspects of MCP: (a) policies about mathematics curriculum, the "what"? (b) agents who are engaged in policy-making, the "who"? (c) factors that influence the design of MCP within a particular "environment", and (d) future directions of MCP. We will illustrate these four aspects by citing our experiences with MCP in three Asian countries, namely, Japan, Korea, and Singapore. Further research in mathematics curriculum policy can be stimulated through in-depth descriptions of intra-national experiences of policy formulation and implementation and inter-national analyses of similar experiences.

Keywords Mathematics curriculum policy · Japan · Korea · Singapore · Policy-making

Introduction

Policies matter. They are statements, actions, or decisions that apply to a well-defined group of people to serve a fairly long-term goal in terms of years rather than weeks or months. They are "designed to bring about desired goal" (Trowler

K.Y. Wong (✉)
National Institute of Education, Nanyang Technological University, Singapore, Singapore
e-mail: khoonyoong.wong@nie.edu.sg

M. Koyama
Hiroshima University, Hiroshima, Japan

K.-H. Lee
Seoul National University, Seoul, Korea

Y. Li, G. Lappan (eds.), *Mathematics Curriculum in School Education*,
Advances in Mathematics Education, DOI 10.1007/978-94-007-7560-2_5,
© Springer Science+Business Media Dordrecht 2014

2003, p. 95). Policies should be differentiated from expedient administrative acts or quick fixes that may not be aligned with these goals and espoused principles.

Curriculum policies specifically direct *what* to teach in schools, *how* to teach it, *who* does the teaching, and *who* the learners are. Mathematics curriculum policies are discipline specific and overlap with general curriculum policies in broad education and socio-political contexts within a country. They include policies about those aspects of mathematics curriculum that differ from policies for other disciplines such as sciences, languages, and arts.

However, "mathematics curriculum policy" (MCP) is less written about than mathematics curriculum. Mathematics curriculum (MC) has been studied extensively in terms of intended standards, textbooks and curriculum materials, implemented classroom practices, and achieved outcomes. This disparity in coverage between MCP and MC becomes quite evident as we are not able to locate seminal papers about MCP from literature and search engines. In this chapter, we attempt to fill this "gap" by proposing a framework to cover four aspects of MCP: (a) policies about mathematics curriculum, the "what"? (b) agents who are engaged in policy-making, the "who"? (c) factors that influence the design of MCP within a particular "environment", and (d) future directions of MCP. We will illustrate these four aspects by citing our experiences with MCP in three Asian countries, namely, Japan, Korea, and Singapore. However, space for this chapter does not allow us to discuss the implementation of these policies: dissemination of policies to the target audiences and their buy-in, training of teachers and curriculum leaders to implement the policies, processes for monitoring compliance of policies, refinement of policies with time as a new cycle of policy-making or their repeal, and other related matters.

Contents of Mathematics Curriculum Policies: The "What"?

In the past two decades, international comparative studies such as the Trends in International Mathematics and Science Study (TIMSS) and the Programme for International Student Assessment (PISA) have stimulated major reforms in mathematics curriculum in many countries. Reports on high performing school systems such as the two McKinsey reports (Auguste et al. 2010; Barber and Mourshed 2007) have advanced important issues that are relevant to MCP, such as the recruitment of qualified teachers. National reports from several countries have also highlighted the importance of joining the global movement to define 21st century literacy and skills for future generations of students who will grow up in the digital world. Examples include The Partnership for 21st Century Skills in the United States (http://www.p21.org/overview), the Japan! Rise again! (http://www.mext.go.jp/english/elsec/index.htm), and the 21st Century Competencies (21CC) in Singapore (http://www.moe.gov.sg/media/press/2010/03/moe-to-enhance-learning-of-21s.php). These frameworks call for the inculcation of creative thinking and problem solving, use of information and communication technologies

(ICT), and communication and collaboration skills. These competencies are expected to be included in the mathematics curriculum, and they form crucial items in MCP.

In addition to the generic 21st century competencies mentioned above, some policies specific to the mathematics curriculum in Japan, Korea, and Singapore are listed in Table 1. They constitute the "contents" or "what" of MCP. This list is not exhaustive but it does highlight some important policies that are common to the three countries. Some of these policies may be more important in some countries than others, and paying attention to differential details in similar policies can help educators search for new possibilities for their own countries.

Agents and Policy Formulation of Mathematics Curriculum Policies: The "Who"?

In these three countries, different agents are responsible for formulating MCP. Table 2 is a framework we have designed to highlight and compare the main agents and their roles and responsibilities in the three countries.

These agents work at different levels of the country's education system and their responsibilities likewise vary considerably across the countries. The roles included in this framework cover the development of vision statements, values, and contents of the policies, negotiating between conflicts of these values and contents among different stake-holders, sourcing for evidence to support certain policies, proposing guidelines for policy implementations, producing curriculum documents, obtaining buy-in from other relevant parties, and so forth. The framework summarises the agents at five organisational levels, viz. nation, regions, teacher education institutes, schools, and classrooms. However, we will concentrate on official education agents, acknowledging that in some countries, non-official and non-education agents, such as professional associations, textbook publishers, commercial providers of ICT resources, politicians, journalists, community leaders, and even parents may play significant roles in debating curriculum matters, including the allocation of resources to support curriculum implementation and reforms.

In Table 2, the scope and levels of the responsibilities of respective agents towards MCP at a specific organizational level are indicated by three numbers: 1 = Low, 2 = Moderate, 3 = High. These levels, though quite crude, allow for rough comparisons of the relative degrees of involvement in MCP across the three countries. A more refined approach will contribute toward more in-depth comparative analyses of these agents and roles in other countries.

In Japan, the Course of Study (CS) for mathematics as a national mathematics curriculum has been revised and reissued approximately once every ten years since the establishment of the Japanese Constitution and the Fundamental Law of Education in 1947. The history of mathematics education in Japan seems to follow the worldwide trends of mathematics education, like a pendulum swinging back and forth, with its own specific features in each period reflecting the Japanese culture

Table 1 Some key mathematics curriculum policies in Japan, Korea, and Singapore

No.	Mathematics Curriculum Policies	Japan	Korea	Singapore
1.	Mathematics is taught in …	• Japanese.	• Korean.	• English.
2.	Mathematics is a compulsory subject.	• Grades 1 to 10. • About 5 hours per week at primary and about 3.5 hours per week at lower secondary levels. About 1500 hours of instruction in mathematics in 10 years. • Choices of different syllabuses from Grade 11 onwards.	• Grades 1 to 10. • About 4 hours per week at primary and 4 hours per week at secondary levels. About 1500 hours of instruction in mathematics in 10 years. • Choices of different syllabuses from Grade 11 onwards.	• Grades 1 to 10. • About 5 hours per week at primary and 4 hours per week at secondary levels. About 1600 hours of instruction in mathematics in 10 years. • Choices of different syllabuses from Grade 5 onwards. • Grades 11 & 12, about 95 % of students take mathematics.
3.	Mathematics curriculum is guided by a framework.	• The Course of Study with "mathematical activities" at the centre, facilitated by four components: concepts, skills, mathematical thinking, and attitude.	• "Creativity and Character-building" facilitated by mathematical process, consisting of problem solving, reasoning, and communication.	• "Pentagon" framework with problem solving at the centre, facilitated by five components: concepts, skills, processes, metacognition, attitude.
4.	Use of calculators and ICT in mathematics teaching and assessment.	• ICT including calculators and computers needed for teaching but not for assessment/ public examination.	• Grade 7 onward for teaching not assessment	• Scientific calculator compulsory for Grade 5 onward for teaching and public examination. • Grades 11 & 12; graphic calculator for teaching and public examination. • ICT is widely used in teaching.

Table 1 (Continued)

No.	Mathematics Curriculum Policies	Japan	Korea	Singapore
5.	Mathematics teachers are "specialist" in mathematics.	• Primary: generalist.	• Primary: generalist	• Primary: generalist (3 subjects) and specialist (2 subjects).
		• Secondary: specialist.	• Secondary: specialist	• Secondary: specialist (2 subjects).

and economic situation surrounding mathematics education at that time (Koyama 2010). For each revision, a Central Council for Education in the Ministry is established to discuss and advise on educational policy in general for changing/reforming education in Japan. This Council is made up of 30 members who are representatives from various agents such as universities, boards of education, schools, parent-teacher associations, regional governments, sports organizations, journalists, and industry. Then, a Curriculum Subdivision of the Council is established to advise on the development of national standards according to the Central Council's advice. After receiving the Curriculum Subdivision's advice and the input from special working groups for each school subjects, the Ministry compiles the CS for schools. Furthermore, the Ministry compiles curriculum guides in which the objectives and contents of each school subject are explained in detail, and instructional materials in which teaching methods are suggested. Any revisions to the CS have to be based on the basic national education policy of "education for all" established in the Japanese Constitution and also with the goals and principles of education prescribed by the Fundamental Law of Education. In 1998, the Curriculum Council submitted the final report to the Minister of Education for revising the 1989 CS under the slogan "Zest for Living" put up by the Central Council for Education. As a result of this revision, the Ministry added such new items into the CS for mathematics as "through mathematical activities," "enjoy mathematical activities" and "cultivate their basis of creativity through mathematical activities" (Ministry of Education, Japan 1999). On the other hand, in order to introduce the so-called five-day week schooling system and create a time period for "integrated study" as a new course, the number of hours for mathematics was reduced by about 15 %, and about 30 % of the mathematical content was removed so as to foster students' positive attitude toward mathematics and provide students with time for doing mathematical activities that might promote their creative thinking in the limited time. However, in February 2006, the Japanese Government changed the Fundamental Law of Education slightly to include an item for explicitly emphasizing the importance of "acquiring basic knowledge and skills, cultivating thinking-judging-representing ability, and fostering positive attitude toward learning" in education. Then, in March 2008, the Ministry of Education, on the basis of a final report submitted by the Central Council for Education, revised the 1998 CS (Ministry of Education, Japan 2008). In the latest CS, the standard number

Table 2 Roles of agents and organizations in mathematics curriculum policies in Japan, Korea, and Singapore

No.	Organizational Levels	Japan	Korea	Singapore
1.	Macro-level: Nation	• Central Council for Education authorized by Ministry of Education, Culture, Sports, Science and Technology determines national curriculum policy (3).	• Curriculum Planning and Development Board (CPDB) authorized by Ministry of Education, Science and Technology (MEST) and National Curriculum Division at MEST design national curriculum to cover primary to pre-university levels (3).	• Curriculum Planning and Development Department of the Ministry of Education; its subject specialists design national curriculum to cover primary to pre-university levels (Grades 1 to 12) (3).
		• Curriculum Council designs the framework for curriculum and assessment to cover primary to pre-university levels (Grades 1 to 12) (3).	• University Admission Division at MEST and Division for Educational Evaluation at Korea Institute for Curriculum and Evaluation (KICE) determine assessment policies of public examinations (3).	• Singapore Examinations and Assessment Board (SEAB) determines assessment policies of public examinations (3). These assessment standards are aligned with the curriculum standards.
		• Ministry of Education subject specialists with some professors and teachers design national curriculum for each school subject (3).		
2.	Meso level, intermediate: Regions	• Municipal Education Board encourages and monitors each school to implement curriculum and assessment policies (2).	• Municipal Education Board encourages and monitors each school to implement curriculum and assessment policies (1).	• Zone and cluster superintendents (1). They do not determine policies but are charged to implement them in local schools. They often initiate new projects such as Action Research for schools in their zones and clusters.

Table 2 (Continued)

No.	Organizational Levels	Japan	Korea	Singapore
3.	Meso level: Teacher education institutes	• More than 50 national institutes and more private institutes for primary and secondary teacher education; some educators are members of Curriculum Council (2).	• 11 national institutes for primary teacher education; 14 national institutes for secondary teacher education and 23 private institutes for secondary teacher education; some educators are members of CPDB (2).	• National Institute of Education is the sole teacher education institute; its educators are members of curriculum review committees (2).
4.	Meso level: Schools	• Principal and subject teachers plan scheme of work (2).	• Principal and subject teachers plan scheme of work (2).	• Heads of departments and committee plan scheme of work (3).
5.	Micro-level: Classrooms	• Teachers implement curriculum and assessment policies (1).	• Teachers implement curriculum and assessment policies (1).	• Teachers plan and implement daily lessons to comply with national policies (1).

of hours for school mathematics is increased and students' mathematical activities are emphasized more than before. These changes to the Fundamental Law of Education and the CS necessarily forced teachers to reflect seriously on their educational philosophy and teaching methods for school mathematics.

The Korean national mathematics curriculum has been revised nine times since the establishment of the Republic of Korea in 1948. The main agent for reform is vested in the hands of the Curriculum Planning and Development Board (CPDB) authorized by the Ministry of Education, Science, and Technology (MEST). This Board is comprised of mathematicians and mathematics educators from teacher education institutes, mathematics teachers, and curriculum officers at the MEST. The consulting committee comprises engineers, economists, chief executive officers, parents, mathematicians, and educators and they offer advice on mathematics curriculum revision. Most revisions were influenced by worldwide trends: for example, the 3rd curriculum announced in 1973 (Grades 1–9) and 1974 (Grades 10–12) was heavily influenced by the "New Math movement" (Paik 2004; Park 2011). The 7th curriculum was announced in 1997 and had been implemented by 2006. This curriculum was characterized as a "differentiated curriculum" based on ability grouping. After the 7th curriculum, two revisions were completed: one in 2007 and one in 2011. Both revisions were named for the year the curriculum was announced; "the revised curriculum in 2007" and "the revised curriculum in 2011". The revised mathematics curriculum in 2011 was dubbed the "creativity-oriented mathematics curriculum". Consequently, creativity development is considered a crucial goal in this revised curriculum (MEST 2011). "Mathematical process" covering problem solving, reasoning, and communication was introduced as an independent dimension to combine with content in the revised curriculum in 2011. The "grade band" system is adopted to provide textbook editors with more leeway for organizing contents. The Korean mathematics curriculum has been uniformly maintained and its overall revision process has been determined by national level planning and development based on feedback from teachers. However, compared to other countries, Korea has a very short history of modern mathematics education and a short curriculum revision term while adopting worldwide trends. Hence, one major concern of Korean mathematics educators is to build their own philosophy of mathematics curriculum to match the unique Korean education environment.

In Singapore, the first national mathematics curriculum for primary and secondary levels was introduced after self-government in 1959 (Ministry of Education, Singapore 1959). This curriculum unified different branches of mathematics (Arithmetic, Algebra, Euclidean Geometry, and Trigonometry) into a single subject that "knows no racial barriers" (McLellan 1957). Since then, the contents of the secondary mathematics curriculum have been dominated by the examination syllabuses of the Singapore-Cambridge GCE Ordinary Level (O-Level) and the Advanced Level (A-level) examinations. In 1990, the Ministry of Education developed the "pentagon" mathematics curriculum framework with problem solving as its central focus, and this became widely known internationally as a key feature of so-called "Singapore Math." The curriculum is regularly reviewed by the Ministry of Education. To do this, the Curriculum Planning and Development Division of the Ministry of Education forms syllabus review committees comprising senior curriculum officers at the Ministry, mathematics educators from the NIE, polytechnic lecturers, and senior mathematics teachers from selected schools. These committees also gather feedback using questionnaires and focus-group discussions with mathematics teachers and look at mathematics standards from many countries, both East and West, including translations of curriculum documents from other languages into English. The revised curriculum must also be aligned with other initiatives introduced by the Ministry at that time, for example, to promote thinking through the "Thinking Schools, Learning Nation" initiative in 1997 and engaged learning with the "Teach Less, Learn More" projects in 2004. Minor revisions were implemented in 2000 and 2006 (Wong and Lee 2009). Another revision is likely to be implemented in 2013, and this latest version will probably give stronger emphasis to everyday applications of mathematics and mathematical modelling and will extend the "pentagon" framework to Junior College (JC) level. To help teachers provide differentiated instruction in mathematics lessons, this latest edition will include a collection of learning experiences for mathematics lessons, compiled from submissions by school teachers and other educators. This regular revision helps to keep Singapore's curriculum up-do-date with changes in national policies and international best practices.

Factors Influencing Mathematics Curriculum Policies: The "Environment"

Policy-making is a complex process involving the balance and trade-off of numerous factors. It also depends on who are involved in policy making at the time. These factors have different impacts on the policy-making process in different countries, and it is not easy to distinguish between Eastern and Western factors. These factors include the following:

- Historical, such as current policies might have been designed and in use for many years and found to be effective; how one particular policy has changed over the years and why?
- Mathematics curriculum policies embedded within the overall education system.
- Curriculum policies respond to emerging social, cultural, political, demographic, and economic changes in the country.
- Resources such as textbooks, budget; this might affect policies about using calculators and ICT.
- Number and quality of mathematics teachers.
- Internationalisation or globalisation, e.g., changes in policies in response to TIMSS and PISA.
- Theories and beliefs about learning including traditional folk psychology.
- Research from local and international, evidence-based policy-making; to what extent research has been considered by the agents? Do they engage in new research?

This chapter does not allow for an extensive treatment of these factors in each country. Hence, we have decided that each country will elaborate on one factor that is particularly influential in that country for further deliberation.

In Japan, it is very important for mathematics curriculum policy that the Japanese Government amends the Fundamental Law of Education to include an item that explicitly emphasizes the importance of "acquiring basic knowledge and skills, cultivating thinking-judging-representing ability, and fostering positive attitude toward learning" in education. There is no doubt that the issues concerning mathematics curriculum and students' mathematical performance identified by the TIMSS and PISA (National Institute for Educational Policy Research, Japan, 2004) influenced the changes of educational law and general curriculum policy in Japan. The latest curriculum revision in the general curriculum policy emphasizes three points: (a) fostering "Zest for Living", (b) balancing the acquisition of basic knowledge and skills with the cultivation of a thinking-judging-representing ability, and (c) fostering an open mind and healthy body by enriching moral and physical education. The latest 2008 CS emphasizes mathematical activities in the teaching and learning of mathematics so that through their mathematical activities, students acquire basic mathematical knowledge and skills, cultivate their thinking-judging-representing ability, and foster their positive attitude toward learning mathematics. In particular, for the first time, the CS incorporates mathematical activities into the mathematics curriculum from Grades 1 to 10 as "content" to be taught and learned. For example, in the case of lower secondary school mathematics, in learning each content of "numbers and algebraic expressions", "geometrical figures", "functions", and "making use of data", and in learning the connection of these contents, students should be provided with opportunities to do mathematical activities like the following: (a) activities for finding out and developing the properties of numbers and geometrical figures based on previously learned mathematics, (b) activities for making use of mathematics in daily life and society, and (c) activities for explaining and communicating to each other in an evidenced, coherent and logical manner by using mathematical representations (Ministry of Education, Japan 2008). This description explains how mathematics curriculum policy is embedded within the overall education system and how the policy changes in response to TIMSS and PISA from the perspective of internationalization or globalization.

In Korea, the revised mathematics curriculum of 2011 was designed based on the detailed discussion about Korean students' specific performances in recent TIMSS and PISA. This illustrates how Korean mathematics curriculum policy is strongly influenced by results of international mathematics assessments. Firstly, while Korean students had a high level of achievement in the assessments, the percentage of correct answers for constructed response items was relatively low. Secondly, the students showed negative attitudes toward mathematics (MEST 2011). To deal with these issues, teaching and learning that emphasizes mathematical process and mathematical creativity is now encouraged in the curriculum. Appropriate mathematics education should consider students' differing levels and propensities for learning and encourage "mathematical processes", and these themes are explicitly included in the curriculum document. Furthermore, the reason for adopting "grade band" is to allow authors to write textbooks that take note of the students' differing ability levels. Many students in Korea traditionally attend private educational institutes (tuition classes or cram schools) for drilling in problem solving and advanced learning. This practice has increased the burden on students and their parents and weakened the role of public education. To address this problem, Korea has decreased the amount of learning content and emphasized a more interesting introduction of mathematical contents for students through the use of concrete materials since the 4th mathematics curriculum (MEST 2011; Shin and Han 2010). This example shows how socio-cultural factors have influenced Korean mathematics curriculum policy. In addition, given the rapid changes in the ICT environment such as internet and mobile phone, teaching and learning methods utilizing these technological tools are highly recommended in the revised mathematics curriculum in 2011.

A brief history of Singapore's mathematics curriculum has already been given above. In an earlier analysis (Wong et al. 2001), a situated socio-cultural model was proposed to explain the development of mathematics education in Brunei Darussalam, Malaysia, and Singapore over the past five decades in terms of historical background, key political events, language issues related to medium of instruction (English and mother tongue languages in Singapore), education structure and aims, cultural mores, and global influences. This section examines a systemic level factor that addresses the issue of providing diverse pathways for students through the education system. For students in Singapore Junior Colleges (JC,

Grades 11–12) that provide pre-university education, this diversity was tackled in the review of the JC curriculum in 2002. It led to the current curriculum which was first implemented in 2006. This curriculum stresses breadth and flexibility (http://www3.moe.edu.sg/cpdd/alevel2006/). There are 12 JCs, with about 20,000 students and 1,800 teachers. To cater to the different needs and aptitudes of JC students, most subjects—including Mathematics—are offered at three levels: H1, H2, and H3. H1 Mathematics is taken by students who wish to study business, economic, and social sciences in the university. Its contents, to be delivered over 120 hours, cover Functions and Graphs, Differential and Integral Calculus of one variable, Probability, Binomial and Normal Distributions, Sampling and Hypothesis Testing (normal), Correlation, and Linear Regression. H2 Mathematics prepares students for university study of Mathematics, Physics, and Engineering. It includes all the topics in H1 Mathematics and the additional topics: Sequences and Series, Complex Numbers, Permutations and Combinations, and Poisson Distribution. It requires 240 hours of study. H3 Mathematics is for students who have a special aptitude and passion for mathematics. There are two main options: (a) to study topics in Graph Theory, Combinatorics, and Differential Equations taught by the respective JC and take the Singapore-Cambridge GCE A-Level in H3 Mathematics, or (b) to take a module in Numbers and Matrices or Linear Algebra taught and assessed by the local universities. The emphasis of H3 Mathematics is on mathematical modelling and proofs. Students must take H3 Mathematics together with H2 Mathematics. The required curriculum hours for H3 Mathematics vary from 120 to 240 hours. This description explains how mathematics curriculum policy has been embedded within the overall education reform at the systemic level.

Future Directions about Mathematics Curriculum Policies

In this section, we will briefly examine two approaches to developing future research and conceptualisation of MCP in order to address the lack of research in mathematics curriculum policies as reported in the literature and to stimulate development of this field of inquiry.

The first approach is to focus on one or two future directions in MCP within each country according to the author's own observations and interpretations of what is likely to be significant in his/her own country in the coming years. These analytic analyses should begin with in-depth descriptions of the intra-national contexts using constructs that are readily understood in international discourse about policies and standards. The framework in Table 2 and the discussions above could be taken as embryonic forms of this kind of analysis. New systemic and reliable data about MCP should be gathered to enrich such comparative analyses.

The second approach is to translate important local documents from the country's language into English for wider international dissemination and discussion. These documents often provide important insiders' perspectives of the respective systems, and their translations by educators who are conversant in the local languages and have worked in the respective systems will enable outsiders to gain access to these perspectives and nuances of policies and practices. We have made use of documents in the Japanese and Korean languages that are not readily available to the international mathematics education community to explicate the policies in those two countries. Unlike Japan and Korea, Singapore has used English extensively in education and such translation is not a major issue there.

Summary and Conclusions

Policies and practices are intricately related. The same policy can be implemented in different ways, as illustrated by several examples described above. An imperative lesson to learn from the numerous factors that impinge in different ways on the translation of policies into practices as discussed above, is to pay special attention to the context under which the practices are designed and implemented at the micro, meso, and macro levels. We believe that this insight is valid for policies and practices in East and West mathematics education systems, although this claim would be more credible with inclusion of cases from the West.

An important aspect of mathematics curriculum policies is reflected in the curricular materials developed to articulate the intended curriculum standards, contents, and goals. Current analyses of these documents, as evident in the TIMSS and other comparative studies, take the form of categorization of curricular elements and the frequencies of occurrence. There are limited attempts to link these results back to the intended policies, some of which might have to be inferred from documents. More sophisticated methodologies need to be developed to study these links. In addition, curriculum documents are the outcomes of much discussion and negotiation that have taken place at numerous committees and meetings but are never reported for public information. To spur further research and gather more in-depth data for scholarly analysis, key agents of MCP should be interviewed to understand their assumptions, views about mathematics values in the national education system, and personal experiences. This is akin to conducting task-based interviews to understand student's mathematical thinking, an approach that has led to sound practical implications about teaching and learning. Thus, a similar methodology to probe policy formulation could bring about significant knowledge concerning MCP and its practices, in particular, new ways to promote effective teaching and meaningful learning of mathematics for students in the 21st century. Likewise, policymakers who are charged with formulating policies that impact these students need to be cognizant of the assumptions and evidence that underpin the policies that they may wish to bring about.

From a policy perspective, several obstacles to enhancing student achievement need attention: translating evidence-based findings into policy statements; determining the levels of policy implementation that work best (local, regional, national); obtaining international collaboration such as memorandum of understanding (MOU) between countries or institutes; identifying resources and cost constraints for policy implementation; and establishing priority options. These are just some of the numerous issues that constitute the "contents" of the MCP that need to be addressed. Indeed, MCP is an exciting field of inquiry waiting to be developed, and we hope that this chapter with its three case studies will stimulate this development.

Authors' Disclaimer The views expressed in this chapter are those of the authors' and do not necessarily reflect the official views and policies of the respective ministries of education.

References

Auguste, B., Kihn, P., & Miller, M. (2010). Closing the talent gap: Attracting and retaining top-third graduates to careers in teaching: An international and market research-based perspective. McKinsey & Company Social Sector Office. Retrieved from http://www.mckinsey.com/clientservice/Social_Sector/our_practices/Education/Knowledge_Highlights/Closing_the_talent_gap.aspx.

Barber, M., & Mourshed, M. (2007). *How the world's best-performing school systems come out on top*. London: McKinsey & Co.

Koyama, M. (2010). Mathematics curriculum in Japan. In F. K. S. Leung & Y. Li (Eds.), *Reforms and issues in school mathematics in East Asia: sharing and understanding mathematics education policies and practices* (pp. 59–78). Rotterdam: Sense Publishers.

McLellan, D. (1957). Foreword. In *Ministry of education (1959), syllabus for mathematics in primary and secondary schools*. Singapore: Ministry of Education.

Ministry of Education, Culture, Sports, Science and Technology, Japan (1999). *Guidebook for the lower secondary school mathematics in the course of study (1998)*. Osaka: Osakashoseki Publisher (in Japanese).

Ministry of Education, Culture, Sports, Science and Technology, Japan (2008). *The courses of study for elementary and lower secondary school* (in Japanese). Retrieved from http://www.mext.go.jp/a_menu/shotou/new-cs/index.htm.

Ministry of Education, Science, and Technology, Korea (2011). *Mathematics curriculum*. Seoul: Author.

Ministry of Education, Singapore (1959). *Syllabus for mathematics in primary and secondary schools*. Singapore: Author.

National Institute for Educational Policy Research, Japan (2004). *Report on the international result of the OECD 2003 PISA survey*. Tokyo: Gyosei Corporation (in Japanese).

Paik, S. Y. (2004). *Mathematics curriculum in Korea*. Paper presented at ICME 10, Copenhagen, Denmark.

Park, K. M. (2011). Mathematics curriculum in Korea. Book chapter submitted.

Shin, H., & Han, I. (2010). The revise curriculum of school mathematics in Korea. In F. K. S. Leung & Y. Li (Eds.), *Reforms and issues in school mathematics in East Asia: sharing and understanding mathematics education policies and practices* (pp. 79–90). Rotterdam: Sense Publishers.

Trowler, P. (2003). *Education policy* (2nd ed.). London: Routledge.

Wong, K. Y., & Lee, N. H. (2009). Singapore education and mathematics curriculum. In K. Y. Wong, P. Y. Lee, B. Kaur, P. Y. Foong, & S. F. Ng (Eds.), *Mathematics education: the Singapore journey* (pp. 13–47). Singapore: World Scientific.

Wong, K. Y., Mohd Taha, Z., & Veloo, P. (2001). Situated sociocultural mathematics education: vignettes from Southeast Asian practices. In B. Atweh, H. Forgasz, & B. Nebres (Eds.), *Sociocultural research on mathematics education: an international research perspective* (pp. 113–134). Mahwah: Lawrence Erlbaum.

Decision Making in the Mathematics Curricula among the Chinese Mainland, Hong Kong, and Taiwan

Hak Ping Tam, Ngai-Ying Wong, Chi-Chung Lam, Yunpeng Ma, Lije Lu, and Yu-Jen Lu

Abstract As in many other places, the mathematics curricula in the Chinese mainland, Hong Kong, and Taiwan underwent reform at the turn of the millennium, addressing the various political, social, and educational needs of these regions. These reforms were not smooth and resulted in many heated debates and, recently, attempts have made to adjust the mathematics curricula in response to these debates. The initiation of change, strong reactions, and adjustments by the policy makers can be better understood by looking into the decision-making system and process of curriculum development in these three educational systems. In this chapter, we shall look at decision making in the mathematics curriculum among the three educational systems from three different perspectives: how curriculum decisions are

H.P. Tam (✉) · Y.-J. Lu
Graduate Institute of Science Education, National Taiwan Normal University, Taipei, Taiwan
e-mail: t45003@ntnu.edu.tw

Y.-J. Lu
e-mail: hitachi6@gmail.com

N.-Y. Wong · C.-C. Lam
Department of Curriculum and Instruction, The Chinese University of Hong Kong, Shatin, Hong Kong

N.-Y. Wong
e-mail: nywang@cuhk.edu.hk

C.-C. Lam
e-mail: chichunglam@cuhk.edu.hk

Y. Ma · L. Lu
Department of Curriculum and Instruction, Faculty of Education, Northeast Normal University of China, Changchung, China

Y. Ma
e-mail: mayp@nenu.edu.cn

L. Lu
e-mail: lvlj@nenu.edu.cn

Y. Li, G. Lappan (eds.), *Mathematics Curriculum in School Education*,
Advances in Mathematics Education, DOI 10.1007/978-94-007-7560-2_6,
© Springer Science+Business Media Dordrecht 2014

made in these regions; what issues they aim to tackle; and why the implementation of curriculum changes has been problematic.

The historical development of the mathematics curricula in these three regions will first be portrayed. Building on this background, the general curriculum decision-making mechanism in these three regions will be delineated and implementation problems discussed. At the end of the chapter, the authors will attempt to draw lessons one can learn from these historical accounts.

Keywords Mathematics curriculum · Curriculum reform · Curriculum decision making · Curriculum implementation · Education in Chinese regions

How a Curriculum Is Developed and then Implemented in the Classroom

The Chinese mainland, Hong Kong and Taiwan have all followed a center–periphery curriculum development system (Association for Curriculum and Instruction of Taiwan 2000; Ma 2008; Morris 1996; Morris and Adamson 2010) for a long time. Though the situation varies across systems, the school curriculum is developed by an agency in the government and then disseminated to schools for implementation at the classroom level; or a special committee is commissioned to be responsible for developing the curriculum that must then be approved before it can be made official. Under this center–periphery system, the official curriculum development agency is given the responsibility of designing a curriculum for a large number of schools.

Among the three educational systems, Hong Kong is by far the smallest in terms of geographical size, number of schools, and student population. Nevertheless, it still has over 800 primary schools and nearly 500 secondary schools. Students come from very diverse backgrounds, with different levels of academic motivation, interest and competency. Catering to this learning diversity in Hong Kong is a serious challenge to the curriculum developers (Lam and Chan 2011). It is not at all difficult to appreciate the severity of this challenge also in the other two educational systems, which are much bigger in size with a much wider range of physical terrain and social composition. Indeed, the demand for a school curriculum that better caters to the diverse needs of the students has become a major issue in all three systems (Lam et al. 2012; Lin 2004).

The Chinese Mainland

Before 2000, the mathematics curriculum of the Chinese mainland was based on centralized decisions in which the government played a leading role (Ma 1998). There were seven editions of mathematics syllabi published from 1949 to 1992. Only a few experts took part in the decision-making process, which was led by the educational administration department. In June 1985, the Department of Elementary Education and the Department of Secondary Education of the State Education Commission made an in-depth study in various areas, including the local economy, education, the status of culture development, current teaching plan, teaching outline, textbooks, and teaching situation (Ma 1992). Accordingly, the *Instructional Plan for Compulsory Primary School and Junior High School* (*draft*) was prepared. The document was then sent out to the educational administrative departments and schools in all provinces, autonomous regions and municipalities in order to gather feedback. After gathering their views, the document was revised repeatedly and the (*draft*) *Instructional Plan* was finalized and submitted to the Party Group members of the Department of Secondary Education for endorsement. Furthermore, instructional plans based on the draft were developed by experts organized by the Department of Secondary Education for all subjects. In 1990, the Basic Education Department again organized expert panels to revise the *Instructional Plan*. During the revision process, principals, teachers, and scholars were invited to offer suggestions and the draft was published in the *China Education Daily*, soliciting recommendations and feedback from the public. Subsequently, the *Instructional Plan for Compulsory Primary School and Junior High School* was eventually worked out. So, one can clearly see that the *Compulsory Education Curriculum Plan* and the instructional syllabi were developed by a few experts working in government department.

The Basic Education Curriculum Reform, which took place in 2000, was also led and organized by the government educational administrative department. The only difference was procedural; experts of different fields were invited to participate in the analyses and discussion at various stages of the development, without waiting till the final stage. The curriculum designers, including university academics, teaching-researchers, in-service teachers from primary and junior high schools, scientists, and sociologists all contributed views from their professional perspectives. Each task group, the mathematics subject group included, began with the nature of individual subjects, then made analyses of the status quo, conducted comparative studies, and investigated both societal and children's needs. All these procedures laid the theoretical foundation of curriculum development. In the subject of mathematics, the expert think tank included mathematicians, mathematics curriculum experts, and mathematics teachers from both the primary and secondary education sectors. Finally, after more than a year's discussion, the *Mathematics Curriculum Standards for Compulsory Education* (*Trial version*) were crafted.

The curriculum implementation process also underwent changes. In the early days, the documents were simply sent out for implementation across the country. Teachers were seen as not having the knowledge or skills to implement new changes so teacher training was organized so as to help teachers understand the curriculum and teaching better. However, as maintained by Guskey (2002), this kind of deficiency model for teacher development seldom works.

The implementation was further complicated by the fact that China is a vast country, with very diverse levels of economic and social development (Ma et al. 2006). Having one universal curriculum with a single set of textbooks for the whole country made instruction very difficult for practicing teachers. Therefore, beginning in the 1980s, the government allowed more publishers to develop textbooks. Having a variety of textbooks helped teachers adapt the curriculum for their students, though this was not a panacea. All these moves increase the chance of the curriculum being implemented in the classroom, though there is still a large gap between the intended and implemented curricula.

Taiwan

The educational system in Taiwan adopts a one-size-fits-all official curriculum policy for general students. Different departments within the Ministry of Education (MOE[1] Taiwan) have always been responsible for overseeing all matters in relation to the development of the official curricula at the school level. However, there is no special division within the MOE (Taiwan) that is in charge of the actual development and write-up of school curricula for any subject. Instead, such duties are basically delegated to external groups that are responsible for designing and writing the new curricula. Though the actual procedures for curriculum development may vary across time, there is commonality with respect to the underlying mechanisms. Typically, the process starts off with the MOE (Taiwan) summoning a group of scholars and administrators to form a steering committee to take care of setting up general principles and operational guidelines for curriculum development. Meanwhile, several scholars will be appointed by the MOE (Taiwan) with each of them playing the role as a convener for a school subject according to his/her expertise. Each convener will then assemble a group of scholars and teachers to serve on the sub-committee for the subject under his/her responsibility. The typical size of a sub-committee amounts to about fifteen members. After a consensus has been reached about the coverage of topics as well as their contents, several members will be commissioned to write up various portions of the curriculum and then everything is compiled into a draft document. All documents must then be submitted to the MOE (Taiwan), which will appoint a review committee to audit the manuscripts for approval. After all curricular documents for a learning stage have been approved, the curriculum will be made official via a decree from the MOE (Taiwan) for subsequent implementation in schools. Developmental procedures for the 1993 primary curriculum in the format of a flow chart is used as a concrete example and presented in Fig. 1.

In the past, the production of textbooks in Taiwan was under the authority of the National Institute for Compilation and Translation (NICT), which is the agency responsible for the compilation and translation of all academic and cultural materials. All students used the same set of textbooks and teaching materials. However, starting in 1991, the MOE (Taiwan) began to allow primary textbooks for the Arts and Activities courses to be compiled by interested parties other than the NICT. This measure was extended to the other subjects at primary level in 1996. Later, in 1999

---

[1] Since the government bodies concerned across the strait are both called Ministry of Education, we add 'China' and 'Taiwan' to distinguish them.

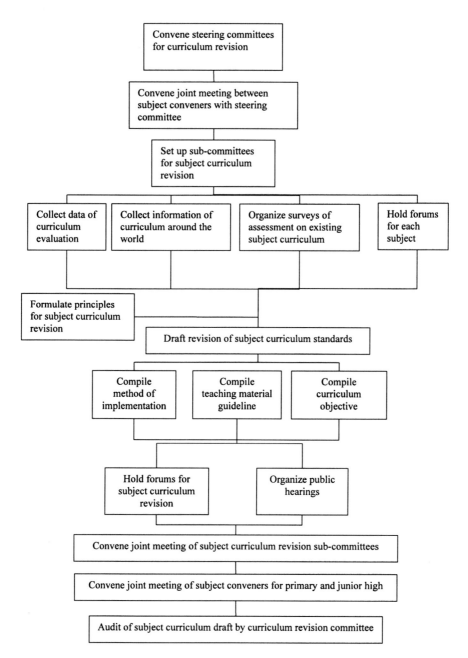

Fig. 1 Development procedures for the 1993 primary mathematics curriculum in Taiwan (MOE Taiwan 1993)

and 2000, the policy was extended to junior and senior high schools. This policy is now known as the *one guide—multiple sets of textbooks* policy under the current curriculum, which opened up the responsibility of developing textbooks to commercial publishers and practicing teachers. One of the main purposes behind this policy was to give teachers the freedom to select their own school-based textbooks according to the needs of their classrooms. Accordingly, the NICT changed its role to simply auditing the manuscripts submitted by commercial publishers for their suitability to be used as textbooks (Tam 2010).

For a new curriculum to be successfully implemented in classrooms, supporting efforts must be provided by various concerned parties towards this end. Moreover, such measures must help emphasize the characteristics of the curriculum and facilitate the achievement of its objectives. For example, the 1993 mathematics curriculum is more child-centered and allows for individual differences in learning. Therefore, some educators promoted the idea of using problem posing, group discussion, questioning, and argumentation between students and teachers, as well as coming to a consensus regarding the knowledge they were trying to learn in the classrooms (Wu and Lin 1997). Since these practices were quite different from those in the previous curriculum, many training materials, in the form of instructional handbooks and videos, were produced. However, professional development workshops that supported the then new curriculum were scant. This curriculum will be further discussed in a later section.

Hong Kong

All the school curricula are developed and issued by the Curriculum Development Council (CDC), an advisory body set up by the government to oversee school curriculum matters. Though theoretically these documents are only recommended for use, in reality schools are expected to adopt them. Besides the curriculum document, there are other means to actualize this, including school inspections, textbook control, and high stakes examinations. Another means is government subsidy. Most schools in Hong Kong are 'subsidized' schools, not run by the government but by religious bodies or non-government organizations; their funding, however, comes from the government. Schools may adapt these centrally developed curricula into 'school-based curricula'; however, they have to do so along the CDC guidelines. So curriculum development is centralized.

However, this does not mean that the CDC is the only force shaping the school curriculum. There are other organizations and stakeholders who can influence the planned and implemented curriculum in the school sector. For example, high level education advisory bodies, such as the Education Commission, which is responsible for the formulating of education policies in Hong Kong, could have a strong say in the school curriculum. In fact, it was the Education Commission that suggested the new academic structure of three-year junior high, three-year senior high and four-year undergraduate study in 2004. After the adoption of this new academic structure, the senior secondary mathematics curriculum was developed, though all these recommendations have to be channeled back to the CDC for the actual design.

The basic CDC structure was established in 1972. At that time, it was named the Curriculum Development Committee, under which were the primary and secondary level mathematics CDCs of which the principal inspectors automatically became chairs. It was reconstructed into the Council in 1988. At its lower level were a number of coordinating committees, three of which were responsible for primary, secondary, and sixth form level curricular matters. These coordinating committees were chaired by school principals, with officials providing administrative support. Under each coordinating committee were a number of subject committees. These subject committees were responsible for the development of subject curricula. In the case of mathematics, there were a total of three subject committees, namely primary, secondary, and sixth form. The subject committees were chaired by practicing teachers, the officials taking up the role of vice-chair and providing secretarial support. Most of the members were practicing teachers. This can be viewed as a gesture of democratization and a response to the emergence of a great number of pressure (concern) groups due to the rise of local awareness in the 1970s. The colonial government tried to incorporate these forces into the establishment by inviting some of these key persons into these committees, though they attend these committees in a personal capacity only (Tang et al. 2007).

Theoretically, CDC members, whether official or non-official, were vested with the power to decide curricular matters. In reality, they functioned more as consultation bodies, feeding the governmental inspectorate advice on curriculum development. Morris (1996) pointed out that these subject committees were in the hands of the officials for a number of reasons. First, all non-official members were recommended and appointed by the government. Second, the non-official members had limited terms, usually no more than six years, while officials served the committees for longer, giving them a stronger influence. Moreover, being the only full-time members, the officials set the agenda and carried out all the groundwork.

With the establishment of the Curriculum Development Institute in 1993, an administrative department under the Education and Manpower Bureau,[2] the Curriculum Development Council was further restructured in 1999. First, all the subjects were grouped under eight Key Learning Areas (KLA). For example, subjects such as geography, history, Chinese history and economics were grouped into the Personal, Social and Humanities KLA. Mathematics, fortunately, was treated as an independent KLA. Secondly, the line between primary and secondary was broken—the mathematics Curriculum Development (KLA) Committee takes care of the mathematics curricula from primary up to senior high levels. The moderating committees were trimmed away. The three-tier system was condensed to two tiers. When there was a need, for example developing a new curriculum or a new form of assessment,

---

[2]There were various restructurings of the government body taking care of education, bearing different labels at different times. For simplicity's sake, we can treat 'Education Department,' 'Education and Manpower Bureau,' and 'Education Bureau' as synonyms.

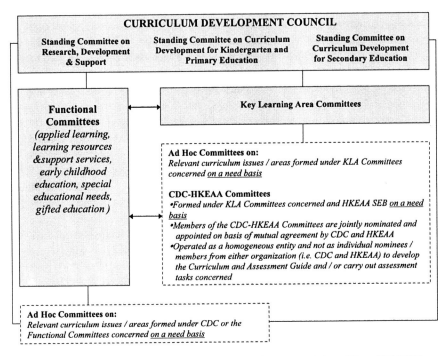

Fig. 2 The Hong Kong Curriculum Development Council structure (adapted from CDI 2009)

a task force would be set up under the KLA committee. Once the task was completed, the task force would be dissolved. Such change allowed the officials to have
an even stronger say in the actual design of curriculum matters because the task
forces were all ad hoc. The present structure is shown in Fig. 2.

There is another line of curriculum development, via public examinations. In earlier days, there was an Examination Section within the Education Department, taking care of various public examinations except for matriculation.[3] The Hong Kong
Examinations Authority was then established in 1977, taking over public examinations gradually, including Certificate and matriculation levels. For mathematics,
there are now subject committees at various levels. Their job is to review the examination syllabi, set regulations and directions for examination papers, and conduct
post-mortem reviews. It was renamed the Hong Kong Examinations and Assessment
Authority (HKEAA) in 2002, indicating that it also takes care of ('internal') assessments as well as public examinations. In subsequent years, the subject committee
underwent 'downsizing,' and fewer academics were incorporated.

To ensure the examination syllabi are aligned with the official school curriculum, when a curriculum is to be included in the public examination—say for exam-

---

[3] At the time the matriculation examinations were in the custody of the universities.

ple the Diploma of Secondary Education Examination—a 'One-committee' which comprises members from both the CDC Working Group and the HKEAA subject committee will be set up to work out the curriculum and assessment guides.

To many teachers, textbooks, rather than the official curriculum and assessment guides, are the 'curriculum documents,' as they rely heavily on textbooks in their teaching. Interestingly, textbooks are not produced by the government. In Hong Kong, textbooks are produced by merchants (publishers). Though there were originally textbook censorships, the target was Chinese language and civic education rather than the more politically neutral subject of mathematics (Wong and Tang 2012). Nevertheless, textbooks are still written according to the official curriculum guide since the Education Bureau has a list of recommended textbooks. There have been incidents where textbooks can still pass the review (and be put onto the recommended list) without following the curriculum guides strictly, and also schools can choose textbooks not on the list. However, to play it safe, textbook producers would obviously try their best to keep the textbooks in line with the official curriculum and assessment guides.

Another means by which the government influences the implemented curriculum is through the high stakes examinations. Students' performances in public examinations have significant impact on their further studies and career. Hence, both students and parents are very concerned about performance in public examinations. If teachers do not teach according to the test, they may be challenged. This inserts indirect control on textbook production too. In a sense, teachers use textbooks to help students pass examinations. To get the market share, textbook developers will naturally try their best to gear the contents of their books to the examination syllabus, which is in fact a shadow of the curriculum document. In sum, the government is controlling the curriculum, textbooks, and day-to-day teaching via high stakes examinations. This proves to be very effective (Fig. 3).

Summary

When designing a curriculum, the developers have to accommodate the demands of various stakeholders. In the case of mathematics, these include, for example, the societal expectations of the competency of the school leavers, the interests and needs of the students, the expectations of the parents, and the views of the mathematicians and mathematics educators. People very often hold different curriculum ideologies (Eisner 2002; Schiro 2008). Some adopt a social efficiency view towards the school curriculum, while others see the important role of the school curriculum in transmitting discipline knowledge. How to accommodate these different demands or orientations is a challenge to curriculum developers.

Since the 1990s, there has been a demand on the schools to prepare the younger generation for the challenges posed by globalization and the advent of the knowl-

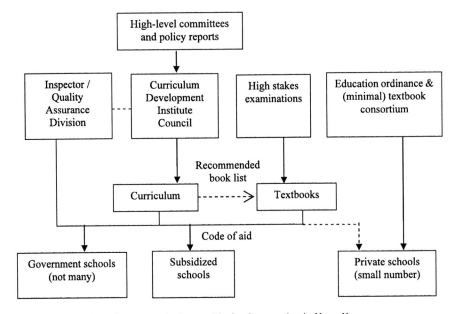

Fig. 3 Forces influencing the curriculum and its implementation in Hong Kong

edge society in these three educational systems (Lam et al. 2012; MOE China 2001; Wu 2003). Internationally, there has been a strong voice promulgating the importance of nurturing generic skills[4] (see, for example, Delors et al. 1996; Wong et al. 2004). Hence, in the 1990s, the three educational systems, in the Chinese mainland and Hong Kong in particular, were facing a series of problems in mathematics teaching and learning that include learner diversity, child-centeredness,[5] and nurturing of non-mathematics-specific generic skills to varying degrees.

To understand these challenges and the potential conflicts in meeting these demands, it is necessary to briefly review the historical development of the mathematics curricula in these three systems.

---

[4]In Hong Kong, the generic skills of collaboration, communication, creativity, critical thinking, information technology, numeracy, problem solving, self-management, and study skills were identified (CDC 2002).

[5]In brief, we aim at facilitating students to become active learners and owners of learning. 'Teacher-led' and 'student-centeredness' may not be in total conflict (Huang and Li 2009; Wong 2004). More recent discussions have focused on 'learning-centeredness' rather than 'learner-centeredness' (Watkins 2008). For simplicity, in this chapter we treat student-centeredness, learner-centeredness, and child-centeredness as synonyms though there could be subtle differences among these terms.

The Evolution of the Mathematics Curricula in the Three Educational Systems

The Chinese Mainland

Background

In the Chinese mainland, education was under strong Russian influence in the 1950s because of the strong political ties between China and Soviet Russia during that period. Computation skills and basic mathematics knowledge were highly emphasized. In particular, the 1963 syllabus was a landmark of the *Two Basics*. During the Cultural Revolution (1966–1976), schooling was disrupted. A series of new curriculum initiatives were launched in the mid-1980s and the 1990s as a way to relieve students' learning burden and to modernize the curriculum in light of international trends. Another trend was to loosen the rigid, centralized control. In 1992, the policy of *one curriculum—diversified sets of textbooks* was implemented. A variety of teaching materials were used in class. More than six different sets of textbooks, each with its own characteristics, were published. By 1997, this decentralized policy was further extended to *diversified curricula—diversified textbooks*. Zhejiang province and Shanghai were granted the autonomy to develop their own curricula (Wong et al. 2004). However, despite these changes, the mathematics curriculum in the mid-1990s was still highly academic and discipline-oriented. The examination pressure exerted on students was still high. Most teachers saw teaching as helping students jump over examination hurdles instead of developing their innate potential. Curriculum was highly centralized and teaching was conventional (Shi and Ma 2009).

There have been ten different versions of the mathematics curriculum since 1949, as shown in Table 1. From this table, we see educational opportunities opening up to the public and allowing diversity across the country. The mathematics curriculum went from the earlier versions of the pro-Russian curricula in the 1950s to the re-vitalized curriculum in the mid-1970s after the cultural revolution and then subsequent revisions in the 1980s. The curriculum underwent another major reform in 2000 to meet the needs of compulsory education. While the details of this history can be found in Shi and Ma (2009) and Lam et al. (2012), we will focus our attention on the latest round of curriculum reform in 2000.

Curriculum Reform at the Turn of the Millennium

There were several missions of the *Mathematics Curriculum Standard of the Compulsory Education* published in 2001. It tried to align the primary and secondary mathematics curriculum into a coherent set for the nine-year compulsory education. Furthermore, students' all-round development was stressed. Affects, values, and abilities were addressed as well as mathematical knowledge and skills. Separate sections were devoted to knowledge and skills, mathematical thinking, problem

Table 1 The evolution of the mathematics curriculum in the Chinese mainland

Primary School	Junior Secondary School
1950: Primary School Temporary Arithmetic Curriculum Standards (Draft)	1950: A concise outline of Mathematical textbook (Draft)
1952: Primary School Arithmetic Teaching Program (Draft)	1952: Junior Secondary School Mathematics Teaching Program (Draft)
1956: Primary School Arithmetic Teaching Program (Revised Draft)	1954: Junior Secondary School Mathematics Teaching Program (Revised Draft)
1963: Full-time Primary School Arithmetic Teaching Program (Draft)	1963: Full-time Junior Secondary School Mathematics Teaching Program (Draft)
1978: Primary School Mathematics Teaching Program (Trial)	1978: Ten-year Full-time Junior Secondary School Mathematics Teaching Program (Trial)
1986: Full-time Primary School Mathematics Teaching Program	1986: Full-time Junior Secondary School Mathematics Teaching Program
1992: Full-time Primary School Mathematics Teaching Program of Nine-year Compulsory Education (Trial)	1992: Full-time Junior Secondary School Mathematics Teaching Program of Nine-year Compulsory Education
2000: Full-time Primary School Mathematics Teaching Program of the Nine-year Compulsory Education (revised version)	1996: Full-time Regular Senior Secondary School Mathematics Teaching Program (Trial)
2001: Mathematics Curriculum Standard of the Compulsory Education (experimental version)	
2011: Mathematics Curriculum Standard of the Compulsory Education (revised version) (ready for implementation)	

solving, and affective attitudes. Connecting mathematics with the real world, developing cultural values, mathematics communication, and thinking processes were emphasized. Along this line, four basic abilities were identified: basic knowledge, basic skills, basic thinking ability, and basic activity experience.

During the experimentation process, however, the original ten-year implementation plan for nationwide curriculum reform was shortened to five years to speed up the change process. Textbook development and teacher preparation failed to cope with the rapid pace of dissemination and implementation. Though the reform did bring about changes in student learning, it encountered opposition from practicing teachers and criticisms from scholars. The debate reached its climax as another renowned mathematician, Boju Jiang, a professor at the Peking University and a Fellow of the National Science Academy, put forth a petition during the National People's Congress and Chinese People's Political Consultative Conference in 2005, calling for a halt to the implementation of the new mathematics curriculum (Lam et al. 2012).

In response to this, the Ministry of Education of China reviewed the situation. After extensive deliberations, the above *four basics* were once again reaffirmed (Shi and Liu 2007). In the course of discussion, the long-standing *product–process* issue, including how to nurture non-mathematical (cross-subject) abilities through mathematics, was once again a focus of attention. The product–process debate can be traced back at least to the 1970s when the Modern Mathematics reform went downhill. The former refers to mathematical contents and the latter the learning process, including the so-called 'process abilities' (higher-order thinking skills or generic skills).[6]

Taiwan

Background

Nine-year compulsory education has been in place in Taiwan for more than 40 years. Although it was stated in the official curricular documents that the primary and secondary mathematics curricula should be connected, they were, for many years, developed separately. Careful alignment was therefore called for. From 1949 to 2003, the primary and junior high school mathematics curricula have been revised seven and eight times respectively. The changes in curricula have been quite rapid, especially in recent years. In brief, Taiwan followed the *Modern Mathematics Movement* in the 1960s; the use of teaching aids (manipulative) was advocated in the reform in the 1970s; and child-centeredness was the theme of the reform in the 1990s. The curriculum introduced in 1993, often referred to as the *constructivist curriculum*, aroused heated debate about its effectiveness. In 2000, Taiwan started to implement a new single mathematics curriculum, the *Grade 1–9 curriculum (temporary edition)*. The major aims of the new curriculum included organizing the content for the nine-year compulsory period as an integrated whole (Chung 2005; Tam 2010) as well as simplification of coverage and level of difficulty from the previous curriculum.

A Microcosm of the Reform in Taiwan

Rather than spreading thinly the discussion of changes to various curricula, this section will focus on discussing the transition into and out of the 1993 curriculum as a microcosm of the reform in Taiwan. This curriculum is chosen because of its relevancy to constructivism, which is deemed more familiar to international readers. Moreover, the transitions with respect to this curriculum were quite strongly related to changes in the social environment and the expectations of various parties. In Table 2, major events that were relevant to various curricula are presented so as to build up a context for subsequent discussion.

   After martial law was lifted in 1987, an environment that fostered pluralistic thinking towards various political and social issues surfaced. Over time, ideas regarding educational reforms began to take shape. In 1988, the Ministry of Education (Taiwan) announced its decentralization of textbook policy. This liberalization also spread into the realm of curriculum design.

---

[6]Refer to Wong et al. (2004) for more details.

Table 2 The timeline of transition of various elementary and junior high school curricula in Taiwan

Curricula		Year	Major events
Elementary	Junior high		
1968 edition	1968 edition	1968	• Implementation of nine years compulsory education
	1972 edition	1972	
1975 edition			
	1983 edition	1983	
	1985 edition		
		1987	• Lifting of martial law
			• Civil educational reform groups began to form
		1989	• Beginning of the decentralization of textbooks policy (starting with art and skill related subjects at the junior high level)
			• Announcement of a new elementary mathematics curriculum standards to be released in 1993
1993 edition		1993	• Release of the 1993 curriculum standards
		1996	• Implementation of the 1993 edition and the beginning of constructive math in elementary school
			• Beginning of the decentralization of textbooks policy for primary mathematics
2000 Grade 1–9 curriculum (temporary edition)		2000	• Nine Year Curriculum (temporary edition) was announced, which would be implemented by stages starting from Grade 1 in 2001
		2002	• Beginning of the decentralization of textbooks for junior high mathematics
			• Nine year curriculum temporary edition was initiated in Grade 7
			• MOE halted the constructive math approach in elementary school
2003 Grade 1–9 curriculum (formal edition)		2003	• Formal edition of the Nine Year Curriculum was launched

At that time, demand for educational reform began to surface from the society at large. Moreover, the 1975 curriculum had been around for quite some time. Thus in 1989, the MOE (Taiwan) announced that a new edition of primary mathematics curriculum would be made public in 1993 and be implemented in 1996. Towards this end, the convener of the 1975 mathematics curriculum design sub-committee was again appointed by the MOE (Taiwan) to serve as the convener for the 1993 curriculum (Pan 2007). This committee was entrusted with full autonomy to devise the curriculum. Whereas the 1975 curriculum was organized according to Piaget's cognitive theory, classroom instruction was teacher-centered and oriented towards the use of manipulatives. The main focus of the 1993 curriculum was not on constructivism either, as can be observed from the fact that only the verb form of 'construct' appeared in the curriculum standards (MOE Taiwan 1993). Moreover, it only appeared in three places in the 42-page manuscript. Though there were arguments that constructivist approaches were only advocated in the corresponding textbooks rather than in the curriculum itself, higher-order thinking skills (connections, communications, etc.) were inevitably the heart of the reform.

Later, in 1991, the convener of the curriculum committee was being recruited to serve as the chief editor for compiling the standard version of mathematics textbooks. In order to promote the idea of student-centeredness, the new textbooks presented different tactics for students to solve the same problems. Some of these tactics might look clumsy on the surface, but they were not meant to be an end in themselves but rather were intended to become the stepping stones for students to learn formal mathematics (NICT 2002a, 2002b). Since this arrangement deviated significantly from past practices, teaching manuals with detailed explanation were prepared at various times to supplement the 1993 curriculum. Some of these documents were very thick; one even amounted to over 700 pages. At that time, the decentralization policy was at its beginning stage. With few experienced textbook writers to be found, commercial publishers had to refer to the standard version while compiling their own version of textbooks. Furthermore, there were not enough training workshops organized for in-service teachers to support the then new curriculum.

Complaints by parents to the MOE (Taiwan) began to surface in the year 2000 (MOE Taiwan 2003). In 2002, serious doubts concerning the effectiveness of the 1993 curriculum were mounted by various parties, including parents, academics, and legislators. Debates on its relative merits and problems were launched on specific websites, in newspapers, and in open forums organized by the MOE (Taiwan). The weaknesses commonly raised included 'constructivist mathematics dumb down students' and 'it made simple computations into complicated procedures' (Pan 2007). An important reason for this impression was that many teachers required their students to strictly follow the tactics presented in the textbooks. Apparently, some of them did not realize that those tactics should later yield to the formal approach of doing mathematics. Insufficient teacher training unfortunately contributed to the ousting of the 1993 curriculum.

Hong Kong

Background

Modern mathematics was brought into the Hong Kong secondary school mathematics curriculum in the 1960s. In line with the Western trend of *back to basics*, the unified mathematics syllabus was released in 1985 (Wong and Wong 2001). As for primary mathematics, Hong Kong extended the original arithmetic curriculum to a mathematics curriculum in 1967 and brought in various notions of child-centeredness based on initiatives such as Nuffield mathematics in the United Kingdom. This was further enhanced by the promotion of the metric system in 1973.

Table 3 The evolution of the mathematics curriculum in Hong Kong

Year	Primary	Secondary
1964		Modern Mathematics
1967	From arithmetic to mathematics	
1973	Metric system	
1975		Syllabus published by Curriculum Development Committee (draft)
1983	Syllabus published by Curriculum Development Committee: Activity approach	
1985		Basic mathematics curriculum
1995	Target Oriented Curriculum	
1997	Holistic review of the mathematics curriculum	
2001	New primary and secondary mathematics curriculum and assessment guides	
2009		New senior secondary school system

The reduction of complex computations in the inter-conversion of units left further room for hands-on activities. After accumulating some years of experience through experimentation, the 1983 version of the primary school mathematics curriculum was finally established. In this version, teaching strategies were recommended for each topic, clearly directing teachers toward the child-centered approach (Tang et al. 2007). To tackle a range of problems arising from the implementation of free and compulsory education, the Target Oriented Curriculum, which was basically an outcome-based curriculum, was proposed. That aroused heated debate and resulted in a holistic review of the mathematics curriculum. The evolution of the Hong Kong mathematics curriculum is depicted in Table 3.

The Dispute that Arose from the Target Oriented Curriculum

As elite education was shifted to universal education in the late 1970s, various issues such as learning motivation and students' deviant behaviors arose in the mid-1980s. In particular, learning diversity was deemed one of the major issues. To address this, the Target Oriented Curriculum was put forth, which involved a standardization of the curriculum (Wong et al. 2004). Theoretically, individual learners could advance their learning step-by-step at their own pace, with diagnosis in every step. This initiated heated debates, the foci of which were fragmented learning and frequent assessments (which were often high stakes). Most seriously, individual subjects were structured to conform to a cross-subject curriculum framework, penalizing subject autonomy.

The Target Oriented Curriculum debate culminated in a group of academics (mathematics educators) publishing their statements in a press conference, which was rather rare in Hong Kong (Wong 2010; Wong et al. 2004; Wong and Tang

2012). Government officials responded very positively and launched a holistic review of the mathematics curriculum from primary up to senior secondary level in 1997. Two research studies (one on international comparison and one on the views of various stakeholders) were commissioned. Hearings were held and with the drafting of 10 position papers, the final report was published at the end of 1999. The whole process lasted two and a half years, which changed the general impression that curriculum reforms were often done in haste. Furthermore, the curriculum development was based on solid scientific research and consultations. Along with the review, two new syllabi, one for the primary level and one for the secondary level, were issued (Wong 2010).

The Millennium Educational Reform

Just as the mathematics holistic review was about to publish its report, a group of education policy makers (above the subject level) initiated a bigger educational reform, which involves restructuring the education system, curriculum structure, and assessment mechanisms. The underlying ideas are learning to learn, stressing process abilities, and decompartmentalizing. Since many of these changes are structural and fundamental, it overrides some of the recommendations of the mathematics holistic review. In particular, the trimming down of subjects is one of its objectives and the original senior secondary curriculum structure (which allows students to take 5–10 subjects) is changed to '4 + (2 to 3X)'. The '4' refers to the four compulsory subjects, Chinese, English, mathematics and Liberal Studies, and the X's are the electives. Other curriculum initiatives include school-based assessment, the use of ICT, project learning, and the grouping of physical education, visual arts, music, service learning, and conventional extracurricular activities into a slot called *Other Learning Experience* (CDC 2002). There are ongoing debates on various issues and we still need time to evaluate the effectiveness of the educational reform and how it actually affects learning and teaching (Wong 2010).

Summary

From the portrayal of the evolution of the mathematics curricula in these three regions, it can be seen that there are some similarities in the desired direction of mathematics curriculum and the underlying conflicts. The *product–process* dichotomy is one. Others include subject-specific objectives and the development of cross-disciplinary generic skills. This involves power hierarchy as well (see discussions below). Child-centeredness is another central issue, which relates to how much should be included in the curriculum (Cai and Wong 2012). How much freedom should be given to the teachers, or do modes of teaching need to be specified in the curriculum documents? Obviously textbooks are another focus of discussion. These issues are not new and not confined to the latest round of curriculum reform.

Different extents of these discussions can be seen throughout the history of mathematics curriculum development among these three educational systems, as will be discussed in the following section.

What Lessons We Can Learn from these Three Regions

The Process of Curriculum Making

Curriculum theorists such as Schiro (2008) have pointed out that people hold different conceptions of curriculum. As people have diverse views and expectations of what curriculum goals should be and what the means of achieving educational goals are (Pajares 1992), curriculum planners often face the challenge of how to accommodate these diverse views and even conflicting demands. The cases of these three systems illustrate the same kind of challenges. The curriculum concerns the high stakes of various parties, including government officials, practicing teachers, educators, mathematicians, and even parents. Accommodating them has been a challenge.

As seen above, curriculum development is highly centralized in all three educational systems. In Hong Kong, for example, curriculum policies are held firmly in the hands of the Education Bureau and the advisory bodies including the Education Commission and the CDC. These central agencies' moral and political roles are negotiating a compromise between the demands and expectations of the various stakeholders such as politicians, business people, teachers, academics, students, and parents. The majority of CDC members are principals, in-service teachers, university academics, and leaders from various walks of life. By having representatives from a number of sectors, it is hoped that the views of various stakeholders will be represented and hence considered in the process. Further views will be solicited through informal consultation when there is a need. However, research studies have shown that officials dominate through control of the membership and the agenda of the curriculum development process (Fok 2005; Morris 1996).

On the Chinese mainland, the hot debate in the mid-2000s on what kinds of mathematics should be taught and what teaching strategies should be adopted also reflects the conflict of values between different stakeholders. After the implementation of the mathematics curriculum in 2001, divergent views surfaced and, as mentioned above, the debate reached its climax in 2005. These views reflected very different perspectives and beliefs towards both mathematics and mathematics education. That includes the value, purpose, content, teaching, and assessment method of the mathematics curriculum. For instance, some people disagreed on the arrangement of mathematics content and insisted that putting the curriculum contents into the four strands of number and algebra, shape and space, statistics and probability, practice and integrative application in fact fragmented mathematical knowledge. Some reflected that the teaching methods were too complicated. The spiral approach slows down those who are talented, underestimating students' abilities (He 2006; Jiang 2005). This reflects a subtle shift of target audience ('end user' of the curriculum) too: from basically nurturing potential mathematicians and scientists to 'mathematics for all.'

There are several features of the curriculum-making process worth noticing in Taiwan. First of all, the MOE (Taiwan) delegates a great deal of freedom to the curriculum design committee to decide the coverage and content of the curriculum according to their expert judgment. Such autonomy and freedom reflects the MOE (Taiwan) policy of respecting the professionals. It was only during rare situations that mathematicians and mathematics educators could not resolve the dispute over the coverage of the Grade 1–9 curriculum and the MOE (Taiwan) stepped in to make a decision. The current situation is that different scholars have different philosophies of how the curriculum should be assembled, thus each curriculum will represent a particular ideology that might not be agreeable to other groups. In order to minimize unnecessary ideological clashes later, it would be most helpful if the curriculum design committee could post a draft for review by various stakeholders before finalizing it.

Secondly, it is observed that changes in the social environment together with expectations from the concerned parties have played non-trivial roles in influencing curriculum development in Taiwan. On one hand, this reflects that the MOE (Taiwan) has paid more attention to opinions from external groups. Yet the worry is that too much influence might be enacted on educational policies from various pressure groups. Currently, social pressure has contributed to rapid changes in curricula within a short period of time. A mechanism should hence be set up to weigh various opinions for their values. In addition, a blueprint is needed for long-term curriculum development.

Thirdly, the termination of the 1993 curriculum illustrated the well-known claim that teachers' preparation is the key to the success of a curriculum. Even though instructional guides had been compiled for teachers, they did not guarantee successful implementation of a new curriculum, nor did they replace the need for full-scale teacher training. Furthermore, mere dissemination of teaching manuals was not enough to enable teachers to understand how the curriculum should be implemented in the classrooms, particularly when some manuals amounted to over 700 pages. This reading was simply too demanding for busy teachers. Instead, systematic in-service teacher development programs should be organized for teachers prior to and during the institution of a new curriculum. These should be planned during the curriculum-making process.

The Consultation Mechanism

As curriculum development in all three systems is highly centralized, consultation is of utmost importance in generating a curriculum that is acceptable to, if not welcomed by, the stakeholders. Curriculum designers have to make sure that implementation is possible when it comes to the hands of the teachers. The change in the curriculum development process (of involving experts and practicing teachers at the stage of development rather than waiting till the final product) in the 2000 revision in the Chinese mainland addressed this issue. In Hong Kong, there have been a number of advisory bodies such as the CDC, but the 'chemistries' in meetings become crucial. As mentioned above, the ways in which the members are identified and appointed essentially decide the outcome. Furthermore, whether members are given ample opportunities to express their views, whether their voices are sufficiently heard, and how officials dominating the agendas and discourse also affect the outcome of the decision-making process are important questions. Some have pointed out the limitations of the so-called 'elite consultation' where the elite and those articulate in speech essentially dominate the floor in public 'town-hall consultations.' The same may be true within committees. Practicing teachers who feel they are of inferior social status and academic standing very often do not have the courage or chance to voice their preferences and demands.

For the curriculum developers, basing curriculum development on solid ground is important too. As seen above, in the Chinese mainland, baseline research is traditionally done before designing a new curriculum. The research might include cross-national curricular comparisons, in-depth investigations on the nature of individual subjects and the status quo of the society as well as children's needs. However, not enough emphasis has been laid on empirical studies. In most cases, including those not confined to the Chinese mainland, no formal needs analyses are performed when a new subject curriculum is designed. As mentioned above, the holistic review of the mathematics curriculum in Hong Kong in the late 1990s served as the needs analysis of the design of the new curriculum in the early 2000s. The holistic review not only reviewed other countries' state of mathematics curriculum, but also identified teachers' and mathematicians' views, the learning problems and behavior of the students, the supports provided by the parents to their children, and parents' and employers' views of youngsters' mathematics competencies through a number of large-scale surveys as well as interviews. The findings of the holistic review provided food for thought in guiding the direction of the curriculum reform. This may explain, in part, why the Hong Kong mathematics curriculum reform led to less controversy in the early 2000s (for details, refer to Wong 2010).

The Subject and the Generic: Conflict or Cooperation

At the turn of the millennium, higher-order thinking was once again stressed. The subject-based curriculum was seen as compartmentalizing knowledge taught in schools. As mentioned earlier, this *product–process* issue is not new (Wong 2010; Wong et al. 2004). Though there had been arguments that individual **subjects** have full capacity to nurture the so-called generic skills, **cross-subject** abilities earned higher regard. This is not solely an academic matter when there is a top-down power relationship in the curriculum policy-making mechanism. Subject committees are always placed under the leadership of general committees. What makes the matter worse is that the high-level officials responsible for curriculum reforms are generalists rather than subject specialists. In Hong Kong, the subject-level committees have been busy fulfilling the orders of the high-level committees for the past twenty years. Such top-down decisions happened from the launching of the Advanced Supplementary Level Curriculum, that of the core curriculum (later turned into the 'Tailored syllabus'), the Target Oriented Curriculum in the 1990s, down to the grosser educational reform in the 2000s, including the New Senior Secondary School curriculum, the Basic Competency Assessment, and the School Based Assessment (though the School Based Assessment has been postponed in the subject of mathematics). These might have distracted the subject curriculum developers' attention from delving into the core mission—improving the subject curriculum.

There had always been a call for 'doing away with mathematics' under the influence of educational progressivism (Morris 1996), though sometimes the voice was louder and other times not as loud. The creation of the new compulsory subject Liberal Studies in Hong Kong shows the belief that this newly created subject is more effective in training generic skills than other well-established subjects. In a sense, subject curricula are means to meet the goals of building up students' generic skills and thus often receive a lower regard. If this kind of mentality prevails, the quality of the mathematics curriculum may suffer in the future.

There is an issue that Hong Kong did not come across: the role of mathematicians in curriculum development. There is always an impression that those who failed to become mathematicians became mathematics teachers/educators. Though this assertion is not without challenge, it seems to be a common belief around the world. However, Hong Kong is a small place where mathematicians and mathematics educators generally live in harmony. There have frequently been collaborations between them. Apparently this is not the case in many other parts of the world. The California Math War, in simplistic terms, was a struggle between mathematicians and mathematics educators. The same is true for other 'math wars,' such as the ones in the Japanese and the Chinese mainland (though some refrain from calling the Chinese situation a war) (Lam et al. 2012). This is also the case in Taiwan when the mathematics curriculum within the *Grade 1–9 Curriculum* transited from the temporary edition to the formal one. One should not dispute the importance of the subject matter in curriculum development. The views of the mathematicians should be respected. However, as pointed out earlier, different sectors (including mathematicians) have to realize that the target users of the school curriculum have been expanded as school education becomes part of general education. Besides maintaining a mathematics flavor in the school mathematics curriculum, it should serve to build a path of mathematization, allowing students to depart from the world around them and gradually progress into the mathematics world (Wong et al. 2004). There is, nevertheless, a positive aspect that lies beneath this apparent conflict. This conflict reflected that both the mathematicians and mathematics educators cared very much about what and how mathematics was taught in classrooms. What is needed is a way to communicate and work together smoothly.

The Curriculum (Document)—A Starting Point or a Consolidation of Experimentation

In the above sections, we repeatedly emphasize that curriculum policy-making in these educational systems is top down and show that the government is dominating the whole process. One may see this from another angle. Are practicing teachers mature enough to bring up ideas for the betterment of classroom teaching? Professional bodies ought to serve a crucial role too. Do we have a professional body that takes a role beyond mere teacher unions? Would it be better for the government to work hand in hand with schools? In Hong Kong, during the heat of the Target Oriented Curriculum debate, the Hong Kong Association for Mathematics Education published an *unofficial curriculum* (Fung and Wong 1997), which was beneficial to the moving forward of the mathematics curriculum. Ideas were shared in seminars and workshops and among the teachers. Through better exchange of ideas, the central curriculum may accommodate the preferences of the teachers, and also build in elements that facilitate its implementation.

Furthermore, after a new curriculum is designed, it is usually sent to the schools in the form of an official document. Teachers are expected to be implementers of curriculum policies decided by the central agencies. Even though teachers in three different systems might view their autonomy and professional view differently, school-based curriculum development in major subjects, mathematics being one, rarely exists (Lam and Yeung 2010), except perhaps in the case of Taiwan where it is explicitly specified in the *Grade 1–9 Curriculum* (MOE Taiwan 2003). Under such a center–periphery curriculum development model, implementation of the new curriculum has been far from smooth (Lin and Zhang 2006) despite the fact that some supporting measures, such as teacher training, were provided.

Preparing teachers for implementing a new curriculum is a headache. One of the crucial issues that hindered the Modern Mathematics curriculum's implementation in Hong Kong in the 1960s was that there were so many teachers, and teacher training could not be done overnight. There were not enough workshops and some teachers could only learn new things in the evening and had to teach the next morning (Wong and Wong 2001). The problem is even more serious in the other two systems where the teacher community is much bigger. Rushing through the teacher preparation process in the Chinese mainland in the early 2000s was detrimental to the curriculum reform. Teachers were seen as lacking the pedagogical skills to enact the reform and hence were required to attend short courses on how to deliver the curriculum reform initiative. Such courses are seldom effective in helping teachers change their beliefs and teaching approaches (Guskey 2002). Furthermore, the feedback loop from the practicing teachers on the curriculum reform to the curriculum planners and government officials was not effective, thus adversely affecting the chance of timely adjustments to the new curriculum.

Conclusion

The three educational systems have undergone a series of curriculum reforms over the past fifty years. The design and implementation processes have never been smooth. Nevertheless, it is evident that a more democratic process of curriculum development involving more people before and during various reforms has emerged. This alone does not guarantee a smooth implementation process; indeed, building consensus is not easy at all. A curriculum development system that allows more stakeholders to share their opinions may help, but the professional input in the needs analysis is also essential.

Designing a curriculum at the policy level is only the first step. It is the teacher who needs to implement the curriculum. Teacher professionalization is essential (Stigler and Hiebert 1999). All other factors, textbooks included, are means to facilitate this. One of the main purposes of curriculum reform should be the nurturing of a learning community among the teachers. Nevertheless, more and more attention is paid to teachers' competence, including knowledge and beliefs. We believe that all these play a more crucial role than producing the curriculum document itself (Cai and Wong 2012).

References

Association for Curriculum and Instruction of Taiwan (2000). *Basic rationale and implementation strategies for school-based curriculum development: Doubt in elementary school mathematics education* [in Chinese]. Taipei: Ministry of Education.

Cai, J., & Wong, N. Y. (2012). Effective mathematics teaching: Conceptualisation, research and reflections. In W. Blum, R. B. Ferri, & K. Maaß (Eds.), *Mathematikunterricht im Kontext von Realität, Kultur und Lehrerprofessionalität* (pp. 294–303). Wiesbaden: Springer Spektrum.

Chung, J. (2005). On the change of the school mathematics curricula in the recent decade [in Chinese]. *Journal of Educational Research, 133*, 124–134.

Curriculum Development Council, Hong Kong (2002). *Basic education curriculum guide: Building on strengths (primary 1–secondary 3)*. Hong Kong: Education Department.

Curriculum Development Institute (2009). *The CDC structure*. Retrieved Jan 15 2013 form http://cd1.edb.hkedcity.net/cd/cdc/download/others/CDC%20Structure_en_090115.pdf.

Delors, J., Mufti, A., Amagi, I., Carneiro, R., Chung, F., Geremek, B., Gorham, W., Kornhauser, A., Manley, M., Quero, M. P., Savané, M., Singh, K., Stavenhagen, R., Suhr, M. W., & Zhou, N. (1996). *Learning: the treasure within*. Paris: UNESCO.

Eisner, E. W. (2002). *The educational imagination: On the design and evaluation of school programs* (3rd ed.). Upper Saddle River: Merrill Prentice Hall.

Fok, P. K. (2005). Curriculum advisory bodies in Hong Kong: Structure, characteristics and critique [in Chinese]. *Educational Research Journal, 20*(2), 265–287.

Fung, C. I., & Wong, N. Y. (1997). *Unofficial mathematics curriculum for Hong Kong: P.1 to S.5*. Hong Kong: Hong Kong Association for Mathematics Education.

Guskey, T. R. (2002). Professional development and teacher change. *Teachers and Teaching: Theory and Practice, 8*(3–4), 381–391.

He, X. (2006). Reactions to Boju Jaing's 'What does mathematics lesson lose under the new curriculum standard' [in Chinese]. *Guangdong Education, 6*, 55–57.

Huang, R., & Li, Y. (2009). Pursuing excellence in mathematics classroom instruction through exemplary lesson development in China: A case study. *ZDM—The International Journal on Mathematics Education, 41*, 279–296.

Jiang, B. (2005, March 16). What does mathematics lesson lose under the new curriculum standard [in Chinese]. *Guangming Daily*. http://www.gmw.cn/content/2005-03/16/content_197119.htm. Accessed 15 January 2013.

Lam, C. C., & Chan, K. S. J. (2011). How schools cope with a new integrated subject for senior secondary students: An example from Hong Kong. *Curriculum Perspectives, 31*(3), 23–32.

Lam, C. C., & Yeung, S. S. Y. (2010). School-based curriculum development in Hong Kong: An arduous journey. In E. H. F. Law & N. Nieveen (Eds.), *Schools as curriculum agencies: Asian and European perspectives on school-based curriculum development* (pp. 61–82). Rotterdam: Sense Publishers.

Lam, C. C., Wong, N. Y., Ding, R., Li, S. P. T., & Ma, Y. (2012). Basic education mathematics curriculum reform in the greater Chinese region—trends and lessons learned. In B. Sriraman, J. Cai, K. Lee, L. Fan, Y. Shimuzu, L. C. Sam, & K. Subramanium (Eds.), *The first sourcebook on Asian research in mathematics education: China, Korea, Singapore, Japan, Malaysia, & India*. Charlotte: Information Age Publishing.

Lin, P. H. (2004). The study of the context of school-based curriculum development [in Chinese]. *Journal of National Taipei Teachers College, 17*(2), 35–56.

Lin, Z. Z., & Zhang, S. (2006). An analysis of the curriculum reform implementation strategies in Hong Kong [in Chinese]. *Exploring Education Development, 12A*, 8–13.

Ma, L. (1992). Some clarifications on 'nine-year compulsory education full-time primary and middle school curriculum planning (try out)' [in Chinese]. In Basic Education Department, MOE (Ed.), *Guidelines for nine-year compulsory education curriculum planning*. Beijing: People's Education Press.

Ma, Y. (1998). Retrospect and outlook on the development of mathematics curriculum in the Chinese mainland, Hong Kong and Taiwan [in Chinese]. *Education Journal, 26*(1), 131–148.

Ma, Y. (2008). The strategies and characteristics of curriculum implementation in the Chinese mainland. In P. K. Fok, Z. Y. Yu, H. X. Xu, K. W. Chu, K. L. Hui, F. Chiang, T. S. Lee, C. C. Tsui, Y. P. Ho, H. S. Hon, J. J. Wang, M. R. Zhao, & Y. G. Lin (Eds.), *Curriculum and instruction: The journey of research and practice* (pp. 164–172). Chongqing: Chongqing University Press.

Ma, Y., Lam, C. C., & Wong, N. Y. (2006). Chinese primary school mathematics teachers working in a centralized curriculum system: A case study of two primary schools in North-East China. *Compare, 36*(2), 197–212.

Ministry of Education, China (2001). *Full time free education mathematics curriculum standard (Trial edition)* [in Chinese]. Beijing: Beijing Normal University Press.

Ministry of Education, Taiwan (1993). *Elementary school curriculum standards* [in Chinese]. Taipei: Author.

Ministry of Education, Taiwan (2003). *Enjoyment of learning mathematics: K-9 mathematics instruction brochure* [in Chinese]. Taipei: Author.

Morris, P. (1996). *The Hong Kong school curriculum*. Hong Kong: Hong Kong University Press.

Morris, P., & Adamson, B. (2010). *Curriculum, schooling and society in Hong Kong*. Hong Kong: Hong Kong University Press.

National Institute for Compilation and Translation, Taiwan (2002a). *Elementary school mathematics: Book 4* [in Chinese]. Taipei: Author.

National Institute for Compilation and Translation, Taiwan (2002b). *Elementary school mathematics teaching guide: Book 4* [in Chinese]. Taipei: Author.

Pajares, M. F. (1992). Teachers' belief and educational research: Cleaning up a messy construct. *Review of Educational Research, 62*(3), 307–332.

Pan, H. L. (Ed.) (2007). *Empowering teachers* [in Chinese]. Taipei: Psychology Publishing.

Schiro, M. S. (2008). *Curriculum theory: Conflicting visions and enduring concerns*. Thousand Oaks: Sage.

Shi, N., & Liu, H. (2007). Quality-oriented education: Fundamental objective and implementation approach [in Chinese]. *Educational Research, 8*, 10–14.

Shi, N., & Ma, Y. (2009). *Mathematics curriculum for basic education: The design, implementation and outlook of the reform* [in Chinese]. Nanning: Guangxi Education Publishing House.

Stigler, J., & Hiebert, J. (1999). *The teaching gap: Best ideas from the world's teachers for improving education in the classroom*. New York: Free Press.

Tam, H. P. (2010). A brief introduction of the mathematics curricula of Taiwan. In F. K. S. Leung & Y. Li (Eds.), *Reforms and issues in school mathematics in East Asia* (pp. 109–128). Rotterdam: Sense Publishers.

Tang, K. C., Wong, N. Y., Fok, P. K., Ngan, M. Y., & Wong, K. L. (2007). Hong Kong primary mathematics curriculum development in the past five decades and its implications for future mathematics curriculum development [in Chinese]. *Journal of Basic Education, 16*(1), 115–131.

Watkins, D. A. (2008). *Learning-centered teaching: An Asian perspective*. Keynote address at the 2nd International Conference on Learner-centered Education, Manila, the Philippines, February.

Wong, N. Y. (2004). The CHC learner's phenomenon: Its implications on mathematics education. In L. Fan, N. Y. Wong, J. Cai, & S. Li (Eds.), *How Chinese learn mathematics: Perspectives from insiders* (pp. 503–534). Singapore: World Scientific.

Wong, N. Y. (2010). The Hong Kong mathematics curriculum: 1997 × MATH × ED = Period of Change. In F. K. S. Leung & Y. Li (Eds.), *Reforms and issues in school mathematics in East Asia* (pp. 33–57). Rotterdam: Sense Publications.

Wong, N. Y., & Tang, K. C. (2012). Mathematics education in Hong Kong under colonial rule. *BSHM Bulletin: Journal of the British Society for the History of Mathematics, 27*, 1–8.

Wong, N. Y., & Wong, K. L. (2001). The process of the modern mathematics reform and the lessons we learn on contemporary mathematics education [in Chinese]. In N. Y. Wong (Ed.), *The long path of mathematics education in Hong Kong: Modern mathematics as the opening chapter* (pp. 9–111). Hong Kong: Hong Kong Association for Mathematics Education.

Wong, N. Y., Han, J., & Lee, P. Y. (2004). The mathematics curriculum: Toward globalization or westernization? In L. Fan, N. Y. Wong, J. Cai, & S. Li (Eds.), *How Chinese learn mathematics: perspectives from insiders* (pp. 27–70). Singapore: World Scientific.

Wu, C. S. (2003). *Knowledge economics and educational development* [in Chinese]. Taipei: Shita Books.

Wu, R. X., & Lin, W. S. (1997). Conceiving constructivistic pedagogy in primary mathematics classroom [in Chinese]. *Journal of Educational Resources and Research, 18*, 44–50.

Potential Impact of the Common Core Mathematics Standards on the American Curriculum

Hung-Hsi Wu

Abstract In June of 2010, the Common Core State Standards in Mathematics (CC-SSM) were introduced in the U.S. Long before the advent of the CCSSM, American schools had a *de facto* national mathematics curriculum, namely, the curriculum dictated by school mathematics textbooks. While there are some formal differences among these books, the underlying mathematics is quite similar throughout. The resulting curriculum distorts mathematics in the sense that it often withholds precise definitions and logical reasoning, fails to point out interconnections between major topics such as whole numbers and fractions, and employs ambiguous language that ultimately leads to widespread non-learning. The CCSSM make a conscientious attempt to address many of these problems and, in the process, raise the demand on teachers' content knowledge for a successful implementation of these standards. This article examines, strictly from an American perspective, some of the mathematical issues (primarily in grades 4–12) that arise during the transition from the *de facto* curriculum to the curriculum envisioned by the CCSSM. Although the CC-SSM would seem to be strictly an American concern, these mathematical issues transcend national boundaries because there are very few deviations in the K-12 curriculum across nations (for the K-8 curriculum, see p. 3-31 to p. 3-33 of National Mathematics Advisory Panel 2008).

Keywords Common Core Standards · Curriculum · Content knowledge · Definition · Reasoning

Introduction

In the unending search for improvement in mathematics education in the U.S. for the last half century, one thing seems to have been consistently overlooked; namely, the fact that there has been a *de facto* American mathematics school curriculum since the demise of the "New Math" in the early 1970s. This is the curriculum encoded

H.-H. Wu (✉)
Department of Mathematics #3840, University of California, Berkeley, CA 94720-3840, USA
e-mail: wu@berkeley.edu

Y. Li, G. Lappan (eds.), *Mathematics Curriculum in School Education*,
Advances in Mathematics Education, DOI 10.1007/978-94-007-7560-2_7,
© Springer Science+Business Media Dordrecht 2014

in school textbooks. There are many textbooks, of course, and they are guided by quite different philosophical outlooks ranging from "traditional" to "reform". Nevertheless, the underlying mathematics is, overall, quite similar. While such a claim may startle some, the element of surprise will disappear the minute one considers for instance, the uniform lack of emphasis in school textbooks on giving precise *definitions* to concepts[1] and, even more significantly, the same lack of emphasis on basing logical reasoning on precise definitions. If even this does not drive home the point, consider further the ambiguity of the meaning of fraction, multiplication or division of fractions, "variable", congruence, similarity, etc. How many textbooks explain how to multiply two fractions strictly on the basis of the definition of a fraction?[2] How many textbooks explain why any two circles are similar *using a precise definition of similarity?* And so on. This body of mathematical knowledge, contained in an overwhelming majority of school textbooks, will be henceforth referred to as **Textbook School Mathematics (TSM)**. (See Wu 2011a and 2011c, for a fuller discussion.) It will be seen from subsequent discussion that TSM, in the words of the Common Core State Standards for Mathematics (2010),[3] page 3, "distorts mathematics and turns off students". More pertinent is the fact that much of the recent mathematics education crisis can be traced to the omnipresence of TSM in the school curriculum. The purpose of this article is to critically examine, *strictly from an American perspective*, several key areas of this *de facto* national curriculum from the vantage point of the CCSSM, highlight the deleterious effect of TSM, and give an indication of how the CCSSM—if they are faithfully implemented—might lead us out of the TSM jungle.

This *de facto* national curriculum has not been part of national dialog thus far for at least two reasons. The obvious one is the large grain size that is normally used in such general discussions. The other reason is very germane to this article: until recently, the issue of *content* in school mathematics education has not been on the frontline of this dialog. The failure to recognize this existence of the *de facto* national curriculum does carry serious consequences, however. In the writing of state or national mathematics standards, for example, the focus has always been on the optimal placement of standard mathematical topics in a certain grade band, e.g., addition of fractions in grades 4–6, solving linear equations in middle school, triangle congruence criteria in high school, etc. The general expectation is that if the statement of the desired outcome (e.g., learn the addition of fractions and use it to solve problems) is phrased correctly, clearly, and in a grade-appropriate manner, and if it is faithfully implemented, progress will ensue (see, e.g., Carmichael et al.

---

[1] It should be understood that *this article is primarily concerned with the mathematics in textbooks of grades 4–12*. The need for correct and grade-appropriate definitions is no less acute in K-3; for example, one does not want young children to be taught that a **decimal** is a number with a decimal point. Nevertheless, a short article such as this cannot adequately attend to all the instructional subtleties in those early grades.

[2] As an illustration of how definitions can be effectively used in mathematical reasoning even in a topic as elementary as fraction multiplication, one may consult Chap. 17 of Wu (2011b).

[3] Hereafter referred to simply as CCSSM.

2010, especially the Foreword). Such expectations ignore the havoc that has been wrought by TSM in the school curriculum. Take, for example, the 2000 standards in grade 5 of California on the addition of fractions (p. 53 of Mathematics Framework for California Public Schools 2006):

> 2.0 Students perform calculations and solve problems involving addition, subtraction, and simple multiplication and division of fractions and decimals:
> 2.3 Solve simple problems, including ones arising in concrete situations, involving the addition and subtraction of fractions and mixed numbers (like and unlike denominators of 20 or less), and express answers in the simplest form.

The statement of this standard is mathematically correct,[4] and its placement in grade 5 is pedagogically unassailable, but now look what happens when it passes through the TSM melting pot and re-emerges in school textbooks:

1. Students are told to add fractions without being told precisely what *adding fractions* means, partly because there is no definition of a fraction as a *number* (this is universal practice).
2. Students learn the skill of adding fractions, either by drawing pictures but not given a formula (cf. Lappan et al. 1998a), or by being given a formula that uses the Least Common Denominator (Bennett et al. 2001; Andrews et al. 2002). The reasoning is either not given or not given with focus and clarity.
3. When students are presented with a problem such as "How much water is in the bucket if you first pour in $2\frac{3}{7}$ gallons and then another $3\frac{2}{9}$ gallons", they dutifully use the method in step 2 only because "addition" is *supposed to be* used on account of the word "and", not because they know why.

There is a discussion in Wu (2011b), p. 221 and p. 228, about the correct definition of fraction addition and the reason why the Least Common Denominator should not be used to define the addition of fractions.

In any case, this is a glaring illustration of how good mathematical intentions are undermined by TSM-based implementations. There are countless examples of this, three major ones will be discussed at some length in a later section. The moral is that, until we eradicate TSM from the school curriculum, any mathematical standard that calls for the teaching of a mathematical topic in a certain grade will do nothing but rearrange the *mathematically flawed* presentations in TSM. Though not entirely appropriate, the proverbial "rearranging the deck chairs on the Titanic" does come to mind: it captures the zeitgeist of the situation.

The need to confront TSM in writing a set of standards was unimagined until the CCSSM came along. Anticipating the usual thinking of TSM, the CCSSM succeed, on the whole, in prescribing how each topic should be taught in a mathematically acceptable way. For example, here is how the CCSSM treat the addition of fractions: they ask that this skill be spread out through three grades. With drastic oversimplification, the CCSSM prescription goes something like this:

---

[4]Although one may quibble with the restriction on the denominators used.

In **Grade 3**, understand a fraction as a number on the number line and interpret $\frac{m}{n}$ as m copies of $\frac{1}{n}$; represent fractions on a number line diagram and explain equivalence of fractions in special cases, e.g., $\frac{1}{3}$ is the same point on the number line as $\frac{2\times1}{2\times3}$.

In **Grade 4**, explain why a fraction $\frac{a}{b}$ is **equivalent** to a fraction $\frac{n\times a}{n\times b}$ by observing that they are the same point on the number line. Also define addition of fractions as joining parts referring to the same whole. Then for two fractions with the same denominator, $\frac{m}{n} + \frac{k}{n} = \frac{m+k}{n}$.

In **Grade 5**, add and subtract fractions with unlike denominators by replacing given fractions with equivalent fractions, so that we have fractions with the same denominator. For example, $\frac{2}{3} + \frac{5}{4} = \frac{8}{12} + \frac{15}{12} = \frac{23}{12}$, which is joining copies of $\frac{1}{12}$ together.

Altogether, these standards guide students through three grades in order to help them understand the *meaning* of adding fractions. (For a more detailed presentation of how these standards can be implemented in the school classroom, one may consult pp. 9–13, 19–28, and 24–28 in Wu 2011d.)

The end result is that addition *is* putting things together, even for fractions, and this mathematical development ends with the formula,

$$\frac{a}{b} + \frac{c}{d} = \frac{ad + bc}{bd},$$

with no mention of Least Common Denominator. What is obvious is that this presentation on adding fractions does not distort mathematics, and cannot be accused of turning students off because adding fractions is now seen to be no different from adding whole numbers: it's *just putting things together*.

In order to overcome TSM, the CCSSM *have* to be prescriptive, but the unprecedented prescriptive nature of CCSSM has provoked, not surprisingly, concerns about the possibility of stifling innovation and individualization (see, for example, page 6 of Institute for Research on Mathematics and Science Education 2010). My interpretation of the situation is that, if all the innovations of the past decades could not produce a curriculum that does justice to mathematics, then it is time to try to *prescribe a way out of this predicament*. If we succeed in implementing the CCSSM and eliminating TSM in the process, then the time will come for a hundred flowers to bloom.

In a short article such as this, it is not possible to discuss TSM in detail, much less also discuss how the CCSSM try to counteract the ill effects of TSM. What I will do is to describe—in the broadest terms—some of the most salient features of TSM in the next section, and then discuss in greater detail three specific examples of how the CCSSM have responded to the challenge of TSM in the following section. The last section will contain a few comments about the potential impact of these proposed changes on teachers.

Now a word about citations of literature. To the extent that I am putting the whole system of school mathematics education under a microscope, any explicit citation in support of a particular statement is bound to give the false impression that I am targeting an author or a book. If I had a choice, I would rather not give any citations. However, the minimum requirement of scholarship dictates that I must, and the only way I can deal with this requirement is to enforce the policy of not citing any one source more than twice. Because this is a sensitive subject, I must add two more remarks in order to round off the picture. My citations were guided largely by what happened to be available to me at the time of writing, so that the presence or absence of a particular textbook or textbook series in the list of references has no significance beyond this fact. In addition, the quality of the cited textbooks varies, and it must not be assumed that each of them has all, or even most, of the flaws that are discussed in this article. I hope the reader will keep the last fact in mind.

Overview

The purpose of this section is to give a *brief* indication of some of the problems with TSM in the K-12 curriculum.

The main topics of grades K-4 are place value and the whole number algorithms. In the *de facto* national curriculum, too often the standard algorithms are presented as *faits accomplis* that require neither motivation for their learning nor a clear explanation of why they provide the correct answers. More recently, these algorithms are downplayed in various ways: they are either buried in a host of other algorithms, or all the ingredients that lead to them are presented but the ultimate conclusions (the algorithms themselves) are not singled out, or they are de-emphasized in favor of invented algorithms (e.g., Bell et al. 2008 and Kliman et al. 2006). Consequently, the fluent execution of the standard algorithms is also de-emphasized. What all these misguided approaches have in common is their failure to recognize the main *mathematical* message of these algorithms, which is to *reduce all whole number computations to single-digit computations*. The standard algorithms reduce a complicated task (the computation with multi-digit numbers) to a series of simple tasks (the computation with single-digit numbers) through the skillful use of place value. When the standard algorithms are taught from this perspective, they become a conduit to learning about two fundamental aspects of mathematics, namely, the need for logical reasoning and the fact that mathematics thrives on the reduction of the complex to the simple. See, for example, Chap. 3 of Wu (2011b).

The CCSSM provide a remedy for the existing situation to a large extent. Concerning the multiplication algorithm, for example, they begin with a (too often neglected) *definition* of multiplication as repeated addition, e.g., 5×7 as $7 + 7 + 7 + 7 + 7$ (Standard 3.OA 1 in CCSSM 2010), and then ask for the multiplication table to be committed to memory (Standard 3.OA 7 in CCSSM 2010) in grade 3. The three basic laws of operation (commutative, associative, and distributive) are also introduced in grade 3. In grade 4, the CCSSM ask for the multiplication of "a whole number of up to four digits by a one-digit whole number," and the multiplication of "two two-digit numbers, using strategies based on place value *and the properties of operations*" (emphasis added; see Standard 4.NBT 5 in CCSSM 2010). Finally in grade 5, students learn to multiply any two whole numbers. When the multiplication algorithm is taught in three grades as described, so that each step of this sophisticated algorithm is given ample time to be internalized by students, there is less of a chance that the teaching will be done by rote. This is all that one can ask for in a set of standards.

As mentioned earlier, the underpinning of these algorithms is *place value*, the fact that, for example, the 3 in 372 represents 300 and 7 is 70 while 2 is 2. From a mathematical perspective, it may be more effective to explain to students, in a pedagogically appropriate way, the real reason that place value is needed: namely, to make it possible to count to any number, no matter how large, by limiting ourselves to the use of *only* ten symbols: 0, 1, 2, ..., 8, 9 (see Chap. 1, Sect. 1.1 in Wu 2011b). Thus place value is a property of the Hindu-Arabic *numeral system* we use and *not* a property of whole numbers. Exposing children to this fact at an early age would reinforce the importance of reasoning in mathematics. This is an idea that is worth exploring in the future.

The dominant topics of grades 4–6 (roughly) are fractions, decimals, and elementary geometry. There is no better illustration of the failure of the *de facto* national curriculum than the teaching of fractions. Fractions are students' first serious entry into abstractions. In their learning progressions, this is the first time that they can no longer rely on counting with their fingers (as they used to do with whole numbers) to relate what they are learning to their tactile experiences. They need detailed and careful guidance—including precise definitions of all the concepts as well as persuasive reasoning—in order to compensate for the loss of reliance on their fingers. Unfortunately, the response of the *de facto* national curriculum is to offer information that is at once confusing (e.g., a fraction is a part of a whole, a ratio, *and* a division) and misleading (the arithmetic operations on fractions bear no relation to those on whole numbers). In place of the precise definition of a fraction, it offers analogies, i.e., a fraction is *like* a piece of pizza or a shape in pattern blocks. In place of precise definitions for the arithmetic operations of fractions, it offers only algorithms and (of course) little explanation because it is impossible to explain anything that has not been precisely defined. The situation as described is so universal that no citation need be given: just open any school textbooks and this is all there is to see.

The same story is pretty much true of the teaching of decimals. Teaching decimals as an extension of whole numbers by the use of tenths, hundredths, etc.—but separate from fractions—is just another form of teaching-by-analogy. (Once again, this practice is so universal that no citation is necessary.) Indeed, this kind of teaching is only good for decimals with at most two decimal digits (pennies and dollars), so students do not get a precise conception of what a decimal is. In addition, such teaching is intellectually dishonest because, even for decimals with only three decimal digits such as 0.127, the nomenclature of "one tenth and 2 hundredths and 7 thousandths" hides the fact that 0.127 is by definition a *sum* of fractions:

$$0.127 = \frac{1}{10} + \frac{2}{100} + \frac{7}{1000}$$

Unfortunately, TSM has never been careful to teach decimals only after the addition of fractions has been defined. Historically, as well as conceptually, a decimal is a fraction whose denominator is a power of 10. Once decimals have been integrated in this way into the domain of fractions, everything becomes simpler, be it the comparison of decimals or the computational algorithms with decimals, especially multiplication and division. (One can consult Sects. 12.3, 13.4, 14.2, 15.3, 17.2, and 18.4 of Wu 2011b.)

If I fault the *de facto* national curriculum for the flawed instruction on fractions, it is because the instruction is incommensurate with our expectations that students acquire a *robust* knowledge of fractions. If all we ask of students is that they achieve a passing acquaintance with the terminology of fractions, know roughly what they are, and be able to use them in simple everyday situations, then what TSM has to offer may just be good enough. Unfortunately, sophisticated word problems involving percent, ratio and rate await students in the sixth and seventh grades, and students need a thorough understanding of the division of fractions for their solutions, which in turn requires a solid foundation in the multiplication of fractions. The *de facto* national curriculum simply does not support this kind of learning. What we have is therefore a situation in which TSM teaches students only a little, but expects them to learn a lot. This sets students up perfectly to fail.

This fraction-decimal situation calls for change, and again the CCSSM have met this challenge to a large extent. Although fractions are introduced informally in grades 3 (as it should be), the recognition that a fraction is a point on the number line is encouraged from the beginning and the various basic theorems such as equivalent fractions are explained on this basis. Likewise, the arithmetic operations on fractions are defined and their algorithms explained in terms of the number line. The amount of details about the teaching of fractions that one finds in the CCSSM is unprecedented, and it raises the hope that a more sensible school curriculum on fractions will follow. As for decimals, the CCSSM state explicitly in grade 4, "Understand decimal notation for fractions, and compare decimal fractions." In other words, students are asked to learn that 0.127 is just a *notation* for the fraction $\frac{127}{1000}$. Thanks to the CCSSM, the teaching of decimals is now firmly integrated into the teaching of fractions. (For the details for both fractions and decimals, consult Wu 2011b, Part 2.)

The other major topic of grades 4–6 is geometry, which is devoted mainly to the introduction of the basic vocabulary and the derivations of basic formulas pertaining to area and volume. The *de facto* national curriculum turns geometric instruction in these grades into a vocabulary-memorizing ritual, and not a very accurate one at that (see, for example, Andrews et al. 2002, or Bennett et al. 2001). For example, the statement in the CCSSM about "classifying two-dimensional figures in a hierarchy *based on properties*" (italics added; Standard 5.G 4) is a pointed reminder that the controversy about whether a square is a rectangle or whether a parallelogram is a trapezoid should be laid to rest. On the other hand, one of the most glaring omissions in the TSM presentation of area and volume formulas is the explanation of why the area of a rectangle with *fractional* side lengths is the product of the side lengths. This theorem, which is critical to the understanding of the concept of area as well as the concept of fraction multiplication in school mathematics (see pp. 62–64 of Wu 2010a), seems to be missing in all existing textbooks and standards (e.g., Bell et al.

2008; National Council of Teachers of Mathematics[5] 2000, and NCTM 2006). It is to the credit of the CCSSM that they explicitly call for this explanation (standard 5.NF 4). Along this line, let it be mentioned that there is a common error in the proof of the area formula for a triangle:

$$\text{area} = \frac{1}{2} \,(\text{base} \times \text{height})$$

The argument given in textbooks, in an overwhelming majority of the cases, is only valid when the altitude meets the base, but not when the altitude falls outside the base, i.e., meets the line containing the base at a point outside the base (cf. Fuson 2006, and Kliman et al. 2006). Unfortunately, if the area formula for a triangle is not known to hold in the latter case, i.e., when the altitude falls outside the base, it would be impossible to derive the area formula for a general trapezoid (see, for example, Wu 2012, pp. 33–36 for the details). Corrections on this level are beyond the capability of a set of standards, even the CCSSM, but such curricular issues point to the overall logical oversight in TSM. An additional contribution of the CCSSM is their attempt to give at least an informal definition of area and volume. See Standard 5.NF 4 and Standard 5.MD 3 of CCSSM. Length and area are usually presented *only* as intuitive concepts in TSM in the elementary and middle grades, and this fact may be the cause of the well-known confusion concerning perimeter and area among students.

The emphases in grades 6–7 are on word problems involving percent, ratio, rate, and rational numbers. Before discussing these word problems, one must point out a grievous omission in the *de facto* national curriculum: the failure to make explicit the so-called Fundamental Assumption of School Mathematics (FASM), see Chap. 21 of Wu (2011b). In essence, this is the statement that, although we only know how to compute with fractions (and later on, rational numbers) at this point, we can extrapolate formally the computational algorithms to all positive real numbers (respectively, all real numbers). FASM is conceptually important in the context of real-world problems about ratio and rate, and especially in algebra. The former often explicitly brings up numbers that are not necessarily fractions (e.g., the ratio of the circumference to the diameter of a circle). As to the latter, even the simplest identity such as

$$\frac{1}{x-1} - \frac{1}{x+1} = \frac{2}{x^2 - 1}$$

begs the question: what does this mean when (for example) $x = \pi$ if students are only taught the division of one *rational* number by another? (In this instance, one has to point out that FASM is not made explicit in CCSSM either.)

Problems involving percent, ratio, and rate are notorious for the amount of misunderstanding they elicit from students. The research on the probable cause of nonlearning in ratio and rate has led to the emphasis on so-called *proportional reason-*

---

[5]Hereafter referred to as *NCTM*.

ing. As this will be discussed at some length in the example on *Rate and Proportional Reasoning* in the next section, we will merely mention the fact that, because these concepts have never been clearly explained (defined) in the *de facto* national curriculum, students cannot be in any position to provide solutions based on mathematical reasoning. Indeed, if there is no definition, there can be no valid reasoning. As the computer dictum goes: *Garbage in, garbage out.*

It must be pointed out that, although the CCSSM try valiantly to make some sense of this whole circle of ideas, they have not made any positive contributions in this direction. See the standards in 6.RP of grade 6 and 7.RP of grade 7. On the other hand, the CCSSM have made great strides in elucidating another murky concept in the *de facto* national curriculum: the concept of an "expression". It would, however, be more appropriate to discuss this during the discussion of algebra below.

The teaching of rational numbers[6] hinges on how negative numbers are integrated into students' knowledge of fractions. The *de facto* national curriculum relies mainly on manipulatives (e.g., the use of counters of different colors to represent positive and negative *integers*), analogies, and patterns (Usiskin et al. 1998, or Collins et al. 1998). The CCSSM acquit themselves particularly well in this regard by their insistence on the use of the number line and reasoning based on the general laws of operations (commutative, associative, and distributive laws) rather than patterns or manipulatives. See Standards 6.NS 5 and 6, and 7.NS 1 and 2. This is particularly true of the careful guided tour through the treacherous terrain of multiplication and division of rational numbers in Standard 7.NS 2. If so desired, one can consult Wu (2011c) for a leisurely discussion of teaching $(-a)(-b) = ab$ that is consistent with the CCSSM.

Grade 8 is a pivotal grade in the school mathematics curriculum, because it is in this grade that a decision is usually made as to whether the whole grade should be devoted to so-called Algebra I or simply make a beginning towards algebra. Now it must be said that there is no natural law that says students' learning of mathematics would suffer irrevocably if all the standard topics of Algebra I were not covered in grade 8. Moreover, what has been glossed over in any such discussion is the fact that the teaching of Algebra I in grade 8 according to TSM is accomplished at an unconscionable cost: it omits any mention of similar triangles, thereby cutting out the mathematical underpinning that connects the geometry of lines to the algebra of linear equations. Consequently, students are forced to learn by rote that one can get the slope of a line by choosing *any* two points on the line, and they are also forced to memorize by brute force the four forms of the equation of a line (often without success). We will examine further this issue in the example on *Slope of A Line* in the next section.

In addition to the omission of any serious discussion of similar triangles, the middle school geometry curriculum according to TSM is a mélange of informal

---

[6]In the education literature, the term *rational numbers* is generally taken to mean *fractions*. In mathematics, the term means *positive and negative fractions*. Because *rational number* is one of the most basic concepts in mathematics, it is best that people in education do not arbitrarily change accepted mathematical terminology.

and disconnected discussions of diverse topics. Thus the concepts of translations, reflections, and rotations are taught as fun activities that heighten our sensibilities in art appreciation, e.g., Escher's prints. But are they relevant to mathematics? That is not so clear (see, e.g., Chap. 9 of Davison et al. 2001 or Eicholz et al. 1995). Congruence is just "same size and same shape", and its relationship with translations, reflections, and rotations may or may not be mentioned in passing (cf. Larson et al. 1999). Likewise, similarity means "same shape but not necessarily the same size", and no effort is made to show how this definition is related to the definition of similar triangles in terms of equal angles and proportional sides. In the rare event that such an attempt is made, it is not done in a mathematically disciplined way (cf. Lappan et al. 1998b).

The above discussion points to two serious gaps in the *de facto* national curriculum: an explanation of why the graph of a linear equation of two variables is a line, and a smooth transition from middle school geometry to the high school geometry. Given the traditional curricular structure of the Algebra I-Geometry-Algebra II sequence in high school, the CCSSM had to solve the knotty problem—in the standards of grade 8—of how to restructure the middle school geometry curriculum so that it provides a geometric foundation to fill both of these gaps. We now give a brief description of the restructuring (it is entirely consistent with the one given in Wu 2010a).

The CCSSM accomplish this goal by asking for an intuitive exploration and discussion of translations, reflections, and rotations and for a definition of congruence as a finite composition of these *rigid motions* in the eighth grade (Standards 8.G 1–3). The CCSSM also call for an intuitive exploration and discussion of dilations, and the definition of a similarity transformation as the composition of a dilation and a congruence; then they call for an informal proof, in grade 8, that two triangles are similar if two pairs of angles are equal (Standards 8.G 4–5). The latter is the critical fact needed for the proof that the definition of the slope of a line is well-defined, and that the graph of a linear equation in two variables is a line (see, for example, Wu 2010b, Sect. 4). Then in high school, the definitions of translations, reflections, rotations, and dilations are formalized and congruence and similarity transformations are defined as in the eighth grade. These precise definitions can now serve to prove the usual criteria for triangle congruence (Standards G-CO 5 in high school geometry) and triangle similarity (Standards G-SRT 2–3 in high school geometry). At this point, the usual development of Euclidean geometry may be pursued if so desired. In particular, translations, reflections, rotations, and dilations—basic concepts in advanced mathematics—are now fully integrated into school geometry as foundational concepts rather than as afterthoughts, and the proofs of theorems in plane geometry are now grounded in the tactile concepts of these basic transformations rather than in a set of abstract axioms. See Wu (2010a and 2012).

In the context of teaching algebra, grade 8 is, of course, more than just the teaching of linear equations. This is also where other foundational algebraic concepts are developed and, among these, none is more basic than the proper use of symbols. It can be said that the *de facto* national curriculum really goes astray at this juncture: instead of making a smooth transition from arithmetic to algebra by carefully introducing the concept of generality and showing why the use of symbols is inevitable, this curriculum places the spurious *mathematical* concept of a "variable" front and center. On this shaky foundation, it introduces the concepts of algebraic expression, equation, and solving equations. This curricular development in TSM leads to misconceptions that make the learning of algebra unnecessarily difficult. To a very large extent, these misconceptions have been removed in the CCSSM. Specifically, the preamble to the high school algebra standards on p. 62 of CCSSM (2010) states:

> An expression is a record of a computation with numbers, symbols that represent numbers, arithmetic operations, exponentiation, and, at more advanced levels, the operation of evaluating a function.

Back in grade 6, standards 6.EE 2c and 6.EE 6 already begin to clarify what a *variable* really is (i.e., a descriptive piece of terminology for a *symbol*) and what an *expression* is. Furthermore, standard 6.EE 5 clarifies what an *equation* is and standard A-REI (in high school algebra) explains what it means to *solve an equation*. These will be further discussed in the example on *Solving Equations* in the next section (for the details, see Wu 2010b, Sects. 1–3). Because of the ubiquity of equations and expressions in introductory algebra, these are genuine contributions to improving student learning.

We only have space to briefly mention the high school curriculum. It goes without saying that the *de facto* national curriculum has its usual share of flaws, e.g., lack of clarity and purpose in presenting the laws of exponents (e.g., Chaps. 7 and 9 of Hoffer et al. 1998, and Chap. 8 of Larson et al. 2007), failure to define a parabola correctly (e.g., Chap. 8 of CME Project: Algebra 1 2009, and Chap. 5 of Hoffer et al. 1998), failure to underscore the importance of completing the square in the study of quadratic functions (e.g., Chap. 5 of Holliday et al. 2008, or pp. 215–220 and 491–504 in Murdock et al. 1998), lack of clarity in presenting inverse functions and logarithms (e.g., Sects. 7-2, 9-1, and 9-2 in Holliday et al. 2008, or Sect. 7.4 in Murdock et al. 1998), etc. But let us address the global problems. In most schools, the traditional curriculum of Algebra I-Geometry-Algebra II is used, while some others follow the *American integrated curriculum*.[7] While the artificial separation of the former into a full year of algebra or geometry is undesirable in principle, the latter has also been criticized for its imprecision, mathematical incoherence, and lack of mathematical closure, at least judging by what has been produced thus far (see e.g., Gray undated and Wu 2000). The CCSSM chose to stay neutral on this issue by listing only what they call "conceptual categories" and leave the precise articulation of the high school curriculum to each state. This then leaves room for a third kind of curriculum that could possibly avoid both kinds of pitfalls, namely, one that is aligned with what is done in Japan (see, e.g., Kodaira 1992, 1996, 1997) and other Asian countries in the Far East. To achieve this goal, one has to be aware of the need to structure mathematical topics in the CCSSM coherently. Moreover, one

---

[7] It is sometimes claimed that, because other nations adopt an *integrated curriculum*, so should we. This claim is misleading because the integrated curriculum of other nations is very different from the American integrated curriculum. The former is organized according to the internal development of mathematics whereas the latter seems to revolve around applications or "real world" problems.

must be aware of the omissions of some standard topics in the conceptual categories of the CCSSM, e.g., the concept of the discriminant of quadratic polynomials, the explicit definitions of certain key concepts such as similarity and inverse functions, the fundamental algebraic properties of the exponential and logarithmic functions, etc. A full discussion of these issues would require a separate article.

Some Examples

The purpose of this section is to give a more detailed discussion of three key topics in school mathematics to illustrate the main difference between TSM and the curriculum envisioned by the CCSSM. In the first two of these (Solving Equations and Slope of A Line), the CCSSM excel, but in the third (Proportional Reasoning and Rate), the CCSSM do less well. I hope the choices I have made reflect my desire to give a balanced view of the CCSSM.

Solving Equations

What does it mean to solve an equation? To simplify the discussion, let us take a simple linear equation $4x - 3 = 2x$. According to TSM, solving an equation requires a confrontation with a "variable". From a typical textbook, we have the following:

> A **variable** is a letter used to represent one or more numbers. An **algebraic expression** consists of numbers, at least one variable, and operations. An **equation** is a mathematical sentence formed by placing the symbol "=" between two algebraic expressions. A **solution of the equation** is a number so that when it is substituted for the variable in the equation, the equality is true. (Collins et al. 1998, pp. 800–808)

In this view of algebra, a *variable* is something distinct from *numbers*. Since all that students know up to this point are numbers (and geometry), a variable is a mysterious object. That said, here are the usual steps for solving $4x - 3 = 2x$:

Step 1: $-2x + (4x - 3) = -2x + 2x$.
Step 2: $2x - 3 = 0$
Step 3: $(2x - 3) + 3 = 0 + 3$
Step 4: $2x = 3$
Step 5: $x = \frac{3}{2}$

How do we justify Step 1 (adding $-2x$ to [...], for example, if we don't know what a *variable* is? Since a variable is [...] he equality $2x - 3 = 4x$ is even more of a mystery. Adding the "variab[...] both sides deepens the mystery.

There seem to be three strategies [...] deal with this mysterious step of removing $2x$ from both sides. *First:* [...] e principle (first enunciated by Euclid) that *equals added to equals rema[...] equal* (Larson et al. 2007, p. 154). This is comforting until one asks what is "equal"? If we don't know what either side means, how do we know they are "equal"? *Second:* Use algebra tiles to "model" this solution of $4x - 3 = 2x$. Thus let a green rectangle model a variable and a red square model -1. Then it seems "*natural*" that, if we remove two green tiles on the left (i.e., adding $-2x$), we should also remove two green tiles on the right (Bellman et al. 2007, p. 133).

Third: Use a balance scale to "model" the equation $4x - 3 = 2x$. It seems "*obvious*" that if we remove $2x$ (whatever it is) from both weighing pans, the pans will stay in balance (Larson et al. 1999, p. 66).

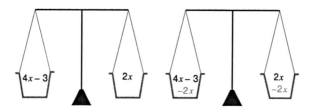

The other steps are justified in exactly the same way, making analogies using the intuitive meaning of "equality", algebra tiles, or balance scales.

These analogies are useful psychological ploys to win students' trust, but mathematics has to *explain* why something is true by logical reasoning, not by making sly suggestions about why it might be true because of analogies. By replacing reasoning with analogies, TSM guarantees that the *fear of variables* will live on.

The correct way to solve equations is well-known and very simple (cf. Wu 2010b, Sect. 3), but it took the CCSSM to finally incorporate it into a set of standards:

- (Grade 6, EE 5) *Understand solving an equation or inequality as a process of answering a question: which values from a specified set, if any, make the equation or inequality true? Use substitution to determine whether a given number in a specified set makes an equation or inequality true.*
- (High school Algebra, A-REI 1.) *Explain each step in solving a simple equation as following from the equality of numbers asserted at the previous step, starting from the assumption that the original equation has a solution. Construct a viable argument to justify a solution method.*

Let us see what it means to solve an equation from this perspective. The key idea is what may be called the **Basic Protocol in the use of symbols**: What a symbol stands for must be clearly stated when a symbol is introduced (Wu 2010b, p. 9). Armed with this idea, we can start anew. *Let x be a real number.* An **equation with x**, such as $4x - 3 = 2x$, is a *question* asking whether the two numbers $4x - 3$ and $2x$ are equal *as numbers*. It could be true, or it could be false. **To solve the equation $4x - 3 = 2x$** is to determine all the numbers x for which the equality is true.

We now show how to correctly solve $4x - 3 = 2x$, but the principle holds in general (e.g., for polynomial equations). *We first assume that there is a solution*, i.e., there is a number x_0 so that $4x_0 - 3 = 2x_0$. Because we are now dealing with numbers, the previous five steps make perfect sense. Thus, starting with $4x_0 - 3 = 2x_0$, we get:

Step *i*: $-2x_0 + (4x_0 - 3) = -2x_0 + 2x_0$.
Step *ii*: $2x_0 - 3 = 0$ (by use of the assoc. law *for numbers*)
Step *iii*: $(2x_0 - 3) + 3 = 0 + 3$
Step *iv*: $2x_0 = 3$ (by use of the assoc. law *for numbers*)
Step *v*: $x_0 = \frac{3}{2}$

Are we done? No. We have not proved that $\frac{3}{2}$ is a solution of $x - 3 = 2x$, only that *if* there is a solution, it must be equal to $\frac{3}{2}$. Having narrowed down the possible candidates to $\frac{3}{2}$, we can now complete the solution process by *proving* that $\frac{3}{2}$ is a solution with a simple computation:

$$4\left(\frac{3}{2}\right) - 3 = 2\left(\frac{3}{2}\right)$$

because both sides are equal to 3. This shows that the previous Steps 1–5 are a *procedurally correct* way to solve the equation. More importantly, this shows that **Steps 1–5 actually make sense** provided they are taught, not as computations with a mysterious quantity called a *variable*, but as computations with *numbers*.[8]

According to TSM:

> Understanding the concept of variable is crucial to the study of algebra, and that a major problem in students' efforts to understand and do algebra results from their narrow interpretation of the term. (NCTM 1989, p. 102)

On the contrary, *a variable* is not a **mathematical** concept. Imposing it on students as a mathematical concept can only obstruct their learning of algebra.

---

[8] Although our purpose is to expose the mathematical flaws of TSM, a side remark about the related pedagogical issue of how to implement the correct mathematics in the school classroom may not be out of place. In the context of solving equations, one may ask whether school students must solve equations in this formal and turgid fashion *each time an equation is solved*. The simple answer is no, because pedagogical common sense must be exercised. One suggestion is to explain in great detail—the *first* time an equation is solved—what the process described in Steps i–v is all about. When the teacher feels comfortable that the students have understood the process, then they should be allowed to abbreviate their work more or less as in Steps 1–5 on page 130 above.

Slope of a Line

The concept of the *slope of a line* is a staple of grade 8 mathematics. In TSM, the definition of **slope** is the following: Let L be a nonvertical line in the coordinate plane and let $P = (p_1, p_2)$ and $Q = (q_1, q_2)$ be distinct points on L. Then the **slope** of L is defined to be $\frac{p_2 - q_2}{p_1 - q_1}$.

Is this *well-defined*, i.e., does it make sense? *Not yet*, because if $A = (a_1, a_2)$ and $B = (b_1, b_2)$ are also on L, is the slope of L equal to $\frac{a_2 - b_2}{a_1 - b_1}$?

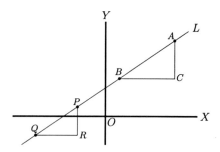

In other words, is it true that $\frac{p_2 - q_2}{p_1 - q_1} = \frac{a_2 - b_2}{a_1 - b_1}$?

This question must be answered because *slope* is supposed to be a property of the line L and not of the two points P and Q on L that happen to be chosen. Students need the assurance that, if they happen to choose A and B on L, they still get the same number. Unfortunately, this question is not even raised in TSM, much less answered.

The proof of the equality $\frac{p_2 - q_2}{p_1 - q_1} = \frac{a_2 - b_2}{a_1 - b_1}$ requires the concept of similar triangles: $\triangle ABC \sim \triangle PQR$. Assuming this similarity, then the proportionality of corresponding sides says

$$\frac{PR}{AC} = \frac{QR}{BC}.$$

Since the length of PR is $p_2 - q_2$, the length of AC is $a_2 - p_2$, etc., the equality is seen to be equivalent to the previous equality at least when the line L is slanted to the right, as shown. If L is slanted to the left, then the proportionality of the corresponding sides translates into the equality of the *negative* of the slopes, and the same conclusion prevails.

The TSM definition of slope confuses **the slope of two chosen points on L** with **the slope of L**.

This kind of teaching-by-rote of slope has serious consequences in mathematics learning. According to a recent survey of students' understanding of straight lines in algebra by Postelnicu and Greenes (2012), the most difficult problems for students are those requiring the identification of slope of a line from its graph. One can well imagine that if students do not realize they can use *any* two points on the line to compute its slope, they would be confused about "how to measure rise and run" (Postelnicu and Greenes, *ibid.*). The need for better teaching of the concept of slope is therefore real. Moreover, without a correct definition of slope, one cannot show that the graph of a linear equation $ax + by = c$ is a (straight) line and the connection between the *geometry* of the line and the *algebra* of the equation will remain undeveloped. Students are therefore reduced to memorizing, by brute force, how to write down the equation of a line. Many are not successful.

The CCSSM prescribe a way out of this impasse. The standards **in grade 8** ask that the following be done to make sense of "slope" as well as lay a foundation for high school geometry.

- Introduce rotation, reflection, translation (in the plane) and their compositions *intuitively* through hands-on activities, and define **congruence** as a composition of (a finite number of) rotations, reflections, and translations.
- Introduce *dilation intuitively* through hands-on activities, and define **similarity** as the composition of a dilation followed by a congruence.
- Give informal proofs of the basic criteria of triangle congruence.
- Give an informal proof of the *AA criterion of similar triangles*: if two triangles have two pairs of equal angles, then they are similar.
- Use the AA criterion to show that the slope of a line is well-defined.
- Use the AA criterion to prove the Pythagorean Theorem.

See Chaps. 4–6 in Wu (2010a), and the discussion of grade 8 in Wu (2012), for details.

The purpose of the emphasis on *intuitive geometry* is for students to gain the necessary geometric intuition as a preparation for the more rigorous course of high school geometry.

Rate and Proportional Reasoning

Proportional reasoning is supposed to be the "capstone of elementary school mathematics and the gateway to higher mathematics" (National Research Council 2001, p. 242). This term has come to mean "understanding the underlying relationships in a proportional situation" (p. 241 of National Research Council 2001). Mathematics is about making explicit assumptions and then drawing logical conclusions from those assumptions. Unfortunately, what happens in TSM is that the "relationship in a proportional situation" is often hidden from students, thereby making it impossible for learning to take place. For example, consider the following prototypical problem in proportional reasoning:

> *A group of 8 people are going camping for three days and need to carry their own water. They read in a guide book that 12.5 liters are needed for a party of 5 persons for 1 day. How much water should they carry?* (NCTM 1989, p. 83)

Students cannot reason proportionally if they are not told that *each person is assumed to drink roughly the same amount of water every day*. Indeed they know from personal observations that different people drink different amount of water each day (at least before they get brainwashed by TSM), and therefore, without such an explicit assumption, they cannot possibly "think proportionally". Once this assumption is made explicit, however, students can experiment with, or can be shown, the numerical pattern in order to achieve some conceptual understanding of the situation. For example:

> Let ℓ be the number of liters each person drinks each day, then two persons drink $\ell + \ell = 2\ell$ liters a day, three persons drink $\ell + \ell + \ell = 3\ell$ liters a day, ..., persons drink $\ell + \ell + \ell + \ell + \ell = 5\ell$ liters a day. Since we are given $5\ell = 12.5$, we have $\ell = 2.5$ liters. Thus 8 people would need roughly $8 \times 2.5 = 20$ liters per day, so that they should carry $3 \times 20 = 60$ liters for three days.

This solution may not appear to be related to "relationships in a proportional situation", but, because it can be reformulated as follows, it is: For every positive integer n,

$$\frac{\text{what } n \text{ persons drink in 1 day}}{n} = \frac{n\ell}{n} = \ell.$$

Since the ratio ℓ is independent of n, we see that

$$\frac{\text{what 5 persons drink in 1 day}}{5} = \frac{\text{what 8 persons drink in 1 day}}{8},$$

as both are equal to ℓ. We now see explicitly the equality of two ratios. In particular, making use of the given fact that 5 persons drink 12.5 liters, we get

$$\frac{12.5}{5} = \frac{\text{what 8 persons drink in 1 day}}{8}.$$

Therefore, what 8 persons drink in one day $= (8 \times 12.5)/5 = 20$ liters. In three days, 8 persons drink $3 \times 20 = 60$ liters, as before.

In retrospect, we see that the correctness of the following proportion,

$$\frac{\text{what } m \text{ persons drink in 1 day}}{m} = \frac{\text{what } n \text{ persons drinks in 1 day}}{n},$$

for *any* positive integers m and n is *a matter of logical reasoning once the needed assumption is revealed to students*, but it is not any kind of *a priori* conceptual understanding that students can develop outside the mathematical framework. If we want students to learn to reason proportionally, then we should cleanse the curriculum of TSM and accord reasoning its rightful place.

A second kind of defect in the teaching of proportional reasoning is the inattention to precise definition. For example, here is another prototypical problem:

> *Which is the better buy: 12 tickets for $15.00 or 20 tickets for $23.00? (NCTM 2000, p. 221)*

Students need to be told, either in the problem itself or in general, the following two pieces of information: (i) all tickets in each price group cost the same amount, and (ii) "better buy" means "the lower price per ticket". While neither is worth mentioning to an adult, an adolescent may well be learning his or her way in life at this point and therefore may not be aware of this information (or at least not the latter). In mathematics, one must strive for total clarity. Again, once these two facts are made explicit, students will see that,

> if one ticket costs d dollars, 2 tickets cost $d + d = 2d$ dollars, ..., and 12 tickets cost $12d$ dollars. Thus if $12d = 15$, then $d = 1.25$ dollars. Similarly if another ticket costs s dollars, 2 tickets cost $s + s = 2s$ dollars, ..., and 20 such tickets cost $20s$ dollars. Thus if $20s = 23$, then $s = 1.15$ dollars.

It follows that 20 tickets for $23.00 is the better buy.

In both cases, TSM is guilty of withholding information and forcing students to make guesses. Mathematics is not about making the right kind of guesses, only about logical reasoning on the basis of an explicitly given hypothesis. It is also manifest that, once the proper information is supplied and students can see the *reasoning* behind such proportional reasoning problems, the solutions become entirely straightforward and therefore learnable. Let us therefore focus on removing these artificial obstacles imposed by TSM on learning.

The preceding problems are examples of a whole class of *discrete* problems on proportionality, in the sense that there is a "natural unit" to use in each problem (namely, one *person* or one *ticket*) and, furthermore, it is not necessary to go beyond this "natural unit" (there is no such thing as "0.3" person or $\frac{3}{4}$ ticket). For such discrete problems, the CCSSM do passably well by isolating the natural unit and the *unit rate*; see Standards 6.RP 1, 2, and 3a. However, there is another class of problems on proportionality, the so-called *continuous problems* where there is no natural unit; they are exemplified by constant speed, constant rate of water flow, constant rate of lawn mowing, etc. We can easily appreciate why there is no "natural unit" to measure time, for example: hour, minute, second, milli-second, micro-second, pico-second, etc., are all legitimate units to use for this purpose. These problems are special cases of what are known as "rate problems". For convenience, we will use **rate** to mean *continuous* rate in the rest of this article.[9] We now turn our attention to these rate problems.

There are serious mathematical issues with the way rate problems are treated by TSM. The fact is that TSM conflates *rate* with *constant rate*. To understand this statement, we begin with a description of the underlying mathematics of the situation, one that requires calculus and is therefore not one that we can use with middle school students. For the sake of clarity, we will use speed exclusively in this discussion, but the idea is of course the same for other kinds of rate. Let $f(t)$ be the function that describes the distance of an object at time t, traveling along a (straight)

---

[9]Note that we treat "rate" as a generic term that refers to a class of phenomena; each of the phenomena will have to be defined individually but there is a good reason not to try to define what "rate" means. Indeed, the general definition of "rate" as the derivative of the "work function" (a function of time) requires calculus; see the discussion of speed in the next paragraph. TSM makes believe that a term that requires calculus for its definition can nevertheless be bandied about in K-12 as a *precise* concept. This is the reason why "rate" problem inspires such fear and loathing in schools.

line, from a fixed point O. Then the **speed** of the object at time t is the derivative $f'(t)$; the object is said to have **constant speed** s if s is a fixed number and $f'(t) = s$ for all values of t. What is worth observing is that if the speed is not constant, the speed $f'(t)$ varies with t and there is no hope of expressing the speed ("rate") as the ratio of two numbers. On the other hand, if the speed is a constant s, then one can describe the "constant speed s" for middle school students without resorting to calculus, as follows. Define the **average speed over a time interval $[u, v]$** to be

$$\frac{\text{difference in distance at time } u \text{ and at time } v \text{ from } O}{\text{length of the time duration from } u \text{ to } v} = \frac{f(v) - f(u)}{v - u}.$$

Then an equivalent definition for the object to have **constant speed** s is that its average speed over *any* time interval is equal to s. If we know that the speed is constant and is equal to s, then we can simply refer to s as **the speed** of the object. In case of constant speed, then (and only then) is the rate (speed) the ratio of two quantities, as in the preceding equation.

With this understood, we can now gain a better understanding of how "rate" is mishandled by TSM. The following is a sample of some attempts to define "rate" by various textbooks; please take note that *constant rate is implicitly assumed in each case.*

> A **rate** is a ratio that involves two different units. A rate is usually given as a quantity per unit such as miles per hour. This is called a **unit rate**. (Eicholz et al. 1995, p. 232)

> A quantity is a rate when its unit contains the word "per" or "for each" or some synonym. (Usiskin et al. 1998, p. 493)

> A *rate* can be thought of as an extended ratio, a ratio which enables us to think beyond the situation at hand, to imagine a whole range of situations in which two quantities are related in the same way. (Lamon 1999, p. 204)

> A rate is a comparison of the measures of two different things or quantities. The measuring unit is different for each value. (Van de Walle 1998, p. 293)

In TSM, rate problems have to be done by assuming the constancy of rate, but because *constant rate* is never defined in TSM, no reasoning is possible in the solution of these problems. Instead, students are asked to memorize the following trinity of formulas,

$$\text{speed} = \text{distance/time}$$

$$\text{time} = \text{distance/speed}$$

$$\text{distance} = \text{time} \times \text{speed}.$$

What is not commonly realized is that there is in fact no need to memorize anything in this situation, because the first is the definition of speed (*when it is known to be constant*), and the other two are consequences of the *definition* of division. Moreover, the resulting solution-by-rote is completely unnecessary because once "constant speed" is precisely defined, the solution can be obtained by *mathematical reasoning*. As illustration, consider the following problem:

John's grandpa enjoys knitting. He can knit a scarf 30 inches in 10 hours. He always knits for 2 hours each day.

1. *How many inches can he knit in 1 hour?*
2. *How many days will it take Grandpa to knit a scarf 30 inches long?*
3. *How many inches long will the scarf be at the end of 2 days?*
      Explain how you figured it out.
4. *How many hours will it take Grandpa to knit a scarf 27 inches long? Explain your reasoning.*

It is clear that, as is, the problem cannot be solved (except for part 2). Indeed, without knowing how much he knits in each of the ten 1-hour intervals, there is no way to answer part 1. Now, suppose we use the above definition of constant rate of knitting, and *add the assumption that grandpa knits at a constant rate.* Let us say he knits ℓ inches in a particular 1-hour interval, then the average rate of his knitting over this 1-hour interval would be $\frac{\ell}{1} = \ell$ inches per hour. But his average rate of knitting over a 10-hour interval, according to the given data, is $\frac{30}{10} = 3$ inches per hour. By the assumption of constant rate, the two average rates are equal and therefore $\ell = 3$ inches in that 1-hour interval and, by assumption, in *any* 1-hour interval. The other parts can be solved similarly. We have therefore solved the problem by use of reasoning when the assumption of constant rate is added (perhaps this is what proportional *reasoning* means in TSM?).

Observe the commonality between the problem of knitting and the previous problem of 8 people camping: both become solvable only after the assumption of constant rate has been added.

To summarize, I hope I have explained clearly the flaws of "proportional reasoning" as it is understood in TSM. I wish I could say that the CCSSM are forceful and emphatic in exposing the need for a precise definition of constant rate as well as prescribing a remedy, but it must be said that while the CCSSM try to make sense of this circle of ideas, they have not made any serious headway. See Standards 6.RP 3b and 3c, and Standards 7.RP 1 and 2. I should also add that there is no need for the CCSSM to be perfect in order to be worthy of support.

The previous remark concerning the need to add an assumption that all rates are constant rates might give the impression that the *de facto* national curriculum tries to make believe that every rate is constant in the real world. This is in fact not the case, because it does try to make students aware that even "speed" need not be constant. One cannot give a better illustration of this fact than to quote a 2011 test item for grade 8 in NAEP (National Assessment of Educational Progress undated):

3. *For 2 minutes, Casey runs at a constant speed. Then she gradually increases her speed. Which of the following graphs could show how her speed changed over time?*

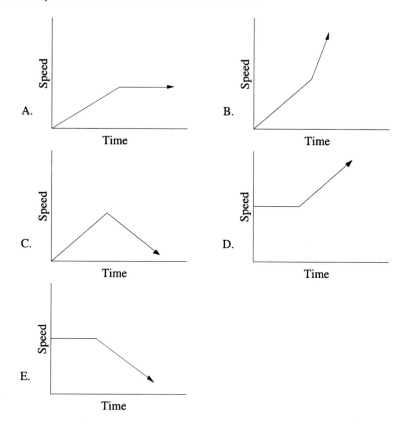

Here, the "speed" in the phrase "she gradually increases her speed" is clearly not one that is constant (regardless of the fact that the concept of variable speed cannot be defined in K-12). Thus TSM treats speed as automatically constant on the one hand, and wants students to be aware of non-constant speed on the other. Such blatant inconsistency is among the many reasons that TSM has to go.

Concluding Remarks

To recap, we may describe the state of the American school mathematics curriculum as follows. For several decades, there has been a *de facto* national mathematics curriculum: the curriculum articulated in the school textbooks. The mathematics in these books is quite uniform in terms of its violation of the basic principles of mathematics (cf. the prefatory article *To the Reader* in Wu 2011b), and we call it *Textbook School Mathematics* (TSM) to distinguish it from *mathematics*. For a long time, the school mathematics curriculum in each state has been drawn from TSM, so any significant curricular improvement will be difficult as long as TSM is recycled from generation to generation the way it is at present. Because commercial interests control textbook publishing, a direct attempt to change textbooks may be impossible without some outside stimulus. The CCSSM could be that needed stimulus. If they can spearhead a vigorous professional development program—nationwide—that allows our teachers to solidify their content knowledge, teachers will ultimately reject textbooks based on TSM. Then we can look forward to TSM's demise.

Such guarded optimism, however, is predicated on the assumption that the CCSSM are here to stay. The collapse of the "New Math" movement in the 1970's is a warning that unless the CCSSM can be implemented effectively in schools by knowledgeable teachers, the collapse of the CCSSM will also be inevitable. The survival of the CCSSM is therefore contingent upon our ability to produce a sufficiently large corps of mathematically knowledgeable teachers. To all who are dedicated to making good school mathematics education a reality, the inter-dependence of the survival of the CCSSM and the availability of knowledgeable teachers should spur us to fight for serious, content-based professional development across the nation. We may add that the professional development must be one that can help teachers overcome their prolonged immersion in TSM.

Thus far, *there seems to be little awareness of the seriousness of the problem in both the education and mathematics communities, much less the will to bring about this kind of professional development*. The difficulty of such an undertaking cannot be overstated. Given that our teachers are brought up on TSM in schools, and given that colleges and universities have done little to help preservice teachers realize that TSM is not mathematics, there is not likely to be significant change in the teacher pipeline anytime soon. As to teachers in the field, they are doubly betrayed: first by the sudden shift in our demand on their content knowledge, and then by our refusal to offer assistance. They are asked by the CCSSM to offer definitions to concepts that have never been properly defined for them: fractions, decimal, percent, expression, congruence, similarity... They are asked to offer explanations for skills that they were forced to learn by rote, such as invert and multiply, $(-a)(-b) = ab$, $\frac{-a}{b} = \frac{a}{-b} = -\frac{a}{b}$, writing the equation of a line, locating the minimum of a quadratic function... They are asked to teach certain facts as definitions and others as theorems, and they are uncertain which is which because TSM has never drawn a clear line between the two e.g., which of the following is a theorem and which is a definition?

$$\frac{a}{b} = a \div b,$$

$$\frac{k}{\ell} \times \frac{m}{n} = \frac{km}{\ell n},$$

$$a^0 = 1,$$

$$0! = 1,$$

two lines are perpendicular if the product of their slopes is -1,

the graph of a quadratic function is a parabola.

They are also asked to look for *structure* in mathematics (p. 8 of CCSSM 2010), but they have always been taught to consider whole numbers, fractions, and rational numbers as "different numbers" rather than as an orderly progression; length, area, and volume as distinctly different concepts rather than as special cases of geometric measurements; algebra as a separate subject from arithmetic rather than as a natural extension... They stand helpless, and our inaction keeps them helpless.

We can either wait for the inevitable collapse of the CCSSM, or we can firm up our resolve and confront the beast that is professional development. Which will it be?

Acknowledgement   I am grateful to Larry Francis for his corrections and useful suggestions.

References

Andrews, A. G., et al. (2002). *Harcourt math. Grade 5. Grade 6. (California edition)*. Orlando: Harcourt.

Bell, M., et al. (2008). *California everyday mathematics. Teachers' lesson guide. Grade 4*. Chicago: McGraw Hill/Wright Group.

Bellman, A. E., et al. (2007). *Prentice Hall mathematics. Algebra 1*. Boston: Pearson/Prentice Hall.

Bennett, J., et al. (2001). *Scott Foresman California mathematics. Grade 4. Grade 5*. Glenview: Scott Foresman.

Carmichael, S. B., Wilson, W. S., Porter-Magee, K., & Martino, G. (2010). *The state of state standards—and the common core—in 2010*. Washington: Thomas B. Fordham Institute. Retrieved from http://www.edexcellence.net/publications/the-state-of-state-of-standards-and-the-common-core-in-2010.html.

CME project: algebra 1. (2009). Boston: Pearson/Prentice Hall.

Collins, W., et al. (1998). *Glencoe algebra 1*. New York: Glencoe/McGraw-Hill.

Common Core State Standards for Mathematics (2010). Retrieved from http://www.corestandards.org/the-standards/mathematics.

Davison, D. M., Landau, M. S., McCracken, L., & Thompson, L. (2001). *Pre-algebra. California edition*. Needham: Prentice Hall.

Eicholz, R. E., et al. (1995). *Addison-Wesley mathematics. Grade 7. Grade 8*. Menlo Park: Addison Wesley.

Fuson, K. C. (2006). *Teacher's edition: Houghton-Mifflin math expressions. Grade 5*. Boston: Houghton-Mifflin.

Gray, L. F. (undated). A sample list of errors in core plus materials. Retrieved from http://www.math.umn.edu/~gray/errors.html.

Hoffer, A. R., Koss, R., et al. (1998). *Focus on advanced algebra*. Menlo Park: Addison Wesley.

Holliday, B., et al. (2008). *Glencoe McGraw-Hill algebra 2*. New York: McGraw Hill.

Institute for Research on Mathematics and Science Education (2010). Research in mathematics education: where do we go from here? Retrieved from http://irmse.msu.edu/2010/11/16/washington-d-c-kick-off-event/irmse-proceedings-mathematics-ed/.

Kliman, M., Russell, S. J., Turney, C., & Murray, M. (2006). *Investigations in number, data, and space in grade 5: building on numbers you know*. Glenview: Scott Foresman.

Kodaira, K. (Ed.) (1992). *Japanese grade 7 mathematics. Japanese grade 8 mathematics. Japanese grade 9 mathematics*. Chicago: University of Chicago.

Kodaira, K. (Ed.) (1996). *Mathematics 1*. Providence: American Mathematical Society.

Kodaira, K. (Ed.) (1997). *Mathematics 2*. Providence: American Mathematical Society.

Lamon, S. J. (1999). *Teaching fractions and ratios for understanding*. Mahwah: Lawrence Erlbaum.

Lappan, G., et al. (1998a). *Connected mathematics: bits and pieces I and II*. Menlo Park: Dale Seymour.

Lappan, G., et al. (1998b). *Connected mathematics: stretching and shrinking*. Menlo Park: Dale Seymour.

Larson, R., et al. (1999). *Passport to algebra and geometry*. Evanston: McDougall Littell.

Larson, R., et al. (2007). *McDougall Littell algebra 1*. Evanston: McDougall Littell.

Mathematics framework for California public schools (2006). Sacramento: California Department of Education.

Murdock, J., Kamischke, E., & Kamischke, E. (1998). *Advanced algebra through data exploration*. Berkeley: Key Curriculum Press.

National Assessment of Educational Progress (undated). NAEP questions tool: mathematics. Retrieved from http://nces.ed.gov/nationsreportcard/itmrlsx/search.aspx?subject=mathematics.

National Council of Teachers of Mathematics (1989). *Curriculum and evaluation standards for school mathematics*. Reston: Author.

National Council of Teachers of Mathematics (2000). *Principles and standards for school mathematics*. Reston: Author.

National Council of Teachers of Mathematics (2006). *Curriculum focal points*. Reston: Author.

National Mathematics Advisory Panel (2008). *Foundations for success: reports of the task groups and sub-committees*. Washington: U.S. Department of Education. http://www.ed.gov/about/bdscomm/list/mathpanel/reports.html.

National Research Council (2001). *Adding it up*. Washington: National Academy Press.

Postelnicu, V., & Greenes, C. (2012). Do teachers know what their students know? *National Council of Supervisors of Mathematics Newsletter*, *42*(3), 14–15.

Usiskin, Z., et al. (1998). *UCSMP transition mathematics* (2nd ed.). Glenview: Scott Foresman Addison Wesley.

Van de Walle, J. A. (1998). *Elementary and middle school mathematics*. New York: Addison Wesley Longman.

Wu, H. (2000). Review of the interactive mathematics program (IMP). Retrieved from http://math.berkeley.edu/~wu/IMP2.pdf.

Wu, H. (2010a). Pre-algebra. Retrieved from http://math.berkeley.edu/~wu/Pre-Algebra.pdf.

Wu, H. (2010b). Introduction to school algebra. Retrieved from http://math.berkeley.edu/~wu/Algebrasummary.pdf.

Wu, H. (2011a). Professional development and textbook school mathematics. Retrieved from http://math.berkeley.edu/~wu/AMS_COE_2011.pdf.

Wu, H. (2011b). *Understanding numbers in elementary school mathematics*. Providence: American Mathematical Society.

Wu, H. (2011c). Phoenix rising. Bringing the common core state mathematics standards to life. *American Educator*, *35*(3), 3–13. Also: http://www.aft.org/pdfs/americaneducator/fall2011/Wu.pdf.

Wu, H. (2011d). Teaching fractions according to the common core standards. Retrieved from http://math.berkeley.edu/~wu/CCSS-Fractions.pdf.

Wu, H. (2012). Teaching geometry according to the common core standards. Retrieved from http://math.berkeley.edu/~wu/Progressions_Geometry.pdf.

Brief Considerations on Educational Directives and Public Policies in Brazil Regarding Mathematics Education

Antonio Vicente Marafioti Garnica

Abstract Taking into consideration the historical context, this chapter considers Brazilian public policies related to mathematics teaching as they are embedded in broader educational policies, while also reflecting on how Brazil has been influenced—more in the past than the present—by foreign models. For a brief overview, we turn first to the curricular directives and the changes they have undergone. This discussion will reveal how education policies in Brazil have suffered from a lack of continuity of programs aimed at developing, implementing, and monitoring these policies, as well as regional inequalities in a country where income inequalities are huge and the cultural diversity is immense. Finally, in general terms, we discuss some points of convergence and divergence between mathematics education research in Brazil, its application within schools, and its effect on the public policies that shape the Brazilian educational system.

Keywords Educational public policies · Brazil · Mathematics education · History · National reforms and programs · Curriculum · Math teachers formation

The Proposal of This Text

Public policies related to education and mathematics education cannot be studied appropriately without taking into consideration the historical context and socio-cultural influences of the field from which they originated and to which the policies apply. The case is no different for Brazil or on the international scene, nor is it different in regard to mathematics teaching in the various courses that compose school programs.

Thus, the present chapter considers public policies related to mathematics teaching as they are embedded in broader educational policies, while also reflecting on

This paper was translated from the Portuguese by Anne W. Kepple.

A.V.M. Garnica (✉)
São Paulo State University (UNESP), São Paulo, Brazil
e-mail: vgarnica@fc.unesp.br

Y. Li, G. Lappan (eds.), *Mathematics Curriculum in School Education*,
Advances in Mathematics Education, DOI 10.1007/978-94-007-7560-2_8,
© Springer Science+Business Media Dordrecht 2014

how Brazil has been influenced by foreign models, perhaps more in the past than the present.[1]

For a brief overview of public policies in Brazil related to mathematics teaching, we turn first to the curricular directives and the changes they have undergone. This discussion will reveal how education policies in Brazil have suffered from a lack of continuity of programs aimed at developing, implementing, and monitoring these policies, as well as regional inequalities in a country where income inequalities are huge and the cultural diversity is immense. Finally, in general terms, we discuss some points of convergence and divergence between mathematics education research in Brazil, its application within schools, and its effect on the public policies that shape the Brazilian educational system.

An Overview of Curriculum Development for Mathematics Teaching in Brazil

The Brazilian educational model only became consolidated as a "system"—a broad network of actors, institutions, constructions, and circumstances that act according to general guidelines dictated by specific legislation for different levels of schooling[2]—in the 1950s. However, evidence can be found of the beginnings of an educational policy for the primary level at the end of the 19th century, with the constitution of the so-called School Groups, clearly based on the American teaching model of three R's—"Reading, wRiting, and aRithmetic"—and also in the 1930s with the establishment of the first university, the University of São Paulo.[3] Mathematics teaching at the secondary and university levels followed mainly French models, as the didactics manuals clearly attest. Primary school teachers were educated in

---

[1]The consolidation of solid educational and mathematics education research centers in Brazil, mainly in the final decades of the 20th century, appears to have at least challenged this external theoretical dependence by encouraging thinking about education that, despite being an open dialogue with sources from various origins and schools of thought, contributed to questioning its own processes. An overview of the development of mathematics education research in Brazil, in particular, can be found in D'Ambrosio and Borba (2010).

[2]In general, the progressive grade system in Brazilian schools underwent few structural changes with respect to programs and courses, despite frequent changes in nomenclature and classifications. In this chapter, to facilitate understanding of the system by foreign readers, we use the expressions "primary education" to signify the first five years of school (the initial grades, which consisted of only four grades until 2009), "secondary education" to signify the seven years following the primary grades, and "higher education" to refer to the university level. "Basic education" in Brazil refers to the first nine years of schooling, and "middle school" refers to the last three years (high school) which precede the university level.

[3]The first Brazilian university, in the sense of an educational complex of higher learning composed of a significant number of different fields managed under a single organizational model, was founded in 1934 in the city of São Paulo, the capital of the state which until today is the largest economic power in the country. Prior to this, there was a small and disperse network of higher education institutions that offered mainly the "classic" fields of engineering, law, and medicine, although it was common at the time for sons of the upper class to study in Europe.

Normal Schools in the 19th century (so called because they were institutions where the norms of civility were to be promoted). Courses for secondary and university level teachers only became available in the 1930s and were based more on the programs aimed at primary level teachers than on the teacher education program at the first Brazilian university.

At least thirty years passed between the time the first university program was established to educate secondary level teachers and the consolidation of such programs in universities throughout Brazil. The number of secondary schools grew at a dizzying pace in the 1950s before there were enough teachers to meet the demand, and the proliferation of universities with teacher education programs only occurred in the 1960s.[4]

Mathematics education in secondary schools in Brazil was divided among three basic courses until the end of the 1930s—algebra, arithmetic, and geometry—with no "mathematics" course, as such. Historians of mathematics education agree that the first movement to modernize mathematics teaching in Brazil took place when these three courses were unified and came to be known in the schools by a single name: "mathematics." The three subjects were to be taught at the same time, with the unifying thread being the concept of function. For the teaching of geometry, Euclides Roxo, a central figure in this 1931 reform, proposed that the deductive focus should be preceded by a practical approach. In addition to the reformulation of the program, this reorganization was characterized by a well-founded series of didactic guidelines for teachers and school administrators. The 1931 reform provided the basis for the elaboration of a collection of textbooks, written by the same Euclides Roxo, in which the links between the three components of the mathematics curriculum essentially followed the guidelines proposed. However, the reform, as well as the textbooks that were a reflection of it, was short-lived. Little more than a decade later, in 1942, changes in public policy dismantled Roxo's initial proposal, which, according to Pires (2008), illustrated how curricular decisions in Brazil have historically been marked by questionable procedures on the part of some groups or individuals, influenced by political issues.

The second half of the 20th century was characterized, according to Pires (2008), by three very distinct phases: the first, from 1960 to 1980, corresponds to the period in which the Modern Math Movement (MMM)[5] euphorically established itself in Brazil, introduced by groups promoting a "new" educational reform; the second, from 1980 to the mid-1990s, is characterized by the emergence, in some states, of a discourse contrary to the MMM, leading to some reformist activities (essentially a counter-reform movement) based on this counter-discourse; and, finally, a third phase which began in 1995 with the publication, at the national level, of the first set of systematic directives developed for the Brazilian school system.

---

[4]Until the end of the 1960s and beginning of the 1970s, emergency teacher training programs were common, for primary as well as secondary level teachers, but the lack of secondary school teachers was conspicuous.

[5]In some countries, *Modern Mathematics Movement* is also known as *New Math Movement*.

The MMM was implemented in Brazilian schools through an intense policy of production and distribution of textbooks. Thus, it was mainly thanks to a set of teaching manuals that the MMM directives effectively entered the classroom. The MMM was presented to teachers and school administrators in short courses that were insufficient to meet the demand and maintain the expected pace, as there were few teachers prepared to face the demands imposed by the new contents and approaches. The criticisms faced by the MMM on the international scene were intensified internally at a time when the schools were still coping with the mere technical implementation of the proposal. Working with Modern Math at that time meant "teaching set theory." Teachers did not comprehend the idea behind Modern Math, much less the criticisms of it.

It was this general climate of discontent that allowed the emergence of the proposals, most of them regional, that guided mathematical curricula in the 1980s and 90s for the primary grades and the initial secondary level grades. Mathematics came to be seen—at least in the programs and directives during these two decades—as having a double function: "as necessary for practical activities that involve quantitative aspects of reality—such as those that deal with sizes, counting, measurement, and calculation techniques—and as being necessary for the development of logical reasoning, ability to abstract, generalize, and transcend what is immediately perceivable"[6] (Pires 2008, p. 22). Integration of the contents was also sought and, inspired by Bruner, the spiral approach to teaching was defended. The directives stated that evaluation should not be limited only to passing or failing, but should diagnose the learning process to suggest changes in teaching activities. Nevertheless, Pires concludes that the new discourses that condemned repetitive practicing of skills and memorization of algorithms while defending problem-solving as a methodological basis, comprehension of concepts and procedures, and balance between arithmetic, geometry, and algebra encountered implementation difficulty due to deeply rooted conceptions, such as mathematics learned through repetitive practice and solving exercises based on a given model. These "new" curricula were regionalized, proposed by states and cities. If, on the one hand, this strategy favored greater flexibility and allowed curricula to attend to different needs in different contexts, on the other hand it also clarified regional differences, and the regions characterized by greater social and economic development, like the south and southeast, proved to be more capable of developing alternative curricular approaches based on current academic research. "Thus, it was found that the deep social segmentation that resulted from the unequal distribution of income in Brazil was also an obstacle to access to education and to the development of contemporary, high quality teaching programs" (p. 25).

Only in the 1990s did national curricular directives emerge for all levels of teaching that aspired to break the limiting mechanisms detected in the earlier policies. Still, implementation of these proposals met with yet other serious obstacles. According to Pires:

> Very decisive factors, such as low teacher salaries, turnover of school personnel, and especially poor teacher education interfered negatively in the development of the process. One

---

[6]Quotes translated from the original in Portuguese.

of the marks of Brazilian public policies relative to curricular issues is the lack of actions aimed at curricular implementation, as though the new ideas would be transformed into practice with a wave of the magic wand. Another mark is the lack of monitoring and evaluation of the innovations proposed, which makes it impossible to judge them adequately and document mistakes and correct moves. These gaps have provoked a sort of 'eternal' situation characterized by prescriptive curricula (the official ones) and real curricula (those implemented by teachers in the classroom). Thus, a phenomenon common to the different levels of the educational system (federal, state, and municipal) is the periodic introduction of curricular changes that are supported neither by preceding concrete experiences nor the involvement of teachers who are the protagonists of their implementation. (Pires 2008, pp. 39–40)

So in practical terms, then, how are the curricular directives for education in Brazil operationalized? The curricular proposal determined by federal legislation in the National Curricular Parameters for Basic and High School Teaching is still enforced. These documents establish the directives for all schools in the country and function as a national curriculum in the sense of outlining, based on the literature, themes and ways of approaching the contents of all the disciplines composing the school programs at each grade level.

With respect to mathematics, the Curricular Parameters for the basic education level indicate a need to move beyond the linear organization of contents and interconnect them, inspired by the metaphor of constructing knowledge like a web. Contents are addressed in blocks (Numbers and Operations; Space and Form; Sizes and Measures; Information Handling[7]), and general didactic guidance is provided, including discussion of possible obstacles to learning and ways to overcome them. The Curricular Parameters for the middle and high school level approach mathematical contents as instruments for developing abilities and competencies. The competencies should be organized according to three principal aspects: "Representation and communication, aimed at developing communication skills; Investigation and comprehension, with the objective of developing the ability to question natural and technological processes, identifying regularities, presenting interpretations, and laying the groundwork for the development of reasoning and the capacity to learn; and Sociocultural contextualization, aimed at understanding and using science as an element for interpretation and intervention, and technology as systematic knowledge of practical sense" (Pires 2008, p. 235).

The mathematical contents addressed in the schools remain essentially very similar to previous programs: the curriculum proposes a new way of addressing them and even changes the sequencing, but does not fundamentally change the themes. The Modern Math Movement played an important role in this sense when it included in the list of "classic" contents some themes considered to be "current" in the 1960s such as the discussion of matrices and a more contemporary approach to geometry and equation systems, which is still used today. More recently, the emphasis on themes related to the block "Information Handling" led to the emergence of

---

[7]"Information Handling" ("Tratamento da Informação" in Portuguese) is how is known a block of content that covers statistics, probability, and combinatorial analysis, similar to what in the NCTM Principles and Standards is called "Data Analysis and Probability" (Campos and Lima 2012).

approaches and contents that had previously been somewhat overlooked in elementary education, and there was a significant parallel increase in research on statistics education. In general, the contents are not addressed using a radically formal model; the emphasis in textbooks and curricular guides is not on formal demonstrations or rigorous proofs. Greater emphasis has been given to the processes of conjecture, experimentation, testing, exemplification, and validation. In the earlier grades, principally, the attempt is to work in a way that approximates students to the mathematical contents using operationalization and problem-solving more than rigor in language and formal argumentation. This approach continues into high school, with the appropriate modifications.

While the official documents at the federal level address more general questions related to teaching the various disciplines, the regional curricular guides (state or municipal) have fulfilled the role of operationalizing these directives, providing teachers with strategies for specific interventions and theoretical details that complement the general guidelines and effectively prepare them for the classroom.

Finally, it is worth noting that "debate and research about curricular questions are not yet a tradition in the community of mathematics educators" (Pires 2008, p. 39). While some research has been conducted in this field, studies have either focused on very general questions, such as the need for and/or appropriateness of official curricula, or more specific issues, such as those that address the teaching of specific contents and ways of implementing given approaches (for example, research on the use of information and computer technology, the emphasis to be given to a given specific mathematical content, or the importance and potential of strategies involving problem-solving).

School Makes a Difference

Evaluation of educational systems focuses on strategies to improve teaching systems, results, and impacts, endeavoring to support public policy in education. Among other findings, data collected on the Brazilian system of basic education—implemented beginning in 1995—revealed "a persistent disparity among the conditions in schools attended by students of different social and ethnic origins," despite significant improvements with respect to the "universalization of the school[8] and democratization of the composition of the study body." According to Ortigão (2008), evaluations have nevertheless shown that "school makes a difference" in Brazil, contrary to studies carried out in the 1950s and 60s, which suggested that "students' performance was strongly determined by their socio-economic context and schools could do little or nothing to change this reality." In general, evaluations of the Brazilian educational system suggest that (a) the physical conditions of the school and the

---

[8]Ninety-seven percent of children aged 6 to 14 years have access to the educational system today in Brazil.

school environment have a considerable impact on student outcomes;[9] (b) the simple habit of requesting and correcting homework implies improvements in students' mean results; (c) in those schools where teachers have higher educational levels, students with higher socio-economic levels benefit more from this characteristic; and (d) when teachers emphasize problem-solving as a teaching strategy in mathematics class, students tend to perform better in this subject.[10] In summary, the research on the Brazilian education system as a whole shows that schools differ not only in the diversity of pedagogical and administrative approaches adopted, but mainly in the variety of internal practices and structures such as the environment, the level of teachers' commitment, and the emphasis given to teaching and learning processes. School makes a difference, and in a country characterized by clear socio-cultural differences, public policies should pay closer attention to the differences among the schools.

A Research Project to Update the Debate

According to D'Ambrosio and Borba:

> The participation of Brazil in World War II as part of the so-called Allied Forces was decisive for the strong pursuit of national unity. Measures were adopted in this period that resulted in the unification of the entire educational system, including religious schools and schools maintained by communities of German, Italian, and Japanese immigrants. The result was the emergence, in the second quarter of the twentieth century, of a homogeneous educational system, subordinating public, private, and religious schools to official programs defined by special commissions of the National Ministry of Education, to be applied throughout the country, from the Amazon region to the prairies of Rio Grande do Sul. These programs, aiming at cultural unification, disregarded seasonal specificities (school periods were the same), cultural and environmental contexts (the program was rigorously the same), and labor and professional needs, according to specificities of the productive sectors. For example, the extractive economy of the north would follow the same programs of the rural south or the industrialized central east. This standardization was applied at all educational levels, from elementary school to higher education. This scenario started to change in the fourth quarter of the twentieth century. (D'Ambrosio and Borba (2010), p. 274)

This standardization, which undervalued the cultural and economic differences among the various regions of this vast country, certainly implied the need for adjustments, which one moment may manifest themselves as subversions of public policy, and another moment express possible ways to carry out this standardization. Preliminary results of a research project that has been underway since 2002, aimed at un-

---

[9]"Differently from what one observes in more developed countries, the conditions of infrastructure and environment of the schools constitute relevant factors for raising academic outcomes" (Ortigão 2008, p. 85).

[10]It has been shown that an emphasis on problem-solving results in improved mathematical knowledge appropriation by students. However, this knowledge is not appropriated by everyone in the same way—students with above-average socio-economic levels benefit more, obtaining better results than their classmates of lower socio-economic status.

derstanding the mechanisms behind public policies related to teacher education, re-inforces the belief that the Brazilian education system is hostage to socio-economic inequalities. The project[11] strives to document the conditions under which mathematics teacher education and practice occurred, or are occurring, the different ways teachers are/were engaged in their teaching practice, how they appropriate(ed) and use(d) teaching materials, and how they either follow(ed) or subvert(ed) the legislation in force. It is a broad mapping process involving a large number of researchers and a great diversity of information, given that historical records can contribute to understanding regarding the centers and the extremes when one considers the socio-cultural aspects that require the consideration of teachers, students, other workers, and lawmakers.

According to Garnica (2010), three findings from this project are important for the study of public policy in Brazil related to mathematics education: (a) the lack of an identity for mathematics teachers and, consequently, the impossibility of classifying their trajectory in "cycles"; (b) the characterization of processes of teacher education for mathematics teachers in Brazil as resulting from policies designed to meet urgent needs, in which transience becomes a constant; and (c) the erroneous discourse of teacher education policies which says teaching is founded on conditions of equality, when in fact opportunities are very unequal.

Regarding the teacher's identity, it is necessary to point out that we begin with the assumption that every identity is a reading, and that, therefore, there is nothing like "the identity" of someone or something. There is a plurality of perspectives according to which we "read" the other, and in this reading we attribute an identity to him/her. Each subject is, in itself, multi-identity. I attribute a given identity to someone according to the lens through which I view the world. Thus, it becomes impossible to group mathematics teachers under a single heading, as though one could define a stable identity capable, therefore, of being subjected to global policies and pressures of the same nature and intensity. Testimonies from teachers throughout Brazil clearly show the diversity of difficulties they face, of the successes they promote, of the challenges they face daily in the classroom. Each region, city, and

---

[11]The project "Mapping of mathematics teacher education and practice in Brazil" (Garnica et al. 2011) is being conducted by a group of researchers with the objective of understanding the way policies related to teacher education and practice are effectively implemented in different regions of the country. It is characterized by distinct methodologies, among them oral history. What is known today as "oral history" is a research methodology which, in Brazil, has been widely used in the field of cultural studies by sociologists, anthropologists, and historians. In Brazil, although there are earlier records of research developed using this approach (the Brazilian Association of Oral History was founded in 1975, and the application of this resource by universities and other institutions became quite evident in the 1980s), only recently—in the first years of the 21st century—does oral history emerge as a method applied to mathematics education research. A certain ambiguity should be noted with respect to the expression "oral history" which, at first glance, induces one to place this rigorous research procedure specifically within the territory of history. In Brazil, it would be more correct to refer to it as a "qualitative research approach that links orality and memory," given that, in this country, the influence of historians (who are still arguing over whether oral history is a field, a technique, or a method) is relative, given the influences coming from the social sciences, for example.

school imposes very special conditions for classroom practices, for the ways meaning is attributed to everything surrounding these practices, and for the way textbooks are employed. We must therefore use caution when speaking of THE mathematics teacher, and it would be more prudent to specify, for each study and for each proposed intervention, WHICH teacher we are talking about, WHICH teachers will be our spokespersons, and to WHICH teachers certain public policies are directed.[12] This would preclude us, for example, from considering a priori, as being the target of public policies, an idealized teacher, devoid of geographic, sociological, political, economic, and personal specificities. Studies regarding elements/characteristics that are common to what we refer to as mathematics teachers remain the order of the day, as do studies about different types of interventions (for example, the development of textbooks that meet diverse geo-socio-cultural needs as well as "common" or "minimal" curricular directives) that take into account the multiplicity of mathematics teachers that we hope to reach in a national education system.

With respect to the urgency that has historically characterized the implementation of teacher education programs in Brazil, one of the more important initiatives that stands out is the Campaign for the Improvement and Dissemination of Secondary Education (*Campanha de Aperfeiçoamento e Difusão do Ensino Secundário*—CADES), a mathematics teacher education program implemented in the 1950s to meet the demand resulting from the expansion in secondary education at a moment when the educational system was becoming consolidated in Brazil. Teachers educated at Normal Schools (and therefore prepared to teach only at the primary school level), and professionals from various other fields (such as engineering, accounting, pharmacy), enrolled in specific courses during the school vacation and, upon passing the necessary exam, were allowed to teach at the secondary school level until specific, university-level teacher education programs became available in their regions. Since the few universities existing at that time were unable to meet the demand,[13] CADES was, in fact, an extremely efficient model for mass teacher education from a quantitative point of view and because of its agility. It was not successful in the education of teachers, in a strict sense, as its activities were limited to "formalizing" teaching practice by regularizing the situation of professionals and ended up promoting the continuity of practices that were anachronistic and inconsistent in the face of the demands imposed by curricular changes, for example. The interruption of CADES led to increasing competition for openings in special weekend courses which were offered by some private institutions mainly in the 1970s and 80s, but which later lapsed. This model of "teacher education," characterized by urgency and a lack of human, conceptual, and technical resources, still exists today in various states in Brazil, albeit under different names.

---

[12]Therefore, thinking of a "life cycle" of Brazilian teachers becomes a futile exercise in fiction. In the not-so-distant past, this expression served to categorize teachers' practice from the beginning to the end of their careers, temporally and linearly, with important consequences for educational research.

[13]There are records of serious teacher shortages in official bulletins at the end of the 1960s, more than 30 years after the founding of the first Brazilian university.

Discourses defending equality are common throughout the history of education in Brazil—equal access as well as quality of teaching offered in the various modes of education for teachers and students. Such discourses indicate a lack of awareness of the differentiations promoted implicitly by educational policies, and the expression "equal conditions" always echoes very positively: students in rural schools were provided with the "same conditions" as students in urban areas; technical school students would have the "same conditions" to face the demands of life as regular middle school students; students living in the Northeast would have the same conditions as students in the Southeast with respect to jobs and wages as long as they passed through the school system. It can be noted, however, that the discourse of equal conditions was never accompanied by the implementation or defense of strategies that promote equal opportunities.[14]

On the Other Hand ...

Despite the negative aspects of public policy in Brazil related to education, and mathematics education in particular, some successful strategies have made it possible to circumvent the fragility of Brazil's relatively new educational system. The continental dimensions of the country and the marked cultural differences of the states that compose it, as well as the schools which reflect this diversity, have not prevented the State from implementing actions such as the free distribution of textbooks that have undergone rigorous evaluation by the federal government. The National Textbook Program (*Plano Nacional do Livro Didático*—PNLD) is one of the public policy success stories in Brazil.

The first commission formed in Brazil with the objective of paving the way for the production, importation, and utilization of textbooks was created in 1938 (Carvalho 2008). Today the evaluation of school textbooks in all fields of knowledge is carried out in partnership with universities and is based on the quality of the materials produced and on the synchronicity between the relevant legislation, modern trends in teaching, and the conceptual correctness of the contents. Publishers submit their books to the PNLD for evaluation and, if approved, they are recommended and purchased by the federal government, which distributes them for free to all public schools in the country. One of the largest programs for free textbook distribution in the world, the PNLD delivered 105 million "recommended" books to 140,000 schools in 2009. Evaluation of mathematics textbooks is based on current trends

---

[14] The history of teaching in rural schools in Brazil is an excellent example of this disparity between "having conditions" and "giving opportunities." In the past, students living in rural areas had the conditions to enroll in primary school AS LONG AS they were able to get to the city to complete the last year of primary education; and they were evaluated with the same rigor and depth as students in urban schools, by the same teachers, EVEN THOUGH the percentage of repeating grades was much higher in rural schools, EVEN THOUGH rural students rarely managed to finish all the grades, EVEN THOUGH the urban authorities and public policies never took into consideration the different "times" and "ways" of living in rural areas.

in research regarding mathematics teaching and learning, and involves researchers and teachers at various teaching levels, coordinated by mathematics educators. Naturally, the evaluation conducted by PNLD was based on recommendations in the official documents, and focused not on minimum contents, but rather on the determinations regarding the competencies and abilities to be developed in each grade.

Graduate programs in Brazil are also evaluated by a specific agency of the federal government, the Coordination for the Improvement of Higher Education Personnel (*Coordenação de Aperfeiçoamento de Pessoal de Nível Superior*—CAPES), which was founded in 1951, the same year the National Council for Scientific and Technological Development (*Conselho de Desenvolvimento Científico e Tecnológico*—CNPq) was created. Both federal agencies evaluate and fund research projects, and most states also have governmental agencies dedicated to this end. The first graduate program in mathematics education in Brazil was created in 1983 at the State University of São Paulo (UNESP) in the city of Rio Claro. Today there is a considerable network of research centers in the field, many of which offer specialized and graduate-level studies aimed not only at preparing researchers, but also providing continuing education for practicing teachers. Currently, graduate programs are associated with both public and private universities and have been submitted to systematic evaluation since 1976. They are based on the teaching and scientific productivity of the students and professors, which emphasizes the vital need for researchers to be engaged in regional efforts that promote the growth and development of research centers to better serve the population. In the specific case of graduate programs in mathematics education, special attention is given to serving schools that provide basic education, and the involvement in research activities of students enrolled in undergraduate teacher-education courses is highly encouraged. Policies regarding teacher education for all levels of teaching have been carefully taken into account by mathematics education researchers in Brazil, a concern which is reflected in the rapid development of lines of research that focus directly on preparing teachers.

There is, however, an established common-sense discourse that claims research in mathematics education has been ineffective in provoking significant changes in the state of affairs in national education with respect to the mathematics classroom and the teaching and learning of mathematics. In my opinion, this is a pseudodiscourse that does not hold up in the face of the facts.

The history of the educational system in Brazil is characterized by various changes in legislation and program proposals for the different teaching levels, and today the system and the strategies being implemented are very different from those of the past. Today, the graduate programs in mathematics education are perfectly integrated with international research agendas and Brazilian researchers are involved in defining the directives for preparing teachers at all levels. The time of importing theories and materials is behind us, as we have abandoned the role of mere consumers and assumed the role of partners and participants in the international centers that, until recently, disseminated guidelines that we followed unquestioningly. Today we are aware of our own needs. These changes in the educational scene are the result of the efforts of a wide range of actors, including members of the research community who, despite the lack of a clear, consolidated directive and the absence of a strong professional society that intervenes in a critical and politically significant manner, have participated in the definition of public policy, programs, textbooks, and teaching strategies.

Not everything has changed as we would have liked, however. History, which teaches us how things stay the same or change over time, clearly reveals the points at which advances have been made and those characterized by stagnation or retreat. The difficulties that plague the national educational system in Brazil and affect public policies related to the teaching of mathematics are many and varied, although one advantage of the current situation is that we have the maturity to face the issues and diagnose the problems. Below, I outline, in general terms, some of the issues currently underlying the public policy problems in Brazil today related to education and mathematics education, with an emphasis on the aspects that contribute to the disconnection between research proposals and reality in the classrooms:

(a) The practices and discourses currently in force in the classroom are strongly characterized by conservatism. Teachers and administrators in the school system, as a general rule, consider it impossible or undesirable to step outside their comfort zone and abandon well-known, familiar practices. The school is, in this sense, subversive: it subverts recommendations for changes in legislation and educational directives. The array of alternatives offered to the schools as possible ways of countering existing negative situations are incorporated and adapted to the predominant conceptions in the educational institutions, rather than serving to change them. Curiously, these "subversive" day-to-day practices are not addressed by research in the fields of education and mathematics education.

(b) There is little research on public schools in Brazil.[15] Considerable research is conducted IN the public schools, with data collected IN the public schools, pointing to changes FOR the public schools, but little research is conducted ABOUT public schools related to education as well as mathematics education. Even fewer studies have been conducted regarding the public school as a workplace, as a space inhabited daily by the professionals educated in the university

---

[15]The educational system in Brazil is free; public education at the elementary, high school, university, and graduate level is free and administered by a complex network of secretariats and agencies. However, there is a distortion with respect to the quality of public education that often escapes the eyes of foreigners: the distinction regarding quality (or the discourse about quality) when the public system is compared with the private system. Public elementary and high schools are often characterized negatively. Speaking about public schools brings to mind a series of problems, such as: violence (physical as well as symbolic); poor student performance in state, national, and international assessments; poorly prepared teachers, which leads directly to poorly prepared elementary students; poor infrastructure; and low teacher salaries. The private elementary and high school system is considered to be far superior. At the university level, however, the situation is radically different: the public universities (state and federal) are institutions of excellence in teaching and research. Students undergo highly competitive exam processes to gain entrance. The private university system is considered very inferior, with the exception of a few more traditional institutions. One of the phases of this distortion is reflected in the fact that a large proportion of the students who studied in public schools, who tend to be from the lower income brackets, do not gain admission to the public universities, which end up serving predominantly students who studied in private schools and are, therefore, mostly from the more privileged classes.

programs which have been the subject of considerable research in the field of mathematics education.

(c) In addition to the public school being a work "place" or "space" that has been the subject of little research, it is also a "place/space" of work that is not homogenous, neither in terms of its physical premises nor in relation to the community it serves, its organizational and administrative structures, location, and identity of the teachers.[16] Thus, public schools are not a singular entity, which has many implications for research, including the impossibility of approaching public schools using standardized or generalist conceptions, theories, and methodologies.

(d) There are no movements or effective, consolidated political entities in Brazil that bring mathematics educators together to interfere more decisively in education policy. Such institutions, rather than seeking consensus, could serve to promote discussion, create representative forums of debate, and generate positions—albeit mutable and dynamic—as a way of defining directives that consider the diverse actors in the mathematics education scene in Brazil. While we may have influenced public policy, we have not done so in a systemic, legitimate, and representative manner.

(e) It should also be considered that conceptions do not change from one moment to the next. We note that, since the 1830s, in the middle of the debate regarding the need to expand schooling in Brazil, teacher education has been pointed to as a constraint to the quality of schools. So it is no accident that it was at this moment in history, specifically 1835, that Normal Schools were created.[17] Has anything changed in the teacher education scenario since then? Certainly there have been changes, but the crucial issues discussed at that time are still debated today. Despite being one of the more economical strategies to achieve quality education in the schools, teacher education is addressed carelessly in educational policy. I am not speaking here of blaming only the system (which is normally considered a large and abstract administrative monster), but ourselves as well: university researchers who have done little or nothing, in our graduate

---

[16]It should be pointed out that the national system, given the territorial expanse of the country and the enormous social, cultural, and economic differences of each region, is composed of small, medium, and large schools located in small, medium, and large cities, rural and urban areas, serving communities of different economic levels, administered by directors with varying expectations based on gaps in the legislation and the biases present in the directives emanating from the State. Because of the low salaries, teachers generally work in more than one school, often being forced to adapt to systems that are clearly distinct, as in the case of private and public schools. Teachers are unable to complete all of their work in school given the time limitations and difficult conditions.

[17]Normal schools were secondary educational institutions that prepared teachers for the primary school levels—teachers who were expected to know the "norms" (therefore, the name Normal School) for teaching scientific, technical, and moral principles to children. The Normal School model adopted in Brazil was parallel to the École Normale model in France, born during the French Revolution, but later re-created during Napoleon Bonaparte´s time. The first university-level Teaching Licensure programs in Brazil, aimed at educating teachers for the high school and university levels, were not modeled after the directives of the first university, but rather the old Normal Schools.

programs or even teacher education programs, to intervene in policies related to the careers, working conditions, and salaries of elementary and high school teachers. This discussion escapes us. These interventions are removed from our concerns, with negative consequences for the relationship between researchers and the schools.

Transitory, but Possible, Conclusions

Education policies in Brazil, and specifically those related to mathematics teaching, suffer from various problems. In this brief history of the re-structuring of curricula in Brazil, one can easily perceive the transitory nature of the decisions and difficulties of implementation that quickly render them outdated. The standardization of programs and curriculums is also a serious problem that must be faced in a country of such great dimensions and cultural diversity and such glaring inequalities in income distribution. In essence, it is more urgent to promote reforms to minimize the huge regional inequities than it is to promote specific educational reforms. While it is true that various researchers in Brazil, known for their competence in the fields of education and mathematics education, have participated in the development, implementation, and monitoring of public policies, reflecting the most recent trends and scientific developments in mathematics education, it is also true that this has occurred in a more or less individualized manner, given that there is no consistent system that organizes these interventions based on the community. From this perspective, we have acted contrary to what we have declared is needed: we have failed to listen to mathematics educators and to teachers so that policies are implemented in a way that everyone agrees on, giving legitimacy to our proposals, and perhaps increasing their chances for success.

References

Campos, M. A., & Lima, P. F. (2012). *Introdução ao Tratamento da Informação nos Ensinos Fundamental e Médio*. São Carlos: SBMAC—Sociedade Brasileira de Matemática Aplicada e Computacional.

Carvalho, J. B. P. (2008). Políticas Públicas e o Livro Didático de Matemática. *BOLEMA, Bulletin of Mathematics Education, 21*(29), 1–11.

D'Ambrosio, U., & de Borba, M. C. (2010). Dynamics of changes of mathematics education in Brazil and a scenario of current research. *ZDM—The International Journal on Mathematics Education, 42*, 271–279.

Garnica, A. V. M. (2010). Presentificando ausências: a formação e a atuação de professores de Matemática. In M. C. R. Fonseca (Ed.), *Convergências e tensões no campo da formação e do trabalho docente* (pp. 555–569). Belo Horizonte: Autêntica.

Garnica, A. V. M., Fernandes, D. N., & Silva, H. (2011). Entre a Amnésia e a Vontade de nada esquecer: notas sobre Regimes de Historicidade e história oral. *BOLEMA, Bulletin of Mathematics Education, 25*(41), 213–250.

Ortigão, M. I. R. (2008). Avaliação e Políticas Públicas: possibilidades e desafios para a Educação Matemática. *BOLEMA, Bulletin of Mathematics Education, 21*(29), 71–98.

Pires, C. M. C. (2008). Educação Matemática e sua influência no processo de organização e desenvolvimento curricular no Brasil. *BOLEMA, Bulletin of Mathematics Education, 21*(29), 13–42.

The *Australian Curriculum: Mathematics*—How Did it Come About? What Challenges Does it Present for Teachers and for the Teaching of Mathematics?

Max Stephens

Abstract The Australian Curriculum: Mathematics which incorporates the content descriptions and proficiencies from Foundation Year to Year 10 came into being in December 2010 when all Australian governments—the national government and the governments of the eight States and Territories—gave their approval to the draft which had been in circulation for nearly two years. Prior to that, each State and Territory had responsibility for developing and implementing its own curriculum. In 2008, an Australian Curriculum and Reporting Authority (ACARA) was also established to coordinate and oversee the development of national curricula in all areas of compulsory schooling, and to move towards an agreed upon national curriculum for Years 11 and 12. The formation of ACARA and the adoption of an Australian Curriculum: Mathematics (2010) are interpreted as a result of major transformations of an Australian federalist model over the past twenty years, shaped in large degree by the demands of national assessment and school reporting. This chapter examines how this came about, what has been achieved within Australia's ongoing federalist framework, and also points to some future challenges for teachers in implementing the national curriculum in mathematics.

Keywords Mathematics · National curriculum · Australia · Policy

---

The current Ministerial Council for Education, Early Childhood Development and Youth Affairs (MCEECDYA) has changed its name several times over the years relevant to this chapter. At the time of the Adelaide Declaration (1989), it was known as the Ministerial Council for Education, Employment and Training and Youth Affairs (MCEETYA). These changes in nomenclature reflect changing responsibilities and alignments of portfolio description of Ministers of Education in the Commonwealth and State Governments. For example, Early Childhood Education is now typically included under school education, whereas Training has been shifted to another portfolio. However, the one constant has been school education. My short-hand references to the "Council of Ministers" or simply "the Ministers" are my way of encompassing these various changes over time. These truncated references do not refer to some separate entity.

M. Stephens (✉)
Graduate School of Education, The University of Melbourne, Parkville, Australia
e-mail: m.stephens@unimelb.edu.au

Y. Li, G. Lappan (eds.), *Mathematics Curriculum in School Education*,
Advances in Mathematics Education, DOI 10.1007/978-94-007-7560-2_9,
© Springer Science+Business Media Dordrecht 2014

Setting the Australian Context

It is important to understand some key features of the Australian governmental and educational context in which the *Australian Curriculum: Mathematics* was developed in the period from 2008 through 2010, and in which it will continue to be framed. At the most basic level, Australia is a federation of six States and two Territories with an over-arching Commonwealth (Australian) government based in Canberra. These constitutional arrangements clearly distinguish Australia from countries like Singapore, Japan, England and China where the curriculum is framed and promulgated at a national level by an agency established by and responsible to the respective national government. On the other hand, Australia operates quite differently from the USA, where despite a union between Washington and the fifty States, 15,000 local school districts are responsible for the day-to-day administration of school education and contribute an important share of the funding of schools through local property taxes. In Australia, for over 140 years, responsibility for public education including the curriculum has remained with the States, following the passing of various State Education Acts in the 1870s providing for free, compulsory and secular public education. The funding of public education is largely contained with State budgets, even though taxation, principally through income taxes and company taxes, is controlled by the Commonwealth government, and disbursed to the States and Territories under agreed upon funding formulae. Property taxes exist at local level but play no role in the funding of school education.

Until the 1960s, the Australian government played virtually no role in public elementary and high school education—there being no minister responsible for school education and no national education authority. Since that time, the Australian federal model has seen a shift in the balance of powers between the States and the Commonwealth, with the national government taking a more active role in policy development and national accountability for educational expenditure, in partnership with the States and Territories, with the creation and steady growth in importance of a federal Department of Education, Employment and Training (DEET). These changing relationships make Australia different, in my opinion, to Canada which also operates a federal model but where individual Provinces appear to retain a greater degree of independence in the running of schools and in deciding what will be taught.

However, the emergence of an Australian Curriculum, and in particular of an *Australian Curriculum: Mathematics*, does not imply that the States and Territories have been edged out of school education. Each State will be responsible for the implementation of the *Australian Curriculum: Mathematics* in all schools. Several states commenced implementation, in part, during 2011 and others will begin during 2012, with all State and Territories agreeing to implement the Australian Curriculum (Mathematics) by 2013.

Since the *Australian Curriculum: Mathematics* is not intended to occupy all available teaching time, State Education authorities may wish to add additional content, where necessary. This is likely, for example, in providing for different courses in Years 9 and 10 to suit different cohorts of students—some of whom may be planning to specialise in Mathematics in the remaining two years of high school, whereas other students will be expected to continue with mathematics through to the end of school as part of their general education. Moreover, State and Territory curriculum, assessment and certification authorities continue to be responsible for the structure and organization of their senior secondary courses and will determine how they will integrate the Australian Curriculum content and achievement standards into their courses. Australian senior secondary courses, taken in Years 11 and 12, serve a dual purpose: first to certify the successful completion of secondary school, and second to provide the principal—and usually the sole—basis of selection into universities and university courses, as well as entry into courses of continuing technical and vocational education. In contrast to many other countries, Australian universities do not conduct their own entrance examinations.

Federalist Approaches to the Mathematics Curriculum

Starting in the late 1980s, the various levels of state and national government began working together to create more consistent approaches to the teaching and learning of mathematics. It was argued, for example, that a lack of consistency in the timing in which mathematical content was introduced and taught created problems for those children who moved from one state's jurisdiction to another in the course of their schooling. In addition, the growing status and importance of international assessments such as TIMSS provided a rationale for more coherent approaches across the states and Territories. However, any move to develop a national curriculum was not taken seriously. In December, 1990, for example, *A National Statement on Mathematics for Australian Schools* was completed as a joint project of the States, Territories and the Commonwealth of Australia. This project had been initiated by the Australian Educational Council with the purpose of providing a framework around which all school systems and schools might review and build their own mathematics curricula. Over the next twenty years, various working groups, representative of all levels of governments and of the non-government schools, continued to develop statements of consistency for the mathematics curricula of the States and Territories in the absence of a national curriculum. A major impetus for this continuing work was the growing importance given to State-based assessment and reporting of student achievement in Mathematics and English, and the use of these assessments as a condition of federal funding of education.

From the early 1990s, with eight different forms of State-based achievement testing (initially at Years 3 and 5, and subsequently extending to Years 7 and 9), the then federal Minister decided to develop benchmarks of achievement that could be used to provide a consistent reporting base to the national government as a basis for its funding of education. The debate and policy focus on a national curriculum, student assessments and school reporting was re-invigorated in 2005 when State and Territory education authorities were required by the national government to implement Statements of Learning in subject areas, such as Mathematics, which had been agreed to by the Ministerial Council for Education, Employment, Training and

Youth Affairs (MCEETYA), along with other requirements for student assessment and school reporting (Australian Government 2004).

The Schools Assistance Bill 2008, which provided Australian Government funding for non-government schools contained similar conditions of funding. These conditions were also embedded in National Education Agreements for Australian Government funding for government school systems. What was significant in these new arrangements was the additional requirement for reports about individual school performance, as determined by the Minister. It was no coincidence that this was the year in which the State and Territory governments, along with the Australian Government, agreed to establish ACARA with a mandate to develop an agreed upon national curriculum in all school subjects, with mathematics being in the first group to be so developed. To readers who are not familiar with this new federalist model, it is important to identify some of the key steps along the way.

These federalist approaches over the past twenty five years cannot be viewed as the province of any one Australian political party. From the late 1980s, they were moved forward by a national Labor government, and then from 1996 to 2007 by a Liberal/National Coalition government, which was followed by a returned Labor government, still in office at the time of writing. Over the same twenty-five year period, the political complexions of the various State and Territory governments were also changing.

Three Declarations on the Way to an Australian Curriculum (1989–2008)

The establishment of ACARA in 2008 was the culmination of a long period of policy debates—in the case of the national curriculum, the debates date back to the 1980s when the then Minister for Employment, Education and Training called for a common curriculum framework that would set out 'the major areas of knowledge and the most appropriate mix of skills and experience for students in all the years of schooling' (Dawkins 1988).

Three important declarations or statements by the Ministers of Education representing the eight States and Territories and the national (Commonwealth) government of Australia the first being the Hobart Declaration in 1989, the next the Adelaide Declaration in 1999, and the last the Melbourne Declaration in 2008, show significant changes in thinking about the meaning of "national curriculum" and "national assessment". The first was the Hobart Declaration on Schooling (MCEECDYA 1989) named after the city in which the Australian Education Council met that year for its sixtieth meeting. In that statement, the ministers agreed for the fist time to improve Australian schooling within a framework of *national collaboration* which embraced:

- Common and agreed upon national goals for schooling in Australia
- (An) Annual National Report on schooling
- National collaboration on curriculum projects

- Establishing the Curriculum Corporation of Australia
- The goal of a common age of entry for Australian schools
- Improving the quality of teaching.

The Curriculum Corporation was intended to be a clearing house for publications to be shared among the States and Territories and to commission new publications. It had no role in curriculum development. Indeed, the very notion of a "national curriculum" is entirely absent from the Hobart Declaration, with its clear commitment to *collaboration* among the States, Territories and the Commonwealth. Among the above goals that directly relate to the teaching and learning of mathematics, one of the stated goals of schooling was "to develop in students skills of numeracy, and other mathematical skills". The term 'numeracy' was not defined, but was generally taken to refer to an ability to use mathematics purposefully in other school subjects, in contexts outside school, and for older students in relation to their future work and life. Indirectly, the Annual National Report on schooling was intended to monitor schools' achievement and their progress towards meeting the agreed upon national goals. It was intended to report on school curriculum (for this, read *what the individual States were doing*), participation and retention rates, student achievements, and the application of financial resources to schools. Reporting on student achievement would rely entirely on whatever measures of achievement were in place at the time in individual State and Territories.

In particular, the Ministers reported that "work has been proceeding through a working party to seek to attain the highest standards of national curriculum, common principles and agreed areas of national collaboration. These will now be defined *for the Mathematics curriculum* taught in Australian schools (i.e. *as taught by the individual States and Territories*). The statement of common principles will identify the knowledge and skills to which all students are entitled, recognize areas of strength and weakness in the mathematics curriculum, and develop recommendations for future collaborative action" (MCEECDYA 1989). The Ministers said that the findings of this process would be presented for public discussion. Significantly, they added: "Their use will *not be compulsory* (my emphasis) but where agreement is reached after full consideration then it is likely that government and non-government systems and schools will use them" (MCEECDYA 1989). It was also agreed that further mapping would continue in the "key curriculum areas of Science, Technology, and English Literacy."

The Hobart Declaration was superseded ten years later by the Adelaide Declaration on National Goals for Schooling in the Twenty-First Century (MCEECDYA 1999). The spirit and letter of federalist collaboration evident in the Hobart Declaration is maintained in this relatively brief declaration. The Ministers' Adelaide Declaration set out eight agreed upon key learning areas through which students were expected to attain high standards of knowledge, skills and understanding in the compulsory years of schooling. These key learning areas were specified as: the Arts, English, Health and Physical Education, Languages other than English, Mathematics, Science, and Studies of Society and Environment. The Ministers' only other direct reference to Mathematics was to say that in terms of the curriculum, "students should have attained the skills of numeracy and English literacy, such that every student should be numerate, able to read, write spell and communicate at an appropriate level" (MCEECDYA 1999). Responsibility for monitoring and reporting on students' attainments *in all these respects* was left to the States and Territories using their own particular forms of assessment and testing.

However, by 2008, the preceding federalist model was transformed and national agreement on *action* was strikingly evident when, in their Melbourne Declaration on Educational Goals for Young Australians (MCEECDYA 2008), the Ministers agreed to take definite steps to *"promoting world class curriculum and assessment"* (my emphasis). Absent from this statement are references to non-binding agreements, as in the Hobart and Adelaide Declarations. In a wide-ranging 20-page document, the Ministers stated that "State, Territory and Commonwealth governments will work together with all school sectors to ensure world class curriculum in Australia" (p. 13). This will require different levels of implementation: a national curriculum, together with curriculum specified at State and Territory, and at local levels. In recognition of the continuing roles of States and Territories, the Ministers said that "schools and school systems are responsible for delivering curriculum programs" (p. 14) that reflect agreed upon learning areas with appropriate flexibility, and the same paragraph singles out English and Mathematics "as being of fundamental importance in all years of schooling and as the primary focus of schooling in the early years" (p. 14).

The Melbourne Declaration makes an explicit reference to national assessment for the first time when it says: "To ensure that student achievement is measured *in meaningful ways* (my emphasis), State, Territory and Commonwealth governments will work with all school sectors to develop and enhance national and school level assessment that focuses on assessment for learning, assessment as learning and assessment of learning to assess student achievement against goals and standards" (p. 14). This statement is followed immediately by a commitment to strengthen accountability and transparency, justified in terms of supporting schools and students, for informing parents and families and the community, and also for governments in order to "analyse how well students are performing, identifying schools with particular needs, to determine where resources are most needed to lift attainment, and to conduct national and international comparisons of approaches and performances" (p. 17). The Ministers reference to measurement "in meaningful ways" could be read in the context of difficulties experienced in the years following the Hobart Declaration (1989) when the eight State and Territory governments tried to compare students' achievement nationally, while still using their own forms of testing. It may also be an implied reference to instances where student achievement appeared to rise over time when smaller States changed from one assessment instrument to another. In 2008, National Assessment of Performance in Literacy and Numeracy (NAPLAN) commenced, replacing all current individual assessment regimes of the States and Territories. It can be argued that. NAPLAN made a national curriculum inescapable.

Prior to the Melbourne Declaration (2008), a National Curriculum Board (NCB) was created by the Australian Government in 2007 to be responsible for carrying forward the initiatives for developing "world class curriculum and assessment". The

NCB was essentially a committee of officials with no statutory power. In October 2008, the Australian Curriculum, Assessment and Reporting Bill (Parliament of Australia 2008) was introduced and enacted creating the Australian Curriculum and Reporting Authority (ACARA) as "an independent statutory authority" which "will manage the creation and implementation of the national curriculum, national student assessment and reporting of school education outcomes" (p. 1). As an independent statutory authority, ACARA derives its plan of work from the Ministerial Council representing all Australian governments and all school sectors. The Ministerial Council approves ACARA's budget with 50 % coming from the Commonwealth and the other 50 % coming from the States and Territories. This ensures that ACARA is independent of any one government. ACARA, which is not an agency of the national (Australian) government acting alone, reflects a new Australian federalist model where responsibility for curriculum and assessment is no longer the exclusive responsibility of the States and Territories. This evolutionary shift gives the national government, acting through ACARA, a greatly enhanced role.

Key Features of the *Australian Curriculum: Mathematics*

In implementing the *Australian Curriculum: Mathematics*, there is a consensus that it should not be too prescriptive and that there needs to be flexibility in order to cater to local needs (Kelly 2008). The States and Territories, in their proposal for a national curriculum, successfully argued that:

> …a national curriculum will benefit if there is flexibility for states and schools to innovate and adapt and to share their experiences of what approaches achieve the best results. A level of autonomy for individual schools and teachers to make professional decisions about curriculum drives the high performance level of a large number of government, Catholic and Independent schools across jurisdictions.

> …whatever common curriculum standards (that is, what students are expected to achieve in mathematics, science etc.) are adopted by jurisdictions, it is important to allow for flexibility in schools catering for different groups of students to achieve these standards in different ways. This is not an argument for lower standards for some students. On the contrary, it is an argument for flexibility in teaching approach and, in some cases, content in order to reach the standards in different settings. (Council for the Australian Federation 2007).

The federal Minister of the time, Julia Gillard, moved to address these concerns, assuring schools that the national curriculum will 'allow teachers the flexibility to shape their classes around the curriculum in a way that is meaningful and engaging for students' (Gillard 2008). Minister Gillard also recognised particular concerns:

The national curriculum, once agreed upon and completed, will be compulsory. But it will not mean that every school will be required to teach the same subjects, line by line, in the same way (Gillard 2008).

The *Australian Curriculum: Mathematics* does not set out in detail how lessons should be taught each day. This would require a very large and intricate document, which would be difficult to apply across the range and variety of schools and students' backgrounds. State and national curriculum documents serve a variety of purposes. They are intended to express an expectation or broad agreement about what should be taught and in what order, and how some key ideas are to be developed. They are intended to set out what children are expected to know and be able to do' and so provide an agreed upon framework for school and system-wide assessments. They are not recipes for teaching in any day-to-day sense. There is always a gap between what is expressed in curriculum documents and how teachers give shape to their lessons. Occasionally, these documents may recommend or suggest particular ways of teaching particular topics. For example, to support its teachers to implement the *Australian Curriculum: Mathematics*, the State of New South Wales—Australia's most populous State—has produced a five-hundred page syllabus document (Board of Studies 2012). This document can be accessed by teachers in other parts of Australia should they wish to use it. On the other hand, the State of Tasmania—Australia's smallest State—has implemented the *Australian Curriculum: Mathematics* from 2012 using the document in its ACARA format. In yet a further example of federalist approaches to implementation, the State of Victoria has "re-badged" the *Australian Curriculum: Mathematics* for its teachers as *AusVELS* (Victorian Curriculum and Assessment Authority 2012).

Content Areas and Priories in Australian Curriculum: Mathematics

How does the *Australian Curriculum: Mathematics* differ from its preceding State and Territory documents? A nationally-funded review by Donnelly (2005) and others showed inconsistencies in depth of treatment and the ways in which content was specified across Year levels in the various State and Territory curriculum documents. In curriculum documents prepared by the majority of Australian States and Territories, mathematical content was present in Bands or Levels which were intended to cover two years of schooling. As a result, the level of detail sometimes appeared scanty or too general when compared with the Mathematics curricula of Japan (Japan Society for Mathematical Education 2000) and Singapore (Ministry of Education 2007). By contrast, the *Australian Curriculum: Mathematics* specifies content according to each year level from the Foundation Year to Year 10. Nevertheless, it is important to understand that the *Australian Curriculum: Mathematics* is a consensus document within a continuing federalist model.

One of the key features of the *Australian Curriculum: Mathematics* (2010) is that content is described for each year level, from Foundation Year to Year 10, using three common content categories: Number and Algebra, Measurement and Geometry, and Statistics and Probability. In addition, four Proficiency Strands, Understanding, Fluency, Problem-solving, and Reasoning, are expected to guide teaching and learning at all year levels, across all areas of content.

The following section will compare the content descriptions of the *Australian Curriculum: Mathematics* with related sections from one of the State-based curriculum documents, namely the Victorian Essential Learning Standards (VELS,

Table 1A Australian curriculum—foundation year, measurement and geometry

Content descriptions	Elaborations
Use direct and indirect comparisons to decide which is larger, heavier or holds more and explain reasoning in everyday language (CMMG006)	Comparing objects directly by pacing one object against another to determine which is larger or longer or by pouring from one container to the other to see which one holds more using suitable language associated with measurement attributes, such as "tall" and "taller", "heavy" and "heavier", "holds more" and "holds less"

Table 1B VELS level 1, measurement, chance and data

Learning focus	Standards
(S)tudents learn to compare common objects using terms such as longer, heavier, fuller and hotter	Students compare length, area, capacity and mass of familiar objects using descriptions such as longer, taller, larger, holds more and heavier. They make measurements using informal units such as paces for length, hand spans for area, glasses for capacity and bricks for weight.

DEECD 2008). As discussed earlier, the VELS is typical of other State-based documents in using Levels, covering a two-year period, instead of year-by-year elaborations. Each level of the VELS is organized according to Learning focus and Standards of performance. The VELS Mathematics domain is organized in five dimensions: Number, Space, Measurement, Chance and Data, Working Mathematically, and Structure. The *Australian Curriculum: Mathematics* uses three content descriptions—Number and Algebra, Measurement and geometry, and Statistics and Probability—to describe the knowledge, skills and processes that teachers are expected to teach and students expected to learn. These descriptions do not prescribe approaches to teaching, but "are intended to ensure that learning is appropriately ordered and that unnecessary repetition is avoided" (ACARA 2010, p. 3). Content elaborations are also given "to illustrate and exemplify content and assist teachers to develop a common understanding of the content descriptions. They are not intended to be comprehensive content points that all students need to be taught" (ACARA 2010, p. 4).

Tables 1A and 1B compare what the two documents prescribe in Measurement for the first year of school. There is a high degree of consistency. Both descriptions are detailed, unambiguous, and measureable (Donnelly 2005). VELS Level 1 is also intended to apply to the first year of school only. Interestingly, VELS includes an informal comparison of areas which is not explicitly included in the *Australian Curriculum: Mathematics* until Year 2.

Tables 2A and 2B compare the two documents in terms of how students in Year 3 are expected to relate knowledge of number facts and relationships for single-digit numbers to mental computation involving larger numbers. This is clearly and unambiguously explained in the *Australian Curriculum: Mathematics*, where the expression "always result in the same answer" is intended to introduce the idea of equiva-

Table 2A Australian curriculum—year 3, number and algebra

Content descriptions	Elaborations
Recall addition facts for single digit numbers and related subtraction facts to develop increasingly effective mental strategies for computation (ACMNA055)	Recognise that certain single digit number combinations always result in the same answer for addition and subtraction, and using this knowledge for addition and subtraction of larger numbers using suitable language associated with Combining knowledge of addition and subtraction facts and partitioning to aid computation [for example $57 + 19 = 57 + 20 - 1$]

Table 2B VELS level 3, structure

Learning focus	Standards
(Students) learn to use number properties to support computations (for example, the use the commutative and associative properties for adding or multiplying three numbers in any order or combination	Students understand the meaning of "=" in mathematical statements and technology displays (for example to indicate either the result of a computation or equivalence). They use number properties in combination to facilitate computation [for example, $7 + 10 + 13 = 10 + 7 + 13 = 10 + 20$]

lence. The elaborations illustrate how this might be applied to developing effective mental strategies. While the VELS expressly refers to equivalence, its references to "number properties" are more general. But the link to computational efficiency is quite clearly shown. This content is expected to be covered by VELS in Years 3 and 4.

In Statistics and Probability, the *Australian Curriculum: Mathematics*, as shown in Table 3A, encourages the use of secondary data from the media and elsewhere to examine how statistics is used to convey messages and how these messages need to be examined carefully with respect to the claims being made and the assumptions made in collecting data, particularly through sampling. On the other hand, VELS Level 4 (covering Years 5 and 6)—shown in Table 3B—treats sampling only indirectly in relation to the collection of primary data through questionnaires and surveys. Incidentally, VELS level 5 Measurement, chance and data has a reference to "Students take samples in order to make inferences and predictions about a population" (DEECD 2008, p. 27). Explicit treatment of the distinction between a sample and its population is given by VELS Level 6, intended for Years 9 and 10 (DEECD 2008, p. 36). These differences could be considered variations in timing and emphasis, but the *Australian Curriculum: Mathematics* places a stronger emphasis on utilising case studies and illustrations from the media and advertising to support the study of Statistics and Probability in the upper primary and early secondary years.

In its treatment of linear and non-linear relations, the *Australian Curriculum: Mathematics* provides more detailed advice than VELS. Tables 4A and 4B set out the content descriptions and elaborations for linear and non-linear relations for Year 9 and Year 10. VELS Level 6 is intended to cover both these year levels. Teachers will see continuities between the content described in Table 4C from VELS Level

Table 3A Australian curriculum—year 6, statistics and probability

Content descriptions	Elaborations
Interpret secondary data presented in digital media and elsewhere (ACMSP148)	developing an understanding of sampling and the ability to interpret secondary data in order to critique data-based claims made in the media, advertising and elsewhere investigating data representations in the media and discussing what they illustrate and the messages the people who created them might want to convey considering the need for sampling and recognising when a census of an entire population is not possible or not necessary, and identifying examples of sampling in the media

Table 3B VELS Level 4, Measurement, chance and data

Learning focus	Standards
Students plan and conduct questionnaires to collect data for a specific purpose	Students recognise and give consideration to different data types in forming questionnaires and sampling

6 and what is recommended for Year 9 and 10 in the *Australian Curriculum: Mathematics*. However, differences between the two documents are more pronounced in this respect: not only does the latter provide greater detail, it also recognizes a need for more challenging content at this Year level for some students. The *Australian Curriculum: Mathematics* achieves this by providing an additional level of content, entitled Year 10A, which while optional "is intended for students who require more content to enrich their mathematical study whilst completing the common Year 10 content" (ACARA 2010, p. 6). Year 10A content descriptions in regard to Linear and non-linear relationships include: Describe, interpret and sketch parabolas, hyperbolas, circles and exponential functions and their transformations (ACMNA267); Solve simple exponential equations (ACMNA270); Apply understanding of polynomials to sketch a range of curves and describe the features of these curves from their equation (ACMNA268); and Factorise monic and non-monic quadratics expressions and solve a wide range of quadratics equations derived from a variety of contexts (ACMNA269). These descriptions recognise that at Year 10 some students require considerably more challenging content than is contained in the "common Year 10" descriptions. This is clearly a limitation of VELS Level 6.

The *Australian Curriculum: Mathematics*, by opting for Year-by-Year descriptions of content, has an advantage over State-based documents which are, in most cases, based on Levels covering two years. Teachers reading the *Australian Curriculum: Mathematics* are intended to see clear continuities between what is currently prescribed in their current State curricula, but they can also expect more detail, less scope for ambiguity, and some definite changes of emphasis. Two areas of changed emphasis are discussed in the following section.

Table 4A Australian curriculum—year 9, linear and non-linear relationships

Content descriptions	Elaborations
Find the distance between two points located on a Cartesian plane using a range of strategies, including graphing software (ACMNA214)	investigating graphical and algebraic techniques for finding distance
Find the midpoint and gradient of a line segment (interval) on the Cartesian plane using a range of strategies, including graphing software (ACMNA294)	investigating graphical and algebraic techniques for finding midpoint and gradient
Sketch linear graphs using the coordinates of two points (ACMNA215)	determining linear rules from suitable diagrams, tables of values and graphs and describing them both using words and algebra
Sketch simple non-linear relations with and without the use of technology (ACMNA296)	sketching parabolas, hyperbolas and circles

Challenges for Teachers and Teaching

This section will examine two content Strands, (Number and Algebra, and Probability and Statistics) and their implications for different approaches to teaching and learning. (The third Strand of Measurement and Geometry may present fewer challenges for teaching and learning since it largely reiterates the content prescribed in preceding State and Territory curricula.) As mentioned before, the inclusion of these two strands from Foundation Year to Year 10 reflects similar efforts to promote a closer integration between Number and Algebra evident in many other national curriculum documents, and an increased emphasis on the teaching of Statistics and probability which is also present in a number of national curriculum documents—the USA (see NCTM 2006) and China (see, Ministry of Education 2001, 2011) providing just two examples.

Number and Algebra

A more coherent and integrated treatment of Number and Algebra in the elementary and junior high school years raises some challenges for teachers and teaching. Several questions are uppermost in this analysis. How is this expectation interpreted by teachers? Does it imply, as some elementary teachers may think, that there is now less time for teaching Computation? What advantages does a more integrated treatment of Number and Algebra offer students to understand more deeply numbers and number operations, especially in the middle and upper elementary years? And how is this more unified treatment of Number and Algebra intended to assist students to make a smoother transition to a more formal study of algebra in the

Table 4B Australian curriculum—year 10, linear and non-linear relationships

Content descriptions	Elaborations
Solve problems involving linear equations including those derived from formulas (ACMNA235)	solving equations that are the result of substitution into common formulas mathematics and elsewhere, including those that involve rearrangement
	checking the solution by substitution into the equation
Explore the connection between algebraic and graphical representations of relations such as simple quadratics, circles and exponentials using digital technology as appropriate ACMNA239	identifying, matching and describing algebraic and graphical representations of parabolas, rectangular hyperbolas, exponential functions and circles, including those that have undergone a single transformation sketching the graphical representations of parabolas, exponential functions and circles
Solve linear equations involving simple algebraic fractions (ACMNA240)	solving a wide range of linear equations, including those involving one or two simple algebraic fractions, and checking results by substitution representing word problems, including those involving fractions, as equations and solving them to answer the question
Solve simple quadratic equations using a range of strategies (ACMNA241)	developing an understanding that many relationships are non-linear and that these can also be represented graphically and algebraically identifying the connection between algebraic and graphical solution of equations (for example understanding that the x-intercepts are the solutions of $f(x) = 0$ exploring the method of completing the square to factorise quadratic expressions and solve quadratic equations

secondary school? To illustrate these points, let us examine how teachers might approach teaching the following two elements of the Number and Algebra Strand in Year 4 and in Year 5:

> Year 4: Use equivalent number sentences involving addition and subtraction to find unknown quantities (ACMNA083)

> Year 5: Use equivalent number sentences involving multiplication and division to find unknown quantities (ACMNA121)

Two contrasting teaching approaches will be discussed. The first might be called a minimalist teaching approach; where the emphasis is focussed on using computation and equivalence to obtain a correct answer to number sentences, involving subtraction such as $39 - 15 = 41 - \Box$, for instance, or a sentence involving multiplication such as $5 \times 18 = 6 \times \Box$. In this minimalist approach, teachers would encourage students to simplify each number sentence by calculating the value of the known pair of numbers, [24 in the subtraction sentence, and 90 in the case of the multiplication sentence] and then ask what unknown number on the right hand side will be needed to give these results, leading to 17 for the subtraction sentence and

Table 4C   VELS level 6, structure

Learning focus	Standards
Students work with functions (for example, linear, quadratic, reciprocal, exponential) simple transformation of these functions, their graphs, and related algebraic properties.	Students identify and represent linear quadratic and exponential functions by table, rule and graph (all four quadrants of the Cartesian coordinate system) with consideration of independent variables, domain and range. They distinguish between these types of functions by testing for constant first difference, constant second difference or constant ration between consecutive terms ... They use and interpret the functions in modelling a range of contexts.
	They recognise and explain the roles of the relevant constants in the relationships $f(x) = ax + c$, with reference to gradient and y axis intercept, $f(x) = a(x + b)^2 + c$, and $f(x) = ca^x$

15 for the multiplication sentence. Some teachers might think that this is all that is needed to *use equivalent number sentences involving subtraction (or multiplication)* to find unknown quantities. However, this minimalist approach omits important opportunities to extend students' understanding of equivalence and its embodiment in different operations.

A mathematically richer approach would be to look more deeply at the structure of these and related equivalent number sentences; noticing especially at how the direction of compensation changes according to the operations involved. In this alternative approach, students are encouraged to refrain from calculating and to look at the numbers either side of the equivalent sign. Some students will express their reasoning verbally, using rich and varied forms of mathematical thinking such as: "*Because 41 is two more than 39, I have to put a number that is two more than 15 in order to keep the same difference*". Other students will express their thinking by using arrows to connect related numbers, 39 to 41 and 15 to the unknown number, concluding that it has to be two more than 15. Other students may write A_1 beneath 39 and A_2 beneath 41, and place B_1 under 15 and B_2 under the unknown number, reasoning that "*Since A_2 is two more than A_1, B_2 has to be two more than B_1*". Some students will explicitly use words such as "equivalent" or "to keep both sides equivalent". In all these cases, students know that they are dealing with *equivalent differences*. These students also know that the direction of compensation used the case of subtraction or difference operates in the opposite way to sentences involving addition. Likewise, for the multiplication sentence, students can be encouraged to notice that since 18 is three times the value of 6, the missing number has to be three times 5 in order to maintain equivalence. The fact that the 6 is one more than 5 in the multiplication sentence is not important, whereas the multiplicative relationship between 6 and 18 is all important to reaching a solution.

Unlike the minimalist approach discussed earlier, these approaches focus on important and generalizable features of sentences involving the same number operations. These features are intended to support students' computational fluency, and also to prepare them for algebraic thinking. Research, such as by Carpenter and

Franke (2001) and by Mason et al. (2009), endorse this approach. These possibilities will be quite new to many Australian elementary and junior secondary teachers. Implementation of the *Australian Curriculum: Mathematics* will need to open up teachers' vision to these ideas.

Statistics and Probability

For the Statistics and Probability Strand, different challenges arise for teachers and teaching. The precedence given to Statistics in the title underscores a difference with *Chance and Data* as used in the National Statement on Mathematics for Australian Schools (AEC 1990), and with the various State curricula, where, for example, VELS (DEECD 2008) uses a content heading *Measurement, chance and data*. Many teachers in the upper elementary and junior high school years, who have been accustomed to thinking about probability from a purely theoretical or computational perspective, will need help to develop their understanding of variability and the effects of sampling, which are consequences of the new emphasis on interpreting secondary data presented in digital and printed media. Research by Watson and Nathan (2010) and by Stephens and Zhang (2011), show how teachers can be assisted to think about the effects of sample size on variability of data, and to connect their teaching of probability and statistics to key mathematical ideas such as ratio and proportion. For elementary teachers, in particular, the focus needs to move away from merely collecting and recording data, and to attend more to developing different ways of representing and interpreting data. All teachers will need a clearer appreciation of the key idea of variability and its impact on interpreting data that has already been gathered.

These two illustrations are intended to show that, while the *Australian Curriculum: Mathematics* contains no radical innovations, it has clearly moved beyond existing State and Territory documents; and it can be expected to challenge current levels of practice and mathematical understanding of many teachers. That is its challenge and opportunity for the teaching and learning of mathematics in Australian schools.

What Does the *Australian Curriculum: Mathematics* Offer to Teachers and Schools?

For the first time in Australian school education, an agreed upon national curriculum sets out clearly for all schools what should be taught and assessed in Mathematics at all levels of schooling from Foundation Year (Kindergarten) to Year 10. Across these eleven years, three continuous content strands—Number and Algebra, Measurement and Geometry, and Statistics and Probability are used. Four Proficiency strands also run across the eleven years with specific elaborations at each year level in Understanding, Fluency, Problem solving, and Reasoning.

The decision to elaborate the curriculum year by year represents a clear departure from the practices of almost all of the States; which had generally used their curriculum documents to describe standards of achievement or outcomes which might be attained by most students over a period of two years. These previous documents, the Victorian Essential Learning Standards (VELS) for instance (DEECD 2008), used six levels to describe the curriculum from Foundation Year (Level 1) to Year 10 (Level 6) using two-year intervals encompassing Years 1 and 2, Years 3 and Year 4, and so on. In England and Wales, the National Curriculum Mathematics (Department of Education 2010) uses only four Key Stages or levels to describe its content for students from the beginning of school to age 16.

While the Content described under Numbers may have been evident in many State-based documents, the joining of Number and Algebra in the primary school years is an important new emphasis. Likewise, the important place given to Statistics and Probability gives a more consistent emphasis to statistical representation and the introduction of probability in the primary years than has been the case in many State-based documents. Some State-based documents included a separate strand on Mathematical thinking. The three Proficiency Strands of the Australian Curriculum are intended to achieve the same purposes.

Smaller States and Territories, which in the past may have experienced difficulty in resourcing the development and updating of their own curriculum, now have access to an agreed upon national curriculum. All States and Territories will also have access to supporting publications and associated teacher development resources. Publishers also can be confident in producing for a national market. In the past, any publisher aiming for a national market had to make significant adjustments in content, timing and terminology to account relatively small differences in curriculum between the States and Territories, which were still significant in terms of teacher acceptance.

Finally, in ACARA there is an independent statutory agency that can undertake systematic evaluations of the current curriculum and initiate revisions in a planned and systematic manner. In the former State-based regimes, reviews and revision were subject to government priorities and changes of government where previously agreed upon priorities might easily be swept aside.

What Have Been Some Drawbacks of the Current Process?

The *Australian Curriculum: Mathematics*, while an undoubted national achievement, has been the result of a consensus process by representatives of government and non-government schools, who were subject as well to inevitable time constraints. The final statement had to be more or less consistent with what was already contained in the pre-existing State documents; no big departures from current practice could be expected. Moreover, the input of the mathematics education research community which was subject to the same government set timelines was uneven. In Australia the mathematics education research community is not adept at dealing with short response timelines set by bodies such as ACARA.

Is the *Australian Curriculum: Mathematics* the "world class curriculum" that was promised in the 2008 Melbourne Declaration? Given only two years to prepare, it is unreasonable to expect something world class to be prepared in this time using a federalist consensus process. World class Mathematics curricula, such as those of Singapore, China and Japan, are developed over much longer time cycles—up to ten years—with careful input from teachers and schools and usually in the hands of a highly expert group of specialists nominated by respective Ministries of Education. Australia needs to learn from the processes used in these other countries.

What Lessons Can Be Learned for the Future?

While 2012 has seen the trialling of the *Australian Curriculum: Mathematics* in several of the States, all States and Territories have agreed to fully implement the new curriculum from 2013. Already several publications in the area of assessment, such as *Rich Assessment Tasks in Mathematics: Years 5 to 8*, published by the Catholic Education Office of Melbourne (2011), have aligned student performances with the Content Descriptions of the *Australian Curriculum: Mathematics* and the Standards currently used in the VELS. This has reassured teachers of the high degree of consistency and continuity between current assessment practice based on VELS and what the *Australian Curriculum: Mathematics* expects students to learn.

The fact that Australian Curriculum and Assessment Authority (ACARA) has successfully worked with the States and Territories to develop common and agreed upon courses in Mathematics for the final two years of school does not replace the various State-based assessment and certification procedures. These courses are to be implemented by the States and Territories during 2015–2016. There are no proposals for a national system of certification and assessment. The Results of the final-year high school assessments, across the States and Territories, are currently moderated in a national system which allows students to apply for entry into any Australian university regardless of their state of origin; and those arrangements will continue.

However, the four agreed upon courses in Mathematics for Years 11 and 12 (ACARA 2012), to be implemented in 2015–2016, will be important in reducing current variations in content and in the range of Mathematics courses on offer to senior high school students in the different States. One course, entitled Mathematical Methods, includes algebra, introductory calculus, trigonometry and statistics, and is intended to provide a broad course for the majority of students who wish to undertake university courses in the mathematical sciences, science and economics. A second course, entitled Specialist Mathematics, which must be taken in conjunction with the first is intended to provide more advanced treatment of these topics, especially in calculus, for a subset of students who intend to undertake more specialised mathematical and statistical studies beyond school. A third course, entitled General Mathematics, has a strong foundation in descriptive statistics and in non-calculus applications of mathematics. It is intended to support those students who may wish to pursue courses in business, and the humanities. A fourth course, entitled Essential

Mathematics, is intended to support students who need to apply basic mathematical techniques in their other school subjects and to support future vocationally oriented studies and training. In the past, this latter group of students may have ceased to study any Mathematics after Year 10, and many may have "dropped out" of school altogether. Continuing to engage these students implies that Essential Mathematics be taught in more vocationally oriented contexts and using very different teaching and learning approaches than from what might be expected in the first three courses.

The adoption by ACARA of these four nationally agreed upon courses for Mathematics in the senior high school years (Years 11 and 12) will require some differentiation of content for students in Year 10, and possibly Year 9, to reflect their different academic pathways, and who need to make appropriate choices about the kind of mathematics that is most likely to be relevant to their continuing studies and aspirations beyond school.

The fact that ACARA is funded 50 % by the Commonwealth and 50 % by the States and Territories exemplifies the new federalist model and is intended to ensure that ACARA is robust enough to weather any changes of government at national or state level in the next five years. ACARA will continue to reflect a balance of responsibilities between the States, Territories, and the Australian (Commonwealth) governments, being especially responsive to the needs of schools and students across Australia; and fostering high quality mathematics education in all Australian schools.

References

Australian Curriculum and Reporting Authority (2010). *Australian curriculum mathematics.* Sydney: ACARA. http://www.australiancurriculum.edu.au/Mathematics/Curriculum/F-10, accessed on 10 January, 2013 [to view one year level per page with elaborations, press the E icon in VIEW on the cover page; Senior Secondary Courses can be accessed through the control bar at the top of the page].

Australian Curriculum and Reporting Authority (2012). *Draft senior secondary Australian Curriculum: Mathematics*, November 2012. Sydney: ACARA. http://www.acara.edu.au/verve/_resources/Consultation_Report_on_the_Draft_Senior_Secondary_Australian_Curriculum__Mathematics.pdf, last accessed 25 September 2013.

Australian Education Council (1990). *A national statement on mathematics for Australian schools.* Melbourne: Australian Education Council.

Australian Government (2004). Schools assistance (learning together—achievement through choice and opportunity) act 2004, paragraphs 14(1)(f) and 14(1)(g) and subsections 31(f) and 31(g). http://www.comlaw.gov.au/ComLaw/Legislation/ActCompilation1.nsf/current/bytitle/B42223A296758099CA257314001D59DD?OpenDocument&mostrecent=1, Accessed on 18 August 2011.

Board of Studies (2012). *NSW syllabuses for the Australian curriculum: mathematics K-10.* Sydney: Board of Studies. http://syllabus.bos.nsw.edu.au/mathematics/mathematics-k10/content/ Accessed on 14 January 2013.

Carpenter, T. P., & Franke, M. L. (2001). Developing algebraic reasoning in the elementary school: generalization and proof. In H. Chick, K. Stacey, J. Vincent, & J. Vincent (Eds.), *Proceedings of the 12th ICMI study conference. The future of the teaching and learning of algebra* (pp. 155–162). Melbourne: University of Melbourne.

Catholic Education Office Melbourne (2011). *Rich assessment tasks in mathematics: years 5 to 8.* Melbourne: Author.

Council for the Australian Federation (2007). *Federalist paper 2: the future of schooling in Australia* (pp. 13–14). Melbourne: Department of Premier and Cabinet. rev. ed. http://dpl/Books/2007/FederalistPaper2_SchoolingInAustraliaRevEd.pdf. Accessed on 31 August, 2011.

Dawkins, J. S. (1988). *Strengthening Australia's schools: a consideration of the focus and content of schooling.* Canberra: Minister for Employment, Education and Training. http://dpl/Books/2008/StrengtheningAustSchools.pdf. Accessed on 8 August 2011.

Department of Education (2010). *National curriculum for mathematics (England).* London: Department of Education.

Department of Education and Early Childhood Development (DEECD) (2008). *Victorian essential learning standards (mathematics).* Melbourne: DEECD. http://vels.vcaa.vic.edu.au/downloads/vels_standards/velsrevisedmathematics.pdf, last accessed 6 February, 2012.

Donnelly, K. (2005). *Benchmarking Australian primary school curricula.* Canberra: Department of Education, Science and Training. http://www.dest.gov.au/NR/rdonlyres/B6E3D22B-6E60-4A1F-920A-EFAB3E5C45FA/7940/benchmarking_curricula_report2.pdf, last accessed 6 February, 2012.

Gillard, J. (2008). *Second reading speech: Australian curriculum, assessment and reporting authority bill 2008.* Canberra: Parliament of Australia, Department of Parliamentary Services. http://www.aph.gov.au/library/pubs/bd/2008-09/09bd060.pdf, accessed on 2 September 2011.

Japan Society of Mathematical Education (2000). *Mathematics program in Japan: elementary, lower secondary and upper secondary schools.* Tokyo: JSME.

Kelly, P. (2008). Labor plan is modest progress on education, *Australian*, 26 September 2008, p. 16, http://parlinfo.aph.gov.au/parlInfo/search/display/display.w3p;query=Id%3A%22

Mason, J., Stephens, M., & Watson, A. (2009). Appreciating mathematical structure for all. *Mathematics Education Research Journal, 21*(2), 10–32.

Ministerial Council for Education, Early Childhood Development and Youth Affairs (MCEECDYA) (1989). The Hobart declaration on national goals for schooling in the twenty-first century. http://www.mceetya.edu.au/mceecdya/hobart_declaration,11577.html, accessed on 2 February, 2012.

Ministerial Council for Education, Early Childhood Development and Youth Affairs (MCEECDYA) (1999). The Adelaide declaration on schooling. http://www.mceetya.edu.au/mceecdya/adelaide_declaration,11576.html, accessed on 2 February, 2012.

Ministerial Council for Education, Early Childhood Development and Youth Affairs (MCEECDYA) (2008). Melbourne declaration on educational goals for young Australians. http://www.mceetya.edu.au/mceecdya/melbourne_declaration,25979.html, accessed on 2 February, 2012.

Ministry of Education of People's Republic of China (2001, 2011). *Mathematics curriculum standards for compulsory education.* Beijing: Beijing Normal University Press.

Ministry of Education of People's Republic of China (2011). *Mathematics curriculum standards for compulsory education (2011 version).* Beijing: Author.

Ministry of Education, Singapore (2007). *Primary mathematics syllabus.* Singapore: Author.

National Council of Teachers of Mathematics (2006). *Curriculum focal points for prekindergarten through grade 8 mathematics: a quest for coherence.* Reston: Author.

Parliament of Australia: Parliamentary Library (2008). Bills digest no. 60 2008-09: Australian curriculum, assessment and reporting authority bill. http://www.aph.gov.au/library/pubs/bd/2008-09/09bd060.htm, accessed 2 February, 2012.

Stephens, M., & Zhang, Q. (2011). Teacher capacity as a key element of national curriculum reform in mathematics: an exploratory comparative study between Australia and China. In *Mathematics: tradition and [new] practices, joint AAMT-MERGA conference*, Alice Springs, Northern Territory, July 3–7 (pp. 702–710).

Victorian Curriculum and Assessment Authority (2012). *AusVELS: mathematics*. Melbourne: VCAA. http://ausvels.vcaa.vic.edu.au/Mathematics/Overview/Mathematics-across-Foundation-to-Level-10, accessed on 13 January, 2013.

Watson, J., & Nathan, E. (2010). Biased sampling and PCK: the case of the marijuana problem. In *Shaping the future of mathematics education, 33rd annual conference of the mathematics education research group of Australia*, Fremantle, Western Australia, July 3–7 (pp. 610–617).

Part III
Curriculum Development and Analysis

Preface

Learning and Sharing of Best Practices in Curriculum Development

It is now common knowledge that curriculum varies across educational systems and also affects mathematics teaching and learning. For example, TIMSS curriculum studies revealed remarkable differences in content topic and requirement inclusion across education systems (e.g., Schmidt et al. 1997, 2002). However, few may consider the possibility of identifying and learning best practices in curriculum design and development, which is often operated behind content topic selection and presentations. In fact, curriculum design and development are often taken as normal practice but not a topic for research that examines possible ideas behind practice. Much remains to be studied and understood about curriculum design and development that are in operation across education systems and possible best practices in developing curriculum. Chapters published in this part provide us great opportunities to learn diverse ideas and practices in curriculum development, textbook design, and changes in curriculum development over the years in different system contexts.

In Chapter 10, Roger Howe proposes an integrated approach for first grade arithmetic. Howe emphasizes the importance of building a solid foundation during first grade for students learning mathematics. He highlights the coordinated development of three pillars: conceptual understanding of addition and subtraction through word problems, computational skills based on place value understanding, and the coordination of counting numbers and measurement numbers. The development and use of these ideas are not restricted by specific system contexts. Instead, Howe points out that these ideas are built upon what we can learn from mathematics textbooks in East Asia and are also consistent with the Common Core State Standards in Mathematics in the United States. Howe also provides a sketch of the possible development of these ideas after the first grade.

Chapter 11, contributed by Judy Anderson, highlights changes in curriculum development from state control to increased central control and accountability measures in Australia. The first national curriculum in mathematics has been developed, together with national testing in grades 3, 5, 7 and 9. This presents a shift similar to the movement in the U.S., where a de-centralized education system adopts a more centralized approach in developing curriculum and monitoring the results of curriculum implementation. Given the fact that states are still responsible for curriculum implementation, new opportunities and challenges are clearly in place for improving students' achievement with new curriculum as expected.

Marc van Zanten and Marja van den Heuvel-Panhuizen focus on textbooks as part of curriculum development in Chapter 12 to illustrate dramatic differences in opportunities provided to students in learning mathematics. They analyze two Dutch textbook series on the topic of subtraction up to 100, in terms of their alignment with the intended curriculum on content and performance expectations. According to the authors, textbooks provide a day-to-day guideline for mathematics teaching and learning in classrooms. However, the Dutch government does not regulate textbook development and publishing, except to specify broad content coverage in the intended curriculum. The inconsistence and difference suggest that textbooks should be carefully considered in the process of curriculum development.

The three follow-up chapters in this part relate to three education systems in East Asia. Chapter 13 by JeongSuk Pang focuses on curriculum changes in South Korea and highlights the trends and challenges in curriculum development over the years in the Korean context. Ngan Hoe Lee outlines curriculum development practices in Singapore evolved from a deductive approach to a mixed model approach in Chapter 14. Possible advantages and contributing factors to the success of the mixed model approach are specified through three case studies. In Chapter 15, Yeping Li, Jianyue Zhang and Tingting Ma focus on mathematics textbook design and development practices in China. With the important role of textbooks in guiding daily instruction, textbook development and its alignment with the intended curriculum have been seen as a critical part of curriculum development over the years in China. Specific textbook design practices and on-going improvements present an interesting case for others to know and use to reflect on their own practices.

Common features across these three education systems in East Asia include (a) they all have a centralized education system, and (b) students in these three education systems consistently show high mathematics performance in large-scale international comparative studies. But are there possible best practices in curriculum development that can be identified and learned from these three education systems? While we believe that readers can learn much more from reading all six chapters included in this part, we would like to share the following two points.

(1) Curriculum is a system-cultural artifact that is developed with specific policy guidance and cultural values in an education system. For example, centralized education systems (e.g., China) specify common curriculum requirements that may put certain restrictions on curriculum design, but tend to provide some flexibility at the local level for curriculum development (e.g., Liu and Li 2010). It is not feasible to examine curriculum design and development, at a macro level, out of its system-cultural context. Thus, it is important to take a holistic approach to examine and understand curriculum design and development as situated in each of the selected system contexts.

(2) At a micro level, curriculum design and development (including textbooks) play an important role in shaping what is taught and learned in classrooms in many education systems (e.g., Howson 1995; Schmidt et al. 1997, 2002). Relevant efforts to examine mathematics textbooks have led to research interest in various aspects

of textbook content presentation and organization. Results from previous studies revealed possible similarities and differences in mathematics curriculum development (e.g., textbooks) in multiple dimensions that ultimately present different opportunities and challenges for teaching and learning (e.g., Leung and Li 2010; Li 2008). Thus, the chapters included in this part provide readers with a platform to cross-examine possible similarities and differences in curriculum design and development across these selected education systems.

As the chapters in this part provide rich information about different aspects of curriculum design and development in different system contexts, readers should be able to learn much from reading these chapters. At the same time, readers still need to justify whether specific practices in curriculum development in a specific system context may be feasible (or can even be taken as the best practice) in one's own system context.

Texas A&M University, USA   Yeping Li
Michigan State University, USA   Glenda Lappan

References

Howson, G. (1995). *Mathematics textbooks: a comparative study of grade 8 texts*. Vancouver: Pacific Educational Press.

Leung, F. K. S., & Li, Y. (Eds.). (2010). *Reforms and issues in school mathematics in East Asia—sharing and understanding mathematics education policies and practices*. Rotterdam: Sense Publishers.

Li, Y. (2008) Transforming curriculum from intended to implemented: what teachers need to do and what they learned in the United States and China. In Z. Usiskin & E. Willmore (Eds.), *Mathematics curriculum in Pacific Rim countries: China, Japan, Korea, and Singapore* (pp. 183–195). Charlotte: Information Age Publishing.

Liu, J., & Li, Y. (2010). Mathematics curriculum reform in the Chinese mainland: changes and challenges. In F. K. S. Leung & Y. Li (Eds.), *Reforms and issues in school mathematics in East Asia—sharing and understanding mathematics education policies and practices* (pp. 9–31). Rotterdam: Sense Publishers.

Schmidt, W. H., McKnight, C. E., Valverde, G. A., Houang, R. T., & Wiley, D. E. (1997). *Many visions, many aims (Vol. 1): a cross-national investigation of curricular intentions in school mathematics*. Dordrecht: Kluwer Academic Press.

Schmidt, W. H., McKnight, C. E., Houang, R. T., Wang, H., Wiley, D. E., Cogan, L. S., et al. (2002). *Why schools matter: a cross-national comparison of curriculum and learning*. San Francisco: Jossey-Bass.

Three Pillars of First Grade Mathematics, and Beyond

Roger Howe

Abstract An integrated approach to first grade arithmetic is described. It consists of a coordinated development of the three pillars of the title, which are (i) strong conceptual grasp of the operations of addition and subtraction through word problems, (ii) computational skill that embodies place value understanding, and (iii) coordination of counting number with measurement number. The ways in which these three parts interact and reinforce each other is discussed. This approach is highly consistent with CCSSM standards recently released in the United States by the Council of Chief State School Officers.

In a second part, a sketch is given of a further development of these key ideas in later grades. Increasing understanding of the arithmetic operations leads to increasing appreciation of the sophistication and underlying structure of place value notation, eventually making links with polynomials. Linear measurement becomes the basis for developing and exploiting the number line, which later supports coordinatization. Throughout, consistent attention should be given to interpreting and solving increasingly involved word problems. Successful intertwining of these three strands supports the later learning of algebra, and its links to geometry.

Keywords Word problems · Place value · Counting-measurement coordination · Number line

For nearly all students, first grade is the beginning of dedicated intensive instruction in mathematics. Since later mathematics learning builds on earlier learning, getting started right is important. Since arithmetic is the main focus of mathematics education in elementary school, first grade should concentrate on giving students a good start in arithmetic. Some would argue that geometry or data or early algebra should also get attention, and there is probably room time to do something about some of these (and the Common Core State Standards in Mathematics (CCSSM) (CCSSO 2011) calls for some), but starting arithmetic off right is the essential task of first grade.

R. Howe (✉)
Mathematics Department, Yale University, New Haven, USA
e-mail: howe@math.yale.edu

Y. Li, G. Lappan (eds.), *Mathematics Curriculum in School Education*,
Advances in Mathematics Education, DOI 10.1007/978-94-007-7560-2_10,
© Springer Science+Business Media Dordrecht 2014

This is not as simple as it might sound. Getting going in arithmetic involves more than learning how to compute. It entails developing a broad conception of the operations of addition and subtraction, one that includes all the main contexts where these might be used, and one that supports thinking of addition and subtraction as well-defined things with specific properties, about which we can reason. It also entails going beyond situations that are described by counting, to see how arithmetic applies to the arena of measurement. The connection of arithmetic to geometry through measurement both enlarges the conception of arithmetic and provides concrete and conceptual tools to help students think about arithmetic.

In the domain of computation, the overarching idea is that of place value. The standard conception of place value in the U.S. tends to be rather limited: it is frequently treated as a vocabulary issue, that students should know the value of each place in a multi-digit number. However, the principle of place value controls essentially all aspects of arithmetic computation and estimation. Students should eventually come to appreciate and be able to exploit the ubiquitous influence of place value. A good start in first grade can help students reach that goal.

The discussion below of computation and place value is substantially influenced by our reading of East Asian texts and education literature. In particular, we emphasize the value of *addition and subtraction within 20* (Ma 1999) as a context for learning the addition and subtraction facts. This also has been recognized by CC-SSM, which has this topic as an explicit standard at grades 1 and 2.

These considerations lead to three main ingredients that are key to starting off right in arithmetic. They are:

(I)   A robust understanding of the operations of addition and subtraction.
(II) An approach to arithmetic computation that intertwines place value with the addition/subtraction facts.
(III) Making connections between counting number and measurement number.

Below we enlarge on each of these topics. In two supplemental sections, we will sketch ways in which these basic themes might extend to later grades.

A Robust Understanding of the Operations of Addition and Subtraction

Addition is often described as combining and subtraction as taking away, but the types of situations in which these operations are used are more varied than these brief descriptions would suggest. Mathematics educators have articulated a taxonomy of one-step addition and subtraction word problems.

The CCSSM has adopted a version that recognizes 14 types. The types fall into three main categories: *change*, in which some number changes over time; *comparison*, in which the difference between two quantities plays a role; and *part-part whole*, in which some quantity or collection of objects made up of two parts. These broad classes are similar to those discussed in *Adding It Up* (Kilpatrick et al. 2001), based on *Children's Mathematics* (Carpenter et al. 1999), and also to the discussion in Fuson's paper (2005).

Each of the first and second types can be divided into two subtypes. In problems involving change over time, the initial quantity can either increase or decrease. Similarly, in comparisons of quantities, one quantity can be described either as more or less than the other one. In part-part whole problems, the two parts play equivalent roles, so these form just one family.

Finally, for each of the four subtypes of change or comparison problems, one can pose three different questions, according as to what is unknown. Thus, for change-increase problems, one can ask to find the final total, the amount of change, or the initial amount. For comparison problems, one can ask to find the larger quantity, the smaller quantity, or the difference. For part-part-whole problems, since the two parts play equivalent roles, there are only two questions: what is the size of the whole, or what is the size of an unknown part. In all, this gives $2 \times 2 \times 3 + 2 = 14$ types.

Here are examples of selected types:

Change-increase, total unknown: Shana had three toy trucks. For her birthday, she got four more toy trucks. How many toy trucks did she have then?

Comparison-more, smaller unknown: Shana has seven toy trucks. She has four more toy trucks than her friend Molly. How many toy trucks does Molly have?

Part-part whole, part unknown: Shana has a collection of seven toy trucks. She keeps them on two shelves in her bedroom. There are four trucks on the top shelf. How many trucks are on the lower shelf?

The full taxonomy, with all 14 subtypes (plus a fifteenth, of a different nature), is given as table I on page 88 of the Common Core State Standards (CCSSO 2011).

Although an adult may think of these types of problem as quite similar, mathematics educators have shown that young children find them quite different (Carpenter et al. 1999). For example, consider the problem

Change-increase, original amount unknown: Shana had some toy trucks. For her birthday, she got four more toy trucks, and then she had seven. How many toy trucks did she have before her birthday?

This type of problem turns out to be difficult for many young students to think about, because they are unsure how to model it. To solve the **Change-increase, total unknown** problem, they can count out three tokens, then four more tokens, then count all the tokens to find the answer. To deal with the **Change-increase, change unknown**, they can proceed similarly after some thought. They lay out seven counters to represent the total, and three next to them to represent the original amount. Then they count the unmatched counters in the total. (Effectively, they have converted the change problem to a comparison problem.) However, with the **Change-increase, original amount unknown**, they have trouble getting started. At this stage, the fact that a sum does not depend on the order in which the addends are combined (the *commutative* property of addition), is still to be learned.

The importance of presenting all types of addition and subtraction problems is clear if we take into account that a tremendous amount of learning takes place through examples. Children acquire vocabulary at the rate of several words each day (for passive vocabulary; see http://en.wikipedia.org/wiki/Vocabulary). Mostly, they do not look them up in the dictionary. Rather, they learn them by seeing them used in context, that is, through examples of how a word is used. It is important to obey the maxim of *example sufficiency*, especially in teaching abstract concepts, which are the main content of mathematics. By example sufficiency, I mean giving a broad enough array of examples to provide a well-rounded representation of the concept. A famous example of example insufficiency is the case of triangles. In brief presentations of the concept of triangle, frequently only one example, that of an equilateral triangle with a horizontal base, is given. Perhaps then it should not be surprising that studies have found that many second or third grade students will not identify non equilateral triangles, or even equilateral triangles with non-horizontal bases, as being triangles. With foundational concepts, such as addition and subtraction, which will form the base on which many further ideas are built, it is especially important to present a well-rounded collection of situations where addition or subtraction can be used. Thus, care should be taken in first grade to introduce all types of one-step addition/subtraction word problems, and to use them all repeatedly throughout the year with larger numbers as student technique in symbolic calculation improves.

Sometimes, the use of only a limited number of the simplest problem types is justified on the basis that young students have limited reading skills, and that mathematics must be presented in ways that they can understand. This point of view might seem to have increased validity today, when so many students are classified as ELL (English-language learners). However, I would argue that mathematics word problems are as important for their potential to improve reading skills and thinking skills as they are for teaching arithmetic technique. In fact, word problems are the glue that binds mathematics to the real world, and studying them from a language arts point of view, as passages that we want to understand, is as important as solving them. Oral presentation and class discussion can be a vehicle for this, as well as individual reading.

In class discussion, comparative analysis may be an effective tool. Comparing and contrasting pairs of problems, then discussing all three of one of the triples of problems, and ending with comparison of pairs of triples, may give students a sense for the territory of addition and subtraction in a way that just solving problems one at a time could not achieve. A somewhat subtle side benefit of this kind of activity may be that some students come to think of addition and subtraction as having an existence independent of calculation, that is, they may realize that the expression $3 + 8$ is a valid name for a number whether or not we calculate to find that it is 11. This kind of understanding supports algebra.

Comparison problems require a special note of caution. In almost all uses of numbers that occur in everyday life, numbers function as adjectives: two hats, or two dollars, or two train rides all can be interpreted readily; however, "two" by itself does not have a clear meaning. Without a unit to refer to, the meaning of "two" is incomplete. Correspondingly, when we discuss addition, we understand (usually tacitly) that the numbers we are adding all refer to the same unit. The statement "3 dimes and 4 nickels equals 2 quarters" is perfectly intelligible. However, the equation $3 + 4 = 2$ violates our usual understandings of arithmetic. The source of the problem here is that each number is referring to a different unit. To write an equation that expresses the desired relationship, we should make sure that all terms are denominated in the same unit. For example, if we express each coin, nickel, dime and quarter in terms of their value in pennies, we can write a correct equation:

$$3 \times 10 + 4 \times 5 = 2 \times 25.$$

Since ignoring the unit is usually does not cause trouble when dealing with whole numbers, units may often be suppressed in first grade and second grade texts. This can even serve a positive purpose, by emphasizing that arithmetic is independent of the unit: 4 apples and 3 apples make 7 apples, and likewise, 4 trucks and 3 trucks make 7 trucks. However, lack of unit awareness can wreak havoc during the study of fractions.

If they are not formulated carefully, comparison problems may seem to violate the same-unit principle. In such problems, one is often asked to compare the number of birds with the number of worms, or the number of children with the number of cookies. It may then seem that we are subtracting birds from worms, or the other way around, in contravention of the consistent unit principle. What is going on in these problems is more complicated. The problem scenario implicitly sets up a correspondence between the two sorts of things being compared, at some rate (often one-to-one). This implicit correspondence converts (implicitly, of course!) one of the quantities to the other, and subtraction takes place among the quantities of the type that is in abundance. However, this under-the-table correspondence may well be too subtle or confusing for young students to grasp. For this reason, it is advisable to formulate comparison problems so that they are about quantities of essentially the same type. For example, it is easier to assimilate "green apples" and "red apples" under the umbrella unit "apple" than it is to think of "tickets" and "people" as being essentially the same. Note that in the comparison example given above, all numbers referred to toy trucks.

An Approach to Arithmetic Computation that Intertwines Place Value with the Addition/Subtraction Facts

Place value is the central concept of arithmetic computation. It is not simply a vocabulary issue, of knowing the ones place, the tens place, and so on; it is the key organizing principle by which we deal with numbers. Place value, together with the Rules of Arithmetic, specifies the key aspects of how we perform addition/subtraction and multiplication/division (i.e., the algorithms of arithmetic). The vital role of place value is attested to by this quotation from Carl Friedrich Gauss (1777–1855), often named the greatest mathematician since Newton:

> The greatest calamity in the history of science was the failure of Archimedes to invent positional notation. (Eves 2002)

Two-digit numbers, and their addition and subtraction, is the topic where students first engage seriously with place value. The main ingredients in learning two-digit addition and subtraction are:

(a) learning the addition/subtraction facts: knowing the sum of any two digits (that is, the numbers 0, 1, 2, 3, 4, 5, 6, 7, 8, 9), and, given the sum and one of the digits, knowing the other digit;
(b) understanding that a two-digit number is made of some tens and some ones; and
(c) in adding or subtracting, you work separately with the tens and the ones, except when regrouping is needed.

Specifically, item (c) comprises two situations:

(i) in adding, when you get more than 10 ones, you convert 10 of them into a ten, and combine that with the other tens; or
(ii) in subtracting, if the ones digit you want to subtract is larger than the ones digit you want to subtract from, you must convert a ten into 10 ones, and subtract from the resulting teen number.

The main US method for teaching this topic has been

(a) learn the addition/subtraction facts by memorization; and
(b) learn the column-wise algorithm for performing the operations.

These are often treated separately, with little or no rationale given for either, and no connections between the two. In recent years, increased use of base ten blocks has probably increased understanding of the regrouping process for some students. However, the learning of the addition facts remains primarily a memorization process, unconnected with the other parts of the package, in particular with regrouping. It is desirable and possible to combine the two key steps in such a way that they support each other, and are both connected to the fundamental principle of place value. We sketch the main steps in this development.

(1) Learn the addition and subtraction facts to 10.

This learning should be fluent, robust and flexible. This means understanding that $3 + 4 = 7$, and $7 - 4 = 3$, and also, that, if you have 4 and want 7, you need 3; and being able to produce any of these statements more or less automatically. (In the U.S., these variants are sometimes referred to as "related facts".) Instruction should be accompanied by many concrete and pictorial illustrations of the relationships involved.

In learning the facts to 10, it is valuable to spend time thinking about all the possible ways to decompose a given number, for example to note that

$$5 = 4 + 1 = 3 + 2 = 2 + 3 = 1 + 4.$$

Besides improving fluency, this work highlights structural facts, such as the commutative rule for addition, which reveals itself here in the symmetry of the possible expansions of 5: each decomposition is paired with another in which the addends are in the opposite order. (Problems that call for all the possible ways to decompose a whole number into two smaller whole numbers are recognized as a fifteenth type of addition and subtraction problem in the Table I of the Common Core Standards, as cited above.)

(2) Learn the teen numbers as a 10 and some ones.

In Chinese this is quite easy, because the number names express this directly: ten and one, ten and two, ten and three, and so on, up to two tens, and onward. It will involve more work in the US, since the number names are not as helpful. There will have to be class discussion about hearing the 10 in "teen", and hearing the 3 in "thir", so that students can think "ten and three" when they hear "thirteen". Similar work will have to be done with the other teen numbers. There will probably have to be some special talk about how "eleven" and "twelve" are pretty dumb names, but you just have to live with them, and think "ten and one" quietly to yourself when you hear "eleven".

Besides the names, the notation will need explicit attention. The fact that the 1 in 13 stands for ten, and the 3 stands for the three additional ones will probably have to be taken note of repeatedly. We agree not to write the 0 in the ten, to save time and space, but we put the 1 on the left of the three, and this is just a short way of writing $10 + 3$. If our number names reinforced this, learning would probably be quicker and easier, but with sufficient reminders, we can hope that students will retain the idea.

Some amount of work with the teen numbers should be done to help students become comfortable with them. Adding and subtracting a teen number and a single digit, not involving regrouping, asking which number comes just before or just after, asking which of two teen numbers is larger, are examples of exercises to increase familiarity. With regard to ordering, and adding that does not cross decades, students may observe spontaneously that only the ones digit is involved, and that, as far as this digit is concerned, everything is "just like" the parallel single digit behavior. If no student offers this, pointing it out may be helpful.

(3) Learning the higher addition facts.

This is known in East Asia as "addition and subtraction within 20" (Ma 1999). The importance of this topic for providing important connections in the learning of place value is recognized by the adoption of this term in the Common Core Standards in grades 1 and 2 (CCSSO 2011).

Now that the teen numbers are understood in terms of their base 10 structure, the focus returns to single-digit addition and subtraction, and learning the addition and subtraction facts when the total exceeds 10. Here the key point is *not* memorization of the higher addition facts, but understanding how to produce them, and their connection to place value notation. So, for example, to add $6 + 7$, a student should think in terms of making a 10. From stage (1), it is known that starting from 6, one needs 4 more to make 10. One gets the 4 from the 7, and since one also knows that $4 + 3 = 7$, there are 3 left over from the 7, so one gets 10 and 3 more, or 13. The formal expression of this in terms of symbolic manipulation uses the Associative Rule of addition to change the form of the sum:

$$6 + 7 = 6 + (4 + 3) = (6 + 4) + 3 = 10 + 3 = 13.$$

However, at this stage, such niceties can be ignored. Similarly, in subtracting a one-digit number from a two-digit number, one may have to unmake or break apart the 10. There are (at least) two different ways that a student might think about this; either one is valid. These are illustrated in the following computations.

$$13 - 7 = 13 - (3 + 4) = (13 - 3) - 4 = 10 - 4 = 6,$$

or

$$13 - 7 = (10 + 3) - 7 = (10 - 7) + 3 = 3 + 3 = 6.$$

(4) Learn that two-digit numbers are made of some tens and some ones.

When students are fairly fluent in the addition/subtraction facts and making/un-making 10, attention can then move to larger numbers. The key understanding is that a two-digit number is made of some tens and some ones.

Thus, $43 = 40 + 3$ is 4 tens and 3 ones. The main work is probably in getting students to think of each -ty number as indicating a certain number of tens. Then the general two digit number is gotten by appending some ones, and this is fairly clearly indicated in the name. Again students need to learn to think beyond the names: "twenty" is 2 tens; "thirty" is 3 tens; "forty" is 4 tens; and so forth. The names and what they mean should again be connected with the notation: the 10s digit tells the number of tens, and the 1s digit tells the number of ones.

For many students, a fair amount of counting with verification, that indeed 20 is 2 tens, forty is 4 tens, and so forth, may be required to solidify confidence in the equivalence. As the counting is being done, the benefits of grouping by some manageable amount, which for us is 10, should be promoted. In fact, if counting gets interrupted, the advantage of having made groups of 10 should be evident, in greatly reducing the amount that must be recounted. A hundreds chart can also be useful in this work. In working with a hundreds chart, it may be helpful to point out that a given number tells the number of spaces in the chart up to and including that number. This observation can also be helpful when studying computation (step 5 below), especially in interpreting the effect of adding 1 or adding 10 to a general two-digit number. Some educators advocate having a hundreds chart in which the numbers with a given tens digit run down a column (rather than across a row, which seems to be the more common form).

Manipulatives such as 10-rods and 1-cubes may be helpful in making two-digit numbers tangible and accessible. Often such manipulatives are handled by arranging them in loose groupings, on a mat or other area designated for the work. However, it is probably a good idea to have students do some of this work in the context of linear measurement, with the 10-rods and cubes arranged into a linear train. Among other advantages, this will emphasize that the various rods and cubes are indeed united into a single quantity, with length corresponding to the size of the number. The measurement model for numbers is discussed further below.

Attention should also be paid to ordering two-digit numbers—thinking about which of two numbers is larger. Here the simple principle is, that the 10s digit determines the relative size of two two-digit numbers, except when both numbers have the same 10s digit, in which case, you look at the 1s digit. Since the size difference between the 10-rods and the cubes is starkly apparent when all are assembled into a train, the measurement or length model of numbers, constructed by trains of 10-rods and cubes, can provide a physical and visual way of thinking about the relative sizes of numbers and the order relation.

(5) Add/subtract two-digit numbers by combining tens with tens and ones with ones.

This can be done in stages: add and subtract 1 or 10 from a two-digit number, add/subtract single digit numbers or multiples of ten from a two-digit number, add/subtract two-digit numbers without regrouping, add/subtract single digit numbers to or from two-digit numbers when regrouping is required, and finally, the general case of adding or subtracting two-digit numbers with regrouping. When adding (or subtracting) a single-digit number to (or from) a general two-digit number, if regrouping is required, the corresponding addition fact should be emphasized. Both the reasoning and the mechanics of regrouping have already been learned while learning the addition facts beyond 10.

Manipulatives such as 10-rods and cubes can of course be used to model addition and subtraction. Again, arranging these rods and cubes into trains and working in terms of the length model for numbers can help students think about addition and subtraction. See section "Making Connections Between Counting Number and Measurement Number" for more details.

The ability to work independently with the tens and the ones should enable many students to do two-digit addition and subtraction mentally. To find $53 + 29$, a student could say "$50 + 20$ is 70, and $3 + 9$ is 12, and $70 + 12$ is 82." To compute $64 - 36$, one could subtract 30 from 64 to get 34, reducing to the problem $34 - 6$, which is $20 + 14 - 6$, which one knows is $20 + 8 = 28$, since one has learned how to compute $14 - 6$ as part of addition and subtraction within 20. (We note that this subtraction method, in which the largest place is subtracted first, will work in general. Of course, it may involve more rewriting than the standard algorithm; but for two-digit numbers, it seems quite manageable.)

It should be mentioned that many of the activities in steps 4 and 5 are present in various U.S. curricula, though perhaps without the unifying viewpoint provided by addition and subtraction within 20 (step 3). They are also presented in teacher training courses (Beckmann 2008; Van de Walle 2006).

Making Connections Between Counting Number and Measurement Number

One of the main arenas of application of mathematics is in measurement. Numbers used in measurement, in contrast to counting, may not be whole numbers. They can be rational numbers (meaning quotients of whole numbers), usually represented by fractions (possibly also with a negative sign), or even stranger numbers.[1]

Geometrical measurement is so different from the context of counting, that the classical Greeks did not think of the numbers involved in measurement as numbers, and reserved the term *ratio* for numbers in the context of geometrical figures (Klein 1992). It was only after the invention of symbolic algebra by Francois Viète around 1600 that the notion of number was expanded to include the numbers that arise in measurement. A few decades later, this development led to the invention of the coördinate plane by René Descartes, and to the strong linkage between number and geometry that we take for granted today.

The history of mathematics can be a good guide to what is important and what is difficult in learning mathematics. The difficulties evinced by the Greeks, combined with our post-Renaissance understanding that they are joined at the hip, indicate that it is necessary to help students explicitly to bridge the intuitive gap between number and geometry, and that this should start early. There are several benefits to starting in first grade. In particular, this can already help students think geometrically about two-digit numbers. Also, it can help prepare students to appreciate the metric nature of the number line (or ray), the use of which is called for explicitly by CCSSM in second grade.

In the course of civilization, people have learned to measure a huge variety of quantities, and several of the most important (area, volume, weight, time, speed, etc.) are dealt with in school. The most basic and probably simplest type of measurement is *linear measurement*: measurement of length or distance. Most adults probably think of linear measurement in terms of using a ruler. However, one should first lay a foundation by getting students to think of length or distance in terms of the familiar counting numbers, and to model addition by *concatenation of length*— laying rods end to end. (This can be viewed as a case of the part-part-whole aspect of addition.)

This process lends itself well to work with manipulatives in first grade. The basic materials needed are a collection of unit cubes, and rods with the same cross section as the cubes, but of various lengths. All whole number lengths from 1 to 20 would afford exploration of addition and subtraction within 20, in other words, a measurement analog of the addition and subtraction facts. Cuisenaire rods can probably be useful, but they don't have the full range of lengths, and their colors may be a distraction. Besides cubes, a generous supply of rods of length 10 is desirable. Unifix cubes might also be used, although these do not come with the ready-made larger

---

[1] Irrational numbers, which, with a few exceptions such as some square roots, π and e are not encountered by non-mathematicians, but which can be articulated into an elaborate hierarchy.

lengths. It might be a productive class activity to assemble cubes into rods of various lengths, which could then serve as templates for activities related to addition.

A first activity would be just measuring the length of various rods in terms of the cubes. It might be a good exercise to see if students could learn to recognize various lengths without having to measure. The rods might be marked with their lengths to facilitate later work (or if Cuisenaire rods are being used, many students will probably learn to associate lengths with the colors).

In learning to measure, students should come to appreciate the importance of lining up the cubes carefully, face to face, with no gaps. For some students, this may require a substantial amount of practice. If Unifix cubes are used, it could be instructive to have several groups of students produce bars with the same number of cubes, and to compare their lengths, noting the importance of having the cubes fit tightly for consistent length.

After students have gained familiarity with measuring the rods, and have come to associate a definite length with a given rod, along with associated ideas of order— that longer rods have greater measured lengths—addition and subtraction can be studied. Students should get used to the idea that addition corresponds to putting bars together end-to-end, aka the combination of lengths. Subtraction corresponds to the comparison of lengths: placing two rods side-by-side, and measuring the un- matched part of the longer rod. After a reasonable amount of work like this, the rea- sons for these correspondences between length measurement and arithmetic should be discussed. Ideally, a student will volunteer the basic reason: we have defined length in terms of measurement by unit lengths, and the collection of units needed to measure a combination of lengths is just the union of the collections that measure each of the individual lengths. Similar reasoning applies to subtraction.

Once addition and subtraction are interpreted in terms of lengths, one can begin to use the length model to bolster understanding of place value. One can introduce 10-rods as a convenient way to simplify the measuring process. The ease of laying down one 10-rod instead of carefully lining up ten unit cubes should be apparent to students. The expression of the teen numbers as a 10 and some 1s is readily modeled with a 10-rod and some cubes, and the modeling of the addition and subtraction facts beyond 10, as well as the making (in addition) and unmaking (in subtraction) of a 10 can be illustrated concretely in terms of length.

At some point, the possibility of measuring other lengths—lengths of pencils, lengths and widths of book covers, various body parts, and anything else that attracts class attention—should be explored. Longer things can be measured as students become accustomed to dealing with larger numbers. (Such activities might also be used as part of introducing larger numbers.) At least some measurement should be done using unit cubes only, so that the huge savings in effort afforded by use of 10-rods instead of only using unit cubes is made evident. Reporting of results of measurement should include units—so many cubes long. If the cube sides are of a standard length, such as a centimeter, this term could be used. Whether it is necessary or advisable at this point to consider different units of length needs study.

Objects in the class environment will typically not be exactly whole numbers of units in length. Often it is advocated to have students say that a given object is "about 14" units long. However, I would favor reporting the length as "between 14 and 15" if it is more than 14, or "between 13 and 14" if less. This kind of language serves to highlight the need for more numbers than whole numbers in the realm of measurement. Indeed, a teacher could tell students that later they will learn about other numbers (fractions, mixed numbers, rational numbers) that can be used to measure more accurately. If the length model for addition and subtraction (and better, its interpretation in terms of the number line, to be introduced later) is well absorbed, it can serve as an anchor for interpreting addition and subtraction of fractions, because although the symbolic representation of addition is substantially more complicated for fractions than for whole numbers, the geometric representation in terms of combination of lengths is uniform.

When students are used to thinking of addition in terms of combining lengths, and are familiar with 10-rods, the length model for addition can be coordinated with base 10 notation. Students can make trains consisting of 10-rods and cubes, to represent two-digit numbers. The convention should be established that the standard way to do this is always to have the 10-rods together on one side of the train (say the left), and the cubes together on the other (the right). This arrangement best displays the base ten structure of the number.

When numbers so represented are added by combining the trains end-to-end, students will probably observe that the resulting train is not in standard form: the 10-rods of the train on the right are to the right of the cubes of the train on the left. To put the train in standard order, these rods and cubes must be rearranged. The resulting train will be seen, perhaps after sufficient teacher direction, to be the result of "combining the tens and combining the ones", just as in the other contexts where two-digit addition is studied. Also, if the sum has more than ten cubes, the regrouping process can be modeled physically by replacing ten of the cubes by one 10-rod. If students fail to do so, it probably should be explicitly noted by the teacher that this process preserves the total length.

The analog of this process for subtraction should also be done carefully. When no regrouping is required, the trains of 10-rods and cubes can be compared to each other, and it should be checked that this yields the same answer as the full train comparison. When regrouping is required, one can convert a 10-rod to cubes to supplement the cubes in the minuend, before comparing with the cubes in the subtrahend. As with addition, the results of the separate comparison processes for the 10-rods and the cubes should be verified to give the same result as the whole train comparison.

This kind of work with lengths can strengthen the learning of arithmetic by reinforcing symbolic work and work with unstructured collections of objects. Equally important, it should get children used to the idea that measurement is a natural domain for application of number ideas. It should prepare them well for introduction of the number line, whose concrete realization is the ruler, as a tool that can be used to measure anything without the need to form trains at all, in second grade.

Beyond First Grade

Above we have argued that coördinated attention to word problems, place value issues in base ten arithmetic, and linear measurement as a domain for number and arithmetic, can form the core of first grade mathematics instruction that gives students a good start. In the remainder of this note, we will sketch how these three topics might continue to develop and support further mathematics learning in later grades.

Second Grade

In many ways, second grade is a continuation and consolidation of first grade, and completes the first stage of mathematics learning. The 3 pillars discussed above remain highly relevant.

The study of addition and subtraction continues, the main advances being progression to more complex problems, and to 3 digit numbers. This is the next stage of a gradual increase in the number of digits students are expected to cope with. CCSSM calls for 4th grade students to deal with numbers up to 1 million, and 5th grade students to also handle decimal fractions to thousandths. CCSSM is superior to many of the state standards that it has replaced, in calling explicitly for students to "Understand the place value system" in fifth grade.[2]

Word Problems   Use of the full array of one-step addition and subtraction word problems should continue, amplified by the introduction of some two-step problems. Some problems might ask for addition of three or even four numbers. For example, for her birthday, Shana could get toy trucks from two or even three different people; or she could get some toy trucks for her birthday, and then some more for Christmas; or both.

The reader may convince him/herself by experimentation, that of the 14 types of one-step addition and subtraction problems discussed above, most pairs can be combined to make a two-step problem, so that there are potentially almost 200 ($14 \times 14 = 196$) two-step addition and subtraction problems. This should make obvious the futility of any "key word" approach to dealing with word problems, and also indicate the rich potential, both for mathematics and language arts, that analysis of multistep problems affords.

Place Value   In dealing with 3-digit addition and subtraction, one should continue to develop the ideas introduced in first grade:

---

[2] However, the final stage of understanding, in which the base ten units are written as powers of 10 using exponential notation, linking place value notation with polynomial algebra, can not take place before 6th grade, when exponential notation is first introduced (6.EE 1).

(i)   Work with expanded form, adding the 1s, the 10s, the 100s independently, with regrouping at the end, as needed. The point should be made that regrouping from 10s to 100s is strictly parallel to regrouping from 1s to 10s, because 100 is made of ten 10s.

(ii) Work with addition and subtraction in parallel, and observe that regrouping in a subtraction problem just reverses the regrouping in the corresponding addition problem.

(iii) The situations that require regrouping are considerably more varied than in the two-digit case, and probably require some systematic study. There may be no regrouping; regrouping only from ones to tens; addition of multiples of ten requiring regrouping of tens to hundreds; addition of general numbers with no regrouping of ones, but regrouping from tens to hundreds; regrouping of both ones and tens; and the most complicated case, when the tens add to 90, and then a carry from the ones place makes this exactly 100, leaving a zero in the tens place of the sum. This last situation may be called "rollover", by analogy with the change in mechanical odometers when 1 is added to a number with 9 in the 10s place (and perhaps larger places also). This should be studied explicitly, along with the corresponding subtraction situation, which requires "borrowing past a zero". Second grade may be a good time to consolidate addition and subtraction algorithms (although CCSSM waits until 3rd grade to ask for fluency). It probably would be a good idea to delay algorithm development until all these different cases have been considered, and then discuss how the usual right-to-left addition procedure handles all cases in one comprehensive method. Subtraction of course is considerably less comfortable, because of the rollover/borrowing past a zero issue, and more discussion of alternative approaches might be helpful.

(iv) Work with manipulatives should include base ten block work (ones cubes, ten-rods and hundred-flats) for student seat work, but also, in some whole class work, with cubes, ten-rods and hundred-rods (meter sticks can double as these) for forming linear trains representing 3-digit numbers. The same kind of rearranging and trading that was done for two-digit numbers should be continued here, including some of the more difficult symbolic cases, such as borrowing past a zero. One big advantage of forming trains to represent 3-digit numbers is that it emphasizes the size relations between 100s and 10s, as well as 10s and 1, making very visible that the 100s are the dominant part of any such number. This point should be made explicitly. Working with trains also shows that arithmetic can take place wholly in terms of the line—two dimensions (or 3, later used for blocks representing 1000 in the standard base ten block sets) are not a necessity, only a convenience, allowing easy manipulation of the blocks.

(v)   In comparing numbers, students should learn that the number of 100s determine which of two numbers is larger, except when both numbers have the same number of 100s, in which case the 10s must be considered, and the 1s only when both numbers also have the same number of 10s.

The Linear Measurement Connection   The counting-linear measurement connection should be strengthened and elaborated. We have already mentioned above that trains of 100-rods, 10-rods and 1-cubes should be created to represent three digit numbers, and combined to illustrate addition, and compared for subtraction. However, in second grade, linear measurement should become a major topic (see CCSSM Standards (2.MD.1 through 6)) and the number line (actually, the number *ray*, since at this stage, it will go only in one direction from the zero or base point or origin, which will be on one end of the stick or rod that embodies the line) should be introduced, essentially as a ruler.

The connection of the number ray with measurement should be emphasized. Especially, the idea that a number on the number ray *represents a length*—the distance from the origin (the end), as a multiple of the unit length—should be carefully established in students' minds. To bring home the necessity to choose a unit, number lines based on several different unit lengths should be used at various times, with explicit attention to specifying the unit. Taking the centimeter as unit will probably afford maximum compatibility with base-ten manipulatives. In the linear measurement context, the effect the choice of unit length has on the number obtained by measurement should also get attention—the larger the unit, the smaller the associated number, for a given length. A dramatic example would be that a single digit number of meters is also hundreds of centimeters. In the U.S., taking the inch as unit will afford a good tie-in with commonly encountered measurements, and later on, converting from feet or yards to inches, or from miles to feet or yards, can provide a source of multiplication and division problems.

The number ray should be used in conjunction with addition by lining up trains of base-ten blocks, and it can be observed that, if you position the trains along the ray with so that the end point of one train coincides with the end of the ray, then the other end of the second train will fall on the number that gives the sum—the number line functions as a computer! (This could be the first stage in rediscovering the slide rule, which could make a great manipulative in the later grades.)

Introducing the number ray and relating it to length is a main task of second grade, a key stage in a long learning trajectory that culminates with Cartesian coördinates and infinite decimal expansions. Some later stages in this development are discussed below.

Another key job of second grade that prepares for later work is to raise the consciousness of students concerning units. Linear measurement is a context where this issue clearly needs addressing, but it is relevant in many other contexts also. As we have discussed above in connection with comparison word problems, in everyday life, we don't really encounter naked numbers, but rather, any number we meet has a unit attached, and it expresses quantity in relation to that unit. In the early stages of learning addition, it may be advisable to suppress attention to units, in order to concentrate on the number relationships being established. Also, when dealing with whole numbers, the relevant unit is often clear and does not need to be pointed out.

However, attention to units is essential when learning fractions. Many fallacies, including claims of the sort

$$1/2 + 1/3 = 2/5 \quad \text{(not!)} \tag{1}$$

involve lack of attention to the unit. The error in this statement is analogous to our discussion of nickels, quarters and dimes in section "A Robust Understanding of the Operations of Addition and Subtraction". An equation like (1) is often justified with a picture such as

$$AB + ABB = AABBB \tag{2}$$

The first group is taken to represent $1/2$ (the number of As compared to the total number of symbols), the second is taken to represent $1/3$, and the last collection represents $2/5$. Addition is taken as union of sets.

What is wrong with Eq. (1)? A grouping such as AB can provide one reasonable way to represent a fraction, but to avoid confusion, it is essential to see that the $1/2$ refers to the first collection as unit, the $1/3$ refers to the second collection as unit, and the $2/5$ refers to the third collection, the union of the first two, as unit. In order to use a consistent unit, we could choose a single symbol as the unit. Doing this, we see that the above equation of sets translates to the numerical fact

$$(1/2) \times 2 + (1/3) \times 3 = (2/5) \times 5,$$

or

$$1 + 1 = 2,$$

which is indeed a true equation.[3]

In summary, both for purposes of learning the basics of linear measurement, and in preparation for dealing successfully with fractions in third grade, a major duty of second grade is to develop in students an awareness of units, especially, the predilection to ask and the ability to keep track of what the unit is in a given context, and to use units in a consistent fashion.

Third Grade and Later

Third grade, in contrast to second, presents a profusion of new ideas: multiplication and division; fractions; and area measurement. The relations between these new concepts must be presented in carefully orchestrated ways to promote successful learning of each. It is beyond the scope of this essay to detail the key relationships that need exploration, or even the key features of each of the new ideas. We will limit ourselves to sketching how our trio of fundamental constituents of first grade mathematics continue to support learning in this new and richer environment.

---

[3] Alternatively, if we select the 5-element set as the unit, then the first two sets represent $2/5$ and $3/5$ respectively, and the equation would read

$$(1/2) \times (2/5) + (1/3) \times (3/5) = 2/5,$$

which is also a true equation, representing $2/5$ as a weighted average (*not* a sum!) of $1/2$ and $1/3$.

Word Problems   To give students a good perspective on the uses of multiplication and division, a varied collection of one-step multiplication and division problems should be presented, with discussion and analysis, mirroring what was done for addition and subtraction in grades 1 and 2. Page 89 of CCSSM gives a table of common multiplication and division situations, and all should be represented in word problems.

Multiplication and division are subtler operations than addition and subtraction and harder for students to internalize. In particular, although as a numerical operation multiplication is commutative, the two factors typically play different roles, and may well have different units attached.[4] Even in the simplest context, usually used in giving the first definition of multiplication, that of combining equal groups, one factor counts the number of things in one group, and the other factor counts the number of groups. In the standard interpretation of, say 3×5 as the combination of equal groups, the 5 represents the number in each group, and the 3 represents the number of groups. In this interpretation of multiplication, it is far from obvious that 3 groups of 5 have the same number as 5 groups of 3. Thus, on a conceptual level, the commutativity of multiplication is somewhat surprising. The fact that multiplication is indeed commutative should receive explicit attention. A good way to justify it is to use arrays, observing that a, say, 5 by 3 array becomes a 3 by 5 array when rotated by 90°.

Corresponding to the distinct roles of the two factors in multiplication, mathematics educators recognize two types of division. One is *partitive*, or sharing, division, in which a quantity is to be divided into a given number of groups, and the question is, what size will these groups be. The other is *quotative*, or measurement division, in which the size of the groups is specified, and the question is, how many groups can be formed. Parallel problems of the two types with the same numbers should be given, and it should be observed, that the numerical value of answer to both types of question is the same, although what the answer designates will be different. In this work, careful attention to units is especially relevant.

Third grade should also see large numbers of two-step problems, including some that involve any pair of the four operations. There are several hundred different possible types already for two-step problems, so the work required for understanding the problem will increase. Discussions of how to figure out what the problem is asking for, and what needs to be done to answer it, will have to be an important part of instruction, and ongoing as the problems become more complex. The work of Lieven Verschaffel and colleagues (Verschaffel et al. 2000) has documented the worldwide failure of mathematics instruction to enable students to adequately interpret word problems.

Later grades should see problems of increasing complexity, eventually arriving at word problems that require algebra for their solution by 7th or 8th grade. In fact, the boundary between arithmetic and algebra is somewhat fuzzy, and problems that might seem to require algebra can often by solved using only arithmetic supported

---

[4]The unit attached to the product is then the product of the units attached to the factors.

by a sufficiently insightful analysis (Howe 2010). It may be valuable for students to consider such problems, and to see parallel solutions. The Singapore bar model method (Singapore Ministry of Education 2009) is another approach to solving a broad class of problems that in the U.S. are most commonly handled by algebra. Singapore students start learning how to use this method in 3rd grade, when they are given problems such as

> There are 36 students in a class. There are 8 more boys than girls.
> How many girls are in the class?

Some Singaporean students become so skilled at using bar models that it is difficult to get them to abandon the model method in favor of symbolic algebraic approaches (Singapore Ministry of Education 2006). Something similar could happen with students who become highly skilled at solving word problems using arithmetic methods. Such students should be challenged with problems of increasing difficulty, until they reach a point when the systematic nature of symbolic algebra becomes so advantageous that they use it willingly.

Place Value and Computation   Acquisition of multiplication allows students to deepen their understanding of place value, eventually revealing its depth and its connection to polynomial algebra.

In grades 1 and 2, students work with the expanded form, such as

$$243 = 200 + 40 + 3,$$

and learn that, in addition and subtraction, they can combine the parts of like magnitude, using only the single-digit addition and subtraction facts, followed by any necessary regrouping. We will call the numbers like 200 and 40 and 3, with only one non-zero digit, *single place numbers*. Thus, the expanded form of a base ten number expresses it as a sum of single place numbers.

Once students start learning about multiplication, they can begin to appreciate the multiplicative structure of single place numbers. In third grade, they can realize that each single place number is a multiple of a *base ten unit*, which is a single place number whose non-zero digit is 1. Thus, $200 = 2 \times 100$ and $40 = 4 \times 10$ and $3 = 3 \times 1$. This allows students to refine the expanded form to

$$243 = 200 + 40 + 3 = 2 \times 100 + 4 \times 10 + 3 \times 1.$$

Thus they would now think of 243 as being made of two 100s, and four 10s, and three 1s. They were in effect using this structure in adding and subtracting, but now they have a language to express what they were doing.

In fourth grade, students should refine their understanding of the base ten units, seeing the ones larger than 10 as repeated products of 10s. Thus,

$$100 = 10 \times 10, \qquad 1{,}000 = 10 \times 10 \times 10, \qquad 10{,}000 = 10 \times 10 \times 10 \times 10,$$

and so forth.[5]

Understanding the structure of base ten units supports the appreciation of the quantity aspect of place value: each base ten unit is ten times as large as the next smaller unit (the place to the right), and only $1/10$ as large as the next larger one (the place to the left). In particular, as one moves to the right in the places, the value of the unit shrinks by 10 at each step. This can support the idea of continuing places to the right of the 1s place, and making

$$1/10 = (1/10) \times 1, \qquad 1/100 = (1/10) \times (1/10), \qquad 1/1000 = (1/10) \times (1/100),$$

and so forth; thus it prepares for thinking about and dealing with decimal fractions.

The final stage of understanding the place value system can be presented in sixth grade, when whole number exponents are introduced. This allows the shorthand notation

$$1 = 10^0, \qquad 10 = 10^1, \qquad 100 = 10^2, \qquad 1000 = 10^3,$$

and so forth. In combination with the earlier work on the structure of single place numbers, this permits the last stage in the progression

$$
\begin{aligned}
243 &= 200 + 40 + 3 \\
&= 2 \times 100 \qquad\quad +4 \times 10 \ +3 \times 1 \\
&= 2 \times (10 \times 10) +4 \times 10 \ +3 \times 1 \\
&= 2 \times 10^2 \qquad\quad +4 \times 10^1 +3.
\end{aligned}
$$

The last stage in this progression shows that a base 10 number can be regarded as a "polynomial in 10". In 6th grade, it probably would serve mainly as an application or example of the use of exponential notation. However, it also highlights the sophistication involved in base ten place value notation, which implicitly uses all the operations of algebra (addition, multiplication, exponentiation), just to write numbers. The full implications of the final expression can be profitably investigated in 8th grade when the algebra of polynomial expressions is discussed. Students can verify that, if a base ten number is turned into a polynomial, by the recipe

$$243 \rightarrow 2x^2 + 4x + 3,$$

and if calculations (addition, subtraction, multiplication) are done with the resulting polynomials, and then 10 is substituted for x, the usual numerical answer will be

---

[5]At this point, it might be a good idea explicitly to discuss the issue of associativity of multiplication, that it does not matter how we group the factors in these (or any) repeated multiplications, the result will not depend on the grouping. Thus, $10,000 = 10 \times 1000$, but just as well, $10,000 = 100 \times 100$. In fact, associativity of multiplication is a somewhat subtle property, and its justification using geometric models involves volumes of 3 dimensional bricks. See for example (Epp and Howe 2008) for a fuller discussion.

obtained. For some students, this observation can provide an "Aha!" moment that will tie together eight years of study of mathematics.

The discussion above of course is quite standard mathematics, and in earlier years this author tended to treat the five-stage progression above as common knowledge. However, there is evidence that many students arrive in college without even stage 2, the basic expanded form, as part of their intellectual toolkit (Thanheiser 2009), and the value of making this progression explicit, and to give it emphasis in the curriculum is supported by Teachers of India (2012). Also, the lack of understanding even of the basic meanings of the places by mid-elementary students was documented by Kamii (1986) long ago.

Linear Measurement and the Number Line The connections of arithmetic with linear measurement developed in grades 1 and 2 are the beginnings of a long development of the intimate relationship between number and geometry. In third grade, the basic understanding of the number ray established in second grade would allow studying the nature of fractions from a geometric viewpoint. Although the array and area models will play an important role in helping students understand and work with fractions, the number line can also contribute.

The understanding that the numbers on the number ray tell distances from the endpoint/origin provides a sound basis for placing fractions on the line. The CCSSM advocates understanding fractions as multiples of unit fractions. Thus,

$$2/3 = 2 \times (1/3), \qquad 5/3 = 5 \times (1/3),$$

and so forth. To locate $1/3$ on the number line, one should divide the unit interval into 3 equal parts. Then the other end of the part with one end at 0 is $1/3$ of the way from 0 to 1, and so should be labeled as $1/3$. Then $2/3$ is the point that is two $1/3$ intervals from 0, and $5/3$ is the point that is five $1/3$ intervals away from 0. Repeating this process for all multiples of $1/3$, one finds that they form a system of equally spaced points, very much like the whole numbers, except three $1/3$s fit inside each unit interval—we could say they are three times closer together, or three times as dense, or only $1/3$ as far apart. It is of course the same for whole number multiples $n/d = n \times (1/d)$ of any fixed unit fraction $1/d$. They form a system of equally spaced points on the number line, each one at distance $1/d$ from its neighbors, with d intervals inside the unit interval. Thus, the number line affords a compelling visualization of the systematic nature of the multiples of a fixed unit fraction.

Two ideas crucial to understanding and working with fractions are

(i) repeated subdivision, and
(ii) reconstitution.

Repeated subdivision involves understanding that a unit fraction such as $1/5$, which resulted from subdividing the original unit into 5 equal pieces, constitutes a new unit that can itself be subdivided. The result of the subdivision will then be a unit fraction, with denominator equal to the product of the two denominators. Thus, if we divide $1/5$ into fourths, the result will consist of $(1/4) \times (1/5) = 1/20$. The general relationship is

$$(1/e) \times (1/d) = 1/ed$$

Reconstitution is the reverse process to repeated subdivision. Just as 4 copies of $1/4$ make 1, the unit, so also 4 copies of $1/20 = (1/4) \times (1/5)$ make $1/5$. In symbols, we would write $4 \times (1/20) = 1/5$. The general relationship is

$$e \times (1/ed) = 1/d, \quad \text{or} \quad e/ed = 1/d.$$

The second form of the relationship shows that reconstitution is the justification for the symbolic move of "canceling the same factor from numerator and denominator".

These relationships should be illustrated in a variety of contexts so that students can see how they work and get used to working with them. The number line can be one of those contexts, and the regular subdivisions of the line provided by the whole number multiples of a unit fraction can be used to show many examples of repeated subdivision and reconstitution, by considering the relationship between the subdivision given by the multiples n/d of a given unit fraction $1/d$, and the multiples m/ed of a unit fraction whose denominator is a multiple of d. This study can also contribute to the understanding of how to add fractions. For example, if one works with $1/6$, then since $6 = 3 \times 2$, reconstitution would tell us that $1/2 = 3/6$. Since also $6 = 2 \times 3$, reconstitution would also tell us that $1/3 = 2/6$. Thus, we could conclude that

$$1/2 + 1/3 = 3/6 + 2/6 = 5/6.$$

This kind of formula can also be shown explicitly on the number line. An important pedagogical consideration here is that the linear measurement interpretation of fraction addition is exactly the same as whole number addition: it is combination of lengths. Similarly, subtraction of fractions amounts to comparing lengths. This consistency over different types of numbers, when the symbolic representations and the necessary manipulations may seem dissimilar, can provide a firm basis for understanding and reasoning.

With the introduction of signed numbers, the number ray must become the number line, that is, it must be (in principle) infinite in both directions. Currently, the typical practice is not to distinguish between the number line and the number ray, and to use the term "number line" for both, but if the distinction were made, the change in terminology could provide a signal that something new is going on.

On the doubly infinite line, the origin loses its distinguished position as the endpoint, because there is no endpoint. Thus, the origin must now be specified explicitly. That done, we see that distance from the origin no longer specifies a unique point—for each distance, there are two possibilities, on either side of the origin. To distinguish between them, we must introduce the idea of *orientation*: left, right, or positive, negative. The need for specifying orientation should be given a lot of emphasis, including the use of 'trick' problems such as

James, Randolph and Rebecca live on Elm Street.

If James lives 2 blocks from Randolph, and Rebecca lives 3 blocks from James, how many blocks does Rebecca live from Randolph?

To deal successfully with signed numbers, several conceptual changes in student thinking about numbers are necessary. The most obvious, of course, is the understanding that a number no longer simply gives information about magnitude, but also about direction (which in one dimension reduces to a dichotomy: left, right; plus, minus). This necessary revision gives rise to another surprise: addition and subtraction become merged into a single operation, with subtraction of a given number amounting to addition of its *additive inverse* (aka *negative* or *opposite*). Thus, we think of $2 - 6$ as $2 + (-6)$. Also, for the first time, subtraction can be performed with *any* two numbers: $1 - 2$ now makes as much sense as $2 - 1$.

Signed numbers are introduced in CCSSM in 6th grade, which is also the grade in which simple algebraic expressions are introduced. Thus, in 6th grade, students are asked to understand expressions such as

$$2 + x, \quad \text{and} \quad 2x,$$

as meaning "Pick a number x and add 2 to it", and "Pick a number x and multiply it by 2"; or somewhat more colloquially, "Add 2 to any number," and "Multiply any number by 2". The change in point of view is perhaps somewhat subtle, but it is highly significant, and it must be given enough attention to ensure that students grasp it. Instead of thinking of addition, or multiplication, as a binary operation, something we do with two numbers, we are asked to think of "adding 2"or "multiplying by 2" as a *unary operation*, something we do to *any* single number.

Thinking of "adding 2" as an operation on any number allows us to think of it as a *transformation of the number line*, a recipe that takes each point, corresponding to some number x, and moves it to the point corresponding to $2 + x$. If students study what this operation does to many points, they may be able to formulate themselves what this transformation does: it moves each point 2 units in the positive direction (to the right, in the usual orientation of the number line). In other words, it is a *translation* of the number line through 2 units to the right. Similar work with adding -2 should reveal it as a translation of the number line through 2 units to the left. This provides a graphic understanding of the fact that adding -2 undoes adding 2, so that it is the same as subtracting 2.

This transformational view of addition can be reinforced by use of a slide rule to add and subtract numbers, by sliding one copy of a number line along a parallel copy. Care should be taken to correlate this new perspective on addition and subtraction with the original understandings of combining and comparing lengths. For adding or subtracting any given pair of numbers, they amount to essentially the same thing. The difference is, when thinking of "adding 2" as a transformation, we are fixing one addend, and letting the other vary.

The operation of "multiplying by 2" likewise can be visualized as a transformation of the number line. Again, by looking at many examples, we can see that it takes any number and moves it to a number that is twice as far away from the origin.

Thus, "times 2" is a stretching of the number line by a factor of 2, from the origin (which does not move). Also, it preserves direction: positive numbers go to positive numbers, and negatives go to negatives. Students should be made to notice that by this transformation, the length of every interval is doubled, not just the intervals with one end at the origin. This is the geometric embodiment of the Distributive Rule.

When this transformational interpretation is extended to fractions, it provides a way of seeing that multiplying by $1/d$ is the same as dividing by d, so that, in the rational numbers, multiplication and division are two aspects of the same operation. More precisely, division by a given number is the same as multiplication by its reciprocal.[6] This relationship is built out of two more basic ones:

(i) For a whole number d, division by d is the same as multiplication by $1/d$; and
(ii) Multiplication by a fraction n/d amounts to multiplication by n, and multiplication by $1/d$, and it does not matter which is done first.

Combining statements (i) and (ii) produces: multiplying by n/d amounts to multiplying by n and dividing by d, in either order.

The ideas that

(i) division by a given number is the inverse of multiplication by that number, and
(ii) division by a given number may be accomplished by multiplication by the reciprocal, which combine to
(iii) division by a given number is the same as multiplication by the reciprocal,

are the key ingredients in the "invert and multiply" rule for division by fractions.

Multiplication by negative numbers, a well-known trouble spot, fits easily and elegantly into the transformational viewpoint (Friedberg and Howe 2008). The main observation is that multiplication by -1 is reflection across the origin. Every number goes to its negative. Then multiplication by -2 would be multiplication by 2, followed by reflection across the origin (or the other way around—it doesn't matter, since multiplication is commutative). In this picture, it is clear why the product of two negative numbers is positive: reflecting twice across the origin leaves orientation unchanged. For many students, this geometric insight into the nature of multiplication by negative numbers may be more convincing than a formal symbolic argument.

These geometric/transformational interpretations of the operations, and their connections with the basic algebraic expressions are not explicitly emphasized in the CCSSM, and the ability of students to grasp the transformational viewpoint is not well documented. However, the picture afforded by these ideas is quite compelling, and the connections to more advanced mathematics are also strong. In particular, this viewpoint fits very well with the CCSSM emphasis on transformations in geometry. It seems possible that some students could benefit from the "multiplication is stretching" idea from the time multiplication is introduced, in 3rd grade,

---

[6]Unfortunately, this basic principle is not explicitly enunciated in the CCSSM. One hopes that this defect will be remedied in the next revision.

and that it could form a useful supplement to the "repeated addition" and array/area interpretations that are explicitly recommended by CCSSM.

A final place where the number line can provide a useful interpretation of a numerical construction is in decimal expansions. In fact, it is hard to imagine developing a firm grasp of decimal expansions without invoking the number line. Essentially, decimal expansions provide an address system on the number line. We should think of successive digits in a decimal expansion as providing successively finer information about the location of a point on the line. As an example, consider the decimal

$$3.14159265358979323\ldots.$$

The whole number part of this number, namely 3, locates the point somewhere in the interval [3, 4] from 3 to 4 (including the endpoints, 3 and 4). The digits to the right of the decimal place are instructions about how to locate this number more precisely. To interpret the 1 just to the right of the decimal place, we should picture the interval between 3 and 4 as being divided into 10 equal subintervals, namely

[3.0, 3.1],   [3.1, 3.2],   [3.2, 3.3],   [3.3, 3.4],   [3.4, 3.5],

[3.5, 3.6],   [3.6, 3.7],   [3.7, 3.8],   [3.8, 3.9],   [3.9, 4.0].

The .1 in this decimal expansion tells us that the number belongs in the second interval, [3.1, 3.2], from 3.1 to 3.2. To use the next digit, we should further subdivide the interval [3.1, 3.2] into ten equal subintervals, namely

[3.10, 3.11],   [3.11, 3.12],   [3.12, 3.13],   [3.13, 3.14],   [3.14, 3.15],

[3.15, 3.16],   [3.16, 3.17],   [3.17, 3.18],   [3.18, 3.19],   [3.19, 3.20].

Then the 4 in the second place to the right of the decimal point tells us that the number is somewhere in the fifth of these intervals, namely in the interval [3.14, 3.15] from 3.14 to 3.15. Each succeeding decimal digit has an analogous interpretation. Any initial segment of the decimal expansion locates the number in a certain interval. We then should break up this interval into 10 equal subintervals, and the next digit in the decimal expansion tells us in which of these 10 subintervals the number lies. If students carry out this process for some examples, they should come to appreciate that the first few decimal places locate the number to sufficient accuracy for most simple purposes, and indeed, that it is rather difficult to resolve an interval into ten subintervals after only a few steps of this procedure, and essentially impossible after only a few more. Our most powerful microscopes allow us to continue the process for several more places, but after 10 to 20 places, depending on how large the starting size was, the remaining decimal places lose physical meaning. A conclusion that should be made explicitly is that it is quite remarkable that our symbolic computational system is capable of producing arbitrarily long decimal expansions for many of the numbers that arise in the course of computation, including $\pi, e, \sqrt{2}$, 1/3, etc.

References

Beckmann, S. (2008). *Mathematics for elementary teachers*. Upper Saddle River: Pearson Addison Wesley.

Carpenter, T., Fennema, E., Franke, M., Empson, S., & Levi, L. (1999). *Children's mathematics*. Portsmouth: Heinemann.

CCSSO (Council of Chief State School Officers) (2011). Common core state standards for mathematics. http://www.corestandards.org/the-standards/mathematics.

Epp, S., & Howe, R. (2008). Taking place value seriously. http://www.maa.org/pmet/resources/PVHoweEpp-Nov2008.pdf.

Eves, H. (2002). *In mathematical circles*. Washington: Mathematical Association of America.

Friedberg, S., & Howe, R. (2008). The rule of signs. https://www2.bc.edu/~friedber/RuleofSigns (Howe-Friedberg)19nov08.pdf.

Fuson, K. (2005). Description of children's single-digit addition and subtraction solution methods. In J. R. Milgram (Ed.), *The mathematics pre-service teachers need to know* (pp. 140–145). Stanford: Stanford University. http://hub.mspnet.org/index.cfm/13083/.

Howe, R. (2010). From arithmetic to algebra. *Mathematics Bulletin—A Journal for Educators, 49*(special issue), 13–21.

Kamii, C. (1986). Place value: an explanation of its difficulty and educational implications for the primary grades. *Journal for Research in Mathematics Education, 17*, 75–86.

Kilpatrick, J., Swafford, J., & Findell, B. (Eds.) (2001). *Adding it up: helping children learn mathematics*. Washington: National Academies Press.

Klein, J. (1992). *Greek mathematical thought and the origin of algebra*. New York: Dover Publications.

Ma, L. (1999). *Knowing and teaching elementary mathematics*. Mahwah: Erlbaum Associates.

Singapore Ministry of Education (2006). Oral communication.

Singapore Ministry of Education (2009). *The model method for learning mathematics*. Singapore: Marshall Cavendish Int (S) Pte Ltd.

Teachers of India (2012). http://www.teachersofindia.org/en/article/five-stages-place-value.

Thanheiser, E. (2009). Preservice elementary school teachers' conceptions of multidigit whole numbers. *Journal for Research in Mathematics Education, 40*, 251–281.

Van de Walle, J. (2006). *Elementary and middle school mathematics: teaching developmentally* (6th ed.). Needham Heights: Allyn & Bacon.

Verschaffel, L., Greer, B., & DeCorte, E. (2000). *Making sense of word problems*. Lisse: Swets & Zeitlinger.

Forging New Opportunities for Problem Solving in Australian Mathematics Classrooms through the First National Mathematics Curriculum

Judy Anderson

Abstract Although the Federal government in Australia has tried on previous occasions to exert a greater influence on curriculum development, curriculum development was the responsibility of each of the eight states and territories until quite recently. The new Labour Government in 2007 has employed increased central control and accountability measures, with national testing in grades 3, 5, 7 and 9 from 2008, publication of school results on a MySchool website, and the development of the first national curriculum in English, Mathematics, Science and History. States are still responsible for implementation, but the new funding model means they must comply with national curriculum implementation up to grade 10. Developing the first national curriculum for mathematics has been a challenge, but a plan of mathematics learning for each grade level organised into three content strands has now been developed. In addition, four proficiency (or process) strands describe the actions associated with doing mathematics. Since problem solving has been a key component of previous curriculum documents and there is evidence of limited use of complex problem solving in some Australian mathematics classrooms, the representation of problem solving in curriculum documents is examined in this chapter to explore whether the new national curriculum for Australia forges new opportunities for teachers and students.

Keywords National curriculum · Historical perspectives · Problem solving · Proficiencies · Teacher interpretation · Authentic problems

How difficult can it be to develop a national mathematics curriculum in a country with fewer than 23 million people? The Australian experience over the past 50 years exposes a rocky road to success. However, this has not deterred the Federal government who, in 2008, began yet another attempt to develop the first national curriculum in English, Mathematics, Science and History—designed to improve quality, equity and accessibility (McGaw 2010). After much debate and consternation, the

J. Anderson (✉)
The University of Sydney, Sydney, Australia
e-mail: judy.anderson@sydney.edu.au

Y. Li, G. Lappan (eds.), *Mathematics Curriculum in School Education*,
Advances in Mathematics Education, DOI 10.1007/978-94-007-7560-2_11,
© Springer Science+Business Media Dordrecht 2014

first national curriculum for mathematics was endorsed by state and territory Ministers of Education in December 2010. The development of this curriculum required navigating the obstacles of divided responsibilities for education between the state and Federal governments, as well as negotiating many stakeholder concerns.

This chapter presents a brief historical account of the development of the first national mathematics curriculum in Australia, and outlines the challenges presented at various phases of the curriculum development process. For clarification, I use the term 'curriculum' to represent the official policies or plans of mathematics content to be taught in schools—also referred to as "the intended curriculum" (Robitaille et al. 1996) or the "specific set of instructional materials that order content" (Clements 2007, p. 36).

Because of its importance in mathematics teaching and learning (Schoenfeld 2007) and because there is evidence of limited use of complex problem solving in Australian classrooms (Hollingsworth et al. 2003), this chapter also examines the ways problem solving has been described and presented to teachers in previous curriculum documents and reports research identifying teachers' interpretation of the curriculum advice about teaching problem solving. Finally, the chapter considers whether the first national curriculum for mathematics provides new problem-solving opportunities for Australian students and teachers, particularly since "problem solving is one of the most fundamental goals of teaching mathematics, but also one of the most elusive" (Stacey 2005, p. 341).

The Australian Context

Before the national curriculum was developed, each of the eight Australian states and territories used state-developed curriculum documents. Some were broad frameworks allowing for school-based curriculum development (e.g., South Australia) while others were more detailed and highly prescriptive (e.g., New South Wales [NSW]). Usually separate curriculum documents were developed for the elementary grades (the first six or seven years of schooling), the secondary grades (in most states from grades 7 to 10), and the senior secondary grades (11 and 12). There is no middle school structure in Australia, although some independent schools that cater to students from the first years of schooling to grade 12 have used state-based curriculum to design alternative experiences for students in the middle years (typically grades 5 to 8).

Usually state-based curriculum documents in Australia present the school mathematics curriculum as lists of topics or 'content' and a set of 'processes'. Content includes the fundamental ideas of mathematics, historically grouped into such topics as number, algebra, measurement, geometry, and chance and data. While processes include the actions associated with using and applying mathematics to solve a range of problem types including applications of mathematics in authentic contexts and other non-routine problems.

Problem solving is recognised as an important life skill involving a range of processes including analysing, interpreting, reasoning, predicting, evaluating, and reflecting. It is either an overarching goal or a fundamental component of the school mathematics curriculum in many countries (Stacey 2005). One of the challenges in curriculum development is to present the mathematics curriculum in a way which encourages teachers to embrace reforms or new approaches to teaching and learning. One new approach was the introduction of problem solving into curriculum documents in Australia in the late Eighties but there has been limited evidence of complex problem-solving opportunities in elementary classrooms (e.g., Anderson et al. 2004) or in secondary classrooms (e.g., Hollingsworth et al. 2003). Because of the diversity of curriculum documents in the Australian context, in this chapter I examine the evolution of problem solving in one state (New South Wales [NSW]) context and compare this with the new Australian curriculum approach.

Historical Perspective of Australian Curriculum Development

I present a brief historical perspective to set the context for the development of the first national Australian curriculum since as Kennedy (2005, p. 1) notes, "the school curriculum is tightly bounded by the social, political and economic contexts in which it is located". This overview is necessarily brief and seeks to identify key drivers of curriculum change, particularly those impacting mathematics.[1]

In Australia, the constitutional responsibility for curriculum resides with the state and territory governments who have "jealously guarded their curriculum sovereignty, overtly or passively resisting attempts to engineer national approaches" (Reid 2005, p. 39). However, curriculum has become a "state and Commonwealth [Federal] political football" (Yates et al. 2011b, p. 4) with the Federal government making several unsuccessful attempts at implementing a national curriculum. Reid (2005) argues the lack of success goes beyond the political agenda to the lack of an adequate rationale for a national curriculum, a failure to develop a rigorous theoretical base for the curriculum, and a failure to consider key aspects of managing curriculum change. Others have argued there has also been a lack of consultation with key stakeholders (e.g., Ellerton and Clements 1994). Reid (2005) outlines four phases in the move towards a national curriculum, particularly after 1963 when the Federal government in Australia began to fund aspects of school education.

In the first phase (1968–1988) the Federal government sought to influence the state-based curriculum using 'indirect' approaches by funding projects for the production of resources for teachers and students. During this phase, the *Mathematics Curriculum and Teaching Program* [MCTP] (Lovitt and Clarke 1988) was developed to address concerns about the teaching of mathematics in Australia and in particular, to address issues about students' attitudes to mathematics

---

[1]For a more detailed historical account of curriculum development in Australia, I recommend Yates et al. (2011a) and Marsh (2010). Both volumes describe case studies of curriculum change in particular states and territories as well as the prevailing political agendas leading to the rejection of earlier attempts at national curriculum development.

and the diversity of students' needs, as well as shallow teaching and narrow assessment practices (Lovitt and Clarke 2011). To support teacher professional development, the program identified and captured good practice in a collection of exemplary lessons—these resources have been sold internationally and are now available online through the Maths300 website (http://www.maths300.esa.edu.au/). While widely recognised as an outstanding resource, it is debatable how much influence this resource has had on addressing the concerns and issues mentioned above, particularly given these same issues continue to be raised (see for example the *AAMT Position on National Curriculum in Mathematics* at http://www.aamt. edu.au/Publications-and-statements/Position-statements/National-Curriculum).

The second phase of national curriculum development (1988–1993) saw the design of *Statements* and *Profiles* in each of eight key learning areas including mathematics. A detailed historical account of the failure of the Australian Education Council [AEC] to develop and then endorse the national curriculum is contained in *The National Curriculum Debacle* (Ellerton and Clements 1994). Through reference to meeting minutes, letters, and personal accounts of events over this period, Ellerton and Clements describe the key issues associated with the failure of this enterprise as:

- the lack of a strong and agreed upon theoretical base, in particular the use of an outcomes-based education approach which the authors align with behaviourist principles suggesting this was "totally at odds with the directions and findings of mathematics education research over the past two decades" (p. 7);
- a lack of consultation with key stakeholders in the curriculum development process, in particular lack of involvement with mathematicians and mathematics educators; and
- being guided by the national curriculum approach in the United Kingdom, which was reported in 1994 as 'disastrous'.

While Ellerton and Clements argue that the approach was strongly influenced by developments in the United Kingdom [UK] at that time, there was a significant difference between the two countries regarding curriculum control. The UK Government had "the constitutional authority to impose a national curriculum" whereas the Australian Government did not and had to "negotiate and persuade" (Piper 1989, p. 22). According to Ellerton and Clements, if the AEC had more closely considered the national *Curriculum and Evaluation Standards for School Mathematics* (National Council of Teachers of Mathematics [NCTM] 1989) developed in the United States of America, the approach would have been far more acceptable to those who were so strongly opposed to the enterprise.

The first stage of development of the *Statement* and *Profiles* began with mathematics and involved a mapping of state and territory curriculum documents to identify similarities and differences. At the time there were

> … large differences in the ways in which school mathematics was organised in the different states and territories. For example, four systems (Victoria, South Australia, Tasmania, and the Australian Capitol Territory) did not mandate any aspect of the mathematics curriculum, and in these systems, centrally issued guidelines served as the basis for school-based

curriculum development for primary school mathematics. In New South Wales, Queensland and Western Australia, however, the aims and content of primary school mathematics were centrally specified, mandatory, and were backed up by centrally specified notes and suggestions. (Ellerton and Clements 1994, p. 52)

While this attempt at developing a national curriculum failed, the mathematics *Statements* and *Profiles* were used as a framework to guide curriculum development in some states. Identified legacies from these documents include an increased emphasis on mental computation, an increased focus on probability and statistics, and the articulation of a separate strand of 'processes' in most state and territory curriculum documents (Morony 2011). These processes tended to be included in a 'working mathematically' strand (e.g., Board of Studies NSW 2003), which also included reference to problem solving. Further elaboration of the approaches taken to embed problem solving into curriculum documents in NSW is examined later in this chapter.

The third phase (1993–2003) witnessed a return to indirect Federal government involvement where significant funds were devolved to schools to support professional development in the move towards a national curriculum, similar to the first phase. Through the *Australian Government Quality Teaching Program* [AGQTP], projects were funded to focus on literacy, numeracy, mathematics, science and/or technology. This phase led to many school- and system-based projects focused on numeracy and/or mathematics throughout Australia (Vincent 2004).

The fourth phase began in 2003 with the Federal Minister for Education suggesting the need for a common school starting age, common assessments for grade 12, and the need for a common curriculum in all states and territories. Another mapping exercise was undertaken to identify overlap and difference between state and territory curriculum documents, leading to the development of four *Statements of Learning* in English, Mathematics, Science and Civics. These 'statements' introduced the notion of 'national curriculum consistency' guiding national testing in literacy and numeracy from 2008 in grades 3, 5, 7 and 9.

The rationale for one curriculum for *all* Australian students was to improve quality, equity and accessibility. The rhetoric suggested "a national curriculum would play a key role in delivering quality education" and that it would be "world class" (ACARA 2010a). Further, one curriculum would mean:

- a united focus on how student learning can be improved to achieve national goals;
- greater attention devoted to equipping students with skills, knowledge and capabilities necessary to enable them to effectively engage with and prosper in society;
- more efficient development of high quality resources; and
- greater consistency for mobile student and teacher populations. (ACARA 2010a)

The curriculum development process began in 2008 with four academics writing framing papers in English, Mathematics, Science and History—Professor Peter Sullivan from Monash University was the author of the early papers for mathematics and a lead writer for the first Australian mathematics curriculum. A brief account of the development of the first national curriculum for mathematics is presented in the next section with the outcome of the process of development in this phase achieving more than in any earlier attempt.

The Development of the First Mathematics Curriculum in Australia

The process of development of the first national curriculum for mathematics by the National Curriculum Board [NCB] began with a *Framing Paper for Mathematics* (NCB 2008). Based on stakeholder feedback, the *Shape of the Australian Curriculum: Mathematics* (NCB 2009) guided the writing of the curriculum with content for each year of schooling, and achievement standards presenting a continuum of typical growth. The *Shape* paper outlined the goals, key terms and structure of the new curriculum. The structure included three content strands—Number and algebra, Measurement and geometry, and Statistics and probability—as well as four proficiency (or process) strands—understanding, fluency, problem solving, and reasoning (adapted from Kilpatrick et al. 2001).[2]

Three key issues were to be addressed in the development of the first Australian mathematics curriculum. First, improve quality and address concerns about the 'syndrome of shallow teaching' (Hollingsworth et al. 2003) by engaging more learners with complex problem solving. Second, improve equity and address differential mathematics achievement among particular groups of students. For example, from PISA 2009 data, differences in performance were related to socio-economic status, geographical location and cultural background (particularly between non-Indigenous and Indigenous students) (see Thomson et al. 2010). Third, increase accessibility with "a commitment to ensuring that all students experience the full mathematics curriculum until the end of Year 10" (NCB 2009, p. 10). This third effect challenges the common practice of 'streaming' or 'tracking' which typically leads to offering a limited mathematics curriculum for groups of students considered not able to learn more challenging mathematics content. For example in NSW, earlier curriculum documents differentiated the mathematics curriculum in grades 9 and 10.

The drafted mathematics curriculum for grades up to 10 was released for consultation in May 2009. Also during this period, the National Curriculum Board became a statutory body, the Australian Curriculum, Assessment and Reporting Authority [ACARA], responsible for curriculum and associated accountability processes including national testing. Feedback to ACARA on the draft curriculum was extensive with many recommendations supported by evidence from research. For example, Siemon (2011) indicated the 'number' content did not clearly identify and articulate the 'big ideas', including numeration. She suggested there were inconsistencies in content sequencing and language, particularly because different people wrote different sections of the draft document. Sadly, as can often occur with curriculum development, Siemon suggested the task "became one of managing competing interests rather than making hard, futuristic decisions based on research and practical experience" (p. 68).

---

[2]For a more detailed account of the development of the first national mathematics curriculum document, see Anderson et al. (2012), and for a detailed critique of sections of the curriculum document, see Atweh et al. (2012a, 2012b).

Table 1 The definitions for each of the proficiencies (ACARA 2010b, p. 3)

Understanding	Students build a robust knowledge of adaptable and transferable mathematical concepts. They make connections between related concepts and progressively apply the familiar to develop new ideas. They develop an understanding of the relationship between the 'why' and the 'how' of mathematics …
Fluency	Students develop skills in choosing appropriate procedures, carrying out procedures flexibly, accurately, efficiently and appropriately, and recalling factual knowledge and concepts readily. Students are fluent when they calculate answers efficiently, when they recognise robust ways of answering questions, when they choose appropriate methods …
Problem Solving	Students develop the ability to make choices, interpret, formulate, model and investigate problem situations, and communicate solutions effectively. Students formulate and solve problems when they use mathematics to represent unfamiliar or meaningful situations …
Reasoning	Students develop an increasingly sophisticated capacity for logical thought and actions, such as analysing, proving, evaluating, explaining, inferring, justifying and generalising. Students are reasoning mathematically when they explain their thinking, when they deduce and justify strategies used and conclusions reached …

Additional concerns included the inadequate representation of the proficiency or process strands in the content descriptions, the need for further reduction of content to provide time for more problem solving and modelling, the poor sequencing of some content, and the need to further consider current research (AAMT 2010; Mathematics Education Research Group of Australasia 2010; Siemon 2011). In addition, the consultation process was limited to feedback from teachers at large on only one draft of the curriculum, suggesting a lack of transparency (Morony 2011). However, it should be noted here that ACARA regularly consulted with small numbers of teachers who represented a broad range of professional associations and systems.

After revisions, the *Australian Curriculum: Mathematics* was released online in December 2010 with opportunities for schools to trial some aspects of the curriculum and provide feedback to the writers so that revisions could be made during 2011 (ACARA 2010b). The final document presents mathematics for Foundation (the first year of schooling) to Year 10. There is evidence that some issues raised during the consultation have been addressed with a review of the sequencing of concepts within the three content strands, and organisation of content into sub-strands. In addition, the embedding of the proficiency strands was revised with the use of more 'actions' at the beginning of content statements. The definitions of each of the proficiencies (see Table 1) highlight the types of verbs used to represent the actions recommended.

Atweh et al. (2012a, 2012b) argue that while the proficiencies are described as 'actions', their descriptions as presented in Table 1 suggest a different interpretation. They state, "these articulations imply that the proficiencies describe dimensions of student performance within mathematics rather than a type of experience they have in its study" (p. 7). This may be because the proficiencies were informed by the work of Kilpatrick et al. (2001) who explained, "proficiency" was used to describe what "it means for anyone to learn mathematics successfully" (p. 5). The language used in the proficiency descriptions describes the outcomes of successful learning rather than the potential actions or experiences. Clearly it is still up to teachers to determine how this might occur and what experiences will be necessary to support the development of these proficiencies.

While the initial *Framing Paper* and the subsequent *Shape* paper articulated a vision for mathematics curriculum few would disagree with, many now feel "there is little to distinguish it from the content of 20 years ago" (Morony 2011, p. 64). Coupled with this, Thornton (2011) argues that in the curriculum documents for mathematics,

> ... the rationale and aims do little to convey a sense of what the practice of mathematics is really like and continue to promote an absolutist view of mathematics as a body of knowledge that needs to be taught and has little or no room for questioning. (p. 75)

Atweh and Goos (2011), and Siemon (2011) question whether the curriculum is 'futures oriented' and prepares young Australians for a 21st Century world. Irrespective of these criticisms, Australia now has a national mathematics curriculum for the first eleven years of schooling.

It is unclear whether this first national curriculum has addressed the challenges of improving quality, equity, and accessibility. As noted above, the final product does present content that is similar to the documents used previously by some states and territories so the question remains as to whether the quality has improved. Producing equitable learning outcomes and improving accessibility will depend very much on how the curriculum is implemented by teachers at the local school level (Atweh and Singh 2011)—clearly teachers will need more support if any real change is to ensue and differential outcomes are to be addressed. Sullivan (2012) argues that

> ... the challenge of equity can be addressed by focusing on depth of learning rather than breadth, by specifically supporting the learning of those students who need it and by extending more advanced students within the content for that level rather than isolating such students into different classes. (p. 175)

However, the embedding of the proficiencies (which include problem solving) into the content statements offers some hope. This may assist teachers in overcoming the 'syndrome of shallow teaching' if they follow the recommendations and provide students with increased opportunities to engage in complex problem solving. The *Melbourne Declaration on Educational Goals for Young Australians* (MCEETYA 2008, p. 8) also informed the development of the national curriculum. Goals for 21st Century learners suggested they "are creative, innovative and resourceful, and are able to solve problems". One way to engage and motivate students in mathematics is through problem solving and investigations (Schoenfeld 2007).

The following sections of this chapter examine the evolution of problem solving in curriculum documents from one Australian state, NSW, and consider whether the national curriculum approach to problem solving forges new opportunities for students and teachers in mathematics classrooms. I draw on Lester's (1994) reflections of 25 years of problem-solving research in reviewing this evolution.

The Evolution of Problem Solving in NSW Curriculum Development

Curriculum documents typically promote reform-oriented approaches and recognise the importance of engaging students in worthwhile mathematics through a range of actions or processes. For example, the *Principles and Standards for School Mathematics* (NCTM 2000) includes standards related to five processes—problem solving, reasoning and proof, communication, connections, and representations. Similar processes have been included in NSW curriculum documents with the most recent including a range of processes under the umbrella term "Working Mathematically". This section documents the evolution of problem solving in the curriculum documents in NSW, and examines some of the research into teachers' knowledge and understanding of the curriculum approach to problem solving in that state.

In NSW, problem solving was made explicit for the first time in the mathematics curriculum documents or syllabuses developed and introduced into elementary (NSW Department of Education 1989) and junior secondary (Board of Secondary Education [BSE] NSW 1989) classrooms in the Eighties. In the introduction to the elementary syllabus, problem solving and applications were described as important components of mathematics teaching and learning and a *problem* was described as having three characteristics:

- there is a goal to be reached
- an obstacle prevents ready solution
- the solver is motivated to reach a solution. (NSW Department of Education 1989, p. 22)

In both the elementary and the lower secondary curriculum documents, advice was provided on how problem solving could be implemented including the possibilities associated with teaching *for* problem solving, teaching *about* problem solving and teaching *through* problem solving (Siemon and Booker 1990). The lower secondary document included problem solving as one of six strands and included examples of problem types. It also advised that problem solving should involve interpretation, use of a range of heuristics, and evaluation of solutions. To support teachers, textbook writers developed chapters devoted to practising particular problem-solving strategies (e.g., Barry et al. 1988) or they presented problems associated with particular content at the end of each chapter.

Alongside the development of the curriculum, teaching support documents were produced to assist the implementation of problem solving in classrooms. However, implementation was limited (Anderson 1996, 1997)—a popular approach in lower secondary contexts was to timetable one lesson a week on 'problem solving' with sets of problem-solving tasks set up in a special classroom or 'laboratory'. Students referred to their lessons as either 'mathematics' or 'problem solving' so that problem solving was viewed as an add-on to the curriculum and not integrated into regular mathematics lessons as a way of learning and a way of doing mathematics. Perhaps this situation was mirrored in the USA as reflected in Lester's (1994) comments.

To date, no mathematics program has been developed that adequately addresses the issue of making problem solving the central focus of the curriculum. Instead of being given coherent programs with clear direction, teachers have had to be satisfied with a well-intentioned melange of story problems, lists of strategies to be taught, and suggestions for classroom activities. (p. 661)

A revised curriculum for grades 9 and 10 was released in NSW in 1996 with three differentiated courses (advanced, intermediate, and general). Curriculum documents provided advice about problem-solving processes and heuristics with the introductory pages referring to problem solving as "a major aspect of mathematics" accompanied by the recommendation for teachers to consider "four important elements of solving problems" (BOS NSW 1996, p. 14), mirroring Polya's (1945) phases. Instead of a problem solving strand, the curriculum writers adopted the term *mathematical investigations* with the advice students should undertake an investigation associated with *Chance and data* as well as "one other, longer investigation which might take up to five hours" (p. 173).

The term 'working mathematically' was also introduced into NSW curriculum at this time. This introduction appeared to be informed by the document *Mathematics—A Curriculum Profile for Australian Schools* (Curriculum Corporation 1994) where *working mathematically* was described as comprising six processes—investigating, conjecturing, using problem-solving strategies, applying and verifying, using mathematical language, and working in context, each with their own outcomes and presented as a developmental continuum across all of the years of schooling. However, the term 'working mathematically' in the NSW grade 9 and 10 syllabus was presented as an objective with no clear description of the associated knowledge, skills or understandings.

The content was presented in each strand as detailed statements with 'applications, suggested activities and sample questions'. These sample questions represented activities not typically found in available textbooks, thus providing opportunities for students to engage in higher-level thinking tasks and investigations of mathematical ideas (see the example presented in Fig. 1). As Anderson (2002) notes, this appeared to be an attempt to align problem solving with the content in a more explicit manner.

In revisions to NSW curriculum in the late Nineties when an outcomes-based approach was adopted (BOSNSW 1998, 1999), *working mathematically* was also introduced into the elementary grades curriculum. More clearly aligned to the *Profile* document (1994), *working mathematically* was described as encompassing the processes of questioning, problem solving, communicating, verifying, reflecting and using technology (BOSNSW 1998). There was no similar list in mathematics curriculum documents for the secondary grades. It is evident from Table 2 that, because of the development of each of these curriculum documents at different times, the approach to mathematics curriculum design for the first 11 years of schooling in NSW was inconsistent, sending mixed messages to teachers of mathematics, particularly in relation to the implementation of problem solving.

At this stage, I pause to include a reflection from Lester (1994) on what should occur in mathematics classrooms to address the lack of engagement with problem solving. Based on his review of the research into problem solving, Lester suggested there were five clear messages about improving this situation for teachers and students.

N2: Consumer Arithmetic Content	N2: Consumer Arithmetic Applications, suggested activities and sample questions
iv) Consumer Problems Learning experiences should provide students with opportunity to: • identify best buys • compare the cost of loans using flat and reducible interest for a small number of repayment periods • find the value of an item after certain time period of depreciation or appreciation • …	**iv) Consumer Problems** Students should: • devise and compare strategies to determine best buys in a realistic context • compare the cost of the same item in different sizes: does the ratio of cost to size remain constant as the size of the item increases? • Use a spreadsheet and graph to investigate the effect of different repayment schedules on the cost of a housing loan • …

Fig. 1 Content and applications for Consumer Arithmetic from the Number strand of the Advanced Years 9 and 10 Syllabus (BOS NSW 1996, pp. 80–81)

Table 2 Names of the strands for the elementary and secondary school curriculum documents in NSW

Grades K to 6 (BOSNSW 1989)	Grades 7 and 8 (Board of Secondary Education NSW 1989)	Grades 9 and 10 (BOSNSW 1996)
Working Mathematically	Problem solving	Working Mathematically
Number	Number	Number
	Algebra	Algebra
	Statistics	Chance and data
Space	Geometry	Geometry
Measurement	Measurement	Measurement (including trigonometry)

1. Students must solve many problems in order to improve their problem-solving ability.
2. Problem-solving ability develops slowly over a prolonged period of time.
3. In order for students to benefit from instruction, they must believe that their teacher thinks problem solving is important.
4. Most students benefit greatly from systematically planned problem-solving instruction.
5. Teaching students about problem-solving strategies and heuristics and phases of problem solving does little to improve student's ability to solve mathematics problems in general. (p. 666)

To send clear messages to teachers, Lester's list suggests problem solving needs to be embedded in curriculum documents from the early years of schooling, with recommendations for regular, well-planned learning experiences for students. While there was considerable advice in the NSW curriculum documents of the late Eighties and the Nineties, problem solving was still presented as a separate strand or included as a process of *working mathematically*, and was usually represented within

Table 3 Working mathematically processes (BOSNSW 2003, p. 16)

Process	Description of the Process
Questioning	Students ask questions in relation to mathematical situations and their mathematical experiences
Applying Strategies	Students develop, select and use a range of strategies, including the selection and use of appropriate technology, to explore and solve problems
Communicating	Students develop and use appropriate language and representations to formulate and express mathematical ideas
Reasoning	Students develop and use processes for exploring relationships, checking solutions and giving reasons to support their conclusions
Reflecting	Students reflect on their experiences and critical understanding to make connections with, and generalisations about, existing knowledge and understanding

content strands as examples of activities or 'good questions'. Depending on one's view of what problem solving is, this was not necessarily visible to teachers (Anderson 2005). The curriculum documents in NSW listed problem-solving strategies and heuristics and emphasised the phases of problem solving—none of these approaches were supported by the research into improving students' problem-solving competence according to Lester (1994).

Beginning in 2000, all of the mathematics curriculum documents from Kindergarten to grade 10 were revised together to ensure "consistency, continuity and coherence" (Anderson 2002, p. 14). Led by the author, the curriculum development process began by mapping content from the three existing sets of curriculum documents, removing overlap and repetition, and realigning content based on research into developmental continua of learning (e.g., Harel and Confrey 1994). Mathematical ideas for all curriculum documents up to grade 10 were grouped into the content strands—number, algebra, data, geometry, and measurement. One process strand, *working mathematically*, was used to describe the mathematical actions or processes associated with doing mathematics. The overarching description of *working mathematically* included reference to problem solving:

> Students will develop knowledge, skills and understanding through inquiry, application of problem-solving strategies, including the selection and use of appropriate technology, communication, reasoning and reflection. (BOSNSW 2003, p. 12)

The *working mathematically* processes included questioning, applying strategies, communicating, reasoning and reflecting (see Table 3 for a description of each process). Anderson and Bobis (2005) argued that when teachers use rich tasks in mathematics lessons so that students are engaging with all of these processes, the students are likely to be experiencing more complex problem-solving situations.

While much of the mathematical content remained the same as in previous curriculum documents, the new curriculum approach required teachers to review their practice by:

Area	Key Ideas
MS3.2 Selects and uses the appropriate unit to calculate area, including the area of squares, rectangles and triangles	Select and use the appropriate unit to calculate area Recognise the need for square kilometres and hectares Develop formulae in words for finding area of squares, rectangles and triangles
Knowledge and skills	**Working Mathematically**
<ul><li>recognising the need for a unit larger than the square metre</li><li>identifying situations where square kilometres are used for measuring area eg a suburb</li><li>recognising and explaining the need for a more convenient unit than the square kilometre</li><li>measuring an area in hectares eg the local park</li><li>using the abbreviations for square kilometre (km^2) and hectare (ha)</li><li>recognising that one hectare is equal to 10 000 square metres</li><li>selecting the appropriate unit to calculate area</li></ul>	<ul><li>apply measurement skills to everyday situations eg determining the area of the basketball court (*Applying Strategies*)</li><li>use the terms 'length', 'breadth', 'width' and 'depth' appropriately (*Communicating, Reflecting*)</li><li>extend mathematical tasks by asking questions eg 'If I change the dimensions of a rectangle but keep the perimeter the same, will the area change?' (*Questioning*)</li><li>interpret measurements on simple plans (*Communicating*)</li><li>investigate the areas of rectangles that have the same perimeter (*Applying Strategies*)</li></ul>

Fig. 2 Content for the Measurement strand, Area sub-strand for grades 5 and 6 (BOSNSW 2003, p. 123)

1. assessing students' current knowledge and planning learning experiences informed by the developmental continuum regardless of the grade they were in at school;
2. designing programs that enabled students to be extended in their learning rather than stopping at some predetermined endpoint which occurred in the previous curriculum with its differentiated three course structure for grades 9 and 10;
3. designing lessons that integrated the process strand, *working mathematically*, with the content so that problem solving became a central focus of learning; and
4. using a range of assessment strategies that included assessment *for* learning as well as assessment *of* learning (BOSNSW 2003).

To encourage teachers to integrate the *working mathematically* processes into everyday learning experiences for students, examples were listed beside the appropriate content in the curriculum document—see Fig. 2 for an example for the Measurement strand, Area substrand. Each example was labelled with one or more processes to assist teachers in their understanding of each term.

Beginning in 2004 the revised curriculum was implemented in NSW classrooms. Extensive professional development was provided by school system personnel, professional associations, and private providers including the University of Sydney (Anderson and Moore 2005). Professional learning experiences focused on the new curriculum approach, particularly how embedding *working mathematically* into mathematics lessons would provide students with increased problem-solving opportunities.

To investigate if teachers understood this approach and whether it assisted them in the integration of *working mathematically* into classroom practice, Cavanagh (2006) interviewed 39 secondary mathematics teachers of grades 7 to 10 from a range of school contexts across NSW. While a small number of teachers had embraced the *working mathematically* approach, most had limited understanding and reported few changes to their practice. In the elementary school context, Anderson and Bobis (2005) surveyed 40 teachers of Kindergarten to grade 6 to evaluate their understanding of *working mathematically*. Based on their responses to open-ended questions about the *working mathematically* processes, only two teachers appeared to have a comprehensive understanding of all five processes with another five teachers revealing a good understanding of most. Eight teachers who reported planning *working mathematically* experiences for their students in most lessons were also interviewed to confirm their knowledge and understanding of the curriculum. While these studies explored the curriculum knowledge of a small number of teachers, they revealed the majority of teachers had a limited understanding of *working mathematically* and problem solving as they were represented in the NSW curriculum documents.

To summarise, in the NSW context, problem solving has been described in curriculum documents since 1989. Problem solving was first represented as a separate strand with accompanying advice about teaching problem-solving processes, heuristics and the phases of problem solving. Examples of problems were frequently presented. During the Nineties, problem solving was included in a *working mathematically* strand and typically described as a set of processes. To assist the integration of problem solving with content, curriculum documents presented lists of 'good questions' or 'activities'. Given this evolution of representations, there is still limited evidence of implementation in mathematics classrooms in NSW. Similar changes have occurred in the curriculum documents in other states and territories in Australia with mixed success (for further information see Clarke et al. 2007; Stacey 2005). Therefore, a valid challenge in developing the first national curriculum was to determine how problem solving should be represented to assist teachers and increase the level of implementation in classrooms. Handal and Herrington (2003) argue

> Successful curriculum change is more likely to occur when the curricular reform goals relating to teachers' practice take account of teachers' beliefs. (p. 65)

While I acknowledge teachers' beliefs filter curriculum advice, I also agree with Kennedy (2009) who states curriculum should articulate the "valued knowledge, skills and beliefs that will benefit young people in the future" (p. 278). Most teachers believe problem solving is an important life skill and that it should be included in the school curriculum (Anderson 2003, 2005; Anderson and Bobis 2005; Cavanagh 2006). Our challenge is to find effective ways to represent problem solving in curriculum documents so that teachers feel better equipped to respond positively to the advice (Stacey 2005; Sullivan 2012). The challenge for curriculum developers

Table 4 The proficiencies in the Australian national mathematics curriculum matched to the names used by Kilpatrick et al. (2001)

Australian Curriculum Proficiency Strands	Mathematical Proficiencies (Kilpatrick et al. 2001)
Understanding	Conceptual understanding
Fluency	Procedural fluency
Problem solving	Strategic competence
Reasoning	Adaptive reasoning
	Productive disposition

is to clearly articulate the expected standards for both content and problem solving at each grade level and to assist teachers by integrating the content with problem solving so that problem-solving approaches to teaching and learning mathematics are explicit and easily understood.

The Approach to Problem Solving in the First Australian Mathematics Curriculum

As reported earlier in this chapter, the Australian curriculum for mathematics has three content strands (Number and algebra, Measurement and geometry, Statistics and probability) and four process strands which are based on four of the five proficiencies described by Kilpatrick et al. (2001) (see Table 4). In this section, the approach taken to embed problem solving into the new national curriculum will be reviewed to determine whether it provides new opportunities for teachers and students.

As noted in the *Shape of the Australian Curriculum: Mathematics* (NCB 2009, p. 5) document, the term 'working mathematically' was not considered to adequately represent the full range of actions so the new proficiencies have been adapted from the mathematical proficiencies proposed by Kilpatrick et al. (2001). Sullivan (2012) argues

> … the four proficiencies … provide a clearer framework for mathematical processes than "working mathematically" and are more likely to encourage teachers and others who assess student learning to move beyond a focus on fluency, however, there will need to be support for teachers if they are to incorporate them into the curriculum. (p. 175)

While there needs to be a balance of the proficiencies in mathematics classrooms (Sullivan 2011), if problem solving and reasoning are to be promoted as important components of the curriculum it is necessary to reconsider the advice from Lester in 1994 and the types of problems used by teachers in mathematics lessons must be carefully considered (Clarke 2009; Sullivan 2011). Curriculum developers recognise that providing problem-solving experiences is critical if students are to be able to use and apply mathematical knowledge in meaningful ways. It is through problem solving that students develop deeper understanding of mathematical ideas, become more engaged and enthused in lessons, and appreciate the relevance and usefulness of mathematics.

In the new *Australian Curriculum: Mathematics* (ACARA 2012) problem solving is described as follows.

> Students develop the ability to make choices, interpret, formulate, model and investigate problem situations, and communicate solutions effectively. Students formulate and solve problems when they use mathematics to represent unfamiliar or meaningful situations, when they design investigations and plan their approaches, when they apply their existing strategies to seek solutions, and when they verify that their answers are reasonable. (p. 6)

For students to become the successful problem solvers that this description suggests, they will need to actively engage with a range of important processes during mathematics lessons. For this to occur teachers will need to select tasks, which allow for student choice about the mathematics they might use and the problem-solving strategies they select to model and investigate mathematical situations. Importantly, they also need to be able to effectively communicate their solutions. According to the NCTM *Standards* (2000, p. 52) "problem solving means engaging in a task for which the solution method is not known in advance". So problem solving frequently involves investigating new and somewhat challenging situations that require time and effort. Problem solving needs to be more than just doing questions that are applications of the mathematics students are learning right now.

To aid teacher understanding of the proficiencies in the Australian curriculum, the following statement is presented at each grade level:

> The proficiency strands Understanding, Fluency, Problem Solving and Reasoning are an integral part of mathematics content across the three content strands Number and Algebra, Measurement and Geometry, and Statistics and Probability. The proficiencies reinforce the significance of working mathematically within the content and describe how the content is explored and developed. They provide the language to build in the developmental aspects of the learning of mathematics.

Under this statement, a brief description is presented for each of the proficiencies, which is appropriate to the grade level. While there is a statement for every grade level, Table 5 presents the description for problem solving for some levels.

These statements include actions associated with learning mathematics and combine types of problem-solving tasks with the content relevant for the particular grade. Several of these statements mention "authentic problems" or "authentic situations", neither of these terms is defined for teachers so while the statements generally suggest engagement with problem-solving experiences, they may not be necessarily clear. Atweh and Goos (2011) offer the suggestion that "authentic activities" would involve "using examples from the real world of the student". At the grade 10 level, problem solving refers to applying formulae and procedures. Depending on student understanding, these could be routine applications and have limited opportunity for problem solving as defined in the curriculum document.

In addition to these problem-solving statements, the content descriptions also include some reference to solving problems. This was the strategy used by the curriculum writers to embed problem solving into the content and to address the concern that teachers believe problem solving is an added extra. Table 6 presents some examples for the Number and Algebra strand at different grade levels.

Table 5 Problem-solving statements at the beginning of several grades (ACARA 2012)

Grade	Problem Solving statement
Foundation	Problem solving includes using materials to model **authentic problems**, sorting objects, using familiar counting sequences to solve unfamiliar problems, and discussing the reasonableness of the answer
2	Problem solving includes formulating problems from **authentic situations**, making models and using number sentences that represent problem situations, planning routes on maps, and matching transformations with their original shape
4	Problem solving includes formulating, modelling and recording **authentic situations** involving operations, comparing large numbers and time durations, and using properties of numbers to continue patterns
6	Problem solving includes formulating and solving **authentic problems** using numbers and measurements creating similar shapes through enlargements, representing secondary data and calculating angles
8	Problem solving includes formulating and modelling, with comparisons of ratios, profit and loss, authentic situations involving areas and perimeters of common shapes and analysing and interpreting data using two-way tables
10	Problem solving includes calculating the surface area and volume of a diverse range of prisms, finding unknown lengths and angles using applications of trigonometry, using algebraic and graphical techniques to find solutions to simultaneous equations and inequalities, and investigating independence of events and their probabilities

Table 6 Examples of embedding problem solving into content descriptions in Number and Algebra at several grade levels (ACARA 2012)

Grade	Content descriptions in Number and Algebra which refer to problem solving
1	Represent and solve simple addition and subtraction problems using a range of strategies including counting on, partitioning and rearranging parts.
3	Apply place value to partition, rearrange and regroup numbers to at least 10 000 to assist calculations and solve problems
5	Solve problems involving multiplication of large numbers by one- or two-digit numbers using efficient mental, written strategies and appropriate digital technologies
7	Recognise and solve problems involving simple ratios
9	Solve problems involving simple interest
10	Solve problems involving linear equations, including those derived from formulas

Table 6 reveals that there has been an attempt to embed problem solving into content, but it is possible teachers may interpret these statements as 'simple word problems'. Anderson (2005) found many teachers believed they were implementing problem solving as required in the curriculum by presenting students with a range of word problems—many of the examples teachers provided were lower order applications requiring little mathematical thinking for students who were able to read and interpret the language in the problem.

It should be noted here that a review of the content descriptions and their elaborations across all grade levels reveals "a heavy focus on" the first two proficiencies of understanding and fluency and "to a lower level on reasoning and problem solving" (Atweh and Goos 2011, p. 221). Atweh et al. (2012a, 2012b) analysed all of the content elaborations for grade 8 and found that while 56 % related to fluency, only 12 % related to problem solving and 7 % to reasoning. Further, they suggest that the problem solving elaborations are limited in their scope and "may not inspire teachers to appreciate the importance of these proficiencies and to think of valuable and exciting ways in which they can be used or developed in the classroom" (p. 9).

The Australian national curriculum does provide advice about problem solving that is different to previous documents, particularly when compared to the NSW context. There is an overarching definition of problem solving, there are statements about problem solving at each grade level, and problem solving has been embedded into several content descriptions. This may provide new opportunities for teachers to engage their students with more problem solving in mathematics lessons. At this early stage of implementation of the new Australian curriculum, no research has been published into teachers' use of the new curriculum documents. It will be critical to examine the impact of this approach to determine whether it assists teachers and improves the level of engagement with problem solving in Australian mathematics classrooms.

It is certainly true that Australia does have its first national curriculum for mathematics and it was implemented in some schools in some jurisdictions in 2012. However, how it is being implemented in each state and territory differs. Several states (e.g., NSW and Victoria) are using the new national curriculum as a framework to develop their own curriculum documents. Implementation in these locations will follow in 2013 or 2014. Others are providing teachers with extensive professional development to use the national curriculum as a planning document for school-based curriculum (e.g., Australian Capital Territory). Given that the responsibility for curriculum implementation rests with the state and territory governments, it is not surprising the approaches to curriculum delivery and teacher support varies. It is historically difficult to change deeply held beliefs and practices, so the implementation of the national curriculum varies depending on which state you visit.

While there appear to be new opportunities for Australian teachers and students to engage in more complex problem solving in the new national curriculum, the fundamental issue of clarity on the meanings of 'problem' and 'problem solving' appears to remain—although research is needed to ascertain whether this is the case. From her review of problem solving in the mathematics curriculum documents from several countries as well as some Australian states in 2005, Stacey recommended:

> Research could examine whether and how these curriculum structures from different countries influence teachers' understanding of the goals of teaching mathematics, and whether these different understandings make a real difference in the attention that teachers give to mathematical problem solving beyond the routine. (p. 345)

It is a shame this recommendation was not heeded—it would have assisted the curriculum developers of the first national curriculum in Australia. But it is not too late to further explore the ways problem solving is represented in other countries and whether alternative approaches may better support teachers' understanding.

References

ACARA (2010a). *Australian curriculum information sheet: why have an Australian curriculum?* Sydney: ACARA.

ACARA (2010b). *Australian curriculum: mathematics F to 10*. Sydney: ACARA.

ACARA (2012). Australian curriculum: mathematics, version 3.0. Downloaded 3rd February 2012 from http://www.australiancurriculum.edu.au/Mathematics/Curriculum/F-10.

Anderson, J. (1996). Some teachers' beliefs and perceptions of problem solving. In P. Clarkson (Ed.), *Technology in mathematics education, Proceedings of the 19th annual conference of MERGA* (pp. 30–37). Melbourne: Deakin University Press.

Anderson, J. (1997). Teachers' reported use of problem-solving teaching strategies in primary mathematics classrooms. In F. Biddulph & K. Carr (Eds.), *People in mathematics education, Proceedings of the 20th annual conference of MERGA* (pp. 50–57). Melbourne: Deakin University Press.

Anderson, J. (2002). Development and overall changes to the K_10 mathematics syllabuses. *Reflections, 27*(4), 14–20.

Anderson, J. (2003). Teachers' choice of tasks: a window into beliefs about the role of problem solving in learning mathematics. In L. Bragg, C. Campbell, G. Herbert, & J. Mousley (Eds.), *Mathematics education research: innovation, networking, opportunity, Proceedings of the 26th annual conference of the mathematics education research group of Australasia*, Geelong, Victoria (pp. 72–79).

Anderson, J. (2005). Implementing problem solving in mathematics classrooms: what support do teachers want? In P. Clarkson, A. Downton, D. Gronn, M. Horne, A. McDonough, R. Pierce, & A. Roche (Eds.), *Building connections: theory, research and practice, Proceedings of the 28th annual conference of the mathematics education research group of Australasia*, Melbourne, Victoria (pp. 89–96).

Anderson, J., & Bobis, J. (2005). Reform-oriented teaching practices: a survey of primary school teachers. In H. L. Chick & J. L. Vincent (Eds.), *Proceedings of the 29th conference of the international group for the psychology of mathematics education* (Vol. 2, pp. 65–72). Melbourne: PME.

Anderson, J., & Moore, M. (2005). Evaluating the professional learning of secondary mathematics teachers: reflecting on their reflections! In *Proceedings of the Australian association for research in education's 35th annual international education research conference*, Sydney, Australia (ISSN 1324-9320). Published at http://www.aare.edu.au/05pap/and05154.pdf.

Anderson, J., Sullivan, P., & White, P. (2004). The influence of perceived constraints on teachers' problem-solving beliefs and practices. In I. Putt, R. Faragher, & M. McLean (Eds.), *Mathematics education for the third millennium: towards 2010, Proceedings of the 27th annual conference of the mathematics education research group of Australasia* (pp. 39–46). Townsville: MERGA.

Anderson, J., White, P., & Wong, M. (2012). Mathematics curriculum in the schooling years. In B. Perry, T. Lowrie, T. Logan, A. MacDonald, & J. Greenlees (Eds.), *Research in mathematics education in Australasia 2008-2011* (pp. 219–244). Rotterdam: Sense Publishers.

Atweh, B., & Goos, M. (2011). The Australian mathematics curriculum: a move forward or back to the future? *Australian Journal of Education, 55*(3), 214–228.

Atweh, B., Goos, M., Jorgensen, R., & Siemon, D. (Eds.) (2012a). *Engaging the Australian curriculum mathematics: perspectives from the field*. Online publication of MERGA. http://www.merga.net.au/sites/default/files/editor/books/1/Book.pdf.

Atweh, B., Miller, D., & Thornton, S. (2012b). The Australian curriculum: mathematics—world class or déjà vu? In B. Atweh, M. Goos, R. Jorgensen, & D. Siemon (Eds.), *Engaging the Australian curriculum mathematics: perspectives from the field* (pp. 1–18). Online publication of MERGA http://www.merga.net.au/sites/default/files/editor/books/1/Book.pdf.

Atweh, B., & Singh, P. (2011). The Australian curriculum: continuing the national conversation. *Australian Journal of Education, 55*(3), 189–196.

Australian Association of Mathematics Teachers [AAMT] (2010). *AAMT response to the draft K-10 Australian curriculum: mathematics.* Adelaide: AAMT.

Barry, B., et al. (1988). *HBJ year 6 mathematics.* Sydney: Harcourt Brace Jovanovich.

Board of Secondary Education NSW (1989). *Syllabus years 7–8.* North Sydney: Board of Secondary Education.

Board of Studies NSW [BOSNSW] (1996). *Mathematics years 9–10 syllabus—advanced, intermediate and standard courses.* Sydney: BOS NSW.

Board of Studies NSW (1998). *Mathematics K-6 outcomes and indicators.* Sydney: BOS NSW.

Board of Studies NSW (1999). *Mathematics years 7–8 syllabus outcomes.* Sydney: BOS NSW.

Board of Studies NSW (2003). *Mathematics years 7–10 syllabus.* Sydney: BOS NSW.

Cavanagh, M. (2006). Mathematics teachers and working mathematically: responses to curriculum change. In P. Grootenboer, R. Zevenbergen, & M. Chinnappan (Eds.), *Identities, cultures and learning spaces, Proceedings of the 29th annual conference of the mathematics research group of Australasia* (pp. 115–122). Adelaide: MERGA.

Clarke, B. (2009). Using tasks involving models, tools and representations: insights from a middle years mathematics project. In R. Hunter, B. Bicknell, & T. Burgess (Eds.), *Crossing divides. Proceedings of the 32nd MERGA annual conference* (Vol. 2, pp. 718–721). Palmerston North: MERGA.

Clarke, D., Goos, M., & Morony, W. (2007). Problem solving and working mathematically: an Australian perspective. *ZDM Mathematics Education, 39*(5–6), 475–490.

Clements, D. H. (2007). Curriculum research: towards a framework for research-based curricula. *Journal for Research in Mathematics Education, 38*, 35–70.

Curriculum Corporation (1994). *Mathematics—a curriculum profile for Australian schools.* Carlton: Curriculum Corporation.

Ellerton, N., & Clements, M. (Ken) (1994). *The national curriculum debacle.* Perth: Meridian Press.

Handal, B., & Herrington, A. (2003). Mathematics teachers' beliefs and curriculum reform. *Mathematics Education Research Journal, 15*(1), 59–69.

Harel, G. & Confrey, J. (Eds.) (1994). *The development of multiplicative reasoning in the learning of mathematics.* Albany: State University of New York Press.

Hollingsworth, H., Lokan, J., & McCrae, B. (2003). *Teaching mathematics in Australia: results from the TIMSS 1999 video study.* Camberwell: Australian Council of Educational Research.

Kennedy, K. (2005). Charting the global contexts of the school curriculum: why curriculum solutions are never simple. In C. Harris & C. Marsh (Eds.), *Curriculum developments in Australia: promising initiatives, impasses and dead-ends* (pp. 1–14). Deakin West: Australian Curriculum Studies Association.

Kennedy, K. (2009). The idea of a national curriculum in Australia: what do Susan Ryan, John Dawkins and Julia Gillard have in common? *Curriculum Perspectives, 29*(1).

Kilpatrick, J., Swafford, J., & Findell, B. (Eds.) (2001). *Adding it up: helping children learn mathematics.* Washington: National Academy Press.

Lester, F. K. (1994). Musings about problem-solving research: 1970–1994. *Journal for Research in Mathematics Education, 25*(6), 660–675.

Lovitt, C., & Clarke, D. (1988). *Mathematics curriculum and teaching program (MCTP) activity bank—volumes 1 and 2.* Canberra: Curriculum Development Centre.

Lovitt, S., & Clarke, D. (2011). The features of a rich and balanced mathematics lesson: teacher as designer. *Educational Designer, 1*(4), 1–25.

Marsh, C. (Ed.) (2010). *Curriculum over 30 years: what have we achieved?* Canberra: Australian Curriculum Studies Association.

Mathematics Education Research Group of Australasia [MERGA] (2010). MERGA response to the Australian curriculum (mathematics), MERGA, May 2010. http://www.merga. net.au/node/49.

McGaw, B. (2010). President's report: transforming school education. *Dialogue, 29*(1). Available: www.assa.edu.au/publications/dialogue/2010_Vol29_No1.php.

Ministerial Council of Education, Employment, Training and Youth Affairs [MCEETYA] (2008). *Melbourne declaration on educational goals for young Australians*. Carlton Sth: MCEETYA.

Morony, W. (2011). Messages about progress to date on the Australian curriculum: mathematics. *Curriculum Perspectives, 11*(1), 62–65.

National Council of Teachers of Mathematics [NCTM] (1989). *Curriculum and evaluation standards for school mathematics*. Reston: NCTM.

National Council of Teachers of Mathematics [NCTM] (2000). *Principles and standards for school mathematics*. Reston: NCTM.

National Curriculum Board (2008). *National mathematics curriculum: framing paper*. Barton: NCB.

National Curriculum Board (2009). *Shape of the Australian curriculum: mathematics*. Barton: NCB.

NSW Department of Education (1989). *Mathematics K-6*. Sydney: NSW Department of Education.

Piper, K. (1989). National curriculum: prospects and possibilities. *Curriculum Perspectives, 9*(3), 3–7.

Polya, G. (1945). *How to solve it*. Princeton: Princeton University Press.

Reid, A. (2005). The politics of national curriculum collaboration: how can Australia move beyond the railway gauge metaphor? In C. Harris & C. Marsh (Eds.), *Curriculum developments in Australia: promising initiatives, impasses and dead-ends* (pp. 39–51). Deakin West: Australian Curriculum Studies Association.

Robitaille, D., Schmidt, W., Raizen, S., & McKnight, C. (1996). Curriculum frameworks for mathematics and science.

Schoenfeld, A. H. (2007). Problem solving in the United States, 1970–2008: research and theory, practice and politics. *ZDM Mathematics Education, 39*(5–6), 537–551.

Siemon, D. (2011). Realising the 'big ideas' in number—vision impossible? *Curriculum Perspectives, 31*(1), 66–69.

Siemon, D., & Booker, G. (1990). Teaching and learning FOR, ABOUT and THROUGH problem solving. *Vinculum, 27*(2), 4–12.

Stacey, K. (2005). The place of problem solving in contemporary mathematics curriculum documents. *Journal of Mathematical Behaviour, 24*, 341–350.

Sullivan, P. (2011). *Teaching mathematics: using research-informed strategies*. Camberwell: Australian Council for Educational Research.

Sullivan, P. (2012). The Australian curriculum: mathematics as an opportunity to support teachers and improve student learning. In B. Atweh, M. Goos, R. Jorgensen, & D. Siemon (Eds.), *Engaging the Australian curriculum mathematics: perspectives from the field* (pp. 175–189). Online publication of MERGA http://www.merga.net.au/sites/default/files/editor/books/1/Book.pdf.

Thomson, S., De Bortoli, L., Nicholas, M., Hillman, K., & Buckley, S. (2010). *Challenges for Australian education: results from PISA 2009*. Melbourne: Australian Council for Educational Research.

Thornton, S. (2011). In search of uncertainty. *Curriculum Perspectives, 31*(1), 74–76.

Vincent, J. (2004). The numeracy research and development initiative projects. *Australian Primary Mathematics Classroom, 9*(4), 4–9.

Yates, L., Collins, C., & O'Connor, K. (Eds.) (2011a). *Australia's curriculum dilemmas: state cultures and the big issues*. Carlton: Melbourne University Press.

Yates, L., Collins, C., & O'Connor, K. (2011b). Australian curriculum making. In L. Yates, C. Collins, & K. O'Connor (Eds.), *Australia's curriculum dilemmas: state cultures and the big issues* (pp. 3–22). Carlton: Melbourne University Press.

Freedom of Design: The Multiple Faces of Subtraction in Dutch Primary School Textbooks

Marc van Zanten and Marja van den Heuvel-Panhuizen

Abstract Mathematics textbook series largely determine what teachers teach and consequently, what students learn. In the Netherlands, publishers have hardly any restrictions in developing and publishing textbooks. The Dutch government only prescribes the content to be taught very broadly and does not provide guidelines on how content has to be taught. In this study, the consequences of this freedom of design are investigated by carrying out a textbook analysis on the topic of subtraction up to 100. To examine the relationship between the intended curriculum and the potentially implemented curriculum, we analyzed the mathematical content and performance expectations of two Dutch textbook series. In order to get a closer view of the learning opportunities offered, the learning facilitators of the textbook series were also analyzed. The results of the analysis show that the investigated textbook series vary in their agreement with the intended curriculum with respect to content and performance expectations. The textbook series reflect divergent views on subtraction up to 100 as a mathematical topic. Furthermore, they differ in the incorporated ideas about mathematics education, as shown in the learning facilitators they provide. Consequently, the examined textbook series provide very different opportunities to students to learn subtraction up to 100.

Keywords Textbook analysis · Subtraction up to 100 · Mathematical content · Performance expectations · Learning facilitators · Intended curriculum · Potentially implemented curriculum

M. van Zanten (✉)
Freudenthal Institute for Science and Mathematics Education, Faculty of Science, Utrecht University, Utrecht, The Netherlands
e-mail: M.A.vanZanten@uu.nl

M. van den Heuvel-Panhuizen
Freudenthal Institute of Science and Mathematics Education, Faculty of Science & Faculty of Social and Behavioural Sciences, Utrecht University, Utrecht, The Netherlands

Y. Li, G. Lappan (eds.), *Mathematics Curriculum in School Education*,
Advances in Mathematics Education, DOI 10.1007/978-94-007-7560-2_12,
© Springer Science+Business Media Dordrecht 2014

Introduction

Textbooks are of great importance in mathematics education. They mediate between the intended curriculum (the statutory goals of education) and the implemented curriculum (the actual teaching in classrooms). Therefore, textbooks are referred to as the potentially implemented curriculum (Valverde et al. 2002). Mathematics textbook series largely determine what teachers teach and, consequently, what students learn (Stein and Smith 2010). Although teachers' teaching is not always in alignment with the textbook they use (Weiss et al. 2002), the textbook is for many teachers the decisive source to realize their mathematics teaching. In the Netherlands, textbooks have a determining role in daily teaching practice. In recent studies it was found that 94 % of the teachers indicate that a textbook is the main source of their teaching (Meelissen et al. 2012) and at least 80 % of primary school teachers are following more than 90 % of the textbook content (Hop 2012).

The intended curriculum and what shows up in a textbook series is not always the same. Textbooks are not only influenced by educational goals, but also by other factors such as commercial considerations, concerns about underprepared teachers (Weiss et al. 2002) and the existence of different ideas about the nature of mathematics that should be emphasized, as well as what instructional approaches should be applied (Reys and Reys 2006). Differences may appear during the transition from the intended curriculum to the potentially implemented curriculum, particularly in countries where there is no centralized textbook design.

In the Netherlands, there is no authority which recommends, certifies or approves textbook series before they are put on the market. Thus, publishers have hardly any restrictions in developing and designing textbook series. In order to investigate the consequences of this freedom of design, we examined in two textbook series how the Dutch intended curriculum is 'translated' into content in the form of tasks, performance expectations, and learning facilitators. To unambiguously determine the possible consequences of this freedom of design, we chose an apparently simple and straightforward mathematical topic for our analysis: subtraction up to 100.

Context and Focus of the Study

Textbook Development in the Netherlands

Freedom of educational design in a way follows from the Dutch constitutional 'freedom of education'. Originating from an arrangement that gave parents the right to found schools in accordance with their religious views, freedom of education has been laid down in the Constitution since 1917. Nowadays, it also allows schools to be founded based on particular pedagogical and instructional approaches.

Because of the freedom of education, the government is rather restrained in giving instructional prescriptions. This means that the Ministry of Education prescribes only the 'what', the subject matter content to be taught, and not the 'how', the way in which this content is to be taught. Not having guidelines for the 'how' gives textbook authors the opportunity to bring in their own views and ideas on teaching mathematics.

There is another reason why textbook authors can express their own interpretations. For several years the 'what' in the intended mathematics curriculum was only described very broadly in the Core Goals for primary school (OCW 1993, 2006). It was not until 2009 that the Core Goals were extended with the Reference Standards (OCW 2009), describing in more detail what students should be able to at the end of primary school. However, there is still room for interpretation. For example, the Reference Standards state that students should learn to calculate using a standard method, but they do not prescribe what standard method should be taught.

There are ten textbook series[1] for teaching primary school mathematics on the market in the Netherlands. The newest have all been released between 2009 and 2012. Several have a history of earlier editions, including two that date back to the 1970s and 1980s,[2] when a reform movement in mathematics education was being enacted in the Netherlands. This reform movement was aimed at developing an alternative for the then prevailing mathematics education, which had a very mechanistic character, and in which teaching began at a formal, symbolic level. To give children a better basis for understanding mathematics, Freudenthal and the Wiskobas group developed a new approach to mathematics education in which, among other things, the use of contexts to encourage insight and understanding played a crucial role. This reform, which was later called 'Realistic Mathematics Education' (RME) (e.g., Van den Heuvel-Panhuizen 2001), was largely supported by reform-oriented textbook series.[3] Until recently all Dutch textbooks series were based more or less on this approach to teaching mathematics and they were all labeled by their publishers as 'realistic'. However, due to a debate that has taken place in the Netherlands since 2007 criticizing the RME approach in favor of a return to the traditional, mechanistic approach (Van den Heuvel-Panhuizen 2010) some textbook series have adapted their content (more emphasis on algorithms[4]) and teaching approach (more attention to repetition[5]) in their new editions. Moreover, new textbook series have been released that are presented as an alternative for realistic textbook series, that restore the traditional mechanistic approach with only one calculation method for each

---

[1] 'De Wereld in Getallen', 'Pluspunt', 'Rekenrijk', 'Alles Telt', 'Talrijk', 'Wis en Reken', 'Wizwijs', 'Reken Zeker', 'Rekenwonders' en 'Het Grote Rekenboek'.

[2] 'De Wereld in Getallen' developed from 1975 on, and Pluspunt, the development of which started in 1985.

[3] This underlines the crucial role that mathematics textbooks have in the Netherlands.

[4] A folder released for the textbook series 'De Wereld in Getallen' (4th edition) and 'Pluspunt' (3rd edition) says "Algorithms get more attention and are gradually built up until the classic long division appears." (All translations of folders and examples from textbooks are done by the authors of this chapter.)

[5] A folder released for the textbook series 'De Wereld in Getallen' (4th edition) and 'Pluspunt' (3rd edition) says: "There is much more room for practice, repetition and automatization."

operation and a step-by-step approach with a focus on repetition.[6] Furthermore, a new textbook series which is a Dutch version of a textbook series developed in Singapore[7] was published. Thus, as a result of the debate about mathematics education, the corpus of Dutch mathematics textbooks series has become very diverse.

Subtraction in the Dutch Intended Curriculum

According to the current Dutch Core Goals for primary school mathematics, children have to "learn to use mathematical language and have to gain numeracy and mathematical literacy" (OCW 2006, p. 37). Mathematical language includes arithmetical and mathematical terms and notations. Mathematical literacy and numeracy refer to, among other things, coherent insight in numbers and a repertoire of number facts and calculation methods. Furthermore, the Core Goals indicate that children "learn to ask mathematical questions and formulate and solve mathematical problems [...] and explain the solutions in mathematical language to others" (OCW 2006, p. 39). Concerning the basic operations, the Core Goals mention that students learn to calculate both in smart ways and using standard methods (OCW 2006, p. 43). Specifically concerning subtraction up to 100, the Core Goals state that children "learn to quickly carry out the basic calculations in their heads using whole numbers, at least up to 100, with additions and subtractions up to 20[...] known by heart" (OCW 2006, p. 43).

The Dutch Reference Standards for mathematics (OCW 2009) distinguish three types of knowing: 'knowing-what', 'knowing-how' and 'knowing-why'. With this in mind, the Standards can be considered a description of what Valverde et al. (2002, p. 125) call "expectations of performance" which refers to "what students should be able to do with content." 'Knowing-what' relates to knowledge of number facts and calculation methods. Subtraction up to 100 includes mental calculation, both using standard methods and using properties of numbers and operations. Furthermore, students learn to subtract both by taking away and by determining the difference. 'Knowing-how' refers to making functional use of particular number facts and calculation methods, including using standard methods with insight in real-life situations and converting context situations to bare number problems. 'Knowing-why' refers to understanding. This includes, for example, knowledge about the operations, such as knowing that the commutative property does not apply to subtraction as it does to addition.

---

[6] A folder released for the textbook series 'Reken Zeker' says: "Practice, practice and more practice", "One strategy for all children". A folder released for the materials of 'Het Grote Rekenboek' says: "This textbook series gives an answer to the recent criticism on mathematics education."

[7] A folder released for the textbook series 'Rekenwonders' says: "This is the Dutch edition of an extremely successful and internationally praised Singaporean textbook."

A Mathedidactical Analysis of Subtraction up to 100

Subtraction as a Mathematical Concept

Relationships between whole numbers can be additive and multiplicative. These relationships ensure that one can think of and reason within an interrelated number system instead of having to deal with an innumerous set of individual loose numbers (Kilpatrick et al. 2001). The additive and multiplicative relationships interconnect, combine, and generate numbers.

Addition and subtraction refer to additive number relationships. This implies that the numbers involved reflect a part-whole relationship. Combining parts into a whole can be considered an addition, whereas taking a part from a whole can be considered a subtraction. Furthermore, the operation of subtraction is the inverse of addition: subtraction undoes addition and vice versa (if $a + b = c$, then $c - b = a$).

Although subtraction is mostly associated with removing a part from a whole, it has two phenomenological appearances: taking away and determining the difference (Van den Heuvel-Panhuizen and Treffers 2009). The two manifestations of subtraction reflect two meanings of subtraction. These two different semantic structures can nevertheless be expressed by the same symbolic representation: $c - b = a$. Written as a minuend minus a subtrahend it can literally stand for taking away b from c, but it can also represent comparing c and b to find the difference, for example, by adding on. So, depending on the semantic structure behind the symbolic representation, the answer to a subtraction problem can have two different meanings: a remainder and a difference (Usiskin 2008).

Just like the minus symbol in the symbolic representation $c - b = a$ does not always mean taking away, the operation of subtraction is not exclusively restricted to problems in which the minus symbol appears (Freudenthal 1983). For example, problems with a + symbol in the form of $\cdots + b = c$ and $a + \cdots = c$ can be solved by a subtraction operation. These latter problems are actually subtraction problems in an addition format (Selter et al. 2012).

Calculation Methods for Subtraction up to 100

The methods that can be applied for carrying out subtractions up to 100 can be described from both the number perspective and the operation perspective (Van den Heuvel-Panhuizen 2012; Peltenburg et al. 2012) (see Fig. 1).

From the operation perspective, subtraction problems up to 100 can be solved by (1) taking the subtrahend away from the minuend, (2) adding on from the subtrahend until the minuend is reached, and (3) taking away from the minuend until the subtrahend is reached. These procedures are respectively called: direct subtraction (DS), indirect addition (IA), and indirect subtraction (IS) (De Corte and Verschaffel 1987; Torbeyns et al. 2009).

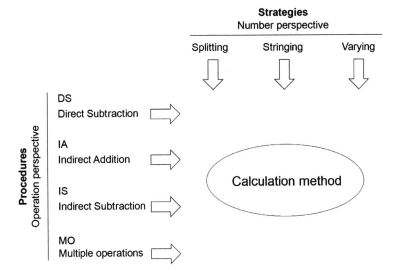

Fig. 1 Two perspectives for describing calculation methods for subtraction up to 100

The number perspective describes how the numbers involved are dealt with. Roughly speaking, there are three strategies: splitting, stringing, and varying. Although researchers do not always use the same wording—for example, other expressions can be found in Klein et al. (1998) and Torbeyns et al. (2009)—there is broad agreement about the general meaning of these strategies. In the splitting strategy, the minuend and the subtrahend are split into tens and ones and then the tens and ones are processed separately. In the stringing strategy, the minuend is kept intact and the subtrahend is decomposed in suitable parts which are subtracted one after another from the minuend. When a varying strategy is applied, the minuend and/or the subtrahend are changed to get an easier subtraction problem. Although in theory all three strategies can be combined with each of the four procedures, not all combinations are common or suitable (see for a more detailed discussion, Peltenburg et al. 2012).

DS can be applied with both splitting (e.g. $67 - 41$ is solved by $60 - 40 = 20$ and $7 - 1 = 6$, followed by $20 + 6 = 26$) and stringing (e.g. $67 - 41$ is solved by $67 - 40 = 27$ and $27 - 1 = 26$). Both the IA and IS procedures can also be combined with splitting and stringing. For example, in the case of $67 - 41$, applying IA with a splitting strategy means calculating $40 + 20 = 60$ and $1 + 6 = 7$, and then $20 + 6 = 26$. Combining IA with a stringing strategy means calculation is $41 + 9 = 50$ and $50 + 10 = 60$ and $60 + 7 = 67$, followed by $9 + 10 + 7 = 26$. Although this latter method can require more steps (when there is a large difference between minuend and subtrahend), the advantage of the stringing strategy is that the problem is not split into two problems. The starting number is kept as a whole.

For subtraction problems that require crossing the ten, applying a DS procedure combined with splitting easily leads to the mistake of reversing the ones (e.g., in the case of $75 - 38$, $70 - 30$ is frequently incorrectly followed by $8 - 5$). This mistake does not happen when DS is combined with stringing. Even more convenient is applying an IA or IS procedure combined with stringing, for example, when there is a small difference between the minuend and the subtrahend, such as in the case of $62 - 58$. Solving these problems by a stringing strategy combined with IA ($58 + 2 = 60$ and $60 + 2 = 62$, followed by $2 + 2 = 4$) or with the less common IS procedure ($62 - 2 = 60$ and $60 - 2 = 58$, followed again by $2 + 2 = 4$) are easier methods that are less sensitive to errors.

Finally, the varying strategy implies multiple operations. Applying this strategy means that a problem is solved through changing it into another problem by making use of properties of numbers and operations. For example, a problem like $77 - 29$ can be solved by first calculating $77 - 30$, followed by $47 + 1 = 48$.

Learning Facilitators for Subtraction up to 100

According to Kilpatrick et al. (2001), mathematical proficiency involves five interwoven and interdependent components, including conceptual understanding; procedural fluency; formulating, representing and solving mathematical problems; having the capacity for reflection and justification; and seeing mathematics as useful and worthwhile. Following this interpretation of mathematical proficiency—which is also reflected in the Dutch intended curriculum—implies that performance expectations should not be restricted to carrying out routine procedures, but also include flexible application of calculation methods, strategy choice, and contextual interpretation of outcomes (Verschaffel et al. 2007).

Applied to the learning of subtraction up to 100, this means that students should be offered opportunities to build a broad mental constitution of subtraction, including the different semantic structures, symbolic representations, and calculation methods of subtraction. Textbooks can contribute to this broad constitution of subtraction by including didactical support in their exposure to subtraction up to 100, such as sufficient contexts and models.

Contexts   First of all, contexts can present students with situations in which subtraction emerges as a mathematical concept in a rather natural manner. The role of contexts is to add meaning to this mathematical concept in order to support the development of understanding. This can happen especially when the contexts that are used are not restricted to word problems in a stereotyped text frame, but instead come in a variety of forms and refer to students' real-life knowledge (De Corte and Verschaffel 1987). Thus, students can become aware that subtraction can apply to all kinds of situations, reflecting different meanings of subtraction. For example, eating cookies and ascertaining how many are left, filling an album with photos and determining how many can still be included, and figuring out how many centimeters a particular person is taller than another person. These contexts which refer to different semantic structures of subtraction can prompt students to use either the DS or the IA or IS procedure.[8] By manipulating the variety in contexts, textbooks can support students' understanding of the different semantic structures of subtraction and learning various calculation methods to solve subtraction problems (see also Fuson 1992). We refer to this use of contexts as 'contexts for supporting understanding', which we distinguish from the use of contexts for just applying subtraction methods. The latter reflects a performance expectation rather than a form of didactical support. To make a clear distinction between these two functions of contexts, in this study we interpreted contexts for supporting understanding as contexts that serve as a source for something new to be learned, such as a new calculation method.

Models Besides contexts, models are also important to support students' learning of subtraction up to 100. This is especially true for carrying out calculation methods and specifically applies to the strategies that are used. A requirement for making this support of models effective is that the models that are used match the strategies used (Van den Heuvel-Panhuizen 2008). Models and strategies should be epistemologically consistent. This means that, for example, the splitting strategy and the stringing strategy each have their own supporting models. The splitting strategy, which is strongly related to the cardinal aspect of numbers, can best be supported by a group model that also reflects the cardinal aspect, like base-10 arithmetic blocks. Likewise, the stringing strategy, which is strongly related to the ordinal aspect of number, finds its supportive model equivalent in line models such as a number line. A line model is also suitable for visualizing and supporting a varying strategy. For example, in the case of $78 - 29$ this means first making a backward jump of 30, followed by a forward jump of 1. As stated earlier, solving $78 - 29$ by a splitting strategy easily leads to the mistake of reversing the ones. A line model would not help to overcome this difficulty, because dealing separately with the 70 and the 20, and the 8 and the 9 on a number line does not make sense. In other words, in teaching calculation methods, strategies and models should match, otherwise models do not have the supportive function they are assumed to have. Consequently, depending on the strategy that is intended, textbooks should give more attention either to group models or to line models.

Symbolic Representations Building a broad mental constitution of subtraction also requires that students are offered various symbolic representations of subtraction. Besides the standard representation $c - b = \cdots$, students should also have opportunities to deal with alternative symbolic representations such as $c - \cdots = a$ and $a + \cdots = c$. These problems make it clear that the operation symbol in a problem can have different meanings (Fuson 1992), and is not per se equivalent to the operation that can be applied to find the solution of that problem. The different symbolic representations reflect the part-whole aspect of additive number relationships

---

[8]This use of contexts should fade away after some time. After all, even though a context can steer a certain calculation method, in term, in the decision what calculation method will be used, not the context, but the numbers involved play a key role.

and the link between addition and subtraction. Furthermore, it supports the understanding that the = symbol does not only mean 'results in' but also 'is equivalent to'. According to Fuson (1992), textbooks do not always pay much attention to the different meanings of the equal and operation symbols.

Research Questions

The purpose of this study is to reveal the consequences of freedom of design for Dutch textbooks as the potentially implemented curriculum for primary school and for the learning opportunities that students are offered. Focusing on subtraction up to 100, we came up with the following research questions:

1. Do Dutch mathematics textbooks reflect the *content* of the Dutch intended curriculum concerning subtraction up to 100?
2. Do Dutch mathematics textbooks reflect the *performance expectations* of the Dutch intended curriculum concerning subtraction up to 100?
3. What *learning facilitators* for learning subtraction up to 100 are incorporated in Dutch mathematics textbooks?

Method

To answer the research questions, a textbook analysis was carried out in which we examined two Dutch textbooks series. The analysis focused on three perspectives: the mathematical content, the performance expectations and the learning facilitators.

Textbook Materials Included in the Analysis

To include the full scope of didactical approaches in the Netherlands in our analysis we examined two recently developed textbook series that, although from the same publisher, are clearly positioned in two contrasting approaches to mathematics education (see section "Textbook Development in the Netherlands"). The first textbook series, called 'Rekenrijk' (RR) (Bokhove et al. 2009), is a RME-oriented textbook series. The name 'Rekenrijk' means both 'kingdom of arithmetic' and 'rich arithmetic'. The second textbook series, called 'Reken Zeker' (RZ) (Terpstra and De Vries 2010), is a new textbook series that is presented as an alternative for realistic textbook series. The name of this textbook series means 'arithmetic with certainty'.

Because subtraction up to one hundred is mainly taught in grade 2, the textbook analysis was carried out with textbook materials from this grade only. We analyzed all materials for grade 2 that are meant for all students. Textbook materials meant for evaluation, and subsequent optional lessons for repetition or enrichment, were not included in our analysis.

Perspective	Category	Subcategory	
Content	Types of problems	Prerequisite knowledge	Decomposing numbers up to 10
			Backwards counting with tens
		Subtraction up to 10	
		Subtraction up to 20	Without bridging the ten
			Bridging the ten
		Subtraction up to 100	Without bridging a ten
			Bridging a ten
	Format of problems	Bare number problems	
		Context problems	
	Semantic structure of problems	Subtraction as taking away	
		Subtraction as determining the difference	
Performance expectations	Knowing subtraction facts	Knowing subtraction facts up to 10	
		Knowing subtraction facts up to 20	
	Carrying out subtractions	Using standard methods	
		Using alternative methods	
	Applying subtractions	Using subtraction methods in context problems	
	Understanding subtraction	Giving explanations	
		Choosing an appropriate method	
Learning facilitators	Degree of exposure	Number and distribution of tasks	
	Structure of exposure	Sequence in types of problems	
		Sequence in level of abstraction	
	Didactical support in exposure	Use of contexts for supporting understanding	
		Use of models	
		Use of various symbolic representations	
		Use of textual instructions	

Fig. 2 Framework for textbook analysis

Framework for Textbook Analysis

To analyze the textbook materials we developed a framework containing the perspectives of content, performance expectations, and learning facilitators (see Fig. 2). Most categories within these three perspectives were initially formulated on the basis of the Dutch intended curriculum for subtraction (see section "Subtraction in the Dutch Intended Curriculum") and our mathedidactical analysis of subtraction up to 100 (see section "A Mathedidactical Analysis of Subtraction up to 100"). Several subcategories were established after an initial round of the analysis, based on what we actually found in the textbook series.

Content

The perspective of content involves problem types, problem formats, and semantic structures of the problems presented in the textbook materials. Regarding the problem types we made a subdivision based on the number domain involved. We incorporated relevant prerequisite knowledge for subtraction: decomposing numbers up to 10 and counting backwards with tens. For the format of the problems we made a distinction between bare number problems and context problems. The semantic structure of problems refers to the two phenomenological appearances of subtraction.

Performance Expectations

Regarding performance expectations, we included knowing subtraction facts, carrying out subtractions, applying subtractions and understanding subtraction. The first two categories correspond to 'knowing-what', the third to 'knowing-how' and the fourth to 'knowing-why', as described in the Dutch Reference Standards. Knowing subtraction facts is subdivided into knowing subtraction facts up to 10 and knowing subtraction facts up to 20. Carrying out subtractions is subdivided into using standard calculation methods (DS combined with splitting or stringing) and alternative calculation methods (e.g., IA combined with stringing or MO combined with a varying strategy). This distinction is in agreement with the Dutch intended curriculum. Applying subtractions refers to using already learnt subtraction facts and calculation methods in context problems. For the category 'understanding' we distinguished 'giving explanations' and 'choosing an appropriate method', based on performance expectations found in the first round of analysis, that go beyond knowing, carrying out and applying subtractions, and unambiguous apply to understanding.

Learning Facilitators

With respect to learning facilitators, we included degree and structure of exposure, based on the importance of the amount and sequencing of content in textbooks (Valverde et al. 2002). We included didactical support in exposure based on our mathedidactical analysis. The subcategory 'use of textual instructions' was added after the first round of the textbook analysis, again based on what we found in the textbook series that can also be considered as supporting learning.

Unit of Analysis

In both textbooks series, the content is organized in lessons meant for one mathematics hour. These lessons are subdivided into sets of tasks. In our study, we use the term 'task' to refer to the smallest unit that requires an answer from a student. Because the amount of tasks vary per set of tasks (see Fig. 3), and content and performance expectations may vary per single task, we used the task as unit of analysis.

Analysis Procedure

First, we identified all subtraction-related tasks. After an initial round of analysis was carried out, we added the following subcategories: 'giving explanations', 'choosing an appropriate method' and 'use of textual instructions'. Then, the first

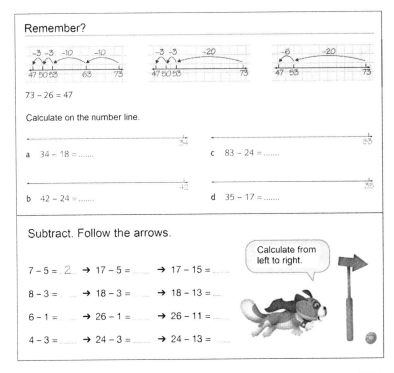

Fig. 3 RR set of 4 tasks (above, RR-book 4b-1, p. 30) and RZ set of 11 tasks (below, RZ-book 4c, p. 26). In the Netherlands, K1, K2, grade 1 and grade 2 are respectively called group 1, 2, 3 and 4

author of this chapter coded all subtraction-related tasks according to the final version of our framework. Each task received several codes. For the content, a code was given for the problem type, the problem format, and the semantic structure of the problem. For the performance expectations, each task was first coded as knowing subtractions facts, carrying out subtractions or applying subtractions. If neither of these sub-categories was applicable, no code was given. Next, for each task, if applicable, a code was given for the category understanding of subtractions. For the learning facilitators, the degree of exposure was determined from the number of tasks. Because the tasks were counted in consecutive lessons, we got an overview of the distribution of the subtraction-related tasks. This also made it possible to reveal the structure of exposure, i.e., the sequence in types of tasks and in level of abstraction. Finally, for each task it was checked which subcategories of didactical support were applicable.

A reliability check of the coding was based on an independent coding by two teacher-trainees. To that end we used a selection of about one tenth of all subtraction-related tasks in which all categories of the framework were included. The two teacher-trainees reached a 93 % agreement. The agreements between each of the teacher-trainees and the first author were respectively 93 % and 95 %.

Results

Content

A substantial difference between the two textbook series for grade 2 is the number of tasks included. The total number of tasks in RR is 5331, whereas RZ has 7051 tasks. However, of these amounts of tasks the proportion of subtraction-related tasks is about the same in both textbooks: RR contains 22 % subtraction tasks (1166 tasks) and RZ 20 % (1440 tasks).

Types of Problems

Both grade 2 textbook series concentrate more on tasks involving subtraction between 20 and 100, and less on tasks involving subtraction up to 10 and up to 20 (see Table 1). Regarding subtraction up to 20, RR offers more tasks that require bridging the ten than RZ. Within subtraction tasks up to 100, the number of tasks that require bridging a ten is larger in RZ, but relatively RR offers more tasks concerning this type of problem (in RR: 378 out of 572 tasks, is about 66 %; and in RZ: 480 out of 1096 tasks, is about 44 %).

The amount of attention to the prerequisite knowledge for these problems differs. Regarding decomposing numbers up to 10, RR has a substantial number of such tasks and RZ almost none. For counting backwards with tens (e.g., 46; 36; 26), RR has very few tasks, while RZ has none. When we checked whether, for example, decomposing numbers up to 10 is already dealt with in grade 1, we found that both textbook series did indeed put more of an emphasis on this prerequisite knowledge in grade 1 than in grade 2. However, the RR booklets for grade 1 have 418 such tasks, while RZ offers only 167 in its first-grade booklets. So, with respect to providing prerequisite knowledge for subtraction up to 100, there is a large difference between the two textbooks series.

Format of Problems

Both textbook series contain far more bare number problems than context problems (see Table 2). However, RR encloses much more context problems than RZ, both relatively and absolutely, even though in RZ the total number of subtraction tasks is larger than in RR.

Semantic Structure of Problems

In both textbook series, only a minority of the tasks reflect a clearly distinguishable semantic structure. Both textbook series address subtraction as taking away, but subtraction as determining the difference is only dealt with in RR (see Table 3).

Table 1 Types of problems in subtraction-related tasks in RR and RZ in grade 2[a]

Types of problems	RR-tasks		RZ-tasks	
	f	%	f	%
Prerequisite knowledge	130	11 %	5	0 %
Decomposing numbers up to 10	107	9 %	4	0 %
Backwards counting with tens	23	2 %	1	0 %
Subtraction up to 10	153	13 %	78	5 %
Subtraction up to 20	311	27 %	261	18 %
Without bridging the ten	79	7 %	135	9 %
Bridging the ten	232	20 %	126	9 %
Subtraction up to 100	572	49 %	1096	76 %
Without bridging a ten	194	17 %	616	43 %
Bridging a ten	378	32 %	480	33 %
Total number of subtraction-related tasks	1166	100 %	1440	100 %

[a]Some percentages do not seem to add up to 100. This is due to rounding off

Table 2 Format of problems in subtraction-related tasks in RR and RZ in grade 2

Format of problems	RR-tasks		RZ-tasks	
	f	%	f	%
Bare number problems	1026	88 %	1415	98 %
Context problems	140	12 %	25	2 %
Total number of subtraction-related tasks	1166	100 %	1440	100 %

Table 3 Semantic structure of problems in subtraction-related tasks in RR and RZ in grade 2

Semantic structure	RR-tasks		RZ-tasks	
	f	%	f	%
Taking away	210	18 %	403	28 %
Determining the difference	53	5 %	0	0 %
Both taking away and determining the difference	28	2 %	0	0 %
No distinguishable semantic structure	874	75 %	1037	72 %
Total number of subtraction-related tasks	1166	100 %	1440	100 %

Performance Expectations

Both textbook series contain tasks that clearly focus on certain performances. RR contains 1081 and RZ contains 800 clearly distinguishable performance expecta-

Table 4 Performance expectations reflected in subtraction-related tasks in RR and RZ in grade 2[a]

Performance expectations	RR-tasks		RZ-tasks	
	f	%	f	%
Knowing subtraction facts	346	32 %	229	29 %
Knowing subtraction facts up to 10	258	24 %	55	7 %
Knowing subtraction facts up to 20	88	8 %	174	22 %
Carrying out subtractions	513	47 %	546	68 %
Using standard methods	413	38 %	546	68 %
Using alternative methods	100	9 %	0	0 %
Applying subtractions	111	10 %	25	3 %
Understanding subtraction	111	10 %	0	0 %
Choosing an appropriate method	74	7 %	0	0 %
Giving explanations	37	3 %	0	0 %
Total number of performance expectations	1081	100 %	800	100 %

[a]In some tasks we distinguished two performance expectations (e.g., carrying out a subtraction and explaining the calculation method). See also Table 1 note

tions (see Table 4). In both textbook series, most emphasis lies on performance expectations related to carrying out subtractions, followed by knowing subtraction facts. RR contains more expectations on applying subtractions than RZ. Expectations regarding understanding were only found in RR.

Knowing Subtraction Facts

RR contains more performance expectations for knowing subtraction facts than RZ. In RR, most emphasis is on knowing subtraction facts up to 10. In RZ, most emphasis is on knowing subtraction facts up to 20.

Carrying out Subtractions

Using Standard Methods   In both textbook series students are expected to learn one standard method for carrying out subtractions up to 20 and up to 100, namely DS combined with stringing. However, the textbook series differ in the way that students are supposed to notate their calculations. In the case of tasks that involve bridging a ten, both textbooks suggest the notation of in-between steps or in-between answers. In RR this is done by writing down under the subtrahend how it is decomposed or by keeping track of the taken-away steps on an empty number line (see Fig. 4).

In RZ, the students have to notate the first in-between answer directly after the = symbol, which is supposed to be followed by the remaining part that has to be

Fig. 4 DS combined with stringing in RR (RR-book 4b-1, p. 57)

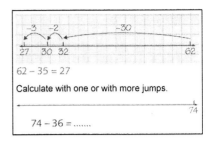

taken away (see Fig. 5). Although the symbolic representation that results in the end is mathematically correct (in fact it describes two equivalent subtractions), notating the calculation in this way implies that students have to perform several in-between steps mentally.

Using Alternative Methods   Only in RR are students expected to learn alternative subtraction methods also, namely, the procedures IA and IS and a varying strategy (see Fig. 6). Although RZ contains missing number tasks (e.g., $28 - \cdots = 23$) which could prompt IS, this textbook series does not otherwise pay attention to this procedure or to any alternative method.

Applying Subtractions

In both textbook series, contexts are used for the application of calculation methods that are presented earlier. RR offers such contexts more than four times as often as RZ (see Table 4). Both textbook series use contexts that refer to real life situations. In RZ all contexts concern taking-away situations, presented by a series of similar sentences. RR offers contexts referring both to taking away and determining the difference, presented in various ways (see Fig. 7).

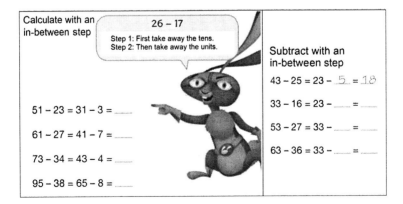

Fig. 5   DS combined with stringing in RZ tasks up to 20 and up to 100 (RZ-book 4c, p. 71; p. 74)

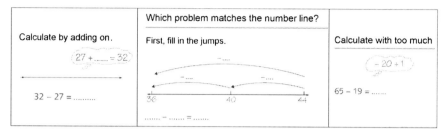

Fig. 6 IA (*left*), IS (*middle*) and a varying strategy (*right*) in RR tasks (RR-book 4b-2, p. 61; 4b-1, p. 2; 4b-2, p. 78)

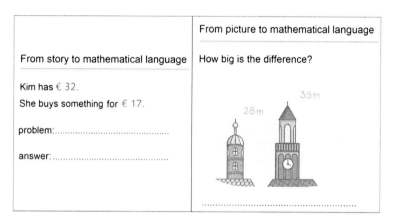

Fig. 7 Context problems in RR reflecting taking away (*left*) and determining the difference (*right*) (RR-book 4b-2, p. 37; p. 78)

Understanding Subtraction

In RR, we found 111 tasks explicitly offering directions or questions to prompt students' reasoning (see Table 4). These tasks include questions for students to explain their thinking (e.g., 'Hoe heb je dit uitgerekend?' [How did you calculate this?]), visualize their calculation method or choose an appropriate calculation method for a given subtraction with certain numbers (see Fig. 8). In RZ, we did not find clearly distinguishable performance expectations regarding understanding.

Learning Facilitators

Degree of Exposure

As mentioned before, RZ provides more subtraction-related tasks (1440) than RR (1166). Figure 9 displays how these tasks are distributed over time (covering the

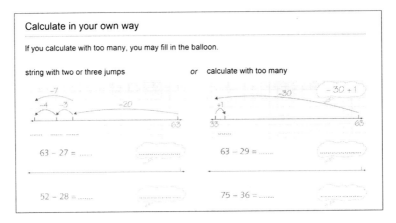

Fig. 8 RR tasks that prompt students to choose an appropriate strategy (RR-book 4b-2, p. 64)

36 weeks of a school year). Both textbooks provide five mathematics lessons each week. The bars in the diagram indicate the number of subtraction tasks per lesson. Every third week in RR and every fourth week in RZ are not filled in (the gray areas). These weeks are meant for evaluation, followed by repetition or enrichment work, and were not included in our analysis.

In RR, the degree of exposure varies: in weeks 1, 7 and 34 relatively more attention is paid to subtraction than in other weeks. In week 1, this concerns the repetition of prerequisite knowledge presented in grade 1, namely number decomposing up to 10. In weeks 7 and 34, a new step in the learning of subtraction is taken. Week 7 is the first time that students encounter subtraction up to 100 and week 34 is the first time that IA is applied to subtraction up to 100. RZ has a fixed pattern of weekly lessons in which 50 to 70 subtraction tasks are offered, with the exception of two periods of three weeks in which almost no attention is paid to subtraction.

Structure of Exposure

Sequence in Types of Problems   Table 5a and 5b show how the main types of tasks are distributed over the school year. The gray shading indicates the number of certain types offered: the darker the gray, the larger the number of tasks. The tasks in both textbook series increase in difficulty during the course of the school year. RZ reaches the most difficult types of tasks earlier than RR.

Sequence in Level of Abstraction   Both textbook series provide bare number problems, context problems (see Table 2) and tasks with supporting models (see Table 6). However, there is a difference regarding the provided context problems. Both textbook series contain context problems to apply earlier learned subtraction methods (which we consider a performance expectation), but only RR also contains contexts for supporting understanding of subtraction (see Table 6).

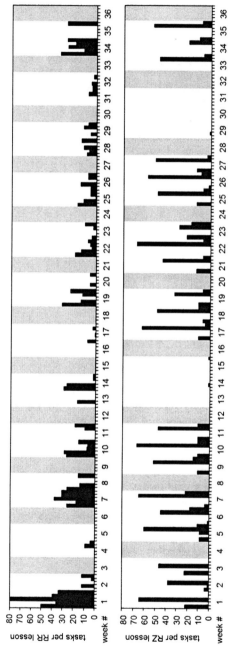

Fig. 9 Distribution of subtraction-related tasks over the school year in RR (*above*) and RZ (*below*)

Table 5a Sequence in types of problems in subtraction-related tasks in RR

Types of problems	Number of RR-tasks								
Subtraction up to 100, bridging a ten					50	54	84	45	145
Subtraction up to 100, without bridging a ten	3		70	49	22	10	31	5	4
Subtraction up to 20	58	173	25	24	23	1	7		
Subtraction up to 10	111	27		12	3				
Prerequisite knowledge	107		21	1	1				
Month #	1	2	3	4	5	6	7	8	9

Table 5b Sequence in types of problems in subtraction-related tasks in RZ

Types of problems	Number of RZ-tasks								
Subtraction up to 100, bridging a ten	4	3	138		25	97	115		98
Subtraction up to 100, without bridging a ten		166	58	1	150	107	88	1	45
Subtraction up to 20	151	57	29	1	13	3	2		5
Subtraction up to 10	39	18	12		9				
Prerequisite knowledge	4					1			
Month #	1	2	3	4	5	6	7	8	9

To get an image of the sequence in level of abstraction, we zoomed in on one particular type of task, namely subtraction up to 20 bridging 10. Figure 10 shows the sequence in level of abstraction of this type of task in the first ten lessons in which it is included. Every black box represents one set of these tasks. Figure 10 illustrates that the sequence in level of abstraction differs between the two textbook series. RR starts with contexts for supporting understanding, followed by tasks with models and then contexts for application. Only in the sixth lesson are bare number tasks provided for the first time. RZ has a different sequence in which bare number tasks and tasks with models are alternated. In contrast with RR, the textbook series RZ begins with bare number tasks. Another difference is that RR provides students with context problems for application several times, while RZ does this only once within the first ten lessons.

Didactical Support in Exposure

Both textbook series offer tasks that provide some form of didactical support. In RR, this is the case in 821 of the total of 1166 subtraction-related tasks (about 70 %) and

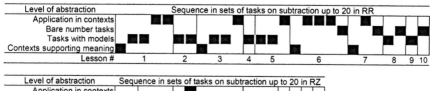

Fig. 10 Sequence in level of abstraction regarding subtraction up to 20 bridging 10 in RR (*above*) and RZ (*below*)

Table 6 Types of didactical support in RR and RZ in grade 2[a]

Didactical support	RR-tasks		RZ-tasks	
	f	%	f	%
Use of contexts for supporting understanding	29	4 %	0	0 %
Use of models	423	52 %	108	39 %
Arithmetic rack	102	12 %	0	0 %
Arithmetic blocks	0	0 %	98	35 %
Number line (structured)	11	1 %	10	4 %
Number line (empty)	305	37 %	0	0 %
Number strip	5	1 %	0	0 %
Use of textual instructions	369	45 %	172	61 %
Instructions how to solve the task	186	23 %	108	39 %
Choices offered for solving the task	146	18 %	64	23 %
Reflection-eliciting questions	37	5 %	0	0 %
Total number of tasks with didactical support	821	100 %	280	100 %

[a]See Table 1 note

in RZ, this is the case in 280 of the 1440 subtraction-related tasks (about 19 %) (see Table 6).[9]

Use of Contexts for Supporting Understanding   Although both textbook series contain context problems, only in RR do some of the provided contexts serve as a source for new topics to be learned, thus supporting understanding of subtraction (see Table 6). An example is shown in Fig. 11, in which subtracting as adding on (IA) is introduced and related to taking away (DS).

---

[9]The use of various symbolic representations of subtractions was not included in this count, because by definition every bare number task has some form of symbolic representation.

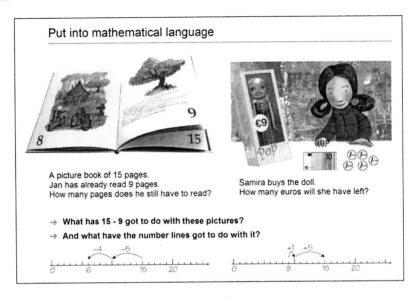

Fig. 11 Relating IA and DS in RR (RR-book 4a, p. 24)

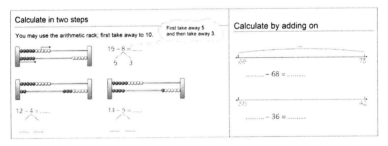

Fig. 12 RR use of the arithmetic rack for subtraction up to 20 (*left*) and the empty number line for subtraction up to 100 (*right*) (RR-book 4a-1, p. 58; 4b-2, p. 78)

Use of Models RR uses the arithmetic rack as the dominant model for subtraction up to 20 and the empty number line for subtraction up to 100 (see Fig. 12). RR uses the empty number line for all calculation methods: stringing combined with DS; IS; IA; and varying (see Fig. 4, Fig. 6, and Fig. 8). In the case of IA, the visualization on the empty number line does not always match the symbolic representation (in 18 of 48 tasks), as can be seen in Fig. 12 (right). In this example, the students are invited to apply an adding on procedure (IA), but the number line (that refers to $73 - \cdots = 68$ or to $68 + \cdots = 73$) and the symbolic representation $\cdots - 68 = \cdots$ do not match to this procedure nor to each other.

RZ uses (pictures of) base-10 arithmetic blocks as the only model for subtraction up to 100 (see Fig. 13). For subtraction up to 20, the structured number line is used also. Although base-10 blocks and the stringing strategy are not epistemologically consistent, RZ uses base-10 blocks as its only supporting model to provide DS combined with stringing, which is the only calculation method that is taught in this textbook series (see section "Carrying out Subtractions"). Furthermore, RZ does not always use this model consistently; sometimes the base-10 structure is not used for subtracting tens (in 11 of 43 tasks, see Fig. 13 [middle]) while at other times it is (in 32 of 43 tasks, see Fig. 13 [right]).

Use of Various Symbolic Representations   Besides the standard representation $c - b = \cdots$, both textbook series present little alternative symbolic representations of subtractions. Only RR contains subtraction-related tasks in an addition format (12 of 1166 tasks), to relate subtraction and addition and to elicit subtraction as adding on (IA) (see Fig. 6 [left]). On the other hand, missing number subtractions (e.g., $19 = 20 - \cdots$ and $26 - \cdots = 21$) are only dealt with in RZ (44 of 1440 tasks).

Use of Textual Instructions   Both textbooks provide students with textual instructions on how to solve subtractions and offer choices for solving tasks. Reflecting-eliciting questions were only found in RR (see Table 6).

Textual instructions on how to solve subtractions that were found are instructions to use a specific calculation method or how to carry out a specific calculation method. In RR, most of these instructions (120 out of 186) concern subtractions up to 20, and include first subtracting down to 10 and then subtracting the rest (e.g., "First take away to ten", see Fig. 12 [left]). In RZ, most of the instructions (35 out of 108) concern subtractions up to 100, and are about first subtracting the tens and then subtracting the units (e.g. "Step 1: First take away the tens. Step 2: Then take away the units", see Fig. 5 [left]).

Both textbook series offer students choices on how to perform certain tasks. A choice that both offer is whether or not to use a model for solving the task (in RR 53 out of 146 choices offered and in RZ 21 out of 64). The other choices that are offered are rather different in nature. In RR this involves choosing an appropriate calculation method: for instance, to use either a stringing or a varying strategy (see Fig. 8) or to take more or less jumps when using the stringing strategy (in the remaining 93 out of 146 choices offered). In RZ, the remaining 43 (out of 64) choices concern whether or not to use scrap paper.

Questions that prompt students to think and reason about tasks were only found in RR. Examples are: "How did you calculate this?"; and "What has $15 - 9$ got to do with these pictures?" and "And what have the number lines got to do with them?" (see Fig. 11).

Concluding Remarks

Our analysis revealed that freedom of design can result in varying agreement of the potential implemented curriculum with the intended curriculum. In our framework, seven categories—covering content and performance expectations—are related to the intended curriculum. With respect to subtraction up to 100, in three of these

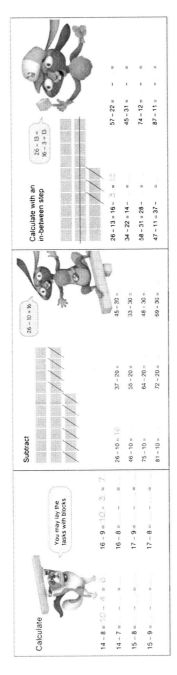

Fig. 13 RZ use of base-10 blocks for subtraction up to 20 (*left*) and up to 100 (*middle* and *right*) (RZ-book 4a, p. 9; 4c p. 25; p. 39)

		Intended curriculum	RR	RZ
Content	Types of problems	Subtraction up to 100	Both RR and RZ offer subtraction up to 100.	
	Format of problems	Context situations	Both RR and RZ offer context situations and bare number problems.	
		Bare number problems	RR offers more context problems than RZ.	RZ offers more bare number problems than RR.
	Semantic structure of problems	Subtraction as taking away	Both RR and RZ present subtraction as taking away.	
		Subtraction as determining the difference	RR presents subtraction as determining the difference.	RZ does not present subtraction as determining the difference.
Performance expectations	Knowing subtraction facts	Knowing subtractions up to 20 by heart	RR puts most emphasis on knowing subtraction facts up to 10.	RZ puts most emphasis on knowing subtraction facts up to 20.
	Carrying out subtractions	Subtraction by standard methods	Both RR and RZ expect students to learn one standard method, namely stringing combined with DS.	
		Subtraction in smart ways	RR expects students to learn IA, IS, and varying strategies.	RZ does not expect students to learn alternative calculation methods.
	Applying subtractions	Using standard methods with insight in real-life situations	Both RR and RZ expect students to apply subtraction methods in context problems.	
			RR offers context situations with various forms and both semantic structures.	RZ offers context situations with one text form and one semantic structure.
	Understanding of subtraction	Understanding of the operation subtraction	RR expects students to explain their thinking, visualize their calculation method and choose appropriate calculation methods.	RZ does not offer clearly distinguishable performance expectations regarding understanding.

Fig. 14 Agreement of RR and RZ with the Dutch intended curriculum regarding subtraction up to 100

categories (types of problems, format of problems and knowing subtraction facts), the textbook series RR and RZ are comparable in their agreement with the Dutch intended curriculum. However, in the other four categories, the fit of RR to the intended curriculum is closer than that of RZ. Figure 14 summarizes our findings.

Regarding the content (research question 1), both textbooks series present subtraction problems up to 100, and both textbook series offer bare number problems as well as context problems. RZ offers more bare number tasks and RR offers more context problems. In deviation of the intended curriculum, RZ only addresses one semantic structure of subtraction. In contrast, RR deals with both.

The degree in which the two textbook series reflect the performance expectations of the intended curriculum (research question 2) also differs. RR offers more tasks on knowing subtractions in total, but RZ presents more tasks on knowing subtractions up to 20. In both textbooks, students are expected to learn the standard calculation method of DS combined with stringing. Only RR expects students to learn alternative calculations methods as well. The way that RZ notates in-between answers can easily lead to incorrect notations (e.g. $12 - 3 = 12 - 2 = 10 - 1 = 9$ instead of $12 - 3 = 10 - 1 = 9$), especially when students interpret the = symbol

		RR	RZ
Degree of exposure	Number of tasks	In both RR and RZ about 20% of all tasks in grade 2 addresses subtraction up to 100.	
		In absolute numbers, RR offers considerably less subtraction-related tasks.	In absolute numbers, RZ offers considerably more subtraction-related tasks.
Structure of exposure	Sequence in types of problems	Both RR and RZ have a structure of increasing difficulty in the course of the school year.	
		RR spends more tasks on prerequisite knowledge.	RZ reaches more difficult types of tasks at an earlier stage.
	Sequence in level of abstraction	RR uses contexts for supporting understanding as the first step in the sequence of level of abstraction.	RZ uses bare number tasks as the first step in the sequence of level of abstraction.
Didactical support in exposure	On the whole	RR offers considerably more tasks with didactical support.	RZ offers considerably less tasks with didactical support.
	Use of contexts for supporting understanding	RR uses contexts for supporting understanding of subtraction.	RZ does not use contexts for supporting understanding of subtraction.
	Use of models	RR uses the empty number line, both for stringing and for alternative methods. In some tasks, the visualization on the empty number line does not match the symbolic representation.	RZ uses (pictures of) base-10 blocks for stringing, the only calculation method it offers, even though this model is not epistemologically consistent with this strategy.
	Use of various symbolic representations	Both RR and RZ provide the standard symbolic representation c-b=...	
		RR provides subtractions in addition format ($a+...=c$).	RZ provides missing number subtractions ($a=c-...$ and $c-...=a$).
	Use of textual instructions	Both RR and RZ provide textual instructions on how to carry out a specific calculation method.	
		RR uses textual instructions for choosing an appropriate calculation method and eliciting reflection.	RZ uses textual instructions for choosing whether or not to use scrap paper.

Fig. 15 Learning facilitators for subtraction up to 100 in RR and RZ

only as 'results in' and not as an equivalence symbol. Both textbook series employ context problems for application of subtraction, but only in RR is this done by presenting various forms of contexts and by including both semantic structures of subtraction. Finally, only RR contains explicit performance expectations regarding understanding of subtraction.

The two textbook series also differ in the learning facilitators they offer students (research question 3). Figure 15 summarizes our findings on this research question.

RZ offers a larger amount of subtraction-related tasks and reaches more difficult types of tasks at an earlier stage. However, RR spends more tasks on prerequisite knowledge and uses contexts for supporting understanding as the first step in the sequence of level of abstraction, resulting in offering a solid base for the learning of subtraction up to 100. Furthermore, RR offers almost three times as much didactical support compared to RZ. This includes forms of didactical support that are absent in RZ, namely contexts for supporting understanding, textual instructions for choosing appropriate calculation methods, and reflection-eliciting questions. Another shortcoming of RZ is that it uses base-10 arithmetic blocks for supporting stringing, which means that model and strategy are not epistemologically consistent.

To a certain degree, a similar inadequacy applies also to RR when using a particular symbolic representation of subtraction which does not match the presentation on the empty number line. Both examined textbook series do only provide very few tasks involving various symbolic representations of subtraction. The textbook series differ with respect to the textual instructions they provide. RZ offers instructions on how to proceed, whereas RR provides instructions that prompt students to reflect.

Our analysis made it clear that freedom of design can result in a potential curriculum that may deviate from the intended curriculum. The two examined textbook series differ noticeably in their view on subtraction up to 100 as a mathematical topic. RZ reflects a limited view including one semantic structure, one meaning, and one calculation method. RR supports students' development of a broad mental constitution of subtraction, including both meanings and both semantic structures, as well as various calculation methods. Furthermore, our results show that the incorporated ideas of the two textbook series about mathematics education (RR is presented as a RME-oriented textbook series and RZ as an alternative to this approach) actually result in different learning opportunities for students. It really makes a difference for students whether or not they are offered a broad mental constitution of subtraction, whether or not they are given reflection-eliciting questions, and whether or not there is a match between models and symbolic representations or calculation methods.

Of course, what is in the textbook is not necessarily similar to what is taught in class. However, following Valverde et al. (2002, p. 125), we think that "how content is presented in textbooks (with what expectations for performance) is how it will likely be taught in the classroom." Therefore, textbook analysis can provide an inside view in how a subject might be taught. As such, textbook analyses are a crucial tool that can preserve us from having teaching practices not in agreement with the intended curriculum and that do not offer students the desired learning opportunities. How necessary such analyses are was shown when a textbook analysis disclosed that higher-order problem solving is lacking in Dutch mathematics textbooks (Kolovou et al. 2009), even though it is part of the Dutch intended curriculum.

In the present textbook analysis on the topic of subtraction it was again revealed that the textbook matters. The examined textbook series contain different learning opportunities. Disclosing these opportunities is as important as examining the efficacy of textbooks. After all, when students cannot encounter particular content along with sufficient learning facilitators, we cannot expect them to learn this content.

References

Bokhove, J., Borghouts, C., Kuipers, K., & Veltman, A. (2009). *Rekenrijk*. Groningen: Noordhoff Uitgevers (student books for grade 2).

De Corte, E., & Verschaffel, L. (1987). The effect of semantic structure on first graders' strategies for solving addition and subtraction word problems. *Journal for Research in Mathematics Education, 18*(5), 363–380.

Freudenthal, H. (1983). *Didactical phenomenology of mathematical structures*. Dordrecht: Reidel Publishing Company.

Fuson, K. C. (1992). Research on whole number addition and subtraction. In D. A. Grouws (Ed.), *Handbook of research on mathematics teaching and learning* (pp. 243–275). New York: MacMillan.

Hop, M. (Ed.) (2012). *Balans van het reken-wiskundeonderwijs halverwege de basisschool 5. Periodieke Peiling van het Onderwijsniveau (PPON)5. [Balance of mathematics education halfway primary school. Periodic assessment of the education level (PPON) 5].* Arnhem: Cito.

Kilpatrick, J., Swafford, J., & Findell, B. (2001). *Adding it up. Helping children learn mathematics.* Washington: National Academy Press.

Klein, A. S., Beishuizen, M., & Treffers, A. (1998). The empty number line in Dutch second grades: realistic versus gradual program design. *Journal for Research in Mathematics Education, 29,* 443–464.

Kolovou, A., Van den Heuvel-Panhuizen, M., & Bakker, A. (2009). Non-routine problem solving tasks in primary school mathematics textbooks—a needle in a haystack. *Mediterranean Journal for Research in Mathematics Education, 8*(2), 31–68.

Meelissen, M. R. M., Netten, A., Drent, M., Punter, R. A., Droop, M., & Verhoeven, L. (2012). *PIRLS en TIMSS 2011. Trends in leerprestaties in Lezen, Rekenen en Natuuronderwijs [PIRLS and TIMSS 2011. Trends in achievement in reading, mathematics and science].* Nijmegen/Enschede: Radboud University/Twente University.

OCW (1993). *Kerndoelen basisonderwijs. [Core goals primary education].* OCW: Den Haag.

OCW (2006). *Kerndoelen basisonderwijs. [Core goals primary education].* OCW: Den Haag.

OCW (2009). *Referentiekader taal en rekenen. [Reference standards language and mathematics].* OCW: Den Haag.

Peltenburg, M., Van den Heuvel-Panhuizen, M., & Robitzsch, A. (2012). Special education students' use of indirect addition in solving subtraction problems up to 100—a proof of the didactical potential of an ignored procedure. *Educational Studies in Mathematics, 79,* 351–369.

Reys, B. J., & Reys, R. E. (2006). The development and publication of elementary mathematics textbooks: let the buyer beware! *Phi Delta Kappan, 87*(5), 377–383.

Selter, C., Prediger, S., Nührenbörger, M., & Hußmann, S. (2012). Taking away and determining the difference—a longitudinal perspective on two models of subtraction and the inverse relation to addition. *Educational Studies in Mathematics, 79,* 389–408.

Stein, M. K., & Smith, M. S. (2010). The influence of curriculum on students' learning. In B. J. Reys, R. E. Reys, & R. Rubenstein (Eds.), *Mathematics curriculum. Issues, trends, and future directions* (pp. 351–362). Reston: National Council of Teachers of Mathematics.

Terpstra, P., & De Vries, A. (2010). *Reken Zeker.* Groningen: Noordhoff Uitgevers (student books for grade 2).

Torbeyns, J., De Smedt, B., Stassens, N., Ghesquière, P., & Verschaffel, L. (2009). Solving subtraction problems by means of indirect addition. *Mathematical Thinking and Learning, 11,* 79–91.

Usiskin, Z. (2008). The arithmetic curriculum and the real world. In D. de Bock, B. Dahl Søndergaard, B. Gómez Alfonso, & C. Litwin Cheng (Eds.), *Proceedings of ICME-11-topic study group 10: research and development in the teaching and learning of number systems and arithmetic* (pp. 11–16). Retrieved from https://lirias.kuleuven.be/bitstream/123456789/224765/1/879.pdf.

Valverde, G. A., Bianchi, L. J., Wolfe, R. G., Schmidt, W. H., & Houang, R. T. (2002). *According to the book. Using TIMSS to investigate the translation of policy into practice through the world of textbooks.* Dordrecht: Kluwer Academic Publishers.

Van den Heuvel-Panhuizen, M. (2001). Realistic mathematics education in the Netherlands. In J. Anghileri (Ed.), *Principles and practices in arithmetic teaching: innovative approaches for the primary classroom* (pp. 49–63). Buckingham: Open University Press.

Van den Heuvel-Panhuizen, M. (2008). Learning from "Didactikids": an impetus for revisiting the empty number line. *Mathematics Education Research Journal, 20*(3), 6–31.

Van den Heuvel-Panhuizen, M. (2010). Reform under attack—forty years of working on better mathematics education thrown on the scrapheap? No way! In L. Sparrow, B. Kissane, & C. Hurst (Eds.), *Shaping the future of mathematics education: proceedings of the 33rd annual conference of the mathematics education research group of Australasia* (pp. 1–25). Fremantle: MERGA.

Van den Heuvel-Panhuizen, M. (2012). *Mathematics education research should come more often with breaking news*. Lecture on the occasion of receiving the Svend Pedersen Lecture Award 2011. Retrieved from http://www.mnd.su.se/polopoly_fs/1.75423.1328790378!/menu/standard/file/svendPedersenLecture_120205.pdf.

Van den Heuvel-Panhuizen, M., & Treffers, A. (2009). Mathe-didactical reflections on young children's understanding and application of subtraction-related principles. *Mathematical Thinking and Learning, 11*(1–2), 102–112.

Verschaffel, L., Greer, B., & De Corte, E. (2007). Whole number concepts and operations. In F. K. Lester (Ed.), *Second handbook of research on mathematics teaching and learning*. Charlotte: NCTM.

Weiss, I. R., Knapp, M. S., Hollweg, K. S., & Burill, G. (Eds.) (2002). *Investigating the influence of standards*. Washington: National Academic Press.

Changes to the Korean Mathematics Curriculum: Expectations and Challenges

JeongSuk Pang

Abstract This chapter provides an overview of mathematics curriculum development and explores the key features of the recent curricular changes in Korea. As such, it first presents a brief history of Korean mathematics curriculum development and highlights the key characteristics. This chapter then elaborates on the most recent curricular changes and trends in terms of why teach mathematics, what to teach in mathematics, how to teach mathematics, and when to teach mathematics. The underlying factors behind such changes and trends are reflected upon. This chapter closes with a discussion of the expectations and significant challenges pertaining to the recent curriculum development and implementation in the Korean context.

Keywords Mathematics curriculum · Curricular change · Mathematics education in Korea · Objective of teaching mathematics · Instructional methods · Curriculum implementation

Introduction

Korean students have demonstrated their superior mathematics achievement in recent international comparative studies such as TIMSS and PISA (e.g., Mullis et al. 2012; Organisation for Economic Co-operation and Development 2010). Many factors may account for the high achievement, such as well-developed curricular materials, high-quality teachers, an exam-driven culture, and parental support of education.

Mathematics curriculum plays a crucial role in students' learning mainly because it describes what is to be taught in school mathematics. This is especially true for countries like Korea where a national curriculum is developed and textbooks must be aligned with the curriculum in order to be approved by the government (Pang 2008). As most Korean teachers use mathematics textbooks as their main instructional resources, it is important to develop high-quality textbooks on the basis of a sound national mathematics curriculum.

J.S. Pang (✉)
Korea National University of Education, Cheongwon, Korea
e-mail: jeongsuk@knue.ac.kr

Y. Li, G. Lappan (eds.), *Mathematics Curriculum in School Education*,
Advances in Mathematics Education, DOI 10.1007/978-94-007-7560-2_13,
© Springer Science+Business Media Dordrecht 2014

The mathematics curriculum in Korea has been altered by various driving forces over time. Such adjustments, similar to those in other countries, reveal the ever-changing values of teaching and learning of school mathematics (Liu and Li 2010; National Council of Teachers of Mathematics [NCTM] 2000; Shin and Han 2010). For instance, practicing routine mathematical skills for optimal performance was the focus of an earlier curriculum, but this became problematic, because it is not as meaningful for students. More recently, the mathematics curriculum has emphasized students' sense-making processes over achieving skill automaticity.

The purpose of this chapter is to introduce mathematics curriculum development in Korea with an emphasis on recent curricular changes for grades 1 to 12. This chapter first presents a brief history of Korean mathematics curriculum development and changes, highlighting the key characteristics at each iteration. It then elaborates the most recent curricular changes and underlying factors. This chapter probes some characteristics of Korean mathematics curriculum development and discusses expectations as well as several challenges with regard to curriculum development and implementation.

A Brief History of the Korean Mathematics Curriculum

This section provides a brief but concise review of the Korean mathematics curriculum from the first teaching syllabus in 1946 to the most recent revisions in 2011. Table 1 summarizes the history of Korean mathematics curriculum (Ministry of Education [MOE] 1997; Ministry of Education and Human Resources Development [MEHRD] 2007; Ministry of Education, Science, and Technology [MEST] 2011; Park 1991). As seen in Table 1, Korean mathematics curricula have undergone many alterations and modifications, sometimes influenced by educational movements in other countries such as the United States of America [USA].

Each curriculum reveals characteristics which were valued in teaching and learning mathematics at that time. For instance, the first mathematics curriculum in the 1950s was centered on everyday life situations. Mathematical content needed to be directly related to real-life problems so that students were expected to calculate everyday problems associated with purchasing items. The second mathematics curriculum in the 1960s emphasized the structure of mathematics over the previous practical usefulness. The third curriculum in the 1970s continued to promote the new mathematics emphasis on a well-structured approach based on the abstract and deductive nature of mathematics. The fourth curriculum in the early 1980s prioritized the acquisition of accurate knowledge and skills over understanding mathematical logic. Both the fifth mathematics curriculum in the late 1980s and the sixth mathematics curriculum in the early 1990s added problem-solving ability to the acquisition of basic mathematical concepts and skills as the centerpiece of school mathematics. The name of the subject was changed from *arithmetic* to *mathematics* in this period, suggesting that learning mathematics should go beyond practicing basic numerical skills, toward developing logical thinking in multiple content areas and application ability.

Table 1 Brief history of Korean mathematics curriculum with key characteristics

Curriculum	Announcement	Characteristics
Teaching syllabus	1946	• Syllabus listed the main topics to be taught
		• Difficult and excessive content for students
1st	1955	• Subject matter-centered curriculum
		• Mathematics in everyday life emphasized
2nd	1963	• Experience-centered curriculum
		• The system of mathematics emphasized
3rd	1973	• Discipline-centered curriculum
		• Influenced from the 'new math movement' in the USA
4th	1981	• Nature and structure of mathematics emphasized
		• Influenced from the 'back to basics movement' in the USA
		• Mathematics content reduced
		• The importance of problem solving highlighted
5th	1987	• Problem solving-centered curriculum
		• Mathematics content further reduced
		• Rigid use of symbols de-emphasized
6th	1992	• Preparation for information society
		• Mathematics content still further reduced
		• Multiple assessment methods emphasized
7th	1997	• Learner-centered curriculum with level-based differentiated structure
		• Mathematics content rationalized
		• Students' activity, interest, and confidence emphasized
		• Multiple learning tools, instructional methods, and assessment methods emphasized
revision	2007	• Mathematics content further rationalized
		• Mathematical thinking and communication ability emphasized
		• Various values of mathematics and affective aspects of learning mathematics emphasized
revision	(2009) 2011[a]	• Creativity-centered curriculum
		• Students' character-building emphasized
		• Mathematical process strengthened
		• Mathematics content reduced
		• The structure of grade bands suggested

[a]The revision in 2009 was related mainly to the management of the overall curriculum. Subject curriculum, including mathematics curriculum, was announced only in 2011

The seventh mathematics curriculum in the late 1990s was substantially different from previous curricula in that it had a level-based differentiated structure (MOE 1997). The national curriculum consisted of two parts: (a) common core (or compulsory) curriculum for all students from the first to the tenth grade with a total of 20 different levels, and (b) selective curriculum with different topics and difficulty levels in the last two years of high school (e.g., practical mathematics, probability and statistics, or differentiation and integration). This change was driven by the increased concern regarding substantial differences between students in terms of mathematical ability, and the desire to better cater to individual learning needs (MOE 1998). Lew (1999) regarded the seventh mathematics curriculum as ground-breaking compared to previous curricula.

The seventh curriculum was progressively revised in 2007, 2009, and 2011. Note that the mathematics curriculum was changed only in 2007 and 2011, because the revision in 2009 dealt with the overall direction and management of all national curricula across subject matters. For instance, in order to raise the creative talent required in a future society, the 2009 revision called for re-examining the effectiveness of learning in school, nurturing students' character, reinforcing students' core competencies, and supporting schools' diversity (MEST 2009). That is to say, the mathematics curriculum, like other subject-matter curricula, was revised in 2011 so as to be aligned with the national curriculum announced in 2009. For convenience, the term the '2011 revision' or '2011 curriculum' is used for this chapter. As these recently revised curricula are important to understand the trends in the development of Korean mathematics curriculum, a detailed description and analysis will follow in next section.

Recent Changes and Trends in the Korean Mathematics Curriculum

This section elaborates on the recently developed mathematics curricula. One of the big issues in revising a mathematics curriculum is selection and sequence of content. However, the focus here is not to list key changes in each mathematics content area across grade levels (see Lew 2008 for the seventh curriculum; see also Shin and Han 2010 for the 2007 curriculum; see also Lew et al. 2012 for the 2011 middle school curriculum), but to analyze curricular changes and their underlying factors. For this purpose, this section consists of four sub-sections dealing with significant changes and underlying motives in terms of objectives, content, instructional methods, and sequence across grades of school mathematics.

Changes in Why Teach (Objectives)

There are three main objectives of teaching mathematics in Korea, which have been consistently emphasized over curricular changes:

(a) the acquisition of mathematical knowledge and skills,
(b) the enhancement of mathematical thinking ability, and
(c) the cultivation of problem-solving ability and attitude (MOE 1998; MEST 2008).

In the 2007 and 2011 revisions, the following four objectives were added to these main objectives.

First, **mathematical communication** ability was added through the 2007 revision. To be clear, mathematics communication ability was mentioned in the seventh curriculum as an ability to foster students' mathematical power, but it was not explicitly emphasized as one of the main objectives of teaching mathematics (MOE 1998). Although mathematical communication ability is necessary to deepen one's mathematical thinking and to discuss one's ideas with others, it is often reported that Korean students were silent and passive in mathematics lessons in comparison to their USA and Australian counterparts (Clark and Hua 2008). The increased concern about the lack of mathematical communication in the classroom led its promotion as one of the main objectives of teaching mathematics.

Second, students' **positive attitude** toward mathematics was highlighted through the 2007 revision. Korean mathematics curricula have focused more on the cognitive aspects than the affective aspects of teaching mathematics. In fact, affective dimensions such as interests in and concerns of mathematics were addressed only from the fifth curriculum in the late 1980s (MEST 2008). However, fostering students' attitudes toward mathematics was only secondary to developing their cognitive abilities. This tendency in school mathematics went through considerable condemnation with the release of data from the *Trends in International Mathematics and Science Study* [TIMSS] (e.g., Kim et al. 2008; Mullis et al. 2008; Park et al. 2004) and the *Programme for International Student Assessment* [PISA] (e.g., OECD 2007, 2010). These international comparative studies showed that Korean students consistently achieved high scores not only in mathematical skills and procedures but also in problem-solving, but had very low interest and confidence in mathematics. Such negative attitudes toward mathematics have been problematic. This led curriculum developers to highlight that students need to appreciate the value of mathematics and develop positive dispositions toward mathematics as articulated in the objectives of school mathematics (MEST 2008).

Third, **mathematical creativity** is emphasized in the 2011 revision. This is a natural consequence because the term creativity has been highlighted as a way to secure national competitiveness, resulting in the slogan of the national curriculum in 2009 (MEST 2009). To be clear, *creativity* per se has been mentioned since the seventh mathematics curriculum (MOE 1997) but it was not made explicit in the objectives of school mathematics until 2011. Creativity, which was emphasized mainly for gifted students, is now reconsidered for all students. Differentiating it from general creativity, the construct of mathematical creativity has been studied (Kim et al. 2009). Problem-solving, communication, and reasoning are described as three key sub-abilities, necessary for fostering students' mathematical creativity (MEST 2011).

Finally, students' **character-building** through school mathematics has been added in the 2011 revision. This is also a natural consequence of the 2009 revision of national curriculum intended to strengthen education by building students' character. In fact, the Presidential Advisory Council on Education, Science, & Technology urged us to raise global, creative, and cultured person and emphasized not only creativity but also character as the key constructs of curriculum revision (Hwang et al. 2011). Given the characteristics of the discipline of mathematics, the main discussions in revising the curriculum were related to the nature of mathematical creativity rather than students' character-building (Kim et al. 2009). However, a 'creative experience-activity' which has been introduced since 2009 for building students' character on the basis of sharing and caring was not enough. Such an activity was regarded as subordinate and incidental to subject matter which occupies most of the school learning. If we meant to raise students' character through school education, such expectation needs to be explicitly included in all subjects including mathematics (Jeong and Kang 2011). In addition, as school violence has recently become a serious social issue in Korea, the curricular emphasis on students' character-building is expected to be addressed in every subject. The nature of character which can be raised through school mathematics has been studied. For instance, Kwon and her colleagues (2011) suggested honesty, responsibility, consideration, courage, possession, patience, fairness, cooperation, and harmony.

Changes in What to Teach (Content)

Revisions of mathematics curriculum documents are frequently related to changing the content. As seen in Table 1, a consistent and noticeable direction of revisions to Korean mathematics curricula since the fourth curriculum has been to reduce learning content. However, actual changes in the curriculum were related to shifting grade levels according to the difficulty of the content to be taught rather than to reducing the total amount of content per se. For instance, in the seventh curriculum as much as 30 % reduction of mathematical content was originally intended to allow for optimization of student learning, but the mathematics curriculum developers were not able to comply with the general policy (Paik 2004). To make matters worse, optional topics provided for mathematically advanced students were taught to all students because such topics appeared in the textbooks and it has been a common belief that all content in the textbooks should be covered in mathematics lessons (Pang 2002). Consequently, it is reported that the amount of content to be mastered in school mathematics has always been perceived as excessive, resulting in a heavy studying-load for students and a high teaching-load for teachers (Hwang et al. 2011; MEST 2008).

Given this, the 2007 revision presented only the core content which would be taught to all students, so the amount of mathematics content was reduced by omitting any optional topics for either advanced or underachieving students (MEHRD 2007). The teacher was instead expected to adapt the content in the curriculum to meet with various levels of students' mathematical knowledge and understanding, their varying future study plans, and the particular conditions of the given school contexts (MEST 2008).

Two additionally compelling factors led to the reduction of the learning content in the recent mathematics curriculum. First, as the school week has been reduced from 6 days to 5 days, a significant reduction of learning content was necessary. Second, the total amount of mathematical content needed to be reduced in order to enhance students' mathematical thinking, communication skills, and creativity. It has been reported that teachers typically rush to cover all topics in the limited time available (Kim et al. 2009). Teaching fewer mathematics topics in greater depth, instead of teaching more topics in a cursory manner, is preferred.

Given this, as much as 20 % of the learning content was reduced in the 2011 revision. There have been many discussions to determine what to reduce in the mathematics curriculum (Hwang et al. 2011). Some topics that only appeared once in the grade level or were disconnected across grade-levels were omitted from the curriculum. This included figures in a position of line symmetry and point symmetry, finding patterns with building-blocks, addition and subtraction of length, volume conversion, relationship between volume and capacity, continued ratio, approximation, binary system, cumulative frequency, and flow charts (MEST 2011).

Another strategy used to reduce the total amount of the learning content was the reconstruction of the mathematics topics to be taught. For instance, in the 2011 revision both three-digit and four-digit numbers are introduced in grade bands 1–2 as a way to foster students' understanding of the principle of decimal notation (see the section 'changes in when to teach' with regard to grade bands). This is a sharp contrast to the 2007 revision where the numbers up to 100 were addressed in grade 1, those up to 1000 were addressed in grade 2, and those up to 10000 were in grade 3. Consequently, addition and subtraction within the specific range of numbers were bound to the specific grade levels in the previous curriculum. However, the 2011 revision enables us to deal with numbers more effectively and to focus on the meaning of place-value and operations applicable to multi-digit numbers. In a similar vein, integers and rational numbers are addressed simultaneously by considering the characteristics of the number system and its operations in grade bands 6–8. Mathematical concepts such as equations or inequalities and their application to solving various real-life problems are integrated into the same strand, instead of presenting them separately.

Whereas some topics were omitted or reduced in the 2011 revision, as described above, other topics were further elaborated. Such topics included number sense over mere calculation, operational sense through estimation over complex computation, understanding of the principles of calculation over practicing skills, effective use of calculator over complicated calculation, understanding of measurable attributes over calculation related to such attributes, addressing the concept of possibility instead of probability at elementary grades, and mathematical justification instead of formal rigorous proof in geometry (Shin et al. 2011).

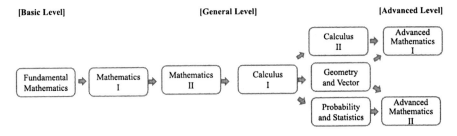

Fig. 1 Hierarchical structure among mathematics subjects in high school

Another significant change in what to teach occurred in the selective curriculum in grades 11 and 12. Note that in the seventh curriculum the common curriculum was applied to all students from the first to the tenth grade, while the selective curriculum was designed for students of grades 11 and 12. The selective curriculum included 'Practical Mathematics', 'Mathematics I', 'Mathematics II', 'Calculus', 'Probability and Statistics', and 'Discrete Mathematics' (see Paik 2004 for the content of these subjects). In principle such curriculum differentiation was intended to tailor the mathematics content to students' needs and capabilities. In practice, however, students tended to choose their mathematics subjects in a way that would allow them to achieve the highest scores possible in the high-stakes college entrance examination, rather than to prepare for their career path and future study (Choi et al. 2004). This led us to make significant changes in terms of mathematics subjects and the paths to those subjects in the 2007 revision. For instance, high school students who plan to study liberal arts or social sciences at university are expected to take 'Mathematics I' followed by 'Calculus and Basic Statistics', whereas others who plan to study natural sciences are expected to take 'Mathematics I', 'Mathematics II', followed either by 'Integral and Statistics' or by 'Geometry and Vector' (Shin and Han 2010).

However, these new mathematics subjects were criticized from the beginning because of their lack of mathematical hierarchies and connections, unnecessary repetitions, and difficulties in implementation in schools (Park et al. 2010). This led us to reconstruct the hierarchical structure among mathematics subjects in high school (MEST 2011). Given the differences in students' mathematical abilities, three levels (i.e., basic, general, and advanced) were presented and their corresponding subjects recommended. In the basic level for students who have difficulties in learning general high school mathematics, 'Fundamental Mathematics' is suggested. In the general level for typical high school students, six mathematics subjects are suggested such as 'Mathematics I' and 'Probability and Statistics'. For the advanced level students, 'Advanced Mathematics I' and 'Advanced Mathematics II' are suggested. Figure 1 summarizes the designated levels and their corresponding mathematic subjects with the suggested learning paths (Park et al. 2010).

Changes in How to Teach (Instruction)

As mentioned above, major revisions in mathematics curriculum are usually related to changes in content. However, recent consecutive revisions focus on how to teach mathematics or pedagogy. Such remarks are closely connected to the changes in the objectives of teaching school mathematics.

For more than a decade, four instructional aspects have been consistently emphasized in mathematics curriculum documents (MOE 1997; MEHRD 2007; MEST 2011). First, **meaningful questions** as a basis for productive mathematical communication need to be raised in mathematics lessons. It is recommended that teachers use appropriate open-ended questions to provoke students' creative responses.

Second, mathematical **concepts and principles** need to be emphasized in lessons. Mathematical constructs need to be addressed using various real-life, social, or natural phenomena. It is also recommended that students discover mathematical constructs for themselves by using manipulative materials or exploratory activities. One of the main reasons students believe mathematics is difficult and not interesting results from a prevalent teaching approach in which mathematics is taught in an abstract, disconnected collection of facts and procedures to be learned and reproduced on command (MEST 2008). This led us to emphasize the importance of students' investigating mathematical situations using their own methods in mathematics classrooms, even though such methods may sometimes include ineffective or unproductive processes.

Third, **problem-solving ability** needs to be fostered in mathematics lessons. For this purpose, the following elements are emphasized:

(a) problem-solving is taught across all content strands;
(b) students need to investigate problem contexts and employ appropriate methods on the basis of mathematical knowledge and thinking strategies to solve a given problem;
(c) the methods and processes employed during problem–solving and problem–posing are just as important as finding solutions; and
(d) students need to investigate mathematical concepts and principles, and generalize them while solving problems.

Finally, students' **positive disposition** toward mathematics, specifically their interest and confidence in mathematics, needs to be nurtured through mathematics lessons. Students are also expected to acknowledge the value and necessity of mathematics by exploring mathematics through various contexts. Given that students' perceptions of the value of mathematics are limited to a set of tools to use in other subjects and for future study or for everyday practical purposes as in the mathematics topics learned in elementary grades (Kim and Pang 2007), a more proactive treatment to increase students' appreciation of mathematics has been called for.

In the 2007 revision of mathematics curriculum, two more instructional remarks were added (MEHRD 2007). First, the following three methods were suggested to enhance mathematical communication ability:

(a) students understand and use correctly mathematical representations such as terms, symbols, tables, and graphs;
(b) students communicate efficiently with others by explaining mathematical ideas with verbal and writing activities and by representing them visually; and
(c) students acknowledge that communication is crucial in learning and using mathematics by clarifying and reflecting on their thinking through representing and discussing mathematics.

These instructional methods were added to specify the new objective; fostering students' communication ability in mathematics. One of the greatest challenges in Korea has been to change the prevalent teaching style from teacher presentations of mathematics as a highly structured subject to be learned and reproduced by compliant, quiet students (Pang 2009; Park and Leung 2005), to an emphasis on mathematical communication in the curriculum especially for secondary school teachers.

Second, the following two methods were suggested to enhance mathematical thinking and reasoning ability:

(a) students infer mathematical facts with induction or analogy, and justify or prove them; and
(b) students analyze mathematical facts or statements, organize mathematical relations, and reflect on their own thinking process.

Although the enhancement of mathematical thinking ability has been a consistent objective of school mathematics, its implementation was only explicitly described in the 2007 revision.

In the 2011 revision of the mathematics curriculum, two additional instructional remarks were added (MEST 2011). First, the following four cautionary notes were implied to nurture mathematical creativity:

(a) mathematics instruction should emphasize mathematical problem solving, reasoning, and communication ability;
(b) mathematical tasks producing various ideas are to be used to stimulate students' divergent thinking;
(c) students solve a given problem with various methods and then compare them; and
(d) students recognize the necessity of mathematical concepts or terms and define them, instead of receiving them by the teacher.

Note that in Korea mathematical creativity has been recommended mainly for gifted students. As the new curriculum is intended to foster mathematical creativity for all students through school mathematics, instructional suggestions need to be further developed and disseminated to support implementation.

Second, the following three methods were suggested for students' character-building:

(a) students respect different solution methods and opinions posed by their peers;
(b) students cultivate literacy as democratic citizens by representing logically their mathematical ideas and by making reasonable decisions; and

(c) students acknowledge that the process is of great significance in solving a mathematics problem.

As students' character-building is a new objective in the mathematics curriculum, instructional suggestions also need to be further investigated.

Changes in When to Teach (Progression)

A significant change in the mathematics curriculum in Korea has involved the gradual introduction of greater flexibility as to when specific mathematics topics are to be taught. As an example, Table 2 shows how the recent three mathematics curricula allocated the topics of number and operations in grades 1 and 2. Whereas the 1997 curriculum specified grades and semesters for each topic, the 2007 curriculum recommended only the grades. For instance, in the 1997 curriculum, numbers up to 100 were to be taught in the second semester of the first grade, but in 2007, the same topic can be taught in either semester. Furthermore, the 2011 curriculum uses grade bands so that the same topic can be taught at any time during grades 1 and 2.

One of the most significant changes to the 2011 Korean mathematics curriculum is the presentation of the mathematics content in 5 grade bands, 1–2, 3–4, 5–6, 7–9, and 10–12. The use of grade bands in other countries such as the United Kingdom [UK], China, Hong Kong, Singapore, and the USA was reviewed (Kim et al. 2009). The grade bands were addressed in Korea to increase the effectiveness of mathematics learning on the part of students and to provide flexibility in constructing and implementing a school curriculum on the basis of mutual connection and cooperation across grades (MEST 2009).

The use of these grade bands is expected to provide textbook developers with greater flexibility in topic organization. In fact, similar topics in previous mathematics textbook series were often separated inefficiently across grades due to the specified grade levels according to each content strand (Pang 2008). This problem is expected to be solved by the use of grade bands. That is to say, the Ministry sets up core topics per each grade band on the basis of curriculum studies (i.e., Kim et al. 2009; Hwang et al. 2011; and Shin et al. 2011 in order for the 2011 curriculum). Textbook authors can determine when each topic is introduced in each semester for their textbooks.

The idea of grade bands may have greater impact on secondary than elementary students. Whereas only one mathematics textbook series is used in the elementary schools in order to serve as the bottom-line for instruction, various textbook series are available in the secondary schools. Note that even secondary mathematics textbooks have to be assessed and certified by the government who has already specified the guidelines for what is to be included. On one hand, this policy would prevent secondary students from experiencing a major difficulty in their transition from elementary school so far as textbook usage is concerned. On the other hand, such specific guidelines resulted in rather similar secondary textbooks in nature (Pang 2008).

Table 2 Curriculum placement of particular number and operations topics for grades 1 and 2 in three mathematics curricula

Curriculum	Grade-Semester	Topics in the Strand of Number & Operations
1997	1-1	• Numbers up to 50
		• Addition & subtraction with simple numbers
		• Use of addition & subtraction
	1-2	• Numbers up to 100
		• Use of various methods of counting numbers
		• Addition & subtraction with one-digit numbers
		• Addition & subtraction with two-digit numbers (without regrouping)
		• Use of addition & subtraction
	2-1	• Numbers up to 1000
		• Addition & subtraction with two-digit numbers
		• Introduction of multiplication
		• Use of addition & subtraction
	2-2	• Multiplication facts
		• Addition & subtraction with three-digit numbers
		• Use of addition, subtraction, & multiplication
2007	1	• Numbers up to 100
		• Addition & subtraction with simple numbers
		• Addition & subtraction with two-digit numbers
	2	• Numbers up to 1000
		• Addition & subtraction with two-digit numbers
		• Addition & subtraction with three-digit numbers
		• Multiplication
		• Understanding of fraction
2011	1 ∼ 2	• Numbers up to four-digits
		• Addition & subtraction with two-digit numbers
		• Multiplication

For the alignment to the 2011 mathematics curriculum, the policy of textbook development is changed from government-certified to government-approved. This is expected to result in variations of the types of mathematics textbooks that are developed. For instance, middle school students may learn mathematics through content-specific textbooks such as a 'function' or 'geometry' textbooks in place of 'mathematics for the seventh grade'. Similarly, high school students may choose different academic tracks and complete different mathematics subjects according to their needs and interests.

Another noteworthy aspect is that the difficulty or challenge of a specific mathematics topic influences when to teach such content. For instance, understanding of the relationship among various quadrilaterals, which was previously taught in the fourth grade, has been moved to middle school. Similarly, the concept of sets and their operations, which was taught in the middle grades, is now placed in the high school levels.

Not only has the difficulty in learning a specific topic been considered, but also the mathematical arrangement among related topics. For instance, fractions as equal partitioning of continued quantity, which were previously taught in second grade, have been moved to grade band 3–4 in order to meet with students' understanding and to be integrated with other meanings of fractions such as equal partitioning of discrete quantity. Similarly, the concept of equations and their basic properties, which was taught in sixth grade, has been moved to grade band 7–9 so as to be combined with linear equations at middle school. Stem-and-leaf plots, which were taught independently in the fifth grade, have been moved to grade band 7–9 in order to be taught with other statistical graphs.

Conclusion and Discussion

Similar to other countries, national mathematics curriculum development in Korea has embraced reform initiatives. For more than a half century, the Korean mathematics curricula have sought to encourage the implementation of significant changes with sometimes conflicting emphases. The main changes in any particular curriculum have reflected what was valued in school mathematics at the particular time it was developed. This section examines some characteristics of recent curricular changes in Korea and discusses challenges in the future.

First, a thorough review of content in the mathematics curriculum has been called for. The recent revision of mathematics curriculum includes significant changes in the scope and range of content. For instance, calculation skills for mathematical proficiency that have been traditionally emphasized in elementary mathematics are substantially less emphasized and the concepts of sets and its operations that have been taught in middle school are now introduced in high school. It is unclear whether these changes to placement of content in the curriculum are sound, so systematic research is required to assess the efficacy of these changes and their impact on students, teachers and schools.

Second, the process of actively engaging in doing mathematics has been emphasized in recent revisions. Up to the sixth curriculum, problem-solving was emphasized. Since then, however, other aspects of mathematical processes such as mathematical thinking, communication, and creativity have been added to the curriculum. These changes were informed by studies on the key competencies required in future society as well as a review of mathematics curricula in other countries such as USA, UK, Japan, Hong Kong, and Singapore (Kim et al. 2009). Up to now, mathematical processes have been described as educational objectives and their related instructional notes have been mentioned at the end of the curriculum document. However, they are neither positioned equally with the content domains nor specified in terms of expectations across grade bands. Given this, a major challenge for teachers will be how to promote such mathematical processes as well as emphasize the mathematical content.

Third, since the seventh curriculum in 1997, the 'learner-centered' curriculum has been a consistent slogan. What students need to learn and how they learn mathematics, beyond which mathematical topics are important, have been important factors in the curriculum design (Hwang et al. 2011). As described, students' overall understanding and difficulty in learning a mathematical concept has been the basis for organizing and positioning the concept in the curriculum. In addition, students' various mathematical abilities have been a big concern in the curriculum design. In particular, in the seventh curriculum, teaching mathematics according to students' ability groups was seriously introduced but gave rise to many problems in implementing it in secondary schools such as psychological resistance to the special complimentary courses for underachieving students and lack of mathematics teachers who could teach different groups of students in terms of their mathematical abilities and levels (MEST 2008). This led us to withdraw students' level-based differentiated structure in the 2007 revision and to give individual schools and teachers more flexibility in organizing mathematics instruction tailored to their students' specific needs and levels in the given school context. Given this change, systematic and comprehensive surveys on students' learning of mathematics are required to analyze the strengths and weaknesses of the recent curriculum in comparison with the previous one.

Fourth, not only cognitive aspects in learning mathematics but also affective dimensions have been emphasized in recent curricular revisions. We do not anticipate any substantial change in the near future in students' negative disposition toward mathematics because of continuing learning pressure on the subject and the high-stake examination-driven culture. Given the traditional proverb; a person who knows something cannot beat a person who likes it, and the person who likes it cannot beat a person who enjoys it, consideration of students' affective dimensions in mathematics learning will continue in the curriculum design.

Fifth, the national mathematics curriculum is to be specified through instructional materials such as textbooks, workbooks, and teacher manuals. The most recently developed curriculum offers more flexibility for textbook developers than before. It will be challenging for textbook authors to arrange mathematics topics and present them efficiently within and across the new grade bands. As the policy for secondary mathematics textbooks has changed into a government-approval system, various types of textbooks are expected. Emerging issues in the review and selection of mathematics textbooks will need to be examined in the Korean context.

Sixth, the alignment of a mathematics curriculum to other related elements is important. Developing an effective mathematics curriculum is just a starting point. It needs to be connected to quality instructional materials, efficient classroom teaching by well-educated teachers, and students' performance measured by appropriate assessment methods (Reys et al. 2010). Since the most recently revised curriculum is implemented step-by-step in schools from 2013, the outcomes are yet to be measured. Because of the challenging nature of the updated curriculum, many issues will be raised in specifying it through instructional materials, implementing it in the classroom, and assessing its impact on students' mathematical learning. We need to take serious consideration of how to assess the effectiveness of the curricular changes specifically with regard to students' mathematics achievement.

The Korean national curriculum has been perceived as a vital factor contributing to students' superior performance in mathematics in international comparative studies. In fact, OECD (2010) reports Korea as an outstanding case showing that students' achievement can be further enhanced over the current top-ranked level on the basis of effective implementation of educational policies. Among many contextual factors, high expectations of students' achievement and full support from parents as well as the overall quality of teachers (Park 2010; Shin and Han 2010) will continue to be the solid foundation of implementing a deliberate and ambitious national mathematics curriculum agenda in school. However, like other countries in East Asia, we must also deal with long-pending problems such as boosting students' self-confidence in mathematics and promoting their positive attitude toward mathematics. This chapter is expected to provoke more discussion on the similarities and differences with regard to the curriculum development and underlying factors across different education systems.

References

Choi, S., Park, M., Park, S., Lee, D., Lee, B., Cho, Y., et al. (2004). *Analysis of implemented mathematics curriculum and study on the future revision*. Seoul: Korea Institute for Curriculum and Evaluation (in Korean).

Clark, D., & Hua, X. L. (2008). Mathematical orality in Asian and Western mathematics classrooms. In O. Figueras, J. L. Cortina, S. Alatorre, T. Rojano, & A. Sepulveda (Eds.), *Proceedings of the joint meeting of PME 32 and PME-NA XXX* (Vol. 2, pp. 337–344). Mexico: Cinvestav-UMSNH.

Hwang, S. W., Hwang, H. J., Paik, S. Y., Lew, H. C., Park, H. S., et al. (2011). *Draft of the creativity-focused mathematics curriculum for the future*. Seoul: Korea Foundation for the Advancement of Science and Creativity (in Korean).

Jeong, J. Y., & Kang, C. Y. (2011). The development of creativity and character education program model through interdisciplinary integration of curriculum in the elementary school. *Journal of Learner-Centered Curriculum and Instruction, 11*(4), 373–391 (in Korean).

Kim, D. H., Park, H. S., Lee, J. H., Kim, H. J., Paik, S. Y., Park, K. M., et al. (2009). *A study on the model of future-oriented mathematics curriculum focusing on creativity*. Seoul: Korea Foundation for the Advancement of Science and Creativity (in Korean).

Kim, K., Kim, S., Kim, N., Park, S., Park, H., & Jung, S. (2008). *Findings from trends in international mathematics and science study for Korea: TIMSS 2007 international report in Korea*. Seoul: Korea Institute for Curriculum and Evaluation (in Korean).

Kim, S., & Pang, J. S. (2007). Why study mathematics? Focused on the elementary school students' conception. *School Mathematics, 17*(4), 419–436 (in Korean).

Kwon, O. N., Park, J. H., & Park, J. S. (2011). Model lessons of mathematical practice focus on creativity and character education curriculum. *The Mathematical Education, 50*(4), 403–428 (in Korean).

Lew, H. C. (1999). New goals and directions for mathematics education in Korea. In C. Hoyles, C. Morgan, & G. Woodhouse (Eds.), *Rethinking the mathematics curriculum* (pp. 218–227). Philadelphia: Falmer Press.

Lew, H. C. (2008). Some characteristics of the Korean national curriculum and its revision process. In Z. Usiskin & E. Willmore (Eds.), *Mathematics curriculum in Pacific Rim countries: China, Japan, Korea, and Singapore* (pp. 37–71). Charlotte: Information Age Publishing.

Lew, H. C., Cho, W. Y., Koh, Y. M., Koh, H. K., & Paek, J. S. (2012). New challenges in the 2011 revised middle school curriculum of South Korea: mathematical process and mathematical attitude. *ZDM Mathematics Education, 44,* 109–119.

Liu, J., & Li, Y. (2010). Mathematics curriculum reform in the Chinese mainland. In F. K. S. Leung & Y. Li (Eds.), *Reforms and issues in school mathematics in East Asia: sharing and understanding mathematics education policies and practices* (pp. 9–31). Rotterdam: Sense.

Ministry of Education (1997). *The 7th mathematics curriculum.* Seoul: The Author.

Ministry of Education (1998). *Commentary on the elementary curriculum: mathematics, science, and practical education.* Seoul: The Author (in Korean).

Ministry of Education and Human Resources Development (2007). *Revision of the 7th mathematics curriculum.* Seoul: The Author.

Ministry of Education, Science, and Technology (2008). *Commentary on elementary mathematics curriculum.* Seoul: The Author (in Korean).

Ministry of Education, Science, and Technology (2009). *Elementary and secondary school curriculum.* Seoul: The Author.

Ministry of Education, Science, and Technology (2011). *Mathematics curriculum.* Seoul: The Author.

Mullis, I. V. S., Martin, M. O., & Foy, P. (2008). *TIMSS 2007 international mathematics report.* Chestnut Hill: Boston College.

Mullis, I. V. S., Martin, M. O., Foy, P., & Arora, A. (2012). *TIMSS 2011 international results in mathematics.* Chestnut Hill: TIMSS & PIRLS International Study Center, Boston College.

National Council of Teachers of Mathematics (2000). *Principles and standards for school mathematics.* Reston: Author.

Organisation for Economic Co-operation and Development (2007). *PISA 2006 science competencies for tomorrow's world: analysis* (Vol. 1). Paris: Author.

Organisation for Economic Co-operation and Development (2010). *PISA 2009 results: what students know and can do—student performance in reading, mathematics, and science* (Vol. 1). Paris: Author.

Paik, S. (2004). *School mathematics curriculum of Korea.* Paper presented at the ICME-10, Copenhagen, Denmark, July 2004.

Pang, J. S. (2002). Difficulties and issues in applying the seventh mathematics curriculum to elementary school classrooms. *School Mathematics, 4*(4), 657–675 (in Korean).

Pang, J. S. (2008). Design and implementation of Korean mathematics textbooks. In Z. Usiskin & E. Willmore (Eds.), *Mathematics curriculum in Pacific Rim countries, China, Japan, Korea, and Singapore* (pp. 95–125). Charlotte: Information Age.

Pang, J. S. (2009). Good mathematics instruction in South Korea. *ZDM Mathematics Education, 41,* 349–362.

Park, H. S. (1991). *The history of Korean mathematics education.* Seoul: Tae-Han Textbooks (in Korean).

Park, J., Jeong, E., Kim, K., & Han, K. (2004). *Findings from trends in international mathematics and science study for Korea: TIMSS 2003 international report in Korea.* Seoul: Korea Institute for Curriculum and Evaluation (in Korean).

Park, K. (2010). Mathematics teacher education in Korea. In F. K. S. Leung & Y. Li (Eds.), *Reforms and issues in school mathematics in East Asia: sharing and understanding mathematics education policies and practices* (pp. 181–196). Rotterdam: Sense.

Park, K., & Leung, F. K. S. (2005). Mathematics lessons in Korea: teaching with systematic variation. In D. J. Clarke, C. Keitel, & Y. Shimizu (Eds.), *Mathematics classrooms in twelve countries: the insiders' perspective* (pp. 247–262). Rotterdam: Sense.

Park, S. K., Kim, M. Y., Kim, S. A., Nam, M. W., Park, S. H., Paik, K. S., et al. (2010). *Study on the reconstruction of optional subjects in high school according to the revised curriculum in 2009. report to the Ministry of Education, Science, and Technology* (in Korean).

Reys, B. J., Reys, R. E., & Rubenstein, R. (Eds.) (2010). *Mathematics curriculum: issues, trends, and future directions*. Reston: NCTM.

Shin, H., & Han, I. (2010). The revised curriculum of school mathematics in Korea. In F. K. S. Leung & Y. Li (Eds.), *Reforms and issues in school mathematics in East Asia: sharing and understanding mathematics education policies and practices* (pp. 79–90). Rotterdam: Sense.

Shin, L. S., Hwang, H. J., Kim, D. W., Lee, D. H., Song, M. H., Shin, H. G., et al. (2011). *Research on the mathematics curriculum according to the revised curriculum in 2009*. Seoul: Korea Foundation for the Advancement of Science and Creativity (in Korean).

The Singapore Mathematics Curriculum Development—A Mixed Model Approach

Ngan Hoe Lee

Abstract Singapore has a history of having a national mathematics curriculum, which is produced and disseminated by the Ministry of Education, exemplifying a deductive approach towards mathematical curriculum development (Olivia, Developing the curriculum, 2009). This Chapter presents, through three case studies of school-based curriculum innovations, how the development of mathematics curriculum in Singapore has evolved from a deductive to containing elements of both the deductive and inductive approaches—a mixed model approach. Through the eyes of the three case-studies, advantages to such a mixed model approach towards mathematics curriculum development will be presented. Key contributing factors for the success of such a mixed model approach will be elicited through an analysis of these case studies as well.

Keywords Singapore mathematics curriculum · Models of curriculum development · School-based curriculum innovation

Introduction

As observed by Olivia (2009, p. 126), models of curriculum development may generally be classified as deductive or inductive. Deductive models of curriculum development proceed "from the general (e.g., examining the needs of society) to the specific (e.g., specifying instructional objectives)" (Lunenburg 2011a). Tyler's (1949) classic work provided an apt example of a deductive model of curriculum development. On the other hand, inductive models of curriculum development start with the actual "development of curriculum materials and leading to generalization" (Lunenburg 2011b). Taba's (1962) Five-Step Sequence to curriculum development exemplifies an inductive model.

Lee's (2008a) analysis of the impact of National Building Initiatives on the Singapore Mathematics Curriculum Development leads one to believe that the devel-

N.H. Lee (✉)
Nanyang Technological University, Singapore, Singapore
e-mail: nganhoe.lee@nie.edu.sg

Y. Li, G. Lappan (eds.), *Mathematics Curriculum in School Education*,
Advances in Mathematics Education, DOI 10.1007/978-94-007-7560-2_14,
© Springer Science+Business Media Dordrecht 2014

opment of Singapore's National Mathematics Curriculum may have taken a deductive approach. This belief is further reinforced by the fact that Singapore's National Mathematics Curriculum is centrally controlled by Singapore's Ministry of Education, which produces and disseminates the Curriculum. This is not surprising, as Lunenburg (2011a) observed that most curricular makers adhere to this approach to curriculum development. The deductive approach allows the broader needs of society to be addressed in the curriculum, reflecting the generally held essentialist philosophy towards education. As Olivia (2009, p. 160) pointed out, the essentialists seek to adjust men and women to society. With Singapore being a young nation, a deductive approach toward curriculum development will help ensure the necessary changes to the education system are effected in order to meet nation-building needs (Lee 2008a).

However, as intellectual capital increasingly becomes the basis for competitive advantage of companies and nations, Singapore's Ministry of Education (MOE) announced in 1999 (The Straits Times, 10 July 1999) that Singapore would "move towards ability-driven education to help the individual pupil recognize and make use of his talents and abilities". To further encourage teachers to focus on the development of the individual pupil, the Prime Minister, Mr. Lee Hsien Loong called on Singapore teachers to "teach less, so that our students could learn more" at the National Day Rally in 2004. In response to this call to "Teach Less, Learn More" (TLLM), many school teachers have embarked on a number of interesting school-based curricular innovations to cater to the specific needs of the pupils in their respective schools. To better support and catalyze such school-based curriculum innovations (SCIs), the Ministry of Education has developed a yearly package to participating schools, and which is available to all schools to apply for over a period of 3 years (Ministry of Education 2008, January 8). The package includes monetary funding as well as training in research methodology of a teacher, called the Research Activist (RA), from each participating school. The RAs worked with curriculum specialists to explore and document the innovations in their respective schools. Such SCIs, which were referred to as Ignite! Projects, appear to be more aligned with an inductive approach to curriculum development. As Lunenburg (2011b) noted, the inductive approach has incorporated "a postmodern view of curriculum, because they are temporal and naturalistic".

The centrally controlled National Mathematics Curriculum coupled with school-based mathematics curriculum innovations have created a new mathematics curriculum that is evolving in some Singapore schools. This new mathematics curriculum starts with the actual development of curriculum materials to target the specific needs of the pupils from the respective schools, but that is also aligned with the National Mathematics Curriculum. The development of such mathematics curriculum appears to have element of both deductive and inductive approaches—a mixed model approach.

The work of three schools, presented as case studies, will provide some insights to the process involved in this mixed model approach.

Case Study 1—The Role of Multiple Intelligences in the Mathematics Classroom

The first case study traces the extensive work carried out by one primary school in an effort to develop a school-based curriculum initiative into a school programme over a three-year period to meet the needs of its pupils (Lee and Abdul Rasip 2010).

It was generally observed in the year 2007 that the motivational level of pupils to learn mathematics was relatively low. The school's performance in mathematics in the national examination was also below the national average. An initiative was then spearheaded by relevant members of the School's Senior Management Committee (comprising the Principal, two Vice-principals, the Head of Mathematics Department as well as senior Mathematics teachers) to investigate how teacher-developed activities based on Gardener's theory of multiple intelligences (MI) (Gardner 1985, 1993) could better address the interest of the pupils in learning mathematics.

The timing of the Initiative enabled it to be considered one of the Ignite! Projects funded by the Ministry of Education package to support and catalyse such efforts in schools (Ministry of Education 2008, January 8). The funding not only allowed the school to purchase necessary services to aid implementation of the initiative, it also allowed the school to assign an RA to take charge of the implementation of the Ignite! Project. The officially appointed RA was provided with time allowance and opportunities for professional development in the area of planning, implementing, and evaluating of the Ignite! Projects, which were mainly planned and managed by the Ministry of Education. The professional development included areas such as curriculum development and research methodology.

The planned Ignite! Project, which was carried out as an action research in the first semester of 2008, sought to provide insight to the research question: Will the use of Multiple Intelligences in the teaching of Mathematics result in an increase in pupils' motivation and engagement, and a positive impact on their attitude and achievement in the subject? To better manage and evaluate the Project, which was new to the teachers in the school, and after considerations were given to timetable constraints, only four classes of Primary 4 pupils were involved—2 experimental and 2 comparison classes. The intervention was also confined to the teaching of the topic "Fractions". The dominant MIs of the four classes of pupils were first determined by using the Branton Shearer's Multiple Intelligences Developmental Assessment Scales (MIDAS). MIDAS helps to provide individual and class profiles of strengths and limitations in the various MIs as proposed by Gardner. While the 2 comparison classes continued with their lessons as usual, the teachers for the 2 experimental classes, together with the RA and a mathematics curriculum consultant, planned, implemented and evaluated mathematics lessons that tapped on dominant MIs of the respective experimental classes using the class profile generated from MIDAS.

At the same time, with the help of experts in psychometrics, MOE developed a new instrument- the PETALS™ Scale, which is a localized context to measure pupils' engagement levels in the classrooms. The Scale has three subscales, namely

Table 1 Comparison of pretest and post-test mean scores for the PETALS™ scale

Engagement Subscale	Mean / SD		Standardized Mean Difference (SMD)
	Post-test	Pretest	
Behavioral	78.1 / 18.2	75.4 / 15.1	0.18
Cognitive	77.0 / 15.8	72.4 / 16.9	0.27
Affective	81.1 / 15.0	76.4 / 17.7	0.31

Behavioral, Cognitive, and Affective engagement levels. The RAs were trained to administer as well as analyze the scores for their own respective Ignite! Projects.

Consequently, the school decided to use the PETALS™ Scale as a proxy measurement of the level of engagement of the pupils from the two experimental classes. A comparison of the pretest and post-test mean scores for the PETALS™ Scale is shown in Table 1.

As seen in Table 1, though the Behavioral Subscale only reflected a slightly greater than small effect size[1], the other two subscales indicated that the SCI might have contributed to a medium effect size on the Cognitive and Affective Engagement levels.

To examine the impact of the SCI on the mathematical achievement of the pupils, a comparison of the scores for the experimental classes and the comparison classes in a review test on "Fractions", which was conducted at the end of the intervention, was made. To check for equivalence, the pupils score in the end-of-year mathematics examination in 2007 was used (refer to Table 2). As the school was also interested in examining possible differential impact on the different ability groups (the classes were made up of low- and middle-ability pupils, as reflected by their mathematics examination scores), the analysis was carried out by grouping the pupils into Low- and Middle-Ability.

As the effect size for the comparison of the 2007 end-of-year mathematics examination mean scores for the experimental and comparison classes is generally small, the experimental and comparison classes may be considered as equivalent in terms of mathematics achievement, for both the Low-ability and Middle-ability groups.

Table 2 Comparison of 2007 end-of-year mathematics examination mean scores

	Low-Ability Group		Middle-Ability Group	
	Experimental Classes ($N = 30$)	Comparison Classes ($N = 32$)	Experimental Classes ($N = 38$)	Comparison Classes ($N = 40$)
Mean / SD	33.3 / 12.1	30.8 / 12.9	63.5 / 9.7	64.6 / 10.7
SMD		0.19		−0.10

---

[1] According to Cohen (1988, pp. 284–288), SMD = 0.10 is a small effect size, SMD = 0.25 is a medium effect size, and SMD = 0.40 or larger is a large effect size.

Table 3 Comparison of mean scores for the review test on fractions

	Low-Ability Group		Middle-Ability Group	
	Experimental Classes ($N = 30$)	Comparison Classes ($N = 32$)	Experimental Classes ($N = 38$)	Comparison Classes ($N = 40$)
Mean / SD	34.6 / 19.8	22.6 / 16.9	71.5 / 14.8	62.1 / 17.1
SMD		0.71		0.55

Table 4 Comparison of engagement mean scores for the PETALS™ scale between experimental and comparison classes

Engagement Subscale	Mean / SD		Standardized Mean Difference (SMD)
	Experimental Classes	Comparison Classes	
Behavioural	78.1 / 18.2	66.6 / 17.3	0.66
Cognitive	77.0 / 15.8	62.2 / 20.6	0.72
Affective	81.8 / 15.0	71.0 / 17.9	0.60

Table 3 provided a comparison of the mean scores in the Review Test on Fractions for the experimental and comparison classes, for both the Low- and Middle-ability groups.

Table 3 reflected a large effect size for both the Low- and Middle-Ability Groups, with a much larger effect size for the Low-Ability Group. It appeared that the impact of the planned Project on the Low-Ability Group is much greater than that on the Middle-Ability Group. The result prompted the School to extend the Project for the second semester of 2008 and to involve both the experimental and comparison classes in another round of the Project planned around the teaching of the second semester topic "Decimals" (Lee et al. 2008). The purpose of the extended Project was to evaluate the long-term effect of the Project, and to examine for the likelihood of a Hawthorne effect. Consequently, a comparison of the engagement levels and performance in a Review Test on Decimals between the experimental classes and comparison classes at the end of the extended Project were carried out, as shown in Tables 4 and 5 respectively.

As reflected in Tables 4 and 5, all the comparisons registered large effect sizes, pointing to a high level of likelihood that the Project has a long term positive impact on pupils' engagement levels and mathematics achievements; it is unlikely that the impact was merely a case of a Hawthorne effect.

In fact, the Project livened up the mathematics classrooms of the experimental and comparison classes so much that it captured the attention of parents and teachers who made requests for the SCI to be extended to other classes and levels. The Principal, Vice-principals, and Head of the Mathematics Department decided, after considering the feedback and working around the constraints, that the Project be rolled out as part of the School's mathematics programme to all the classes at Primary 1, 4, and 5 in 2009. Classes at the Primary 4 level were chosen to further extend the Project carried out in 2008 so that the teachers involved could build on

Table 5 Comparison of mean scores for the review test on decimals between experimental and comparison classes

	Low-Ability Group		Middle-Ability Group	
	Experimental Classes ($N = 30$)	Comparison Classes ($N = 32$)	Experimental Classes ($N = 38$)	Comparison Classes ($N = 40$)
Mean / SD	61.1 / 17.4	46.1 / 16.1	84.7 / 7.5	76.4 / 13.6
SMD		0.93		0.61

the earlier resources developed for the topics "Fractions" and "Decimals" to other topics. Classes at the Primary 5 level in 2009 included the four classes of pupils in the experimental and comparison classes for the Project conducted in 2008. It was a way for the school to ensure continuity in the mathematics curriculum for this group of pupils when the programme got rolled out to the Primary 5 classes in 2009. A teacher who was directly involved in the Project conducted in 2008 was also tasked to lead the teachers in rolling out the programme to the Primary 5 classes in 2009 as a way to build on the existing expertise that then resided in the school. Primary 1 classes were also involved as the Primary 1 mathematics teachers felt that the way the existing Primary 1 mathematics lessons were structured resembled closely the principles of the Project. Because the roll-out of the Project as part of the School's mathematics programme to Primary 1, 4 and 5 classes was well-supported by the School's Senior Management Committee, and relevant expertise—both outside and within the School's context—was made available arising from the Project implemented during the previous years, this new element in the School's mathematics curriculum was well received by all concerned: pupils, teachers and parents. Consequently, the school decided to fully roll out the Project as part of the School's mathematics curriculum in 2010, with the exception of the Primary 6 mathematics classes. The key consideration in excluding the Primary 6 pupils was the fact pupils at this level, all pupils would need to take the national examination—Primary School Leaving School Examinations (PSLE) to proceed to Secondary Schools. As much of the content would have been covered during the first five years in Primary Schools, most of the Primary 6 teachers concentrated more on helping pupils to consolidate their learning.

Multiple Intelligences in Mathematics is now featured prominently on the School's website as one of the key features of the School's Mathematics Curriculum—reflecting a 3-year evolution of a Project to part of the School's Mathematics programme. In fact, the school, with special encouragement from the Principal herself, has also carried out a longitudinal study of the pupils involved by tracking the School's passing rate for mathematics in the national examination (PSLE), and noted a 20 % increase when the first batch of pupils who were exposed to the MI approach graduated in 2010 (Engaging Multiple Intelligences in the Math Classroom 2011).

Fig. 1 The framework for the Singapore mathematics curriculum (Ministry of Education 2006, p. 12)

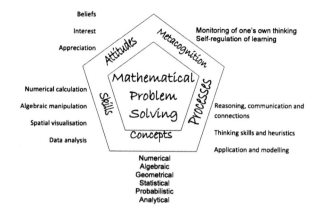

Beliefs
Interest
Appreciation

Monitoring of one's own thinking
Self-regulation of learning

Numerical calculation
Algebraic manipulation
Spatial visualisation
Data analysis

Reasoning, communication and connections
Thinking skills and heuristics
Application and modelling

Numerical
Algebraic
Geometrical
Statistical
Probabilistic
Analytical

Case Study 2—Multi-model Representation and Pupils' Conceptual Understanding

The second case study traces the continual work of a primary school to develop a school-based mathematics curriculum that promotes the multi-modal representations to improve pupils' conceptual understanding in mathematics.

At the end of 2009, as part of the school's needs assessment to improve on the teaching of learning of mathematics, teachers observed that, although pupils at the lower primary may be able to reproduce the required "answers" during assessment, there was usually a lack in depth of conceptual understanding in Mathematics. This has been reflected by pupils' inability to explain and justify their answers when solving mathematics problems in their daily work, as well as during tests and examinations. In fact, the Singapore Mathematics Curriculum advocates the importance of addressing conceptual understanding through the national Mathematics Curriculum Framework, as depicted in Fig. 1.

The Singapore Mathematics Curriculum Framework summarises the essence of mathematics teaching and learning in Singapore schools:

> Mathematical problem solving is central to mathematics learning. It involves the acquisition and application of mathematics concepts and skills in a wide range of situations, including non-routine, open-ended and real-world problems. The development of mathematics problem solving ability is dependent on five inter-related components, namely, Concept, Skills, Process, Attitudes and Metacognition. (Ministry of Education 2006, p. 12)

The Curriculum (Ministry of Education 2006, p. 13) advocates that "[S]tudents should develop and explore the mathematics ideas in depth, and see that mathematics is an integrated whole, not merely isolated pieces of knowledge". Wong (2004) pointed out the importance of the multi-modal representation approach to promote such deeper understanding of mathematics concepts. In fact, the concrete-pictorial-abstract (C-P-A) development of concepts, which encourages the use of concrete, pictorial and abstract representations of concepts in mathematics, is advocated in the Singapore Primary School (Ministry of Education 2006, p. 7). However, it was generally agreed among the teachers that the promotion of concrete representations

Fig. 2 Folder for the curriculum package (case study 2)

in the mathematics classroom was lacking. Furthermore, Ng (2009) pointed out, and teachers agreed, that when concrete materials are used to cater to the needs of the concrete learners at the Primary levels, "great care must be demonstrated to show how the concrete representations are linked to their abstract forms". In an effort to address these issues with appropriate funding, the teachers submitted their idea for an appropriate SCI for consideration as an Ignite! Project in 2010, for which approval was granted.

Under the leadership of an appointed RA from the school, who was also a mathematics teacher, the teachers came together in the early part of 2010 to develop and tailor-make a set of concrete manipulatives, along with accompanying lesson plans, to facilitate the teaching of fractions at the Primary 2 level for three weeks at the beginning of Semester 2. The planned Ignite! Project aimed to improve the conceptual understanding of fractions at the Primary 2 level by promoting the use of and emphasizing linkages between concrete, pictorial, and abstract representations of concepts. As part of the curriculum package for the project, a Folder (Fig. 2) was developed to facilitate the teachers to adopt such an approach so as to encourage a greater level of acceptance by the teachers concerned.

The Folder allowed the teachers to get pupils to place concrete manipulatives, trace the outline of the manipulatives, and write the abstract symbol on it—thus encouraging not only the use of concrete, pictorial, and abstract representations of concepts, but also facilitating the comparison and linkage of the different representations of concepts. At the same time, a pictorial representation of the fraction strips with the corresponding abstract representation of the respective representation in symbols was included as a permanent feature of the folder as the teachers felt that this was much needed for the intended content to be covered under the Project.

As in Case Study 1, the RA was provided with time allowance and opportunities for professional development in the area of planning, implementing and evaluating of the Project. Armed with the new-found knowledge in conducting action research, the RA led his team of teachers to adopt the Comparison Group Post-test research design. As the RA was teaching a Primary 2 Class, his class of mixed abilities pupils was conveniently assigned as the experimental class and another class of mixed ability was assigned the comparison class. The equivalence of the two classes was checked using their pupils' end-of-year Primary 1 mathematics examination scores in 2009. As reflected in Table 6, the SMD of 0.05 gives a small effect size;

Table 6 Comparison of 2009 end-of-year primary 1 mathematics examination mean scores

	Experimental Class (N = 29)		Comparison Class (N = 29)
Mean / SD	82.9 / 13.7		82.0 / 17.2
SMD		0.05	

Table 7 Comparison of mean scores for fractions post-test

	Experimental Class (N = 29)		Comparison Class (N = 29)
Mean / SD	22.1 / 3.7		22.0 / 4.1
SMD		0.02	

in other words, the two classes could be considered as equivalent in terms of their mathematical achievements.

A 30-mark 21-item pen-and-paper Fraction Post-test consisting of multiple choice and open-ended questions was administered to determine the difference in the two classes' conceptual understanding of fractions. The questions included in this Post-test, which required pupils to interpret the concept of fractions in various modes of representation, are closely related to the concepts learnt and exercises assigned during the 3-week intervention period of the Project. A comparison of the mean scores for the two classes in this Post-test is shown in Table 7, as the two classes were considered to be equivalent in terms of mathematical achievement.

The SMD of 0.02 in Table 7 shows that there is only a negligible effect size in terms of the difference in the mean scores for the Fractions Post-test. The RA attributed the negligible difference in performance in the Fractions Post-test to the short duration of the Project, albeit a positive effect size. And, in anticipation of such an outcome, he has also included as part of the data collection reflective journal entries for all pupils from both classes to complete at the end of each lesson during the intervention period. The Journal required pupils to write a letter to his/her friend to tell him/her about the mathematics lesson that the pupil had in school. As observed by Tan et al. (2011)

> Pupils in experimental group showed the ability to write "richer" reflections. They were able to describe with more details and their reflections were more focussed and were evidently related to the learning outcomes of the lessons.

In fact, the Team also observed that pupils in the experimental class not only remembered the manipulatives that were used during the lesson, they were also able to describe their learning using these manipulatives. This provides further evidence of a possible positive impact of the concrete manipulatives on pupils' conceptual understanding of fractions.

As in Case Study 1, the team also included the use of the PETALS™ Scale, the instrument that all the RAs were trained to administer and analyze for their respective Ignite! Projects, as a proxy measurement to compare the level of engagement

Table 8 Comparison of engagement mean pre-scores for the PETALS™ scale between experimental and comparison classes

Engagement Subscale	Mean / SD		Standardized Mean Difference (SMD)
	Experimental Class	Comparison Class	
Behavioral	85.1 / 15.3	83.8 / 15.0	0.09
Cognitive	77.3 / 23.0	78.6 / 19.0	−0.07
Affective	84.6 / 23.4	85.6 / 18.3	−0.05

Table 9 Comparison of engagement mean post-scores for the PETALS™ scale between experimental and comparison classes

Engagement Subscale	Mean / SD		Standardized Mean Difference (SMD)
	Experimental Class	Comparison Class	
Behavioral	88.3 / 10.5	83.5 / 17.5	0.27
Cognitive	82.4 / 14.9	80.4 / 20.0	0.10
Affective	88.5 / 13.9	89.3 / 14.9	−0.05

of pupils from the two classes. Tables 8 and 9 provided comparisons of the Engagement Mean Pre- and Post-scores for the PETALS™ Scale between Experimental and Comparison Classes as the instrument was administered to both classes before and after the intervention.

The SMDs obtained in Table 8 indicated a negligible effect size for all the 3 subscales of the PETALS™ Scale, pointing towards a reasonable assumption that both classes are equivalent in terms of the three types of engagement. It is thus reasonable to compare simply the Mean Post-scores for the PETALSTM Scale between experimental and comparison Classes for some insight to the impact of the intervention on the engagement levels of the pupils (Table 9). An SMD of −0.05 for the Affective Engagement subscale indicated a negligible effect size of the intervention on Affective Engagement of the pupils. As pointed out by the RA, this could have been contributed by the short duration of the intervention which may not have sufficient time to impact the pupils affectively. On the other hand, the SMD for the Behavioral and Cognitive subscales registered a positive but medium and small effect size respectively. The intervention appeared to have a positive though small impact on the cognitive engagement of the pupils, and a positive and reasonable level of impact on the behavioral engagement of the pupils on their mathematics learning.

The Team even went on to look for longer term impacts of the intervention on the pupils' mathematics achievement by comparing the 2010 mean end-of-year mathematics examination scores for the two classes (Table 10). An SMD of 0.2 reflected a small to medium effect size, pointing towards a reasonable level of longer term impact of the intervention on the pupils' mathematics achievement. Given that the difference in the mathematics achievement between the two classes were negligible prior to the intervention (Table 6) and the team has good knowledge of what transpired between the mathematics lessons of the two classes during the second semester of 2010, the team expressed confidence in attributing the improvement in the mathematics achievement of pupils in the experimental class to the Project.

In fact, the RA was so encouraged by the outcome of the project that he decided to embark further to help his pupils in the learning of fractions in the following year. With the ease and availability of information and communication technology (ICT), the RA looked towards tapping on the use of ICT tools to further enhance the C-P-A approach in promoting conceptual understanding and engagement of his pupils in learning fractions. Ng (2009) observed that the range of ICT, including virtual manipulatives, is available to help motivate and engage children in learning process. Mindellhall et al. (2008) observed that virtual manipulative as a virtual representation of a physical manipulative and through various dynamic processes may help develop mathematical conceptual understanding. Thus, in 2010, the RA embarked on an extension of the project to determine the impact of the use of virtual manipulatives on the learning of fractions (Lee and Ferrucci 2012).

Despite the completion of the Ignite! Project in 2009, the RA sought clearance and support from the School's Senior Management Committee to continue his work on the extension of the Project. Equipped with the skills for implementing and evaluating of SCIs and the support of the Curriculum Advisor (CA) as a result of the previous year's involvement in the Ignite! Project, he was able to secure approval to continue with his extended Project. However, as the Ignite! Project was formally completed; he would have to continue with the work without a team assigned to him. Consequently, the RA decided to work around the Primary Three mathematics classes under his charge in 2010, in which were some of the pupils involved in the original Ignite! Project. This, as the RA pointed out, would provide some continuity in the way fractions are taught to these pupils.

In the extended Project, the RA, with the guidance of the CA, made use of the virtual manipulative *Fractions* (Collars et al. 2007) to introduce the Primary 3 pupils to the concept of equivalent fractions. In the planned lesson for this extended project, the teacher, who is also the RA, used a laminated circle as a concrete material to first introduce the concept of equivalent fractions, and then linked the concrete representation of equivalent fractions with the virtual representation using the virtual manipulative *Fractions*. The teacher also constantly linked the representations to the pictorial and abstract representations of equivalent fractions, in both cases.

As the RA was interested in investigating for a possible differential impact of the intervention with different ability pupils, the lesson was conducted to two of the RA's Primary 3 classes, one of higher (3A) and one of lower (3F) mathematics ability, as reflected by their 2009 end-of-year mathematics examination scores. As

Table 10 Comparison of 2010 mean end-of-year mathematics examination scores	Experimental Class ($N = 29$)	Comparison Class ($N = 29$)
Mean / SD	75.9 / 16.9	71.5 / 21.9
SMD	0.2	

Table 11 Comparison of fraction pre-test mean score for the two classes

	3A (N = 40)	3F (N = 38)
Mean / SD	18.8 / 1.7	16.7 / 2.2
SMD	1.0	

Table 12 Comparison of mean number of equivalent fraction of $\frac{1}{3}$ listed by pupils of the two classes

	3A (N = 40)	3F (N = 38)
Mean / SD	5.6 / 3.2	4.3 / 2.9
SMD	0.4	

the concept of fractions was first introduced at Primary 2, a Fraction Pre-test, based on concepts in fractions taught in Primary 2 was administered to both classes to determine if the two classes are indeed different in their entering behavior for the lesson. Table 11 provided a comparison of the Fraction Pre-test mean scores for the two classes. The SMD of 1.0 reflected a large effect size, indicating that the two classes were indeed different in terms of achievement in the entry-level knowledge for the planned lesson, with 3A achieving a higher level than 3F.

As a measure of the level of mathematics achievement of the pupils after the intervening lesson, the pupils in both classes were required to use either the concrete manipulative or the virtual manipulative to find 8 equivalent fractions of $\frac{1}{3}$. Table 12 provided a comparison of the mean number of equivalent fraction of $\frac{1}{3}$ that pupils of the two classes listed for the given task.

The SMD of 0.4 in Table 12 did reflect a large effect size of the mathematics achievement between the two classes after the intervention, measured by proxy using the number of equivalent fractions of $\frac{1}{3}$ that the pupils were able to list. However this effect size is much smaller than that when comparing the Fraction Pre-test mean scores for the two classes (Table 11). It appeared that the use of the virtual manipulative may have narrowed down the achievement gaps of the two groups.

To determine the level of engagement of the pupils, an Engagement Survey was conducted. The Survey is a modified version of the PETALS™ Scale. The RA has decided to modify the PETALS™ Scale based on the experience of using it for the Ignite! Project in 2010. The items in the Scale were not changed in content, but the language was simplified for some and the Likert 11-point Scale is reduced to one with only 3 points so as to cater to the language and cognitive needs of the targeted pupils. As there were 5 questions for each subscale, the maximum score for each subscale is 15. Table 13 gave a breakdown of the mean scores for the 3 subscales in the Engagement Survey for the 2 classes.

The engagement level for the 3 subscales as shown in Table 13 is in agreement with the observation made by the RA during the lessons; both point toward a high level of engagement among the pupils in the 2 classes. As more than 90 % of the pupils chose to use the virtual manipulative over the concrete manipulative, the RA

Table 13 Breakdown of the mean score for the 3 subscales in the engagement survey for the 2 classes

Engagement Subscale	Mean / SD	
	3A	3F
Behavioral	13.0 / 0.6	13.3 / 0.5
Cognitive	12.1 / 0.7	13.4 / 0.5
Affective	13.8 / 0.5	14.2 / 0.4

attributed the slightly higher engagement scores of Class 3F to a possible inflated self-report score due to the use of the virtual manipulative. The RA also observed that the virtual manipulative facilitated the process of trial and error in finding the equivalent fractions of $\frac{1}{3}$—an encouragement for the weaker pupils who often do not succeed at their first trial with problems. This might have also contributed to the narrowing achievement gaps between the two groups.

The RA has expressed that he was much encouraged by the outcome of the extended project and would continue to source for ways to improve the school's mathematics curriculum so as to further enhance pupils' conceptual understanding and engagement in mathematics learning. He was also excited about the school's acquisition of a classroom set of iPads in the year 2012, and he has been looking at the possibilities of making use of the ease and dynamism that such an electronic device could offer in classrooms to better facilitate the multi-modal representation of mathematical concept to help enhance conceptual understanding of his pupils further. He also shared that the professional development he acquired from the initial involvement in the Ignite! Project has equipped him well in planning, implementing, and evaluating SCI. However, he felt that his lone effort, coupled with teaching and administrative responsibilities was limiting his desire in his work in this area. In order to rally more teachers to join him in his pursuit, he felt that the key pedagogical approach—the C-P-A development of concepts, needed to be re-examined in the light of the availability of such pedagogically rich ICT tool. In other words, the C-P-A approach needed to be reframed to include the role of virtual representations to better allow teachers to appreciate and integrate the use of virtual manipulatives in promoting conceptual understanding in the mathematics classrooms.

Case Study 3—Developing a Metacognitive Scheme to Help Pupils Kick-Start Mathematics Problem Solving

The third case study provides an insight to the impact on SCIs that the structure and culture left behind by the legacy of Ignite! Projects. It described the holistic and continuous approach by a primary school to develop a metacognitive scheme to help their pupils kick-start mathematics problem solving.

As in Case Study 2, during school's needs assessment to improve on the teaching of 1 mathematics at the end of 2010, the teachers observed that although pupils were explicitly taught problem-solving heuristics, they consistently fared poorly in solving non-routine problems. It was reflected by the often blank spaces left by pupils when they encountered such tasks in their daily work, tests or examinations. This often eventually took a toll on pupils' mathematics achievement scores, as marking of pupils' working is structured in such a way that credit will be awarded to both the process and product for such tasks. Thus, the teachers felt strongly that there was a need to help pupils to kick-start their mathematics problem solving.

Polya, who is probably best known for making mathematics problem solving as the focus of mathematics instruction, proposed the following four-phase model for mathematics problem solving (1957):

1. Phase 1: Understanding the problem
2. Phase 2: Devising a plan
3. Phase 3: Carrying out the plan
4. Phase 4: Looking back

As such, helping pupils to kick-start their problem solving processes would probably require an address of the first two of Polya's four-phase model. In fact, in a study of Singapore students by Kaur (1995), she found that students encountered the following difficulties in mathematics problem solving:

• Lack of comprehension
• Lack of strategy knowledge
• Inability to translate the problem into a mathematical form

Lee (2008b) found that the Problem Wheel (Fig. 3) could serve well as a metacognitive scheme to help pupils kick-start their problem solving processes and hence boost their confidence in solving problems. The Wheel provided pupils with the necessary prompts (Table 14) to better ask relevant questions and be more aware of and monitor their comprehension, and hence understanding of, the problem posed. It also helped pupils to regulate the use of their resources, in terms of knowledge and skills that they have learnt, to translate the problem into a mathematical form and to develop a plan to solve the problem.

Given the relevance of the Problem Wheel in addressing the needs of the school and the fact that the Wheel also addresses the issue of metacognition in the mathematics classroom—a key component of the Singapore Mathematics Curriculum (Fig. 1), the School decided to embark on an SCI by adapting and refining the Wheel to meet the needs of the School. In an effort to secure necessary funding to embark on the SCI, the School submitted the idea for an appropriate SCI for consideration as an Ignite! Project in 2011, for which approval was granted.

A team was formed to oversee the Ignite! Project. As in the previous two Case Studies, the team comprised of an officially appointed RA from the school, who was also a mathematics teacher—new to the profession but an enthusiastic teacher. He was supported by three other key members in the team—an experienced mathematics teacher as well as the Vice-principal and the Head of the Mathematics Department of the School. The Team examined the Problem Wheel further and decided to modify it into the STARtUP (STARt Understand and Planning) Scheme as shown in Fig. 4 (Hong et al. 2012).

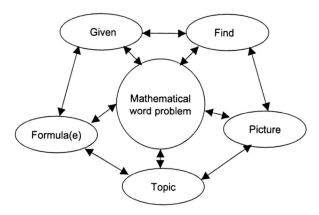

Fig. 3 The problem wheel (Lee 2008a, 2008b)

Table 14 Examples of generic question prompts pupils were encouraged to use for each component of the problem wheel

Component of the Problem Wheel	Examples of Question Prompts
Given	What is / are given to us in this problem?
	What do we know about the problem?
	What value(s) is / are given to us in this problem?
Find	What are we supposed to find in this problem?
	Which value(s) is / are we supposed to find as the answer to this problem?
Picture	Can we draw a picture to represent this problem?
	What would we draw to represent this problem?
Topic	Which is / are the topic(s) that we have learnt might help us to solve this problem?
	Can you list the topic(s) that we have learnt which would help us to solve this problem?
Formula(e)	Which formula(e) we have learnt that might be needed for us to solve this problem?
	Can we list the formula(e) that we have learnt which would help us to solve this problem?

As pointed out by Hong et al. (2012), "The 'Topic' and 'Formula(e)' components in the original Problem Wheel were replaced with 'Heuristic(s)' and 'Start' in STARtUP as non-routine problems are generally not topic-specific and there are few, if any, formulae to be learnt at Primary Four. 'Start' was added as a motivating slogan".

After looking into the constraints of timetabling and teacher involvement, it was decided that the Project would involve pupils at the Primary 4 level. Two intact

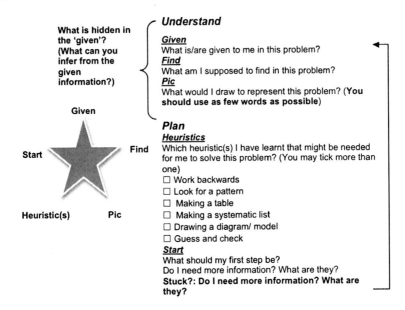

Fig. 4 The STARtUP scheme (Hong et al. 2012)

mixed ability classes, one to serve as the experimental and the other the compari-son class, participated in the study. The Project sought to determine the impact of the Scheme on these pupils' problem solving performance. The pupils in the Ex-perimental Class were exposed to 6 sessions, spanned over a 6-week period—one session per week, on the use of the STARtUP Scheme to solve non-routine prob-lems. In the first session, the Experimental Class was explicitly taught Polya's 4-phase approach towards problem solving as well as the various components of the Scheme. For each of the subsequent 5 sessions, the pupils in the Experimental Class were encouraged to use the Scheme to kick-start their problem solving process for the task assigned to them. The same tasks were used for pupils in the Comparison Class during these 6 weeks of intervention, and Polya's 4-phase approach was also explicitly taught to these pupils. However, pupils in the Comparison Class were not introduced to the Scheme.

As a measure of the impact of the Project on pupils' problem solving perfor-mance, a problem-solving test comprised of 5 non-routine problems tasks was ad-ministered both as a pre- and post-test to both the Classes. The level of understand-ing and planning exhibited by the pupils were each assessed via the aggregate scores based on a set of rubrics adapted from Charles et al. (1987), with scores ranging from 0 to 2, applied to each of the tasks. Success in problem solving was measured by the total score obtained in the Test out of the full score of 20 marks. The marking scheme for the Test was structured as in normal tests and examinations in the local context, whereby credit will be awarded to both the process and product for such problems. Tables 15 and 16 provided a comparison of the mean scores obtained by the two classes for all three measures in the pre- and post-test respectively.

Table 15 Comparison of mean pre-scores for the problem solving test between experimental and comparison classes

Measure	Mean / SD		Standardized Mean Difference (SMD)
	Experimental Class (N = 31)	Comparison Class (N = 32)	
Understanding	4.3 / 2.3	4.4 / 2.6	−0.04
Planning	4.0 / 2.5	3.8 / 2.7	0.07
Success	6.9 / 4.8	7.2 / 5.2	−0.06

Table 16 Comparison of mean post-scores for the problem solving test between experimental and comparison classes

Measure	Mean / SD		Standardized Mean Difference (SMD)
	Experimental Class (N = 31)	Comparison Class (N = 32)	
Understanding	5.0 / 2.7	4.4 / 2.4	0.25
Planning	4.9 / 2.9	4.2 / 2.6	0.27
Success	8.2 / 5.5	7.0 / 4.7	0.26

The SMDs obtained in Table 15 reflected negligible effect sizes for all the measures associated with the problem solving pre-test. In other words, the two classes could be considered as in equivalent for these measures. Consequently, a comparison of the mean scores of these measures for the problem solving post-test would be sufficient to examine the impact of the intervention. Table 16 showed that there was a medium effect sizes for all these measures associated with the problem solving post-test. There appeared to be positive and reasonable level of impact of the intervention on pupils' level of understanding and planning phases during problem solving as well as their problem solving achievement. As pointed out by Hong et al. (2012), though the STARtUP Scheme does not guarantee success in helping pupils of all abilities to solve all kind of mathematics problems, it appeared to have helped pupils to kick-start their problem solving processes, and in fact seemed to have also contributed to the overall success of the pupils' problem solving performance.

Again, as in Case Studies 1 and 2, the team also included the use of the PETALS™ Scale—the instrument that all the RAs were trained to administer and analyze for their respective Ignite! Projects, as a proxy measurement to compare the level of engagement of pupils from the two classes. Tables 17 provided comparisons of the Engagement mean scores for the three PETALS™ subscales between Experimental and Comparison Classes when the instrument was administered to both classes before the intervention as a pre-test.

As reflected in the SMDs obtained in Table 17, except for the Affective Engagement subscale, which registered a small effect size, the other two subscales both registered large effect sizes. Consequently, the two classes may not be considered equivalent for the two Engagement subscales: Behavioural and Cognitive. For these

Table 17 Comparison of engagement mean pre-scores for the PETALS™ scale between experimental and comparison classes

Engagement Subscale	Mean / SD		Standardized Mean Difference (SMD)
	Experimental Class	Comparison Class	
Behavioral	69.0 / 16.3	76.7 / 18.8	−0.41
Cognitive	67.9 / 21.4	74.9 / 18.2	−0.38
Affective	78.9 / 16.5	81.5 / 17.3	−0.15

two subscales, a comparison of the respective mean gain scores, albeit with a greater error margin, when the PETALS™ Scale was administered as a post-test will be made to examine the impact of the intervention on these two measures. Table 18 provided a comparison of the relevant mean post-scores for the three PETALS™ subscales between Experimental and Comparison Classes.

The SMDs obtained in Table 18 reflected a medium to large effect size for the Behavioral subscale, a medium effect size on Cognitive subscale, while a negligible one on the Affective subscale of the PETALS™ Scale. It appeared that the intervention has resulted in a positive way to the behavioral and cognitive engagement but no apparent difference in the affective engagement of the pupils.

The apparent lack of the impact the intervention had on the affective engagement of the pupils might have resulted in the observed short-term impact of the Scheme on the pupils. Despite the encouraging performance in the Problem Solving post-test by the pupils in the Experimental Class, these pupils did not seem to have internalized the Scheme after the intervention. Though some found the Scheme to be helpful in capturing the key information of a problem solving task to kick-start the process, some expressed that they found it a hassle to write down the information given in the problem and what is to be found (Hong et al. 2012). It appeared that the pupils may not have been able to appreciate the value of such a Scheme in kick-starting their problem solving process, and thus did not consciously put the Scheme to practice.

Consequently, the Team decided to embark on further efforts to improve on the Scheme as well as the teaching of the Scheme to help pupils better develop it into part of their productive problem-solving habits of mind. Despite the completion of the Ignite! Project, the Team remained intact, still comprised of the Vice-principal,

Table 18 Comparison of the relevant mean post-scores for the PETALS™ subscales between experimental and comparison classes

Engagement Subscale	Type of Score	Mean / SD		Standardized Mean Difference (SMD)
		Experimental Classes	Comparison Classes	
Behavioral	Gain Score	1.2 / 18.5	−6.3 / 24.1	0.31
Cognitive	Gain Score	−0.3 / 16.4	−5.9 / 23.4	0.24
Affective	Post-Score	78.4 / 18.2	78.0 / 22.0	0.02

the Head of the Mathematics Department, the Senior Mathematics teacher and the RA, and tasked to tackle the problem as an SCI for 2012. With the support of the Curriculum Advisor (CA), each of team members maintained the same role as before—the Team functioned essentially as in the case when they were handling the Ignite! Project: The Vice-principal as the key administrative resource person, the Head of Mathematics Department as the key curriculum resource person, the Senior Mathematics teacher as the key pedagogical resource person, and the RA as the key research resource person. The structure and culture in implementing, planning, and evaluating SCIs laid down by the Ignite! Projects appeared to have taken roots in the school.

Observations and Discussion

The examination of the three Case Studies revealed that all these SCIs needed to address the A-B-C-D-E-F of school-based curriculum development (Lee 2008b):

Analysis of Needs   In all the three cases reviewed, the SCIs started with an analysis of the pupils' needs—the first in the Taba's (1962) Five-Step Sequence to curriculum development that exemplifies that of an inductive model. In Case Study 1, the motivational level of the pupils in the School to learn mathematics was identified as relatively low. On the other hand, Case Study 2 diagnosed that pupils at the lower primary is lacking in depth of conceptual understanding in Mathematics. Finally, in Case Study 3, teachers observed that although pupils were explicitly taught problem-solving heuristics, they consistently fared poorly in solving non-routine problems, and felt strongly that there was a need to help pupils to kick-start their mathematics problem solving. These, as Taba (1962) pointed out, reflected the "gaps, deficiencies, and variations in [pupils'] backgrounds" that are diagnosed by the teachers concerned.

Bridging of Theory and Practice   For each of the needs identified in the three Case Studies, there were conscious and explicit attempts made by the respective teams to source for the relevant and appropriate theoretical underpinnings to explain and close up the gaps in the teaching and learning of mathematics. The Team involved in Case Study 1 looked into the literature on teaching and learning styles before they chanced upon the theory of multiple intelligences to address the motivational level of the pupils in the learning of mathematics (Lee et al. 2008). The role of representation theory in promoting conceptual understanding was the focus of the theoretical background that motivated the Team in Case Study 2 to consider the explicit and contextual use of concrete and virtual manipulatives in the mathematics classroom (Tan et al. 2011, and Lee and Ferrucci 2012). The search for a tried and tested scheme that helped pupils kick-start their problem solving prompted the Team in Case Study 3 to use the Problem Wheel as a basis to develop such a scheme (Hong et al. 2012). All these demonstrated the efforts of the practitioners, who were spearheading these SCIs, to bridge the gap between theory and practice in the mathematics curriculum development.

Fig. 5 Intra-&
inter-organisational factors
contributing to the
sustainability of school-based
curriculum initiatives (Lee
and Abdul Rasip 2010)

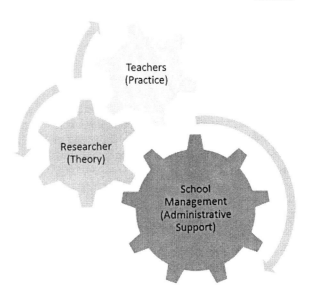

Collaborators Identification   Lee (2008b) pointed out that "for successful school-based curriculum development to occur, it is important to identify a collaborator in the school who not only takes on a personal interest in such an endeavor, but is also able to rally and lead a team of teachers in such a process". It appeared that in all the three cases, the RA, who was not only given time and opportunities to develop himself/herself professionally in but when the Projects have been completed, also taken on the leadership role of planning, implementing and evaluating SCIs in the respective schools. However, as Lee and Abdul Rasip (2010) observed, the intra- and inter-organisational factors also contributed to the sustainability of SCIs (Fig. 5). The bridging of theory to practice established by the inter-organizational linkage of the RA and the CA must also be facilitated by the administrative support provided by school management personnel within the context of the school concerned for SCIs to be sustainable. The active and direct involvement of the Principal in Case Study 1 and that of the Vice-principal and Head of Mathematics Department in Case Study 3 have, in both cases, equipped the RA with the necessary support to continually improve and work on the SCI within a systematic structure.

Delineating of Objectives   As Olivia (2009, p. 409) observed, "[A]s curriculum planners, we wish changes in education to take place for the better", and "[E]valuation is the means for determining what needs improvement and for providing a basis for effecting that improvement". And, in refining his model of curriculum development, validating curriculum goals and objectives were listed as part of the main types of curriculum evaluation (Olivia 2009, p. 447). In fact, in all the three Case Studies presented, there were clear objectives delineated for each SCI, presented in the form of research questions. Case Study 1, for example, was primary concerned with the level of pupils' engagement. Though there were also efforts to examine the impact of the SCI on the mathematical achievement of the pupils, the

Team was quick to point out that the interest was more of determining the possible impact of an increase in engagement levels of the pupils, if any observed, may have on the mathematical achievement of the pupils. In fact, in one of the meetings to review the progress of the SCI, a teacher in the Team shared her concern if the observed increased level of interest among her pupils during the mathematics class would be translated into higher achievement scores in mathematics. The Principal, who chaired the meeting, was quick to direct the teacher to the primary objective of the SCI—the engagement levels of the pupils, and advised the teacher to focus her work on the primary objective of the SCI. The reassurance from the school management personnel not only helped the Team to focus on the objective of the SCI, it also helped to reassure the Team to move further from what they perceived as a more practice-oriented approach towards teaching mathematics. This example further established the importance of the intra-organisational factor in the sustainability of SCI. However, it must also be emphasized that the evaluation of the primary objective of the SCI has been facilitated by the development of the PETALS™ Scale for the local context. The availability of such contextualized instrument encouraged to venture into SCIs that investigated variables that otherwise might not be easily measurable. This has been observed in all the three Case Studies presented here—engagement levels of the pupils, which otherwise may be an abstract concept to the practitioners, were examined by all the Teams.

Embedding into National Curriculum   In all the three Case Studies presented, the Teams concerned were quick and conscious to ensure that their respective SCIs were well aligned with the Singapore Mathematics Curriculum Framework (Fig. 1). The Team in Case Study 1, when addressing the engagement and motivational levels of the pupils justify their focus via the Attitudes component of the Framework. Case Study 2's focus on promoting conceptual understanding through multi-modal representation sought to focus the Concept component of the Framework. And, finally, Case Study 3's work on equipping pupils with a metacognitive framework to kick-start their problem solving process addressed both the Metacognition and Process components. Lee (2008a) observed that the Singapore Mathematics Curriculum Framework, developed in 1990, survived, with minor modification, the major curriculum review for the 2001 (and in fact also for the 2007) curriculum. One of the key reasons for the Framework's survival, he noted, was its rigour and robustness in presenting the philosophy and principles underlying decisions made about what mathematics education should equip our students with. Thus, as the schools sought to develop their own mathematics curriculum to better meet the needs of their pupils, conscious effort was made to ensure that the school mathematics curriculum was embedded into the national curriculum, with the national curriculum taking on the role of a quality controller.

Framework Establishment for School-Based Curriculum   Lee (2010) referred a curriculum framework as "a succinct description of the philosophy of the curriculum and helps to establish the important aspects of learning and teaching". He pointed out that due to the succinctness of the curriculum framework, it is often conveniently employed as the "ruler' in guiding the implementation curriculum development initiatives. Clearly, the theory of Multiple Intelligences served as a curriculum framework for Case Study 1. In fact, the school has been much encouraged by the role it played in the school's mathematics programme that there were plans to examine the appropriateness of extending it as a possible curricular framework for other programmes in the school. For Case Study 3, the STARtUP Scheme appeared to have taken on the role of the Framework for the SCI, and there was conscious effort on the part of the Team to revised and refine the Framework based on an evaluation of the SCI. Case Study 2 appeared to have tap on the C-P-A pedagogical approach as the Framework for their Ignite! Project. However as the RA consider the role of virtual manipulatives in the extended project, the concern of the RA for a need to reframe the C-P-A approach to better include the role of virtual representation reflected a need for a new Framework to be established to better guide the RA in the implementation of the SCI.

In all the three case studies, the schools analyzed the specific needs of their respective pupils' needs to supplement the National Mathematics Curriculum with learning experiences so as to better cater to the pupils' needs. The National Mathematics Curriculum provided the objectives and content (Ministry of Education 2006), which as pointed out earlier, are deductively derived at. Lunenburg (2011c) observed that curriculum can be organized into three major components: objectives, content, and learning experiences. Learning experience refers to the interaction between the learner and the external conditions in the environment to which he/she can react (Tyler 1949, p. 63). Tyler (1949) outlined five general principles in selecting learning experiences. Of these, one states that the learning experience must "fit" the students' needs and abilities; the teacher must begin where the pupil is ability-wise and that prior knowledge is the starting point for new knowledge. In fact, the inclusion of learning experiences in the Singapore National Mathematics Curriculum is one of the key features in the newly revised curriculum which will be implemented from the year 2013 onwards (Ministry of Education 2012a, 2012b). However, the learning experiences derived from these case studies are different from those reflected in the revised 2013 Singapore National Mathematics Curriculum. The learning experiences reflected in the revised National Mathematics Curriculum are stated "in the mathematics syllabuses to influence the ways teachers teach and students learn so that the curriculum objectives can be achieved". On the other hand, the learning experiences from the three case studies were derived inductively and followed Taba's (1962) Five-Step Sequence to curriculum development closely:

1. Producing pilot units
2. Testing experimental units
3. Revising and consolidating
4. Developing a framework
5. Installing and disseminating new units

Thus, in all the three case studies presented, the development of the mathematics curriculum for each school contains elements of both the deductive and inductive models. The objectives and content that are aligned with the National Mathematics

Curriculum are deductively developed while the learning experiences, which are the key products of the SCIs, are inductively developed. Each of these schools seems to have developed their "unique" school mathematics curriculum through a mixed model.

Conclusion and Implications

This analysis of the three case studies is meant to shed some light to the Singapore's mixed model approach towards mathematics curriculum development in the school. Despite a history of having a national curriculum, deductive in approach and assuming a one-size fits all philosophy, and having performed well in international comparative studies on pupils' mathematics achievement, the evolving needs of society has created a need to re-examine this centrally-controlled system. The effort to encourage teachers to vary the school-based mathematics curriculum within the constraints of the national curriculum called for a more inductive approach that view each pupil as an individual is contradictory to the essence of the national curriculum that teachers are familiar with. However, it appears that the deliberate planning and careful execution of the Ignite! Projects have yielded some positive results in this effort to promote the meeting of the top-down and bottom-up approaches. The result appears to hold the best of both worlds—the quality assurance of a national curriculum and the creativity of school-based curriculum to meet the needs of the learners. Three key areas appear to have contributed to such an effective enculturation of SCIs within this centrally-controlled system:

- Support of the SCIs by school management
- The identification and professional development of a RA to facilitate the process of SCIs within each school
- The development of suitable instruments for evaluation of SCIs

As countries seek to improve on their mathematics curriculum and some begin see the value of a centrally directed mathematics curriculum guidelines, such as Australia's effort to establish a national mathematics curriculum and USA's Common Core State Standards initiative, it is hoped that the case studies presented help to provide some insights, through the Singapore experience, on how the individual pupils' mathematical development need not necessarily be compromised in such a system.

References

Charles, R., Lester, F., & O'Daffer, P. (1987). *How to evaluate progress in problem solving*. Reston: National Council of Teachers of Mathematics.
Cohen, J. (1988). *Statistical power analysis for the behavioural sciences* (2nd ed.). Hillsdale: Erlbaum.

Collars, C., Koay, P. L., Lee, N. H., & Tan, C. S. (2007). *Shaping maths teacher's resource CD-ROM 3*. Singapore: Marshall Cavendish.

Engaging multiple intelligences in the math classroom (2011, November/December). SingTeach. Retrieved from http://www.nie.edu.sg/research-nie/research-publications/singteach?url=http://singteach.nie.edu.sg/.

Gardner, H. (1985). *Frames of mind*. New York: Basic Books.

Gardner, H. (1993). *Multiple intelligences: the theory in practice*. New York: Basic Books.

Hong, S. E., Lee, N. H., & Yeo, J. S. D. (2012). A metacognitive approach in kick-starting the understanding and planning phases of mathematical problem solving. In *ICME-12, the 12th international congress on mathematical education—pre-proceedings, TSG22-3*. Seoul: ICME-12.

Kaur, B. (1995). *An investigation of children's knowledge and strategies in mathematical problem solving*. Unpublished master's thesis, Monash University, Melbourne, Australia.

Lee, N. H. (2008a). Nation building initiative: impact on Singapore mathematics curriculum. In M. Niss (Ed.), *10th international congress on mathematical education proceedings (CD)*. Copenhagen: Roskilde University.

Lee, N. H. (2008b). *Enhancing mathematical learning and achievement of secondary one normal (academic) students using metacognitive strategies*. Unpublished PhD thesis, Nanyang Technological University, Singapore.

Lee, N. H. (2010). The role and nature of curriculum frameworks in mathematics curriculum development initiatives. In Y. Shimizu, Y. Sekiguchi, & K. Hino (Eds.), *Proceedings of the 5th East Asian regional conference on mathematics education (EARCOME5): in search of excellence in mathematics education* (pp. 607–614). Tokyo: Japan Society of Mathematics Education.

Lee, N. H., & Abdul Rasip, A. (2010, August). *Sustainability of school-based curriculum initiatives—lessons drawn from igniting passion in mathematics through multiple intelligences*. Poster session presented at the 5th East Asia Regional Conference on Mathematics Education, Tokyo, Japan.

Lee, N. H., & Ferrucci, B. (2012). Enhancing learning of fraction through the use of virtual manipulatives. *The Electronic Journal of Mathematics & Technology, 6*(2).

Lee, N. H., Abdul Rasip, R., Othman, S., & Sam, H. (2008, November). *School-based curriculum initiative—the case of igniting passion in mathematics through multiple intelligences*. Paper presented at APERA Conference 2008—Educational Research for Innovation & Quality in Education: Policy & Pedagogical Engagements Across Contexts, Singapore.

Lunenburg, F. C. (2011a). Curriculum development: deductive model. *Schooling, 2*(1).

Lunenburg, F. C. (2011b). Curriculum development: inductive model. *Schooling, 2*(1).

Lunenburg, F. C. (2011c). Key components of a curriculum plan: objectives, content, and learning experiences. *Schooling, 2*(1).

Mindellhall, P., Swan, P., Northcote, P., & Marshall, L. (2008). Virtual manipulatives on the interactive whiteboard: a preliminary investigation. *Australian Primary Mathematics Classroom, 13*(1), 9–14.

Ministry of Education (2006). *Mathematics syllabus—primary, 2007*. Singapore: Author.

Ministry of Education (2008, January 8). More support for school's "teach less, learn more" initiatives [Press Releases]. Retrieved from http://www.moe.gov.sg/media/press/2008/01/more-support-for-schools-teach.php.

Ministry of Education (2012a). *O-level mathematics teaching and learning syllabus*. Singapore: Author.

Ministry of Education (2012b). *Primary mathematics teaching and learning syllabus*. Singapore: Author.

Ng, S. F. (2009). The Singapore primary mathematics curriculum. In P. Y. Lee & N. H. Lee (Eds.), *Teaching primary school mathematics—a resource book* (2nd ed., pp. 15–34). Singapore: McGraw-Hill Education.

Olivia, P. F. (2009). *Developing the curriculum* (7th ed.). Boston: Pearson Education.

Polya, G. (1957). *How to solve it* (2nd ed.). Princeton: Princeton University Press.

Taba, H. (1962). *Curriculum development: theory and practice*. New York: Harcourt Brace Jovanovich.

Tan, J., Lim, C. A. C., & Tan, K. C. (2011). *Impact of use of manipulative materials in the concrete-pictorial-abstract approach on pupils' engagement and conceptual understanding*. Poster presented at 4th Redefining Pedagogy International Conference 2011, Singapore.

The Straits Times (1999). *Preparing people for challenges—addenda to the president's address*. Singapore: Singapore Press Holdings.

Tyler, R. W. (1949). *Basic principles of curriculum and instruction*. Chicago: University of Chicago Press.

Wong, K. Y. (2004, July). *Using muti-modal think-board to teach mathematics*. Paper presented for TSG14: Innovative Approaches to the Teaching of Mathematics at ICME-10, Copenhagen, Denmark.

School Mathematics Textbook Design and Development Practices in China

Yeping Li, Jianyue Zhang, and Tingting Ma

Abstract In this chapter, we present and discuss school mathematics textbook design and development in China, with a special focus on high school mathematics textbooks. Textbook development in China has its own history. This chapter highlights several design guidelines and common development practices used in selecting, presenting, and organizing content in mathematics textbooks over time. With the recent curriculum reform in China, we also discuss some new developments in designing high school mathematics textbooks. The implication of these Chinese practices in textbook development are then discussed in a broad context.

Keywords China · Curriculum reform · Mathematics textbook · School mathematics · Textbook design · Textbook development

Introduction

It is generally recognized that developing and using textbooks can serve as an important channel for promoting changes in teaching and learning mathematics (e.g., Ball and Cohen 1996; Beagle 1973; Hirsch 2007; Weiss et al. 2002). Although textbooks' effectiveness in improving classroom teaching and learning relates to many factors, including the teachers who use them (e.g., Kilpatrick 2003; National Research Council [NRC] 2004), the textbook quality itself is often an important concern to many teachers and educators (e.g., American Association for the Advancement of Science [AAAS] 2000; Kulm 1999; Trafton et al. 2001). Efforts to develop new, high-quality textbooks have received ever-increasing attention and sup-

This chapter is built upon an article that formally appeared in ZDM: Li, Y., Zhang, J., & Ma, T. (2009). Approaches and practices in developing mathematics textbooks in China. *ZDM, 41*, 733–748.

Y. Li (✉) · T. Ma
Texas A&M University, College Station, TX, USA
e-mail: yepingli@tamu.edu

J. Zhang
People's Education Press, Beijing, China

Y. Li, G. Lappan (eds.), *Mathematics Curriculum in School Education*,
Advances in Mathematics Education, DOI 10.1007/978-94-007-7560-2_15,
© Springer Science+Business Media Dordrecht 2014

port over time (e.g., Senk and Thompson 2003). In contrast, there are a very limited number of studies available that examine and discuss textbook design and the process of textbook development. In fact, during the 10th International Congress of Mathematics Education (ICME-10) held in Denmark in 2004 (Fan et al. 2008), the development and research of mathematics textbooks was the topic of a Discussion Group for the first time in the history of the International Commission on Mathematical Instruction (ICMI). As textbook development is a process that integrates many different considerations in content and instruction, a better understanding of textbook design and development practices helps enhance the quality of the textbooks being developed. Because many issues related to textbook design and development (e.g., "the relationship between mathematics curriculum standards/syllabi and textbooks" and "possibly good practices and approaches in presenting and organizing content in textbooks") are not restricted to specific regions, in this chapter we focus on the guidelines and practices used in developing mathematics textbooks in China.[1]

China's case becomes especially interesting since textbooks play a very important role in developing effective classroom instruction and teachers' knowledge in Chinese education overall, and especially in mathematics (e.g., Ding et al. 2012; Li and Li 2009; Ma 1999; Wang and Paine 2003). Ma found that Chinese teachers even consider their use and study of textbooks the most important of the factors contributing to their professional growth over the years. Ma's findings suggest that Chinese textbooks have been well accepted and are adhered to by teachers and students for day-to-day classroom instruction, and have been very successful in promoting mathematics teaching and learning in China. The important role of textbooks in mathematics teaching and learning has undoubtedly led to the emphasis placed on developing high-quality textbooks for Chinese education.

Although some studies are now available that reveal various features of mathematics textbooks from China (e.g., Fan et al. 2004; Li 2000, 2007), much remains unknown to outsiders about the design considerations and development practices of mathematics textbooks. Mathematics textbook development in China should provide useful information for curriculum developers and mathematics educators in many other education systems to reflect on their own textbook design and development practices.

The following sections are organized into four parts. In the first part (Section "School Mathematics Textbook Development: Issues and Focuses"), we outline issues and focuses on school mathematics textbook development. Descriptions of some issues in mathematics textbook development in the international context are provided in this part to help outline further discussions of mathematics textbook development in China. The second part (Section "General Characteristics of Mathematics Textbook Development in China Before 2000") provides detailed descriptions of various characteristics of mathematics textbook development in China before the dramatic curriculum reform taking place in 2000. Pre-

---

[1] If not specified otherwise, China refers to the Chinese mainland in this chapter.

vious practices and approaches commonly used in selecting, presenting and organizing content in mathematics textbooks are addressed and discussed. With recent curriculum reform taking place in China, the third part (Section "Developing Secondary Mathematics Textbooks in the Context of the Mathematics Reform After 2000") focuses on the new development in designing and authoring mathematics textbooks, with an emphasis on secondary mathematics textbooks. In the last part (Section "Concluding Remarks"), we conclude the article with discussions on textbook design and development practices in China, as well as possible directions for research.

School Mathematics Textbook Development: Issues and Focuses

Similar to many other education systems, curriculum is a key component in Chinese education. Because of its centralized education system, China uses nationwide unified curriculum standards (previously called the "teaching and learning syllabus") which provide guidelines for all teaching and learning activities at different grade levels and serve as a direct channel for major education reforms. Mathematics textbooks have been developed in alignment with the unified curriculum standards, and play an important role in guiding day-to-day teaching and learning activities in classrooms across the system. Given the large impact that textbooks wield on daily classroom teaching and learning, textbook quality is predictably important in the eyes of education policy makers, schoolteachers, and students.

A recent effort to examine textbook development in the United States has placed a focus on textbook design principles and development processes (Hirsch 2007). In particular, those textbook development teams, funded by the US National Science Foundation (NSF), were asked to contribute and share explicitly how they designed and developed their textbooks. The book edited by Hirsch (2007) includes contributions from four textbook development teams at the primary school level (Kindergarten through Grade 5), four at the middle school level (Grades 6–8), and seven at the high school level (Grades 9–12). The book's emphasis on design principles and development processes for textbooks at all grade levels in school mathematics is consistent with the focuses of Discussion Group on mathematics textbooks (DG14) during the ICME-10 (Fan et al. 2008). Similar focuses were also taken by Pang (2008) when she discussed mathematics textbook design and implementation in South Korea. Thus, in this chapter, we focus on similar issues in the case of China. The following three aspects are used as a guideline to frame our discussion in this chapter.

(1) The typical process of textbook development.
(2) General considerations in textbook structural design and content selection.
(3) General guidelines for authoring textbooks in terms of content organization and presentation.

General Characteristics of Mathematics Textbook Development in China Before 2000

The Typical Process of Textbook Development

Back in the 1950s, the Chinese Ministry of Education (MOE) founded the People's Education Press (PEP): a specialized organization dedicated to studying, authoring, and publishing textbooks for primary and secondary school education as well as a contact for designing and revising the "National Mathematics Teaching and Learning Syllabus". Since then, the PEP, under the direct administration of the MOE, has taken a leading role in curriculum development in China.

Because the PEP played a major role in textbook development before 2000, some common practices were formed along the way. For instance, authoring textbooks had always followed the process of "research, authoring—review, experimental use—revise, publish—experimental use again, review—revise again, ..." strictly. During this process, it was emphasized that great efforts are needed to prepare the text, review and experimentally use it several times.

One major feature in developing textbooks was to learn from other education systems and consider different opinions. For instance, since 1961 researchers and authors have begun to reflect on previous textbook development experiences and, more recently, conducted international comparative studies on teaching requirements, content, and method and content organization (Wei 1996). In the 1980s a national investigation was also conducted to examine the need for mathematics essential knowledge and techniques based on the economic and social development in China. The investigation involved sixteen vocations including engineering, water and electricity, aerospace, and agriculture. Questionnaires on mathematics knowledge requirements were collected from 692 engineers, technicians, or administrators and more than 300 experts from over 60 higher education institutes. Furthermore, 76 journals were randomly selected from 21 categories; and the mathematics knowledge used in the articles of those journals was categorized. Findings indicated that knowledge other than existing mathematics in curriculum materials should be added; including probability, statistics, calculus, optimization, linear programming, vectors, and analytic geometry.

Structural Design of Textbooks—Combination or Separation

There has always been heated discussion on the structure of mathematics textbooks in China, which mainly involves two questions: (1) Which approach is better; a separated, subject linear organization or an integrated, gradual organization? (2) What may be the overall design guideline, in consideration of these two different approaches?

Traditionally, separated content branches such as "algebra", "plane geometry", "solid geometry" and "analytic geometry" have been adopted in Chinese textbooks.

The guidelines for arranging mathematical content in different branches are as follows:

For algebra: content is organized as developing from number → expression → equation → function, constant to variable, concrete to abstract, simple to complex. "Function" is the core concept throughout the textbook.

For plane geometry: content is arranged as going from relationships between lines, equal or unequal relation → circle → similar triangles → solving triangles → measurement (e.g., circumference and area).

For solid geometry: content is organized as developing from lines and planes → polyhedron, evolving shape. If we take relative positions as a theme, contents are then organized from 'line and line' → 'line and plane' → 'plane and plane'.

To connect plane geometry and solid geometry, it is emphasized to extend the main properties of geometry from plane to solid, and from simple to complex.

For plane analytic geometry: content is arranged as emphasizing its transitional function from elementary mathematics to advanced mathematics by focusing on the integration of number and shape and its comprehensive application. It can be placed in a later part of the high school mathematics curriculum. Content organization can be arranged from Cartesian coordinate → polar coordinate; line → conic section; standard equation → general equation.

Since the late 1990s, all the above content divisions have been integrated into one subject—mathematics. The guidelines for the course structure include: reducing the number of mathematical curriculum branches; modernizing the course content; helping students learn the "Two Basics";[2] and facilitating students' application of mathematics knowledge. Principles for content arrangement include: (a) integrating all mathematical branches into one course; (b) proceeding step by step from simple to complex, shallow to deep, based on students' learning curves and abilities; (c) strengthening the systematic characteristic of textbook content; (d) separating the contents into two parts with different emphases for junior and senior high schools respectively; (e) integrating with related science subjects.

Textbook Content Selection

Changes to mathematics curriculum and textbooks have been made frequently. There are various reasons for the changes in Chinese mathematics curriculum and textbooks. One lasting concern is to reduce students' learning burden and improve teaching quality.

General Guidelines of Textbook Content Selection

Standards of textbook content selection that are used in China include the following considerations:

---

[2]"Two Basics" refer to basic knowledge and skills in school mathematics that are often identified and emphasized in Chinese mathematics curriculum (e.g., Zhang 2006).

First, is it the basic knowledge of algebra, geometry, statistics and probability?
Second, is it widely used in everyday life, production and technology activities?
Third, is it prerequisite knowledge for students' future study?
Fourth, is it feasible for students to learn?

The above considerations are generally accepted in many other education systems as well. However, the application of the standards can vary due to different natures of specific content topics and different understanding of the standards. The following sub-section will provide several examples of textbook content changes over the years.

Selection and Arrangement of Examples and Exercise Problems

An important principle in selecting and arranging examples and exercise problems is matching the exercise problems with the provided example problems. Memorizing and understanding basic concepts is highlighted with the use of similar problems and therefore the difficulty of study is reduced.

At present, the textbook differentiates exercise problems by difficulty to meet various students' needs. Problems are divided into group A and group B: A is fundamental and B is focused on applying the "two basics", improving students' ability and meeting high-achieving students' extra needs. Chapter review problems (also in A and B groups) and "self tests" are designed to help students study and examine their progress.

Besides textbooks, there are other additional curriculum materials, such as exercise problem books. In those books, challenging worked-out examples and exercise problems are provided for capable students.

General Guidelines and Highlights for Organizing and Presenting Content in Mathematics Textbooks

Logical Order of Mathematics Knowledge

This is a textbook compilation method: textbook content is arranged according to content logic connections in quantity and spatial forms. For example, in junior high algebra textbooks, rational number, real number, algebraic expression, linear equation and quadratic equation are introduced to prepare students for learning algebra transformations and solving equations. Function is then introduced. In senior high school, knowledge of algebraic expressions, equations, and inequalities are developed first and then the following concepts are introduced: exponential functions, logarithmic functions, trigonometric functions, sequences, induction, permutation and combination, probability and statistics, and basic calculus.

The logical order of mathematical concepts is also emphasized. In textbook development, there is an unwritten rule that states: a mathematical concept without a strict definition cannot be used. Every concept must be defined with previously introduced terms. For instance, concepts such as square roots and real numbers are defined before introducing the Pythagorean Theorem.

Introducing Concepts Clearly

Chinese textbook authors take the understanding of mathematical concepts as a necessary condition to learning mathematics well. Without understanding, students cannot apply concepts to solve problems. Therefore, Chinese textbook authors consider "introducing concepts clearly" the most important feature of textbooks. Various approaches have been developed and used, such as starting from examples of previously learned concepts, explaining concepts with real-world examples, or introducing concepts through comparison with related concepts. For instance, the concept of "irrational numbers" is introduced in a Chinese textbook as follows (Secondary School Mathematics Section 2001a, pp. 154–155):

The textbook begins with the review of "rational numbers can be written in forms of finite decimals or circulating decimals" and provides examples.

Second, $\sqrt{2}$, $\sqrt{3}$, $\sqrt[3]{2}$, $-\sqrt{7}$, and π are used to illustrate the existence of infinite, non-repeating decimals.

Third, infinite, non-repeating decimals are defined as irrational numbers.

Fourth, students are asked to think about the following questions; "Are $\sqrt{4}$, $-\sqrt[3]{27}$ irrational numbers? Are all numbers with radical signs irrational numbers?"

Finally, irrational numbers are classified.

In the above process, the definition of an irrational number is introduced through a comparison of irrational numbers with rational numbers by examples. π is used deliberately, as an example to explain that irrational numbers are not always numbers with radical signs. Questions are also raised to help students understand that "numbers with radical signs are not necessarily irrational numbers". This sequence of steps presents competently the idea of introducing concepts clearly.

Important Points, Hinge Points, and Difficult Points

In textbook development important points, hinge points, and difficult points of content are highlighted.

Important points refer to mathematical knowledge that plays an important role in the current content level and further studies. It is necessary to devote more time and effort to introducing such knowledge. For example, in middle school algebra, important points include rational number computation, solving linear equations, quadratic equations and systems of equations. In plane geometry, the properties of plane figures are important points.

A hinge point indicates significant mathematics content, which influences students' understanding of other relevant mathematics content knowledge to a great extent. Such content points should receive great instructional attention in order to

Fig. 1 Two intersecting lines

foster students' conceptual understanding in depth. For example, identical transmu-
tation of algebra expressions is a hinge point in middle school algebra. The textbook thus places much emphasis on the inclusion of various types of worked-out
examples and a large number of exercise problems with various levels of cognitive
demands.

Difficult points refer to mathematical knowledge that is hard for students to understand. Ways to deal with such contents include the use of more real-life examples,
emphasis on visualization, relevant knowledge preparation in advance, and step-by-
step exercises. For example, proof in plane geometry is a difficult point, which is
demonstrated in textbooks as containing the following several steps across several
content sections (Secondary School Mathematics Section 2001b):

First, in the section of "intersecting lines and opposite vertical angles", "opposite
vertical angles are equal" is derived first from informal reasoning and then through
a formal proof.

As shown in Fig. 1, $\angle 2$ and $\angle 1$ are complementary; and $\angle 3$ and $\angle 1$ are complementary. Because both $\angle 2$ and $\angle 3$ are complementary angles of $\angle 1$, therefore $\angle 2$ is
equal to $\angle 3$ since complementary angles of the same angle are the same. Similarly,
$\angle 1$ is equal to $\angle 4$.

Then a formal proof is introduced:

$\because \angle 2$ and $\angle 1$ are complementary; $\angle 3$ and $\angle 1$ are complementary (Definition of
adjacent complementary angles).

$\therefore \angle 2 = \angle 3$ (Complementary angles of the same angle are equal).

By repeatedly demonstrating the above process from reasoning to proof in the
content of parallel lines, a norm of proving is developed.

Second, in the section of "proposition, theorem, and proof", concepts such as
propositions, true or false propositions, axioms, theorems, and proofs of axioms
and theorems are introduced together with examples of writing formal proof process
(i.e., Known $\rightarrow$ To be proved $\rightarrow$ Analyze $\rightarrow$ Prove).

Third, in the "triangle" chapter, topics such as "theorem of the sum of a triangle's
internal angles" and "congruent triangles" are included and discussed to strengthen
geometrical proving.

Basic Mathematical Skills

Emphasis on basic skills is presented with the inclusion of worked-out examples and
exercise problems. Problem analysis is emphasized in the worked-out examples in
textbooks to show how to analyze and solve them and why certain methods are used.
Problem analysis in worked-out examples is followed by problem solution procedures, which show students a problem's solution step by step. Corresponding basic
skill exercises are provided after worked-out examples so as to consolidate concepts

and methods. For instance, in the section of "Using the method of substitution to solve a binary linear system of equations" (Secondary School Mathematics Section 2001a), worked-out examples and exercise problems are arranged as below:

Example 1 Solve the system of equations

$$\begin{cases} y = 1 - x, & (1) \\ 3x + 2y = 5. & (2) \end{cases}$$

Problem analysis: y is equal to $1 - x$ in Eq. (1); therefore, y in Eq. (2) can be substituted by $1 - x$, which transforms Eq. (2) into a linear equation.

Example 2 Solve the system of equations

$$\begin{cases} 2x + 5y = -12, & (1) \\ x + 3y = 8. & (2) \end{cases}$$

Problem analysis: consider substituting one unknown with an algebraic expression containing the other unknown. In Eq. (2), the coefficient of x is 1, therefore, Eq. (2) can be transformed by denoting x with an algebraic expression of y. Then such a substitution can be put into the Eq. (1).

The above examples introduced the method of substitution. The underlying basic thinking of this method is by means of "substitution" to eliminate one variable. The following procedures are usually used,

(1) Choose one equation containing one unknown with a simpler coefficient from the system of equations and substitute the unknown, for instance, y, with an algebraic expression containing x, that is, the form of $y = ax + b$;
(2) Substitute y for $y = ax + b$ in the other equation and get a linear equation of x;
(3) Solve this linear equation and get the value of x;
(4) Substitute x in $y = ax + b$ with the value of x and then get the value of y to obtain the solution of the system of equations.

Example 3, solving the system of equations with more complicated coefficients, is then provided.

Relevant exercise problems are provided and they can be divided into the following four types:

Type 1, transform $2x + y = 3$, $5x - 2y + 12 = 0$ into the form of denoting y with an algebraic expression that contains x;

Type 2, solve the system of equations;

Type 3, solve word problems that can be transformed into systems of equations;

Type 4, solve non-traditional problems. For example, the solutions to $\begin{cases} ax + by = 8, \\ ax - by = 2 \end{cases}$ are $x = 5$, $y = 3$. What are the values of a and b?

In summary, worked-out examples are first provided with different coefficients that are arranged from easy to difficult. Exercise problems are provided in a large quantity and corresponding to the worked-out examples.

Emphasis on Improving Students' Mathematical Ability

Chinese textbook authors pay close attention to improving students' mathematical abilities, and focus on computation, logic and reasoning, and spatial visualization. Textbook authors believe that students' abilities are developed together with "Two Basics" training and problem solving. In the process of problem solving, students' abilities of observation, comparison, analysis, synthesis, abstraction and generalization and their thinking habits of induction, deduction and analogy are developed through analyzing quantitative relationships in problems and reasoning on various solution methods. In addition, connections between different concepts, for example, solving geometric problems with algebraic methods, or investigating function graphs with geometric knowledge can develop students' mathematical abilities as well. Thus, exercise problems are carefully selected and arranged in textbooks.

System-unified Common Requirements with Elective Contents

With the use of the national teaching and learning syllabus and university entrance examinations in China, textbooks mainly focus on system-unified common requirements, though they are flexible to some extent. Less flexibility and more common requirements are presented in textbooks for middle school than those for high school. The elective contents in middle school textbooks include:

(1) "Reading" for broadening students' knowledge, such as "decomposing quadric trinomial with the method of making square", "complex fraction" and "why $\sqrt{2}$ is not a rational number?"

(2) "Thinking about it" to develop students' thinking and improve their abilities to analyze and solve problems, through enhancing knowledge connections.

(3) "Trying it" to improve students' abilities to handle practical tasks and interests in geometric learning. For example, on a piece of paper, if we draw a line l, and randomly take a point P on it and a point Q not on it. Through folding the paper, we get a perpendicular line l_1 of line l so that line l_1 should (a) pass through point P; or (b) pass through point Q. How many folding lines can we get?

Furthermore, the second group of exercise problems (i.e., group B) is included to strengthen the applications of "Two Basics", improve students' abilities, and meet the needs of high-achieving students.

Summary of Textbook Design and Development Practices Before 2000

Chinese primary and secondary curriculum has adopted a national unified model. Chinese school textbooks were also nationally unified for a long period of time. As a major resource for teachers and students, textbooks played a significant role in Chinese primary and secondary teaching and learning. Consequently, the Chinese government emphasized textbook development through organizing the specialized educational press and convening experts to develop textbooks. Much experience has been accumulated, especially in the following aspects:

(1) It is emphasized that textbooks need to embody mathematics education objectives. That is, "Two Basics", intellectual and ability, and ideological education should all be treated as significant and important, and they should supplement each other.

(2) When developing and selecting instructional objectives and textbook contents, social needs (after graduation, students have to seek jobs or pursue further education) and the intellectual development of students should be the two main considerations. The selected contents must be fundamental, useful for production, science, and technology, and connected with higher education. The content requirements should have a certain flexibility to accommodate individual differences among the students.

(3) Instructional objectives and textbook contents should be updated to align with social and knowledge development, but priority ought to be given to strengthening "Two Basics". Reform can not be completed in one day; instead, textbooks should be relatively consistent during a certain period. It would benefit teachers to master textbooks and use them to improve teaching quality. It is better to "revise" or "supplement" textbooks rather than completely change everything in the textbooks.

(4) The organization of textbook content should consider the connections and relations between mathematics knowledge (e.g., connection and difference between numbers and shapes), and also take into account cognitive and intellectual development of students. With regard to the organization of textbook content, linear curriculum and spiral curriculum content organizations have their own advantages and disadvantages. Linear organization of textbook content avoids repetition, but some content knowledge are not easily obtained by students; spiral organization of textbook content fits students' cognitive development, but may cause unnecessary repetitions. Consequently, linear organization should be taken as the main approach with some difficult contents being arranged spirally.

(5) Textbook authors should pay close attention to the relationship between learning and the application of mathematics knowledge, as well as the implementation of the principle of learning for application.

Developing Secondary Mathematics Curriculum Textbooks in the Context of the Mathematics Reform After 2000

The Need for Developing New Textbooks to Meet Mathematics Curriculum Reform Requirements

At the beginning of the 21st century, China embarked on a new round of basic education curriculum reform. In 1999, the Ministry of Education began to design the new basic education curriculum for the 21st century. School mathematics in China has experienced dramatic changes, especially since 2001. In 2001, the new Curriculum Standards for the nine-year compulsory education were formally established for experimentation. The ongoing "standards-based education reform" specifies the mathematics knowledge and ability requirements for students, advocates the advancement of students' conceptual understanding, basic skills, problem solving simultaneously and the improvement of teaching quality.

Because the previous mathematics curriculum focused on knowledge acquisition, textbooks failed to meet the needs of society's development. Some contents in previous textbooks were "complicated, difficult, insignificant and outdated" with few options available for students. The curriculum implementation lacked flexibility and opportunities for self-directed learning. Because too much attention was paid to the drilling of "Two Basics", students were restricted in the development of creativity and critical thinking. It is advocated that new mathematics textbooks should be fundamental, diversified and selective. The textbooks should help arouse students' interest in learning mathematics, help students to study mathematics actively, develop students' potential in creativity through learning basic knowledge, improve students' mathematical thinking when trying to understand mathematics, and raise students' awareness of applying mathematics knowledge in everyday lives. The new expectations placed on textbooks have inevitably called for changes in textbooks.

New Textbook Development

Purposes

The primary aims of the reform include changes to curriculum systems, structure, and content in order to construct a new basic education curriculum system for teaching and learning development (Liu and Li 2010). There are specific tasks textbook development should include. First, textbook reforms should be oriented towards the exploration of knowledge and student development, based on their prior knowledge and creative teaching. Second, textbook content should meet the requirements of the curriculum standards, embody physical and cognitive development of primary and secondary school students, and reflect social, political, economic and technological needs. Third, textbook contents should be presented in various ways to facilitate students' active engagement in activities such as observation, experimentation, survey, and communication. Fourth, the adoption and use of diversified curriculum materials for primary and secondary schools should be advocated. Education institutions and publishing companies are encouraged to develop textbooks that are aligned with the national curriculum standards.

Diversification of curriculum materials has been achieved by developing new reform-oriented school mathematics textbooks. In particular, nine series of middle school mathematics textbooks and six series of high school mathematics textbooks have been developed with approval from the education administration in China. With the brief history of the development of new textbooks in the context of mathematics curriculum reform, it is difficult to summarize and discuss specific design principles and practices that may be common to different textbook series. To illustrate the diversity of new textbooks, we describe some features of selected reform-oriented high school mathematics textbooks in the following sub-sections.

Features of Selected Reform-Oriented High School Mathematics Textbooks

People's Education Press's High School Mathematics Textbooks (Version A)

A team effort to develop a series of high school mathematics textbooks was carried out by the People's Education Press. The textbook development in this project basically follows the process of "literature review–theoretical framework construction–textbook development–experimental use of textbooks–results and reflection–textbook revision". Based on literature review and relevant researches in this project, the team expects to explore the design and development of mathematics textbooks that can help students learn mathematics in an active way, integrating teacher-guided and student-centered teaching and learning. Specific instructional strategies and methods are designed and integrated in mathematics textbooks to help actively engage students in the classroom. The team develops high school mathematics textbooks, and examines their scientific accuracy, rationality and effectiveness with experimental use. Through analyzing the data collected from the experiments and summarizing feedbacks from teachers and students, the results are used as guidelines for textbook revisions.

Several aspects have been emphasized in developing new textbooks. They include the following four aspects. Some specific examples are also provided to illustrate the changes.

(1) Placing more emphases on context, mathematical thinking, and application.

Introducing context, mathematical thinking and application are intended to integrate mathematical logic and students' thinking. Students' thinking and cognitive development are emphasized as well as the development logic of mathematical knowledge. In this way, mathematics content is not only organized by algorithms, but also by students' cognitive development.

Example: changes in introducing the concept of function.

In previous textbooks, the concept of "function" was introduced through the sequence of "set and corresponding $\rightarrow$ mapping $\rightarrow$ function". Mathematical logic was highlighted such as "mapping is a special case of corresponding", and "function is a special case of mapping". Consequently, students felt that the concept of function was abstract and disconnected from their lives.

In new textbooks, "function" is introduced through "real-life examples" with an emphasis on "function is a mathematical model descriptive of the rules of change in the real world". By going through the process from "analyzing features of real-life examples" to "summarizing common features to understand the concept of function", students learn to apply the concept of function into analyzing and solving problems.

(2) Problematizing mathematics.

Problematizing mathematics in textbooks is intended to improve students' creative spirit and ability in knowledge applications. In the new mathematics textbooks, content introduction is changed from the simple form of 'given' to include some new sections, such as "observation", "think about it", and "exploration" that are set up to pose questions in order to facilitate students' thinking and exploration. During that process, students experience the joy of discovery and creativity in mathematics.

(3) Emphasizing the guidance for developing mathematical reasoning.

The new mathematics textbook authors tried to change the approach from "what is it?" without providing explanation of "why is it?" in the previous textbooks to "guide students' mathematical reasoning".

Example: changes in introducing "the basic properties of inequality".

In previous textbooks, the content was introduced through the following sequence: "stating eight basic properties of inequality → proving the properties of inequality → working through examples → doing exercises".

In new textbooks, an introduction is presented as an advanced organizer: two real numbers, a and b, can have one of the following relationships: $a < b$, $a = b$ or $a > b$. These relationships are represented as: $a < b \Leftrightarrow a - b < 0$; $a = b \Leftrightarrow a - b = 0$; $a > b \Leftrightarrow a - b > 0$. These equivalent forms are called basic facts about the magnitude of real numbers.

Inequality and equality are basic quantity relationships. Equality is described with an equal sign and an unequal sign for inequality. To solve problems involving equality, we need to use the basic properties of equality. Similarly, we need to use the properties of inequality to solve problems involving inequality. Because both "equal to" and "unequal to" refer to relationships of numbers and expressions, we can explore inequality properties with an approach similar to those used in discussing equality properties.

Question #1: can you recall the basic properties of equality?

Question #2: what is the approach used in discussing equality properties? (Hint: "invariance" in operations.)

Question #3: based on the discussion about the basic properties of equality, can you guess the basic properties of inequality?

Question #4: the proof of the basic properties of equality is mainly based on "basic facts" (Note: this permeates axiom reasoning). Can you give the proof based on the "basic facts"?

(4) Emphasizing connections among different content knowledge.

With more emphasis on connections among different content knowledge, students are exposed to various approaches to obtaining conceptual understanding.

Example: changes in presenting and organizing the content of vector.

In previous textbooks, it was directly stated that mathematical operations such as addition and subtraction can be performed with vectors. The addition of vectors satisfies the communicative law and the associative law, etc.

In new textbooks, introduction is first provided as numbers can be operated. In light of the physical features of vector and number operations, the concept of vector operation is introduced.

Then, derived from the concept of displacement in physics and the experiment of the composition of forces, the "addition of vectors" is introduced. A follow-up question is raised to encourage students to think more about it: "Number operations and operation laws are closely connected since operation laws simplify operations and addition satisfies the commutative and associative laws. Are there similar operation laws for vector addition?" Students can then be guided to derive their conclusions.

Hunan Education Press Version of High School Mathematics Textbooks

Features of the Hunan Education Press version of high school mathematics textbooks include: focusing on inter-relationship among different mathematics contents and stressing underlying thinking and methods of various mathematics contents. For instance, other textbooks often lack a common theme for connecting contents such as trigonometry, analytic geometry, and complex numbers. This textbook series treats vectors as a unifying theme. Focusing on the concept of vector, the textbook introduces various contents such as trigonometry, analytic geometry, and complex numbers coherently.

This textbook series also gives prominence to mathematical methods rather than simply deleting contents to reduce students' burden. Newly added contents such as vectors are helpful for students to learn other contents and solve problems. Learning vectors well is useful for plan geometry, analytic geometry, solid geometry, trigonometry, complex numbers and even high school physics. In this way, although students learn new contents, their burden of learning other contents is actually reduced. Sufficient exercise problems are also included in the textbook to further facilitate students' learning of the mathematical methods.

The textbook series stresses the importance of geometry and the inter-relationship between numbers and geometric shapes. Specifically, the textbook emphasizes the importance of geometrical visualization in the introduction and explanation of mathematical reasoning and algebraic operations. For instance, complex numbers are generally introduced as $i^2 = -1$ from the algebraic perspective in mathematics textbooks. However, the Hunan Education Press version textbook introduces complex numbers through geometric transformations. Therefore, students come to know that explorations of geometric transformations can lead to complex numbers. Such an introduction relates numbers and geometry, embodies mathematical thinking and makes the content easier for students to understand.

The textbook series introduces mathematical knowledge through questioning students. In attempting to solve the problems, students learn concepts and algorithms and develop theoretical awareness. The mathematics experiments included in the textbooks involve students in activities. While thinking about and doing mathematics, students realize the needs of mathematical concepts, experience failure or success in exploration and discovery, and trace the development of mathematical knowledge. In this way, students explore more mathematical knowledge by themselves than in being led by teachers.

This textbook series emphasizes the expression of mathematical concepts. Based on practice and research in mathematics education, this series presents rigorous mathematical concepts with easy access. For example, it provides the elementary expression of fundamental theorems of calculus and relatively rigorous proofs. In this way, students can understand the essence of the significant outcome in the history of mathematics, even if they do not have the opportunity to learn more calculus. It is also helpful for students who are going to learn more calculus in their further studies. This series does not decrease the difficulty for easiness nor abandon rigor of mathematics. It does not increase the difficulty for the sake of rigor of mathematics, either.

The textbook series also gives prominence to in-depth thinking on mathematical problems and discovering the fun in mathematics. For example, it raises the possibility of an operation in which 0 is a divisor by introducing a new number. Such a question may promote critical thinking among students about the rules of introducing new numbers in the system of numbers, and thus elevate their mathematical habit of mind.

Last, the textbook series includes and arranges mathematical experiments for high school students. Besides mathematics experiments in the text, the textbook authors also include experiments in the exercises following the text. In this way, students are provided with opportunities to understand the text more deeply through observation, experimentation and induction. This also encourages students to seek evidence to verify the new mathematics knowledge in the text. For example, after introducing the concept of definite integrals, the textbook arranges an experiment to calculate the area of a circle using a computer. Other experiments include extended exercises integrating mathematics and physics. For instance, students are required to draw the reflection of parallel rays through spherical mirrors to observe the light gathering power of spherical mirrors. Another instance is to observe sine curves using spring vibration, based on Hooke's law.

Beijing Normal University Press's Version of High School Mathematics Textbooks

There are several important features for this version of textbooks. They are highlighted as follows.

First, function is taken and used as the core concept connecting almost all content areas in high school mathematics, including function and equations, inequalities, linear programming, algorithms, derivatives and their applications, and random variables in probability and statistics. It is important to understand these content areas from the perspective of functions. At the same time, learning these contents deepen students' understanding of functions.

Second, geometry is used to develop students' abilities of observation and reasoning. In this series, geometry integrates logical thinking and visual imagination using texts, pictures, and graphs. Two parts of geometry content are designed as follows: (1) the content of geometric shapes is designed and arranged as to developing students' visual imagination. (2) logical thinking is integrated into geometric content.

Third, operations are fundamental to mathematics. In this series, operations and methods of operation are significant and indispensable. The textbook introduces two components of operations: first, objects of operation; second, rules of operation. Objects of operation include numbers, variables or algebraic expressions, exponents, logarithms, trigonometric functions, and vectors. Rules of operation include associative law, commutative law, distributive law and "$a + (-a) = 0$". The textbook focuses on operations of various contents, including exponential operation, algorithmic operation, trigonometric function operation, vector operation (including plane and space vectors), complex number operation and derivative vectors.

Fourth, in terms of statistics and probability, the textbook series focuses on the following content areas with students' active involvement: the ability to deal with data, the process of gathering and analyzing data, case studies in statistics, inductive thinking and random sampling in statistics.

Summary of New Textbook Development After 2000

Grounded in Chinese mathematics education traditions, the reform-oriented high school mathematics textbooks discussed above show distinctive features. These newly developed textbook series contain not only specific considerations in content selection and mathematical treatment, but also aspects of students' learning and cognitive development. In a way, these new textbooks embody expectations for teaching and learning that are advocated in the mathematics curriculum reform. In contrast to previous textbook development in China, the involvement of many educators and researchers promotes the development of multiple textbooks available for students and teachers. However, there are no specific studies that have been reported to empirically document possible advantages and disadvantages of these new textbooks.

The most widely adopted and used high school mathematics textbook series is developed by People's Education Press (Version A). Based on the marketing data collected by PEP, more than 60 % of high school students in China are using mathematics textbooks published by PEP (Version A). Yet, this particular series lacks solid empirical evidence to document its effectiveness, though some data collection has been conducted in recent years.

In fact, the development of many new textbooks in China was a bit rushed (Li 2008). With the formal release of the new curriculum standards in 2001, some textbook developers took less than one year's time to develop and publish their new textbooks. The quality of the new textbooks has become a concern. The 'rushed' development of textbooks further suggests the importance of quality control, which can and should be supplemented with empirical data collected from textbooks' experimental uses.

The Integration and Use of Technology in Mathematics Textbooks and Instruction

The above discussion does not provide specific information about the use of technology in mathematics textbooks and instruction. The integration and use of technology did not receive much attention before 2000, but the situation in China changed dramatically after 2000. The integration and use of technology in mathematics instruction in China can be outlined as going through three different stages over the years.

The first stage can be characterized with the use of electric equipment in classroom instruction, such as slide projectors, projectors, and TV sets. The use of such electric equipment helps the presentation of mathematics content, but not necessarily changes the way of how students learn. There are also very limited impacts on students' learning content and their thinking.

The second stage can be characterized as computer-assisted teaching and learning. With the advancement of technology, more and more teachers have changed their views about the use of technology in classroom instruction. Teachers also become used to computers, which provides the base for the follow-up stage of using information technology.

The third stage can be designated as the integration of information technology and mathematics instruction. In addition to scientific calculators and computers, many other technology equipment (e.g., graphing calculators, internet) is also used. Many more software and applications become readily available for teaching and learning almost all contents in high school mathematics. For example, multi-media teaching courseware is made available for selected chapters of People's Education Press version textbook. Teachers are able to use the courseware to teach high school mathematics in interactive ways. In addition, the software of "Scilab" developed collaboratively by China and France is also used as a platform for mathematics teaching and learning. As free software, "Scilab" can be downloaded by teachers and schools from the official website. The publisher plans to develop many more textbook-related courseware that will be free to all teachers and students to download and use. Figure 2 shows the textbook introduction of information technology use for collecting water temperatures and building a function model.

Concluding Remarks

The above discussions and summaries outline a number of guidelines and practices used in developing mathematics textbooks in China. Because textbook development

收集数据并建立函数模型

我们周围的绝大多数变化现象，是难以根据已知理论直接建立函数模型的．但只要能收集到变化过程中变量的数据，利用信息技术就可以建立起能大致反映变化规律的函数模型．

下面就向大家介绍如何用计算机、数据采集器、温度传感器等信息技术工具收集水温变化数据，并建立温度与时间的函数模型．

（1）连接计算机、数据采集器、温度传感器，并在数据采集器上，将要采集的温度个数和每两个温度的间隔时间设置好，然后将温度传感器放入热水杯中．

（2）将计算机和数据采集器中的运行功能打开．这时，计算机和数据采集器上就会同时显示出温度随时间的变化情况（图1(1)，(2)）.

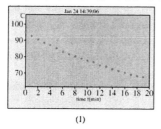

(1)

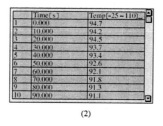

(2)

图1

（3）通过对整个温度变化过程的观察，根据图1(1)，在计算机中选择一个能大致反映其变化规律的函数模型，如 $y = ae^{dt} + c$，计算机便立即画出这个函数的图象并求出其解析式（图2）.

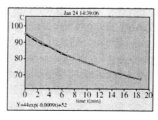

图2

以上建立函数模型的过程简单、方便，形象直观，是传统手段难以比拟的．只要我们掌握好所学的函数模型，利用信息技术，就可以探索复杂现象的变化规律．

Fig. 2 Collecting water temperatures and building a function model (People's Education Press textbook)

was viewed more of a profession before 2000, it is clear that Chinese textbook developers have accumulated many practical experiences in textbook development. These accumulated experiences in textbook development should provide a rich source of information for textbook writers and mathematics educators in other education systems to reflect on their own practices.

At the same time, textbook development itself has undergone many changes in China. Although various changes to textbooks happen all the time, the recent curriculum reform in China has brought the biggest change in textbook development. Before 2000, textbooks were mainly focused on mathematical knowledge itself. Specifically, presentation and organization of mathematics content in textbooks focused on knowledge accuracy and connections. Because textbooks have an important role in guiding day-to-day classroom instruction in China (e.g., Li et al. 2009a), students' high achievement and teachers' textbook use with fidelity suggest that Chinese textbooks were effectively implemented. Although textbooks were developed by a group of professionals housed in a large education press, textbook development was mainly an experience-based practice. It becomes important to elevate accumulated experience in Chinese textbook development for theoretical awareness.

After 2000, however, more attention has been given to students and their needs, which is reflected in textbook development with both content adjustment and considerations for teaching and learning in classrooms. Efforts are needed to focus on meeting the needs of students with diverse socioeconomic background, especially those coming from rural areas.

In contrast to practices before 2000, textbook development and publication is now open to all publishers. It is not only a few full-time professionals housed in a large education press, but experienced teachers and university professors, that become the main working force of textbook development in China. The situation therefore becomes more and more similar to other education systems, such as the United States (Hirsch 2007). As diversity can certainly promote creativity and competition in textbook development, changes in textbook developers would eventually benefit the improvement of textbook quality and thus mathematics teaching and learning in classrooms. Yet, textbook development still remains largely an experience-based practice in China. The successful changes in curriculum reforms in China may require specific strategies and considerations (e.g., Huang 2004). With recent growing interest in the quality and process of textbook development, making textbook development a scientific endeavor becomes a significant challenge to educators and researchers in many education systems, including China.

Knowing and understanding curriculum and textbook development cannot be separated from the social and political contexts of a system (Apple 2004). The situation in China is no exception. Although we intended to focus and frame our discussions on several aspects of textbook development more from an academic perspective (see Section "School Mathematics Textbook Development: Issues and Focuses"), the history of textbook development in China suggests that changes in mathematics textbooks and textbook development are closely related to social and political changes in the system over the years (Li et al. 2009b). Our inclusion and discussion of textbook development in China over the years helps highlight the importance of attending to the contextual changes in the educational system. By doing so, we encourage mathematics educators and curriculum developers in other education systems to reflect on their own practices.

Finally, it is important to point out that textbook development itself is not a result by itself, but a process that aims to produce high-quality textbooks. Textbook development closely relates to textbook studies that examine the quality of textbooks and their impact on teaching and learning mathematics. Efforts to improve textbook development can be informed and facilitated by the ever-growing research interests in examining and documenting teachers' use of textbooks and use of textbooks in students' learning (e.g., Ding et al. 2012; Li et al. 2009a; Stein et al. 2007). Further research is needed on textbook development, the connection of textbook development and textbook use, and the impact of textbook development on teaching and learning mathematics.

References

American Association for the Advancement of Science (2000). *Middle grades mathematics textbooks: a benchmark-based evaluation*. Washington: American Association for the Advancement of Science.

Apple, M. W. (2004). *Ideology and curriculum, 25th anniversary* (3rd ed.). New York: Routledge.

Ball, D. L., & Cohen, D. K. (1996). Reform by the book: what is—or might be—the role of curriculum materials in teacher learning and instructional reform? *Educational Researcher, 25*(9), 6–8, 14.

Beagle, E. G. (1973). Some lessons learned by SMSG. *Mathematics Teacher, 66*, 207–214.

Ding, M., Li, Y., Li, X., & Gu, J. (2012). Knowing and understanding instructional mathematics content through intensive studies of textbooks. In Y. Li & R. Huang (Eds.), *How Chinese teach mathematics and improve teaching* (pp. 66–82). New York: Routledge.

Fan, L., Turnau, S., Dole, S., Gelfman, E., & Li, Y. (2008). DG 14: focus on the development and research of mathematics textbooks. In M. Niss (Ed.), *Proceedings of the 10th international congress on mathematical education* (pp. 485–489). Roskilde: Roskilde University.

Fan, L., Wong, N. Y., Cai, J., & Li, S. (Eds.) (2004). *How Chinese learn mathematics: perspectives from insiders*. Singapore: World Scientific.

Hirsch, C. R. (2007). *Perspectives on the design and development of school mathematics curricula*. Reston: National Council of Teachers of Mathematics.

Huang, F. (2004). Curriculum reform in contemporary China: seven goals and six strategies. *Journal of Curriculum Studies, 36*, 101–115.

Kilpatrick, J. (2003). What works? In S. Senk & D. Thompson (Eds.), *Standards-oriented school mathematics curricula: what does research say about student outcomes?* (pp. 471–488). Mahwah: Lawrence Erlbaum Associates.

Kulm, G. (1999). Making sure that your mathematics curriculum meets standards. *Mathematics Teaching in the Middle School, 4*, 536–541.

Li, J. (2008). Curriculum development in China. In Z. Usiskin & E. Willmore (Eds.), *Mathematics curriculum in Pacific Rim countries: China, Japan, Korea, and Singapore* (pp. 127–140). Charlotte: Information Age.

Li, Y. (2000). A comparison of problems that follow selected content presentations in American and Chinese mathematics textbooks. *Journal for Research in Mathematics Education, 31*, 234–241.

Li, Y. (2007). Curriculum and culture: an exploratory examination of mathematics curriculum materials in their system and cultural contexts. *The Mathematics Educator, 10*(1), 21–38.

Li, Y., & Li, J. (2009). Mathematics classroom instruction excellence identified and promoted through the platform of teaching contests. *ZDM—The International Journal on Mathematics Education, 41*, 263–277.

Li, Y., Chen, X., & Kulm, G. (2009a). Mathematics teachers' practices and thinking in lesson plan development: a case of teaching fraction division. *ZDM—The International Journal on Mathematics Education, 41*, 717–731.

Li, Y., Zhang, J., & Ma, T. (2009b). Approaches and practices in developing mathematics textbooks in China. *ZDM—The International Journal on Mathematics Education, 41*, 733–748.

Liu, J., & Li, Y. (2010). Mathematics curriculum reform in the Chinese mainland: changes and challenges. In F. K. S. Leung & Y. Li (Eds.), *Reforms and issues in school mathematics in East Asia* (pp. 9–31). Rotterdam: Sense.

Ma, L. (1999). *Knowing and teaching elementary mathematics: teachers' understanding of fundamental mathematics in China and the United States*. Mahwah: Lawrence Erlbaum.

National Research Council (2004). *On evaluating curricular effectiveness: judging the quality of K-12 mathematics programs*. Washington: National Academies Press.

Pang, J. S. (2008). Design and implementation of Korean mathematics textbooks. In Z. Usiskin & E. Willmore (Eds.), *Mathematics curriculum in Pacific Rim countries: China, Japan, Korea, and Singapore* (pp. 95–125). Charlotte: Information Age.

Secondary School Mathematics Section, People's Education Press (2001a). *Algebra II for junior high school in nine-year compulsory education*. Beijing: People's Education Press.

Secondary School Mathematics Section, People's Education Press (2001b). *Geometry I for junior high school in nine-year compulsory education*. Beijing: People's Education Press.

Senk, S. & Thompson, D. (Eds.) (2003). *Standards-oriented school mathematics curricula: what does research say about student outcomes?* Mahwah: Lawrence Erlbaum.

Stein, M. K., Remillard, J., & Smith, M. S. (2007). How curriculum influences student learning. In F. K. Lester Jr. (Ed.), *Second handbook of research on mathematics teaching and learning* (pp. 319–369). Charlotte: Information Age.

Trafton, P., Reys, B. J., & Wasman, D. (2001). Standards-based mathematics instructional materials: a phrase in search of a definition. *Phi Delta Kappan, 83*, 259–264.

Wang, J., & Paine, L. (2003). Learning to teach with mandated curriculum and public examination of teaching as contexts. *Teaching and Teacher Education, 19*, 75–94.

Wei, Q. (1996). *The history of the development of secondary school mathematics curriculum and textbooks in China*. Beijing: People's Education Press.

Weiss, I. R., Knapp, M. S., Hollweg, K. S., & Burrill, G. (Eds.) (2002). *Investigating the influences of standards: a framework for research in mathematics, science, and technology education*. Washington: National Academy Press.

Zhang, D. (Ed.) (2006). *Teaching and learning "Two basics" in Chinese school mathematics*. Shanghai: Shanghai Education Press.

Part IV
Curriculum, Teacher, and Teaching

Preface

When leaders of local, regional, or national school systems seek improvement in the yield of their educational efforts, there are several natural opportunities for action. The simplest and most common strategy is to define a new scope and sequence for the intended curriculum. In school mathematics this usually means introducing important new topics of study, changing the order and timing of presentation for familiar topics, and occasionally deleting topics that are judged to be no longer important. A more challenging but very attractive goal is improving the quality of classroom instruction to reflect the latest findings from research on student development, learning, and teaching.

Choosing a course of action is actually the easy part of any school improvement initiative. The real challenge is translating those intentions into everyday classroom reality. The implementation phase of reform requires 'selling' the plans to concerned teachers and the wider school community, preparing appropriate instructional and assessment materials, providing professional development for teachers, and sustaining support for innovations. Then any responsible school improvement actions should be studied carefully to see whether they are achieving their goals.

The six chapters in this section provide a variety of perspectives on the process of improving school mathematics by reform of curriculum and teaching. Through analyses of case studies in Israel, the United States, England, Japan, and China they offer insights into the challenges of developing, implementing, and evaluating change in the content objectives and teaching of K-12 mathematics.

Developing Instructional Materials: Throughout the nineteenth century and much of the twentieth century, classic school mathematics textbooks were typically written by individuals or small author teams, and the books became known by the names of those authors. However, in the past 50 years, that tradition has given way to a more corporate style of text production in which books become known by publisher or curriculum development project name, rather than by the names of contributing authors. Textbooks developed by project teams are now typically the result of collaboration among mathematicians, mathematics education researchers, curriculum development specialists, and teachers. But the role of teachers is mainly to test and react to pilot versions of textbooks written by others.

The first chapter in this section, by Ruhama Even and Shai Olsher, describes a technology-enhanced form of collaborative textbook development *The Integrated Mathematics Wiki-book Project*. With the aim of making teachers more active participants in textbook production, researchers at the Weizmann Institute in Israel developed a web-based process that invited and enabled teachers to contribute ideas and specific suggestions for revision of the first edition of an *Integrated Mathematics* textbook for middle grades.

The Even and Olsher chapter describes the functionality of their Wiki tool and the ways that teachers took advantage of the opportunity to participate actively in its use. It also describes some of the inevitable tensions in a process designed to produce instructional materials that meet the perceived needs of many different kinds of teachers and students and in which ideas of teachers and curriculum development 'experts' clash.

Fidelity of Implementation: Any attempt to improve mathematics education by a change in curriculum or teaching faces a very substantial challenge in also changing the beliefs and practices of teachers. Because most reform initiatives over the past several decades have combined new content objectives with fundamental changes in standard teaching patterns, students of the reform process have paid close attention to the fidelity with which new curriculum materials are implemented.

The second chapter in this section, by Mary Kay Stein, Julia Kaufman, and Miray Tekkumru Kisa, describes a theoretical scheme and a practical research tool for studying teacher learning and changes in practice. It then reports the results from applying the scheme to the study of two specific reform initiatives.

The study tool looks at three main qualities of curriculum use: (1) the extent to which new instructional materials are actually used as the basis of classroom activity; (2) the congruence of classroom activity and the instructional philosophy of the materials; and (3) the quality of enacted instruction. Findings from the application of this curriculum research tool are then used to understand the effects of different curriculum implementation strategies applied in schools and districts. The result is a very insightful description of what it takes to make meaningful changes in curriculum and teaching.

The third chapter of this section, by Margaret Brown and Jeremy Hodgen, recounts experiences in two major reforms of curriculum and teaching in England. The first was a National Numeracy Strategy that attempted a highly prescriptive plan for curriculum content and pacing and a template for daily mathematics lessons. The implementation of the strategy was systematic and standardized in order to reach more than 100,000 teachers in more than 17,000 schools. An accountability program that included external tests with results published in the national press monitored the implementation of reform. The analysis of results from this national initiative provides important insights into the process and prospects of such highly prescriptive top-down reform actions.

The Brown and Hodgen analysis of the National Numeracy Strategy is complemented by their report of findings from a parallel Leverhulme Numeracy Research

Project that studied the effects on teachers and teaching and a Cognitive Acceleration through Mathematics Education project that attempted to change teaching through a 'bottom up' process. Those two research projects reveal the difficulty of making broad and deep changes in long-standing patterns of mathematics teaching at the elementary level, but offer some hope that a school based change process is more feasible than a large-scale systemic strategy.

Content Analysis: The fourth chapter, by Jinfa Cai, Bikai Nie, John Moyer, and Ning Wang, makes the case for careful content analysis as a tool in curriculum design, teaching, professional development, and research. The rationale for this claim is made by contrasting two different approaches to fundamental ideas in algebra, with a focus on the concept of variable.

After describing the conceptions of the variables that underlie typical *Standards*-based and more traditional middle grades curricula, the authors show how those differences shape the definition and development of other important ideas in algebra. They then present research results showing how the two approaches affect classroom teaching and student learning, they discuss the interplay of intended, implemented, and attained curricula, and they describe certain issues in the methodology of curriculum research.

Implementation Strategy: The fifth chapter in this section, by Akihiko Takahashi, addresses the challenges of the effective implementation of change in mathematics curriculum and teaching. It describes the ways that a single public elementary school in Japan used lesson study to introduce mandated changes in the national course of study. Because the new Course of Study emphasized the importance of promoting mathematical thinking and exposition, the lesson study groups focused on production and study of research lessons aimed at that goal. The Takahashi paper describes the resulting lesson study process in great detail.

Textbook Effects: The final chapter in this section, by Rongjin Huang, Z. Ebrar Yetkiner Ozel, Yeping Li and Rebecca V. Osborne, focuses on the role of textbooks in shaping the content and teaching of school mathematics. Through a case study of fraction division in Chinese classrooms, they explored Remillard's ideas about the ways that teachers use and/or interpret curriculum materials.

After reviewing prior theoretical and empirical research on learning trajectories, mathematical tasks, and pedagogical representations, the Huang et al. study examined the ways that a sample of Chinese teachers developed student understanding and skill in fraction division. In particular, the investigators looked for similarities and differences in the ways different teachers approached their instructional task. They looked to see how the observed teaching corresponded to and made use of developments of fraction division in the available text materials. The results of their work offer others some guides to studying the important interactions between teacher judgments and actions and textbook presentations of mathematical ideas.

Taken together, the six chapters of this section offer many insights into the widely varied activities required by development, implementation, and evaluation of reform in curriculum and teaching of school mathematics. Some suggest new ways of thinking about the design of curricula and instructional materials. Others focus on the challenges of implementing innovations effectively. All provide fresh ideas for tackling the central tasks of school mathematics improvement.

University of Maryland, USA   James Fey

Teachers as Participants in Textbook Development: *The Integrated Mathematics Wiki-book Project*

Ruhama Even and Shai Olsher

Abstract This chapter examines how the conventional relationships between teachers and textbooks may be expanded so that teachers become more genuine participants in the process of textbook development. The *Integrated Mathematics Wiki-book Project* is used as a vehicle for investigating this matter. First, the work environment provided for teachers is described. Then, the chapter focuses on the ways in which teachers participated in the joint editing of a textbook they were using in class, during the first year of the project. The analysis focuses on three aspects that characterize the unique work environment provided for the teachers: (1) designing a textbook for a broad student population, (2) preparing a new textbook by making changes to a textbook designed by expert curriculum developers, and (3) consulting with professionals that are not part of the teachers' usual milieu.

Keywords Textbook development · Teachers as curriculum developers · Teachers and textbooks · Wiki-book · Wiki

The relationships between teachers and textbooks are generally associated with curriculum enactment and teachers' use of curriculum materials. Less prevalent is the association of teachers with curriculum development and textbook preparation. The aim of this chapter is to examine how the conventional relationships between teachers and textbooks may be expanded so that teachers become more genuine participants in the process of textbook development. The *Integrated Mathematics Wiki-book Project* is used to examine how this challenge maybe addressed, focusing on the ways in which teachers participated in a unique opportunity made available to them to jointly edit a textbook they were using in class.

After appraising research on the relationships between teachers and textbooks, which provide a basis for conducting this work, we describe the *Integrated Mathematics Wiki-book Project*, in which this research is situated. Then, we report on the ways in which teachers participated in the joint editing of a textbook they were using in class, during the first year of the project. The study reported in this part

R. Even (✉) · S. Olsher
Weizmann Institute of Science, Rehovot, Israel
e-mail: ruhama.even@weizmann.ac.il

Y. Li, G. Lappan (eds.), *Mathematics Curriculum in School Education*,
Advances in Mathematics Education, DOI 10.1007/978-94-007-7560-2_16,
© Springer Science+Business Media Dordrecht 2014

of the chapter focuses not on the changes teachers suggested for the textbook, but instead on teachers' ways of participating in the joint editing of a textbook.

Background

Research on the relationships between teachers and textbooks usually focuses on how textbooks influence classroom instruction. This research examines how teachers use curriculum materials and how a written curriculum is transformed into classroom reality (e.g., Manouchehri and Goodman 1998; Remillard 2005; Remillard et al. 2009; Stein et al. 2007). Accumulating research in a number of countries suggests that curriculum materials, textbooks in particular, considerably influence classroom instruction: teachers often follow teaching sequences suggested by curriculum programs, and base class work mainly on tasks included in textbooks (e.g., Eisenmann and Even 2009, 2011; Grouws et al. 2004; Haggarty and Pepin 2002). Research also reveals discrepancies between the written and the enacted curriculum. For example, Stein et al. (1996) showed that cognitively challenging mathematical tasks tend to decline into less demanding, procedural exercises when implemented in class. Even and Kvatinsky (2010) suggest that teachers who adopt different teaching approaches, to some extent, make different mathematical ideas available for students to learn, even when they use the same textbooks. Such research on the relationships between teachers and textbooks reflects prevalent views and assumptions about the teacher's role, usually regarding the teacher as a curriculum enactor and user of curriculum materials furnished by expert developers.

Yet, in contrast to their central role in curriculum enactment, teachers usually play a rather insignificant role in the development of textbooks. Indeed, some textbook authors are teachers, and as part of the process of curriculum development, selected teachers are often recruited by curriculum developers to teach an experimental version of a new curriculum program in order to gather information about how students deal with the tasks posed, to estimate the time needed to work on tasks in class, and to construct a conjectured learning trajectory (Clements 2002; Cobb 1999; Gravemeijer 1998; Hershkowitz et al. 2002; Schwarz and Hershkowitz 1999; Simon 1995). Still, obviously, only a minute number of selected teachers can actually participate in the development of textbooks in these ways. Thus, the voice of the vast majority of teachers remains unheard and most teachers rarely influence textbook preparation or development.

In reflecting on the insignificant role that teachers play in the development of textbooks and their central role in using them in class, we feel that the conventional relationship between curriculum developers and teachers is basically unidirectional—from curriculum developers to teachers. Teachers' aspirations about desired textbooks as well as adjustments that they make in textbooks—based on their experiences, their knowledge and beliefs about mathematics and its teaching and learning, as well as their acquaintance with the system in which they teach and with their own students—often remain unknown to curriculum developers.

The *Integrated Mathematics Wiki-book Project* aims to expand the traditional unidirectional connection between curriculum developers and teachers into a bidirectional relationship: to stem also from the teachers to the curriculum developers. Thus, it aspires to offer teachers a way to become more genuine participants in the process of textbook development. In the following section we first describe the *Integrated Mathematics Wiki-book Project*. Then we report on a preliminary study that examines teachers' ways of participating in editing and producing a wiki-based revised version of the mathematics textbook they used in class, in an environment offered to them during the first year of the project.

The *Integrated Mathematics Wiki-book Project*

Background

As a country with a centralized educational system, the Israeli school curriculum is developed and regulated by the Ministry of Education. In 2009 the Ministry of Education launched a new national junior-high school mathematics curriculum (Ministry of Education 2009). The new national curriculum comprises three strands: numeric, algebraic, and geometric. It stresses problem solving, thinking, and reasoning for all students, and approaches mathematics teaching in junior-high schools in a spiral approach.

In response to the introduction of the new national junior-high school mathematics curriculum, the mathematics group in the Department of Science Teaching at the Weizmann Institute of Science began developing a new comprehensive junior-high school mathematics curriculum program entitled *Integrated Mathematics* (*Matematica Meshulevet*). The curriculum development team comprises experienced mathematics curriculum developers and mathematics teachers. At the time of this writing, the experimental edition is being used in more than 250 schools throughout Israel, and the team works closely with hundreds of teachers all over the country who need help in adapting to a new curriculum. The *Integrated Mathematics Wiki-book Project* uses the *Integrated Mathematics* textbooks as a point of departure. The first author is the head of the *Integrated Mathematics Project* and the *Integrated Mathematics Wiki-book Project*; the second author is a leading team member of the *Integrated Mathematics Wiki-book Project*.[1]

---

[1]The project is part of the Rothschild-Weizmann Program for Excellence in Science Teaching, supported by the Caesarea Edmond Benjamin de Rothschild Foundation. Other team members include Michal Ayalon, Gila Ozruso-Haggiag, and Edriss Titi.

Project Objectives and Focus

The main objective of the *Integrated Mathematics Wiki-book Project* is to expand the conventional relationships between teachers and curriculum developers, which are mainly unidirectional—stemming from curriculum developers to teachers. To this end, the *Integrated Mathematics Wiki-book Project* invites teachers who use the *Integrated Mathematics Program* to collaborate in editing the textbooks they use in their classes and to produce, as group products, revised versions of these textbooks—wiki-based revised textbooks that are suitable for a broad student population, and not only for students in a particular teacher's class.

An additional goal of the *Integrated Mathematics Wiki-book Project* is to foster teachers' professional development and growth. It is assumed that this kind of teachers' collaborative work has the potential to contribute to improving teachers' understanding of mathematics and the curriculum, to acquaint teachers with the use of a valuable technological tool and resource (Wiki) that allows easy collaborative creation and editing of teaching materials, and to support the development of a professional community whose members work collaboratively with colleagues on authentic tasks of teaching.

The Technological Platform

To enable collaborative textbook editing and the production of a joint revised textbook, we use, with some modifications, the MediaWiki platform and Wikibook templates for constructing the *Integrated Mathematics Wiki-book* website. The project website serves as an online platform for collaborative work on a common database (i.e., a textbook) and for discussions in a forum-like fashion.

Figure 1 shows part of the main page of a textbook on *the Integrated Mathematics Wiki-book* website. (The text in this, as well as in all other figures, is a translation to English of the original Hebrew text.) The main page includes standard MediaWiki tabs (top of the page) that allow performing actions (e.g., editing and requesting change notifications) or viewing pages related to a selected textbook unit (e.g., modifications made and discussions held). An abbreviated textbook table of contents is displayed (on the right) to enable easy access to textbook units. Also included in the main page of a textbook on *the Integrated Mathematics Wiki-book* website (as well as in all other pages) are navigation shortcuts to frequently used pages and tools (e.g., the latest modifications, technical support, and consultation with various professionals) as well as a link to a free-hand drawing applet embedded in the website (on the left).

To assist in the process of textbook editing, we added different kinds of buttons to the standard Wikitext editing toolbar. Some of these buttons were added before the project started, based on the project team's anticipation; other buttons were added as the editing work progressed, in response to participants' requests. One kind of added buttons is buttons that assist in general text editing. For example, a button

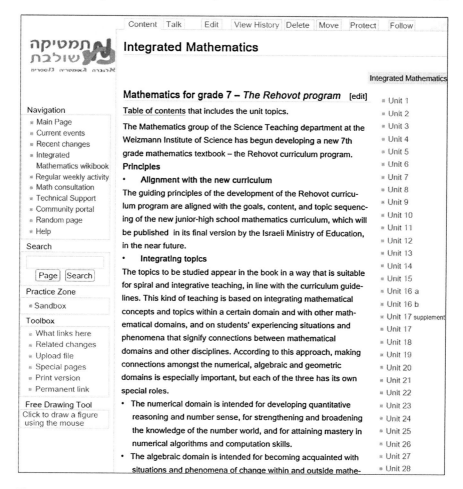

Fig. 1 Part of the main page of a textbook on the *Integrated Mathematics Wiki-book* website

labeled *important* was added in response to participants' requests to easily highlight core parts of a textbook. However, unique challenges are associated with the task of editing a mathematics textbook that are not encountered in most other uses of Wikitext. These challenges are rooted in the need to type mathematical text and the desire to display mathematics problems in specific formats. Therefore, we added buttons to the standard Wikitext editing toolbar that enable the insertion of frequently used mathematical text templates and textbook problem templates. Figure 2 displays customized added templates.

Quite a few buttons were added in order to improve communication among the participants about proposed changes. This kind of buttons includes, for instance, buttons labeled *before* and *after* to signal whether a suggested editing action is based on anticipated or actual classroom teaching; buttons labeled *like* and *seen*

Fig. 2 Customized templates
added to assist in the editing
of a mathematics textbook

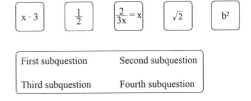

were added to enable easy positive and neutral responses (respectively); and a *smiling face* button was added to enable a softening of the "tone" of written messages.

Operating the Project

The *Integrated Mathematics Wiki-book Project* started in September 2010. At the time of writing this paper it has successfully concluded two years of operation and is embarking on the third year. Participation in this project consists of (1) on-going distance work, and (2) monthly face-to-face whole-group full-day meetings. These are elaborated on next.

The ongoing distance work includes textbook editing, reacting to other participants' suggestions, and discussions of mathematical and pedagogical issues. Figures 3–6 present various kinds of ongoing distance work. Figure 3 shows a Wiki-textbook page in which one of the participating teachers added a task (task 6). The new task asks students to work algebraically and to generalize their previous work on task 5, which involves work on several numeric cases. The teacher explained her suggestion to add a generalization task in the corresponding discussion page:

> I added an additional task following question 5 because in question 5 the students solve several examples regarding which of the figures has a larger area… so I thought to add a generalization question, where the side of the rectangle is x.

Figure 4 shows a teacher's proposal to change the phrasing of tasks in the textbook. In this example, a teacher added an organizational table (the second table in Fig. 4) to an investigation task that involves pattern finding and problem solving related to a series of "buildings" made from matches.

The reactions of other participating teachers to this suggested change in task phrasing were expressed in the corresponding discussion page (see Fig. 5). As shown, the suggestion to add an organizational table (by T1) received "like" responses from two other participants (T2 and T3).

The discussion page in Fig. 5 includes only "like" responses; i.e., concise teachers' responses that require only a small effort. To respond in this way, the teachers needed only to click on a ready-made button. Figure 6 shows a discussion page of a different nature. This discussion page includes a debate among five teachers (T1-T5) regarding whether there was a need to change the structure of a certain unit in the 7th grade textbook.

5. a. Determine, in each drawing, which has a greater area, the rectangle or the triangle. Explain. (The drawings are not to scale)

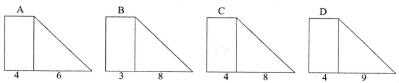

b. In the following drawing, it is known that the area of the rectangle is equal to the area of the triangle.

What is the length of the edge marked with a box? Explain how you found it.

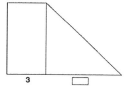

6. One of the edges of the rectangle is marked with an X (see drawing). Write an expression for the length of the edge marked with a box so that:

a. The area of the triangle will be greater than the area of the rectangle?

b. The area of the triangle will be smaller than the area of the rectangle?

c. The area of the triangle will be equal to the area of the rectangle?

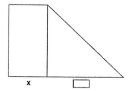

Fig. 3 Edited Wiki-textbook page—adding tasks

The monthly face-to-face whole-group meetings consist of collaborative work on advancing the textbook editing, discussions of mathematical and pedagogical issues, and formulation of community working norms. These meetings are built on the preceding teachers' distance work of textbook editing, and they also serve as departing points for subsequent distance work.

Participating teachers are provided with two kinds of support that accompany both the distance work and the face-to-face meetings. One is technical support in using the technological platform for textbook editing. The aim of this support is to provide a smooth running work environment that enables teachers to perform desired editing without having to deal with, or be constrained by, technological difficulties.

Lesson 1. Building with matches

Finding the rule of a series of match structures and building an algebraic

expression

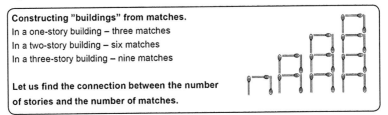

Constructing "buildings" from matches.

In a one-story building – three matches

In a two-story building – six matches

In a three-story building – nine matches

Let us find the connection between the number

of stories and the number of matches.

1. a. How many matches are required for constructing a 5-story building? 11-story building?
How did you find the number of matches?

b. How many matches are required to build a 100-story building? Explain.

c. Complete the table.

Number of matches	Number of stories
	4
	7
30	
	23

d. Yuval has 51 matches, Maayan has 61 matches, Shaked has 71 matches, and Omer
has 72 matches. Each of them is trying to construct a building that is as tall as possible.
Who will not have any matches left? Explain.

Childrens' names	Number of matches	Number of stories	Matches left
Yuval			
Maayan			
Shaked			
Omer			

e. Noa constructed a building from the matches she had. She had two matches left.
Give an example for the number of matches that Noa had.

f. To construct an *x*-story building ,3x matches are required. How many matches are
required for constructing an *a*-story building?
A building requires *3b* matches to be built. How many stories does it have?

Fig. 4 Edited Wiki-textbook page—change of task phrasing

The other kind of support is related to conceptual issues that emerge as part of the
editing work. To address that, participating teachers are offered the opportunity to
consult with various professionals throughout their ongoing distance work and the
monthly face-to-face meetings. The professionals made available for consultation
include authors of the textbooks, a research mathematician, and researchers in the
field of mathematics education. To enable easy access to these professionals, a va-

T1 Correction after a lesson in question 1 part d, I added a table- T1 19:26, 6 November 2010 (UTC) I added another column to the table: number of matches
T1 - T1 19:24, 9 Novmber 2010 (UTC) Correction after a lesson

T2 says: Like

T3 21:09, 4 December 2010 (UTC) says: Like

Fig. 5 Discussion page: "Like" responses to a suggested change in task phrasing

Exercises 9 12, 13 & 14 provide practice for lesson 4 so they should be moved into lesson 4.
T1 21:47, 20 December 2010 (UTC)

I think the exercises are in their correct place. Exercise 9 in the original book provides practice of fractions in algebraic expressions. Same goes for exercises 12, 13, & 14. Lesson 4 deals with substitutions, simplifying algebraic expressions with fractions and review of the whole unit.-- T2 13:41, 28 December 2010 (UTC)

T3 15:37, 28 December 2010 (UTC) says: Like

In my opinion lessons 2, 3, 4 can be learned together, there is no need for a lesson for each of them, therefore the order of the exercises does not matter. -- T4 00:58, 2 January 2011 (UTC)

It is not possible, when considering the length of the lesson to teach those lessons together. Each of these lessons «takes» a whole period, and if there is any time left one could integrate the assignment collection during the lesson. T2 13:48, 2 January 2011 (UTC):Correction after a lesson

I agree with T1 about the place of exercises 9, 12, 13, 14 (especially 9, and then you need to change its part a, since it is the same exercise from lesson 4). I also agree with T2 that it is impossible to teach lessons 2 - 4 in one period due to lack of time. T5 19:25, 5 January 2011 (UTC):Correction after a lesson

Fig. 6 Discussion page: debating the structure of a certain textbook unit

riety of consultation channels are offered via the *Integrated Mathematics Wiki-book* website, regular e-mail, Skype chats and calls, and face-to-face meetings.

Several changes occurred in the project between the first and the ensuing years of operation. During the first year of operation (starting in September 2010), the project team purposely avoided any intervention with, commenting on, or evaluation of the teachers' work, besides instructing the teachers on how to use the *Integrated Mathematics Wiki-book* website. The role of the project team during that year was to provide a smooth running work environment and to moderate, but not direct, the monthly face-to-face meetings. Similarly, during this year, the consultants associated with the project were explicitly instructed not to initiate any intervention with, comment on, or evaluate the teachers' work. Instead, the consultants were directed to respond only when explicitly approached by the teachers, and to address only queries related to the following areas: reasons for specific choices made in the textbook by the textbook authors, the mathematics in the curriculum, and research in mathematics education. In particular, the consultants were instructed not to comment on or evaluate particular teachers' editing suggestions, even when requested to do so by the teachers.

In the second year of the project the participating teachers (some newcomers and some continuing participants) continued to receive an autonomous work environment wherein they could freely edit the textbooks as they wished. However, the work environment was slightly modified. For example, the opportunities to interact with professionals that are not part of the teachers' usual milieu were expanded. Thus, a sizable part of the monthly face-to-face meetings during the second year was devoted to semi-structured discussions with the textbook authors and with the mathematician. Also, the consultants associated with the project were allowed to freely comment on the teachers' editing suggestions and could freely address any query raised by the teachers. Moreover, during the second year of the project the project team initiated various activities that purposely addressed important issues related to the teachers' work, such as aspects of argumentation in mathematics classes. Finally, as the number of participating teachers grew considerably, some of the editing work was conducted in small groups, according to different focus preferences. Each small group had a group leader, who also participated in the planning of the project activities together with the project team. A similar work environment is planned for the third year of the project.

As can be seen, several characteristics of the work environment offered by the *Integrated Mathematics Wiki-book* project are not usually part of teachers' practice. This includes, for example, designing a textbook for a broad student population instead of focusing on the specific student population taught, generating a textbook by making changes to a textbook designed by expert curriculum developers, and consulting with professionals that are not part of the teachers' usual milieu. The next part of the chapter focuses on ways in which the first-year teachers participated in the joint editing of a textbook that they were using in class, in this unique work environment.

First-Year Teachers' Ways of Participating in Textbook Editing

Most of the first-year teachers participated in the distance editing of the textbook on a regular basis. Yet they varied regarding the extent and nature of their work on the *Integrated Mathematics Wiki-book* website. Some used the website extensively, making or suggesting changes, commenting on colleagues' suggestions, or discussing mathematical or pedagogical issues. Others were less active in using the website. All teachers, however, actively participated in the face-to-face monthly meetings; some explained that they could express themselves better in these meetings than on the website.

At the beginning of the year, teachers moved rather hastily from one unit to another, not achieving closure on suggested changes, and leaving some issues raised by other teachers unaddressed. Moreover, different teachers frequently worked on different textbook units, which resulted in less collaborative editing. Therefore, after a few months, the project team included in each monthly face-to-face meeting a session that focused on addressing changes suggested and issues that were raised in previous distance work, in relation to only one or two textbook units.

Next, we present a preliminary study that focused on the ways in which teachers participated in the joint editing of a textbook that they were using in class during the first year of the project, stressing three characteristics that are not usually part of teachers' practice. Where appropriate, we added relevant information from the second year of the project's operation.

Methods

Participants in the first year of the project consisted of nine 7th grade teachers, all of whom used the 7th grade *Integrated Mathematics* textbook (Bouhadana et al. 2009a, 2009b) in class. The teachers came from different parts of the country, from Jewish and Arab sectors, and from orthodox religious and secular sectors. Their teaching experience varied considerably, from 6 to 29 years. All of the participants held a first degree either in mathematics or in a mathematics-related field, such as a B.Ed. with a major in mathematics. Five held a masters' degree, not necessarily in mathematics or mathematics education. None of the participants had any prior experience in editing texts using a wiki-based platform; however, most were familiar with Wikipedia as a source of information. The teachers received grants as well as course credits that would count towards a salary increase.

Data sources include the following: (1) the *Integrated Mathematics Wiki-book Project* website, which contains the wiki-based textbook with all changes made, their corresponding discussion pages, and online forum-like discussions, (2) video-documentation and field-notes of the monthly whole-group meetings, (3) individual semi-structured interviews with the teachers, at the end of that year, (4) individual papers written by the teachers as a final assignment, and (5) a journal kept by the second author in which he documented informal conversations with project participants, and added ideas and reflections.

Data analysis focused on the ways in which the teachers participated in the joint editing of a textbook that they were using in class during the first year of the project. The analysis focused on the following three aspects:

• Designing a textbook for a broad student population.

- Preparing a textbook by making changes to a textbook designed by expert curriculum developers.
- Consulting with professionals that are not part of the teachers' usual milieu.

For each of the first two aspects, we scrutinized the following data sources: discussion pages and online forum-like discussions on the *Integrated Mathematics Wikibook Project* website, field-notes of the monthly meetings, transcripts of the interviews, final papers, and the researcher's journal. We searched for instances related to each of the two aspects. We then examined and interpreted them. We took into account how each instance is connected to others and how it is linked in the overall activity of each relevant teacher and of the whole group of teachers.

For the third aspect, we identified and examined all recorded interactions with a representative of the textbook authors, the research mathematician, and the researcher in mathematics education. We then interpreted those interactions.

Designing a Textbook for a Broad Student Population

The task for the group of nine teachers was to produce, as a group product, one—and only one—wiki-based revised textbook that would be suitable for a broad student population, and not only for students in a particular teacher's class. In general, the first-year teachers embraced this approach and conceived their role as preparing a textbook that would be suitable for any 7th grade class in the country. This is illustrated by the following episode that took place during the third monthly face-to-face meeting. The group of teachers discussed a particular change one of them had suggested. Feeling that the modification suggested might not be appropriate for a general student population, one teacher commented that the textbook they were preparing should be appropriate for the whole population of 7th grade students in the country. Her colleagues agreed with her.

T1: We are making a book that is not suitable for us individually.
T2: [puzzled] Why?
T1: But a book that should be appropriate for the whole country.
T2: Right.

To write a textbook that is suitable for a broad student population, the teachers often introduced, and insisted on adopting changes that emerged from their personal teaching context. For example, one of the teachers that taught only lower-achieving classes for several years continually stated that one of her goals was to make the 7th grade *Integrated Mathematics* textbook more suitable for the low-achieving students in her classes. She consistently suggested modifications based on her teaching experience in those classes. For example, explaining why she revised the table in a textbook task that dealt with the number of marbles a child [Noi] had in a variety of situations, the teacher wrote in the corresponding discussion page that this revision helped students in her class who have difficulties. She also indicated that the change she made would be appropriate for higher-achieving students as well, signaling that she was aware that the textbook needed to be appropriate for other classes too:

I changed Noi's table, I recorded [in the table] the example exercise that the students had to fill in. It was very helpful for students in my class who have difficulties; by the way I think that one example wouldn't harm strong students as well.

Throughout the year this teacher suggested and initiated numerous changes with the goal of making the textbook more suitable for low-achieving students. The majority of these suggestions were rejected by most other participants as not suitable for the broader 7th grade student population. Eventually, to resolve the continual tension that the group experienced when producing a generic textbook and dealing with the requests of one teacher to introduce modifications that specifically attend to the lower-achieving students, the group decided that there was a need for an additional version of the textbook, designed specifically for low-achieving students. The teacher who was interested in this modification began to develop such a version by herself. In the second year of the project she became a leader of a group of teachers who collaborated on editing a version of the 8th grade *Integrated Mathematics* textbook that was intended by the curriculum developers for classes of low-achieving students. She will continue to lead a group of teachers similarly during the third year of the project.

However, another case in which a teacher repeatedly initiated changes that suited her unique teaching context ended up differently. This teacher, who had easy access to a computer lab for her class, stated that her main objective was to find ways to include in the textbook technology-based activities so that her students could use computers as they learned mathematics. Her view, which she continually expressed throughout the year, was that integrating computers into school mathematics is important for all students (i.e., not only for her students). This view was clearly expressed, for instance, in the paper she wrote as a final assignment:

Educators in this country and around the world agree that the mathematics curriculum should address the needs of a modern society in the 21st century, therefore, the right thing to do is to integrate computer technology into the textbooks, technology that will challenge and lead students to better learning. The Wikibook framework promotes the integration of interactive tools that provide intriguing stimuli and provide a sense of control with the learning.

This teacher devoted a great deal of her time to work in this direction during the first year of the project. She continued to do so during the second year as well, in addition to serving as a leader of a small group of participating teachers. The authors of the *Integrated Mathematics Program* liked the applets she developed, and decided to display them on the *Integrated Mathematics Project* website, in her name, making them available to all users of the *Integrated Mathematics Program*.

Unlike the case of attending to the needs of low-achieving students described before, the suggestion to incorporate the use of technological tools into the textbook was embraced by the other participants. They agreed with the teacher who initiated the integration of advanced technological tools that this is important to all students. Thus, they supported revisions in this direction even though the use of computers in mathematics lessons in Israel is sparse. For instance, in her final paper, one of the other teachers wrote:

> It is important to say that not in all schools from which the participants come there is an adequate technological infrastructure for such work, and therefore the integration of technology was irrelevant for them... My feeling is that in this topic, the integration of technological tools into mathematics teaching, there was a consensus about its importance.

Making Changes to a Textbook Designed by Experts

Most teachers actively participated in the joint editing of the textbook. Yet, making changes to a textbook written by expert curriculum developers was a role that not all teachers easily embraced. In the following illustrative excerpt, taken from an interview with one of the participating teachers at the end of the year, the teacher described how she felt at the beginning of the year. Responding to the interviewer's opening question: "Tell me how the project was for you, in general," the teacher replied:

> T: It took some time to get going.
> I: Okay, what does it mean?
> T: It took some time to get going. Uh, I remember that the moment I introduced the first change, I said: 'What? Can I introduce changes? Can I here?' It was not obvious to me. And, at least at the beginning, it took some time [to realize] that you can make...

As the work progressed, the teachers generally seemed comfortable introducing changes to the textbook. Nevertheless, a few episodes occurred later in the year, indicating that teachers sometimes refrained from making changes because of their respect for the decisions and choices of the textbook's authors. For example, commenting on a debate among three teachers regarding several significant changes that they had suggested in a specific textbook unit, another teacher wrote in the discussion page:

> In my opinion the changes are exaggerated here. I would like to emphasize a sentence that was stated in the last meeting and that Shai didn't like: There are professional people who wrote the book with a broader and more secure view. I do believe that change begins in the field but we need a solid basis.

A similar episode occurred during the third whole-group face-to-face meeting. One of the teachers suggested to the group that a label be added to each "owl" icon, to indicate whether it is important or not ("owl" icons were used in the original textbook to signify lesson summaries, definitions, comments, and clarifications). Another teacher objected to labeling some "owls" as unimportant: "I think that if they [the textbook authors] decided to include it in the owl then it is probably important."

Moreover, most teachers introduced changes directly in the textbook, inserting new text, as well as changing or omitting existing text. Yet some teachers tended to suggest changes as ideas, describing them in the discussion pages, or in online forum-like discussions that accompanied the wiki-based textbook. In addition to technical difficulties that were the main source for this behavior at the beginning, sometimes, especially later in the year, this behavior was rooted in the participating teachers' perception of their role in producing the edited textbook. For example, one teacher continually stated that she only suggests ideas for changing the textbook, whereas it is the professional curriculum developers' task to carry them out—if they thought the ideas were good—and execute the actual editing of the book. For instance, in her interview at the end of the year, this teacher said:

> T: Even changes to the textbook… because, really, it's, like, it is difficult for me to make any changes. No, not technically.
> I: Why?
> T: I don't know. Like, who am I, like, it is difficult for me, I don't want, like, to make changes. So I propose, and if it's good then
> I: Then what?
> T: Then they will take this idea.
> I: Who?
> T: The team of curriculum developers…

Consulting with Professionals Not Part of the Teachers' Usual Milieu

The project offered the first-year teachers the possibility of consulting with three professionals that are not part of the teachers' usual milieu: a representative of the textbook authors, a research mathematician, and a researcher in mathematics education. This consultation was restricted to queries related only to the following areas: reasons for specific choices made in the textbook by the textbook authors, the mathematics in the curriculum, and research in mathematics education. There were about twenty explicit requests for consultation during the year, most of which were directed to the representative of the textbook authors; none were directed to the researcher in mathematics education. All but two of the requests for consultation occurred during whole-group face-to-face meetings.

Most of the requests for consultation were directed to the representative of the textbook authors, who played a double role, since she was also a full member of the *Integrated Mathematics Wiki-book Project* team. Thus, she was present in all face-to-face meetings. As intended, almost all the queries to her were related to reasons for specific choices made in the textbook by the textbook authors. For example, teachers asked her why the authors did not provide captions to the different kinds of "owls", whether all the drawings in the textbook are supposed to be precise, what is the role of a specific part of a unit, why there is no definition of function in the textbook, etc. Rarely, teachers also sought approval for their suggested changes. The most salient example was when one teacher, who suggested a complete change in the national curriculum so that it would be based on a functional approach, presented her suggestion in one of the whole-group meetings, and later repeatedly pressed for the textbook writers' opinion.

Seldom did the first-year teachers use the opportunity to consult with the mathematician who, unlike the representative of the textbook authors, was not part of the ongoing work. The teachers met the mathematician only once, when he introduced himself at a whole-group meeting, but he was available to answer questions via email and video chat using Skype. The teachers approached the mathematician three times, using the project team as mediators, mainly as a referee in cases when they strongly disagreed with each other (not necessarily about mathematics per se). For example, when the group of teachers could not reach a consensus regarding which of two textbook problems was more difficult for students, or which definition of the algebraic activity of substituting numerical values into expressions should be included in the textbook, if at all.

Conclusion

In this chapter we used the *Integrated Mathematics Wiki-book Project* to examine how the traditional unidirectional relationships between curriculum developers and teachers can be expanded into a bidirectional relationship: also from the teachers to the curriculum developers. The first year of the project provided an autonomous intervention-free work environment for teachers to freely edit the textbook as they wished, restricting—somewhat artificially—the scope of their interactions with other professionals. Thus, the project team offered extensive technical support but purposely avoided and even impeded any involvement with, commenting on, or evaluation of the teachers' work.

The initial examination of the ways in which the first-year teachers participated in the joint editing of a textbook they were using in class focused on characteristics that are not usually part of teachers' practice. The findings revealed that most teachers accepted the role of preparing a textbook that would be suitable for a broad student population rather easily. To this end, the teachers often used the knowledge that they had acquired from their own teaching experience as a springboard for textbook modifications, but took into account a variety of teaching contexts as well as different needs and preferences of various teachers, students, and the educational system at large (e.g., when considering the needs of both mainstream and lower-achieving classes, and when deciding to integrate the use of computers into the textbook).

Most teachers accepted their role in making changes to a textbook written by expert curriculum developers rather well; yet, a few did not. At times, some teachers refrained from making changes because of their respect for the expertise of the textbook's authors. Those teachers either protested against suggested changes that appeared to contradict the intention of the textbook's authors' (e.g., labeling some "owls" as unimportant) or in general perceived their role as a suggestion maker for changes in the textbook, but leaving the decision of whether and how to carry out those changes to the experts.

The work environment provided to the first-year teachers purposely prevented them from freely interacting with professionals that were not part of the teachers' usual milieu. This kind of environment enables one to study changes that a group of teachers suggest to make in a textbook they use in class, without being intimidated by interventions and criticisms of people who might be perceived by the teachers as authority figures. This is the focus of another study that we are currently conducting. However, the work environment provided to the first-year teachers is rather artificial, and perhaps is not as beneficial, when the second goal of the *Integrated Mathematics Wiki-book Project*, which is promoting teachers' professional development, is considered. Not only might improving teachers' understanding of mathematics and of the curriculum be less successful this way, but this kind of work environment also prevents teachers from interacting with professionals who are not part of the teachers' usual milieu in more authentic ways. As described in this chapter, in the second and third years of the project this deficiency is addressed by modifying the teachers' work environment. Yet the findings of this preliminary study suggest that careful attention should be given in designing the work environment, so that it nourishes teachers' participation in the development of textbooks in ways that help them feel qualified to face other professionals.

The *Integrated Mathematics Wiki-book Project* was founded on the premise that teachers should become more genuine participants in the process of textbook development. The unique design of the *Integrated Mathematics Wiki-book Project* sets the stage for new and exciting ways for all teachers to actively participate in textbook development, and for professional curriculum developers and policy makers to learn about teachers' needs, desires, and aspirations.

This project also provides a unique research setting for examining important issues that presently are not well-understood or easily accessible to study. These include, for instance, teachers' expectations and aspirations for desired textbooks, the types of changes teachers think should be made in textbooks they use, and the contribution of specific work environments to teachers' joint editing of textbooks (affordances and limitations). This chapter lays the groundwork for such future research studies.

References

Bouhadana, R., Friedlander, A., Koren, M., Ozruso-Haggiag, G., Robinson, N., & Taizi, N. (2009a). *Integrated mathematics (Matematica Meshulevet): 7th grade—part A*. Rehovot: Weizmann Institute (in Hebrew).

Bouhadana, R., Friedlander, A., Koren, M., Ozruso-Haggiag, G., Robinson, N., & Taizi, N. (2009b). *Integrated mathematics (Matematica Meshulevet): 7th grade—part B*. Rehovot: Weizmann Institute (in Hebrew).

Clements, D. H. (2002). Linking research and curriculum development. In L. English (Ed.), *Handbook of international research in mathematics education* (pp. 599–630). Mahwah: Laurence Erlbaum.

Cobb, P. (1999). Individual and collective mathematical development: the case of statistical data analysis. *Mathematical Thinking and Learning, 1*(1), 5–43.

Eisenmann, T., & Even, R. (2009). Similarities and differences in the types of algebraic activities in two classes taught by the same teacher. In J. T. Remillard, B. A. Herbel-Eisenmann, & G. M. Lloyd (Eds.), *Mathematics teachers at work: connecting curriculum materials and classroom instruction* (pp. 152–170). New York: Routledge.

Eisenmann, T., & Even, R. (2011). Enacted types of algebraic activity in different classes taught by the same teacher. *International Journal of Science and Mathematics Education, 9*, 867–891.

Even, R., & Kvatinsky, T. (2010). What mathematics do teachers with contrasting teaching approaches address in probability lessons? *Educational Studies in Mathematics, 74*, 207–222.

Gravenmeijer, K. (1998). Developmental research as a research method. In A. Sierpinska & J. Kilpatrick (Eds.), *Mathematics education as a research domain: a search for identity* (Part 1, pp. 277–296). Dordrecht: Kluwer Academic.

Grouws, D., Smith, M., & Sztajn, P. (2004). The preparation and teaching practices of United States mathematics teachers: grades 4 and 8. In P. Kloosterman & F. Lester Jr. (Eds.), *Results and interpretations of the 1990 through 2000 mathematics assessments of the National Assessment of Educational Progress* (pp. 221–267). Reston: National Council of Teachers of Mathematics.

Haggarty, L., & Pepin, B. (2002). An investigation of mathematics textbooks and their use in English, French and German classrooms: who gets an opportunity to learn what? *British Educational Research Journal, 28*(4), 567–590.

Hershkowitz, R., Dreyfus, T., Ben-Zvi, D., Friedlander, A., Hadas, N., Resnick, T., Tabach, M., & Schwartz, B. (2002). Mathematics curriculum development for computerized environments: a designer-researcher-teacher-learner activity. In L. English (Ed.), *Handbook of international research in mathematics education* (pp. 657–694). Mahwah: Laurence Erlbaum.

Manouchehri, A., & Goodman, T. (1998). Mathematics curriculum reform and teachers: understanding the connections. *The Journal of Educational Research, 92*, 27–41.

Ministry of Education (2009). Math curriculum for grades 7-9. Retrieved from http://meyda.education.gov.il/files/Tochniyot_Limudim/Math/Hatab/Mavo.doc (in Hebrew).

Remillard, J. T. (2005). Examining key concepts in research on teachers' use of mathematics curricula. *Review of Educational Research, 75*, 211–246.

Remillard, J. T., Herbel-Eisenmann, B. A., & Lloyd, G. M. (Eds.) (2009). *Mathematics teachers at work: connecting curriculum materials and classroom instruction* (pp. 152–170). New York: Routledge.

Schwarz, B. B., & Hershkowitz, R. (1999). Prototypes: brakes or levers in learning the function concept? The role of computer tools. *Journal for Research in Mathematics Education, 30*, 362–389.

Simon, M. (1995). Reconstructing mathematics pedagogy from a constructivist perspective. *Journal for Research in Mathematics Education, 26*(2), 114–145.

Stein, M. K., Grover, B. W., & Henningsen, M. (1996). Building student capacity for mathematical thinking and reasoning: an analysis of mathematical tasks used in reform classrooms. *American Educational Research Journal, 33*, 455–488.

Stein, M. K., Remillard, J., & Smith, M. S. (2007). How curriculum influences student learning. In F. K. Lester (Ed.), *Second handbook of research on mathematics teaching and learning* (pp. 319–369). Charlotte: Information Age.

Mathematics Teacher Development
in the Context of District Managed Curriculum

Mary Kay Stein, Julia Kaufman, and Miray Tekkumru Kisa

Abstract The purpose of this study was to develop and test the viability of a conceptual framework for analyzing mathematics instruction and mathematics teacher development within the context of policies regarding district-wide adoption of curriculum. The framework takes three dimensions of curriculum-based instruction into account independently: use, congruence (the extent to which instruction aligns with district and curricular guidelines), and quality (the extent to which instruction maintains the cognitive demand of appropriately challenging tasks, takes account of and builds on student thinking, and situates intellectual authority in mathematical reasoning). Based on analyses of multiple observations of 36 teachers across two districts, teachers were classified into one of four implementation profiles (flounderer, mechanical, canonical, maverick) that were created by crossing the three dimensions; in addition, their trajectory through those profiles was traced over a two-year period. Results suggest teachers were more likely to use the district-adopted curricula as the source of their lessons than to align their practice with curricular and district guidelines. Teachers' demonstration of high-quality lessons was less frequent. Differences across the two districts in the percentages of teachers falling into each of the implementation profiles suggests that district actions may have shaped teachers' uptake of the curriculum. Finally, results suggest a more uneven pathway toward high-quality instruction than had been initially conjectured.

Keywords Mathematics teacher learning · Mathematics teacher development · Curriculum · Instructional practice · Mathematics teaching · District policy

An earlier version of this paper was presented at the 2011 annual meeting of the American Educational Research Association, New Orleans. This work was supported by a grant from the National Science Foundation (IERI Grant REC-0228343), as well as support by the Institution of Education Sciences and the U.S. Department of Education (Award R305B1000012). The content or opinions expressed herein do not necessarily reflect the view of the National Science Foundation or any other agency of the U.S. Government.

M.K. Stein (✉) · M.T. Kisa
LRDC, University of Pittsburgh, Pittsburgh, USA
e-mail: mkstein@pitt.edu

J. Kaufman
University of Pittsburgh, Pittsburgh, USA

Y. Li, G. Lappan (eds.), *Mathematics Curriculum in School Education*,
Advances in Mathematics Education, DOI 10.1007/978-94-007-7560-2_17,
© Springer Science+Business Media Dordrecht 2014

Over the past decade, district policies in the United States have become increasingly focused on the improvement of instruction, especially in subjects that are regularly tested under NCLB (Elmore and Burney 1999; Hightower et al. 2002; Hubbard et al. 2006; Supovitz 2006). In mathematics, curriculum[1] has traditionally been viewed as the key policy lever for improving instruction and learning on a large scale. Yet curriculum alone has been shown to have limited influence on teachers' instructional practices (Ball and Cohen 1996; Coburn 2001; Fullan 1991; Fullan and Pomfret 1977; Wilson 1990). While it may be relatively easy to get curriculum materials into the hands of large numbers of teachers, it can be difficult for district leaders to ensure that teachers actually *use* the new materials and more difficult yet to ensure that they use them in a manner that is *congruent* with the pedagogical[2] features of the curriculum (e.g., group work, manipulative use) and with district guidelines for the sequencing and pacing of lessons/units.

To complicate matters further, even the use of curricula in a congruent manner (as described above) still does not guarantee high-quality instruction, especially for standards-based mathematics curricula that are comprised of cognitively challenging instructional tasks.[3] Teachers can set up an instructional task exactly as specified in the curricular materials, yet fail to support students' high-level thinking and reasoning as they actually work on the task (Stein et al. 1996). This is significant because it is not whether students are sitting in groups or using manipulatives or on the right lesson on the right day that matters, rather it is what students are actually thinking about that determines their opportunities to learn.

The purpose of this study was to develop and test the viability of a conceptual framework for analyzing mathematics instruction and mathematics teacher development *within the context of local policies regarding district-wide curriculum adoption and implementation*. Our framework will take *use*, *congruence* and *quality* into account independently as we develop teacher implementation profiles and conjecture pathways of teacher development.

We view the study's contribution as two-fold. First, we believe that our provision of a new framework that takes use, congruence, and quality into account separately represents an advance for the field of research on curriculum implementation and that it can serve as a unifying framework for future studies of large-scale teacher improvement within the context of district managed curricula. The study results suggest that our framework is "up to the task" in that it was able to detect meaningful variation among teachers—variation that appears to be related to the context of the school or district in which they worked. Second, situating the study of teacher development within district reform efforts provides an illustration of how combined

---

[1] In this manuscript, we use the term, "curriculum" to mean a textbook series.

[2] Non-US readers may prefer the term "didactical." The features to which we refer are those that relate to how to teach the mathematics content.

[3] Because the two curricula used in this study were standards-based and at least partially funded by the National Science Foundation, the presumption (supported by some prior analyses [see Stein and Kim 2009]) is that the tasks—as they appeared in the curriculum—were high-quality.

attention to district policies and implementation can make progress on understanding and supporting the improvement of teaching on a large scale.

Theoretical Framework

Most models of mathematics teacher development describe teacher learning without reference to the materials with which they interact on a daily basis or the work environment in which their learning occurs (Fennema and Nelson 1997). The contribution of our framework is that it examines teacher learning in a specific, well-defined context: large-scale, district-mandated improvement efforts that rely heavily on the adoption and implementation of standards-based curricula. These kinds of district-wide improvement efforts have become increasingly prevalent over the past decade in the United States with many large urban districts adopting and supporting one carefully selected curriculum (Hightower et al. 2002; Supovitz 2006).

We propose that teacher learning occurs along one or more pathways or trajectories that can be specified. Similar to current efforts to identify *student* learning trajectories that one would expect to emerge within the context of well-conducted programs of instruction (Clements and Sarama 2004), our long-term goal is to identify teacher learning trajectories that could be expected to emerge within the context of well-conducted district improvement efforts.

District Improvement Initiatives as Context for Teacher Learning

Two key features of district improvement efforts that can impact how teacher learning unfolds are (a) the selected *curriculum*; and (b) the *professional support* provided to teachers and other professionals as they are learning to implement the new curriculum.

Selected Curriculum

Past research suggests that standards-based mathematics curricula can offer both challenges and supports for teacher learning (Davis and Krajcik 2005). They offer *challenges* to teacher learning because they aim for more ambitious, cognitively complex forms of student learning (i.e., conceptual understanding; the capacity to think, reason, and problem solve) than teachers have traditionally been accustomed to. Not only did teachers themselves likely not learn mathematics in this less traditional way, but many have also not learned to teach mathematics in ways that foster students' capacity to think, reason, and problem solve (Borko and Putnam 1995).

When designed well, standards-based curricula can offer *support* for teacher learning (Davis and Krajcik 2005; Stein and Kim 2009). Instead of treating the teacher as an instrument for delivering the curriculum to students, some standards-based curricula invest in the education of the teacher as a critical contributor to the teaching and learning environment. Designers of these so-called *educative* curricula believe that student learning cannot be entirely scripted in advance, but rather unfolds in moment-to-moment, contingent interactions between teachers and students during a lesson; interactions in which materials are a resource for, not the of determinant of, learning. In this view of teaching and learning, the teacher must have sufficient knowledge of the mathematical purpose and learning goals of the instructional tasks in the curriculum and insight into how students might respond to those tasks. This kind of information thus becomes integrated into the curricular materials. Despite the increasing popularity of the idea of educative curricula, recent research suggests that standards-based curricula differ widely in the extent to which they are educative for teachers (Stein and Kim 2009).

Professional Support

In addition to the curriculum materials that they select, districts also vary in the nature and extent of *professional support* offered to teachers in the context of district-wide curricular reform initiatives. Most districts now recognize that teachers need more support than that offered by the typical publisher-provided one-day training session. Common support structures include the provision of coaches (Duessen et al. 2007) and common planning periods for teachers on the same grade level. Because of the system-wide nature of these initiatives, professional support is often arranged at contiguous levels of the system. For example, the district mathematics leadership team might provide some kind of ongoing support for principals, as well as hold monthly meetings with coaches; the coaches, in turn, might meet weekly with their building leadership team as well as hold weekly meetings with teachers. Sometimes district math leaders deliver professional development directly to teachers.[4] It should be noted that, although the above kinds of support structures can be found across many districts, past research suggests that districts vary with respect to *how* these support system are carried out, with some focusing more on operational features such as how to use materials and pacing guidelines and others focusing more on the big mathematical ideas and the underlying intent of the lessons (Stein and Coburn 2008).

Framework for Analyzing Instruction and Teacher Development

Our conceptual framework for analyzing teaching and teacher learning within the context of district-based improvement efforts is based on (a) the extent to which

---

[4]This is possible because, in the context of district-paced implementation, teachers on the same grade level should be implementing the same lessons at roughly the same time, thereby allowing the district to "preview" an upcoming unit to teachers across the district on the same date.

teachers actually *use* the selected curriculum as the source of their lessons; (b) the degree of *congruence* of teachers' instruction to curricular and district guidelines; and (c) the *quality* of teachers' instruction (the extent to which it maintains the cognitive demand of appropriately challenging tasks, takes account of and builds on student thinking, and situates intellectual authority in mathematical reasoning). Each of these is described below.

Use of Curriculum   We conceptualize curriculum use as the extent to which the teacher draws on the selected curriculum as the source of activities in her lessons. It is important to note that this measure says nothing about *how well* the teachers use the curriculum or even the extent to which they follow the curriculum's and district's guidelines for how to run the lesson. Nevertheless, assessments of use are important because curriculum use constitutes a necessary foundation for large-scale teacher learning within a district-led improvement effort. If the curriculum materials remain swathed in shrink wrap in the closet, teachers and students will not be able to avail themselves of the activities and opportunities for learning contained in them. This aspect of curriculum based reform is often assumed in studies of teacher change, but experience suggests that it should not be taken for granted.

Congruence with Curricular and District Guidelines   We conceptualize congruence as the extent to which teachers' instruction aligns with the pedagogical features of the curriculum (e.g., group work, manipulative use) and with district guidelines for the proper sequencing and pacing of lessons/units.[5] Determining congruence can be accomplished with reference to relatively superficial aspects of instruction, for example, items that might appear on a checklist that a principal uses to evaluate teacher adherence to district mandates. Items that would be relevant for determining congruence include features such as directions for how to set up a lesson (including the manipulatives that will be needed), how to group students for various parts of the lesson, and guidelines for pacing. Items not relevant for determining congruence include an examination of the mathematical ideas at play in the lesson or the extent to which students have the opportunity to learn those ideas.

Assessments of congruence are important because they signal a level of teacher effort that goes beyond using the curriculum materials as a source of activities. Congruent use implies that teachers are actually trying to follow the curriculum in a manner that is aligned with the curriculum developers' and the district's expectations.

Instructional Quality   Instructional quality is conceptualized in terms of the affordances for student learning of important mathematical ideas that the instruction provides. Although our criteria for instructional quality adhere to a particular approach to teaching and learning (variously referred to as standards-based, student-centered, or inquiry based), they have not been designed to align specifically with

---

[5] Judgments about congruence are necessarily district and curriculum specific.

any one particular curriculum. However, standards-based curricula, in general (including the two curricula studied herein) are philosophically compatible with this view of teaching and learning.

We've defined instructional quality in terms of three constructs: the maintenance of high levels of cognitive demand, the level and kind of attention that the teacher pays to student thinking, and the extent to which the intellectual authority in the classroom is vested in mathematical reasoning (vs. the text or the teacher). Each of these is described in more detail below.

1. *Maintenance of high-level cognitive demand.* Cognitive demand refers to the level of thinking and reasoning that is required in order to successfully complete a mathematical instructional task (Doyle 1983; Stein et al. 1996).[6] High-level tasks often consist of open-ended problems with limited guidance regarding how to solve them, thus requiring students to engage in complex, non-routine thinking and reasoning such as making and testing conjectures, framing problems, representing relationships and looking for patterns. High-level tasks can also be more constrained by orienting students toward the use of general procedures or multiple representations to solve complex problems, but doing so in such a way that concepts, meaning or understanding are illuminated. Low-level tasks focus students' attention on algorithms and routine procedures without attempts to foster conceptual understanding or on memorizing basic facts or definitions.

The cognitive demands of tasks often change as they pass through different phases (Stein et al. 1996). First, tasks exist in print on the pages of curricular **materials**. Next, as the teacher **sets up** the task in the classroom, she may (knowingly or unwittingly) change the cognitive demand of the task (e.g., by inserting easier numbers into the problem; by providing "hints" regarding what to look for). Finally, the students (sometimes with the teacher's help) go about actually working on or **enacting** the task. It is not unusual for the cognitive demand of the tasks to change at this final phase as well, usually as a result of the teacher "taking over" and doing the thinking for the students instead of allowing them to struggle. Past research has shown that students in classrooms in which teachers are able to maintain the high level of cognitive demand of tasks that appear in standards-based materials perform better on tests of higher level thinking and reasoning (Stein and Lane 1996). Thus, we consider one hallmark of a high-quality lesson to be the teacher's ability to maintain the high cognitive demand of instructional tasks.

2. *The level and kind of attention that teachers paid to student thinking.*[7] Proponents of standards-based instruction stress the importance of teachers paying close attention to what students do and say as they work on problems so as to be able to uncover and understand their mathematical thinking (e.g., Brendehur and Frykholm

---

[6]A mathematical task is defined as a classroom activity, the purpose of which is to focus students' attention on a particular mathematical idea. An activity is not classified as a new or different task unless the underlying mathematical activity toward which the activity is oriented changes. Standards-based lessons typically consist of one or two tasks.

[7]Judgments about teachers attending to student thinking and about intellectual authority were made based on the entire lesson.

2000; Hodge and Cobb 2003; Lampert 2001; Nelson 2001; Schoenfeld 1998; Shifter 2001). This is commonly done by circulating around the classroom while students work (e.g., Boerst and Sleep 2007; Hodge and Cobb 2003; Lampert 2001). An important goal is to identify the mathematical learning potential of particular strategies or representations used by the students, thereby honing in on which student responses would be important to share with the class as a whole during the discussion phase (Brendehur and Frykholm 2000; Lampert 2001; Stein et al. 2008). Thus, we consider another feature of a high-quality lesson to be the extent to which the teacher attends to and builds on student thinking.

3. *Intellectual Authority*. Proponents of standards-based instruction also endorse the view of mathematics classrooms as places where students are 'authorized' to solve mathematical problems for themselves, by employing mathematical reasoning rather than relying on the teacher or text (Engle and Conant 2002; Hamm and Perry 2002; Lampert 1990; Scardamalia et al. 1994; Wertsch and Toma 1995). A learning environment embodying the norm of accountability to the discipline regularly encourages students to 'account' for how their ideas make contact with those of other mathematical authorities, both inside and outside the classroom (see also Cobb et al. 1997). Thus, our final feature of high-quality instruction is the extent to which the teacher fosters students' intellectual authority.

Combining Above Features   The unique feature of our framework is that it combines judgments about use, congruence and quality to arrive at a set of instructional profiles. By crossing *use* and *congruence* with *quality*, we have identified the following "implementation profiles":[8]

- *Canonical Implementer*: High quality, with high use and high congruence. This teacher not only *uses* the district's selected curriculum and aligns her instruction to be *congruent* with curricular and district guidelines, but she also provides students with *high-quality* opportunities to think, reason and problem solve.

- *Maverick*: High quality, with low use or low congruence. This teacher also provides her students with *high-quality* opportunities to learn to think, reason and problem solve; however, she does so without the curriculum. Either she does *not use* the curriculum at all; or she uses it in a manner that is *incongruent* with curricular and district guidelines.

- *Mechanical Implementer*: Low quality, with high use and high congruence. This teacher *does not provide high-quality* opportunities for student learning but she *uses* the curriculum in a manner that is *congruent* with curricular and district guidelines.

---

[8]We have identified 4 profiles instead of 8 possible profiles because only 4 profiles were conceptually meaningful. Two profiles (either high or low quality crossed with low use and high congruence) were unlikely because it is difficult to imagine a teacher implementing materials with pedagogical fidelity without actually using the materials. The other two profiles are actually represented in the flounderer and maverick categories which stipulate that (along with either low [flounderer] or high [maverick] quality) the teacher implements with low congruence and either high or low use. Conceptually the dimension that carries the weight of both the flounder and maverick categories is having low congruence with the pedagogical guidance of the curriculum and district.

• *Flounderer*: Low quality, with low use or low congruence. This teacher is *not providing high-quality* opportunities for student learning and is disregarding the curriculum. Either she does *not use* the curriculum at all; or she uses it in a manner that is *incongruent* with curricular and district guidelines.

As shown by the profiles, this framework separates instructional quality judgments from "following the curriculum" judgments. As such, we are able to differentiate teachers who follow the curriculum in a superficial manner (mechanical implementers) from teachers who follow the curriculum with fidelity to the underlying intent of the curriculum (canonical implementers). In addition, we recognize two different ways of exhibiting high-quality instruction: the canonical implementer and a teacher who sets up and maintains the cognitive demand of appropriately challenging tasks, listens to and challenges student thinking, and encourages students to take mathematical authority, but who does not follow (and may not use) the district-supported curriculum (maverick). In this way, we allow for innovative, high-quality teaching that is not bound to a particular curriculum. Finally, there are also different ways of exhibiting poor-quality teaching: the mechanical implementer who is trying to follow the curriculum, albeit in a superficial manner and the flounderer who is not following (and perhaps not using) the district-supported curriculum but is also not exhibiting high-quality instruction.

Within a well-conducted district-supported implementation, we would conjecture the following pathway for teacher development. The teacher begins by using curriculum materials in *mechanical* ways. That is, she diligently bases her lessons on a set of well-designed curriculum materials and makes a good faith effort to follow the curricular guidelines set forth by her district including what lessons to teach, how quickly to go, what grouping formats to use and so forth. However, the teacher has difficulty delivering on the deeper structure of the curriculum. Over time—if she is well supported by educative materials and by her district—she begins to implement the curriculum in ways that conform to not just the surface features but also the deeper cognitive features that influence how students think and reason (becoming a canonical implementer). Finally, having "learned" a more cognitively challenging, student-centered manner of teaching, she may depart from the standard curriculum and become a maverick, meaning that her teaching is still high quality, but she no longer uses the district-mandated curriculum or she stops adhering closely to the operational guidelines of the curriculum and/or the district.

The purpose of this study was to develop and test the viability of this framework for analyzing mathematics instruction and mathematics teacher development within the context of local policies regarding district-wide curriculum adoption and implementation. The following questions guided this study:

1. How do teachers participating in district-wide curricular-based initiatives vary with respect to use of the mandated curriculum, congruence with curricular and district guidelines regarding how to use the curriculum, and quality of instruction?
2. How do teachers participating in district-wide curricular-based initiatives vary with respect to the framework's four profiles?

3. What within-teacher patterns, if any, emerge with respect to the four profiles as teachers participate in the district-wide initiative over multiple years?
4. In what ways, if any, might the above identified patterns be related to the nature of the curricular materials and/or the nature of the professional support provided by the district?

Methods

Data Sources

Data for the present study come from a large NSF-supported multi-year study of the initial years of district-wide implementation of *Investigations* and *Everyday Mathematics* in two urban districts. In Fall 2003, Greene School District[9] mandated implementation of *Investigations*, whereas Region-Z mandated implementation of *Everyday Mathematics*; both are standards-based elementary (grades K-5) curricula. Six focal teachers in each of 4 case-study schools in each district were selected for observation. Schools were selected to represent the range of schools in each district with respect to teacher capacity and extent of teacher professional communities; teachers were selected to represent the range of talent and grade levels in the building. For this study we used all the teachers for whom we had data for the 2004-05 and 2005-06 school years, which includes19 Greene teachers and 17 Region-Z teachers.

Most teachers were observed six times per year (for 3 consecutive lessons in the fall and 3 consecutive lessons in the spring). All classroom observations were conducted by trained observers who took detailed field-notes and then completed pre-specified, qualitative write-ups upon leaving the classroom.[10] The write ups included a comprehensive lesson summary and answers to a set of questions about cognitive demand, teachers' attention to student thinking, and the location of intellectual authority during the lesson. Answers were required to be backed up by one or more examples from the lesson.

Each lesson was coded by one of a group of four trained Masters- or PhD-level mathematics educators, all of whom were familiar with the first author's prior research on cognitive demand. The sources of data that informed the coding for each lesson included the classroom write up, the artifacts from the lesson, and the transcript of the pre- and post-interview.[11] In order to prevent coding "drift," the coders

---

[9]Pseudonyms.

[10]The individuals who were selected to conduct the observations and create the write ups had expertise in either mathematics education or a social science field that relied heavily on observation (e.g., anthropology). They participated in a 2-day, in-person, group training at the start of the project. This training involved watching videos of mathematics lessons and creating write ups that were critiqued by project leaders and their peers. During the course of the project, the observers were provided feedback on their write-ups and participated in at least one follow up group session.

[11]Because one pre- and one post-interview were conducted per set of 3 contiguous lessons, the coded data based on those interviews is the same across all lessons in one set.

met with the authors on a monthly basis to share codes for a randomly selected lesson. These 1–2 hour meetings produced 10 "consensus coded" documents plus refinements of the decision rules. In addition, another 9 % of the lessons were double coded with an inter-rater reliability of 81 %, 67 %, and 75 % for use, congruence, and quality respectively.[12] For each double-coded lesson, differences were resolved and a consensus code was entered.

In addition to teacher observations, we have copies of all the curricular materials adopted by the two districts, transcripts of teacher pre- and post-lesson set interviews, observations of professional development at different levels of the system, and transcripts of interviews with principals, mathematics coaches and district leaders. We did not analyze these data sources firsthand, but instead drew on previous project analyses that examined (a) the nature of demand and support in the curriculum materials (Stein and Kim 2009; Stein and Kaufman 2010); the nature of district-wide support (Stein and Coburn 2008; Coburn and Russell 2008); differences across schools (Sutherland et al. 2007); and the evolution of reform mandates and supports over time (Kaufman and Stein 2010).

Procedures of Analysis

Our initial analysis focused on characterizing each of the 36 teachers according to use, congruence, and quality across the three observed lessons that they delivered in each of four semesters over the course of two years: Fall 2004, Spring 2005, Fall 2005, and Spring 2006. Each lesson write-up was coded by a mathematics educator according to *use* (on a scale of 0–4 according to the portion of the lesson that used the curriculum as the source of activities in the lesson); *congruence* (an aligned/non-aligned judgment based on the math educators' assessment of the lesson's congruence with the curriculum's and district's guidelines [specifically constructed for each curriculum]); and *quality* (a score of 1 to 8 based on judgments of the levels of cognitive demand at the set-up and enactment phases of the lesson coupled with educators' judgment of where intellectual authority resided and the e   lesson built on student thinking; this coding system builds on   in Stein and Kaufman 2010).

Next, the sco   her's three lessons were averaged across the three observations to   n-year score on each dimension. Finally, teachers' practice was identified   or low use, congruent or non-congruent implementation, and high- or low-quality based on cut scores that were conceptually determined. Each of these analytic phases for use, congruence and quality is described below.

---

[12] Inter-rater reliability was computed as the number of agreements divided by the total number of possible agreements/disagreements.

Curriculum Use

Curriculum use was measured on the following scale:

0 = 0 % of the lesson drew on *Investigations or Everyday Mathematics*
1 = 1–25 % of the lesson drew on *Investigation or Everyday Mathematics*
2 = 26–75 % of the lesson drew on *Investigations or Everyday Mathematics*
3 = 76–99 % of the lesson drew on *Investigations or Everyday Mathematics*
4 = 100 % of the lesson drew on *Investigations or Everyday Mathematics*

High use was defined as a teacher with an average score of 3.0 or higher across the three lessons she taught during each semester, meaning that over 75 % of the time—on average—the teacher would have drawn on curricular materials for the three lessons she taught. Thus, in addition to those teachers who used the selected curriculum the entire time of all of their observed lessons, we also included teachers who used *Investigations* or *Everyday Mathematics* as the source of their classroom activities between 76 and 99 % of the time.[13] Anyone who used *Investigations* or *Everyday Mathematics* 75 % of the time or less, on average, was characterized as a "low" user.

Congruence

We developed two separate checklists—one with indicators of congruent instruction and one with indicators of incongruent instruction—for each curriculum based on an in-depth analysis of the curriculum and the district's expectation of how that curriculum should be implemented. For example, *Everyday Mathematics* relies on a spiral structure where lessons that happen later in the sequence depend upon material that was covered earlier. Because of this design, skipping particular lessons would be considered to be incongruent; whether a teacher skipped a lesson in *Everyday Mathematics* is one of the *Everyday Mathematics* indicators for whether a teacher is incongruent. In contrast, *Investigations* has a modular design. The curriculum does not require that teachers use all units and there is flexibility in the order that units are employed. Because of this different design, skipping a unit would not be considered incongruent and is not part of the set of indicators determining incongruence for *Investigations*.

After a coder completed the checklists for congruent and incongruent indicators, that coder would determine the overall lesson to be "congruent" through a holistic

---

[13]This seemed reasonable because it is not unusual for teachers to do non-textbook activities for a small portion of a class period. For example, they might review a skill such as "telling time" because an early dismissal has been announced for the day. On the other hand—because *Investigations and Everyday Mathematics* are comprehensive curricula with daily lessons—a teacher who failed to use them at all for one or more lessons (of the six observed lessons) would be considered to be an inconsistent user.

judgment of the lesson, using checkmark counts for congruence versus incongru-ence as a source of evidence for making that holistic judgment, as well as taking into account whether the teacher engaged in congruent instruction for the majority of the lesson.

A congruent set of three lessons within a semester is defined as a set of lessons where only one lesson out of three is incongruent. That is, the majority of the lessons within a semester had to be congruent.

Quality

The quality score is comprised of three measures: maintenance of cognitive demand, attention to student thinking, and intellectual authority. Our scale for maintenance of cognitive demand is based upon (1) the extent to which the teacher maintained the same cognitive demand for the primary instructional task from the materials phase to the set up phase; and (2) the extent to which the teacher maintained the same cognitive demand from the set up phase to the enactment phase. For each of these two transitions, we allocated 1–4 points to each teacher's lesson in the following way:

- 1 point—The teacher maintained a low level of cognitive demand from one phase to the next.
- 2 points—The teacher transformed a task from a high level of cognitive demand to a low level of cognitive demand.
- 3 points—The teacher maintained a high level of cognitive demand between two phases but transformed the task from one kind of high-level task into another type.[14] Although the teacher still maintained a high level of cognitive demand, the nature of that cognitive demand essentially shifted in a way that was not con-sistent with the intent of the instructional task. Thus, a teacher received fewer points than if s/he had maintained the same type of high-level cognitive demand from one phase to another.
- 4 points—The teacher maintained the same high level of cognitive demand from one phase to another without transforming a task into another type of high-level demand or to a lower level of cognitive demand.

Through this point system, the maintenance of cognitive demand score could be from 2–8 points.

For scoring for *attention to student thinking*, teachers were assigned a score of 1 to 4 depending on the extent to which they uncovered student thinking and made it available to other students in a way that would help the class's learning as a whole. The guidelines for score assignments were:

---

[14]Either from a "doing mathematics" task to a "procedures-with-connections" task or from a "procedures-with-connections" task to a "doing mathematics" task (Stein et al. 1996).

1 point—The teacher did no work to uncover student thinking.

2 points—The teacher did some work to uncover student thinking, including asking students to publicly share their work.

3 points—In addition to point 2, the teacher purposefully selected some students to share their work.

4 points—In addition to points 2 and 3, the teacher connected or sequenced students' responses in a meaningful way.

Finally, for scoring *mathematical authority*, teachers were assigned a score of 1 to 3 depending on the extent to which students had such opportunities in the lesson. The guidelines for score assignments were:

- 1 point—Judgments of correctness derived from teacher or text.
- 2 points—Judgments of correctness sometimes derived from teacher or text, but also some appeals to mathematical reasoning.
- 3 points—Judgments of correctness derived from mathematical reasoning.

Teachers with high quality instruction are differentiated from teachers with low quality instruction by establishing a "high quality" cut score for each of the three constructs: maintenance of cognitive demand (CD), teachers' work to uncover and productively use student thinking (ST), and the extent to which intellectual authority was vested in mathematical reasoning (IA). For CD, high quality was defined as an average score of 7.0 for teachers' lessons in one semester. For ST, high quality was defined as an average score of higher than 1.0 for all a teachers' lessons in a semester. For IA, we also set the cut score as higher than 1.0 for all a teachers' lessons in a semester. We set these cut scores based on our knowledge of each construct and our own expectations regarding what constitutes a high-quality lesson for that construct. Finally, we judged a teacher as having an overall high-quality set of lessons across the year if s/he scored as "high quality" for CD and *either* ST or IA. We did not require teachers to have a "high quality" score for both ST and IA with the rationale that both constructs equally reflect high-quality instruction and receiving a high score on one of the two constructs alongside a score above the cut for cognitive demand would reflect ample opportunity for student learning.

Assigning Instructional Profiles

For each semester, teachers were classified as flounderers, mechanical implementers, canonical implementers, or mavericks according to their use, congruence, and quality ratings as described on pages 355–356.

Identifying Features of District Improvement Strategies

If patterns of cross-site differences and/or within-teacher development of instructional profiles over time were identified, we consulted findings associated with previously analyzed data to build conjectures regarding why the patterns emerged.

Results

We present the results according to the research questions, beginning with an assessment of the variation across teachers and sites in their levels of use, congruence and quality. The fourth question (contextual features associated with observed patterns) is addressed throughout the results section as patterns are identified.

Teachers' use, congruence and quality

As shown in Table 1, there was variation across the three dimensions of use, congruence and quality; quite noticeable variation between Region Z and Greene teachers; and some variation over time. We discuss each of these in turn.

The data in Table 1 suggest that teachers were more likely to use their respective curricula as the source of their classroom activities than to align their instructional practice with curricular and district guidelines. Approximately 80 %–90 % of the teachers used their curricula to a high degree (i.e., more than 75 % of the time) whereas as few as 53 % of the teachers (and never more than 71 %) exhibited instructional practice that was judged to be highly congruent with curricular and district guidelines. Each of these dimensions, however, exceeded teachers' capacities to demonstrate high-quality lessons. The percentage of teachers with high quality lessons hovered around 25 %, much lower than the first two dimensions.

Perhaps more interesting are the differences between Region Z and Greene in terms of use, congruence and quality. With respect to all three dimensions, Greene teachers exhibited higher levels at all time points except one.[15] The differences are most marked with respect to quality and least marked with respect to use.

Variations over time are more difficult to detect. There do not appear to be strong differences over time in Region Z, but Greene teachers exhibited fairly substantial declines in congruence (from 95 % to 68 %) and in quality (from 53 % to 37 %) between the Spring of 2005 and the Fall of 2005.

What does all of this suggest? Early in these two district-wide initiatives, it appears to have been easier to obtain relatively high levels of use—and to maintain that high level of use over time—than to command greater teacher investments in terms of congruence or quality. In both districts, messages from central office were very clear: teachers were expected to use the new curriculum and principals would be checking to make sure that they were. Thus, mandates appear to work in terms of the lowest levels of compliance, that is, they drive teachers to take books out of their shrink wrap, distribute them to students, and teach out of them. Just one step beyond that, however, mandates are less effective. Many fewer teachers used the materials according to even the most superficial guidelines for their use (i.e., the

---

[15]Fall 2005 where 82 % of Region Z teachers were high users and 79 % of Greene teachers were high users.

Table 1 Teachers' Use, Congruence, and Quality

	Fall 2004 (n = 35)	Spring 2005 (n = 35)	Fall 2005 (n = 36)	Spring 2006 (n = 36)
High Use	**89 %**	**83 %**	**81 %**	**78 %**
(use of mandated curriculum more than 75 % of the time in each lesson, on average)	**(31/35)**	**(29/35)**	29/36	28/36
...Region Z	81 %	75 %	82	71
	(13/16)	(12/16)	14/17	12/17
...Greene	95 %	89 %	79 %	84 %
	(18/19)	(17/19)	15/19	16/19
High Congruence	**71 %**	**66 %**	**53 %**	**58 %**
(practices aligned with features at least 2 out of 3 lessons/semester)	**(25/35)**	**(23/35)**	19/36	21/36
...Region Z	44 %	31 %	35 %	41 %
	(7/16)	(5/16)	6/17	(7/17)
...Greene	95 %	95 %	68 %	74 %
	(18/19)	(18/19)	(13/19)	(14/19)
High Quality	**29 %**	**29 %**	**22 %**	**28 %**
(high quality on cognitive demand and either student thinking or mathematical authority)	**(10/35)**	10/35	8/36	10/36
...Region Z	6 %	0 %	6 %	6 %
	(1/16)	0/16	1/17	1/17
...Greene	47 %	53 %	37 %	47 %
	(9/19)	10/19	7/19	9/19

kinds of markers that principals would be looking for in their classrooms to indicate that teachers are being faithful to the curriculum). Finally, quality was, by far, the most difficult thing to achieve, suggesting that mandates alone cannot dictate transformations of practice. Given that such transformations require teacher learning, additional investments in the professional development of teachers appears to be required.

The differences across Region Z and Greene with respect to quality beg the question of possible differences in how Region Z teachers versus Greene teachers were supported. In earlier analyses of how these two districts created organizational environments to support their respective reforms (Stein and Coburn 2008), we found that Greene was able to create significant opportunities for teacher learning that aligned with reform goals while efforts in Region Z coordinated teachers' actions but failed to spur meaningful opportunities for teacher learning. For example, while coaches played a role in both districts' reform efforts, the selection process used in Greene yielded better coaches. Not surprisingly, the substance of what coaches talked about with teachers and with principals was very different across the two districts. In Greene, coaches' interactions were more substantive and more focused on mathematics teaching and learning; in Region Z interactions primarily focused on how to manage the *Everyday Mathematics* materials, gathering manipulatives and other tools for teachers, and providing general pointers regarding how to plan for and teach a lesson with little or no discussion of mathematical content or student thinking. Similarly interactions in teacher communities in Greene were more likely to move beyond pacing and managing materials to also include more substantive conversations about instructional strategies, student learning, and at times, the mathematics itself. Also, the principals in Greene were more likely to receive training on the mathematics reform and to work closely with their mathematics coaches in assessing and improving instruction in teachers' classrooms. The principals in Region Z, on the other hand, either turned over the mathematics program completely to their coaches or used their coaches for non-mathematics tasks.

Finally, it appears as though use alone does not buy district leaders much if their ultimate goal is high-quality instruction. Despite use levels that were not much lower than Greene's, the vast majority of Region Z teachers' instructional practices were judged to be low quality. On the other hand, the data in Table 1 suggest that congruence may play a more influential role in creating high-quality instruction if for no other reason than substantially greater percentages of Greene teachers exhibit congruent instruction and also exhibit high-quality instruction (although at lower rates).

The decline that occur between the Spring of 2005 and the Fall of 2005 in Greene co-occurred with a policy shift. Specifically, new state-level requirements for teachers' professional development hours related to English as a Second Language instruction necessitated a much larger emphasis on ESL professional development at the district and school level in Greene, which led to many fewer opportunities for teachers to engage in mathematics professional development (Kaufman and Stein 2010). In addition, a newly hired superintendent made it clear that teachers were free to use whatever materials they wished to address learning goals and, especially, ESL concerns. In other words, *Investigations* was no longer a mandated curriculum. Interestingly, from the Spring of 2005 to the Fall of 2005 teachers showed less decline in their use of the curriculum as the source of their daily activities (from 89 % to 79 %) than they did in congruence which dropped quite precipitously (from 95 % to 68 %). Perhaps this reflects the fact that teachers had been forced to relinquish their old curriculum materials and thus had no other materials on hand. Quality declined less, suggesting that teachers had developed some internal capacity to teach mathematics at a high level without necessarily following a specific curriculum.

Table 2 Teachers' instructional profiles

	Fall 2004 ($n = 35$)	Spring 2005 ($n = 35$)	Fall 2005 ($n = 36$)	Spring 2006 ($n = 36$)	Overall
Flounderer	29 %	34 %	42 %	39 %	
	10/35	12/35	15/36	14/36	
...Region Z	56 %	69 %	65 %	59 %	62 %
	9/16	11/16	11/17	10/17	41/66
...Greene	5 %	5 %	21 %	21 %	13 %
	1/19	1/19	4/19	4/19	10/76
Mechanical	43 %	37 %	36 %	31 %	
	15/35	13/35	13/36	11/36	
...Region Z	38 %	31 %	29 %	35 %	33 %
	6/16	5/16	5/17	6/17	22/66
...Greene	47 %	42 %	42 %	26 %	39 %
	9/19	8/19	8/19	5/19	30/76
Canonical	26 %	26 %	17 %	28 %	
	9/35	9/35	6/36	10/36	
...Region Z	6 %	0 %	6 %	6 %	5 %
	1/16	0/16	1/17	1/17	3/66
...Greene	42 %	47 %	26 %	47 %	41 %
	8/19	9/19	5/19	9/19	31/76
Maverick	3 %	3 %	6 %	3 %	
	1/35	1/35	2/36	1/36	
...Region Z	0 %	0 %	0 %	0 %	0 %
	0/16	0/16	0/17	0/17	0/66
...Greene	5 %	5 %	11 %	5 %	7 %
	1/19	1/19	2/19	1/19	5/76

Teacher Profiles

As shown in Table 2, teachers were unevenly distributed across the four profiles. There are—once again—noticeable differences in Region Z teachers versus Greene teachers; and there is some change over time. Each of these is discussed in turn.

Across all four time periods teachers were most likely to be classified as flounderers or mechanical implementers. As noted earlier, these profiles reflect low-quality implementations with the difference being that the mechanical implementers are using the curriculum as the source of activities for the majority of their lesson activities and are attempting to follow curricular and district guidelines regarding how to use the curriculum while the flounderers are not attempting to follow guidelines and, in some cases, were making limited or no use of the materials. There were many fewer canonical implementers, and fewer still, mavericks.

Again, there were differences between the two districts, but also one important similarity. Similar percentages of Greene and Region Z teachers were classified as mechanical implementers (39 % and 33 % respectively). However, despite these similarities, the balance of the teachers in Region Z tended to be flounderers while the balance of the Greene teachers were canonical implementers. Thus, the overall distribution of teachers in each of these profiles looks very different across the two districts.

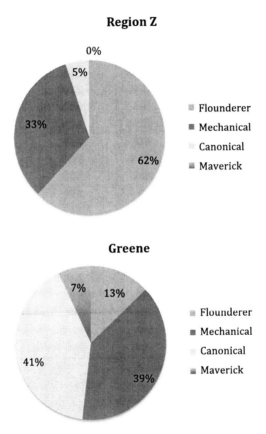

Over time, the largest change appears between the Spring 2005 and Fall 2005 time periods in Greene when the percentages of flounderers increased from 5 % to 21 % and the percentages of canonical implementers decreased from 47 % to 26 %. There were no noticeable changes over time in the Region Z data.

What does all of this suggest? Across the early years of district-wide improvement efforts, the two districts' approaches to mandated, curriculum-based reform appeared to have yielded a lot of flounderers and mechanical implementers, neither of which, according to our definitions, was providing high quality opportunities for student learning. As noted earlier, mandates alone do not appear to work in producing high-quality instruction.

Table 3 Region Z within-teacher instructional profiles

		Fall 2004	Spring 2005	Fall 2005	Spring 2006
Predominantly Flounderer (59%)	EN	Flounderer	Flounderer	Flounderer	Flounderer
	EB	Flounderer	Flounderer	Flounderer	Flounderer
	BT	Flounderer	Flounderer	Flounderer	Flounderer
	SD		Flounderer	Flounderer	Flounderer
	BE	Mechanical	Flounderer	Flounderer	Flounderer
	DS	Mechanical	Flounderer	Flounderer	Flounderer
	BH	Flounderer		Mechanical	Flounderer
	PQ	Flounderer	Mechanical	Flounderer	Flounderer
	QJ	Flounderer	Flounderer	Flounderer	Mechanical
	MD	Flounderer	Flounderer	Flounderer	Mechanical
Flounderer / Mechanical Mix (18%)	UW	Mechanical	Flounderer	Mechanical	Flounderer
	KT	Flounderer	Mechanical	Mechanical	Flounderer
	HQ	Mechanical	Flounderer	Flounderer	Mechanical
Predominantly Mechanical (18%)	OG	Flounderer	Mechanical	Mechanical	Mechanical
	UF	Mechanical	Mechanical	Mechanical	Mechanical
Other (6%)	TT	Canonical	Flounderer	Flounderer	Mechanical
	NC	Mechanical	Mechanical	Canonical	Canonical

Despite both districts having similar numbers of mechanical implementers, however, Greene appears to have been able to foster a non-trivial amount of canonical implementation, meaning that teachers were using the district curriculum to create worthwhile learning opportunities for students. Thus, it appears as though mandates accompanied by support for teacher learning can yield positive outcomes related to quality. Finally, as noted earlier, our proposed pathway of teacher learning suggests that well-supported teachers develop from mechanical implementers to canonical implementers. The data in Table 2 suggest that this *might have* happened in Greene, but not in Region Z. We now turn to a within teacher analysis over time to examine this claim.

Patterns Over Time

Because the patterns over time are so different in Region Z versus Greene we will discuss the teachers in the two districts separately.

As shown in Table 3, across the two-year period, 10 Region Z teachers (59 %) displayed a predominately flounderer profile, never growing out of that profile for more than one time period. However, many teachers who stayed with the curriculum over time—and even tried to follow their guidelines (the mechanical implementers)—also never improved to a canonical profile. As shown in Table 3, a group of three teachers toggled back and forth between the mechanical and flounderer patterns and two teachers by and large remained mechanical implementers throughout the two-year period. Finally, in the "other" pattern, we find one teacher who appeared to actually progress nicely from a mechanical to canonical implementer and another teacher who is hard to classify.

Table 4 Greene within-teacher instructional profiles

	Teacher	Fall 2004	Spring 2005	Fall 2005	Spring 2006
Predominantly Canonical and Maverick (37%)	LH-6	Canonical	Mechanical	Maverick	Canonical
	NQ	Canonical	Mechanical	Canonical	Maverick
	DN	Canonical		Maverick	Canonical
	CD	Canonical	Canonical	Mechanical	Canonical
	BX	Canonical	Mechanical	Canonical	Canonical
	KE	Canonical	Mechanical	Canonical	Canonical
	XN	Canonical	Mechanical	Canonical	Canonical
Canonical Mechanical/ Mix (26%)	FT	Mechanical	Canonical	Flounderer	Canonical
	TS	Mechanical	Canonical	Flounderer	Canonical
	LI	Mechanical	Canonical	Mechanical	Canonical
	NN	Canonical	Canonical	Mechanical	Mechanical
	UN	Mechanical	Canonical	Canonical	Mechanical
Predominantly Flounderer /Mechanical (37%)	KN	Flounderer	Flounderer	Flounderer	Flounderer
	QS	Mechanical	Mechanical	Flounderer	Mechanical
	SH	Mechanical	Mechanical	Mechanical	Mechanical
	DT	Maverick	Mechanical	Mechanical	Flounderer
	SN	Mechanical	Canonical	Mechanical	Flounderer
	LH-7	Mechanical	Canonical	Mechanical	Flounderer
	WH	Mechanical	Canonical	Mechanical	Mechanical

What do these patterns suggest? A closer look at the preponderance of flounderers, who never improved (the first group), reveals that one school contributed 5 out of the 10 teachers. Unlike the rest of our focal schools in Region Z, this particular school was not "on board" with the mandated nature of the mathematics reform. From the start, it was clear that the principal sanctioned a wide variety of materials in addition to—or in place of—*Everyday Mathematics*, often claiming the rationale that there were "rumors" that the district was going to switch to a different curriculum (Sutherland et al. 2007). Moreover, the coach in this school took on a range of duties beyond that of mathematics coach.

The only Region Z teacher who improved over time (NC), came from a school in which there was some degree of conscientiousness about following the curriculum, including the help of a coach who proclaimed to be a new convert to the *Everyday Mathematics* curriculum. However, three of NC's colleagues in the school (HQ, OG, and UF) did not progress as she did, but rather remained trapped in a mechanical profile (OG, UF) or a flounder/mechanical mix (HQ).

As shown in Table 4, the Greene teacher patterns (with the exception perhaps of the final group) are very different than the Region Z teacher patterns. First, there are 7 teachers (37 %) who, for the most part, stay within the two high-quality profiles, either canonicals or mavericks. Interestingly, these 7 teachers appeared to be "strong out of the gate," that is, they displayed a canonical profile at the first data collection point (the reader is reminded however, that the first data collection point was the beginning of the second year of the reform in both districts).

The second group of teachers displayed a mixture of canonical and mechanical profiles. The first three teachers are especially interesting because they began with a mechanical implementation but ended as canonical implementers. The fact that these same three teachers "slipped" into a flounderer or mechanical profile in the Fall of 2005 is interesting because that is when the new superintendent lifted the mandate to use the *Investigations* curriculum. Finally, the third group of Greene teachers appear similar to the Region Z teachers in that (except for KN) they all tried to use the curriculum at some point (there is a preponderance of mechanical implementations), but were rarely able to break into a sustained canonical profile.

What can we make of the Greene patterns? First, the teachers who were predominantly canonical or maverick were never flounderers (the first group). This suggests that perhaps floundering should be a red flag to observers or evaluations. It is sometimes argued that teachers should be permitted to go with their own decisions regarding curriculum; this study suggests that this will not lead to high quality—whether canonical or maverick.[16]

Closer examination of the first consistently good profile (the canonical/maverick group), reveals that 4 out of the 7 teachers came from one school, a school that had a principal who was a former mathematics coach and a consistent supporter of the *Investigations* curriculum. Even when the district pulled back its support of the reform, this school continued to support mathematics teachers with coaching and professional development (Kaufman and Stein 2010).

An optimistic interpretation of the next group—the five teachers labeled as the canonical/mechanical pattern—could be that they are "on the way" to sustained canonical implementations. Four of these five teachers came from the same school. The principal was an advocate of the reform and the *Investigations* curriculum during the early years, but then embraced the freedom to supplement in year 3 when the new superintendent lifted the mandate. Interestingly, at that point in time, four of the teachers slipped into a lower-quality profile; the fact that all but one re-emerged as a canonical implementer suggests that they perhaps had really learned from the earlier years implementing the curriculum and were thus able to reconfigure their practice at that higher level after "flirting" with the freedom from the mandate.

Finally, Greene was not immune from the flounderer/mechanical pattern that only rarely develops beyond low-quality instruction. This group of teachers came from all four of our schools, suggesting that no one school was immune from it as well.

Closer examination of the differences in the patterns *across* the two districts suggests that, perhaps, one leg of our proposed pathway of teacher development—from mechanical to canonical implementer—did indeed occur and it occurred more in Greene than in Region Z. We have already discussed how these two districts organized very different opportunities for teacher learning associated with their respective reforms. We have not, however, examined the curricula that each district selected to anchor their reform. As noted earlier, both were standards-based reforms. Both provided access to high-level, cognitively demanding tasks. However, one (*Investigations*) was found to have substantially more educative features than the other (Stein and Kim 2009). The *Investigations* materials more often identified the big

---

[16]There were no flounderers that led to mavericks.

mathematical idea at play in the lesson (and often provided a brief tutorial on it), thereby allowing teachers to apprehend the purpose of the activities in which they were about to engage their students. These materials also helped teachers to anticipate how students might respond to the many open-ended activities, thus helping them prepare ahead of time for how they might handle divergent and otherwise unexpected student responses. *Everyday Mathematics*, on the other hand, tended to have less open-ended tasks and to channel students and teachers toward a particular route through the problems. Teachers are provided with few in-depth details regarding how students might be expected to respond to the problems.

In short, the two curricula can be viewed as taking different stances toward teacher learning. *Investigations* does not script the teaching and learning that should occur in the classroom believing that student learning is always an emergent phenomenon, one that teachers must be attuned to through their attention to student thinking. As such, it helps teachers to (a) develop a nuanced understanding of the mathematical content to be learned; and (b) ways in which students might address this content. By doing so, it is investing in the teacher as an important element in the teaching and learning equation. *Everyday Mathematics*, on the other hand, appears to place the bulk of the expected learning between the student and the materials, with the teacher acting as a deliverer of those materials. Much less investment in the teacher is provided. Thus, another contributing factor to the greater preponderance of mechanical implementers developing into canonical implementers in Greene may be that the curricular materials provided greater transparency about their intent and potential student responses and, as such, helped teachers to move beyond a superficial, follow-the-directions style of implementation.

Conclusions

This work has implications for research on characterizing mathematics instruction within the context of district improvement strategies that rely on curricula and for research on teacher learning pathways. In addition, local policy makers could use findings generated here to help inform their designs for large-scale, curriculum based reforms.

Characterizing Instruction

The utilization of three dimensions (use, congruence, and quality) to characterize instruction offers a multi-dimensional view of instructional practice within district-wide, curriculum-based reform efforts. The fact that these three dimensions varied independently from one another suggests that each is offering a unique contribution to characterizing the nature of instruction. Yet, most often, only congruence *or* quality is measured. We believe that our framework represents an advance for the field of research on curriculum implementation and that it can serve as a unifying framework for future studies of large-scale teacher improvement within the context of district managed curricula. This includes our method of delineating four profiles of instruction, which our results suggest are viable as well. These profiles (flounderer, mechanical, canonical and maverick) captured variation across the teachers and appeared to be responsive to difference in contexts across the two districts.

Characterizing Teacher Development

The findings do not suggest that we have identified a clear, uniform pathway for teacher development within the context of district-wide, curriculum based reforms. Instead of straightforward development from mechanical to canonical to maverick, some of our data toggled back and forth between two or more different profiles. This raises questions about the instructional profiles as reliable platforms on the road to teacher improvement.

The results suggest a more uneven pathway toward high-quality instruction than we had proposed. First, teachers who achieved a canonical implementation did not always stay at that level of implementation. In most cases, they exhibited mechanical (or even flounderer) profiles after they had achieved a canonical implementation. We conjectured that these "declines" may sometimes have been related to changes in district-level enforcement of the curricular mandate. Another potential contributor could be the topic. Perhaps a mechanical profile was exhibited because the teacher was on a challenging topic (for her) and therefore more comfortable with a procedural, follow-the-book style of implementation. Or perhaps the teacher changed grade level and therefore did not have her earlier command of the conceptual field.

The results do, however, support our notion that teacher pathways are relevant with respect to a particular context. Both districts were in the midst of large-scale, curriculum-based reforms. However, past analyses suggested that the amount and type of support each district provided for teacher learning varied significantly. The present analysis suggests that, under a supportive context, more than half of the teachers may be able to achieve canonical implementations; in a less-supportive context, however, the vast majority of implementations will most probably consist of a mixture of flounderers and mechanical implementations.

Finally, the fact that there were few mavericks suggests that a common concern raised about district-based curricular reforms may not be warranted. Often, critics complain that excellent teachers are muffled by heavy-handed, top-down district reforms that force them to use a particular curriculum. The low incidence of mavericks in our data set (even after the mandate was lifted in Greene in the second year) suggests that this worry may be unfounded. A much larger worry, on the other hand, is the large number of flounderers and mechanical implementers that such reforms may foster.

Implications for Large-Scale District Reform

The findings reported herein suggest that expecting all teachers to implement standards-based curricula places a huge responsibility on the district to—not only monitor where teachers are on any given date—but also to support them as they try out new and often unfamiliar materials. By positioning teacher development against the backdrop of various ways in which teachers implement the district curriculum, this study's findings provide important foundational knowledge for the development of efficient and effective large-scale teacher support systems in environments characterized by district-wide managed curriculum.

Our findings suggest that district policies must go beyond mandates. Alone, mandates delivered only the lowest level of implementation: use. They were relatively ineffective for assuring that teachers implement the curriculum in a way that is aligned with the pedagogical guidelines in the curriculum and with district guidelines. They were not effective in delivering quality. The canonical implementers were almost exclusively in Greene, the district with effective support systems accompanying their roll-out of the new curriculum.

Our study also suggests ways in which our framework might be useful to the design of district support systems. Knowing the profiles of teachers in one's school or district would be useful in planning professional development. Not only do teachers with different profiles require different kinds of professional development (the maverick could be challenged by innovative offerings outside the district while the flounderer needs basic support), but teachers can be paired with one another in ways that take advantage of their differences. For example, a mechanical implementer could learn from a canonical implementer, but leaders would not want to send a flounderer into a maverick's classroom because—although it would be high-quality—without a curricular roadmap, it would be unclear to the flounderer how the teacher accomplishes what she does. Overall, considering various implementation profiles in the context of district-wide, curriculum-based improvement efforts is a promising approach to both diagnosing teachers' needs and identifying and using the strengths already present in the district (the canonical implementers) to address those needs.

References

Ball, D. L., & Cohen, D. K. (1996). Reform by the book: what is—or might be—the role of curriculum materials in teacher learning and instructional reform. *Educational Researcher, 25*(9), 6–8.

Boerst, T., & Sleep, L. (2007). Learning to do the work of mathematics teaching. In M. Lampert (Chair), *Conceptualizing and using routines of practice in mathematics teaching to advance professional education.* Symposium presented at the Annual Meeting of the American Educational Research Association, Chicago, IL.

Borko, H., & Putnam, R. (1995). Expanding a teacher's knowledge base: a cognitive psychological perspective on professional development. In T. Guskey & M. Huberman (Eds.), *Professional development in education* (pp. 35–65). New York: Teachers College Press.

Brendehur, J., & Frykholm, J. (2000). Prompting mathematical communication in the classroom: two preservice teachers' conceptions and practices. *Journal of Mathematics Teacher Education, 3*, 125–153.

Clements, D. H., & Sarama, J. (2004). Learning trajectories in mathematics education. *Mathematical Thinking and Learning, 6*(2), 191–221.

Cobb, P., Gravemeijer, K., Yackel, E., McClain, K., & Whitenack, J. (1997). Mathematizing and symbolizing: the emergence of chains of signification in one first-grade classroom. In D. Kirschner & J. A. Whitson (Eds.), *Situated cognition: social, semiotic and psychological perspectives* (pp. 151–233). Mahwah: Erlbaum.

Coburn, C. E. (2001). *Making sense of reading: logics of reading in the institutional environment and the classroom.* Ann Arbor: University Microfilms.

Coburn, C. E., & Russell, J. L. (2008). District policy and teachers' social networks. *Educational Evaluation and Policy Analysis, 30*(3), 203–235.

Davis, E. A., & Krajcik, J. S. (2005). Designing educative curriculum materials to promote teacher learning. *Educational Researcher, 34*(3), 3–14.

Doyle, W. (1983). Academic work. *Review of Educational Research, 53*(2), 159.

Duessen, T., Coskie, T., Robinson, L., & Autio, E. (2007). *"Coach" can mean many things: five categories of literacy coaches in reading first.* REL Northwest (REL 2007-No. 005). IES: US Department of Education.

Elmore, R., & Burney, D. (1999). Investing in teacher learning: staff development and instructional improvement. In L. Darling-Hammond & G. Sykes (Eds.), *Teaching as the learning profession: handbook of policy and practice* (pp. 263–291). San Francisco: Jossey-Bass.

Engle, R. A., & Conant, F. C. (2002). Guiding principles for fostering productive disciplinary engagement: explaining an emergent argument in a community of learners classroom. *Cognition and Instruction, 20*(4), 399–483.

Fennema, E. & Nelson, B. (Eds.) (1997). *Mathematics teachers in transition.* Hillsdale: Erlbaum.

Fullan, M. (1991). *The new meaning of educational change* (2nd ed.). New York: Teachers College Press.

Fullan, M., & Pomfret, A. (1977). Research on curriculum and instruction implementation. *Review of Educational Research, 47*(2), 335–397.

Hamm, J. V., & Perry, M. (2002). Learning mathematics in first-grade classrooms: on whose authority? *Journal of Educational Psychology, 94*(1), 126–137.

Hightower, A. M., Knapp, M. S., Marsh, J. A., & McLaughlin, M. W. (Eds.) (2002). *School districts and instructional renewal.* New York: Teachers College Press.

Hodge, L. L., & Cobb, P. (2003, April). *Classrooms as design spaces for supporting students' mathematical learning and engagement.* Paper presented at the Annual Meeting of the American Educational Research Association, Chicago, IL.

Hubbard, L., Mehan, H., & Stein, M. K. (2006). *Reform as learning: school reform, organizational culture, and community politics in San Diego.* New York: Routledge.

Kaufman, J. H., & Stein, M. K. (2010). Teacher learning opportunities in a shifting policy environment for instruction. *Educational Policy, 24*(4), 563–601.

Lampert, M. (1990). When the problem is not the question and the solution is not the answer: mathematical knowing and teaching. *American Educational Research Journal, 27*(1), 29–63.

Lampert, M. (2001). *Teaching problems and the problems of teaching.* New Haven: Yale University Press.

Nelson, B. S. (2001). Constructing facilitative teaching. In T. Wood, B. S. Nelson, & J. Warfield (Eds.), *Beyond classical pedagogy: teaching elementary school mathematics* (pp. 251–273). Mahwah: Erlbaum.

Scardamalia, M., Bereiter, C., & Lamon, M. (1994). The CSILE project: trying to bring the classroom into World 3. In K. McGilly (Ed.), *Classroom lessons: integrating cognitive theory and educational practice* (pp. 201–228). Cambridge: MIT Press.

Schoenfeld, A. S. (1998). Toward a theory of teaching-in-context. *Issues in Education, 4*(1), 1–95.

Shifter, D. (2001). Learning to see the invisible: what skills and knowledge are needed to engage with students' mathematical ideas? In T. Wood, B. S. Nelson, & J. Warfield (Eds.), *Beyond clas-*

sical pedagogy: teaching elementary school mathematics (pp. 109–134). Mahwah: Erlbaum.

Stein, M. K., & Coburn, C. E. (2008). Architectures for learning: a comparative analysis of two urban school districts. *American Journal of Education, 114*, 583–626.

Stein, M. K., & Kaufman, J. (2010). Selecting and supporting the use of mathematics curricula at scale. *American Educational Research Journal, 47*(3), 663–693.

Stein, M. K., & Kim, G. (2009). The role of mathematics curriculum materials in large-scale urban reform: an analysis of demands and opportunities for teacher learning. In J. Remillard, G. Lloyd, & B. Herbel-Eisenmann (Eds.), *Mathematics teachers at work: connecting curriculum materials and classroom instruction* (pp. 37–55). New York: Routledge.

Stein, M. K., & Lane, S. (1996). Instructional tasks and the development of student capacity to think and reason: an analysis of the relationship between teaching and learning in a reform mathematics project. *Educational Research and Evaluation, 2*(1), 50–80.

Stein, M. K., Grover, B. W., & Henningsen, M. (1996). Building student capacity for mathematical thinking and reasoning: an analysis of mathematical tasks used in reform classroom. *American Educational Research Journal, 33*(2), 455–488.

Stein, M. K., Engle, R. A., Smith, M. S., & Hughes, E. K. (2008). Orchestrating productive mathematical discussions: helping teachers learn to better incorporate student thinking. *Mathematical Thinking and Learning, 10*(4), 313–340.

Supovitz, J. A. (2006). *The case for district-based reform: leading, building and sustaining school improvement.* Cambridge: Harvard Education Press.

Sutherland, S., Smith, J., & Wallace, C. (2007). *The missing link? The coaches' role in policy translation.* Paper presented at the annual meeting of the American Educational Research Association, Chicago.

Wertsch, J. V., & Toma, C. (1995). Discourse and learning in the classroom: a sociocultural approach. In L. P. Steffe & J. Gale (Eds.), *Constructivism in education* (pp. 159–174). Hillsdale: Erlbaum.

Wilson, S. (1990). A conflict of interests: the case of mark black. *Educational Evaluation and Policy Analysis, 12*(3), 309–326.

Curriculum, Teachers and Teaching: Experiences from Systemic and Local Curriculum Change in England

Margaret Brown and Jeremy Hodgen

Abstract The seminal work of Michael Fullan and his University of Toronto colleagues (e.g. Fullan, Journal of Educational Change 1(1), 5–27, 2000, The New Meaning of Educational Change, 2001; Leithwood et al., Large-Scale Reform: What Works?, 1999) gave rise to a body of research looking into the reform of curriculum and teaching methods, in particular trying to identify the ingredients for successful reform. This chapter reflects on key features of reform in mathematics education by examining the effectiveness of a major system-wide attempt to change curriculum and teaching in English elementary schools, the National Numeracy Strategy. This is then contrasted with a more local intervention, Primary CAME. Process and outcomes in these different cases are considered, and some lessons suggested which can be drawn from them. In particular the notions of superficial change and deep change are used to analyse development in teachers' behaviours and beliefs.

Keywords Curriculum · Deep change · Local reform · Systemic reform

Setting the Context

There had been occasional national and local guidance but no strict requirement about curriculum or pedagogy in English primary schools since 1911. Government ministers started to express concern about national standards of numeracy in the mid-1970s, leading to agreement to recommendations concerning curriculum, teaching methods and assessment in the government-sponsored Cockcroft Report (DfES/WO 1982). A utilitarian curriculum was proposed, supported by more practical work and problem-solving, while students would also undertake mathematical investigations and assume a more active role in classroom discussion. Both curriculum and examinations at the end of compulsory schooling would become more differentiated so as to better meet the needs of students with a wide range of mathematical attainment, and would incorporate coursework to assess practical problem-solving and investigational skills.

M. Brown (✉) · J. Hodgen
King's College London, London, UK
e-mail: margaret.brown@kcl.ac.uk

Y. Li, G. Lappan (eds.), *Mathematics Curriculum in School Education*,
Advances in Mathematics Education, DOI 10.1007/978-94-007-7560-2_18,
© Springer Science+Business Media Dordrecht 2014

The Report had substantial support among policymakers, teachers and education-ists; through connected networks of influence, changes were implemented gradually, consistently, and on the whole in a positive spirit, although clearly at secondary level (age 11–16) the changes in national external assessment provided a strong incentive to conform.

It could be said that the Cockcroft Report addressed the more significant problem of designing a mathematics curriculum and assessment for mass education to age 16 and providing an updated definition of numeracy, rather than focusing narrowly on raised standards.

But after the relatively relaxed days of post-Cockcroft reform in the early 1980s, the repeatedly mediocre performances of England in international comparisons like SIMS and TIMSS (Reynolds and Farrell 1996) triggered further, faster and more prescriptive levels of government intervention, starting with a National Curriculum in the late 1980s, then national tests at ages 7, 11, and 14 in the 1990s, to supple-ment the long-standing external assessment at age 16. Results were then published in school league tables at ages 11 and 16. Finally, when England's international performance still failed to rise, a new Government decided in the summer of 1997 to introduce a National Numeracy Strategy across all year-groups in all elementary schools in 1999/2000 (Brown et al. 2000).

The next three sections will focus on research relating to the processes and out-comes of the implementation of this major top-down national systemic initiative. The following section of the chapter will contrast this implementation with the de-velopment of a curriculum development project, Primary CAME (Cognitive Accel-eration through Mathematics Education) through a local researcher-teacher partner-ship, aimed at building connected mathematical thinking.

The National Numeracy Strategy 1999–2005: Outline

Together with the related National Literacy Strategy which took place a year earlier, the National Numeracy Strategy in England was said by the Canadian team com-missioned to evaluate the initiative to be "the most ambitious large-scale strategy of reform witnessed since the 1960s" (Fullan 2000, p. 19). The implementation of the strategy cost around the equivalent of $150m in the first year (1999/2000), with a further $100m per year for the following 5 years, then finally declining to zero within 10 years.

The objective of the reform was to raise standards of numeracy, in particular in national and international tests. Thus the definition of numeracy used (DfEE 1998, p. 11) was in terms of 'proficiency' with calculation and solution of word problems rather than that used earlier in the Cockcroft Report which related to the ability to apply mathematics in everyday life, further education and employment.

The Strategy was based on a National Numeracy Project funded by the previ-ous government starting in 1996, which was still large-scale by most standards and had focused on schools in 13 localities selected because of low results in national tests. This fore-runner Project was led by a well-regarded national figure, Anita Straker, who had involved most of England's elementary mathematics experts in assisting with the detailed curriculum and recommended didactics (Brown et al. 2003). Nevertheless all were aware that the development had to conform to some political requirements, for example by focusing on calculation, being prescriptive about curriculum and didactics, and involving a high proportion of whole class teaching.

The new Government was not prepared to await the full evaluation of the project before going ahead and rolling it out nationally in the form of the National Numeracy Strategy. However, reactions from teachers were positive, and so were early indications of attainment gains. The materials developed and many of the personnel appointed were carried over to the Strategy with minimal obstacles, thus enabling it to be implemented quickly.

Key aspects of the reform were:

- *an increased emphasis on number and on calculation, especially mental strategies for calculation*, including new methods of teaching number skills, a delayed introduction of written methods, and an encouragement for pupils to select from a repertoire of strategies;
- *a three-part template for daily mathematics lessons*, starting with 10–15 minutes of whole class oral/mental arithmetic practice, then 25–35 minutes of direct interactive teaching, first with the whole class and then with groups, and finally 10 minutes of plenary review;
- *detailed planning using a centrally provided week-by-week framework of detailed objectives*, specified for each year group, which introduced many skills at an earlier stage than previously.

The Strategy claimed to be evidence-based, but there was some question as to how many aspects really were underpinned by research (Brown et al. 1998). There was however much use of successful teaching models (e.g. the empty number line) already used by the Realistic Mathematics Education group based at the Freudenthal Institute in Holland (Anghileri 2001). There were also similarities with some aspects of the 'reform mathematics' movement in the United States, for example the emphasis on discussion and refining of children's own strategies and a focus on mental work rather than formal written algorithms. However calculator use was postponed until the final years of elementary school.

Teachers were discouraged from using sets of textbooks and instead encouraged to devise their own detailed lesson plans using the variety of sources they might have access to, in particular, the extensive examples illustrating each of the large number of lesson objectives which were provided in the teachers' Framework documents (DfEE 1999). In fact the speed of the roll-out meant that it was impossible for publishers to bring out new textbooks matching the Strategy planning templates in time for the first year of implementation. Teachers therefore reported in the first year that they spent many additional hours preparing these new lessons, and found it especially frustrating when some good quality supportive textbooks started to appear in the following years.

The method of implementation was highly systematic and standardised, as it probably needed to be in order to quickly reach more than 100,000 teachers in more than 17,000 schools. It involved a substantial national training programme based on a "cascade" model of capacity-building. This was designed by the national director, together with a group of regional directors, who each trained locally based newly appointed consultants using a standard training package. In turn the local consultants delivered a 3-day training to groups of teachers, one from each school who had been appointed as their school mathematics co-ordinator. Head teachers and school governors (often a parent) attended for part of this time to ensure school managers were properly briefed. Finally each mathematics co-ordinator collected her own package to deliver 3 full days of training, spread over a year, in each school. Each of the training boxes contained videos of several 'exemplary' lessons, PowerPoint slides highlighting key features of the Strategy, including recommended methods of calculation, and guidance booklets to demonstrate 'best practice'.

In addition to the 'cascade' training, each local consultant was required to provide additional in-school coaching for teachers in a group of schools. This included running 5-day courses to boost teachers' subject knowledge. In the first year those schools selected were perceived as needing support because of poor results in national tests at age 11, but over 3 years each school experienced this additional support, and the majority of elementary teachers experienced the 5-day courses.

There were considerable external incentives for schools to quickly and fully implement the National Numeracy Strategy, since it took place within a tight school accountability regime. Statutory testing was in place at ages 7 and 11; at 11 this took the form of externally set and marked tests with results published as league tables in the national press. There was also a strict national inspection regime in place run by Ofsted (Office for Standards in Education). Schools could expect to be inspected at least every three or four years, and even more frequently if they had below average test results. Inspectors observed classes to grade teaching; they had the right to put schools in special measures which required them to improve rapidly or to close. Thus although the National Numeracy Strategy (unlike the National Curriculum) was technically non-statutory, not to implement it thoroughly would have been to risk poor outcomes from inspection.

After the initial implementation, as discussed in more detail in the next section, there were only small rises in national test results, so policymakers felt that a stronger line needed to be taken over control of teaching quality. The central strategy team (national and regional directors, supported by other consultants) were therefore asked to provide a complete year's set of lesson plans available on the internet to match the objectives specified, for all year groups from Grade 2 to Grade 5. The lesson plans were full but not complete—but they mainly required teachers to supply only additional practice examples. There is no national data but pooled personal experience suggests that local consultants strongly encouraged their use and there was a very high take-up, even among schools which had recently invested in new textbooks matched to the Strategy. Some attributed this to the mathematical insecurity of, and fear of inspectors by, teachers—if the lesson observed followed closely a recommended Strategy lesson then they could not be perceived as non-compliant.

Thus within a period of 20 years England had moved from a position where elementary teachers were free to teach in mathematics whatever and however they wished, via gradually more prescriptive steps of a national curriculum, national tests, accountability measures and a national strategy, to a position where almost all teachers of a given grade were teaching exactly the same centrally designed lesson on the same day throughout the country.

The National Numeracy Strategy: Effect on Attainment

Considerable claims have been made for the success of the reform in raising standards of attainment (e.g., Mourshed et al. 2010). Since the National Numeracy Strategy was a reaction to poor results in international comparative surveys, the ultimate evaluation was whether England's rankings improved in TIMSS (Trends in International Mathematics and Science Study) and PISA (Programme for International Student Assessment).

At the elementary level, data is available only from TIMSS Grade 4 comparisons. The results for England have risen gradually from 484 in 1995 to 531 in 2003 and 541 in 2007. England was 7th out of 36 countries in 2007 and was only outperformed by four Pacific rim countries, Russia and Kazakhstan (Sturman et al. 2008). (In view of their bottom position out of 65 countries in PISA the Kazakhstan results are unlikely to be valid.) England had drawn ahead of Australia, New Zealand, Canada and the Netherlands, all countries which previously outranked England. This suggests a significant gain across the period of the Strategy, although the actual gain is likely to be only about half as large as this because in 2003 and 2007 the tests in England alone were sat 3 months later in the year.

There has also been a small rise in TIMSS at Grade 8; after remaining pretty steady at around 498 between 1995 and 2003, the score increased significantly to 513 in 2007. This was for the first TIMSS cohort which would have experienced the National Strategy in elementary schools. England was now 7th out of 49 countries, and only significantly outperformed by five countries, Hungary and four from the Pacific rim (Sturman et al. 2008). In contrast the 2006 and 2009 PISA (age 15) results are low compared with 2000, with England at 20th out of 32 countries in 2009 against 8th out of these same 32 in 2000 (OECD 2001, 2010). This contrast in trends between TIMSS and PISA may make some sense in that TIMSS assesses a more traditional curriculum which might be strengthened by a Strategy which favours number skills whereas PISA assesses mathematical literacy, which was probably stronger under the post-Cockcroft curriculum.

A further indication of the effect of the Strategy on attainment should be the changes in the proportion of children reaching the 'nationally expected' level in national tests at age 11. Here there has been only a very slow gradual improvement of on average 1 % per year, with 69 % of children achieving the level in 1999 and 76 % in 2006. Remarkably similar trajectories were obtained for Science and English results. It was interesting that Science gains during this period (9 %) were very slightly larger than the Mathematics gain (7 %), since although there were National

Strategies for Numeracy and Literacy, there was no such scheme for Science. This suggests that the gains were more closely related to teachers' growing expertise in test preparation pressured by league tables and inspections than to the effects of the Strategy.

It was fortuitous that a large-scale 5-year (1997–2002) research programme on elementary mathematics, the Leverhulme Numeracy Research Programme (LNRP), coincided with the introduction of the National Numeracy Strategy. The LNRP research involved a longitudinal survey tracking children's progression in numeracy based on a nationally representative sample of 40 schools, 10 each from four diverse local authorities (education districts). Additional research foci included a detailed qualitative longitudinal study of children's experiences in mathematics classrooms, an investigation of school leadership in mathematics and numeracy and a study of the effects of the Numeracy Strategy training on teachers. There were two cohorts of children involved, one moving from Kindergarten to Grade 3 and one from Grade 3 to Grade 6. This meant that we had complete Grade 3 (aged 8–9 years) data from 35 out of the 40 schools both in 1997, two years before the start of the Numeracy Strategy, and in 2002, two years after its introduction. The tests used were of the type of numeracy which featured strongly in the Strategy, and the items had been fully trialled in earlier research projects also based at King's College London (Brown et al. 2008).

This comparison of Grade 3 (aged 8–9) children's attainment before and after the introduction of the reform shows that the Numeracy Strategy produced an effect size of 0.18 (Brown et al. 2003; see also Tymms 2004). This was consistent whether the gain was measured at the beginning or the end of the school year. Whilst this effect size is relatively modest (and is somewhat smaller than the increases in national test performance over the same period), it is comparable to effect sizes achieved in similar educational systems (e.g., the recent rise in German performance in PISA mathematics). An idea of what this effect size means in practice is that the difference is the equivalent of about 2.5 months' learning. Alternatively, it meant that just over one in three schools had a lower mean score after the introduction of the Strategy than before, while the remaining two in three had higher mean scores.

Beneath this overall effect, there were differential effects across the attainment range (performance amongst the lowest attaining group of children fell) and in different part of mathematics (attainment on multiplication items did not rise, while number line and addition/subtraction items did). Analysis of the performance of a subset of the children at the end of Grade 6 (their first year in lower secondary school) found that their attainment on the elementary numeracy test was below that at the end of Grade 5, suggesting that the overall gain in attainment was not sustained.

These outcomes suggest that even a carefully developed, well trialled and systematically implemented curriculum change, costing in total around $1billion, may have a relatively small effect on children's attainment.

The National Numeracy Strategy: Effect on Teachers and Teaching

The official evaluation of the implementation of both the National Numeracy and the National Literacy Strategies was commissioned from the Ontario Institute for Studies in Education (Earl et al. 2003), and there were also reports based on school inspectors' observations (Ofsted 2002). These demonstrated that the implementation processes had been very thorough and successful in reaching all teachers as well as in giving coherent and consistent messages. The recommendations were being put into practice faithfully by teachers, in relation to the content of the curriculum, the lesson planning and adoption of centrally provided learning objectives, the specific mathematical didactics (e.g. use of the empty number line for addition and subtraction), and the generic pedagogy (the format of each lesson).

The Leverhulme Numeracy Research Project (LNRP) also had a large database of teacher interviews and observed lessons from before and after the Strategy implementation. Particular attention was paid to the Grade 3 lessons, which were taught in the same 35 schools (but rarely by the same teachers) during 1997/8 and 2001/2. These included about 75 lessons, one from each Grade 3 class, in each of the two years.

In particular the LNRP research was in line with the OISE and Ofsted reports in concluding that the more superficial aspects of the reform were implemented conscientiously by almost all teachers and schools (Millett et al. 2004a). Lessons became objective-driven, and lesson structures, pedagogy, didactics, and curriculum were modified in compliance with the guidance provided.

However teachers' lack of understanding of the mathematics and unwillingness to make independent professional judgements acted as barriers to deeper levels of change. Teachers felt they must stick closely to the objectives and lesson structure since they had been assured that these were research-based and would produce good outcomes, even when they felt that pupils could have benefited from greater flexibility. They rarely felt they had the knowledge or confidence to challenge or adapt the lessons. For example, teachers sometimes expressed a desire to spend longer on a topic or idea until the whole class had consolidated their knowledge, or to omit the plenary session to allow pupils longer to work individually. As intended by the Strategy, the process of teaching seemed to have acquired priority over the process of learning.

We observed some levelling down as well as levelling up of quality in the process of pursuit of compliance. Thus the examples of really inspiring and engaging lessons we had sometimes observed in 1997/8 were no longer there in 2001/2. On the other hand, the fact that teachers were now focusing on prescribed objectives probably explained why by 2001/2 there were far fewer lessons where children's confusion about mathematics seemed to be a consequence of a teacher's lack of clarity over what they were trying to achieve.

However, almost all teachers expressed great enthusiasm for the changes. They felt that both they and the children had a better grasp of the mathematics with the new ways of teaching number and number operations. They were convinced that pupils' achievement was significantly greater than before the Strategy was introduced, in spite of our results which showed that in over a third of schools the results were lower than previously, and in very few schools were they significantly higher. They appreciated the focus on asking children to explain how they tackled problems, although in lesson observations teachers often found it hard to build on children's responses. Instead, keen to achieve the lesson objective, teachers would often simply then show children how they were expected to solve the problem.

Millett et al. (2004b) note:

> In our opinion, the major impact of the Strategy so far on the teaching of mathematics has been in changing the attitude towards mathematics on the part of teachers, and with that the motivation for changing practice ... improvements in the quality of mathematical interactions in the classroom are extremely limited. (p. 204)

These observations seem to explain some of the results on attainment reported in the previous section. For example, the drop in attainment of the lowest attaining children seemed to follow from teachers' reluctance to diverge from whole class teaching on prescribed objectives or to spend longer on a topic than decreed. The fact that there were greater changes in some areas of numeracy than others reflected changes in emphasis and didactics. For instance, more focus on the number line brought significant rises in number line items, whereas some word problem items fell in facility as problem-solving was no longer emphasised. There was not anything like as great an effect size as was anticipated by the politicians because there was not really a change in the quality of classroom interactions between teachers and children.

Primary CAME (Cognitive Acceleration through Mathematics Education): 1997/2001

A significant barrier to the success of interventions at scale is that many of the recommendations made by the mathematics education research community are difficult to communicate to teachers at a distance. For example, systemic interventions face considerable challenges when attempting to encourage teaching that emphasises formative assessment.

We now shift our attention to a curriculum change project, Cognitive Acceleration through Mathematics Education (CAME), which attempted to address this issue (Shayer and Adhami 2007). Specifically, CAME sought to effect "bottom-up" change by working initially at a local level with small groups of teachers, then encouraging their continued involvement through a national support network of teachers.

CAME was one element of a wider programme of research in Cognitive Acceleration that began in Science Education (Adey and Shayer 2002). Central to the CAME approach were lesson outlines in which children were encouraged to grapple with cognitively challenging ideas. Drawing on neo-Piagetian, Vygotskian and other related research into children's conceptual development (Adhami et al. 1995;

Biggs and Collis 1982), the lessons attempted to match the reasoning levels inherent in mathematical tasks with what children might reasonably be expected to achieve, relating this in particular to potential misconceptions and children's naïve understandings of key mathematical ideas (Hart et al. 1981).

Hence, CAME lessons were designed to provide all students in a typical class with opportunities to engage mathematics just beyond their current level. In doing so, the lessons included explicit attention to the key constructs of *concrete preparation, construction, cognitive conflict, metacognition* and *bridging*. These ideas were drawn from the mathematics education literature and are described in some detail elsewhere (Shayer and Adhami 2007).

For the purposes of this chapter, however, we emphasise two key design features of the intervention with teachers. The first important feature relates to conceptual teaching. CAME lessons were introduced to teachers as *"Thinking Maths"* lessons to supplement (and not replace) regular mathematics teaching and to be taught every two or three weeks. This reduced the conflict that teachers often feel in novel approaches between curriculum coverage and covering an issue thoroughly. Thus, it offered teachers the opportunity to explore and think in depth about the CAME approach, while mostly maintaining their previous practice.

The second feature relates to collaboration. Teachers' professional development was built around the teachers doing the CAME mathematical activities themselves, then planning, team-teaching and reflecting on the relevant lesson, before teaching the lesson to their own classes. Hence, collaboration was designed into the professional development specifically around teachers' central professional interest— teaching the lessons. Teachers are often extolled to collaborate, but they need both an opportunity and a reason to collaborate.

CAME has been developed for lower elementary, upper elementary and lower secondary education. The upper elementary work, of Primary CAME was part of the Leverhulme Numeracy Research Programme (LNRP) and hence, although this was not intended, went on alongside the National Numeracy Strategy. This made it difficult to analyse the results, especially while using national test results where some schools focused more than others in coaching their pupils for tests.

The work started with 2 teachers in each of two schools, working as teacher researchers with a local primary mathematics advisor and a group of four university researchers. The aim was to design, trial and refine Grade 4 lessons as explained above. In the second year, the teacher researchers inducted teachers in seven main study schools from the same local district, who trialled the lessons while the research group developed and trialled Grade 5 lessons, which were then introduced to the additional seven schools in the third year.

Hodgen and Johnson (2004) have described the significant changes in beliefs that occurred in some, but not all, of the teacher researchers involved.

Evaluation results for CAME in different phases all showed positive effects. In lower secondary (equivalent to Grades 6 and 7, ages 11–13), gains on an immediate post-test show an effect size of 0.34 on a test of conceptual understanding. In addition and significantly, public examination results at age 16 indicate a "far effect size" of 0.44, three years after the intervention took place (Shayer and Adhami 2007).

In lower elementary (equivalent to Kindergarten and Grade 1, ages 5–7), a group of teachers from 8 schools participated in professional development led by the researchers themselves, whilst a further group of 10 schools participated in professional development led by others (Shayer and Adhami 2010). On an immediate post-test, the group taught by the researchers showed gains equivalent to an effect size of 0.71 with gains for the additional group of 10 schools at 0.60 using a test of conceptual understanding. On a national test conducted five years later, both groups showed gains in comparison to the national sample equivalent to effect sizes of 0.24 and 0.22.

Finally, CAME in upper elementary that is described here was evaluated alongside the introduction of the National Numeracy Strategy (Adhami 2002). These indicate an effect size gain of 0.26 of the intervention classes over the control. Although this is a more modest gain than in lower elementary or upper secondary, we note that this gain was in addition to the effect of the introduction of the National Numeracy Strategy.

Thus there is reasonably good evidence for the efficacy of the CAME intervention both in elementary and in secondary education. Of particular note are the "far" effects indicated by the lower elementary and the secondary evaluations, showing that the effects of the interventions appear to be sustained. However, scaling up and sustaining the approach remains a challenge, an issue that we return to in our concluding discussion.

It is worth noting that in a recent report on good practice in elementary mathematics teaching by the inspectorate, based on observations in many schools (Ofsted 2011), a Primary CAME lesson taught by a teacher who had not been part of the original research was featured as an example of an outstanding lesson, and indeed the chief inspector for mathematics explained that it was the best lesson she had ever observed.

Conclusions

The local project, Primary CAME, had significantly larger effect sizes than the systemic reform. However this may only reflect the smaller scale of these projects, bringing about a greater personal commitment and a potential Hawthorne effect often associated with early adopters. As in the case of other CAME projects it was also clear that not all teachers bought into the system (non-implementation was not a realistic option for the National Strategy).

Nevertheless, Primary CAME is part of a wider and mature cognitive acceleration programme that has shown effects can be sustained (Shayer and Adhami 2010). In contrast to the deep change in teachers' beliefs that can result from these local projects where teachers develop positive relationships with the project leaders and with other teachers involved, commit to the project and play an active role in the development, and often therefore experience a sense of shared ownership of the work, the National Numeracy Strategy produced rather superficial changes, but on a far wider scale. It seems likely that the marginal costs per teacher might be similar, but further work is needed on comparing the relative costs of local and systemic reform (Brown 2010).

We argue that two key deficiencies of systemic development are that it fails to encourage the development of authentic teacher professional networks (which Spillane 1999, argues is key to successful professional change), and it tends to discourage teacher exploration and experimentation (thus discouraging change, Cuban 1993). We are now seeing the lack of long term effect in that since the removal of the National Strategy infrastructure, many of the curricular and didactic features (such as methods of teaching calculation) seem to be fragmenting, leaving a lack of coherence in approach, both between and within schools. Only the more simplistic pedagogic features which probably have a lesser effect on outcomes (like the 'three-part lesson') seem to have survived as part of the nationally agreed definition of 'good practice'. In contrast there are certainly still networks of Primary CAME teachers sustained by a small number of enthusiasts, but it is unclear how long these will survive.

These two case studies suggest that there is no clear winner between local and systemic innovation in mathematics curriculum; they have different development paths and effects. It may be that a system should alternate; for example, after a period of closely prescribed systemic change like the National Numeracy Strategy in England, a "let a thousand flowers bloom" approach of encouraging a wider number of small scale local projects would achieve gains equivalent to that achieved by systemic reforms initiative at a roughly similar cost, but would have the advantage of encouraging a revival of teacher creativity and producing a wider variety of approaches to the teaching of mathematics. The most promising might then be carefully evaluated and considered for wider, maybe even systemic, implementation in the next phase.

References

Adey, P. S., & Shayer, M. (2002). Cognitive acceleration comes of age. In M. Shayer & P. S. Adey (Eds.), *Learning intelligence: cognitive acceleration across the curriculum*, Buckingham: Open University Press.

Adhami, M. (2002). Cognitive acceleration in mathematics education in years 5 and 6: problems and challenges. In M. Shayer & P. S. Adey (Eds.), *Learning intelligence: cognitive acceleration across the curriculum from 5 to 15 years* (pp. 98–117). Buckingham: Open University Press.

Adhami, M., Johnson, D. C., & Shayer, M. (1995). *Cognitive acceleration through mathematics education: an analysis of the cognitive demands of the national curriculum and associated commercial schemes for secondary mathematics*. Paper presented at the Joint Conference of the British Society for Research into Learning Mathematics (BSRLM) and the Association of Mathematics Education Tutors (AMET), 19 & 20 May, 1995, Loughborough.

Anghileri, J. (Ed.) (2001). *Principles and practices in arithmetic teaching: innovative approaches for the primary classroom*. Buckingham: Open University Press.

Biggs, J., & Collis, K. (1982). *Evaluating the quality of learning: the SOLO taxonomy (structure of the observed learning outcomes)*. New York: Academic Press.

Brown, M. (2010). Are we getting better at educating? King's College London Annual Education Lecture.

Brown, M., Askew, M., Baker, D., Denvir, H., & Millett, A. (1998). Is the national numeracy strategy research-based? *British Journal of Educational Studies, 46*(4), 362–385.

Brown, M., Millett, A., Bibby, T., & Johnson, D. C. (2000). Turning our attention from the what to the how: the national numeracy strategy. *British Educational Research Journal, 26*(4), 457–471.

Brown, M., Askew, M., Millett, A., & Rhodes, V. (2003). The key role of educational research in the development and evaluation of the national numeracy strategy. *British Educational Research Journal, 29*(5), 655–672.

Brown, M., Askew, M., Hodgen, J., Rhodes, V., Millett, A., Denvir, H., & Wiliam, D. (2008). Individual and cohort progression in learning numeracy ages 5–11: results from the Leverhulme 5-year longitudinal study. In A. Dowker (Ed.), *Children's mathematical difficulties: psychology, neuroscience and education* (pp. 85–108). Oxford: Elsevier.

Cuban, L. (1993). *How teachers taught: constancy and change in American classrooms 1880–1990* (2nd ed.). New York: Teachers College Press.

Earl, L., Watson, N., Levin, B., Leithwood, K., Fullan, M., Torrance, N., & Volante, L. (2003). *Watching and learning 3: OISE/UT (Ontario Institute for Studies in Education, University of Toronto) final report of the external evaluation of England's national literacy and numeracy strategies.* London: Department for Education and Skills.

Department for Education and Employment (DfEE) (1998). *The implementation of the national numeracy strategy: the final report of the numeracy task force.* London: DfEE.

Department for Education and Employment (DfEE) (1999). *The national numeracy strategy: framework for teaching mathematics from reception to year 6.* London: DfEE.

Department of Education and Science/Welsh Office; Committee of Inquiry into the Teaching of Mathematics in Schools (1982). *Mathematics counts ('The Cockcroft report').* London: HMSO.

Fullan, M. (2000). The return of large-scale reform. *Journal of Educational Change, 1*(1), 5–27.

Fullan, M. (2001). *The new meaning of educational change* (3rd ed.). New York: Teachers College Press.

Hart, K., Brown, M. L., Küchemann, D. E., Kerslake, D., Ruddock, G., & McCartney, M. (Eds.) (1981). *Children's understanding of mathematics: 11–16.* London: John Murray.

Hodgen, J., & Johnson, D. C. (2004). Teacher reflection, identity and belief change in the context of primary CAME. In A. Millett, M. Brown, & M. Askew (Eds.), *Primary mathematics and the developing professional* (pp. 219–244). Dordrecht: Kluwer.

Leithwood, K., Jantzi, D., & Mascall, B. (1999). *Large-scale reform: what works?* Ontario: Ontario Institute for Studies in Education (OISE), University of Toronto.

Millett, A., Askew, M., & Brown, M. (2004a). The impact of the national numeracy strategy in year 4: (II). *Teaching. Research in Mathematics Education, 6,* 191–205.

Millett, A., Brown, M., & Askew, M. (Eds.) (2004b). *Primary mathematics and the developing professional.* Dordrecht: Kluwer.

Mourshed, M., Chijioke, C., & Barber, M. (2010). *How the world's most improved school systems eep getting better.* London: McKinsey & Company.

OECD (2001). *Knowledge and skills for life: first results from the OECD programme for international student assessment (PISA) 2000.* Paris: OECD (Online at: http://www.oecd.org/dataoecd/44/53/33691596.pdf)

OECD (2010). PISA 2009 results: what students know and can do—student performance in reading, mathematics and science (Volume I) (Online at doi:10.1787/9789264091450-en).

Ofsted (2002). *The national numeracy strategy: the first three years 1999–2002.* London: Office for Standards in Education.

Ofsted (2011). *Good practice in primary mathematics.* London: Office for Standards in Education.

Reynolds, D., & Farrell, S. (1996). *Worlds apart? A review of international surveys of educational achievement involving England. Ofsted reviews of research series.* London: HMSO.

Shayer, M., & Adhami, M. (2007). Fostering cognitive development through the context of mathematics: results of the CAME project. *Educational Studies in Mathematics, 64*(3), 265–291.

Shayer, M., & Adhami, M. (2010). Realizing the cognitive potential of children 5–7 with a mathematics focus: post-test and long-term effects of a 2-year intervention. *British Journal of Educational Psychology*, *80*(3), 363–379.

Spillane, J. P. (1999). External reform initiatives and teachers' efforts to reconstruct their practice: the mediating role of teachers' zones of enactment. *Journal of Curriculum Studies*, *31*(2), 143–175.

Sturman, L., Ruddock, G., Burge, B., Styles, B., Lin, Y., & Vappula, H. (2008). *England's achievements in TIMSS 2007: national report for England*. Slough: NFER.

Tymms, P. (2004). Are standards rising in English primary schools? *British Educational Research Journal*, *30*(4), 477–494.

Teaching Mathematics Using Standards-Based and Traditional Curricula: A Case of Variable Ideas

Jinfa Cai, Bikai Nie, John C. Moyer, and Ning Wang

Abstract This chapter discusses approaches to teaching algebraic concepts like variables that are embedded in a *Standards*-based mathematics curriculum (CMP) and in a traditional mathematics curriculum (Glencoe Mathematics). Neither the CMP curriculum nor Glencoe Mathematics clearly distinguishes among the various uses of variables. Overall, the CMP curriculum uses a functional approach to teach equation solving, while Glencoe Mathematics uses a structural approach to teach equation solving. The functional approach emphasizes the important ideas of change and variation in situations and contexts. The structural approach, on the other hand, avoids contextual problems in order to concentrate on developing the abilities to generalize, work abstractly with symbols, and follow procedures in a systematic way. This chapter reports part of the findings from the larger LieCal research project. The LieCal Project is designed to investigate longitudinally the impact of a *Standards*-based curriculum like CMP on teachers' classroom instruction and student learning. This chapter tells part of the story by showing the value of a detailed curriculum analysis in characterizing curriculum as a pedagogical event.

Keywords LieCal project · Standards-based curriculum · Longitudinal study · Curriculum study · Algebra · Variables · Equations · Equation solving · Functional approach · Structural approach

Research reported in this chapter is supported by grants from the National Science Foundation (ESI-0454739 and DRL-1008536). Any opinions expressed herein are those of the authors and do not necessarily represent the views of the National Science Foundation.

J. Cai (✉) · B. Nie
University of Delaware, Newark, USA
e-mail: jcai@math.udel.edu

J.C. Moyer
Marquette University, Milwaukee, USA

N. Wang
Widener University, Chester, USA

Y. Li, G. Lappan (eds.), *Mathematics Curriculum in School Education*,
Advances in Mathematics Education, DOI 10.1007/978-94-007-7560-2_19,
© Springer Science+Business Media Dordrecht 2014

Purpose

The purpose of this paper is to compare the approaches to algebra that are embedded in two types of middle school curricula used in the United States: "*Standards*-based" and "traditional," with a focus on variable ideas. The *Standards*-based curriculum that we analyze in this paper is the Connected Mathematics Program (CMP). It was developed with the support of the National Science Foundation and designed to align with the reform-oriented principles recommended in the NCTM *Standards* (NCTM 1989). The "traditional" curriculum that we analyze is Glencoe Mathematics. The National Science Foundation did not fund the development of Glencoe Mathematics. Although it professes to be *Standards*-based, Glencoe Mathematics is generally considered to be traditional in its approach, rather than reform-oriented. Our goal is not to evaluate these curricula. Instead, our intent is to acquaint the reader with the details of two distinct approaches to the teaching of algebra, as well as the mathematical conceptions that underlie them.

In the past two decades, researchers have begun to explore new conceptions of school algebra (Kieran et al. 1996; Nemirovsky 1996). Curriculum designers often disagree about the organizing themes that should be used to give coherence to algebra across the curriculum. Two ways to conceptually organize curricula written for school algebra are via functions and via structures (Algebra Working Group to NCTM 1997). These two conceptions of school algebra are the basis for two popular approaches to the teaching of school algebra. The central mathematical concept of relation underlies the functional approach, which has been advocated by many mathematics educators (Bednarz et al. 1996). Under the functional approach, the important ideas of change and variation that can be seen in various situations and contexts are used to organize algebraic concepts across the curriculum. The structural approach, in contrast, looks beyond the potentially confounding aspects of real-world contexts. It focuses, instead, on procedures and on underlying structures and patterns. That is, the structural approach requires students to move away from contextual problems and develop the ability to generalize, work abstractly with symbols, and follow procedures in a systematic way.

In this chapter, our analysis shows how these two approaches are implemented in *Standards*-based and traditional mathematics curricula, respectively, with a focus on variable ideas. This chapter has five sections. We first provide background information about the recent curriculum reform in the United States and the LieCal Project on which this chapter is based. Second, we present our detailed analysis of variable ideas in the CMP (*Standards*-based) and non-CMP curricula. The following related questions guided our analysis of the two types of curricula: (1) What are the learning goals for the concept of variable in the two curricula? (2) How is the concept of variable defined and introduced in the two types of curricula? and (3) How is the concept developed across the middle grades in both types of curricula?

Building on the second section, the third section examines how the variable ideas in CMP and non-CMP curricula influence the definition and introduction of other important algebraic ideas, such as equation, equation solving, and function. The fourth section highlights teachers' use of the two types of curricula in classrooms and the ensuing student achievement growth across the three middle school years. Our goal in the fourth section is to show the impact of curriculum on teachers' teaching and student learning.

In the fifth section, the chapter concludes with an in-depth discussion of the complex interplay among three levels of curriculum (intended, implemented, and attained), as well as methodological issues of curriculum studies (Cai 2010). The intended curriculum refers to the formally written documents that set system-level expectations for learning mathematics. The intended curriculum usually includes goals and expectations set by the educational system along with textbooks, official syllabi or curriculum standards, and course objectives. The implemented curriculum refers to school and classroom processes for teaching and learning of mathematics as interpreted and implemented by the teachers, according to their experience and beliefs for particular classes. The attained curriculum refers to what is learned by students and is manifested in their achievements and attitudes. In addition, this chapter provides some insights into the substance of the current reform effort in the United States, which has received widespread attention over the past decade.

Background

Advocates of mathematics education reform often attempt to change classroom practice, and hence students' learning, by means of changes in curricula (Ball and Cohen 1996). This is not a new development since, historically, curricula have been used to convey what students should learn as well as to improve instruction. Therefore, an analysis of curricula can provide insights not only into different philosophies regarding mathematics learning, but also into different approaches to the teaching of mathematics (Cai et al. 2002, 2010; Nie et al. 2009).

In the late 1980s and early 1990s, the National Council of Teachers of Mathematics (NCTM) published its first round of *Standards* documents (e.g. NCTM 1989, 1991, 1995), which provided recommendations for reforming and improving K-12 school mathematics. These *Standards* documents not only specified new goals for school mathematics, but also specified major shifts in teaching mathematics, including movement toward:

- classrooms as mathematical communities—away from classrooms as simply collections of individuals;
- logic and mathematical evidence as verification—away from the teacher as the sole authority for right answers;
- mathematical reasoning—away from merely memorizing procedures;
- conjecturing, inventing, and problem solving—away from an emphasis on mechanistic answer-finding;
- connecting mathematics, its ideas, and its applications—away from treating math as a body of isolated concepts and procedures.

With extensive support from the National Science Foundation (NSF), a number of school mathematics curricula were developed and implemented to align with the recommendations of the *Standards*. The Connected Mathematics Program (CMP) is one of the *Standards*-based middle school curricula developed with funding from NSF. The CMP curriculum was designed to build students' understanding of important mathematics through explorations of real-world situations and problems. It is a complete middle-school mathematics program. Students using the CMP curriculum are led to investigate important mathematical ideas and develop robust ways of thinking as they try to make sense of and resolve problems based on real-world situations.

In this chapter, we compare the approaches to variable ideas in the CMP curriculum to those in the more traditionally-based Glencoe *Mathematics: Concepts and Applications* curriculum (Bailey et al. 2006a, 2006b, 2006c). The Glencoe curriculum is also a complete middle-school mathematics program. Students using the Glencoe curriculum are taught important mathematical skills and concepts principally by studying completely worked out examples with clear explanations that are paralleled by guided practice. As we have stated, mathematics educators consider the Glencoe curriculum to be traditional, rather than *Standards*-based. There is one book for each grade level in Glencoe Mathematics. Unlike Glencoe Mathematics, the CMP curriculum consists of a number of unit booklets for each grade level.

LieCal Project

The research reported here was part of a large research project designed to longitudinally compare the effects of a *Standards*-based curriculum (CMP) to the effects of more traditional middle school curricula on students' learning of algebra. In the large project, *Longitudinal Investigation of the Effect of Curriculum on Algebra Learning* (LieCal),[1] we investigated not only the ways and circumstances under which CMP and other middle school curricula like Glencoe Mathematics did or did not enhance student learning in algebra, but also the characteristics of the curricula that led to student achievement gains (Cai et al. 2011a, 2011b). The LieCal project was conducted in 14 middle schools of an urban school district serving a diverse student population in the United States. Approximately 85 % of the participants were minority students: 64 % African American, 16 % Hispanic, 4 % Asian, and 1 % Native American. Male and female students were about evenly distributed. (See Cai et al. 2011a, 2011b and Moyer et al. 2011 for details about the LieCal Project.)

In particular, the LieCal Project was designed to provide: (a) a profile of the intended treatment of algebra in the CMP curriculum with a contrasting profile of the intended treatment of algebra in non-CMP curricula; (b) a profile of classroom experiences that CMP students and teachers had, with a contrasting profile of experiences in non-CMP classrooms; and (c) a profile of student performance resulting

---

[1] In 2006 and 2009, the CMP authors published revised editions of the CMP curriculum under the name CMP2. CMP3 was published in 2013. This article is based on the original CMP curriculum because the students in the LieCal project used CMP, not CMP2 or CMP3.

from the use of the CMP curriculum, with a contrasting profile of student performance resulting from the use of non-CMP curricula. Accordingly, the project was designed to answer three research questions:

1. What are the similarities and differences between the intended treatment of algebra in the CMP curriculum and in the non-CMP curricula?
2. What are key features of the CMP and non-CMP experiences for students and teachers, and how might these features explain performance differences between CMP and non-CMP students?
3. What are the similarities and differences in performance between CMP students and a comparable group of non-CMP students on tasks measuring a broad spectrum of mathematical thinking and reasoning skills, with a focus on algebra?

While the focus of this chapter is on research question 1, we will also provide some evidence addressing research questions 2 and 3.

Variable Ideas in CMP and Non-CMP Curricula

Importance of Variable Ideas in Algebra

The concept of Variable is one of the most important algebraic ideas (NCTM 2000; Schoenfeld and Arcavi 1988). A major difference between arithmetic and algebra is the involvement of variables in algebra. In algebra, the concept of variable can be understood in different ways. For example, variables can be introduced in a curriculum as quantities whose values may change or vary according to circumstances. From this perspective variables can represent many numbers simultaneously; they have no place value, and they can be selected arbitrarily. In the mathematics education community, we have not had consistent conceptions for the following pairs of concepts: letters and variables, unknowns and variables, place-holders and variables (Janvier 1996). Some educators and curriculum developers believe that both words in each of the pairs mean the same thing, but others believe they represent different concepts. For example, Wheeler (1996) thinks the letter "*x*" can stand for an as-yet-unknown number, a general number, or a variable. From Wheeler's point of view, a letter and a variable are not the same thing, and a variable is different from an unknown and from a general number. As part of a larger study, when Schoenfeld and Arcavi (1988) asked a diverse group of people (mathematicians, mathematics educators, computer scientists, linguists, logicians, and so forth) to describe the concept of variable in one word, and they produced the following list: symbol, placeholder, pronoun, parameter, argument, pointer, name, identifier, empty space, void, reference, and instance. Interestingly, none of the subjects used the word *unknown* to describe the concept of a variable. Schoenfeld and Arcavi (1988) explained that the omission occurred because the word *unknown*, which connotes something that has a fixed value that one does not yet know, did not match the subjects' conception of variable as something that varies or has multiple values. Schoenfeld and Arcavi also listed ten different meanings of variable from a variety of sources, making the point that mathematicians use the term variable differently in different contexts, and that this practice makes it difficult for mathematics educators to define the word variable, and even more difficult for students to learn the concept.

Indeed, there is no consensus in the mathematics education community on a single definition of variable that should be used in algebra textbooks. One reason for this is that there is no consensus on the role that the study of algebra should play in precollege mathematics. Different conceptions of algebra are better served by some interpretations of variable than others (Usiskin 1988). For example, one conception of algebra favored by many educators is that algebra is generalized arithmetic. For this conception, the interpretation of a variable as a pattern generalizer is preferable to other interpretations. Another conception of algebra is that it is the study of procedures for solving certain kinds of problems. In this case, the most useful meaning of variable is that of an unknown or constant. The concept of algebra as the study of relationships among quantities, on the other hand, is best served by emphasizing the use of variables as arguments or parameters. Finally, the conception of algebra as strictly the study of structures is best served if variables act as arbitrary symbols, or marks on a paper.

Since there is no agreement among mathematics educators regarding the definition of the term variable, it is important to determine which, if any, of the commonly used interpretations of a variable align with the goals of the two curricula being analyzed. Variables have been used in middle school mathematics curriculum materials in each of the following three ways (Usiskin 1988):

(1) Variables viewed as pattern generalizers (e.g., in generalizing $3 + 5 = 5 + 3$ to the pattern $a + b = b + a$) or as representatives of ranges of values (e.g., in using $3t + 6$ to represent the possible values that can result when 6 is added to 3 times a quantity);

(2) Variables viewed as placeholders or unknowns in naked equations (e.g., as in $x + 6 = 21$), or in equations translated from a word problem (e.g., "In how many years will your 6-year-old sister be 21?").

(3) Variables used to represent relationships, such as in the use of $y = 9x - 43$ to represent an equation of the line with slope 9 that goes through the point $(5, 2)$, or as in the use of $C = 15N$ to represent the relation between the number of \$15 tickets (N) and their total cost (C).

In our analysis, we examine which of these meanings of variable align with the goals and approaches of the portions of the CMP and Glencoe Mathematics curricula that introduce the concept of variable, and that develop concepts related to algebraic equations and linear functions.

Learning Goals for the Concept of Variable

CMP learning goals can be found in the implementation guide (Lappan et al. 2002c), in the lesson planner (Lappan et al. 2002d), in the Teacher's Guide to each unit, and

Table 1 Focus of the learning goals related to the concept of variable in the CMP and Glencoe mathematics curricula

Conceptions of Variables	CMP	Glencoe
The learning goals characterize variables as pattern generalizers or as being used to represent ranges of values	✓	✓
The learning goals characterize variables as placeholders or unknowns		✓
The learning goals characterize variables as being used to represent relationships	✓	

in the student texts themselves. The learning goals for the Glencoe Mathematics curriculum are given in the teacher's wraparound edition of each course. Table 1 shows the focus of the learning goals related to the concept of variable in the CMP and Glencoe Curricula.

The learning goals related to the acquisition and use of the concept of variable in the CMP curriculum focus on the use of variables to represent relationships. The following learning goals are representative of those related to the concept of variable in CMP: "[to] search for patterns of change that **show relationships** among the variables," (Lappan et al. 2002d, p. 71), "[t]o understand that variable is a quantity that changes and to recognize the variables in the real world," (Lappan et al. 2002d, p. 73), and "[t]o identify variables and determine an appropriate range of values for independent and dependent variables," (Lappan et al. 2002d, p. 103). These learning goals are very explicit in their expectation that students understand that variables are used to represent relationships. We could not find any goal statements in CMP that suggest that variables should be viewed as placeholders or unknowns.

In contrast, almost all the learning goals about the concept of variable in Glencoe Mathematics describe a variable as a placeholder or an unknown. For example, the *Mathematical Content and Teaching Strategies* section of the teacher's wraparound edition says the following about Lesson 1-6 of Course 1: "…students first explore the use of models to stand for unknown quantities. They then transfer this concrete sense to an understanding of the function of variables in algebraic expressions," (Bailey et al. 2006a, p. 4D). Furthermore, the Glencoe learning goals that involve the concept of variable are typically written in an equation-solving context. For example, the following statement refers to Lesson 1-7 of Course 1: "In earlier grades, students were exposed to the concept of missing parts of equations as represented by boxes and circles. They learn how variables serve the same function in an algebraic equation," (Bailey et al. 2006a, p. 4D). Here is a second example, taken from the grade 8 teacher wraparound edition: "A problem like $(\ ) + 6 = 8$ that they might have included in an earlier course is now written with a variable as $x + 6 = 8$," (Bailey et al. 2006c, p. 4C). It is apparent from these examples that an important learning goal in Glencoe Mathematics is for students to understand that variables are placeholders or unknowns.

To complement CMP's emphasis on the use of variables to represent relationships, CMP encourages students to view variables as pattern generalizers or representatives of ranges of values. This is done by requiring students to "...search for patterns of change that show relationships among the variables," (Lappan et al. 2002d, p. 71).

Glencoe Mathematics does not have specific learning goals suggesting that variables should be viewed as pattern generalizers or representatives of ranges of values. However, we can find instances in the Glencoe Mathematics curriculum where variables are used as pattern generalizers. For example, in sixth grade a proportion is defined as "...an equation stating that two ratios are equivalent," and it is accompanied by the following use of variables as pattern generalizers: "$a/b = c/d$, $b \neq 0$, $d \neq 0$," (Bailey et al. 2006a, p. 386).

Defining and Introducing Variable Ideas

Variable in CMP   CMP formally introduces the concept of variable in grade 7, while Glencoe Mathematics introduces the concept of variable in grade 6. Although both curricula formally define the term *variable*, the definitions provided by CMP and Glencoe Mathematics are very different. CMP defines the term *variable* in conjunction with its connection to coordinate graphs: "A **variable** is a quantity that changes or *varies*. ... A **coordinate graph** is a way to show the relationship between two variables," (Lappan et al. 2002a, p. 7). Glencoe Mathematics defines a variable as "...a symbol, usually a letter, used to represent a number," (Bailey et al. 2006a, p. 28). From these definitions, it is clear that CMP uses variables to represent relationships, while variables are viewed as placeholders or unknowns in Glencoe Mathematics.

The CMP curriculum's definition of variable as a quantity rather than a symbol makes it convenient to use variables informally in relationships long before it introduces the concept of variable formally in 7th grade. In Investigation 4 ("Coordinate Graphs") of the 6th grade unit *Data About Us* (Lappan et al. 2002e), students analyze data by constructing coordinate graphs to explore relationships among quantities listed in tables (e.g., distance and time from school, height and foot length). This is done by labeling the horizontal and vertical axes with the names of the quantities, plotting data points, and observing that there is a relationship between the quantities. Sometimes the relationship is qualitative ("Students who live further away from school generally spend more time getting to school" (p. 45)); sometimes the relationship is quantitative ("Height is generally about 6 to 6-1/2 times foot length" (p. 44)).

A year later, when CMP formally introduces the concept of variable in the 7th grade unit *Variables and Patterns* (Lappan et al. 2002a), only the word *variable* is new. This is because the formal use of variables in the first three investigations of the 7th grade unit ("Variables and Coordinate Graphs," "Graphing Change," and "Analyzing Graphs and Tables") is the same as the informal use of quantities in 6th grade. That is, students use quantity names (now called "word names for the variables") as before, to describe relationships in words and to label columns of data tables and axes of coordinate graphs.

CMP	Glencoe Mathematics
The graph below shows the numbers of cans of soft drink purchased each hour from school's vending machine in one day (6 means the time from 5:00 to 6:00, 7 represents the time from 6:00 to 7:00, and so on).	*Evaluate algebraic expressions* *(1) Evaluate 16 + b if b=25;* *(2) Evaluate x-y if x=64 and* *y=27.*

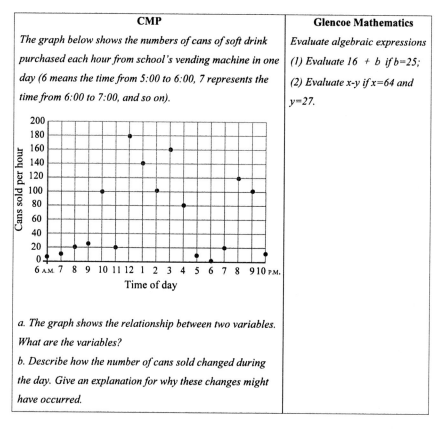

a. The graph shows the relationship between two variables. What are the variables?

b. Describe how the number of cans sold changed during the day. Give an explanation for why these changes might have occurred.

Fig. 1 Sample problems to introduce the concept of variable in CMP and Glencoe Mathematics curricula (Lappan et al. 2002a, p. 11; Bailey et al. 2006a, p. 29)

It is not until Investigation 4 ("Patterns and Rules") of *Moving Straight Ahead* that the students are finally introduced to the use of symbols for variables (Lappan et al. 2002b). Investigation 4 provides the following rationale for using symbols: "A shorter way to write rules using variables is to replace the word names for the variables with single letters," (p. 50). One of the application problems at the end of the investigation that introduces the concept of variable is shown in Fig. 1. Question *a* in the CMP part of Fig. 1 illustrates the curriculum's emphasis on understanding the concept of variable through real-world situations. Question b illustrates how CMP uses scatterplots based on real-world contexts to develop students' informal understanding of variability and the interrelationship of variables.

In CMP, the development of the concept of variable underscores the changing or varying nature of variables, and it emphasizes that expressing relationships between variables is at the heart of algebra. Rather than developing the concept of variable by introducing algebraic equations immediately, CMP introduces the terms *independent variable* and *dependent variable*. Then relationships between independent and dependent variables are emphasized by way of graphs and tables of real world quantities.

Variable in Glencoe Mathematics   Glencoe Mathematics defines a variable as a symbol (or letter) used to represent a number, and the examples that illustrate the definition show students how to evaluate algebraic expressions for given values of the variables. These examples give the impression that variables and numbers can be interchanged. This is because every variable (letter) is assigned only one number. Letters used this way in equations are often called *unknowns*, and are not universally considered to be variables because they are thought of by many as having *fixed* values that we do not yet know (Usiskin 1988; Schoenfeld and Arcavi 1988).

Based on an analysis of the problems used in the introduction of variable in their curricular materials, it is probable that the initial conceptualizations of variable for CMP students and Glencoe Mathematics students will be different. CMP provides an opportunity for students to understand variables using a functional approach by analyzing the relationships between them. However, Glencoe Mathematics imparts a structural perspective to the concept of variable by giving the impression that every variable is a letter that has a fixed value.

Introduction of Equations, Equation Solving, and Functions

In this section, we show how the CMP and Glencoe Mathematics curricula incorporate functional and structural approaches, respectively, into their introduction of the concepts of equation, equation solving, and function. We refer to the previous section's analysis of how these two curricula define and introduce variable ideas to help us understand the approaches to teaching equation solving in CMP and Glencoe Mathematics.

Defining Equations

In the previous section we showed that CMP, with its emphasis on relationships, clearly takes a functional approach to the concept of variable. In contrast, Glencoe Mathematics' focus on variable as a symbol points toward its structural approach. It is not surprising, therefore, that the concept of *equation* is defined functionally in CMP, but structurally in Glencoe Mathematics.

Functional Approach in the CMP Curriculum   In CMP, the concept of equation is functionally based. This approach is a natural extension of CMP's development of the concept of variable described above and is based on the guiding principle that expressing relationships between variables is at the heart of algebra. Representations that express these relationships are introduced incrementally. At the beginning of 6th grade, relationships between quantities are expressed using graphs and tables rather than via algebraic equations. CMP does not even introduce algebraic equations when it formally defines the term *variable* in the 7th grade unit *Variables and Patterns* (Lappan et al. 2002a). Instead, CMP simply prepares for the eventual introduction of equations as descriptors of relationships by introducing the terms *independent variable* and *dependent variable*, which are vital in the language of equations and functions.

Equations themselves are introduced later through contextual examples that give rise to formulas or rules that model a given real life context. An instance of this can be found on page 49 of *Variables and Patterns*:

$$circumference = \pi \times diameter$$

which is later referred to as an example of an equation or a formula. The emphasis in CMP is on using equations to describe real-world situations. Rather than seeing equations simply as objects to manipulate, students are shown that equations often describe relationships between varying quantities that arise from meaningful, contextualized situations. Clearly, this view of *equation* fits within the framework of a functional approach (Bednarz et al. 1996).

The functional approach to introducing the concept of equation is also apparent in CMP's emphasis on multiple ways of representing equations. In the unit *Variables and Patterns*, students study the graphs of various equations using a graphing calculator. In addition, students study tables corresponding to various equations. The intention is to help students to understand relationships among the symbolic, graphical, and tabular representations of equations. It is instructive to note that in CMP, students' initial exposure to equations does not involve solving equations.

Structural Approach in the Glencoe Mathematics Curriculum   As the development of equations in CMP arises naturally from its characterization of variables, Glencoe Mathematics similarly follows a natural path from its definition of variable as a symbol to the use of decontextualized equations and emphasis on procedures for solving equations. These are hallmarks of a structural focus.

Lesson 1-7, entitled "Algebra: Solving Equations," of the Glencoe Mathematics 6th grade textbook (Bailey et al. 2006a), introduces equations shortly before defining them. The lesson begins with a Hands-On Mini-Lab in which students represent single-variable equations on a balance scale. On the scale, a paper cup represents the variable (placeholder), and groups of centimeter cubes represent numerical constants. Students are told that when the amounts on each side of the scale are equal, the scale is balanced. The students place 3 cubes and a cup on one side of the scale and 8 cubes on the other. Then they are instructed to replace the paper cup with centimeter cubes until the scale balances. By way of practice, the students use the scale to model four other equations and find the number of centimeter cubes needed to balance the scale for each. Neither the word *equation* nor the word *solve* is used in the Mini-Lab.

After the Mini-Lab, in Lesson 1-7 itself, Glencoe defines an equation as "...a sentence that contains an equals sign" (p. 34). By way of illustration, the book then provides examples of number sentences (p. 34):

$$2 + 7 = 9 \qquad 10 - 6 = 4 \qquad 4 = 5 - 1$$

However, the text does not explicitly relate these examples to the Mini Lab. Therefore, it is conceivable that these examples actually reinforce erroneous interpretations of the equals sign as a symbol that signifies the result of a computation (e.g., when 2 is added to 7, the result is 9) (Kieran 1981). As a consequence, some students may continue to mistakenly believe that an equals sign means "Write the answer or result of the indicated computation."

Immediately following these arithmetic-based examples of equations, the text illustrates equations that contain variables:

$$2 + x = 9 \qquad 4 = k - 6 \qquad 5 - m = 4$$

Students are told that the way to solve an equation is to replace the variable with a value that results in a true statement. It is worth noting that, at this point in the lesson, the text does not refer to the hands-on Mini-Lab, nor does it make any explicit reference to how the notion of balance relates to equations or equation solving.

An important equation-solving technique in Glencoe Mathematics is to use mental math, e.g. "THINK 12 equals 5 plus what number?" (p. 35). After solving an equation mentally, students are asked to graph the solution on a number line. Almost all of the equations in Chaps. 1–8 of the 6th grade text can be solved using mental addition or subtraction. Equation solutions that require multiplication or division are introduced in Lesson 9-4, Solving Multiplication Equations. Also, the Addition Property of Equality and the Subtraction Property of Equality are formally stated and used in Chap. 9. The Multiplication and Division Properties of Equality are used in this chapter, but not formally stated.

In Grade 7, as in grade 6, the concept of an equation is also introduced using number sentences as examples. However, the number sentences used are quite different from what they were in Grade 6. In the Grade 7 examples, it is more evident that the equals sign does not signify the result of a computation, instead it represents equality or equivalence, e.g. "$4 + 3 = 8 - 1$", "$3(4) = 24/2$" and "$17 = 13 + 2 + 2$" (Bailey et al. 2006b, p. 24).

In order to make the transition from writing algebraic expressions to writing equations, Glencoe Mathematics tells students that "When you write a verbal sentence as an equation, you can use the equals sign ($=$) for the words *equals* or *is*" (Bailey et al. 2006b, p. 151). After showing how to write a phrase as an expression, Glencoe Mathematics provides examples showing how to write sentences as equations, as shown in Fig. 2.

In addition, the reverse situation is described: "write a verbal sentence that translates into the equation $n + 5 = 8$" (Bailey et al. 2006b, p. 151). Students must think critically to come up with a real life scenario that matches the equation given. This is intended to help them see the value of using algebraic equations.

Example 1: Write the phrase *five dollars less than Jennifer earned* as an algebraic expression

Words	Five dollars less than Jennifer earned.
Variable0	Let d represent the number of dollars Jennifer earned.
Expression	$d - 5$

Example 2: **Sentence**   **Equation**
Five more than a number is 20 $n + 5 = 20$
Example 3: Three times Bill's age equals 12 $3a = 12$
Example 4: It is estimated that 12.4 million pounds of potato chips were consumed during a recent super Bowl. This was 3.3 million pounds more than the number of pounds of tortilla chips consumed. Write an equation that models this situation.

Words	Potato chips were 3.1 million more than tortilla chips.
Variable0	Let t = number of million pounds of tortilla chips.
Expression	$12.4 = 3.1 + t.$

Fig. 2 Sample examples of translating written sentences into equations in Glencoe Mathematics (Bailey et al. 2006b, pp. 150–151)

Introduction to Equation Solving

CMP and Glencoe Mathematics use functional and structural approaches, respectively, to introduce equation solving, consistent with the approaches they used to define equations.

Introduction to Equation Solving in the CMP Curriculum   In the CMP curriculum, equations are introduced as descriptors of relationships between variables. In Investigation 1 of *Moving Straight Ahead* (the second algebra unit in 7th grade, Lappan et al. 2002b), the topic of linear equations and functions is formally introduced as "linear *relationships.*" This way of introducing linear equations and functions is aligned with CMP's conception of algebra as the study of relationships. In this first investigation, students do not solve or analyze equations that are provided to them. Rather, they are asked to perform an experiment in which they collect data relating the height of release of a rubber ball to the height of its bounce. Students graph the data on a coordinate graph and look for a relationship between the quantities. This investigation sets the tone for the rest of the unit, in which students use graphs, tables, and equations to analyze the relationships between pairs of contextualized variables and compare the representations with one another.

The initial treatment of equation solving does not involve symbolic manipulation, as found in most traditional curricula. Instead, CMP attempts to introduce students to linear equation solving by making visual sense of what it means to find a solution. Its premise is that a linear equation in one variable is a specific instance of

Table 2 An example of equation solving in the CMP Unit Moving Straight Ahead (p. 55)

Thinking	Manipulating the symbols
"I want to buy a CD-ROM drive that costs $195. To pay for the drive on the installment plan, I must pay $30 down and $15 a month."	$195 = 30 + 15N$
"After I pay the $30 down payment, I can subtract this from the cost. To keep the sides of the equation equal, I must subtract 30 from both sides."	$195 - 30 = 30 - 30 + 15N$
"I now owe $165 which I will pay in monthly installments of $15."	$165 = 15N$
"I need to separate $165 into payments of $15. This means I need to divide it by 15. To keep the sides of the equation equal, I must divide both sides by 15."	$165/15 = 15N/15$
"There are 11 groups of $15 in $165, so it will take 11 months."	$11 = N$

a corresponding linear relationship (or equation in two variables). It relies heavily on the context in which the equation itself is situated, and on the use of a graphing calculator.

Students are first given various equations in two variables, each modeling a real-world context (e.g., $A = 5 + 0.5d$, where A represents dollars owed and d represents number of miles walked). Then various questions are asked in which either a value for A or d is given (e.g., $17 is owed, or someone walked 28 miles), and subsequently, the other value must be found. Initially, students solve these types of problem by graphing the original equation in two variables on a graphing calculator, then finding the value of either the given dependent or the given independent variable on the graph, and finally reading off the other value as the solution. This graphical approach is intended to help students understand the meaning of a solution to a linear equation and the process of solving an equation in one variable.

After equation solving is introduced graphically, the symbolic method of solving linear equations is finally broached (p. 55). It is introduced within a single contextualized example, where each of the steps in the equation solving process is accompanied by a narrative that demonstrates the connection between the procedure and the real-life situation (see Table 2). In this way, CMP justifies the equation-solving manipulations through contextual sense-making of the symbolic method. That is, CMP uses real-life contexts to help students understand the meaning of each step of the symbolic method, including why inverse operations are used.

Introduction to Equation Solving in Glencoe Mathematics In the Glencoe Mathematics curriculum, contextual sense-making is not used to justify the equation-solving steps, as it is in the CMP curriculum. Rather, Glencoe Mathematics first introduces equation solving as finding a number to make an equation a true statement. In fact, solving an equation is described as replacing a variable with a value (called the solution) that makes the sentence true (see Fig. 3).

In 6th grade, Glencoe formally introduces equation solving with inverse operations by way of an activity that uses a cup to stand for an unknown (see Fig. 4).

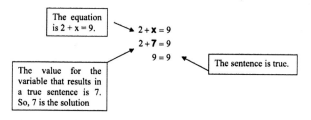

Fig. 3 Meaning of solving an equation in Glencoe Mathematics (Bailey et al. 2006a, p. 34)

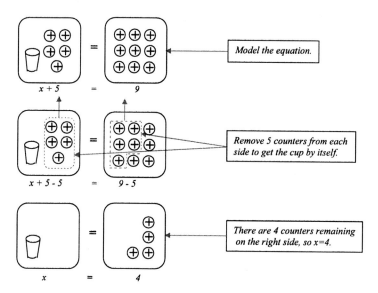

Fig. 4 Introduction of equation solving with inverse operations in Glencoe Mathematics (Bailey et al. 2006a, p. 337)

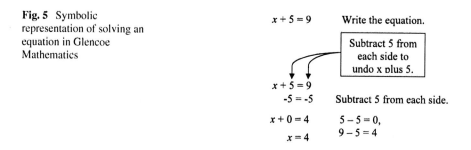

Fig. 5 Symbolic representation of solving an equation in Glencoe Mathematics

The cups and counters used as manipulatives in the activity are direct representations of the symbols. That is, the manipulatives illustrate each step of the symbolic manipulations.

In basketball, each shot made from outside the 3-point line scores 3 points. The expression $3x$ represents the total number of points scores where x is the number of 3-point shots made. ...List the ordered pairs (3-point shots made, total number of points) for 0, 1, 2, and 3 shots made .... Make a table, Graph the ordered pairs... then describe the graph.

x (shots)	$3x$	y (points)	(x,y)
0	3(0)	0	(0,0)
1	3(1)	3	(1,3)
2	3(2)	6	(2,6)
3	3(3)	9	(3,9)

Fig. 6 Connecting a table, formula, and graph in Glencoe Mathematics (Bailey et al. 2006a, p. 322)

Solving the equation using manipulatives, as shown above, is referred to as "Method 1." An illustration of the method is typically placed adjacent to an example showing a corresponding solution that uses "Method 2," the symbolic method. In this way, Glencoe Mathematics illustrates how each manipulative step is comparable to a symbolic step in a solution based on algebraic properties of equality, which is shown vertically. Figure 5 shows an example of how to use Method 2 to solve a one-step equation.

Effort has been made in Glencoe Mathematics to connect tables, formulas, and graphs. For example, the 6th grade curriculum shows the table of values corresponding to an expression as well as the corresponding ordered pairs (see Fig. 6). Then the ordered pairs are graphed, and the graph is described.

Defining and Introducing Function

Consistent with their approaches to variables and equations, CMP and Glencoe Mathematics use functional and structural approaches, respectively, to introduce the concept of function. Their respective approaches can be seen quite clearly in the differences between their stated learning goals for the concept of function. CMP's learning goals for students are (1) that they be able to understand and predict patterns of change in variables, and (2) that they be able to represent relationships between real-world quantities using word descriptions, tables, graphs, and equations. In contrast, Glencoe Mathematics' stated learning goals are (1) that students explore the use of algebraic equations to represent functions, and (2) that they be able to identify and graph functions, calculate slope, and distinguish linear from nonlinear functions.

Connected Mathematics We have already described how CMP informally introduces the concept of variable (identified as a real-world quantity) in 6th grade at the same time that it informally introduces the concept of function (identified as a relationship between real-world quantities). Recall that this is done by requiring students to construct coordinate graphs to explore relationships between real-world quantities listed in tables.

At the beginning of 7th grade, when the concept of variable is formally introduced in the *Variables and Patterns* unit, coordinate graphs are used as a way to "tell a story" of how changes in one variable are related to changes in the other. In an introductory investigation, students graph how many jumping jacks they can do in successive 10-second intervals for two minutes. Then they analyze the graph to determine whether a relationship exists between time and the number of jumping jacks. At the same time, students are exposed to the concepts of "independent variable" and "dependent variable." This is well before the concept of function is formally introduced during the second half of 7th grade in the *Moving Straight Ahead* unit. Although the concept of function is introduced in this unit, the term "relationship" is almost always used instead of the word "function." Furthermore, in the teacher's guide, the term "function" is explicitly identified as "nonessential." In fact, the term "function" is not given any importance in the CMP curriculum until the introduction of quadratic functions in the 8th grade unit *Frogs, Fleas, and Painted Cubes*.

CMP's strategy to solidify the concept of function by exploring relationships between real-world quantities appears to be done explicitly to help students reach a deeper understanding of both variables and functions. This approach to the development of the concept of function in CMP reflects a central algebraic learning principle in the CMP curriculum: "As you study how variables are related, you are learning algebra."

Glencoe Mathematics Glencoe Mathematics informally introduces the concept of function in the preview to lesson 9-6 of 6th grade by having students make a function machine out of paper. The function machine has three key elements: input, output, and operation. The operation, or rule, lies at the core of the function machine, while input and output are external to it. Immediately after the introduction of the function machine, Glencoe Mathematics formally introduces the concepts of function, function table, and function rule in Lesson 9-6. This formal introduction begins with the following situation: "A brown bat can eat 600 mosquitoes an hour." The student is then asked to write expressions to represent the number of mosquitoes a brown bat can eat in 2 hours, 5 hours, and t hours. Finally, the terms function and function table are illustrated, and the term function rule is defined (see Fig. 7). The function rule is characterized as a rule giving the operation(s) that will transform input into output.

Glencoe Mathematics defines function as a relationship where one thing depends on another. However, it treats a function as a process of starting with an input number, performing one or more operations on it, and getting an output number. The main purpose of the function machine and the function table seems to be for students to experience the process of computing the output values from given input values and vice versa. That is, the development of the concept of function in Glencoe Mathematics emphasizes operations on variables rather than the relationship between variables.

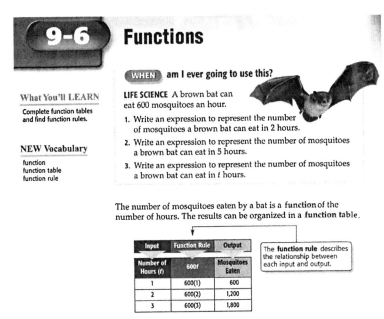

Fig. 7 Formal introduction of functions in Glencoe Mathematics (Bailey et al. 2006a, p. 362)

Types of Problems Involving Linear Equations

The mathematical problems included in a curriculum can reveal not only the instructional goals and principles that the authors espouse, but also the learning opportunities they provide for students. Problems serve to direct students' attention to particular aspects of content, as well as their ways of processing information (NCTM 2000).

In both the CMP and Glencoe Mathematics curricula, the vast majority of equation problems involve linear equations. To obtain a more detailed picture of the situation, we further classified problems involving linear equations in the CMP and Glencoe curricula into three categories:

(1) One equation with one variable—e.g., $2x + 3 = 5$;
(2) One equation with two variables—e.g., $y = 6x + 7$;
(3) Two equations with two variables—e.g., the system of equations $y = 2x + 1$ and $y = 8x + 9$.

Figure 8 shows the percentage distribution of these categories of problems involving linear equations in each curriculum. The two distributions are significantly different ($\chi^2(2) = 1262.0$, $p < 0.0001$). The CMP curriculum includes a significantly greater percentage of "one equation with two variables" problems than the Glencoe curriculum ($z = 35.49$, $p < 0.0001$). On the other hand, the Glencoe curriculum includes a significantly greater percentage of "one equation with one variable" problems than the CMP curriculum ($z = 34.145$, $p < 0.0001$). These results

Fig. 8 Percentage distribution of problems involving linear equations in CMP and Glencoe curricula

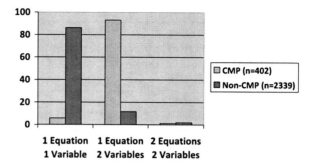

resonate with our finding that the CMP curriculum emphasizes an understanding of the relationships between the variables of equations rather than an acquisition of the skills needed to solve equations. In fact, of the 402 equation-related problems in the CMP curriculum, only 33 of them (about 8 % of the linear equation-solving problems) involve decontexualized symbolic manipulations of equations. However, Glencoe Mathematics includes 1,550 problems involving decontexualized symbolic manipulations of equations (nearly 70 % of the linear equation solving problems in Glencoe Mathematics).

Glencoe Mathematics not only incorporates many more linear equation-solving problems into the curriculum, but it also carefully sequences them based on the number of steps required to solve them. Of 2,339 problems involving linear equations, 1,218 of them (over 50 %) are one-step problems like $x + b = c$, $ax = c$. Nearly 700 of them (or about 30 %) are two-step problems, like $ax + b = c$. Nearly 20 % of the linear equations involve three steps or more, like $ax + bx + c = d$ or $ax + b = cx + d$. Each grade of Glencoe Mathematics includes one-step, two-step, and three-plus-step problems involving linear equations. As the grade level increases, however, the Glencoe Curriculum provides increasingly more comprehensive procedures, suitable for solving all forms of linear equations. For the CMP curriculum, the most common linear equation-solving problem type is one equation with two variables. Over 50 % of these are in $y = ax + b$ form ($a \neq 0$, $a \neq 1$ and $b \neq 0$). Over 30 % of them are in $y = x + b$ form ($b \neq 0$). The rest of the problems are either in $y = c$ form or $y = ax$ form ($a \neq 0$).

Highlights of the Impact of Curriculum on Teaching and Learning

In this chapter, although the focus of our discussion has been on the intended treatment of functions, variable ideas, and equation solving in the CMP and Glencoe Mathematics curricula, it is also important to highlight the impact of their different approaches on teaching and learning. Elsewhere, we have reported that different profiles of classroom instruction and student learning occur when using CMP and non-CMP curricula like Glencoe Mathematics (Cai et al. 2011a, 2011b; Moyer et al. 2011).

Table 3 Ratings for conceptual and procedural emphases in the classroom

	6th Grade	7th Grade	8th Grade	Overall
Conceptual Emphasis				
CMP	14.51	12.52	13.27	13.41
Non-CMP	9.44	10.11	10.61	10.41
Procedural Emphasis				
CMP	11.67	11.70	11.48	11.61
Non-CMP	13.77	14.24	15.41	14.49

The highest possible rating is 20

Effect on Classroom Instruction and Student Learning

Generally speaking, we found that the type of curriculum that teachers use has a significant effect on the teaching that they do. Based on our analysis of the curricula, we have argued that the CMP curriculum may be regarded as a curriculum with a pedagogy that predominantly emphasizes the conceptual aspects of algebra, whereas Glencoe Mathematics may be regarded as a curriculum with a pedagogy that predominantly emphasizes the procedural aspects of algebra. In line with this result, our LieCal investigation of classroom instruction found that CMP teachers emphasized the conceptual aspects of learning significantly more often than the non-CMP teachers. Non-CMP teachers correspondingly emphasized the procedural aspects of learning significantly more often than the CMP teachers (Moyer et al. 2011). Table 3 shows the mean scores of the conceptual and procedural emphases in CMP and non-CMP classrooms.

There was a significant difference across grade levels between CMP and non-CMP instruction in conceptual emphasis ($F(3, 575) = 53.43$, $p < 0.001$). The overall (grades 6–8) mean of the summated ratings on the conceptual emphasis factor for CMP lessons was 13.41, while the overall mean of the summated ratings on conceptual emphasis for non-CMP lessons was 10.06. There was also a significant difference across grade levels between CMP and non-CMP instruction related to procedural emphasis. The procedural emphasis ratings across grade levels for the non-CMP lessons were significantly higher than the procedural emphasis ratings across grade levels for the CMP lessons ($F(3, 575) = 37.77$, $p < 0.001$).

We also found that on open-ended tasks assessing conceptual understanding and problem solving, the growth rate for CMP students over the three years (grades 6–8) was significantly greater than that for non-CMP students (Cai et al. 2011a, 2011b). In fact, our analysis using Growth Curve Modeling showed that over the three middle school years, the CMP students' scores on the open-ended tasks increased significantly more than the non-CMP students' scores ($t = 2.79$, $p < 0.01$). At the same time, CMP and non-CMP students showed similar growth over the three middle school years on multiple-choice tasks assessing computation and equation solving skills. In the 2008–2009 academic year, the LieCal middle school students entered high school as 9th graders. We followed about 1,000 of these students who were enrolled in 10 high schools in the same urban school district. In these high schools, the former CMP and non-CMP students were mixed together in the same mathematics classrooms and all used the same curriculum. Although we are still in the process of analyzing data from these high school students, preliminary results appear to support the hypothesis that the CMP students continue to benefit from their conceptual and problem-solving advantages from middle school (Cai et al. in press).

Conclusion

Two Approaches to Teaching Algebra

How can we effectively teach algebra? In this chapter, we discussed approaches to teaching algebraic concepts such as variables, equations, and functions that are embedded in a *Standards*-based mathematics curriculum (CMP) and in a traditional mathematics curriculum (Glencoe Mathematics). Variable is a very complex concept because it involves different conceptions and meanings, and because it is inextricably tied to the concept of function. Neither CMP nor Glencoe Mathematics clearly distinguishes among the various uses of variables. It might be helpful if curricula distinguished letters, unknowns, and symbols from variables that truly change by clearly pointing out the differences among them. When students begin to learn about linear functions like $3x + 2 = y$, if they only hold the idea that x is an unknown as in the equation $3x + 2 = 5$, how can they understand that the values of x and y can change and then further explore the pattern of the change? Alternately, if students think that variables always vary, how can they reconcile this with the use of variables to solve single-variable equations?

"An understanding of the meanings and uses of variables develops gradually as students create and use symbolic expressions and relate them to verbal, tabular, and graphical representations," (NCTM 2000, p. 225). In line with this view, it is our opinion that, over time, it is desirable for a mathematics curriculum to clearly point out the different ways of using the word *variable* in order to avoid misunderstanding. We recommend that curricula should differentiate truly varying variables from letters, unknowns, and symbols, and we suggest that every algebra curriculum highlight the interpretation that a variable represents a quantity that changes or varies. Therefore, it might not be wise to have a single definition of the term variable. It may be more advantageous to point out to students that the term variable has many different uses, and therefore has many different definitions, each depending on the purpose for which it is used.

We also found that overall, the CMP curriculum uses a functional approach to teach equation solving, while Glencoe Mathematics uses a structural approach to teach equation solving. The functional approach emphasizes the important ideas of change and variation in situations and contexts. It also emphasizes the representation of relationships between variables, which many mathematics educators feel is at the heart of school algebra. The structural approach, on the other hand, avoids contextual problems in order to concentrate on developing the abilities to generalize, work abstractly with symbols, and follow procedures in a systematic way. These abilities are considered by other mathematics educators to be at the heart of school algebra.

The CMP curriculum includes very few equation-solving problems that require the use of conventional symbolic manipulations. Using a functional approach, the CMP curriculum defines variables as quantities that change or vary and that are used to represent relationships. As a natural extension, the CMP curriculum introduces equations as a way of studying relationships. The intent of the CMP curriculum is that students learn to view equations as instruments to describe real-world situations, rather than simply as objects to manipulate. Correspondingly, equation solving is introduced within the discussion on linear relationships. Thus, the vast majority of the linear equations in CMP involve two variables. A two-variable graph is used to introduce students to the meaning of a solution to a linear equation in one variable as well as to the process of solving an equation in one variable. CMP uses real-life contexts to help students understand the meaning of each step of the symbolic method of equation solving.

Glencoe Mathematics, in contrast, formally defines a variable as a symbol (or letter) used to represent a number. It treats variables predominantly as placeholders by using them to represent unknowns in expressions and equations. Maintaining their structural approach, Glencoe Mathematics defines an equation as a statement that contains an equals sign. In the Glencoe Mathematics curriculum, contextual sense making is not used to justify the equation-solving steps. Rather, Glencoe Mathematics introduces equation solving as a process to find a number that makes the statement true.

Equation solving is highly conceptual and highly procedural in nature. It is highly conceptual since it involves an understanding of mathematical relationships. It is highly procedural since it involves performing a series of steps to find solutions to equations. The primary focus of the functional approach in the CMP curriculum is related to conceptual understanding, and the primary focus of the structural approach in Glencoe Mathematics is related to procedural understanding. In this sense, the CMP curriculum may be regarded as a curriculum with a pedagogy that emphasizes predominantly the conceptual aspects of equation solving, while Glencoe Mathematics may be regarded as a curriculum with a pedagogy that emphasizes predominantly the procedural aspects of equation solving. The results reported in this paper not only show the unique features of the CMP and the Glencoe Mathematics curricula, but also present the CMP and the Glencoe Mathematics curricula as concrete examples of functional and structural approaches, respectively, to the teaching of equation solving.

We have characterized the approach to the concepts of variable and equation that CMP uses as functional. The reason we call the CMP approach functional is that the concept of function (i.e., how variables are related) is a central and unifying theme throughout the algebra strand of the CMP curriculum. As such, the CMP view of function colors and/or determines its approach to all the topics in the algebra curriculum. By way of contrast, we have characterized the Glencoe Mathematics approach to the concepts of variable and equation as structural. The structural approach places high priority on the ability to work abstractly with symbols, and to follow procedures in a systematic way. This priority on abstract symbols (variables) and procedures (e.g., equation solving) colors and/or determines its approach to all the topics in the algebra curriculum. In particular, Glencoe's approach to variables and equations determines its approach to the concept of function, rather than the other way around, as it does in the CMP curriculum.

Curriculum as a Pedagogical Event and Teaching as a Curriculum Process

Historically in the field of curriculum studies, decisions about what to include in the mathematics school curriculum evolved at the institutional level, and decisions about how to structure the curriculum evolved at the level of curriculum engineering. Details regarding potential dichotomies between the intended versus the implemented and attained curriculum at the classroom level were often neglected because of the illusion that curriculum could directly and fully regulate teaching. In this chapter, our focus is clearly on the intended curriculum. However, our research does not purposely neglect the implemented and attained curricula. As we indicated before, this chapter reports part of the findings from the larger LieCal research project. The LieCal Project is designed to describe longitudinally the impact of a *Standards*-based curriculum like CMP on teachers' classroom instruction and student learning. This chapter tells part of the story by showing the value of a detailed curriculum analysis in characterizing curriculum as a pedagogical event (Doyle 1992).

Most importantly, our research shows the complex interplay of the three levels of curriculum (Cai et al. 2011a, 2011b). First of all, the ultimate goal of educational reform generally and of curriculum reform specifically is to improve students' learning. Put another way, students' learning of important mathematics should be an important source of information when conducting curriculum research. The findings from the LieCal Project do show that *Standards*-based curricula like CMP have a positive impact on students' learning (Cai et al. 2011a, 2011b). However, the curriculum itself may not have a direct impact on students' learning; it is more likely mediated by instruction. In fact, there is growing consensus that studies of curriculum or of instruction cannot be conducted in isolation. The significance of the integration of curriculum with instruction needs to be considered when attempting to account for curricular effects, since "curriculum [is] a pedagogical event" and "teaching [is] a curriculum process" (Doyle 1992).

Pedagogical features of reform classrooms, such as the use of more conceptual-oriented instruction and the use of more learning tasks of higher cognitive demand, which we documented in the LieCal project, reflect the power of reform curricula to effect pedagogical changes (Moyer et al. 2011). Curriculum and instruction jointly affect the nature and level of student learning. Our research suggests that changes in the nature and quality of classroom instruction are consistently made in response to the innovative features of *Standards*-based curricula like CMP.

References

Algebra Working Group to the National Council of Teachers of Mathematics (1997). *A framework for constructing a vision of algebra: a discussion document*. Reston: NCTM.

Bailey, R., Day, R., Frey, P., Howard, A. C., Hutchens, D. T., McClain, K., et al. (2006a). *Mathematics: applications and concepts*. Columbus: The McGraw-Hill Company (teacher wraparound edition), course 1.

Bailey, R., Day, R., Frey, P., Howard, A. C., Hutchens, D. T., McClain, K., et al. (2006b). *Mathematics: applications and concepts*. Columbus: The McGraw-Hill Company (teacher wraparound edition), course 2.

Bailey, R., Day, R., Frey, P., Howard, A. C., Hutchens, D. T., McClain, K., et al. (2006c). *Mathematics: applications and concepts*. Columbus: The McGraw-Hill Company (teacher wraparound edition), course 3.

Ball, D. L., & Cohen, D. K. (1996). Reform by the book: what is—or might be—the role of curriculum materials in teacher learning and instructional reform? *Educational Researcher, 25*(9), 6–8, 14.

Bednarz, N., Kieran, C., & Lee, L. (Eds.) (1996). *Approaches to algebra: perspectives for research and teaching*. Dordrecht: Kluwer Academic Publishers.

Cai, J. (2010). Evaluation of mathematics education programs. In P. Peterson, E. Baker, & B. McGraw (Eds.), *International encyclopedia of education* (Vol. 3, pp. 653–659). Oxford: Elsevier.

Cai, J., Lo, J. J., & Watanabe, T. (2002). Intended treatment of arithmetic average in U.S. and Asian school mathematics textbooks. *School Science and Mathematics, 102*(8), 391–404.

Cai, J., Nie, B., & Moyer, J. (2010). The teaching of equation solving: approaches in standards-based and traditional curricula in the United States. *Pedagogies: An International Journal, 5*(3), 170–186.

Cai, J., Ni, Y., & Lester, F. K. Jr. (2011a). Curricular effect on the teaching and learning of mathematics: findings from two longitudinal studies in China and the United States. *International Journal of Educational Research, 50*(2), 63–64.

Cai, J., Wang, N., Moyer, J. C., Wang, C., & Nie, B. (2011b). Longitudinal investigation of the curriculum effect: an analysis of student learning outcomes from the LieCal project. *International Journal of Educational Research, 50*(2), 117–136.

Cai, J., Moyer, J. C., Wang, N., Hwang, S., Nie, B., & Garber, T. (in press). Mathematical problem posing as a measure of curricular effect on students' learning. *Educational Studies in Mathematics*.

Doyle, W. (1992). Curriculum and pedagogy. In P. W. Jackson (Ed.), *Handbook of research on curriculum* (pp. 486–516). New York: Macmillan.

Janvier, C. (1996). Modeling and the initiation to algebra. In N. Bednarz, C. Kieran, & L. Lee (Eds.), *Approaches to algebra: perspectives for research and teaching* (pp. 225–236). Dordrecht: Kluwer Academic Publishers.

Kieran, C. (1981). Concepts associated with the equality symbol. *Educational Studies in Mathematics, 12*(3), 317–326.

Kieran, C., Boileau, A., & Garançon, M. (1996). Introducing algebra by means of a technology supported functional approach. In N. Bednarz, C. Kieran, & L. Lee (Eds.), *Approaches to algebra: perspectives for research and teaching* (pp. 257–293). Dordrecht: Kluwer Academic Publishers.

Lappan, G., Fey, J. T., Fitzgerald, W. M., Friel, S. N., & Phillips, E. D. (2002a). *Variables and patterns*. Upper Saddle River: Prentice Hall.

Lappan, G., Fey, J. T., Fitzgerald, W. M., Friel, S. N., & Phillips, E. D. (2002b). *Moving straight ahead*. Upper Saddle River: Prentice Hall.

Lappan, G., Fey, J. T., Fitzgerald, W. M., Friel, S. N., & Phillips, E. D. (2002c). *Getting to know connected mathematics: an implementation guide*. Upper Saddle River: Prentice Hall.

Lappan, G., Fey, J. T., Fitzgerald, W. M., Friel, S. N., & Phillips, E. D. (2002d). *Lesson planner for grades 6, 7, and 8*. Upper Saddle River: Prentice Hall.

Lappan, G., Fey, J. T., Fitzgerald, W. M., Friel, S. N., & Phillips, E. D. (2002e). *Data about us*. Upper Saddle River: Prentice Hall.

Moyer, J. C., Cai, J., Nie, B., & Wang, N. (2011). Impact of curriculum reform: evidence of change in classroom instruction in the United States. *International Journal of Educational Research, 50*(2), 87–99.

National Council of Teachers of Mathematics (1989). *Curriculum and evaluation standards for school mathematics*. Reston: Author.

National Council of Teachers of Mathematics (1991). *Professional standards for teaching mathematics*. Reston: Author.

National Council of Teachers of Mathematics (1995). *Assessment standards for school mathematics*. Reston: Author.

National Council of Teachers of Mathematics (2000). *Principles and standards for school mathematics*. Reston: Author.

Nemirovsky, R. (1996). Mathematical narratives, modeling and algebra. In N. Bednarz, C. Kieran, & L. Lee (Eds.), *Approaches to algebra. Perspectives for research and teaching* (pp. 197–220). Dordrecht: Kluwer Academic Publishers.

Nie, B., Cai, J., & Moyer, J. C. (2009). How a standards-based mathematics curriculum differs from a traditional curriculum: with a focus on intended treatments of the ideas of variable. *ZDM—International Journal on Mathematics Education, 41*(6), 777–792.

Schoenfeld, H. A., & Arcavi, A. (1988). On the meaning of variable. *The Mathematics Teacher, 81*(6), 420–427.

Usiskin, Z. (1988). Conceptions of school algebra and uses of variables. In A. F. Coxford (Ed.), *The ideas of algebra, K-12* (pp. 8–19). Reston: NCTM.

Wheeler, D. (1996). Backwards and forwards: reflections on different approaches to algebra. In N. Bednarz, C. Kieran, & L. Lee (Eds.), *Approaches to algebra: perspectives for research and teaching* (pp. 317–325). Dordrecht: Kluwer Academic Publishers.

Supporting the Effective Implementation of a New Mathematics Curriculum: A Case Study of School-Based Lesson Study at a Japanese Public Elementary School

Akihiko Takahashi

Abstract The Japanese national standards, known as the Course of Study (COS), is revised about every 10 years. After a revised COS is released, Japanese elementary schools usually use lesson study with the entire faculty to seek an effective implementation of the new COS. This chapter, based on a case study, documents how Japanese teachers and administrators in a public school work collaboratively to implement the new curriculum through lesson study, and identifies elements that seem important for connecting the curriculum, teachers, and teaching. The results of the study suggest that Japanese educators' use of school-based lesson study is an effective way to implement a new curriculum. Unlike many lesson study projects outside Japan, which are often conducted by a few volunteers within a school and supported externally, school-based lesson study in Japan is a highly structured, collaborative effort of school administrators, teacher leaders, and all the teachers at the school, with additional support from the local district.

Keywords Lesson study · In-service · School-based · Role of administrators · Course of study · Japan · Professional development · Research lesson · Research steering committee

Introduction

Implementing a new curriculum is always a challenge. Mathematics education researchers and educators have been interested in learning from other countries to see how the intended curriculum and implemented curriculum impact student achievement since the First International Mathematics Study (FIMS) was conducted by the International Association for the Evaluation of Educational Achievement (IEA) in 1964. Recent movements toward establishing nationwide common standards in mathematics in the United States have left mathematics educators with the question

A. Takahashi (✉)
DePaul University, Chicago, USA
e-mail: atakahas@depaul.edu

Y. Li, G. Lappan (eds.), *Mathematics Curriculum in School Education*,
Advances in Mathematics Education, DOI 10.1007/978-94-007-7560-2_20,
© Springer Science+Business Media Dordrecht 2014

of how to implement the curriculum in every school so that every student is provided an equal opportunity to learn mathematics. This requires a lot of effort, not only to develop good curriculum materials, but also to provide effective professional development programs for the teachers to gain the knowledge necessary for teaching the new curriculum, as well as the expertise necessary to support their students in learning mathematics (Common Core State Standards Initiative 2010; National Mathematics Advisory Panel 2008; Stigler and Hiebert 1999, 2009).

Faced with the challenge of bringing a new curriculum into every classroom, Japanese educators use the lesson study process as a vehicle for professional development and for establishing shared knowledge (Takahashi 2011). Various forms of lesson study exist, including district- and national-level lesson study (Murata and Takahashi 2002; Takahashi 2006). This chapter reports on a case of school-based lesson study at a public elementary school in Tokyo to examine how revisions of the national curriculum, known as the Course of Study (COS), get implemented nation-wide.

About the Study

The study was conducted (1) to document how teachers and administrators in a Japanese public school work collaboratively to seek an effective implementation of the new curriculum through lesson study, and (2) to identify possible elements that seem important to seamlessly connect the curriculum, the teachers, and instruction.

During the 2011–2012 school year, from April 2011 to December 2011, the author visited the school more than ten times to observe and document lesson study activities. These activities included six research lessons and post-lesson discussions, lesson planning sessions during summer break, and the school's public open house at the end of the second year of the school research. Also, the author conducted interviews with the school's principal and assistant principal, the chair of the school research steering committee, and the invited "knowledgeable others" who provided feedback and final comments during the post-lesson discussions. All these sessions and interviews were documented using an audio recorder and field notes. All data from communications and interviews with the subjects were collected and analyzed in Japanese and the results were translated into English by the author. In addition, all lesson plans and internal documents that were directly related to the school-based lesson study project were gathered and analyzed in Japanese.

Background

COS Revision Process and Its Implementation

The Japanese COS has been revised approximately every 10 years since 1951. The latest Japanese elementary school COS was announced in March of 2008.[1] In June of the same year, an elaboration of the COS for elementary schools, *Teaching Guide for the Japanese Course of Study: Mathematics*, was released by the Japanese Ministry of Education, Culture, and Sports. Immediately after its release, school districts provided workshops, attended by representatives of the schools, discussing the major changes in the revision. The districts also assigned selected schools to focus their school-based lesson study on the effective implementation of the new COS. This process occurred while the textbook companies were developing new materials based on the new curriculum. The new COS went fully into effect among all the Japanese public elementary schools in April of 2011 (the beginning of the school year). Thus it took three years for the textbook publishers and schools to fully implement the COS.

During this preparation period, even before revised curriculum materials were available, many schools began to seek effective implementation of the new COS. Schools often conduct school-based research, using lesson study, with the entire faculty. The school districts often provide financial support to the schools and encourage them to host a lesson study open house as the culmination of their school-based research to disseminate their findings to other schools in the district. As a result, some schools in the district have open houses before the full implementation of the COS. These lesson study open houses may include several different subject areas and focus on different changes in the COS.

Role of Lesson Study in Implementing the COS

To support teachers in improving their own teaching and learning, the Japanese school system has a systematic professional development approach called lesson study. It is the most common form of professional development in Japan (Lewis 2000; Lewis and Tsuchida 1998; Murata and Takahashi 2002; Takahashi 2000; Takahashi and Yoshida 2004; Yoshida 1999a). In lesson study, a team of teachers studies the COS, reads research articles, examines available curricula and other materials, and designs a lesson. One teacher from the team instructs the lesson publicly, and the team conducts a post-lesson discussion focusing on how students responded to the lesson, in order to gain insights into how students learn and to find ways to improve teaching.

---

[1] An unofficial English translation of the mathematics curricula in the Japanese Course of Study, including objectives and content for grades 1–9, is available at http://www.seiservices.com/APEC/APEC_KB/KBDisplay.aspx?lngPkID=1567.

During lesson study, teachers have the opportunity to look closely at teaching practices and judge, based on student learning, whether the lesson properly supports the students in learning mathematics. Researchers credit Japanese lesson study with enabling the implementation of new approaches to teaching mathematics (Lewis 2002; Lewis and Tsuchida 1998; Stigler and Hiebert 1999; Yoshida 1999b).

Although lesson study is commonly used as a medium of professional development that focuses on teachers and schools improving their teaching and learning, lesson study is also used to seek practical ideas for effective implementation of curricula (Murata and Takahashi 2002).

During the transition period from one COS to a new COS, the Japanese school system provides a variety of supports for schools and teachers, which include a document that elaborates on the focus and the contents of the COS (the *Teaching Guide* mentioned above), and workshops for administrators, district coordinators, and teacher leaders, which provide further information and examples of the contents of the COS. Commercial publishers, including textbook publishers, release teacher resources, curriculum materials, and sample curriculum maps for teachers. These publishers often work closely with teacher leaders to develop materials before the full implementation of the COS.

Among all of the supports that teachers receive during the transition to the new COS, this study focuses on school-based lesson study, which is one of the major professional development components during this important period. The author started documenting one school's lesson study cycles at the beginning of the second year of the school's lesson study-based research project. The author also closely followed the school administrators to investigate how they worked with members of the school steering committee and chairperson to be sure that the school-based research was conducted properly and effectively.

Major Points of Revision of the 2008 COS

The Ministry of Education released the 2008 COS in response to concerns about declining mathematics achievement due to a severe reduction in content and number of class periods in the 1998 revision. As a result, the 2008 Course of Study returned almost completely to the content and the number of class periods of the 1989 COS. Table 1 shows how the standard numbers of class periods required for mathematics by the law has changed. For teachers who previously taught according to the 1989 COS, this change presented little challenge. On the other hand, younger teachers saw this revision as an overwhelming increase to their workload, and it included some mathematics that they may have never taught before.

Another major change of the 2008 COS was to increase the emphasis on mathematical processes such as thinking mathematically and expressing thoughts using mathematical representations such as diagrams and equations. In order to address this, all classroom teachers are expected to regularly provide each student with opportunities to think mathematically and to express their own thoughts.

Table 1 How the standard numbers of class periods required for mathematics by the law has changed over time

Grade	Age	Standard number of class periods per year for mathematics						
		1951	1958	1968	1977	1989	1998	2011
Elementary								
1	6	77	102	102	136	136	114	136 (4 per week)
2	7	123	140	140	175	175	155	175 (5 per week)
3	8	138	175	175	175	175	150	175 (5 per week)
4	9	160	210	210	175	175	150	175 (5 per week)
5	10	160	210	210	175	175	150	175 (5 per week)
6	11	160	210	210	175	175	150	175 (5 per week)
Lower secondary								
1	12	140	140	140	105	105	105	140 (4 per week)
2	13	140	140	140	140	140	105	105 (3 per week)
3	14	140	105-175	140	140	140	105	140 (4 per week)

Table 2 Number of the students by the grades and the class

	Grade 1	Grade 2	Grade 3	Grade 4	Grade 5	Grade 6	Special needs
Class 1	36	37	40	31	31	37	13
Class 2	36	36	40	31	30	37	12
Class 3	35	36	40	32	31	37	
Class 4		37		32	31		

To prepare for these radical changes, the Ministry set a two-year preparation period for schools, teachers, and textbook publishers. All public elementary schools in Japan in the spring of 2008 created a professional development plan to prepare for the full implementation of the new COS in the 2010–2011 school year.

The Case

About the School

A public elementary school in Tokyo was chosen for the case study because it is a typical neighborhood school with a diverse student population. As of May 1, 2011 there were 758 students, 397 male and 361 female, from grades 1 to 6. Table 2 shows the number of classes in each grade and the number of students in each class.

Led by the principal and the assistant principal, 64 teachers and staff worked collaboratively to carry out the school's mission. Among these, there were 35 full-time

Table 3 Distribution of the teaching experience among the full time teachers at the school (2012–2013 school year)

Teaching Experience	Number of the full-time teachers
1 year–less than 5 years	7 (20 %)
5 years–less than 10 years	16 (45 %)
10 years–less than 15 years	2 (6 %)
15 years–less than 20 years	3 (9 %)
More than 20 years	7 (20 %)
Total	35

teachers, which included 22 classrooms teachers, 6 teachers for students with special needs, 4 additional teachers who teach special subjects, 2 school nurses, and 1 dietitian who is responsible for the school lunch menu. There were also several part-time teachers working at the school. Table 3 shows the years of teaching experience among the full-time teachers.

Process of School-Based Lesson Study and Its Supporting Structure at the School

Year 1: April, 2010–March, 2011

After the COS revision was announced in March of 2008, the teachers of the school decided to study the major changes in the COS revision and its effective implementation. Of the various subjects, the teachers decided to focus on mathematics. One motivation for this decision was the requirement that students learn an additional 20 % of mathematics content in grades 1–6. The teachers at the school felt that this content increase would mostly impact the teachers with less than 10 years of teaching experience. Since about 65 % of the full-time teachers had less than 10 years of teaching experience, collaboration among novice and senior teachers would be key for the successful implementation of the revised COS. Another challenge in mathematics was the new emphasis on promoting mathematical thinking and exposition. Teachers would need to consider not only how the amount of content changed but also how to design lessons that would push all students to think mathematically and to communicate with each other in such a way as to learn other ways of thinking mathematically.

After deciding to focus on the effective implementation of the mathematics curriculum, the school submitted a request to the local school district board to support this study. The local school district responded by making a small grant to support a public open house at the end of the study to disseminate the results of the school's work.

The school organized a research steering committee (RSC), which consisted of representatives of each grade level and the math teacher who was in charge of supporting other teachers in regards to teaching mathematics. The chair of the committee worked closely with the administrators to arrange logistics for conducting the school-based lesson study. In order for the faculty at the school to be prepared to begin the school-based lesson study, the RSC began drafting a proposal of the study during the end of the 2009–2010 school year. At the first faculty meeting of the 2010–2011 school year, April 2, 2010, they proposed the following theme and focus:

> **Research theme:** The development of individual thinking and the expression of these thoughts
>
> **Focus of study:** Seeking effective ways to support students' individual problem solving skills and the ideal facilitation of whole-class discussion in teaching through problem solving

The school research theme was intended to address one of the emphases of the revised COS. The RSC decided to focus on improving the quality of lessons based on problem solving, such lessons having been emphasized in Japanese mathematics education for several decades as a way to foster student mathematical thinking (Takahashi 2008, 2011).

The teachers at the meeting concluded that the proposed theme and focus of the school research would be a good starting point, but would be revisited after several research lessons and post-lesson discussions.

Under this tentative theme and focus of study, the full time faculty members were divided into 8 teams: one for each of grades 1 through 6 plus 2 teams consisting of teachers of students with special needs. During year 1, each team developed a lesson plan for a research lesson and conducted the research lesson and its post lesson discussion to address the theme. All full-time teachers and the school nurse and school dietitian observed the lessons and participated in the post-lesson discussions, so each full-time teacher had the opportunity to be a part of 8 research lessons during the school year. In addition to the 8 research lessons, the school invited two distinguished mathematics educators to give lectures, one in the first month of the school year (April) and another during the summer break, about the issues and trends in mathematics education and ideas for implementation of the new COS.

Based on the approved plan and the schedule drafted by the RSC, each team was asked to decide when the team wanted to have their research lesson. Each team examined the curriculum and the schedule of possible dates, and chose a couple of possible topics that they wanted to study in order to address the theme and focus of the school research. Based on each team's preference, the RSC proposed a schedule that was discussed, revised, and approved by the teachers at the faculty meeting on April 7, 2010. Accordingly, the following events occurred during that first school year:

- Friday, April 9. Demonstration lesson by an invited teacher to raise issues related to the theme and school research focus
- Wednesday, April 21. Faculty meeting to discuss and approve the theme of the school-based lesson study
- Wednesday, May 19. Lecture by a leading math educator on the school research theme

- Wednesday, June 16. Research lesson and post-lesson discussion: "various lengths" for a class of special needs students
- Wednesday, June 23. Research lesson and post lesson discussion: "subtraction (1)" by the grade 1 team
- Friday, August 27 (During summer break). A lecture by a leading math educator on the school research theme
- Wednesday, September 22. Research lesson and post-lesson discussion: "area" by the grade 4 team
- Wednesday, October 27. Research lesson and post-lesson discussion: mathematics for students with special needs by the special needs team
- Tuesday, November 24. Research lesson and post-lesson discussion: "multiples and factors" by the grade 5 team
- Wednesday, November 30. Research lesson and post lesson discussion: "enlarged and reduced drawings" by the grade 6 team
- Wednesday, January 26. Research lesson and post-lesson discussion: "addition and subtraction (2)" by the grade 2 team
- Wednesday, February 16. A research lesson and post-lesson discussion: "math sentences using □" by the grade 3 team.

The teachers at the school shared many responsibilities to make the research lessons and discussions go smoothly. For example, for the research lesson held in June, the grade 1 team developed a lesson plan and taught the lesson based on this plan. During the post-lesson discussion, the grade 4 team facilitated the discussion and the team of teachers of special needs students took notes of the post-lesson discussion for the school's official record.

One notable activity that launched the two-year research project was the demonstration lesson by an invited practitioner. With more than 30 years of teaching experience, that person is known as a master teacher. The RSC assigned to their colleagues the following four points of focus for their observations during the lesson:

(1) Ways to organize board writing
(2) Effective key questions
(3) Effective ways to develop ideas based on students' reactions
(4) Ways to support students in developing the ability to explain their ideas and approaches

In selecting these four focus points, the RSC drew upon articles and resources from journals and reference books of mathematics education. According to the chairperson, the RSC hypothesized that having these four focus points would help the faculty develop a shared view about the way in which they might address the school research theme and develop students' ability to come up with their own thinking and to express their thoughts.

From the shared observations and discussions, the school developed a draft concept map of the research theme and focus. The RSC used this draft as a foundation for two years and finalized a concept map as a result of their research. The concept map was included in the research report as the Structure of the Overall Research and was distributed to other schools in the district (see Appendix).

Year 2: April, 2011–March, 2012

The second year of the research program was mostly similar to the first. One major difference between year 1 and year 2, however, was that the schedule in year 2 had a public open house scheduled near the end of the school year, December 1. Having a public open house to disseminate the results of the school's research project is common practice among Japanese public schools. In order to have this event, the school had to complete all research lessons by the middle of the fall and compile their findings as much as possible a few months before the open house. This made the school schedule rather inflexible.

At the first faculty meeting of the 2011–2012 school year, on April 6, 2011, the RSC proposed a change in the research theme based on their reflections on the first year's activities. The first year's theme had emphasized the development of individual students' ability to think and express their thoughts. Now the teachers felt that students were not appreciating the benefits of collaboration—learning from others' ideas and developing better ideas by exchanging and combining ideas. This led to the following new research theme:

> **Research theme:** Mathematics teaching that helps students explain their ideas to each other and learn from each other—learning through problem solving

At the same meeting, the faculty also approved the following schedule of activities for year 2, which the author participated in and documented using field notes:

- Wednesday, April 6. Faculty meeting to discuss and approve the modified theme of the school-based lesson study and set the schedule of research activities
- Friday, April 8. Workshop by a leading math educator about effective lesson observation
- Wednesday, April 20. Research lesson and post-lesson discussion: "symmetry" by the grade 6 team
- Wednesday, April 27. Lecture by a leading math educator
- Wednesday, May 11. Research lesson and post-lesson discussion: "angles" by the grade 4 team
- Wednesday, May 18. Research lesson and post-lesson discussion: "multiplication of decimal numbers" by the grade 5 team
- Wednesday, June 13. Research lesson and post-lesson discussion: "division" by the grade 3 team
- Wednesday, June 21. Research lesson and post-lesson discussion: "subtraction" by the grade 1 team
- Friday, Aug 26. Grade band meetings for developing lesson plans for the public research lessons at the public open house.
- Wednesday, Sep 14. Research lesson and post-lesson discussion: "addition and subtraction" by the grade 2 team
- Thursday, Dec 1. Public open house.

In addition to the these events, the RSC met several times between the research lessons to summarize the ideas that had been proposed by each lesson planning team and addressed during the post-lesson discussion. This was done to make sure that individual learning was consolidated and shared among all teachers at the school. The summary of the RSC's effort was published as a school research newsletter each month. Besides documenting the process of this long-term collaborative effort, these newsletters allowed the teachers to share what was discussed and helped the later teams build off the results of the previous research lessons.

The Structure of the School Research Organization and the Role of the School's Research Steering Committee (RSC)

During the two years of the school research program, all full-time teachers at the school worked within a structure based on existing grade-level groups. Grade-level groups typically exist in Japanese elementary schools to facilitate the sharing of responsibilities for running school events and for academic activities. These responsibilities include preparing curriculum materials for the teachers in the grade to use, preparing school events such as the sports festival and open houses, and planning and conducting events organized by each grade such as field trips and teacher-parent conferences. Most public schools have scheduled time for grade meetings in their weekly schedule, typically about one hour, and have desks in a common work area so that the teachers who teach the same grade level can easily collaborate on a regular basis. It was natural to build off this existing collaborative structure for the school-based lesson study work, and so each grade level group was made responsible for designing a lesson plan for a research lesson, preparing the research and the post-lesson discussion, and supporting the other teams' research lessons. The overall structure of the school research organization is shown in Fig. 1.

Although each grade team developed its own lesson plan, each lesson plan was expected to address the school research theme and to help develop shared approaches to effectively implementing the new curriculum. The RSC had the important responsibility of maintaining cohesiveness of ideas in the lesson plans across the grades.

The RSC comprised a teacher from each grade group, nominated by that group, and a chairperson appointed by the school administrators. According to the principal, the chair was chosen based on his leadership ability and his knowledge of mathematics teaching and learning. The RSC chair was one of the full time special subject teachers at the school, normally in charge of supporting upper grade classroom teachers in teaching mathematics and preparing curriculum materials for the school. As chair, his primary role was to lead the school research in order to maximize teacher collaboration to accomplish the research goals. The chair led the RSC to complete the following tasks:

- Communicate regularly with the principal and the assistant principal to develop a master plan for the school research that included the effective use of resources including time and budget

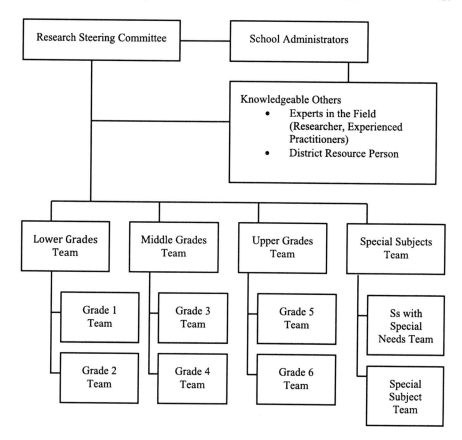

Fig. 1 Structure of the school research organization

- Schedule and lead the monthly RSC meetings to find strategies to address the theme of the research based on the ideas of the teachers
- Lead the preparations and oversee each school research activity such as research lessons and lectures
- Publish a monthly internal newsletter to update the findings of each research lesson and to share important ideas and information for carrying out research activities
- Plan, edit, and publish the school research reports, including the publications for the open house
- Communicate with knowledgeable others for the effective use of their expertise.

As Fig. 1 shows, the school also had the grade-band teams, which consisted of all the teachers from adjacent grades, such as grade 1 and grade 2. The major role of these teams was to discuss and implement strategies proposed by the RSC in each research lesson. Although the responsibility for lesson planning belonged to each grade group, most of the lesson planning was done in grade band meetings, since the teachers felt that the grade level groups, comprising only 3 or 4 teachers, were too small on their own to generate enough variety of ideas to lead to good research lessons. Also, the grade band meetings helped the teachers develop a shared view not only of their students but also of the scope and sequence of the curriculum in adjacent grades, which is important since Japanese elementary school teachers typically teach the same students two consecutive years. Finally, the grade band meetings also provided additional opportunities to participate in research lesson planning, a valuable experience especially for novice teachers not only to learn how to design lessons but also to deepen their understanding of the topics they teach though *kyozaikenkyu* (Takahashi et al. 2005; Takahashi and Yoshida 2004; Watanabe et al. 2008). In these ways, the grade-band teams were a crucial piece of the overall structure supporting the school's lesson study research.

Lesson Plans and Their Development

Based on the faculty's reflections from the year 1 research activities, the RSC provided guidelines for preparing research lessons and lesson plans. Their objective was to aid two new teachers who had joined the school in year 2 and who had little experience with systematic school-based research. The guidelines were as follows:

An example of preparing a research lesson

(1) Decide on the topic of the research lesson and who will teach the lesson. Develop a rough idea of a lesson plan and conduct *kyozaikenkyu* related to the topic.

(2) **Three weeks before the research lesson:** The first lesson-planning meeting is held to discuss the rough draft to check for consistency with other grade groups' approaches.

(3) Develop the first draft of the lesson plan based on the discussion at the first meeting.

(4) **Two weeks before the research lesson:** The second lesson-planning meeting is held to discuss the lesson plan and the team's focus strategies.

(5) Update the draft lesson plan and the focus strategies.

(6) **One week before the research lesson:** Finalize the lesson plan and send it to the invited final commentator of the research lesson (the knowledgeable other) via express mail, including a handwritten letter by the teacher who will teach the lesson.

(7) Print the lesson plan. Share the tasks needed to prepare for the research lesson, including the preparation of materials such as manipulatives, posters, and worksheets.

(8) **On the day of the research lesson:** Conduct the research lesson and the post-lesson discussion. Support the teacher who teaches the research lesson.

Note: Although each grade group is mainly responsible for the preparation and execution of its lesson, the above preparations should be done through the grade band team's collaboration.

Based on these guidelines, each grade group planned a research lesson once during the year. So each teacher was responsible for writing one lesson plan as a member of a grade group and also had the opportunity, as a part of a grade-band team, to be a part of the lesson planning discussion of another grade.

In each stage of lesson plan development, the chair and members of the RSC reviewed the lesson plan and provided feedback to the team. Through this process, the RSC tried to ensure that the lesson plans were of sufficient quality to merit discussion by the entire faculty and contributed to the school's effective implementation of the COS. But, according to the school principal, the quality of the research lesson plans in year 1 was not satisfactory. Based on the principal's suggestion, the RSC developed the following list of criteria for lesson plans and distributed it to each teacher at the beginning of the year 2:

- Does the lesson plan provide sufficient information for the reader to understand the task and the flow of the lesson?
- Does the lesson plan provide sufficient information about how the planning team decided to teach the lesson as described by the plan?
- Do the objectives of the lesson plan clearly address the COS?
- Are the tasks appropriate for the students given the date of the lesson?
- Are the key questions clear? Will they push students to think mathematically and help them complete the task independently?
- Does the lesson plan include reasonable anticipated student responses and indicate how the teachers will help students overcome any misunderstandings?
- Does the lesson plan include a plan for formative assessment and a plan to accommodate individual student differences during the lesson?

These criteria were used not only by the RSC in reviewing the draft lesson plans but also by the teachers themselves during the planning meetings. According to the principal, the lesson plans that were developed for research lessons in year 2 reflected much deeper thought compared to the plans developed in year 1.

One of the unique features of this school's research lesson plans was the inclusion of a two-page summary. Typical research lesson plans are several pages in length—they sometimes run more than ten pages. Faced with such a lengthy plan, teachers with less lesson study experience sometimes have difficulty comprehending the important points of the lesson and preparing to observe it effectively. Also, the final version of a lesson plan was usually distributed to the faculty a day prior to or in the morning of the research lesson, which meant that teachers did not necessarily have a lot of time to read it carefully. So the school decided to include a short summary to help teachers with less experience and teachers cramped for time easily understand what he or she should be looking for while observing the research lesson.

Organization of the Research Lesson and Post-Lesson Discussion

Although each teacher had only one chance each year to develop a lesson plan for a research lesson, he or she had eight opportunities each year to observe a research

Table 4 Schedule for a research lesson and post-lesson discussion	1:30–2:15	Research Lesson
	2:20–2:40	Small Group Discussion (Grade Band Teams)
	2:40–3:45	Post-Lesson Discussion (Entire Faculty)
	3:45–4:30	Final Comments by a Knowledgeable Other
	4:30–4:45	Summary and Next Steps

lesson and discuss the effectiveness of the implementation of the COS. This is a major advantage for teachers of school-based lesson study.

In order for all faculty members at the school to observe these research lessons, the school scheduled most research lessons on Wednesdays. Similar to most public schools in the area, the school scheduled special events every Wednesday afternoon so that students can be dismissed early if necessary. The school used Wednesday afternoons once a month for the research lessons. On the day of the research lessons, all of the classes were dismissed immediately after lunch except the class with which the research lesson would be conducted. In this way, the school freed teachers to observe the research lesson. Table 4 shows the schedule followed by the school on those Wednesday afternoons.

Typically, a post-lesson discussion with the entire faculty is held immediately after the research lesson. The school decided, however, to first hold small-group discussions in grade band teams as a way to provide more opportunities for each teacher, especially for the novice teachers, to share their ideas. In the past, some teachers at the school seemed reluctant to share their honest opinions at the post-lesson discussion because it was formal and in front of the entire faculty. The small-group discussions usually lasted about 20 minutes and were led by the RSC members. The discussions were summarized on small posters and were shared at the beginning of the full faculty discussion.

The full faculty discussion usually began with the principal introducing the final commentator, or knowledgeable other. Then the moderator, a member of a different grade-level team, would invite each grade band to share the issues they identified during the small group discussions. The discussion then focused on how the lesson plan could be improved. In the first year and the beginning of the second year, the discussions were not so active, and only the members of the RSC contributed observations and thoughts about how the lesson plan could be improved. But by the fourth research lesson in June 2011 the dynamic was changing and more teachers, including new teachers, began to contribute to the discussion.

At the end of the discussion, a knowledgeable other, invited from outside the school, would provide a summary of the discussion and offer suggestions not only for improving the particular research lesson from that day but also for carrying out the school research. The school made use of several knowledgeable others over the two-year period, inviting them based on their schedule and the topic of the research lesson, with a few of them giving comments several times. The knowledgeable others were instructional leaders from the area with more than 30 years of teaching experience.

After the final comments by the knowledgeable other, the assistant principal at the school usually offered a summary of the research lesson and its post-lesson discussion by highlighting the issues that were discussed and the major points that all the faculty members should keep in mind in designing future lessons. The assistant principal then formally concluded the discussion by thanking the knowledgeable other, the team who developed the research lesson, and the teacher who taught the research lesson.

Although the post-lesson discussion was at that point formally closed, and the knowledgeable other and administrators left the meeting room, the entire faculty remained to summarize their learning and to discuss next steps. This discussion, usually led by the chairperson of the RSC, helped ensure that each research lesson was not an isolated event, and helped maintain the cohesiveness of the school research. The RSC representative from the group responsible for the next research lesson was specifically charged with making sure that the next lesson would address issues from the discussion.

Disseminating the Results of the School Research

The school used two conduits to disseminate the results of its research: a public open house that offered live research lessons, and a research report published at the end of the two-year project.

Public Open House

The school hosted a half-day public open house on the afternoon of December 1, 2011. All of the district content specialists and principals of other area schools were invited to the open house, and many other schools sent their teachers to the open house. In all, a total of 612 participants, including teachers, administrators, educators, and parents attended. Among these participants, about 60 % of the participants were teachers, administrators, and educators, 35 % from the district and 24 % from outside of the district. Clearly, this school-based research project attracted many educators. According to the participants, one of the major reasons for them to come to the open house was to see the implementation of the revised COS in action. Since all grades from grade 1 to 6 held research lessons on the day, participants could choose which research lesson or lessons they wanted to see from a wide variety of topics and grades. Also notable is that 160 parents came to the open house, about 20 % of the number of students at the school. Parents came to see what the teachers at the school do to improve their teaching. According to the principal, involving parents in the open house builds strong support from the parents even though the open house is designed for professional educators and teachers. Other participants of the open house included people from the local neighborhood, textbook publishers, and retired teachers of the school. Table 5 shows the breakdown of participants.

Table 5 Participants at the public open house on Dec. 1, 2011

Type of participants	Number (%)
Invited guests	23 (4 %)
Administrators from the schools in the district	38 (6 %)
Teachers from the schools in the district	180 (29 %)
Teachers and educators from outside of the district	146 (24 %)
Parents of the school	160 (26 %)
Others	65 (11 %)
Total	611 (100%)

The public open house consisted of three major parts: public research lessons, research presentations by the school's RSC, and a panel discussion by experts in the field of mathematics education who had been involved with the school's research project. The schedule of the open house was as follows:

1:10–1:40 Registration
1:40–2:25 Research lessons in 25 mathematics classrooms, including four mathematics classes for the students with special needs
2:25–2:40 Break
2:40–3:15 Research presentation in the gymnasium
2:15–4:25 Panel discussion by the knowledgeable others
4:25–4:30 Closing remarks by the principal

There were 28 mathematics lessons based on 25 different lesson plans available for the participants to observe at the beginning of the open house. All 25 lesson plans were distributed as a booklet to each participant at registration. The participants were thus able to witness strategies for the effective implementation of the COS in live lessons and were able bring these ideas back to their school as a set of lesson plans.

The presentation given by the members of the RSC informed participants about the philosophy and the rationale behind the strategies for implementing the new COS at the school. The presentation also provided educators from other schools an opportunity to learn how the school conducted its research using lesson study and what the faculty at the school learned.

The panel discussion provided a broad view of the issues and trends in implementing the COS at schools in the area. Because the panelists had served as knowledgeable others for other schools, they were able to highlight unique features of the strategies that this school had come up with through their two-year collaborative efforts and how other schools might adopt these ideas and strategies.

Research Reports

Two sets of research reports were made available for teachers and administrators of other schools as summaries of the school research effort of year 1, 2010–2011, and of year 2, 2011–2012. Since the school used a district grant to produce them, all the research reports were available free. For the summary of year 1, the school compiled one booklet of 102 pages, which included:

(a) the rationale behind the school's choice of research theme;
(b) a concept map of the research theme and focus;
(c) a report on each research lesson, which included the unit plan, lesson plan, and summary of the post-lesson discussion; and
(d) a summary of an assessment of student attitudes and achievement.

In the second year, the school compiled a report covering the entire two-year study. The report was produced as four booklets: three of them were distributed at the public open house and the last was sent to all the schools in the district at the end of the 2011–2012 school year:

Distributed at the public open house:

1. The school research report[2] (20 pages)
2. Lesson plans for the research lessons at the open house lessons (16 lesson plans, 38 pages)
3. Two-page shortened versions of lesson plans of all the research lessons from the two years of the school's research (20 lesson plans, 46 pages)

Distributed at the end of the school year 2011–2012:

4. Report of the public open house comprising reports of each lesson at the open house (28 lesson reports, 57 pages).

According to the principal, these reports, with their large number of lesson plans for all the elementary grades, are not meant to be a collection of best practice. They are expected to be a resource for teachers in the district to draw from as they engage in their own study about effectively implementing the COS. Thus these reports include not only lesson plans but also reflections of the teachers, sharing what they learned from the research lessons. The reports make it clear that the teachers at the school used lesson study as a way to examine their knowledge, ideas, and practice for teaching mathematics—not as a way to come up with perfect lessons.

Findings

In addition to his observations during the second year of the program, the author conducted interviews that provided insights into the thinking of the school administrators and how the project impacted teachers. Based these interviews and on his own observations and those of the persons interviewed, several factors stand out as

---

[2]An English translation of this report is available for download at http://www.impuls-tgu.org/resource/readings/page-26.html.

important to the effectiveness of this project for preparing the teachers to implement the new Course of Study. They are: leadership by the administration and Research Steering Committee; the deliberate importation of new knowledge and ideas from outside; structures to support collaborative learning; and the lesson study process itself.

Shared Leadership

Lesson study has been described as "teacher-led professional development." In this school-based LS project, teachers led the way by developing research lessons in which they proposed and tested strategies for solving common problems. Teachers also took turns handling the logistics of their colleagues' research lessons by facilitating the discussion or taking notes. But important leadership also came from the administration and from the RSC, sometimes "behind the scenes" and sometimes overtly.

Administration

As is common practice, the school made use of the existing grade-level teams as the primary organizational structure for its lesson-study work. When they were making grade-level assignments of teachers, the administrators carefully distributed experience and expertise among the grade-level teams.[3] This meant that each grade band had the teacher leadership needed to conduct thorough *kyozaikenkyu* when developing its research lesson plan.

Even with this distributed knowledge and expertise, the administrators still felt it was important to attend some of the lesson planning meetings as an instructional leader. According to the assistant principal, they attended the lesson planning meetings in order to gauge the teachers' understanding of the content that they planned to teach. He believes that the quality of the lesson plan hinges on the level of understanding of the content and the curriculum. If a team was struggling to understand what the major point is and why students need to learn it, he offered some suggestions. But, to preserve the teachers' sense of ownership, he tried not to provide suggestions too often. The assistant principal said, "We need to carefully monitor what teachers are thinking in order to provide sufficient support. We do not want to give too many suggestions to the teachers. This is just like teaching students mathematics." The assistant principal carefully reviewed all lesson plans line by line before they were finalized.

---

[3] Japanese teachers usually teach a different grade in each year. Classroom teachers often teach the same students multiple years, typically two years. They may request their preferred grades, but the principal makes the final decision.

Another important role for the administrators is to bring knowledgeable others with strong teaching backgrounds who can best help the school address their research theme. Among various experienced educators, such as university professors, leading practitioners, and retired principals, the administrators chose people whom they had seen fill the knowledgeable other role well and who also fit the school's particular needs. As a result, some knowledgeable others were invited several times and some were invited just once during the two years.

Finally, the administrators exercised their leadership through their own participation in the research lessons. The author has never seen any research lessons at the school conducted without the presence of the administrators. Either the principal or the assistant principal—and usually both—observed each research lesson from beginning to end and contributed comments during the post-lesson discussion. Then the principal joined with the planning team, the chair of the RSC, and the knowledgeable other in an in-depth meeting to consolidate the important insights or ideas to carry forward from the research lesson.

Many teachers at the school agreed that hard working teacher leaders and administrators were the key to the success of the school research. According to the principal, school-based lesson study never succeeds if the school administrators are not part of lesson observation and discussion. But for them to make positive contributions, the administrators and teacher leaders should be experts in teaching and learning of the subject matter, or at least be keen about improving teaching and learning for the students at the school, and genuinely interested in studying the students' learning process.

Research Steering Committee (RSC)

Perhaps ironic, one of the most important leadership actions by the administration was to devolve leadership to the teachers by creating a Research Steering Committee. Led by the chairperson, the RSC played an important role in leading the school research project and supporting each team's lesson study effort. Although the chairperson was appointed by the administrators, the committee consisted of representatives of each grade band. The RSC functioned as the hub of interaction among teachers and the driver of the school-based lesson study project. According to the principal, establishing a research steering committee is typical practice among schools in Japan.

The major role of the RSC was to solicit ideas from teachers and make sure that what was learned through the two-year project was shared across the school. That shared knowledge included a deeper understanding of the mathematics that they teach based on the COS, pedagogical ideas for addressing their students' needs, and ideas for improving teaching and learning in general.

The RSC assumed the following responsibilities during the two-year research project:

- Created a draft research proposal with theme and research focus;
- Created a draft calendar of events;
- Created a guideline for the lesson planning process;

- Created criteria for lesson plans as a way to improve their quality;
- Synthesized important points from each post-lesson discussion, published them in a newsletter, and explicitly directed later planning teams to address them, helping to keep the school research program coherent and moving forward;
- Produced the reports at the end of the first and second years.

In addition to these responsibilities, the chair and members of the RSC put a great deal of effort towards facilitating the transfer of ideas and strategies from one research lesson to later research lessons. By its nature, the process of lesson study—planning lessons together and observing the results with their own students—helps create shared knowledge. But the principal argues that the benefits of lesson study can dissipate without regular efforts to summarize teachers' learning. Even though planning teams worked toward a shared objective, if each lesson were built from scratch using the team's unique ideas and strategies, there was significant risk of ending up with an incoherent set of ideas and strategies for implementing the new COS. To keep the work coherent and progressing forward, the school administrators and the chair of the RSC had regular meetings between the research lessons to discuss what knowledge should be shared and what actions might be needed next. The chair of the RSC distributed a monthly internal newsletter based on these meetings to all teachers summarizing what they learned from each research lesson and post-lesson discussion. The RSC also reminded each planning team to address issues from previous lessons.

So administrators and teachers, through the RSC, each played their part in guiding the lesson study project. According to the principal, it is crucial for successful school-based lesson study to plan for this kind of shared responsibility.

Pathways of New Knowledge and Ideas

Even if teachers work hard to seek ways to effectively implement the COS, it is not always realistic to expect them to come up with good strategies without having deep subject matter knowledge or without a broad awareness of issues in improving teaching and learning. According to the assistant principal, the successful implementation of the COS hinges on each teacher's understanding of the contents that they teach, so that they can teach mathematics using textbooks rather than teaching the textbooks (Takahashi 2011). To do this, each teacher must understand what the key elements are in each lesson and why students need to understand them.

The main way teachers develop their understanding of the content they teach is through *kyozaikenkyu*, the careful study of materials for teaching. But some teachers are not accustomed to practicing careful *kyozaikenkyu*. From the administrators' perspective, an important long-term outcome of the school research project would be that teachers would conduct rich *kyozaikenkyu* when preparing their everyday lessons. Thus the planning of the research lessons, the teaching of the lessons, and the post-lesson discussions were not just about the issues explicitly addressed in those lessons, but were also about providing teachers with experiences that would improve their everyday *kyozaikenkyu* and lead to better teaching overall.

The plan created by the RSC was designed to provide teachers with those experiences, and administrators and the RSC monitored the various research activities and provided additional support when necessary. The administrators also took additional actions to enrich the experiences teachers had from the project.

Requesting Support from the District   When they make grants to support school-based lesson study, local school districts routinely provide awarded schools prioritized access to a district curriculum coordinator, and funds for extra resources. The funds can be used not only to purchase books and journals but also to invite outside experts to the research lessons and workshops. Schools also receive additional support from the district to conduct one or more public open houses and to publish the results of their study, to be distributed to all the schools in the district.

Using the district support, the RSC at this school collect resources that were related to the theme of the school research. The district funds also made it possible to have knowledgeable others come more frequently than normal; the administrators worked with the RSC to find appropriate knowledgeable others to serve as lecturers or final commentators for the research lessons.

Hiring Teachers with Experience   Between year 1 and year 2 of the school based research project, the school hired some new teachers with strong subject knowledge, including knowledge of the new COS, and with leadership experience. The addition of these teachers gave other teachers more access to high quality lesson study experience and, according to the principal, raised the level of discussion during lesson planning meetings.

Collaborative Structure to Support Teacher Learning and Growth

As is often done, this school used their existing grade-level groups for research lesson development and as the core of the research project. In addition, the school added the grade-band teams and the RSC as additional structures for better communication throughout the school. The grade-band teams leveraged the limited number of experienced teachers at the school, providing all teachers access to the knowledge of those experienced teachers when designing lesson plans. According to the assistant principal, the idea was to ensure that all teachers, novice and experienced teachers alike, would have multiple paths of access to the knowledge held within the school. For example if a teacher had a question regarding everyday classroom instruction, he/she could ask it during a grade level meeting. If the question were related to specific subject matter, he/she could ask a member of the grade band team. If the question were related to a broader issue of teaching mathematics, the RSC could help direct it to the most knowledgeable teacher at the school or to outside experts. According to the principal, administrators often use a school research project as an opportunity to establish a collaborative structure if the school does not already have one.

The collaborative structures seemed to have the desired effects. Several novice teachers at the school reported that planning a research lesson with their colleagues using the guidelines that the RSC provided helped them learn how to conduct *kyozaikenkyu* in their everyday planning. Also, working with experienced teachers when planning the lesson for their grade-level group research lesson greatly helped them to learn about the different kinds of resources that were available at the school and how to use them when planning the lesson. As a result they gradually developed a habit of thinking about the objective of the lesson in relation to the COS and how to support students in accomplishing the objective.

From those comments, it can be concluded that using existing grade-level groups as a foundation is an effective ways to reinforce a collaborative environment among teachers at the school. Because the teachers could discuss not only the research lessons they planned together but also, with the same group members, issues in everyday teaching, the knowledge and ideas that arose out of the school research project carried over into their conversation of everyday teaching. One classroom teacher reported that the nature of conversation at the regular grade level meetings shifted to focus more on what the differences of expectations were between the previous COS and the new COS. When discussing topics new to the COS, teachers worked together to study resources such as the official teaching guide of COS (Ministry of Education 2008), teacher journals, and lesson plans published by commercial publishers.

The Value of Lesson Study

The research lessons, the core activity of lesson study, are a particularly visible feature of school-based lesson study, but other features are important for supporting steady progress toward implementing the COS. The school has to have a long-term, well-planned timetable for the school research, a structure to support teacher collaboration, and pathways to bring updated knowledge of the curriculum and key ideas for its implementation.

The school used lesson study as the fundamental process for addressing the challenges of implementing the new COS. It is worth considering what can be learned about lesson study itself from this project.

Each teacher was deeply involved in planning only one research lesson per year. This may not seem like enough to support the changes needed for implementing the new COS, but the lesson study process afforded other opportunities to learn. Teachers observed each other's lessons and discussed the issues. Each teacher at the school also had at least two opportunities to critique lesson plans from another team during the planning process through the grade-band meetings. Finally, teachers observed and discussed the lessons of all the other grades at the school. These additional opportunities may have contributed at least as much to the teachers' learning as did their work on their own research lesson.

Lesson study outside of Japan may often focus too much on the teacher who teaches the research lesson and on the team that plans the lesson. Lesson study can be powerful even for teachers who just observe the research lesson and participate in the post-lesson discussion. Thus it may be equally important to think about how to maximize the learning opportunity for the research lesson participants.

Successful school-based lesson study requires leadership for creating a long-term plan connected to a broader perspective of improving mathematics teaching and learning, and for supporting teachers' efforts strategically. Although the administration plays an important leadership role, one of the most important tasks of the administration is to cultivate leadership among the teachers, such as by creating a research steering committee and by deliberately distributing more experienced teachers across the grade levels. The administrators and teacher leaders also need to think about how to create long-term pathways for bringing in new ideas and knowledge, such as by creating a norm of conducting thorough *kyozaikenkyu*. Finally, it is important to think about how the lesson study activities can benefit teachers beyond those on an individual planning team.

Summary

The new COS presented two significant challenges in mathematics for schools throughout Japan: an increased amount of content and a new emphasis on promoting mathematical thinking and exposition. At the same time, many schools had a significant number of teachers retiring and being replaced by novice teachers year after year. At the school examined in this chapter, the faculty and leaders made a decision to address these challenges together through a rigorous, 2-year school research project based on lesson study.

Outside Japan, lesson study has been introduced as teacher-led professional development. In the U.S. and perhaps elsewhere, many lesson study projects have been conducted by a few volunteers within a school with support from outside the school. In contrast, this case study shows that school-based lesson study in Japan is a highly structured, collaborative effort of school administrators, teacher leaders, and all the teachers at the school, with additional support from the local district.

School-based lesson study involves a significant amount of interaction and collaboration among the teachers at the school. There are several levels of meetings included in the school schedule for school-wide study and to prepare for each public research lesson. In addition, many informal voluntary meetings occur. The school administrators also have frequent meetings with teacher leaders to share ideas and concerns in order to make sure all the teachers are progressing toward their common goal. The school administrators and the RSC members of the school frequently communicated with outside experts not only when conducting research lessons, but also when the teachers were preparing lesson plans for their research lessons.

Although this is a single case from one Japanese public elementary school, it illustrates how the staff of a school can work together toward an effective implementation of new standards.

Acknowledgements   The author wants to thank the Project IMPULS at Tokyo Gakugei University that provided generous support to help carry out this study, Thomas McDougal who read and edited numerous revisions, and the anonymous reviewers for their invaluable comments on earlier versions of this chapter.

Appendix: Concept Map of the Research Theme and Focus (English translation by the Project IMPULS at http://www.impuls-tgu.org)

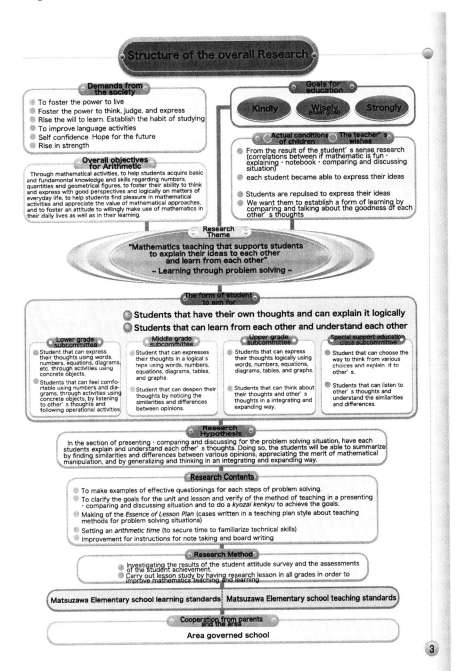

References

Common Core State Standards Initiative (2010). Common core state standards for mathematics. Retrieved 12/27/2010, from http://www.corestandards.org/the-standards/mathematics.

Lewis, C. (2000, April). *Lesson study: the core of Japanese professional development*. Paper presented at the AERA annual meeting.

Lewis, C. (2002). *Lesson study: a handbook of teacher-led instructional change*. Philadelphia: Research for Better Schools, Inc.

Lewis, C. C., & Tsuchida, I. (1998). A lesson is like a swiftly flowing river: how research lessons improve Japanese education. *American Educator, 22*(4), 12–17, 50–52.

Ministry of Education, C., Sports, Science and Technology (2008). The teaching guide of the course of study for elementary school mathematics. Retrieved from http://www.mext.go.jp/a_menu/shotou/new-cs/youryou/syokaisetsu/index.htm.

Murata, A., & Takahashi, A. (2002). Vehicle to connect theory, research, and practice: how teacher thinking changes in district-level lesson study in Japan. In *Proceedings of the twenty-fourth annual meeting of North American chapter of the international group of the psychology of mathematics education* (pp. 1879–1888).

National Mathematics Advisory Panel (2008). *Foundations for success: the final report of the national mathematics advisory panel*. Washington: U.S. Department of Education.

Stigler, J. W., & Hiebert, J. (1999). *The teaching gap: best ideas from the world's teachers for improving education in the classroom*. New York: Free Press.

Stigler, J. W., & Hiebert, J. (2009). Closing the teaching gap. *Phi Delta Kappan, 91*(03), 32–37.

Takahashi, A. (2000). Current trends and issues in lesson study in Japan and the United States. *Journal of Japan Society of Mathematical Education, 82*(12), 15–21.

Takahashi, A. (2006). Types of elementary mathematics lesson study in Japan: analysis of features and characteristics. *Journal of Japan Society of Mathematical Education, LXXXVIII*, 15–21.

Takahashi, A. (2008). *Beyond show and tell: neriage for teaching through problem-solving—ideas from Japanese problem-solving approaches for teaching mathematics*. Paper presented at the 11th International Congress on Mathematics Education in Mexico (Section TSG 19: Research and Development in Problem Solving in Mathematics Education), Monteree, Mexico.

Takahashi, A. (2011). The Japanese approach to developing expertise in using the textbook to teach mathematics rather than teaching the textbook. In Y. Li & G. Kaiser (Eds.), *Expertise in mathematics instruction: an international perspective*. New York: Springer.

Takahashi, A., & Yoshida, M. (2004). Ideas for establishing lesson study communities. *Teaching Children Mathematics, 10*, 436–443.

Takahashi, A., Watanabe, T., Yoshida, M., & Wang-Iverson, P. (2005). Improving content and pedagogical knowledge through kyozaikenkyu. In P. Wang-Ivenson & M. Yoshida (Eds.), *Building our understanding of lesson study*. Philadelphia. Research for Better Schools.

Watanabe, T., Takahashi, A., & Yoshida, M. (2008). Kyozaikenkyu: a critical step for conducting effective lesson study and beyond. In F. Arbaugh & P. M. Taylor (Eds.), *Inquiry into mathematics teacher education. Association of mathematics teacher educators (AMTE) monograph series* (Vol. 5).

Yoshida, M. (1999a, April). *Lesson study [jugyokenkyu] in elementary school mathematics in Japan: a case study*. Paper presented at the American Educational Research Association Annual Meeting, Montreal, Canada.

Yoshida, M. (1999b). *Lesson study: a case study of a Japanese approach to improving instruction through school-based teacher development*. Dissertation, University of Chicago, Chicago.

Does Classroom Instruction Stick to Textbooks? A Case Study of Fraction Division

Rongjin Huang, Z. Ebrar Yetkiner Ozel, Yeping Li, and Rebecca V. Osborne

Abstract In this chapter, we examined the consistency between textbook and its implementation in classrooms. By investigating how two selected Chinese teachers taught fraction division over four consecutive lessons, and making use of an existing study on the treatments of the same content unit in textbooks, it was found that the sample teachers essentially adopted their textbooks. The teachers put great effort into developing students' understanding of the meaning of fraction division and justifying why the algorithm of fraction division works by employing a problem-based approach and using multiple representations. They followed the textbooks regarding the conceptualization of concepts and algorithms, the topic coverage, the sequence of content presentation, the approach to developing the concepts and algorithms, and the selection of problems and exercises. Meanwhile, the teachers also demonstrated certain flexibility in constructing their own problems for introducing new knowledge and consolidating the learned knowledge. Finally, the authors argued that the Chinese strategies of adopting textbooks might be attributed to their teaching culture and professional development practice.

Keywords Fraction division · Mathematics curriculum · Mathematics teaching · Mathematical tasks and representations · Curriculum implementation fidelity · Chinese mathematics teaching and learning

Background

Textbooks are seen as an important factor impacting what teachers do and, therefore, what students learn (Tarr et al. 2008). However, most teachers do not teach all

R. Huang (✉)
Middle Tennessee State University, Murfreesboro, USA
e-mail: hrj318@gmail.com

Z.E.Y. Ozel
Fatih University, Istanbul, Turkey

Y. Li · R.V. Osborne
Texas A&M University, College Station, USA

Y. Li, G. Lappan (eds.), *Mathematics Curriculum in School Education,*
Advances in Mathematics Education, DOI 10.1007/978-94-007-7560-2_21,
© Springer Science+Business Media Dordrecht 2014

topics in their textbooks. They may use the same textbooks but teach vastly different lessons; or, even when similar lessons are taught, assignments from the textbooks may be quite different (Huntley and Chval 2010; Kilpatrick 2003; Tarr et al. 2006; Thompson and Senk 2010). Variation in the implementation of a textbook is often cited as a factor that is likely to contribute to mediation of textbooks' impact on student learning (e.g., Remillard 2005). The differences in the implementation of textbooks are linked to various factors, such as state assessment pressures (Huntley and Chval 2010), lack of clarity in textbooks' intents, teachers' beliefs, teachers' prior experiences as students or as pre-service teachers, teachers' knowledge or understanding of the textbook's content and/or the pedagogy called for in the textbooks, the environment in which teachers work, and students' prior knowledge (e.g., Remillard 2005). It is this complexity that calls for studies on "coherence between the textbook and implemented curriculum; that is, consistency between curriculum and instruction is needed in order to actualize student learning in mathematics" (Tarr et al. 2008, p. 275). A written curriculum cannot fully provide guidance for teaching (e.g., Ball and Cohen 1996), and the same textbook could be implemented unevenly within and across schools (e.g., Kilpatrick 2003). Thus, implementation fidelity, the extent to which there is a match between the written curriculum and teachers' practices in the classroom, has become an important issue (National Research Council 2004). A few studies on coherence between reform-oriented or traditional textbooks and their implementation (Tarr et al. 2006; Thompson and Senk 2010) have questioned the appropriateness of textbook adaptation.

Because Chinese students have repeatedly outperformed their Western counterparts in school mathematics in various international comparative assessments (e.g., Mullis et al. 2008; OECD 2009), an examination of the implementation of Chinese textbooks may provide insight into the discussion on implementation fidelity. There are several studies on Chinese mathematics curricula and textbooks (e.g., Li et al. 2009a, 2009b; Liu and Li 2010) and some research on mathematics classroom instruction in China (Huang and Leung 2004; Leung 2005; Li and Huang 2012). Yet, little attention has been devoted to examining the features of textbook implementation. In general, as argued by Park and Leung (2006), "in many East Asian countries, teachers and students regard the textbook as a 'Bible' which contains all the essential knowledge" (p. 230) due to the centralized curriculum and assessment systems (e.g., Leung and Li 2010; Usiskin and Willmore 2008). However, little empirical research has approved or disapproved this statement. The current study is designed to investigate the learning opportunities provided by a sample of teachers and their relationship with the textbooks used. In order to sharpen the research focus, a common topic of fraction division was selected. In particular, this study is sought to address the following research questions:

(1) How is the content of fraction division presented in the selected Chinese classrooms?
(2) How is the content of fraction division enacted in the selected Chinese classrooms?
(3) How are the content focus and organization in the classrooms related to the textbooks?

Research Background

Textbook Use as Following or Subverting

As suggested by Remillard (2005), there are three different ways of examining curriculum use: use as following or subverting, use as interpretation, and use as participation. The stance of textbook use as following or subverting reviews "the written curriculum as embodying discernible and complete images of practice and examine the degree to which teachers follow these guidelines with fidelity" (Stein et al. 2007, p. 343). The view of curriculum use as interpretation holds that teachers bring their own beliefs and experiences to create their own meanings of textbooks, and they implement textbooks based on their interpretation of the authors' intentions. Thus, this notion assumes that it is impossible to examine the fidelity between written teaching materials and classroom action. The third view of curriculum use as participation suggests that use of curriculum materials is a kind of collaboration with the materials. Central to this perspective is the assumption that teachers and curriculum materials are engaged in a dynamic interrelationship.

Given the nature of our research questions, the stance of textbook use as following or subverting was more suitable. The question that now arises is "how far may teachers go in their adaptations without destroying the spirit and meaning of the curriculum they implement in their class?" (Ben-Peretz 1990, p. 31). Tarr et al. (2006) found that their sample of teachers taught 60 to 70 % of the textbooks. Teachers often supplement the textbook, omit problems or sections, and change the order of the lesson presented in textbooks based on different considerations (Huntley and Chval 2010; Tarr et al. 2006). Thus, the key goal is supporting teachers in making well-informed, purposeful decisions that benefit students' learning of mathematics (Huntley and Chval 2010). An examination of the implementation of textbooks in China, where there is a high-achieving education system, may provide some suggestions.

In a previous study, Li et al. (2009a, 2009b) examined the textbook treatments of fraction division in China, Japan, and the US. Building on their findings, this study will focus on an examination of fraction division teaching and observe the extent to which the characteristics of fraction division teaching in classrooms are in line with the treatments of fraction division in textbooks.

Teaching and Learning of Fraction Division

Learning of Fraction Division Developing a conceptual understanding of the algorithm of fraction division is a difficult task for both students and teachers (e.g., Carpenter et al. 1989; Li and Kulm 2008). Even though teachers can perform computations of fraction division, it is difficult for them, at least in the United States, to explain the computation of fraction division conceptually and with appropriate representations or connections to their mathematical knowledge (Ma 1999). Researchers have suggested different approaches to help students learn how to divide fractions, including (1) providing mathematical justifications for the fraction division algorithm and (2) using concrete or visual demonstrations to explain how fraction division can be computed through extending the whole-number division to fraction division with the measurement interpretation and the partitive interpretation (Li 2008).

Treatments of Fraction Division in Textbooks In their study, Li et al. (2009a, 2009b) examined the ways of dealing with fraction division in Chinese, Japanese, and US textbooks. The researchers examined three Chinese, three Japanese, and four US textbooks in great detail using a two-level framework. At the macro level, they identified how content topics were placed and organized. At the micro level, they examined how fraction division was conceptualized, which focused on the content topic introduction and potential use of representations and/or examples. In addition, the learning progression—the coverage and sequence of topics presented—was also examined.

Li et al. (2009a, 2009b) found that their sample of Chinese and Japanese textbooks developed fraction division as an inverse operation of fraction multiplication and prominently used examples to illustrate the relationship between the two operations using the "one problem, multiple solutions" approach. In contrast, the focus of US textbooks was on the computational process of fraction division by extending previous understandings of division involving whole numbers. In the US, the concept of division of fractions was either explained directly or through the use of pictorial representations. Thus, the Chinese approach emphasized the mathematical structures of and the relationship between fraction division and multiplication, whereas the US approaches emphasized the computation procedures.

Although both Chinese and US textbooks emphasized multiple representations, the US textbooks generally used pictorial representations to demonstrate the computation process of fraction division while the Chinese textbooks primarily used pictorial representations to develop the concept of fraction division and to explain why the algorithm works. In addition, the Chinese textbooks emphasized the problem-solving approach in the presentation of fraction division content and tended to include larger number and more difficult problems than the US textbooks.

A Framework for Examining Classroom Instruction

A variety of theories and approaches could be used to examine classroom instruction (Richardson 2001). Some studies have focused on investigating the nature of mathematics classroom (Clarke et al. 2006; Cobb and Bauersfeld 1995; Hiebert et al. 2003), while others were aimed at characterizing pedagogical contracts (e.g., Boaler 1998). Due to the purposes of the current study (i.e., examining the nature and characteristics of fraction division teaching and their connections to textbooks used), by reference to the framework used by Li et al. (2009a, 2009b), we will focus our literature review on (1) learning progression of fraction division, (2) mathematics tasks (examples and exercises), and (3) representations.

Learning Trajectory   Building on the social constructivist theory, Simon and his collaborators (Simon 1995; Simon and Tzur 2004; Simon et al. 2004) have developed a theory on designing and implementing lessons based on the notion of Learning Trajectory (LT) (Simon and Tzur 2004; Simon et al. 2004). The LT has three components: "the learning goal that defines the direction, the learning activities, and the hypothetical learning process—a prediction of how the students' understanding will evolve in the context of the learning activities" (Simon 1995, p. 136). In the context of fraction division, different conceptualization approaches project different learning trajectories. In the current study, the instructional objectives stated in lesson plans and learning progressions uncovered in the videotaped lessons were examined to depict learning trajectories constructed in classrooms.

Mathematical Tasks and Student Learning   The role mathematical tasks play in engaging students in mathematical thinking and reasoning about substantial concepts and ideas has been realized and investigated for a long time (Doyle 1983, 1988; Hiebert and Wearne 1993; Stein and Lane 1996). Mathematical tasks are fundamental to learning because "tasks convey messages about what mathematics is and what doing mathematics entails" (National Council of Teachers of Mathematics [NCTM] 1991, p. 24). Mathematical tasks can provide a learning environment in which students engage in and develop mathematical concepts and mathematical thinking. Mathematical tasks have potential influences on students' thinking and can broaden, or restrict, their ideas and perspectives on subject matters (Henningsen and Stein 1997). A theory of mathematics teaching, called *teaching with variation*, has been in place for several decades in China (Gu et al. 2004). This theory emphasizes developing knowledge and building essential connections among relevant concepts through working with systematic and interconnected problems that focus on critical features of the objects of learning. Although mathematical tasks generally include projects, questions, constructions, applications, and student exercises, in this study tasks are used to refer to problems (including examples) and exercises. We examined the features of classroom instruction through investigating how teachers developed new knowledge through launching and implementing mathematical tasks.

Pedagogical Representations and Student Learning   In addition to use of mathematics tasks, pedagogical representation is a widely used aspect for exploring classroom instruction. When we speak of pedagogical representations, we mean representations used by teachers and students in the classroom. Pedagogical representations are helpful in explaining or illustrating concepts, connections, relationships, or problem solving processes (Cuoco and Curcio 2001). Some representations may be more powerful than others for teaching particular concepts (Leinhardt 2001). Thus, what representations to use and how to use them are important decisions a teacher makes when selecting instructional strategies for a mathematics classroom.

Recently, an attempt to examine how Chinese and US teachers conceptualized and constructed pedagogical representations for mathematics instruction (Cai 2005; Cai and Wang 2006; Huang and Cai 2011) shed insight into understanding of mathematics instruction. Accordingly, in this study we investigated how teachers taught fraction division through examining how they constructed and used representations in the classroom.

The Current Study

In the current study, we examined how selected Chinese teachers taught fraction division regarding: (1) the structure of fraction division in classroom teaching, namely, instructional objectives and the sequence of content knowledge presentation (answering research question #1); (2) the development of the content by examining mathematics tasks and pedagogical representations (answering research question #2). In addition, we examined the connections between the characteristics of fraction division teaching in Chinese classrooms (findings derived from the current data analysis) and the treatment of division of fractions in Chinese textbooks (findings by Li et al. 2009a, 2009b) (answering research question #3).

Method

Data Sources

The data consisted of eight videotaped lessons taught by two Chinese teachers and their corresponding lesson plans, selected from a larger project investigating cross-cultural (Chinese and US teachers') lesson planning and classroom instruction. A total of seven elementary schools from two Chinese provinces participated in the larger research project (Li et al. 2009a, 2009b). With the guidance of Chinese mathematics education experts, the sample schools were selected so that they represented a large range of school qualities based on their reputations. Each selected school received an invitation to the project and an explanation of the objectives, procedures, and instruments used for data collection. For the current study, we selected two teachers based on the reputation of their schools and their teaching experiences so that they represented an average level of teaching.

Each of the two teachers selected for this study taught four consecutive lessons that were videotaped by one of the researchers. These two teachers were from elementary schools located in two different provinces. The first elementary school was located in a suburban area of a medium-sized city; however, the school was in the process of transformation. The school used to serve a student population mainly from the rural areas adjacent to the city, but it has now started to serve some of the urban areas as well. In terms of the school's location, the community it served, students' test scores, and perceived teachers' quality, the school had an average standing in that province. The teacher from the first school (Teacher A) had 8 years of teaching experience. The second school was located in a rural area in another province; its quality was judged as below average for that province. Teacher B, who was from the second school, was a promising teacher with 19 years of teaching experience. There were roughly 45 students in each class.

Data Analysis

We used the videotaped lessons and transcripts as our data sources. One researcher watched the videos and read corresponding transcripts to get an understanding of the Chinese lessons. Then, the researcher identified the main contents of all of the lessons and developed a concept map of teaching division of fractions. We made a detailed examination of all four consecutive lessons from each Chinese teacher with extra attention paid to the content connection and variation across lessons. We examined the use of mathematics tasks for introducing, developing, and consolidating fraction division. Meanwhile, we also examined how teachers constructed pedagogical representations when solving problems. The types of representations included in the lessons were algebraic/symbolic, numeric/tabular, graphic, and verbal/literal (Cuoco and Curcio 2001).

Results

The results are presented in three sections. In the first section, we report the development of a learning trajectory for division of fractions. The second section concerns common features of fraction division teaching in the sample Chinese classrooms. The third section reports an analysis of the relationship between how division of fractions is taught in classrooms and how it is treated in textbooks.

Learning Trajectory Constructed in the Classrooms

Content Coverage and Instructional Objectives   The two Chinese teachers, Teacher A and Teacher B, spent four lessons teaching fraction division in a similar manner. The content arrangement and relevant instructional objectives based on lesson plans are displayed in Table 1.

Table 1 shows that Chinese teachers covered essentially the same content and instructional objectives: understanding the meaning of fraction division and the relationship between multiplication and division; understanding and mastering the computational rules for dividing a fraction by a whole number (F/WN); understanding

Table 1 The content arrangement and instructional objectives in the Chinese lessons

Teacher	Lesson 1	Lesson 2	Lesson 3	Lesson 4
A	Understanding the meaning of fraction division and the relationship between multiplication and division; Understanding and mastering the computational rules for dividing fractions by whole numbers (F/WN)	Understanding and mastering the computational rules for dividing whole numbers by fractions (WN/F)	Understanding and mastering the computational rules for dividing fractions by fractions (F/F)	Mastering the methods of solving word problems using fraction division; Understanding comparison of fractions
B	The meaning of fraction division; The relationship between multiplication and division; The algorithm of F/WN and its justification	Understanding the meaning and algorithm of WN/F	Synthesizing the algorithm of F/F; Problem posing and problem solving; Solving word problems	Dividing mixed numbers by mixed numbers; Understanding of comparison of fractions.

and mastering the computational rules for dividing a whole number by a fraction (WN/F); understanding and mastering the computational rules for dividing a fraction by a fraction (F/F); and mastering word problem solving and comparison of fractions before and after division by a fraction. Their developments of these contents were also quite similar, except for the minor differences in emphasis.

Learning Progression for Fraction Division

Both lesson plans and videotaped lessons revealed that the teachers followed a pattern (see Fig. 1) explicitly. The two Chinese teachers made efforts to develop fraction division: (1) developing the concept of fraction division based on students' prior knowledge (meaning of whole number division and the relationship between multiplication and division) (Lesson 1); (2) developing the algorithms coherently and systematically from F/WN (Lesson 1), WN/F (Lesson 2), to F/F (Lesson 3), and (3) applying the algorithms to different contexts such as word problems and comparison of fractions (Lessons 3 and 4). The key of learning fraction division was to understand that the meanings of fraction division and whole number division were the same, and that division is the inverse operation of multiplication. Then, ways of learning about the whole number division were analogized and adapted to fraction division. Second, by effectively using the pictorial representation (segment diagram), the meaning of a fraction and the meaning of division were explicated to help students understand WN/F (lesson 1), WN/F (lesson 2), and F/F (lesson 3). In

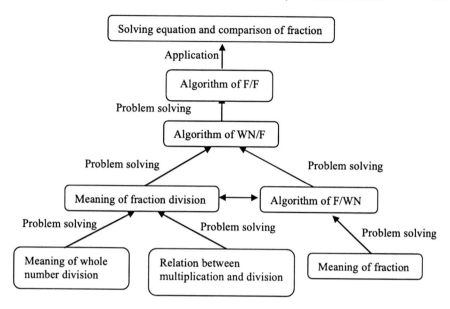

Fig. 1 The concept map of DoF development

this way, the fraction division concept and algorithm were built on and developed from the basic concept of whole number division, the meaning of a fraction, and the relationship between division and multiplication. So, different kinds of knowledge were interconnected. And finally, the new knowledge was linked to problem solving and comparison of fractions. Thus, students' knowledge of fraction division was strengthened and re-structured. This relationship is displayed in Fig. 1.

Characteristics of Fraction Division Teaching

The Lesson Structure

By and large, the two teachers shared a similar teaching pattern, which included (1) reviewing previous lesson's content or relevant knowledge for learning the new topic, (2) introducing the new topic through solving mathematical problems related to everyday life, (3) practicing new knowledge with a variety of interconnected problems and summarizing relevant key points or contents in the lesson, and (4) assigning homework. In the sections that follow, we describe the main procedures of the four consecutive lessons of Teacher A.

Lesson 1   After starting with a review of the meaning of whole number division and doing some relevant mental computations, the teacher posted two word problems with pictorial representations: (1) If each of five people eats half a cake, how

Fig. 2 The segment diagram
representing $(4/5) \div 2 =$
$(4 \div 2)/5$

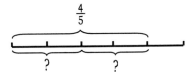

much do they eat in total? (2) Can you pose two division problems based on the
above information? Students produced three numerical expressions ($5 \times \frac{1}{2} = \frac{5}{2}$;
$\frac{5}{2} \div 5 = \frac{1}{2}$; $\frac{5}{2} \div \frac{1}{2} = 5$) as they solved the problems. Students were then led to
discover *the meaning of fraction division* and were subsequently asked to read this
statement from the textbook in chorus.

The class moved on to explore the algorithm of dividing a fraction by a whole
number as they worked on word problems in groups. Four different solutions to the
same problem were discussed: (a) $\frac{4}{5} \div 2 = \frac{4}{5} \div \frac{2}{1} = \frac{4 \div 2}{5} = \frac{2}{5}$; (b) using a segment
diagram to demonstrate the meaning of $\frac{4}{5}$ and to divide it into two parts (of size $\frac{2}{5}$)
(see Fig. 2); (c) using the equivalence, that is "Dividing $\frac{4}{5}$ by 2 is equal to $\frac{1}{2}$ of $\frac{4}{5}$"
(i.e., $\frac{4}{5} \div 2 = \frac{4}{5} \times \frac{1}{2}$); and (d) transformation of the equivalence into a decimal operation (i.e., $0.8 \div 2 = 0.4$). This discussion led to the formulation of two common
strategies: (1) If the numerator of the fraction is a multiplier of a whole-number divisor, then the quotient equals a fraction with a numerator that is dividing the original
numerator by the divisor while the denominator remains the same; and (2) Dividing
a fraction by a whole number is equal to the fraction times the reciprocal of the
whole number.

Students followed with a variation of the previous word problem so that they le-
gitimized that the second strategy was more convenient and applicable. Moreover,
the teacher asked students to read this *computational rule* in chorus (it was emphasized that the divisor cannot be equal to zero). After that, students worked on several
exercises from the textbook and some extra problems as they competed in groups or
as individual seat-work followed by sharing their work in class. Finally, the teacher
summarized the key points of the lesson.

Lesson 2   After reviewing the meaning of fraction division and computational
rules for dividing fractions by whole numbers, two word problems from the textbook were discussed. The purpose of the first problem was to review whole number
division using the quantitative relationship among velocity (V), time (T), and distance (S) (i.e., $S = VT$). The second problem was designed to explore the new
topic, which was dividing whole numbers by fractions ($v = s/t = 12 \div \frac{1}{5}$). Students presented three different ways of computing $12 \div \frac{1}{5}$: (a) $12 \div 0.2 = 60$;
(b) $12 \div \frac{1}{5} = 12 \times 5 = 60$; and (c) using a segment diagram including five equal
parts, each of them presenting the distance in $1/5$ hours (similar to Fig. 2).

Students were also asked to explain different numerical expressions of dividing
whole numbers by fractions (e.g., $7 \div \frac{1}{4} = 28$; $24 \div \frac{3}{4}$) using a segment diagram.
Based on previous discussions, the computational rule of fraction division was sum-

Fig. 3 Diagram representing the relationship between time and distance

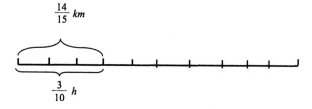

marized. Then, the class worked on several exercises on dividing a whole number by a fraction.

Lesson 3   After a review of the previously learned computational rules of fraction division (i.e., $\frac{4}{5} \div 3 = \frac{4}{5} \times \frac{1}{3}$; $4 \div \frac{1}{3} = 4 \times 3$), students identified the commonality among these rules: changing division into multiplication and changing the divisor into its reciprocal. Then, the teacher asked students to read out a word problem from their textbook (i.e., Xiaoming walks 14/15 km in 3/10 hours, how far does he walk in one hour?), and students were asked to express the relation using fraction division (e.g., $\frac{14}{15} \div \frac{3}{10}$). Students were encouraged to make conjectures on how to perform the fraction operation and to justify their conjectures. By using a segment diagram (the teacher drew on the board, see Fig. 3), students were asked to explain the following procedure:

$$\frac{14}{15} \div \frac{3}{10} = \frac{14}{15} \div 3 \times 10 = \frac{14}{15} \times \frac{1}{3} \times 10 = \frac{14}{15} \times \frac{10}{3}$$

The teacher assigned several exercises from the textbook (such as, $\frac{2}{7} \div \frac{5}{6}$; $\frac{1}{12} \div \frac{4}{15}$); several students were invited to write their solutions on the board, and then students' solutions were discussed in the class.

After completing exercises, students were encouraged to summarize the computational rule of fraction division using different representations: Dividing a number by a fraction is equal to the number multiplied by the reciprocal of the divisor (in word); $A \div B(B \neq 0) = A \times \frac{1}{B}$ (in symbol). In particular, students noted the divisor could not be zero. Then, students were asked to read the computational rule in chorus from their textbook.

Subsequently, the students were asked to do more exercises from the textbook, and some students were invited to write their solutions on the board (the teacher explicitly emphasized that it was necessary to increase their computational speed when mastering computational procedures). Finally, the solutions were discussed, and the teacher summarized some key points.

Lesson 4   Starting with a review of the fraction division rule, students were then asked to change four fraction division problems into multiplication problems orally. Subsequently, the teacher presented the topic for the current lesson: word problems. The teacher presented a problem (If 3/8 of a given number is 1/4, what is the given number?) that required students to use two methods (i.e., $\frac{3}{8}x = \frac{1}{4}$; or $\frac{1}{4} \div \frac{3}{8}$) in the solution. The teacher summarized that there were two methods to solve problems such as "Given a proportion of a number, find out the number."

The teacher then presented four word problems to be solved using equations. Students wrote their solutions on the board, and the teacher commented on the solutions. The teacher then presented four fill in the blank problems for students to solve (e.g., 1/3 is 5/6 of ( )?). Students were asked to compare the fraction division expression with the original dividend (e.g., $\frac{6}{7}$ with $\frac{6}{7} \div 3$; 9 with $9 \div \frac{3}{4}$; $\frac{1}{2}$ with $\frac{1}{2} \div \frac{2}{3}$; $\frac{14}{15}$ with $\frac{14}{15} \div \frac{7}{30}$). With this exercise, it was intended to lead students to realize that dividing by a fraction less than 1 would result in the quotient's increase and dividing by a fraction larger than 1 would result in the quotient's decrease. After that, the teacher assigned similar exercises from the textbook.

The Common Features of Fraction Division Teaching in China

A detailed description of the four lessons by Teacher B can be found in Appendix. After comparing the lessons by the two teachers, we found that there were more commonalities than differences. The common features included: developing students' understanding of the algorithm through solving word problems, consolidating the algorithm through systematic and varying exercises, and deepening students' understanding of the algorithm through purposefully selected representations.

Developing the Algorithm As indicated in the concept map of fraction division (Fig. 1), problem solving is an often-used strategy for introducing, developing, and consolidating knowledge. These two teachers consistently introduced and developed knowledge (concepts and algorithms) by exploring word problems. For example, in lesson 1, in order to explore the meaning of fraction division, both Teacher A and Teacher B used word problems. Both teachers (in lesson 3 by teacher A while in lesson 4 by teacher B) presented word problems that required equations in their solutions, such as "3 times a number is $\frac{2}{5}$. Find the number."

In order to explore the algorithm of F/WN, Teacher A used two word problems: (1) Divide a rope of $\frac{4}{5}$ meter into two equal parts. How long is each part? and (2) Divide a rope of $\frac{4}{5}$ meter into three equal parts. How long is each part?

Again, in lessons 2 and 3, both teachers used word problems to introduce the algorithm of WN/F and F/F. For example, Teacher A used the problem "A pigeon flies 1.2 km in 1/5 hours. What is the velocity of the pigeon?" ($v = s/t = 1.2 \div \frac{1}{5}$) to introduce WN/F, and another word problem, "A butterfly flies 13/14 km in 3/10 hours. How far can it fly per hour? " to explore F/F. Similarly, Teacher B used the word problems "If a train travels 60 kilometers per hour, then how far does it travel in 3/4 hour?" and "If a train travels 45 km in 3/4 hours, how far does it travel per hour?" to introduce WN/F, and another word problem, "One red silk belt measures $\frac{9}{10}$ m. If $\frac{3}{10}$ m red silk belt is needed to make a Chinese tie, how many ties can be made from this belt?" to introduce F/F.

In both teachers' lessons, there was a common effort to encourage students to find multiple solutions to the same problem. Through comparing different solutions, the most reasonable solution was emphasized (usually it was related to an appropriate computational rule). For example, in lesson 1, both teachers explored the computational rule of F/WN through solving word problems. Although students found two strategies, the second strategy (i.e., the rule for F/WN: the fraction times the reciprocal of the whole number) was more convenient and applicable. Thus, the introduction of the rule for F/WN was justified. In lessons 2 and 3, both teachers encouraged students to find different methods to solve the same problem. As a result, new computational rules were discovered, and different concepts and knowledge were applied to develop a deeper understanding. For example, in Teacher B's second lesson, three solutions to the problem "If a train travels 45 km in 3/4 hours, how far does it travel per hour?" were explored:

$$45 \div 3 \times 4 = 45 \times \frac{1}{3} \times 4 = 60 \text{ (km)}; \qquad 45 \div 3 + 45 = 60 \text{ (km)}$$

$$45 \div \frac{3}{4} = 45 \times \frac{4}{3} = 60 \text{ (km)}; \qquad x \times \frac{3}{4} = 45 \text{ (km)}.$$

Thus, $45 \div \frac{3}{4} = 45 \times \frac{4}{3}$ (i.e., the rule of WN/F) was discovered and justified. Also, the relationship between the parts and the whole unit was demonstrated by a segment diagram (similar to Fig. 2).

Consolidating the Algorithm   In each lesson, there were many classroom exercises for enhancing and applying learned knowledge. The following features were found in common: (1) practice problems were mainly selected from the textbook, though some of them were created by teachers; (2) classroom exercises were conducted in various forms, such as individual work, group work, or competition. Usually, the answers were presented on the board and discussed in class; and (3) types of problems varied, with a focus on the learned content. For example, in lesson 3 of Teacher B, classroom exercises included (1) basic exercises (e.g., $\frac{2}{7} \div () = \frac{2}{7} \times \frac{1}{7}$); (2) computation and reasoning (judging if an equation or inequality is tenable: for example, $\frac{1}{2} \div \frac{3}{5} = \frac{1}{2} \div \frac{5}{3}$, $\frac{2}{5} \times \frac{1}{5} < \frac{2}{5} \div \frac{1}{5}$); (3) word problems that required solving equations (e.g., $\frac{1}{3}x = \frac{4}{9}$, $5x = \frac{4}{9}$), and (4) an open-ended problem. The following open-ended problem was presented as group-work:

If the area of the shaded part in the diagram on the right is 28 square meters, what questions can you pose? How can you solve them?

Students, working in groups of four, raised the following questions and solutions:

(1) The area of each shaded block? ($28 \div 7 =$?)
(2) The area of the large rectangle? ($28 \div \frac{7}{9} =$?)
(3) What is the area of the blank part of the large rectangle? ($2 \times (28 \div 7) =$? or $28 \div \frac{7}{9} - 28 =$? or $(28 \div \frac{7}{9}) \times \frac{2}{9} =$?)

When arranging and solving problems, we observed characteristics that were common to both teachers. They developed new problems based on a prototype of problems and encouraged students to search for multiple solutions to problems.

Developing the Algorithms through Purposeful Use of Representations The two teachers purposefully used different representations to develop the algorithm of fraction division. In lesson 1, both teachers basically used verbal and numerical representations to review the meaning of whole number division and to develop the meaning of fraction division. The teachers also used pictorial representations and/or a physical model (for example, Teacher A used a half circle representing half a cake, a segment diagram representing the partitioning of ropes, and a physical rope to demonstrate the partitioning of a rope). In lesson 2, both teachers paid great attention to using segment diagrams to develop the algorithm for WN/F. In lesson 3, the teachers used either a segment diagram (Teacher A) or a pictorial representation (Teacher B) to develop the algorithm and solve problems. In lesson 4, symbolic and verbal representations were extensively used to solve equations and to compare fraction values.

It seems that these two teachers used representations selectively and hierarchically: from physical representations to pictorial representations to symbolic and verbal representations. The pictorial and physical representations were only used to develop the algorithm of fraction division. After the algorithm was discovered and justified, they used symbolic/numerical representations for application.

The Relationship Between Textbooks and Classroom Teaching

We presented the relations between textbooks used and classroom teaching from three aspects: (1) the ways of conceptualizing fraction division; (2) the ways of selecting and using mathematical tasks (examples and exercises); and (3) the ways of using representations.

Teacher A used one of the three textbooks examined by Li et al. (2009a, 2009b), and Teacher B used another of the three textbooks. These teachers not only did directly choose workout examples and class exercises from their textbooks but also asked students to read aloud the computation rules stated in the textbooks. Particularly, Teacher B explicitly required students to read the textbook before class. As a result, there was a strong consistency between the textbooks and classroom instruction. Considering findings of Li et al. (2009a, 2009b) and findings of the current study, we identified the following consistencies.

First, over four lessons both teachers put great efforts to progressively develop students' understanding of the meaning of fraction division, the relationship between division and multiplication, and why the algorithm of fraction division worked. This is fairly consistent with the intention of Chinese textbooks (Li et al. 2009a, 2009b).

Second, the Chinese teachers organized word problem solving activities to guide students to discover and justify the algorithm for division of fractions from simple (F/WN) to complex situations (F/F) using different approaches. They both encouraged students to find multiple solutions to the same problem and to recognize the invariant pattern (i.e., computation rule) through comparing different solutions. This feature reflects Chinese textbooks' design that develop division of fractions as an inverse operation of fraction multiplication through solving problems using multiple methods, namely the "one problem, multiple solutions" approach (Li et al. 2009a, p. 824). Meanwhile, these teachers either had students complete some of the textbook exercises in class and/or assigned them as homework. However, teachers paid close attention to some problems in textbooks. For example, both teachers treated "identifying the relationship between quotient and dividend when the divisor increases or decreases" (Li et al. 2009a, p. 823) as an opportunity to develop students' ability to observe and discover. Moreover, they also deliberately designed some problems based on other published teaching materials or their own lesson plans. The open-ended problem posing and solving given by Teacher B (lesson 3) was one example.

Third, the use of different representations (e.g., psychical, pictorial, numerical) in these lessons was intended to help students understand the process of problem solving and why the algorithm worked, which was in line with the intention of the textbooks (Li et al. 2009a, 2009b).

In summary, textbooks had important influences on Chinese teachers' classroom teaching in terms of content coverage, teaching objectives, principles of developing content/learning trajectories, and teaching strategies. Overall, classroom teaching essentially stuck to the textbooks. However, there were some variations and flexibilities in terms of emphasis on certain content points, selection of problems, and assignment of homework. In particular, the teachers adopted some challenging mathematics problems from other resources or adjusted some classroom exercises to meet students' needs. This situation is coined as a Chinese saying, "Teaching should be derived from textbooks, but exceed textbooks."

Conclusion and Discussion

Based on the analysis of selected Chinese teachers' teaching of fraction division, we came to the following conclusions. The Chinese teachers (1) put great effort into developing students' understanding of the meaning of fraction division and their justification of why the algorithm of fraction division works (as inverse operation of fraction multiplication); (2) adopted a problem-based approach to develop the meaning of fraction division, to justify the algorithm, and then to apply the algorithm; and (3) used multiple representations strategically (i.e., visual representations to scaffold the development of algorithms and symbolic representations for extensive applications of algorithms).

A consistency between textbooks and their implementation in classrooms was found regarding the coverage of contents, content development, and selection and use of problems and exercises. The Chinese teachers followed the fundamental principles of their textbooks, such as conceptualizing fraction division as the inverse operation of fraction multiplication and developing the meanings and algorithms of fraction division through word problems. In addition, pictorial representations were used to show why the algorithm of fraction division worked, which also mirrored the textbook treatment. However, the teachers demonstrated flexibility in selecting and constructing examples and exercises.

Given the fact that textbooks in China are official and mandated (Liu and Li 2010), it is not surprising that the sample teachers taught classes by following their textbook seriously. Interestingly, teachers not only followed the sequence of content presentation in the textbook smoothly but also implemented the fundamental principles presented in textbooks essentially. For example, the teachers conceptualized division of fractions as an inverse operation of fraction multiplication as it was presented in textbooks (Li et al. 2009a, 2009b). The teachers adopted problem-based approach to develop the concept and algorithm of fraction division consistently. Surprisingly, the Chinese teachers put much emphasis on the conceptual understanding of such a procedure-oriented content over four lessons. The practice may imply that the Chinese teachers pay great attention to developing students' conceptual understanding and procedural fluency simultaneously.

Use of the Problem-Based Approach Consistently

Emphasis on solving problems and altering problems to promote multiple perspectives are traditional features of Chinese mathematics classrooms (Cai and Nie 2007; Huang et al. 2006), and these approaches were also valued in textbooks (Li et al. 2009a, 2009b; Sun 2011). The core of teaching with variation, a widely adopted teaching method in China, is to vary problems systematically and strategically to promote students' learning (Gu et al. 2004). The problem-based approach is well-recognized as a mathematics learning and teaching method around the world (e.g., Baroody and Dowker 2003; Shimizu 2009); it may make a difference in creating opportunities for students to learn if this approach is valued in both textbooks and classroom instruction intentionally.

Using Representations Flexibly

This study may provide an explanation to why Chinese students prefer using symbolic representation when solving problems (Cai 2005) because Chinese teachers treat concrete representation as scaffolding for developing algorithms, and then they will use symbolic/abstract representations for application of knowledge. Huang and Cai (2011) found that the Chinese teacher in their study tended to use representations selectively based on the nature of problems, while the U.S. teacher in the study tended to use multiple representations simultaneously. Developing students' ability using multiple representations has been called for decades for the development of mathematics knowledge and problem solving (Cuoco and Curcio 2001; Lesh et al. 1987). The use of representations in Chinese textbooks and classrooms suggest that it is crucial to adopt representations purposefully and flexibly, rather than the multiplicity of representations.

Adaptation of Textbooks Strategically

Let us consider "how far may teachers go in their adaptations without destroying the spirit and meaning of the curriculum they implement in their classes?" (Ben-Peretz 1990, p. 31). Although it is difficult, if not impossible, to answer this question precisely, the Chinese practice may shed light on addressing this issue. Firstly, it is crucial to follow the fundamental principles presented in textbooks, such as conceptualizing fraction division as an inverse operation of fraction multiplication, adopting the word problem-based approach, and using pictorial representations to develop the algorithm. Second, introductory problems, examples, and exercises should be used carefully with attention to their purpose and roles and considering students' knowledge readiness and ability. Third, teachers should be encouraged to construct their own examples and exercise problems based on their knowledge of students and pedagogy to individualize their teaching (such as by decreasing or increasing cognitive demands of problems). Considering these factors may help teachers in adapting textbooks in their classes appropriately without destroying the intents of textbooks.

Developing Knowledge and Capacity in Adapting Textbooks

Responding to the call to support teachers in making "well-informed, purposeful decisions (that is, acceptable adaptation) to benefit students' learning of mathematics " (Huntley and Chval 2010, p. 301), it is necessary to realize the importance of studying teaching materials (Ma 1999). In Ma's seminal work, she attributed Chinese elementary teachers' profound understanding of fundamental mathematics to four main factors, including: studying teaching materials intensively, learning mathematics from colleagues, learning mathematics from students, and learning mathematics by doing it. In China, it is fundamentally important to extensively study teaching materials (including textbooks, teaching and learning frameworks, and teachers' manuals) (Ma 1999). Ding et al. (2012) further found that Chinese teachers' knowledge and understanding of mathematics instructional content is mainly attained through intensive studies of textbooks under a supporting professional development system. The sample teachers in their study viewed the "study of textbooks" as an exploration of knowledge beyond textual information, which included (1) identifying the important and difficult points of teaching a lesson, (2) studying the purposes of each worked example and practice problem, (3) exploring the reasons behind certain textbook information, and (4) exploring the best approaches, from the perspectives of students, to present examples. Such a profound understanding of textbooks may help teachers to make appropriate and effective decisions in adapting textbooks to prompt students' learning.

Methodology of Studying Implementation Fidelity

Previous studies mainly conducted surveys, interviews, and classroom observations (Huntley and Chval 2010; Tarr et al. 2006) as their methodologies to study textbook implementation but paid less attention to the teaching of specific contents. In contrast, this study extends efforts to examine *implementation fidelity* through investigating what really happens in the classroom. Focusing on a specific topic over consecutive lessons may provide an additional way of researching implementation of textbooks.

In conclusion, the sample teachers essentially adapted their textbooks. They followed the textbooks regarding the conceptualization of concepts and algorithms, the topic coverage, the sequence of content presentation, the approach to developing the concepts and algorithms, and the selection of problems and exercises. The teachers also demonstrated certain flexibility in constructing their own problems for introducing and consolidating new knowledge. The strategies of adapting textbooks may be related to their teaching culture and professional development practice. Extensively studying teaching materials may be an effective way to develop teachers' knowledge of and capability in adapting textbooks in their classrooms.

Appendix: Brief Description of Teacher B's Lessons

Lesson 1 Two methods of fraction division were discussed via a word problem. The teacher asked students to state the meaning of fraction division and the relationship between multiplication and division. After explicitly expressing that the meaning of fraction division was the same as the meaning of whole number division, and fraction division was the inverse operation of fraction multiplication, the teacher led the class to discuss the algorithm of dividing a fraction by a whole number.

Then, the teacher asked students to express the algorithm for dividing a fraction by a whole number. To practice this algorithm, students posed several problems related to dividing a fraction by a whole number (e.g., $\frac{2}{7} \div 3$, $\frac{4}{9} \div 2$) and discussed their solutions and justification in terms of two classifications (i.e., when the numerator is divisible by the divisor and when it is not). For example, students explained why the following procedure worked: $\frac{4}{9} \div 2 = \frac{4 \div 2}{9} = \frac{2}{9}$. Students explained the procedure according to the meaning of fraction and whole number division. In order to help students understand why dividing a fraction by a whole number is equal to the fraction times the reciprocal of the whole number, the teacher organized a hands-on demonstration activity: one student was asked to classify 12 magnetic pads into 3 equal groups, and another student was asked to take away one third of the 12 magnetic pads.

Through comparing the two methods of arranging magnetic blocks, students realized that dividing a fraction by a whole number was equal to the fraction times the reciprocal of the whole number. Then, three types of exercise problems were organized: questions for oral answers, word application problems, and competition problems.

Lesson 2 Beginning with a word problem, the class explored the meaning and algorithm of dividing a fraction by a fraction. The problem was used to recall the method of using a diagram to represent the quantitative relationship between a standard (unit) quantity, partial rate, and partial quantity (similar to Fig. 3). The teacher presented another word problem as follows: If a train runs 45 km in 3/4 hours, how far does it run per hour? By using a similar diagram, students found three solutions to the problem and justified $45 \div \frac{3}{4} = 45 \times \frac{4}{3}$.

Based on this discussion, students discovered the algorithm of dividing a whole number by a fraction. Immediately, the teacher assigned a similar word problem for students to solve, and students presented their three solutions on a small board.

Lesson 3 The lesson began with a review of dividing fractions by whole numbers and dividing whole numbers by fractions. The teacher presented one word problem (i.e., There is a red silk strip measuring 9 over 10 meter in length. If making one Chinese tie requires 3 over 10 of a red silk strip, how many Chinese ties can be made using the strip? How can this problem be expressed numerically? The answer to the question resulted in the following numerical expression: $\frac{9}{10} \div \frac{3}{10} = \frac{9}{10} \times \frac{10}{3} = 3$. Then, the teacher asked students to generalize this rule by providing another concrete example. Finally, the rule of fraction division was synthesized in general:

> Dividing a number A by a number B is equal to the number A times the reciprocal of the number B ($B \neq 0$).

After that, students worked on several different types of exercises: basic exercises, comparing sizes of two expressions (e.g., $\frac{1}{2} \div \frac{3}{5} = \frac{1}{2} \div \frac{5}{3}$, $\frac{2}{5} \times \frac{1}{5} < \frac{2}{5} \div \frac{1}{5}$), open-ended problems, and word problem solutions (e.g., $\frac{1}{3}x = \frac{4}{9}$, $5x = \frac{4}{9}$).

Lesson 4 After reviewing the rules of fraction division, the teacher presented several fraction division expressions that included at least one mixed number (e.g., $\frac{7}{8} \div 1\frac{5}{6}$; $4\frac{2}{7} \div 1\frac{11}{14}$). Students worked on these problems individually and shared their solutions (some corrections were made). Then, the rule for division of mixed numbers was summarized: first transforming the mixed number to an improper fraction, then using the rule of fraction division.

Then, some exercises from the textbook were assigned to four student groups to be solved, and the results were checked in class. After that, the class discussed two sets of computation problems to make the following observations: (1) When dividing by a fraction less than 1, the quotients will increase, and when dividing by a fraction larger than 1, the quotients will decrease; (2) When the denominators are the same, the larger the numerator is, the larger the fraction is. On the other hand, when the numerators are the same, the larger the denominator is, the smaller the fraction is.

References

Ball, D. L., & Cohen, D. K. (1996). Reform by the book: what is—or might be—the role of curriculum materials in teacher learning and instruction reform? *Educational Researchers, 25*(9), 6–8, 14.

Baroody, A. J., & Dowker, A. (Eds.) (2003). *The development of arithmetic concepts and skills: constructing adaptive expertise.* Mahwah: Lawrence Erlbaum.

Ben-Peretz, M. (1990). *The teacher-curriculum encounter: freeing teachers from the tyranny of texts.* Albany: State University of New York Press.

Boaler, J. (1998). Open and closed mathematics: student experiences and understandings. *Journal for Research in Mathematics Education, 29*(1), 41–62.

Cai, J. (2005). U.S. and Chinese teachers' constructing, knowing, and representations to teach mathematics. *Mathematical Thinking and Learning, 7*, 135–169.

Cai, J., & Nie, B. (2007). Problem solving in Chinese mathematics education: research and practice. *ZDM—The International Journal on Mathematics Education, 39*, 459–473.

Cai, J., & Wang, T. (2006). U.S. and Chinese teachers' conceptions and constructions of representations: a case of teaching ratio concept. *International Journal of Mathematics and Science Education, 4*, 145–186.

Carpenter, T. P., Fennema, E., Peterson, P. L., Chiang, C. P., & Loef, M. (1989). Using knowledge of children's mathematics thinking in classroom teaching: an experimental study. *American Educational Research Journal, 26*, 499–531.

Clarke, D. J., Keitel, C., & Shimizu, Y. (Eds.) (2006). *Mathematics classrooms in twelve countries: the insider's perspective.* Rotterdam: Sense.

Cobb, P., & Bauersfeld, H. (1995). *Emergence of mathematical meaning: interaction in classroom cultures.* Hillsdale: Erlbaum.

Cuoco, A. A., & Curcio, F. R. (2001). *The roles of representation in school mathematics: 2001 yearbook.* Reston: National Council of Teachers of Mathematics.

Ding, M., Li, Y., Li, X., & Gu, J. (2012). Knowing and understanding instructional mathematics content through intensive studies of textbooks. In Y. Li & R. Huang (Eds.), *How Chinese teach mathematics and improve teaching.* New York: Routledge.

Doyle, W. (1983). Academic work. *Review of Educational Research, 53*, 159–199.

Doyle, W. (1988). Work in mathematical classes: the context of students' thinking during instruction. *Educational Psychologist, 23*, 167–180.

Gu, L., Huang, R., & Marton, F. (2004). Teaching with variation: an effective way of mathematics teaching in China. In L. Fan, N. Y. Wong, J. Cai, & S. Li (Eds.), *How Chinese learn mathematics: perspectives from insiders* (pp. 309–348). Singapore: World Scientific.

Henningsen, M., & Stein, M. K. (1997). Mathematical tasks and student cognition: classroom-based factors that support and inhibit high level mathematical thinking and reasoning. *Journal for Research in Mathematics Education, 8*, 524–549.

Hiebert, J., Gallimore, R., Garnier, H., Givvin, K. B., Hollingsworth, H., Jacobs, J., & Stigler, J. (2003). *Teaching mathematics in seven countries: results from the TIMSS 1999 video study.* Washington: National Center for Education Statistics.

Hiebert, J., & Wearne, D. (1993). Instructional tasks, classroom discourse, and students' learning in second-grade arithmetic. *American Educational Research Journal, 30*, 393–425.

Huang, R., & Cai, J. (2011). Pedagogical representations to teach linear relations in Chinese and U. S. classrooms: parallel or hierarchical. *The Journal of Mathematical Behavior, 30*, 149–165.

Huang, R., & Leung, F. K. S. (2004). Cracking the paradox of the Chinese learners: looking into the mathematics classrooms in Hong Kong and Shanghai. In L. Fan, N. Y. Wong, J. Cai, & S. Li (Eds.), *How Chinese learn mathematics: perspectives from insiders* (pp. 348–381). Singapore: World Scientific.

Huang, R., Mok, I., & Leung, F. K. S. (2006). Repetition or variation: "Practice" in the mathematics classrooms in China. In D. J. Clarke, C. Keitel, & Y. Shimizu (Eds.), *Mathematics classrooms in twelve countries: the insider's perspective* (pp. 263–274). Rotterdam: Sense.

Huntley, M. A., & Chval, K. (2010). Teachers' perspectives on fidelity of implementation to text-books. In B. J. Reys, R. E. Reys, & R. Rubenstein (Eds.), *Mathematics curriculum: issues, trends, and future directions* (pp. 289–304). Reston: National Council of Teachers of Mathematics.

Kilpatrick, J. (2003). What works. In S. L. Senk & D. R. Thompson (Eds.), *Standards-based school mathematics curricula: what are they? What do students learn* (pp. 57–88). Mahwah: Lawrence Erlbaum.

Leinhardt, G. (2001). Instructional explanations: a commonplace for teaching and location for contrast. In V. Richardson (Ed.), *Handbook for research on teaching* (4th ed., pp. 333–357). Washington: American Educational Research Association.

Lesh, R., Post, T., & Behr, M. (1987). Representations and translations among representations in mathematics learning and problem solving. In C. Janvier (Ed.), *Problems of representation in the teaching and learning of mathematics* (pp. 33–40). Hillsdale: Erlbaum.

Leung, F. K. S. (2005). Some characteristics of East Asian mathematics classrooms based on data from the TIMSS 1999 video study. *Educational Studies in Mathematics, 60*, 199–215.

Leung, F. K. S., & Li, Y. (Eds.) (2010). *Reforms and issues in school mathematics in East Asia*. Rotterdam: Sense.

Li, Y. (2008). What do students need to learn about division of fractions? *Mathematics Teaching in the Middle School, 13*, 546–552.

Li, Y., & Huang, R. (Eds.) (2012). *How Chinese teach mathematics and improve teaching*. New York: Routledge.

Li, Y., & Kulm, G. (2008). Knowledge and confidence of pre-service mathematics teacher: the case of fraction division. *ZDM—The International Journal on Mathematics Education, 40*, 833–843.

Li, Y., Chen, X., & An, S. (2009a). Conceptualizing and organizing content for teaching and learning in selected Chinese, Japanese and U.S. mathematics textbooks: the case of fraction division. *ZDM—The International Journal on Mathematics Education, 41*, 809–826.

Li, Y., Zhang, J., & Ma, T. (2009b). Approaches and practices in developing school mathematics textbooks in China. *ZDM—The International Journal on Mathematics Education, 41*, 733–748.

Liu, J., & Li, Y. (2010). Mathematics curriculum reform in the Chinese mainland: changes and challenges. In F. K. S. Leung & Y. Li (Eds.), *Reforms and issues in school mathematics in East Asia* (pp. 9–32). Rotterdam: Sense.

Ma, L. (1999). *Knowing and teaching elementary mathematics: teachers' understanding of fundamental mathematics in China and the United States*. Mahwah: Lawrence Erlbaum.

Mullis, I. V. S., Martin, M. O., & Foy, P. (with Olson, J.F., Preuschoff, C., Erberber, E., Arora, A., & Galia, J.) (2008). *TIMSS 2007 international mathematics report: findings from IEA's trends in international mathematics and science study at the fourth and eighth grades*. Chestnut Hill: TIMSS & PIRLS International Study Center, Boston College.

National Council of Teachers of Mathematics [NCTM] (1991). *Professional standards for teaching mathematics*. Reston: Author.

National Research Council (2004). *On curricular the K-12 evaluating effectiveness: judging quality of K-12 mathematics evaluations*. Washington: The National Academies Press.

Organization of Economic Cooperation Development [OECD] (2009). *Learning mathematics for life: a perspective from PISA*. Paris: Organization of Economic Cooperation Development.

Park, K., & Leung, F. K. S. (2006). A comparative study of the mathematics textbooks of China, England, Japan, Korea, and the United States. In F. K. S. Leung, K. D. Graf, & F. J. Lopez-Real (Eds.), *Mathematics education in different cultural traditions—a comparative study of East Asia and the West: the 13th ICMI study*. New York: Springer.

Remillard, J. T. (2005). Examining key concepts in research on teachers' use of mathematics curriculum. *Review of Educational Research, 75*(2), 211–246.

Richardson, V. (Ed.) (2001). *Handbook of research on teaching* (4th ed.). Washington: American Educational Research Association.

Shimizu, Y. (2009). Japanese approach to teaching mathematics via problem solving. In B. Kaur, Y. B. Har, & M. Kapur (Eds.), *Mathematical problem solving: yearbook 2009, Association of Mathematics Educators* (pp. 89–101). Singapore: World Scientific.

Simon, M. A. (1995). Reconstructing mathematics pedagogy from a constructivist perspective. *Journal for Research in Mathematics Education, 26*, 114–145.

Simon, M. A., & Tzur, R. (2004). Explicating the role of mathematical tasks in conceptual learning: an elaboration of the hypothetical learning trajectory. *Mathematical Thinking and Learning, 6*, 91–104.

Simon, M. A., Tzur, R., Heinz, K., & Kinzel, M. (2004). Explicating a mechanism for conceptual learning: elaborating the construct of reflective abstraction. *Journal for Research in Mathematics Education, 35*, 305–329.

Stein, M. K., & Lane, S. (1996). Instructional tasks and the development of student capacity to think and reason: an analysis of the relationship between teaching and learning in a reform mathematics project. *Educational Research and Evaluation, 2*, 50–80.

Stein, M. K., Remillard, J., & Smith, M. S. (2007). How curriculum influence student learning. In F. Lester (Ed.), *Second handbook research on mathematics of teaching and learning* (pp. 319–370). Charlotte: Information Age.

Sun, X. (2011). "Variation problems" and their roles in the topic of fraction division in Chinese mathematics textbook examples. *Educational Studies in Mathematics, 76*, 65–85.

Tarr, J. E., Chavez, O., Reys, R. E., & Reys, R. J. (2006). From the written to the enacted curricula: the intermediary role of middle school mathematics teacher in shaping student's opportunity to learn. *School Science and Mathematics, 106*, 191–201.

Tarr, J. E., Reys, R. E., Reys, B. J., Chavez, O., Shih, J., & Osterlind, S. J. (2008). The impact of middle-grades mathematics curricula and the classroom learning environment of student achievement. *Journal for Research in Mathematics Education, 39*, 247–280.

Thompson, D. R., & Senk, S. L. (2010). Myths about curriculum implementation. In B. J. Reys, R. E. Reys, & R. Rubenstein (Eds.), *Mathematics curriculum: issues, trends, and future directions* (pp. 249–264). Reston: National Council of Teachers of Mathematics.

Usiskin, Z., & Willmore, E. (2008). *Mathematics curriculum in Pacific Rim countries—China, Japan, Korea, and Singapore*. New York: Information Age.

Part V
Curriculum and Student Learning

Preface

What Mathematics Do Children Learn at School?

The question sounds straightforward, but as the chapters in this section show, there are no easy answers. Part of the complexity lies in the fact that when we ask "What mathematics do children learn?" it is not clear whether we asking about the educational experiences that children receive while at school, or about the outcomes of those experiences.

The educational experiences that are planned for learners are generally collectively described as the curriculum. The term appears to have been first used in Scottish universities in the early seventeenth century as a description of the collection of courses followed by students. In his widely read *Principles of curriculum and instruction* (still in print more than six decades after its first publication), Ralph Tyler proposed that the curriculum should be seen as a means to an end, rather than an end in itself. He identified "four fundamental questions which must be answered in developing any curriculum and plan of instruction" (Tyler 1949, p. 1):

1. What educational purposes should the school seek to attain?
2. What educational experiences can be provided that are likely to attain these purposes?
3. How can these educational experiences be effectively organized?
4. How can we determine whether these purposes are being attained?

One of Tyler's colleagues, Hilda Taba, elaborated on Tyler's model, and in *Curriculum development: Theory and practice* (Taba 1962) proposed a seven step model for curriculum development. Two features of Taba's model are especially important. The first is that she was clear that the curriculum was much more than a list of what was to be taught. She regarded "content" as more than knowledge, and in particular, many important outcomes depended on how things were taught—in other words, that curriculum entailed pedagogy:

the selection and organization of content implements only one of the four areas of objectives—that of knowledge. The selection of content does not develop the techniques and skills for thinking, change patterns of attitudes and feelings, or produce academic and social skills. These objectives only can be achieved by the way in which the learning experiences are planned and conducted in the classroom. [...] Achievement of three of the four categories of objectives depends on the nature of learning experiences rather than on the content (Taba 1967, p. 11)

The second important feature of Taba's model is that, because it entailed considerations of pedagogy, she rejected the idea that curriculum could be developed "top-down." For Taba, all seven stages of the curriculum development model had to be conducted with the involvement of the teachers who would be teaching it.

While the model proposed by Tyler, and to a lesser extent, that of Taba, have been extremely influential, they have also been criticized for being too linear. For example, Kerr (1968) suggested that curriculum was based on four elements: objectives, evaluation, knowledge, and school learning experiences, with the explicit expectation that the elements interact with each other, so that a change in one leads to changes in the others. Kerr also broadened the idea of a curriculum. In much early usage, "the curriculum" referred exclusively to the formally timetabled educational activities in the school—as is clear from the designation of certain activities as "extra-curricular." Kerr proposed that the term curriculum should denote "All the learning which is planned or guided by the school, whether it is carried on in groups or individually inside or outside the school." (p. 16)

Towards the end of the 1960s, there was a vigorous debate in the Anglophone educational research community about whether curriculum should be subordinate to educational aims and objectives or not (above/Equal to?). At the annual meeting of the American Educational Research Association held in Chicago in February 1968, a symposium specifically addressed this issue, and to a large extent, it seems that, to paraphrase Stevens (1946, p. 677), participants left through the door by which they had entered.

One of the most vocal critics of the objectives approach was Lawrence Stenhouse. Drawing on the work of R.S. Peters (1966), Stenhouse suggested that the very idea of basing curriculum on objectives was misguided (Stenhouse 1970). He pointed out that there were aspects of human experience that might be included because of their inherent value rather than because they were instrumental in achieving specified objectives. Moreover, he argued that objectives based instruction becomes simplistic and self-fulfilling, that it works against the exploration of new ideas, and undermines the creativity of students and teachers, not in the least because objectives based approaches place little importance on the desirability of teacher professional development (Stenhouse 1985, pp. 80–81). Within such a model, Stenhouse argued, the teacher is treated as a kind of "intellectual navvy, working on a site plan simplified so that people know exactly where to dig their trenches without knowing why" (Woods 1996, p. 24).

In contrast, Stenhouse suggested that any definition of curriculum should reflect its essentially dynamic nature: "A curriculum is an attempt to communicate the essential principles and features of an educational proposal in such a form that it is open to critical scrutiny and capable of effective translation into practice." (Stenhouse 1975, p. 4). In other words, a curriculum is a proposal for action that not necessarily right, but is reasonable (Toulmin 2001).

Stenhouse proposed that such proposals should consist of three parts: planning, empirical study, and justification, each of which should specify a number of principles and guidance. Stenhouse explicitly rejected the idea that a curriculum could be developed independently of considerations of how it was to be implemented—for Stenhouse, the involvement of teachers was essential. It is also important to note this was not done out of any misguided notion of professional respect, but due to the limitations of the communication process. Because each classroom is different, it is simply not possible to specify a way in which the same proposal could be implemented the exact same way in different classrooms.

An important, and often neglected, feature of Stenhouse's position is that the traditional subject disciplines were essential to effective education. Because of his emphasis on the involvement of teachers, it is sometimes presumed that Stenhouse assumed an "anything goes" approach to teaching but that would allow teachers to impose their values on their students.

> One of the main functional advantages of the disciplines of knowledge and of the arts is to allow us to specify content, rather than objectives, in curriculum, the content being so structured and infused with criteria that, given good teaching, student learnings can be treated as outcomes, rather than made the subject of pre-specifications. Disciplines allow us to specify input rather than output in the educational process. This is fairer to the needs of individual students because, relative to objectives, disciplined content is liberating to the individual. (Stenhouse 1970, p. 77)

Lawton (1975) adopted a slightly different approach to the definition of curriculum. He suggested that:

> the school curriculum (in the wider sense) is essentially a selection from the culture of a society. Certain aspects of our way of life, certain kinds of knowledge, certain attitudes and values are regarded as so important that their transmission to the next generation is not left to chance in our society but is entrusted to specially-trained professionals (teachers) in elaborate and expensive institutions (schools). (p. 7)

The idea that curriculum is a selection from culture is at once both obvious and profound, drawing attention to the fact that what is in the curriculum is the result of choices that have been made during the curriculum development process. Sometimes these choices are explicit, and at other times they are implicit. Sometimes, what is left out speaks as loudly as what is included—what Elliot Eisner calls the "null curriculum:"

> the options students are not afforded, the perspectives they may never know about, much less be able to use, the concepts and skills that are not part of their intellectual repertoire (Eisner 1985, p. 107).

The various aspects of curriculum discussed above can be seen interacting in the chapters of this section. In the chapter by Geiger, Goos, and Dole, we see how the discipline of mathematics—in this case focusing on numeracy—can anchor cross-curricular work so that teachers are able to create student activities that are rigorous as well as being realistic—too often, attempts to incorporate cross-curricular work involve a "dumbing down" of disciplinary work so that it is trivial and undemanding. The idea that students should be able to apply their mathematics outside their mathematics classroom draws attention to the "null curriculum" of many schools, where students learn to think of mathematics as self-contained, and lacking any connection to the "real world" (Boaler 1997). In this chapter, too, we see teachers developing curriculum in the sense envisaged by Stenhouse, and also a respect for the voice of learners as key stakeholders in the process.

Mary Shafer's chapter on the impact of *Mathematics in Context* reminds us that ultimately, what really matters are the outcomes for students. Very few people would suggest that our standardized measures of student achievement in mathematics are the only important outcomes of learning. After all, given the unpredictability of the world in which those currently in school will live their lives, being able to learn will be at least as important (Papert 1998) as.... However, ultimately, all education is about change. If education does not change learners, then it is by definition ineffective, and increases in standardized measures of achievement, though imperfect, are indices of improved outcomes for students. The Mathematics in Context materials were designed to be used in a particular way, and when they were used as intended, perhaps not surprisingly, they worked more effectively. This echoes the point made by Stenhouse about treating teachers like "intellectual navvies." Just telling the navvies where to dig does not equip them with the skills they need to make smart decisions about what to do when the specified location is unsuitable, for example because of the presence of underground cables. In the same way, even if they are not involved in the creation of the materials, teachers need to understand the rationale behind the materials in order to make adjustments in their use in the messy, real world of classrooms.

The chapter by Senk, Thompson and Wernet reminds us of the basic distinction made by Bauersfeld (1979) between the matter "meant," the matter "taught," and the matter "learned" (p. 204) and shows the considerable variation in intended, enacted and achieved curricula even though all the curricula, nominally at least, had the same aim—an understanding of the term "function." To those who espouse the "top-down" model of curriculum development, such variation is likely to be interpreted as lack of fidelity in implementation—an inconsistency to be eliminated through more effective training. To others, the variation of implementation is just an inevitable outcome of the nature of curriculum innovation. Curriculum entails pedagogy.

In the chapter by Fuson and Li, we see how different cultures (in this case those of the United States and China) faced with the same realm of mathematics, have made slightly different selections from that culture in determining what mathematics students should learn, and how they should do so. Some of these selections may be arbitrary, but others may be related to differences in the way in which aspects of culture, such as language, may provide greater affordances for learning (e.g., the idea that some strategies, such as the "make-a-ten" method are more difficult in English because of the structure of number names). The careful analysis presented here shows that some approaches to teaching early number work are likely to be superior to others in common use, which suggests that children's early number learning might be improved by their adoption.

Finally, the chapter by Sinclair and de Freitas points out that the "matter meant" is continually evolving. For many years, it was believed that mathematics was essentially tautological, if not in fact simply a subset of logic (Zermelo 1908). We now know that many aspects of mathematics (e.g., the properties of certain kinds of transfinite cardinals) that are widely accepted as part of mathematics cannot be derived from logical axioms. The addition of two palpably non-logical axioms (the axiom of regularity and the axiom of choice) did generate a viable "creation myth" for mathematics, but even this "repair" to the foundations of mathematics was to be short lived.

In 1900, at the International Congress of Mathematicians in Paris, David Hilbert pronounced that "In mathematics, there is no *ignoramibus* [things we shall not know]"—in other words, that it was possible to prove the truth or falsity of any mathematical statement. Forty years later Kurt Gödel showed that in any mathematical system that was sufficiently complicated to include arithmetic, there were undecidable propositions—in other words, there were mathematical statements that could be made within the system whose truth or falsity could not be determined within the system (Gödel 1940). While some have debated what Hilbert would have made of this, it seems likely that Hilbert would have accepted that he was wrong— there are things that we shall not know in mathematics.

The idea that mathematics is simply additive—that new knowledge simply adds on to what we already know—is therefore inadequate. Our understanding of what mathematics is changes over time, and this seems especially important as digital technology allows us to think about mathematics in new ways. More importantly, our understanding of the nature of mathematical objects will change, and as a consequence, so will the way we teach. Sinclair and de Freitas suggest that it may be appropriate to design a curriculum in which multiplication precedes addition. This may seem bizarre, or just plain wrong. After all, everyone "knows" that we should teach addition before multiplication, but there are plenty of examples of "logical" curriculum sequences that turn out to be no more than historical baggage. In most countries, multiplication is taught before division, because computational skill at the former is a pre-requisite for computational skill at the latter. However, there is now considerable evidence that *conceptually*, division is easier to understand than multiplication (Hart 1981, p. 35). Similarly, in calculus, differentiation is taught before integration, presumably because computational skill at the former is a prerequisite for computational skill at the latter. However, it seems that conceptually, the order should be reversed; the idea of the area under a curve seems much easier to understand than the gradient of a curve at a point (it is certainly the case that in the history of mathematics, the development of integration preceded that of differentiation). The question for propositions such as "should multiplication precede addition" is therefore not "Are they correct?" Such questions are in effect so vague as to be untestable (what Wolfgang Pauli criticized as "Not even wrong"). The question is rather, "Is it generative?" Does it lead to new, more effective kinds of actions in classrooms by teachers and students? This is the powerful question being posed by Sinclair and de Freitas.

None of the chapters have found any definitive answers to the question of "what mathematics do children learn at school?" To those who seek to discover "what works?" in education, this will be seen as a disappointment, or even failure. But to those who see the purpose of educational research to be moving teachers to more effective action—see, for example, Wiliam and Lester (2008)—then this diversity is a source of further theory building and learning. In the spirit of Lawrence Stenhouse, we have five clear "attempts to communicate the essential principles and features of educational proposal in such a form that it is open to critical scrutiny and capable of effective translation into practice."

Institute of Education, University of London   Dylan Wiliam

References

Bauersfeld, H. (1979). Research related to the mathematical learning process. In I. International Commission on Mathematical (Ed.), *New trends in mathematics teaching* (Vol. IV, pp. 199–213). Paris: UNESCO.

Boaler, J. (1997). *Experiencing school mathematics: teaching styles, sex and setting*. Buckingham: Open University Press.

Eisner, E. W. (1985). *The educational imagination: on the design and evaluation of school programs* (2 ed.). New York: Macmillan.

Gödel, K. (1940). *The consistency of the continuum hypothesis*. Princeton: Princeton University Press.

Hart, K. M. (Ed.). (1981). *Children's understanding of mathematics: 11–16*. Eastbourne: Antony Rowe.

Kerr, J. F. (1968). The problem of curriculum reform. In J. F. Kerr (Ed.), *Changing the curriculum* (pp. 13–38). London: University of London Press.

Lawton, D. L. (1975). *Class, culture and the curriculum*. London: Routledge and Kegan Paul.

Papert, S. A. (1998). Child power: keys to the new learning of the digital century. Retrieved on February 15, 2013 from http://www.papert.org/articles/Childpower.html.

Peters, R. S. (1966). *Ethics and education*. London: George Allen & Unwin.

Stenhouse, L. (1970). Some limitations of the use of objectives in curriculum research and planning. *Paedagogica Europaea, 6*(1), 73–83.

Stenhouse, L. (1975). *An introduction to curriculum research and development*. London: Heinemann.

Stenhouse, L. (1985). *Research as a basis for teaching*. London: Heinemann.

Stevens, S. S. (1946). On the theory of scales of measurement. *Science, 103*(2684), 677–680.

Taba, H. (1962). *Curriculum development: theory and practice*. New York: Harcourt Brace Jovanovich.

Taba, H. (1967). *Teacher's handbook for elementary social studies: an inductive approach*. Reading: Addison-Wesley.

Toulmin, S. (2001). *Return to reason*. Cambridge: Harvard University Press.

Tyler, R. W. (1949). *Basic principles of curriculum and instruction*. Chicago: University of Chicago Press.

Woods, P. (1996). *Researching the art of teaching: ethnography for educational use*. London: Routledge.

Zermelo, E. (1908). Untersuchungen über die Grundlagen der Mengenlehre I [Investigations in the foundations of set theory]. *Mathematische Annalen, 65*, 261–281.

Curriculum Intent, Teacher Professional Development and Student Learning in Numeracy

Vince Geiger, Merrilyn Goos, and Shelley Dole

Abstract Numeracy, or mathematical literacy as it is also known, is a major educational goal internationally, and as such, is addressed in the curriculum documents of educational jurisdictions and in national and international testing regimes. This chapter reports on an aspect of a research study which investigated the interrelationship between curriculum intent, teacher professional learning and action, and students' perspectives on their own learning in a 12 month long research and development project. Specifically, this chapter examines the impact upon student learning as a teacher attempted to implement the numeracy requirements of a state based curriculum in an educational jurisdiction within Australia. These attempts were structured through a rich model of numeracy and supported through regular interaction with the project researchers in a collaborative partnership aimed at improving student learning outcomes in alignment with state curriculum objectives. An emergent aspect of the project is the importance of a clear model of numeracy, which outlines essential elements, to changes in a teacher's numeracy practice. These changes in practice led to positive student views on their mathematics learning and to greater connectedness of this learning within and outside of mathematics itself.

Keywords Numeracy across the curriculum · Mathematical literacy · Applications of mathematics · Teacher professional development · Student perceptions of numeracy

Introduction

Numeracy, or mathematical literacy as it is also known, is a major educational goal internationally, and as such, is addressed in the curriculum documents of educational

V. Geiger (✉)
Australian Catholic University, Brisbane, Australia
e-mail: Vincent.Geiger@acu.edu.au

M. Goos · S. Dole
The University of Queensland, Brisbane, Australia

Y. Li, G. Lappan (eds.), *Mathematics Curriculum in School Education*,   473
Advances in Mathematics Education, DOI 10.1007/978-94-007-7560-2_22,
© Springer Science+Business Media Dordrecht 2014

jurisdictions and in national and international testing regimes. Numeracy is increasingly seen as fundamental to developing students' capacities to use mathematics to function as informed and reflective citizens, to contribute to society through paid work, and in other aspects of community life (Steen 2001). This aspect of mathematics education has been recognised internationally through the OECD's *Program for International Student Assessment* (PISA). According to PISA's definition mathematical literacy is:

> an individual's capacity to identify and understand the role mathematics plays in the world, to make well-founded judgments, and to use and engage with mathematics in ways that meet the needs of that individual's life as a constructive, concerned and reflective citizen. (OECD 2004, p. 15)

This chapter reports on an aspect of a research study which investigated the interrelationship between curriculum intent, teacher professional learning and action, and student learning, in a 12 month long research and development project. A focus of this project was on enabling the numeracy dimensions of school subjects across the curriculum. The purpose of this chapter is to examine the impact upon student learning of a teacher's attempts to implement the numeracy requirements of a state based curriculum in an educational jurisdiction within Australia. These attempts were structured through a rich model of numeracy and supported through regular interaction with the project researchers in a collaborative partnership aimed at improving student learning outcomes in alignment with state curriculum objectives.

The chapter is structured in five sections. First, the curriculum context in which the study was situated is described. Second, the theoretical framework which guided our approach to supporting teachers in the development of rich numeracy focused learning experiences is outlined. Third, we summarise the methodological approach we employed when working with students and teachers. Fourth, we present vignettes based on observations of teacher designed classroom activities as well as students' views of their own numeracy development in order to illustrate the nature of students' experiences of numeracy learning. Finally, we discuss the challenges of moving from the intended learning objectives of a curriculum document to the enactment of these objectives in teaching and learning practice.

Curriculum Context

In Australia, numeracy is an educational priority, with the national numeracy strategy being part of government policy since 1997. The launch of the national numeracy strategy was encapsulated in the following statement:

> ...that every child leaving primary school should be numerate, and be able to read, write and spell at an appropriate level. (MCEETYA 1997, p. ix)

This statement resulted in vigorous debate in relation to defining numeracy. After continual discussion, consideration and revision of proposed definitions, educators and policy makers in Australia have embraced a broad interpretation of numeracy similar to the OECD definition of mathematical literacy: "To be numerate is to use mathematics effectively to meet the general demands of life at home, in paid work, and for participation in community and civic life." (AAMT 1997, p. 15). A further outcome of the discussion around a succinct definition that captured the essence of numeracy, and particularly a definition that was broader than facility with basic number and calculation skills, was agreement that mathematics is necessary but not sufficient for numeracy, and that all teachers are teachers of numeracy.

The cross-curriculum and contextual notion of numeracy as an Australian educational goal has further been validated and reiterated by a review of numeracy education undertaken by the Australian government (Human Capital Working Group, Council of Australian Governments 2008), recommending:

> That all systems and schools recognise that, while mathematics can be taught in the context of mathematics lessons, the development of numeracy requires experience in the use of mathematics beyond the mathematics classroom, and hence requires an across the curriculum commitment. (p. 7)

Australia is now moving to implementation of a new national curriculum, and numeracy continues to be a government educational priority. Within the national curriculum numeracy has been included as a General Capability in all subjects. In the case of the Mathematics curriculum documents (Version 3.0), numeracy, in all subjects, is described in the following way.

> Students become numerate as they develop the knowledge and skills to use mathematics confidently across all learning areas at school and in their lives more broadly. Numeracy involves students in recognising and understanding the role of mathematics in the world and having the dispositions and capacities to use mathematical knowledge and skills purposefully.

(Australian Curriculum, Assessment and Reporting Authority 2012a, p. 11)

There is also a specific numeracy statement within each subject. For example, in the Australian National Curriculum: History, it is stated that:

> Students develop numeracy capability as they learn to organise and interpret historical events and developments. Students learn to analyse numerical data to make meaning of the past, for example to understand cause and effect, and continuity and change. Students learn to use scaled timelines, including those involving negative and positive numbers, as well as calendars and dates to recall information on topics of historical significance and to illustrate the passing of time.

(Australian Curriculum, Assessment and Reporting Authority 2012b, p. 10)

Hence, numeracy, from the perspective of the national government, is considered to be a vital element in all students' education across all subjects within schools.

In Australia, however, the responsibility for curriculum development and implementation lies within the individual states of the federation. This means that states have the authority to implement curriculum with a flexibility that allows them to cater for the circumstances of schools and students within their jurisdictions. None-the-less, numeracy remains a priority for all Australian states and territories. In the specific case of the educational jurisdiction that forms the background for the research study reported here, numeracy was viewed as a critical element within all school subjects. Curriculum documents in this state, known as the *Curriculum Standards and Accountability Framework*, include a specific statement on numeracy in relation to each subject. For example, within the Society and Environment subject area numeracy is described through the following statement.

> Learners develop and use operational skills in **numeracy** to understand, analyse, critically respond to and use mathematics in different contexts. These understandings relate to measurement, spatial sense, patterns and algebra and data and number. This learning is evident in society and environment when, for example, students use and understand the concept of time, when they use spatial patterns, locations and pathways in the form of maps, and they gather and analyse data for social decision-making.

> (Department of Education and Children's Services 2005, p. 294)

Numeracy is also seen as an important goal for students in Mathematics.

> Learners develop and use operational skills in **numeracy** to understand, analyse, critically respond to and use mathematics in different contexts. Students' learning in mathematics enables students to explore the relationships between different mathematical ideas and apply mathematical understandings to their learning in all curriculum areas.

> (Department of Education and Children's Services 2005, p. 219)

Even with the support of educational policy makers and curriculum authorities, it has proven difficult to implement effective numeracy practice in Australian schools. Attempts to introduce numeracy practices into schools have sometimes been characterized by a utilitarian approaches that have emphasized basic skills over the capacity to engage higher order thinking. This is in contrast to the growing complexity of the mathematical demand of work in many industries (Hoyles et al. 2002; Straesser 2007). Further, numeracy has often been interpreted as being almost exclusively associated with number, excluding other areas of mathematics, such as geometry and algebra, which can also contribute to an individual's capability to use mathematics to solve problems in contexts outside of mathematics itself. Until recently, few proponents of numeracy practice have acknowledge the important role physical, representational and digital tools play in using mathematics in the outside of school world despite the importance of these tools in working with mathematical ideas and concepts in industry and in life away from the workplace (e.g., see Zevenbergen 2004). Thus, while the view of numeracy as a capability every student should possess is endorsed by educational policy makers and curriculum authorities the implementation of approaches to teaching and learning that foster the numeracy development of students has been problematic. The challenge, therefore, is to find ways to enact the intent of numeracy statements and objectives within curriculum documents into mainstream classroom teaching and learning practice.

Theoretical Framework

While previous definitions capture the broad thrust of the concept of numeracy, they lack the detail necessary for teachers to implement numeracy based approaches in

Fig. 1 A model for numeracy in the 21st century (Goos 2007)

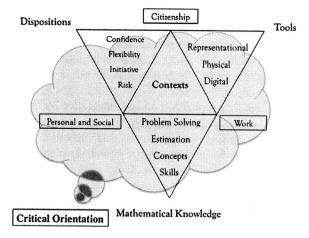

practice. In short, current definitions of numeracy do not appear to convey what is needed to transform what is intended within curriculum documents into what is enacted in school classrooms. More recently, however, Goos (2007) has proposed a model of numeracy (Fig. 1) which encompasses four essential elements: attention to real-life *contexts*, the deployment of *mathematical knowledge*, the use of physical and digital *tools*, and consideration of students' *dispositions* towards the use of mathematics. These elements are embedded in a *critical orientation* to the use of mathematical skills and concepts that emphasises, for example, the capacity to evaluate quantitative, spatial or probabilistic information used to support claims made in the media or other contexts. While the model was intended to be readily accessible to teachers as an instrument for planning and reflection, its development was also informed by relevant research, as outlined below.

At the centre of the concept of numeracy is the key dimension of *context*. According to Steen (2001), numeracy is about the use of mathematics to act in and on the world. Typically, when mathematics is used in a context it is applied in a way different from how it is traditionally taught in school (Noss et al. 2000; Straesser 2007) and so to learn to be numerate individuals must be exposed to using mathematics in a range of contexts (Steen 2001).

Appropriate mathematical knowledge is required to act on problems within a given context. In a numeracy context, mathematical knowledge includes not only concepts and skills, but also higher order thinking—such as problem solving strategies and the ability to make sensible estimations (Zevenbergen 2004). How to interpret a problem outside of mathematics in a mathematical way, and then how to choose which mathematical knowledge needs to be selected to engage with the mathematised problems is a challenge that lies at the intersection of *contexts* and *mathematical knowledge*.

The desire and confidence to apply mathematics in real world contexts is related to the *disposition* of an individual in relation the use of mathematics. The importance of developing positive attitudes towards mathematics is emphasised in national and international curriculum documents (e.g., Australian Curriculum, Assessment and

Reporting Authority 2012a; OECD 2004). Further, Gresalfi and Cobb (2006) argue that it is not sufficient to focus on the mathematical skills and capacities we want students to learn alone, but that teaching must take place with students' dispositions in mind if students are to develop an affinity with a discipline. This affinity is vital for students to be disposed to making use of mathematics in their current lived in worlds and in their future lives (Boaler and Greeno 2000). These dispositions include not just confidence with mathematics but a willingness to think flexibly, to show initiative, and to take risks.

An increasing number of studies identify tools as mediators of meaning making, reasoning and action in relation to mathematical learning (e.g., Pea 2004; Verillon and Rabardel 1995). In school and workplace contexts, tools may be representational (symbol systems, graphs, maps, diagrams, drawings, tables, ready reckoners) and physical (models, measuring instruments), but increasingly tools are digital (e.g., Artigue 2002; Goos et al. 2003).

The elements of the Goos (2007) model are embedded in a critical orientation of the use of mathematical skills and concepts which emphasises the evaluative and judgemental aspects of numeracy practice. We view this critical orientation as a vital capacity for informed and participatory citizenship and for exercising effective and socially conscious decision making in an individual's personal life. Ernest (2002) views social empowerment as an important reason for teaching mathematics. This social empowerment can range from the purely utilitarian skills associated with the mathematics that is needed to function, in the simplest sense, in work and society through to the critical skills that enable individuals to: make decisions and judgements; add support to arguments; or challenge an argument or position. This position is also consistent with that of Frankenstein (2001) and Jablonka (2003) who argue for the need to recognise how mathematical information and practices can be used to persuade, manipulate, disadvantage or shape opinions about social or political issues.

The elements of the model and the critical orientation within which these elements interact are summarised in Table 1.

Table 1 Descriptions of the elements and critical orientation of the numeracy model

Mathematical knowledge	Mathematical concepts and skills; problem solving strategies; estimation capacities.
Contexts	Capacity to use mathematical knowledge in a range of contexts, both within schools and beyond school settings
Dispositions	Confidence and willingness to use mathematical approaches to engage with life-related tasks; preparedness to make flexible and adaptive use of mathematical knowledge.
Tools	Use of material (models, measuring instruments), representational (symbol systems, graphs, maps, diagrams, drawings, tables, ready reckoners) and digital (computers, software, calculators, internet) tools to mediate and shape thinking
Critical orientation	Use of mathematical information to: make decisions and judgements; add support to arguments; challenge an argument or position.

This model has been used as a framework to audit school curricula (Goos et al. 2010) and for analysis of teachers' attempts to design for the teaching of numeracy across the curriculum (Goos et al. 2011). The numeracy model was also used to promote teacher professional learning and, in particular, to assist teachers to reflect upon their own practice. In this chapter the numeracy model will be used to evaluate one teacher's attempts to enhance her numeracy teaching practice by developing richer classroom learning experiences and to analyse her students' perceptions of their own numeracy learning as a result of their teacher's attempts to change her practice.

Research Design

Twenty teachers were recruited from ten demographically diverse schools on the basis of their interest in cross-curricular numeracy education. They came from four primary schools (Kindergarten-Grade 7), one secondary school (Grades 8–12), four smaller schools in rural areas (Grades 1–12), and one school that combined middle and secondary grades (Grades 6–12). The focus on teaching numeracy across the curriculum meant that it was important to include teachers with varying subject area specialisations. Thus, participants included generalist primary school teachers as well as secondary teachers qualified to teach particular subject areas (mathematics, English, science, social education, health and physical education).

The research design was consistent with an action research model with the Loucks-Horsley et al. (2003) framework for professional development underpinning the development aspect of the project. Consistent with this framework, project meetings were followed up with school visits, enabling the research team to provide on-going support to teachers in their efforts to change their numeracy practices, whilst simultaneously providing the means to gather data on the process. Two full action-research cycles were implemented, providing teachers with the opportunity to set new goals and re-plan after the first cycle.

At the first project meeting, teachers came together with researchers and Department personnel to explore the ideas embedded in the numeracy model, to discuss the potential to teach numeracy within the constraints and affordances of the state-wide curriculum framework, and to work through investigations that allowed for the elaboration and clarification of the ideas embedded in the model. In order to stimulate discussion about numeracy demands that existed within the curriculum, teachers were also presented with a numeracy audit of the curriculum framework. The audit was completed by examining the relevant Curriculum Scope and Standards statements within the *Curriculum Standards and Accountability Framework*. Numeracy demands of each subject were evaluated by reference to the elements of the numeracy model in Fig. 1: mathematical knowledge, contexts, dispositions, tools, and critical orientation. The results of the audit indicated that numeracy demands existed within each subject area in alignment with the dimensions of the Goos numeracy model (further detail can be found in Goos et al. 2010). After discussing the demands and opportunities provided by the curriculum framework within the whole group, teachers worked in small groups to adapt presented tasks or to develop new activities they might trial in their own classrooms.

After this initial meeting, teachers were asked to introduce the activities they had begun to develop at the first meeting and/or other activities into their own classroom. After a number of months, teachers were brought together again for a second whole project meeting to present examples of activities they had trialled and to engage in further curriculum planning while being supported by teachers from other schools. During this meeting, the researchers provided input on the way elements of the numeracy model were evident in each of the activities presented. The researchers also provided additional input on the role of critical orientation within the numeracy model as this was an area that was noticeably underdeveloped during the first round of school visits and an aspect that teachers had asked for further advice in particular.

The project concluded with another cycle of trialling activities, visits from the research team and a final presentation to the entire project group.

Between each of the whole project meetings, the researchers visited schools to provide further input and support, and to collect data for the purpose of evaluating the success of the trialled activities from the perspective of students and their teachers. Across the project data were collected via field notes of classroom observations, records of semi-structured interviews with teachers and students, and artefacts such as student work samples and computer files. The data used in this chapter are drawn from one teacher and her class of Grade 8 students (12–13 years of age), which represents a case study from within the larger project. The teacher was selected because her progress through the course of the project revealed a developing capacity to interpret the numeracy demands and opportunities of the *Curriculum Standards and Accountability Framework* in a way that allowed her to create tasks of increasing richness for her students. Her case was also chosen for this chapter because her field of expertise lay outside of mathematics teaching, that is, health and physical education, which demonstrates the across the curriculum possibilities that exist for numeracy learning and teaching practice. The student participants who were interviewed as part of the data collection process where nominated by their teacher as individuals she perceived to have the capacity to articulate their thoughts on classroom activities the teacher had designed for their numeracy learning in a clear, open and honest fashion. As a group, these students' history of mathematic achievement was varied. Interviews lasted approximately 30 minutes and were conducted away from the classroom without the presence of the teacher.

The Development of a Student Oriented Numeracy Practice

In this section one teacher's attempt to design student learning experiences that satisfied the requirements of the *Curriculum Standards and Accountability Framework* within the subject area, Health and Physical Education (HPE), while also meeting the numeracy demands of this framework, is outlined and illustrated. This teacher,

Clare, had volunteered for the project for two reasons. Firstly, she was initially trained as a Health and Physical Education teacher but over time had found she preferred to work with students in the middle school (Grades 6 to 9) where she was required to teach across the curriculum. As a result, she found herself teaching in a subject where she had received no pre-service training and in which she felt less confident. Her engagement with the project was, in part, an attempt to improve her content and pedagogical knowledge in an area she perceived to be a weakness—mathematics teaching. Secondly, she had begun to believe that her approach to teaching, in general, was too direct, and she saw the project as a way of engaging with more inquiry based approaches to teaching and learning.

First School Visit

Clare had worked hard to improve her classroom numeracy practice from the onset of the project but had been disappointed with her initial efforts with a Grade 8 class (12–13 years of age). In the first lesson we observed, Clare attempted to develop students' understanding of the addition and subtraction of directed numbers. She demonstrated the method via a number line drawn on the blackboard, which was also illustrated on a handout distributed to students. Students were to stand on the first number listed and face in the positive direction if the operation was to be addition or the negative direction if the operation was to be subtraction. They were then to walk the number of steps indicated by the second number, walking forward if this number was positive and backwards if it was negative. The number at which they arrived via this process was the answer to the problem. The handout provided a systematically developed list of problems involving adding and subtracting positive and negative numbers, including a "long walk" with seven operations in succession. Two questions then required students to describe any patterns they observed in their walks and to explain some of the rules they discovered while adding and subtracting.

After an initial ten minutes of teacher instruction, students moved outside to complete the activity. One drew a chalked number line and gave instructions to another as this student "walked" a couple of problems. After 30 minutes of outdoor activity the class moved inside and Clare asked students what they had been thinking and feeling during the activity. How did they know if they were on the right track? Students seemed willing to say they were confused; others simply said that the activity was fun. Clare explained to them that they had been using a model that would help them understand the thinking they would be doing in the next few lessons on adding and subtracting directed numbers. She drew their attention to the questions about patterns and rules, and asked them to try a list of additional exercises for homework. She then modelled the number line representations of:

$$-3 + +2 = -1$$
$$-3 + -2 = -5$$
$$-3 - +2 = -5$$
$$-3 - -2 = -1$$

and asked if anyone could describe something about what they saw, reiterating that this was to be done for homework.

Reflecting on this lesson through the lens of the numeracy model, *mathematical knowledge* had a clear focus in the addition and subtraction of directed numbers. At the start of the lesson Clare elicited some of the real life *contexts* in which directed numbers appeared, however, the *context* she used to demonstrate these operations, the chalk number line outside the of classroom, could not be considered to be related to a real-life use of directed numbers. A *representational tool*, the number lines drawn on the blackboard and on the ground, was used to help students discover patterns and explain rules concerning these operations on directed numbers, although Clare did not elicit and evaluate students' ideas during the lesson. Clare attempted to ascertain students' *dispositions* towards mathematics and the learning activity by asking them how they felt about the lesson but students' responses were varied from finding the lesson fun to experiencing confusion in relation to what they were meant to learn. Despite Clare's efforts to design an engaging and thought provoking lesson for her students, there was no opportunity to develop a *critical orientation* to this subject matter.

Clare was disappointed with the lesson and admitted she was struggling, in particular, with critical orientation. She felt there was no scope in the lesson for developing a critical orientation to the subject matter.

After some reflection, Clare decided the only way to improve her practice was to take a very different approach from how she had taught in the past.

> After much reflection I decided to do some things differently… One of the goals I set myself was to take a more exploratory and investigative approach, particularly in dealing with teaching aspects of numeracy across all learning areas.
>
> (Peters et al. 2012, p. 24)

Between School Visits

Clare's first step on the new pathway she had set herself took place between the school visits by the project researchers. In this activity, students in HPE were to investigate media coverage of sports. Clare implemented this activity in preparation for a report at the second teachers' meeting. Her students collected sports reports from a local newspaper each day for a week and then measured and calculated the area of the space devoted to both female and male sports. Clare reported that students found that equal representation was not given to female and male sports in the media and that an interesting discussion had followed. Clare was much happier with the outcome of this lesson as she felt she had begun to address numeracy in HPE and that it seemed to create a deeper student understanding of the concepts and processes covered.

Second School Visit

During our second visit to the school, near the end of the project, Clare had prepared an activity within Health and Physical Education where students investigated the level of their physical activity through the use of a pedometer that they wore during the day for one week. Students entered the number of paces they had walked or run every day into a shared Excel spreadsheet. They were then asked to analyse their own data using Excel and to compare their results with those of other students (see Fig. 2).

Students also had to convert their total daily and total weekly paces into kilometres to gain a sense of how far they typically walked in a day or a week. The task was also designed to help students realize that the distance they walked was not determined by the number of paces alone, as an individual's pace length was also a factor. In order to bring about this conversion, students were required to design a process for determining the length of their own pace. This involved marking out a distance of 100 metres and counting the number of paces they each took to walk this distance. After demonstrating the procedure for obtaining the length of her pace and then converting paces in a day to kilometres from her own personal data, the teacher asked students to complete conversions of their own pace totals to kilometres. She also suggested that students compare their kilometric distances with each other and discuss why they were different.

Clare finished the lesson by indicating the next session would include an investigation of the number of paces Usain Bolt takes during a 100 metre sprint.

This activity provided Clare with the opportunity to promote the elements of numeracy described in the *Curriculum Standards and Accountability Framework* and

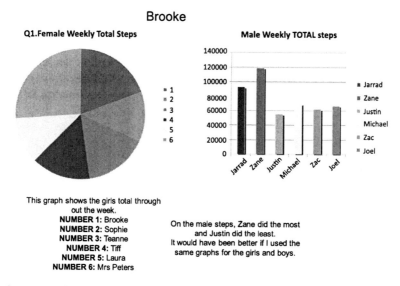

Fig. 2   A comparison of male's and female's weekly total steps

made explicit in the numeracy model employed to guide her practice. In this activity, the elements of numeracy were situated in an authentic *context* (their level of physical activity) in which students were challenged to use a range of *mathematical knowledge* (measurement, conversion of units, representation of data) and to make use of physical (measuring tapes, trundle wheels), digital (pedometers, spreadsheets), and representational *tools* (graphical representations). She encouraged the development of positive *dispositions* in students towards the use of mathematics by designing a task students were personally interested in (their own activity levels). This lesson also incorporated aspects of a *critical orientation* as students made judgments about the reasonableness of results and posed their own questions about meaning that lay within the collected data. Clare indicated that making the desired changes to her practice necessitated a change in teaching practice towards a less directive and more inquiry-oriented approach, a "letting go" process that she found difficult but more effective for enriching students' mathematical knowledge and promoting a critical orientation to evaluating information and answers.

It can be seen though this sequence of events that Clare had attempted to enact the numeracy aspect of the *Curriculum Standards and Accountability Framework* in a rich and engaging way for students. From Clare's perspective, she had been successful in her aim to improve students' dispositions towards mathematics learning that in turn resulted in positive outcomes for her students in all aspects of numeracy. She believed these improvements were due to the changes she had made to her teaching practice. But teachers' perspectives on the benefits to student learning as a result of changes in teaching practice are only one part of the story of realising the intent of a curriculum in practice. In the next section, students' perspectives on the changes they experienced though the year, as part of the project, are presented.

Students' Perspectives on Their Learning Experiences

Students were interviewed in small groups of five during each of the school visits. They were asked to reflect upon the numeracy lessons they had recently experienced and to express their feelings about mathematics or using mathematics in various activities.

First School Visit

During the first visit to the school, we interviewed four students immediately after Clare's lesson on directed numbers. Attitudes towards mathematics varied in this group with some saying it was at the "top" of their favourite subjects and others saying it was at the "bottom".

When asked about the lesson they had just experienced on directed numbers, students were able to explain they were learning how to add and subtract positive and negative numbers. They thought the activity was helpful because it was "step by step" and they could "do it", by which they meant engage with the ideas and concepts through a physical activity. Students' responses varied in relation to what they had learnt from the lesson. One student could not recall if her group came up with any rules about the addition or subtraction of directed numbers based on the activity. Another student, however, recounted that he had worked out that you go "up the number line" if adding positive numbers or subtracting negative numbers and "down the number line" if adding negative numbers or subtracting positive numbers. It would appear that their learning in relation to mathematical knowledge ranged from improved understanding and confidence to that of only limited observations on the key features of the lesson.

Students were also asked about the nature of the activity, not just its content, and how they felt about learning mathematics. Students indicated that they had occasionally gone outside for mathematics lessons, for example, to find shapes nominated by the teacher (rectangles or triangles), or to measure the perimeter of the basketball court. They offered the opinion that these "outside" activities helped them understand mathematics better than when they worked on mathematics in their exercise books while sitting at a desk in the classroom. This was because they felt they "really didn't pay attention to what they were doing" when working in this fashion. While the students were positive about their teacher, they did not express any excitement about their mathematics learning nor indicate that mathematics was being connected to contexts that were interesting to them or relevant to their current or future lives, other than through occasional "outside" activities. It would appear from these comments that the students believed the use of *contexts* was advantageous to their learning but that this approach had been infrequently adopted by their teacher. Further, students' positive attitudes to learning mathematics in ways that varied from traditional classroom bound approaches and their lack of enthusiasm for mathematics taught in this way implies that their *dispositions* towards mathematics and to learning mathematics is influenced by the *context* in which it is presented. During this interview, students made no mention of the use of *tools*, either representational or digital, when learning mathematics.

Second School Visit

During the second school visit we observed a HPE lesson in which students were analysing the data they had collected using pedometers by the use of Excel spreadsheets. Four students were interviewed as a group directly after the lesson. During this discussion students were clear about how they were meant to conduct the activity, what they were meant to investigate, and what they found.

Researcher 1:   *We saw you earlier today—and you were wearing pedometers! What was going on there? What was that all about?*

Student 1:   *We were measuring how many steps we took over a period of one week. From, in effect, Saturday to Friday—measuring how many steps we took.*

Researcher 2: *So, did you have to wear the pedometers the whole time?*
Student 1:   *Yeah, pretty much.*
Student 2:   *And we were told that when we measured our steps it had to be at around the same time everyday. So that you've got an even amount of steps every week day.*
Researcher 2: *So weren't wearing it all day then?*
Student 2:   *Yeah you wore it most of the day.*
Student 1:   *Whenever we walked.*
Researcher 2: *So you didn't have to wear it while sitting on the couch then?*
Students: *Laugh.*

As part of the discussion, students indicated they were enthusiastic about the opportunity to use digital *tools*. They made use of an Excel spreadsheet to graph different representations of the data and then used these graphs (*representational tools*) to draw conclusions about their own and other class members' level of physical activity (*critical orientation*).

Researcher 1: *So, it was interesting seeing that table (referring to the Excel spreadsheet) and one thing that stood out for me was first, if you look at the totals, there are differences between all of you. But did you notice when you were looking at that on different days of the week each of you were walking different numbers of steps?*
Student 2:   *Yeah, Sunday was smallest.*
Researcher 1: *I noticed!*
Student 2:   *I was going to say that Thursday and Saturday probably would have been the biggest too, 'cause that's when we play sport.*
Student 3:   *We did some graphs on the computer too showing two days and I did Saturday and Sunday on a line graph . . .and there was a major difference! Saturday was like this (gesturing to show a large number of steps) and Sunday was like this (gesturing to show a small number of steps).*
Researcher 1: *OK. So when you did this on the computers, you used Excel did you?*
Students: *Yeah (together).*
Researcher 1: *Had you ever used Excel before?*
Student 1:   *Yes—last year we learnt the basics of it.*
Student 2:   *Except this is the new version and not many of us knew how to use it except for me.*
Student 1:   *I think we are getting the hang of it. There haven't been too many complaining about how hard it is, but it is very complicated.*
Researcher 1: *So some of you already knew how to use it and others of you didn't— so how did that work in the classroom when some people knew what to do and others didn't?*
Student 1:   *Well some of us are a bit better with it—like we understand it a lot quicker, so just got help from them.*

Interestingly, and even surprisingly, students were comfortable with having a higher skill level in relation to this type of technology than their teacher and their peers, and were happy to accept the responsibility of providing assistance, where necessary, to their teacher and other class members. This is an indication of both the confidence students had developed with respect to the use of digital *tools* and their willingness to take the lead in assisting all members of the class, their teacher included, in moving forward with their mathematics learning (*dispositions*). It also demonstrates the teachers' new preparedness to take risks by including skill elements in an activity she herself was yet to master and to give over some degree of control to the students in order that they had opportunity to feel responsible for their own and others' learning (*dispositions*).

Student 2:   *And I was trying to help Mrs Clarke as well, so then she knew how to use it to help others.*
Researcher 1:   *That is an interesting thing. Most people think that teachers know all of this stuff and they are meant to help students.*
Student 2:   *Well, she admitted she didn't know how to use it.*
Researcher 1:   *Is that OK, for a teacher to be learning stuff?*
Student 2:   *Yeah* (all students).

Students were conscious of the potential for the use of digital *tools* in other subject areas and in different real-life *contexts*. They were also aware that their teacher was deliberately attempting to provide greater focus on mathematical ideas, skills, and processes, in other school subjects (*contexts*). To illustrate this awareness they recalled a number of instances where mathematics was particularly relevant to their learning in other subject areas.

Researcher 3:   *So do you think it is a program you could use in other subject areas?*
Student 1:   *Definitely!*
Researcher 3:   *Like what?*
Student 1:   *Like we had to do in Science recently, a prac, and it required amounts, graphs and percentages. I haven't done it yet but I'm going to get the percentages and use them on Excel and make a graph out of it.*
Researcher 3:   *And that will be OK with your teacher?*
Student 1:   *Yeah. The idea is to create a graph and on the computer is fine. And it is easier than trying to draw up one.*
Researcher 1:   *So that subject we saw today was PE?*
Students: *HPE!* (together).
Student 1:   *But with a bit of maths integrated.*
Researcher 1:   *Yeah.*

The students were very aware of the teacher's purpose in relation to the "mathematics" in other subject areas (*contexts*).

Student 1:   *That's what out teacher, Mrs Clarke, is trying to do. Trying to get more maths stuff in other subjects.*
Researcher 1:   *Do you think that it is working? Can you see how maths is being integrated into other subjects?*
Students: *Yeah* (together).

Student 2:   *And I think HPE is the best lesson to do it in as well because all of your sports and stuff, you use numbers for your scores. And if you can learn it in different areas as well it helps.*

Researcher 1:   *What about other subject areas. Can you tell us about some examples where Ms C has put more maths there.*

Student 1:   *In Science earlier this year, we done [sic] a test to see how much one plain peanut – how much exercise you have to do to work off that much.*

Student 2:   *It was a cashew!*

Student 1:   *Yes a cashew. And we set fire to it. And then I got it with mathematics to calculate how much. And we came up with seven to eleven minutes of handwriting to work off one plain unsalted cashew!*

With prompting, students realised there was mathematics in English.

Student 3:   *Yeah, remember we were going to do that thing about how many pence in a dollar. Remember reading the Red Dog book?*

Student 1:   *Yeah. When we listened to the recordings of a Fortunate Life (a novel), it was talking about the old currencies and we were going to do some maths on the amounts of pence and pounds.*

Student 3:   *But we ran out of time!*

The students also identified many opportunities to use measurement in their Home Economics class where they were making boxer shorts (mathematical knowledge, tools, context).

Researcher 3:   *What are you doing in Home Ec (Home Economics) at the moment?*

Student 2:   *We're doing a bit of sewing. Tomorrow we're making boxer shorts.*

Student 1:   *Yeah …lots and lots of measuring.*

A number of students also demonstrated that they were able to use mathematics in a critical sense to form judgements within subjects outside of mathematics (*critical orientation*). In Studies of Society and Environment, they described their learning about koala habitats. In this exchange they revealed that they had developed an understanding of the relationship between koalas and specific types of eucalyptus leaves on which they feed.

Student 1:   *And we recently did a section on Koalas and the different types of trees they eat. And we did a percentage table of the different types of trees eaten by a Koala. And we did a pie graph for that.*

Researcher 1:   *Did that lead you to draw some conclusions or report a finding?*

Student 4:   *Koalas are fussy!*

Student 1:   *I'm not sure we found what leaf they eat the most.*

Student 4:   *It was the Madegal! In South Australia at least…and New South Wales.*

Researcher 1:   *So if you say they are fussy, it means they only eat certain types of leaves from certain types of trees. So that makes me think about if we ever get to a situation where there is not enough of those trees—if we cut them down.*

Student 4:   *Yeah, that's what it was basically about. You know it's alright if we cut them down and you try and regrow them for Koalas but if we put them in the wrong spot and they stave because they don't like the trees.*

Towards the end of the interview, students were asked what they thought of their teacher being involved in the project. Students were enthusiastic about their teacher's involvement as they viewed it as a way she was attempting to upgrade her skills in order to help her students' learning.

Researcher 2:   *So what do you think of your teacher being involved in a project like this. Do you think this is a good thing for teachers?*
Students: *Yeah* (together).
Student 2:   *I think it is because sometimes they don't know what we're gonna do during a lesson and in this program they get a chance to know how kids like to learn and whether they learn more out of doing things, showing or doing it themselves.*

In general, students said they enjoyed the numeracy learning experiences, for a variety of reasons: they were allowed to work in groups; they participated in extended investigations; they used technology such as the Internet and Excel spreadsheets and graphs. Many commented that they were learning mathematics without realising it.

Students' comments revealed that they believed Clare's new approach to teaching numeracy provided them with opportunities to engage with *mathematical knowledge* within *contexts* that emerged in other subject areas as well as in mathematics classes. These *contexts* were ones students could identify as related to their current or future lives. They were also aware of the important role physical, representational, and digital *tools* played in developing their understanding of and capacity to use mathematics. Their preparedness to use mathematics to solve problems in context and to take risks when applying mathematics to new situations stood in contrast to what students reported during the interview after the first school visit and indicates a healthy *disposition* towards using mathematics. Students also displayed a capacity to take a *critical orientation* to the use of mathematics within subjects outside of mathematics.

Discussion and Conclusion

The challenges of moving from the intended learning outcomes framed by formal curriculum documents to the enacted practices of teaching and learning, in a way that is faithful to the spirit of the original curriculum design, are well known. This chapter outlines an approach where teachers were supported in implementing an intended cross-curricular practice—numeracy—in a way that provided for rich learning opportunities for students. This approach was mediated by the use of a model that made more explicit the essential elements of numeracy and was supported by social practices in the form of discussions with the project researchers during school visits and interactions with other teachers during whole project meetings.

With a clearer sense of what was intended by numeracy statements within relevant curriculum documents and the support offered by the project researchers, Clare developed adeptness at designing learning experiences that her students found relevant and engaging. This was a gradual process in which Clare found she needed to take the risk of moving away from teacher centred approaches, with which she felt confident, towards approaches where students were challenged to take intellectual risks by engaging with open-ended activities and to look for opportunities to use mathematical knowledge and modes of reasoning in a variety of within school and outside of school contexts. Clare's focus on improving students' numeracy outcomes, the permission to explore numeracy rich topics relevant to students' interests expressed through the numeracy audit, and the personal support offered through the project, encouraged her to move from teacher centred, topic focused modes of teaching practice to a more student focused and inquiry based approach to teaching and learning. This new approach was context rich and aimed at improving students' dispositions towards doing and using mathematics. Clare was now conscious of the need to incorporate the use of digital tools in her teaching practice and to provide opportunity for students to exercise judgements, form opinions, and make decisions based on mathematical evidence.

Students responded to this new approach in ways that demonstrated that they were interested in learning mathematics, provided learning activities were challenging and offered a genuine opportunity to be engaged in their own learning. Students could see their teacher was attempting to create activities where learning was relevant to students' current or future interests and that had a genuine purpose. Clare's approach meant that students learnt about mathematics in classroom contexts that were not specific to mathematics, that is, for example, in Health and Physical Education. In the case of the activity where students investigated their levels of physical activity, students demonstrated that they had acquired new mathematical knowledge, made use of digital tools, and demonstrated positive dispositions to the use of mathematics in inquiring into an issue embedded within a context relevant to students' current interest and well being. The data gathered, as a consequence of this activity, provided students with the opportunity to critically review their personal levels of activity through comparison with those of other members of the class.

This chapter was concerned with how the intent of the numeracy aspect of a curriculum document was enacted in one school classroom through the support of a research and development project. The outcomes reported here appear to be a consequence of the clarity offered by the model employed in the project in relation to the essential elements of numeracy and of the approach to teacher professional learning adopted by the project. These influences have led to positive student views on their mathematics learning and to greater connectedness of this learning within and outside of mathematics itself. Further research is needed, however, in order to demonstrate the effectiveness of this approach on a scale greater than a small group of teachers working within a limited number of project supported schools. In attempting to implement approaches of greater scale, for example, whole school,

school cluster, regional or system wide, the issue of leadership must necessarily be addressed. This implies work must also be done on developing a theory of and vision for numeracy leadership as part of the implementation of curriculum within schools.

References

Artigue, M. (2002). Learning mathematics in a CAS environment: the genesis of a reflection about instrumentation and the dialectics between technical and conceptual work. *International Journal of Computers for Mathematical Learning, 7*(3), 245–274.

Australian Association of Mathematics Teachers (1997). *Numeracy = everyone's business. Report of the numeracy education strategy development conference.* Adelaide: AAMT.

Australian Curriculum, Assessment and Reporting Authority (2012a). Australian curriculum: mathematics. Retrieved 12 March 2012 from http://www.australiancurriculum.edu.au/Australian%20Curriculum.pdf?a=M&l=F&l=1&l=2&l=3&l=4&l=5&l=6&l=7&l=8&l=9&l=10&l=10A&e=0&e=1&e=2&e=3&e=4&e=5&e=6.

Australian Curriculum, Assessment and Reporting Authority (2012b). Australian curriculum: history. Retrieved 12 March 2012 from http://www.australiancurriculum.edu.au/Australian%20Curriculum.pdf?a=H&l=F&l=1&l=2&l=3&l=4&l=5&l=6&l=7&l=8&l=9&l=10&e=0&e=1&e=2&e=3&e=4&e=5&e=6&e=7&x=0.

Boaler, J., & Greeno, J. (2000). Identity, agency and knowing in mathematics worlds. In J. Boaler (Ed.), *Multiple perspectives on mathematics teaching and learning* (pp. 171–200). Palo Alto: Greenwood.

Department of Education and Children's Services (2005). South Australian curriculum, standards and accountability framework. Retrieved 11 March 2012 from http://www.sacsa.edu.au.

Ernest, P. (2002). Empowerment in mathematics education. *Philosophy of Mathematics Journal.* Retrieved from http://www.ex.ac.uk/~PErnest/pome15/contents.htm.

Frankenstein, M. (2001). *Reading the world with math: goals for a critical mathematical literacy curriculum.* Keynote address delivered at the 18th biennial conference of the Australian Association of Mathematics Teachers, Canberra.

Goos, M. (2007). *Developing numeracy in the learning areas (middle years).* Keynote address delivered at the South Australian Literacy and Numeracy Expo, Adelaide.

Goos, M., Galbraith, P., Renshaw, P., & Geiger, V. (2003). Perspectives on technology mediated learning in secondary school mathematics classrooms. *The Journal of Mathematical Behavior, 22*(1), 73–89.

Goos, M., Geiger, V., & Dole, S. (2010). Auditing the numeracy demands of the middle years curriculum. In L. Sparrow, B. Kissane, & C. Hurst (Eds.), *Shaping the future of mathematics education. Proceedings of the 33rd annual conference of the mathematics education research group of Australasia* (pp. 210–217). Fremantle: MERGA.

Goos, M., Geiger, V., & Dole, S. (2011). Teachers' personal conceptions of numeracy. In B. Ubuz (Ed.), *Proceedings of the 35th conference of the international group for the psychology of mathematics education* (Vol. 2, pp. 457–464). Ankara: PME.

Gresalfi, M. S., & Cobb, P. (2006). Cultivating students' discipline-specific dispositions as a critical goal for pedagogy and equity. *Pedagogies: An International Journal, 1*(1), 49–57.

Hoyles, C., Wolf, A., Molyneux-Hodgson, S., & Kent, P. (2002). *Mathematical skills in the workplace. Final Report to the Science, Technology and Mathematics Council. Foreword and Executive Summary.* London: Institute of Education, University of London; Science, Technology and Mathematics Council.

Human Capital Working Group, Council of Australian Governments (2008). National numeracy review report. Retrieved 11 March 2012 from http://www.coag.gov.au/reports/docs/national_numeracy_review.pdf.

Jablonka, E. (2003). Mathematical literacy. In A. Bishop, M. A. Clements, C. Keitel, J. Kilpatrick, & F. Leung (Eds.), *Second international handbook of mathematics education* (pp. 75–102). Dordrecht: Kluwer.

Loucks-Horsley, S., Love, N., Stiles, K., Mundry, S., & Hewson, P. (2003). *Designing professional development for teachers of science and mathematics* (2nd ed.). Thousand Oaks: Corwin Press.

Ministerial Council on Education, Employment, Training and Youth Affairs (MCEETYA) (1997). *National report on schooling in Australia 1997*. Melbourne: MCEETYA.

Noss, R., Hoyles, C., & Pozzi, S. (2000). Working knowledge: mathematics in use. In A. Bessot & J. Ridgeway (Eds.), *Education for mathematics in the workplace* (pp. 17–35). Dordrecht: Kluwer.

OECD (2004). *Learning for tomorrow's world: first results from PISA 2003*. Paris: OECD.

Pea, R. (2004). The social and technological dimensions of scaffolding and related theoretical concepts for learning, education, and human activity. *The Journal of the Learning Sciences, 13*(3), 423–451.

Peters, C., Geiger, V., Goos, M., & Dole, S. (2012). Numeracy in health and physical education. *The Australian Mathematics Teacher, 68*(1), 21–27.

Steen, L. (2001). The case for quantitative literacy. In L. Steen (Ed.), *Mathematics and democracy: the case for quantitative literacy* (pp. 1–22). Princeton: National Council on Education and the Disciplines.

Straesser, R. (2007). Didactics of mathematics: more than mathematics and school! *ZDM. Zentralblatt für Didaktik der Mathematik, 39*(1), 165–171.

Verillon, P., & Rabardel, P. (1995). Cognition and artifacts: a contribution to the study of thought in relation to instrumental activity. *European Journal of Psychology of Education, 10*, 77–103.

Zevenbergen, R. (2004). Technologizing numeracy: intergenerational differences in working mathematically in new times. *Educational Studies in Mathematics, 56*(1), 97–117.

The Impact of a Standards-Based Mathematics Curriculum on Classroom Instruction and Student Performance: The Case of *Mathematics in Context*

Mary C. Shafer

Abstract As standards-based mathematics curricula were introduced in the 1990s, various stakeholders expressed concern about whether these curricula would result in improved student performance. The summative evaluation of one of the middle-school curricula, *Mathematics in Context*, directly addressed this concern using quantitative and qualitative methodologies in both cross-sectional and longitudinal analyses. Beyond the importance of prior achievement, the results show that the ways in which instructional units were taught and the opportunities that students were given to learn from the units influence student achievement. The findings suggest that when implemented well, student achievement does improve in significant ways as a consequence of studying *Mathematics in Context* over two or three academic years.

Keywords Mathematics instruction · Standards-based curriculum · Mathematics curriculum · Middle school · Summative evaluation

In the early 1990s the National Science Foundation (NSF) began funding projects to develop instructional materials that incorporated the reformed vision of school mathematics recommended by the National Council of Teachers of Mathematics (NCTM 1989). In the mid-1990s, as the initial editions of standards-based curricula became available, many stakeholders—from school district administrators to funding agencies—called for reliable, valid evidence that these curricula did improve

The research reported in this chapter was supported by the National Science Foundation REC-9553889 and REC-0087511, by the Wisconsin Center for Education Research, School of Education, University of Wisconsin–Madison, and Northern Illinois University. This chapter draws on the monographs and technical reports from the research (see http://micimpact.wceruw.org/) and the book that followed (Romberg and Shafer 2008). Any opinions, findings, or conclusions are those of the author and do not necessarily reflect the views of the National Science Foundation, the University of Wisconsin–Madison, and Northern Illinois University.

M.C. Shafer (✉)
Northern Illinois University, DeKalb, IL, USA
e-mail: shafer@math.niu.edu

Y. Li, G. Lappan (eds.), *Mathematics Curriculum in School Education*,
Advances in Mathematics Education, DOI 10.1007/978-94-007-7560-2_23,
© Springer Science+Business Media Dordrecht 2014

student performance in mathematics. Information collected during pilot- and field-testing of the curricula was rarely gathered in ways that would support the kind of responses stakeholders requested, as it was frequently used to improve instructional units and teacher guides. Summative evaluations of each new curriculum were needed. Clements (2007) maintained that such evaluations should include various research contexts and data collections through a diverse set of research instruments in order to assess the effect of the implementation of the curriculum on students, their teachers and parents, and programs, and to assess fidelity of implementation in the use of the curriculum. Furthermore, qualitative methodologies should be used in addition to quantitative methods.

In 1996, NSF funded the longitudinal/cross-sectional study of one of the standards-based curricula, *Mathematics in Context* (MiC; National Center for Research in Mathematical Sciences Education & Freudenthal Institute 1997–1998), which was developed at the National Center for Research in Mathematics Education at the University of Wisconsin-Madison in collaboration with the Freudenthal Institute at the University of Utrecht in The Netherlands. Published by Encyclopaedia Britannica, the first edition of MiC materials consisted of 10 instructional units and accompanying teacher guides at each grade level (grades 5–8), assessment materials, and two sets of supplementary materials.

MiC was different from conventional textbooks prevalent in middle schools at that time. In MiC, students are encouraged to deepen their understanding of significant mathematics in algebra, geometry, and probability and statistics in addition to number, while emphasizing connections among mathematical ideas. The principles of Realistic Mathematics Education (RME; Freudenthal 1983) from the Freudenthal Institute in The Netherlands were used in the development of MiC. In RME, mathematics is viewed as a dynamic set of interrelated ideas best learned by applying concepts and procedures in problem contexts and situations that make sense to students. Students are given the opportunity to reinvent significant mathematics under the guidance of their teachers, through interaction with their peers, and through the use of mathematical models introduced and developed during instruction. Initially, students develop a model of a situation in which they use problem contexts and informal reasoning strategies. Such models act as bridges between concrete real-life problems and abstract formal mathematics. Through lessons that allow students to solve problems using a variety of strategies, teachers encourage students to discuss interpretations of problem situations, express their thinking, and react to different levels and qualities of solution strategies shared in the group. Through instruction and discussion, more elaborate models and strategies are introduced. Students solve problems at different levels of abstraction, falling back to more concrete, less abstract strategies whenever they feel the need. As a result of exploration, reflection, and generalization, students theoretically progress from context-specific situations to more abstract mathematical reasoning. This process is called progressive formalization. This type of interaction is far different from that generated by two-page lessons with the worked examples, emphasis on memorization, and independent, quiet seatwork often seen in traditional classrooms.

The goal of the summative evaluation of MiC was to examine the ways in which teachers changed their instructional practices when they implemented MiC, and the effects these changes had on students' achievement in mathematics. The longitudinal/cross-sectional study investigated the relationship between classroom achievement for groups of the students with respect to other variables such as prior achievement, instruction, opportunity to learn with understanding, and the capacity of schools to support and sustain high academic standards for mathematics teaching and learning. In this chapter, selected results of this summative evaluation are described.

Methodology

Researching instructional contexts and fidelity of curricular use is complex and involves multifaceted processes. A structural model was used as the foundation of data collection and research analyses. The model included 14 variables in five categories: prior variables (teacher background and experience, student background, and school cultures); independent variables (teacher knowledge, teacher professional responsibility, curricular content and materials, and the support environment for teachers and students); intervening variables (classroom events, teachers' pedagogical decisions, and student pursuits); and outcome and consequent variables (student knowledge and understanding, application of mathematics, attitudes, and future pursuits). To use the model for analysis of mathematics instruction and fidelity of implementation brought about by using MiC in the schools, an index or scale was created and validated for each variable in order to assess variation across research districts and classrooms. Analysis of the variables involved both quantitative and qualitative approaches to explicate differences in student performance in different groups over time. In this chapter, answers to one of the three research questions are discussed: What is the impact of the MiC instructional approach on student performance? To answer this question, grade-level-by-year studies, cross-sectional comparisons, and longitudinal studies were completed. Select results of these studies are described in this chapter.

The Sample

The longitudinal/cross-sectional study began when MiC was first available in its commercial form. Beginning in the 1997–1998 school year, data were gathered over a three-year period on three cohorts of students in four school districts (one cohort beginning the study in fifth grade, one beginning in sixth grade, and one beginning in seventh grade). School districts were selected on the basis of initiatives for reforming mathematics curriculum and instruction; consideration of district size, location, and demographics; amount of experience teachers had with MiC; and willingness of districts to participate in a study of this nature. District administrators and on-site coordinators were asked to select schools that were representative of the district population, rather than selecting schools with extremely low- or high-achieving groups. Principals of the selected schools chose the study teachers. Teachers, in turn, selected classes of students with average mathematical abilities rather than classes of low ability or classes in honors programs. Middle school teachers selected two classes of students.

In Districts 1 and 2, a comparative study was conducted; students studied either MiC or conventional curricula already available in their schools. Lessons were observed, and teachers completed teaching logs, journal entries, interviews, and questionnaires. District 1 was located in an urban region in the eastern part of the United States. Three elementary schools and four middle schools participated in the study. Six fifth-grade study classes were in self-contained elementary classrooms. The remaining fifth-grade study classes, also in elementary schools, and all middle-school study classes had several subject-matter teachers. The district had a 45 % minority student population with 30 % African American students and 12 % Hispanic students. Approximately 30–40 % of the students in the district were eligible for government-funded lunch programs. District 2 was located in a large urban area in southeastern United States. Three elementary and four middle schools participated in the study. Two of the nine fifth-grade study classes were in self-contained settings in elementary schools. The remaining fifth-grade study classes, also in elementary schools, and all middle-school study classes had several subject-matter teachers. The district student population was predominantly minority, with 33 % African American students and 52 % Hispanic students. Over 50 % of the students in the district were eligible for government-funded lunch programs.

In Districts 3 and 4, teachers in these districts only used MiC. Lessons were not observed, and teachers completed only interviews and questionnaires. District 3 was located in a suburban area of a large western state and was composed of four schools, each specializing in three or four grade levels. Study participants included all fifth-through seventh-grade and most eighth-grade mathematics classes in the district. The six self-contained fifth-grade study classes were in a school for Grades 3–5; Grades 6–8 were in a middle school. One sixth-grade class was self-contained. All other middle-school classes had several subject-matter teachers. The district student population was predominately White. District 4 is one of many districts located in a large urban area in the eastern part of the country. Grades 6–8 were in middle schools in which students had several subject-matter teachers. Study participants were from one middle school in this district. The district student population was predominantly minority with 50 % African American and 37 % Hispanic students. Over 50 % of the students are eligible for government-funded lunch programs.

Research Design

The longitudinal/cross-sectional study used a nonequivalent control-group, quasi-experimental design: The assignment of subjects to the groups was nonrandom, and pretests and posttests were administered to both treatment and control groups. This design allowed the research team to distinguish whether observed group differences on posttests were correlated to a particular curriculum rather than by preexisting group differences on some of the variables in the research model.

When examining data from the first year of the study, colinearity across the variables was found. Because of the inherent interpretation problem, a simplified research model was developed in 1998–1999 at the Center for Advanced Study in the Behavioral Sciences at Stanford University. The statistical working group suggested that composite variables, created from the original 14 variables, could serve as indicators. The simplified model then attributed variation in classroom achievement to variations in preceding achievement, methods of instruction, opportunity to learn with understanding, and the capacity of schools to support high academic standards for mathematics teaching and learning. (For a discussion of the impact of school capacity, see Romberg and Shafer 2008.)

Classroom Achievement

MiC was designed to deepen student understanding of comprehensive mathematics content while emphasizing connections among mathematical ideas. In order to assess the impact of MiC, two assessment systems were developed. The External Assessment System (Romberg and Webb 1997–1998) was designed to measure student performance on multiple-choice and open response tasks that were used by national and international samples of middle-school students. The items were selected from publicly-released items from National Assessment of Educational Progress (NAEP; National Center for Education Statistics 1990, 1992) and the Third International Mathematics and Science Study (TIMSS; International Association for the Evaluation of Educational Achievement 1996). Assessment items addressed four content strands: number, algebra, geometry and measurement, and probability and statistics. In order to analyze growth in mathematical skills over time, a core of the same items was included on each grade-specific assessment. The Problem Solving Assessment System (Dekker et al. 1997–1998) was developed by mathematics educators at the Freudenthal Institute. Assessment items (all open-response) addressed the same four content strands as the External Assessment System. The set of grade-level-specific assessments was designed to align with mathematics content in both MiC and conventional curricula (e.g., more number-related items on the fifth-grade assessment, more algebra items on the eighth-grade assessment). The items were also designed to address three levels of reasoning: conceptual and procedural knowledge; making connections, finding patterns and relationships; and mathematical modeling, analysis and generalization. This balanced approach to assessment in mathematics is used in the Program for International Student Assessment (PISA; Organisation for Economic Co-Operation and Development 1999). Two methods were used to ensure fairness for students who studied MiC and students who studied conventional curricula. First, the external evaluator of the project reviewed all items in both assessment systems with respect to content, reasoning, and impartiality. Second, both assessments were pilot-tested in grade-specific classrooms in which MiC or conventional curricula were used. Analyses suggested that assessment items were appropriate for both groups.

Student responses on all assessment items were used by researchers at the Australian Council for Educational Research to calibrate a single proficiency scale used for the composite index classroom achievement (Turner and O'Connor 2005). The scale and accompanying progress maps were consistent with both the PISA definition of mathematization and with Romberg's (2001) view of mathematical literacy. The proficiency scale for classroom achievement provided a frame of reference for monitoring growth in student performance over one year or multiple years and a way to compare the performances of groups of students.

Prior Achievement

Because random assignment of students or classes of students to treatments was impractical, national percentile rankings of standardized test scores as measures of prior achievement were used in the first study year, with the understanding that the percentile scores came from different tests and different yet presumed similar, norm-populations. In the second and third years, classroom achievement from the previous year was used as a measure of preceding achievement.

Instruction

Data used in characterizing instruction were collected through classroom observation reports, teacher logs, journal entries, interviews, and questionnaires (Shafer 2004, 2005). Although teachers in all four research sites completed interviews, in Districts 1 and 2 classroom observations were conducted, and teachers completed teaching logs and journal entries.

The composite variable Instruction was based on three complementary perspectives for examining instruction in the context of reform: the NCTM *Standards* documents (1989, 1991, 1995); the principles of Realistic Mathematics Education (Gravemeijer 1994); and research on teaching and learning mathematics for understanding (Carpenter and Lehrer 1999; Cohen et al. 1993; Fennema and Romberg 1999; Hiebert et al. 1997). The instruction composite variable included five major categories—unit planning, lesson planning, mathematical interaction during instruction, classroom assessment practice, and student pursuits during instruction—which involved 19 aspects of instruction. For each of the 19 aspects of instruction, three to six levels were outlined through discussion among the research staff. The levels were further described through a review of literature specific to each aspect. Beginning with data from fifth-grade study teachers, the levels were further refined. This process was based on Strauss' (1987) system of open, axial, and selective coding, a process which involved repeated coding of data for interpretive codes. The levels were subsequently refined through coding data from all other teachers. When a code was added, the entire set of data was reread to see whether the new codes were more appropriate for the data. The development of levels, along with examples of each level, is explained in Shafer (2005).

The instruction composite variable was created only for teachers in Districts 1 and 2 for whom there was a complete set of ratings on all 19 aspects of instruction. Thirty-four teachers were included in the analysis for the first year of data collection, 32 teachers in the second year, and 17 teachers in the third year. Some teachers were in the study multiple years. Six levels of Instruction were identified to capture the variation among teachers in different grade levels and treatments. A summary of these levels is shown in Table 1. A full description of the levels, along with examples, is provided in Shafer (2005).

Opportunity to Learn with Understanding

Data used in characterizing the composite variable instruction were collected through classroom observation reports, teacher logs and journal entries, and interviews. The same number of teachers was included in the analysis for the composite variable Opportunity to Learn with Understanding (OTLu) as in Instruction. OTLu is described through curricular content, modification of curricular materials, and classroom events.

Curricular content and modification of curricular materials represents the teacher's decisions in defining the actual curriculum—the topics and instructional units or chapters covered, the supplementary materials used during instruction, and modifications of the intended curriculum. Classroom events represent the interactions among teacher and students that promote learning mathematics with understanding: development of conceptual understanding; student conjectures about mathematical ideas; connections within mathematics; and connections between mathematics and students' daily lives. Attempts to capture student understanding of mathematics content rarely occur in measures of OTL. However, in the Third International Mathematics and Science Study (TIMSS), both content and instruction were considered (Stigler and Hiebert 1999). Hiebert (1999) noted that instruction for U. S. students predominately emphasized computational procedures, and conceptual understanding was given little attention. Furthermore, the results suggested that students learned what they had the opportunity to learn—simple calculation, terms, and definitions—rather than solving non-routine problems and using mathematical processes such as reasoning about complex problems and developing mathematics arguments. In MiC, understanding mathematics receives substantial emphasis. Therefore, in the MiC longitudinal/cross-sectional study, OTL was interpreted more broadly than as a mere gauge of content coverage and was viewed as a student's opportunity to learn mathematics *with understanding* (OTLu). The development of levels for curricular content and modifications of curricular materials followed the same process as for the levels of the composite variable Instruction, and the levels for teaching for understanding were the ones derived for Instruction.

Table 1 Summary of the composite variable instruction

Level 6: Most Reflective of Teaching for Understanding	Level 3. Limited Attention to Conceptual Understanding
Mathematical Interaction Inquiry and lesson presentation • Emphasis on conceptual understanding • Active participation by students with teacher support • Discussion of solutions, generalizations, connections Interactive decisions • Predominantly aligned with understanding • Frequent questions on articulation of thinking, understanding mathematics, or reasonable solutions *Classroom Assessment Practice* • Attention to mathematical processes • Ongoing, purposeful feedback from teacher, students • Feedback: making sense of mathematics, solutions • Student assessment of own work and others' work *Student Pursuits* • Occasional substantive conversation • Student-student conversation about procedures *Lesson Planning* • Student discussion, problem solving, reflection planned	*Mathematical Interaction* Inquiry and lesson presentation • Students use invented or demonstrated strategies • Student explanations focused on procedures Interactive decisions • More reflective of good standard pedagogy • Some attention to articulation of thinking, reasonable solutions • Occasional addition of different context or review *Classroom Assessment Practice* • Evidence from homework, classwork, occasionally student explanations • Teacher feedback: concepts, contexts, *or* procedures, answer format • Student-student feedback: answers *Student Pursuits* • Student-student conversation limited, answers shared *Lesson Planning* • Discussion of vocabulary, steps in procedures planned, not elaboration of thinking
Level 5: Reflective of Teaching Mathematics for Understanding	**Level 2: Focus on Procedures**
Mathematical Interaction Inquiry and lesson presentation • Emphasis on conceptual understanding • Active participation by students and teacher • Discussion of solutions Interactive decisions • Attentive to teaching for understanding • Teacher explanations promote connections *Classroom Assessment Practice* • Student explanations as evidence of mathematical processes *or* procedural understanding • Feedback consistent with Level 6 *Student Pursuits* • Student-student conversation limited, answers shared *Lesson Planning* • Student discussion, problem solving, reflection planned	*Mathematical Interaction* Inquiry and lesson presentation • Predominantly lower order thinking • Students expected to use demonstrated procedures Interactive decisions • Predominantly least aligned with understanding • Limited changes in response to student difficulties, misunderstanding *Classroom Assessment Practice* • Evidence from homework, classwork • Emphasis on procedures, format of answers • Teacher feedback indirectly responsive to students, inattentive to student misconceptions • Student-student feedback: minimal *Student Pursuits* • Student-student conversation limited, answers shared *Lesson Planning* • Discussion anticipated but not planned

Four levels of OTL*u* were identified to capture the variation among teachers in different grade levels and treatments. A summary of these levels is shown in Table 2. A full description of the levels, along with examples, is provided in Shafer (2005).

The Impact of MiC

In this section of the chapter, select results for the following research question are described: What is the impact of the MiC instructional approach on stu-

Table 1 (Continued)

Level 4: Attempt to Teach Mathematics for Understanding	Level 1: Underdeveloped Lessons
Mathematical Interaction Inquiry and lesson presentation • Attempt for conceptual understanding, but focus on procedural understanding • General acceptance of teacher's procedures Interactive decisions • More attentive to good standard pedagogy • Additional exercises, mini-lessons, contexts, review *Classroom Assessment Practice* • Evidence from student explanations • Focus on procedural understanding • Teacher feedback related to concepts, contexts • Student-student feedback: answers, procedures *Student Pursuits* • Engagement mildly enthusiastic, teacher encouraged *Lesson Planning* • Student discussion, problem solving, planned	*Mathematical Interaction* Inquiry and lesson presentation • No formal lesson presentation • Procedures demonstrated to individual students • Student dependence on teacher for mathematical work • Frequent confusion or misunderstanding Interactive decisions • Least likely to support teaching for understanding • Teacher explanations preferred, no changes to address student needs *Classroom Assessment Practice* • Teacher feedback inattentive to student misconceptions, misleading, lacked mathematical substance • Student-student feedback: nonexistent *Student Pursuits:* • Conversation not encouraged *Lesson Planning* • Student discussion, problem solving not considered

Table 2 Summary of the composite variable opportunity to learn with understanding

Level 4: High Level of Opportunity to Learn with Understanding	Level 3: Moderate Level of Opportunity to Learn with Understanding
• Curriculum with attention to all content areas • Few modifications to curricular materials • Portions of lessons focused on conceptual understanding • Student conjectures related to validity of particular statements • Connections among mathematical ideas clearly explained by the teacher • Connections between mathematics and students' life experiences apparent	• Content taught in depth, but limited to one or two content areas • Supplementary activities occasionally used • Limited development of conceptual understanding • Student conjectures related to making connections between anew problem and problems previously seen • Connections among mathematical ideas briefly mentioned • Connections between mathematics and students' life experiences reasonably clear if explained by the teacher
Level 2: Limited Opportunity to Learn with Understanding	**Level 1: Low Level of Opportunity to Learn with Understanding**
• For teachers using MiC: Few content areas taught due to slow pacing • For teachers using conventional curricula: Vast content as disparate pieces of knowledge, laden with prescribed algorithms • For teachers using MiC: Supplementary materials subsumed the curriculum • For teachers using conventional curricula: Few modifications to curricular materials; supplementary activities occasionally used • Limited development of conceptual understanding • Student conjectures related to making connections between a new problem and problems previously seen • Connections among mathematical ideas briefly mentioned • Experiences reasonably clear if explained by the teacher	• Vast content as disparate pieces of knowledge, laden with prescribed algorithms • For teachers using MiC: Supplementary materials subsumed the curriculum • For teachers using conventional curricula: Haphazard presentation of content; no adherence to textbook as guideline • Conceptual understanding not promoted • Student conjectures not observed; connections not encouraged • Connections among mathematical ideas not discussed • Connections between mathematics and students' life experiences not evident

dent performance? This question was explored through grade-level-by-year-studies, cross-sectional comparisons, and longitudinal studies (Romberg and Shafer 2008; Romberg et al. 2005).

Grade-Level-by-Year Studies

Grade-level-by-year studies were extensive investigations of student performance organized by teacher/student groups (students in one elementary class or two middle-school classes taught by the same teacher during a particular school year). Eight studies were conducted: fifth, sixth, and seventh grades in 1997–1998; sixth, seventh, and eighth grades in 1998–1999; and seventh and eighth grades in 1999–2000. In all eight studies, much variation in the Classroom Achievement variable (CA) was evident among the 92 teacher/student groups who used MiC across the four school districts.

Other analyses revealed that District 3 teacher/student groups had higher CA results and District 4 groups often had lower CA results than other districts. Analyses in each district showed that CA scores were not as varied in over half of the teacher/student groups at the same grade level in the same year. In most cases this was also evident in CA scores for the separate content strands (number, algebra, geometry and measurement, probability and statistics). These findings suggested homogeneous grouping (tracking), which was verified in principal and teacher interviews, along with other sources of variation. For example, in District 2 in 1998–1999 Ms. Keeton[1] and Ms. Teague taught MiC in eighth-grade in the same school. In Ms. Keeton's group, 21 students completed study assessments in both spring 1998 and spring 1999. They had an overall mean prior achievement (PA) on the CA proficiency scale of 253.6 and mean CA at the end of the year was 270.6, an increase of 16.4. In Ms. Teague's group, 17 students completed both study assessments each spring. They had PA of 230.2 and mean CA at the end of the year was 244.0, an increase of 13.8. While the increases in mean CA scores were similar between the groups, it is clear that PA was higher in Ms. Keeton's group. In addition, Ms. Keeton's group experienced a higher quality of instruction and a higher level of opportunity to learn with understanding (OTLu) than Ms. Teague's group. Along with differences in PA, the instruction and OTLu these students experienced likely affected their performance.

Percentile scores from the standardized test scores provided by the districts were used to check for consistency with the patterns evident from using the CA index. Because the CA index was developed from student responses to all assessments designed for this study, checking for consistency was important in order to know whether the results of the CA index were idiosyncratic. The pattern of percentile scores generally reflected the patterns of variation in the CA scores in the grade-level-by-year studies. Other analyses suggested a strong correlation between PA and CA.

---

[1] Names of teachers and schools are pseudonyms.

Based on the grade-level-by-year studies, the MiC instructional approach as practiced in the 92 teacher/student groups produced much variation in CA performance. The results showed that some students were able to translate a contextualized or non-contextualized, generally non-routine problem into mathematical terms by applying a formula or relationship or specific mathematical knowledge. Most students primarily solved contextualized problems in which they used simple calculations or they applied routine procedures to standard or familiar contextualized problems. Some students were in the lowest area of the proficiency scale.

Cross-Sectional Studies

Two types of cross-sectional studies were completed: cross-grade comparisons and cross-year comparisons.

Cross-Grade Comparisons   In cross-grade comparisons, the performances of students in different grade levels in the same district were studied for one year with the goal of generating insight into longitudinal performance for a group of the same students over time. The assumptions of cross-grade comparisons are that achievement likely increases over time and students in consecutive grade levels are comparable in the school cultures and instructional practices they experienced. However, these assumptions were problematic in this research, as less variance in some teacher/student groups was attributable to homogeneous grouping and differences in the instruction and OTLu. Other conditions, such as transition of fifth-grade students to middle schools and initiatives for some eighth-grade students to take algebra classes, changed the composition of students from one grade level to the next.

An example of the cross-grade comparisons is from 1998–1999. Performance on the CA index was compared for students in all four districts in sixth, seventh, and eighth grades (see Table 3). The overall scores for the three grades were similar. However, patterns by district were evident. In District 1, a nearly significant decrease in CA means from sixth grade to seventh grade and a significant decrease in mean scores from seventh grade to eighth grade was found. New students were added to the study in the second year to increase sample size, but not in the third year. The quality of instruction and OTLu students experienced were higher in seventh grade than eighth grade, and this likely influenced student performance. In District 2, there was a nearly significant increase in mean scores from sixth grade to seventh grade and a significant increase in mean scores from seventh grade to eighth grade. The quality of instruction and OTLu students experienced were likely factors in the increase in mean scores as teachers "looped" with their students from one grade level to the next. In District 3, the mean CA scores from sixth grade to seventh grade were about the same, but there was a significant increase in performance from seventh grade to eighth grade. In District 4, there was a significant increase in mean CA scores from sixth to seventh grade, but a significant decrease in mean scores from seventh to eighth grade. Initiatives for students to take formal algebra classes

Table 3 Classroom achievement for MiC students, grades 6, 7, and 8 in 1998–1999, overall and by district

		(N)	Mean	SD	95 % Confidence Interval	
					Lower	Upper
Overall						
	Grade 6	550	249.4	56.4	244.7	254.1
	Grade 7	636	248.8	44.9	245.3	252.3
	Grade 8	319	249.0	45.9	244.0	254.0
District 1						
	Grade 6	162	269.7	57.8	260.8	278.6
	Grade 7	121	254.2	44.6	246.3	262.1
	Grade 8	86	237.1	41.0	228.4	245.8
District 2						
	Grade 6	171	222.1	52.7	214.2	230.0
	Grade 7	210	234.2	39.3	228.8	239.5
	Grade 8	92	253.8	31.0	247.5	260.1
District 3						
	Grade 6	115	281.1	42.3	273.3	288.8
	Grade 7	123	280.6	48.4	272.0	289.1
	Grade 8	63	300.5	32.7	292.4	308.6
District 4						
	Grade 6	102	227.1	41.5	219.1	235.2
	Grade 7	182	240.7	37.0	235.3	246.0
	Grade 8	78	214.9	36.1	206.9	222.9

in eighth grade may have resulted in quite different samples for the two years. In District 3, all teachers taught six to seven units, at times teaching portions of MiC units from a previous grade level to support student learning of units specific to their grade levels. In District 3, the instructional context was more aligned with the assumption for cross-grade studies that students had comparable educational experiences. Therefore, the changes in District 3 may provide insight into the impact of MiC on students' performance as they study the curriculum from sixth through eighth grades. By content strand, similar patterns were apparent in Districts 1, 2, and 3. In District 4, the lower eighth-grade CA mean scores were due to the lower mean scores in the algebra and geometry strands.

In summary, in cross-grade comparisons the performances of students in different grade levels in the same district were studied for one year with the goal of generating insight into longitudinal performance for a group of the same students over time. The assumption is that students in consecutive grade levels are comparable in the school cultures and instructional practices they experienced. In the MiC comparisons, the comparability of the groups was problematic, and increased performance across grades was sometimes lacking. However, even when accounting for these situations, there were many instances that performance did increase over the grade levels when students studied MiC.

Cross-Year Comparisons   The cross-year comparisons yielded information about the performance for groups of students in the same district at the same grade level who were exposed to the curriculum over time. For example, at the end of the first year, seventh-grade students had studied MiC one year; at the end of the second year, seventh-grade students had studied MiC for two years; and at the end of the third year, seventh-grade students had studied MiC for three years. The assumption was, with comparable students and instructional practices in each district, the results might generate some insight in the performance of the same group of students as they experience MiC over a period of years.

To illustrate these comparisons, results are shown for all three study years for students in seventh grade in all four districts (see Table 4). Overall scores for all students were not significant when the first and second years were compared, but they increased significantly from the second year to the third year. This was also found for the scores in Districts 1, 2, and 3. In District 4, although the mean scores increased each year, the increases were not significant. Results from the cross-grade studies provide some insight here. In District 1, the means for Year 3 and for the content strands showed similar performance of the group of students in the cross-grade studies. Similarly, results from the grade-level-by-year studies inform the cross-grade studies. In District 2, the results of the cross-year studies were compromised by the different samples each year. In Year 1, students were from Guggenheim and Hirsch Middle Schools, in Year 2, from Guggenheim and Weir Middle Schools, and in Year 3 only from Guggenheim Middle School. Therefore, the increase in scores for Year 3 in District 2 was likely attributable to increases in all content areas, particularly number and probability and statistics.

In summary, cross-year comparisons provided information about the performance for groups of students in the same district at the same grade level who studied the curriculum over time. The assumption was that students and instructional experiences were comparable, but that was not the case particularly in District 2. The goal was to provide insight into the performance of the same group of students as they experienced the MiC instructional approach over a period of years, and because both teachers and students would be more familiar with MiC units and the instructional approach, student performance would increase. The cross-year studies did provide evidence of this, particularly in seventh grade in the third year.

Longitudinal Studies

Longitudinal studies examined changes in performance of cohorts of individual students for two or three consecutive years. The assumption of longitudinal studies is that tracking the growth for individual students is possible. Data were only from

Table 4 Classroom achievement for MiC students, grade 7 in 1997–1998 (year 1), 1998–1999 (year 2), 1999–2000 (year 3), overall and by district

		(N)	Mean	SD	95 % Confidence Interval	
					Lower	Upper
Overall						
	Year 1	507	252.8	49.2	248.5	257.1
	Year 2	636	248.8	44.9	245.3	252.3
	Year 3	267	282.2	52.2	276.0	288.5
District 1						
	Year 1	88	247.2	43.9	238.1	256.4
	Year 2	121	254.2	44.6	246.3	262.1
	Year 3	79	286.8	56.8	274.2	299.3
District 2						
	Year 1	184	240.3	39.8	234.5	246.0
	Year 2	210	234.2	39.3	228.8	239.5
	Year 3	61	259.7	42.6	249.1	270.4
District 3						
	Year 1	127	293.4	40.5	286.4	300.5
	Year 2	123	280.6	48.4	272.0	289.1
	Year 3	94	305.6	42.5	297.0	314.2
District 4						
	Year 1	108	230.8	50.0	221.3	240.2
	Year 2	182	240.7	27.0	235.3	246.0
	Year 3	33	246.1	46.4	230.3	262.0

students who completed both the Problem Solving Assessment and the External Assessment System during each year of participation in the study. Assessment scores were not imputed statistically because the results of these assessments were used in the development of the CA proficiency scale. Longitudinal cohorts were planned for three cohorts of students, one beginning in fifth, sixth, and seventh grade during the first study year. These were Cohorts A, B, and C, respectively. However, the number of students in each cohort was small due to factors that included fifth-grade students were dispersed into many classes as they moved to middle school; some students did not complete both study assessments in a given year; four teachers in District 2 withdrew from the study in the first year; movement of middle school students out of a study school or into classes of non-study teachers; and initiatives for students to take a formal algebra course in eighth grade. Therefore, other cohorts of individual students were created to examine the performance of the same students over time and to use in comparison to the initially planned cohorts.

Cohorts A, F, and H MiC was developed for fifth through eighth grades, in response to the recommendation for the middle grades beginning in fifth grade in the NCTM *Curriculum and Evaluation Standards for School Mathematics* (1989). Cohorts A, F, and H began the study in 1997–1998. Cohort A was in the study for three years, Cohort F was in the study only in fifth and sixth grades, and Cohort H was only in the study in fifth grade (see Table 5). The performance of Cohort A was statistically significant from year to year. At the end of the third year, half the students were able to translate a contextualized or non-contextualized, generally non-routine problem into mathematical terms by applying a formula or relationship or specific mathematical knowledge. Nearly half primarily solved contextualized problems in which they used simple calculations. The performance of Cohort F was lower than Cohort A in the same grade levels. More than half of the students solved contextualized problems in which they used simple calculations. More students applied routine procedures to familiar kinds of problems than Cohort A. In comparison, the performance of Cohort H minimally increased in performance over the school year and was significantly lower than Cohorts A and F.

By district, Cohort A was mostly composed of students from District 3. In that district, student enrollment was the most stable across all three years. The increase in performance of Cohort A in this district was significant from year to year. In District 1, the performance of Cohort A was consistent with the performance in the cross-grade studies. Generally, the quality of instruction was higher at Grade 5 than at Grades 6 and 7 in District 1. Fifth-grade teachers tended to teach for understanding, and students participated more fully in lessons. Also, fifth-grade teachers taught at least six units that included content in all four strands, and they rarely supplemented MiC units with other resources. In contrast, lessons for two of the three sixth-grade teachers were characterized as underdeveloped or focused on procedures. Sixth-grade teachers also taught fewer MiC units than fifth-grade teachers (one to two units each in number, algebra, and geometry). In seventh-grade, one teacher taught six units including all content strands in ways that promoted conceptual understanding, whereas the other teacher taught three units that were heavily supplemented with traditional drill-and-practice exercises on computational procedures. In District 1, the dip in performance in Grade 6 rebounded in Grade 7, but still did not recover to the level of performance in Grade 5. The use of MiC units, the quality of instruction, and opportunity to learn with understanding were very different for students in Grades 5, 6, and 7 in this district.

Results of other analyses provided additional insight into the performance of Cohort A. In Cohort A, both girls and boys showed gains in CA over the three years, and gains were also apparent by content strands. On the standardized tests administered in each district, Cohort A showed a gain from fifth to sixth grade, but a loss from sixth to seventh grade. These results contrast with the gain year to year in CA. Gains from year to year were also evident in performance on nearly all of the common items on the External Assessment System designed for the study. The performance of Cohort A on 80 % of the common items was comparable to or greater than the original eighth-grade samples on national and international assessments. The performance of Cohort F was generally lower on all measures than Cohort A.

Table 5 Classroom achievement for MiC cohorts A, F, and H, overall and by district

		(N)	Mean	SD	95 % Confidence Interval	
					Lower	Upper
Overall						
Cohort A	Grade 5	89	271.6	37.4	263.9	279.4
	Grade 6	89	282.5	43.0	273.6	291.5
	Grade 7	89	304.1	45.2	294.7	313.4
Cohort F	Grade 5	55	265.7	42.4	254.5	276.9
	Grade 6	55	268.1	56.2	253.3	283.0
Cohort H	Grade 5	293	247.4	44.3	242.3	252.5
District 1						
Cohort A	Grade 5	15	290.9	30.4	275.5	306.3
	Grade 6	15	277.1	55.9	248.8	305.4
	Grade 7	15	295.4	54.7	267.7	323.1
Cohort F	Grade 5	28	268.1	43.1	252.1	284.1
	Grade 6	28	257.4	63.1	234.1	280.8
Cohort H	Grade 5	106	247.4	44.3	239.0	255.8
District 2						
Cohort A	Grade 5	6[a]	248.7	33.9	221.6	275.9
	Grade 6	6	239.5	25.0	219.5	259.5
	Grade 7	6	259.9	23.9	240.8	279.0
Cohort F	Grade 5	3	249.2	25.7	220.1	278.2
	Grade 6	3	285.0	48.8	229.8	340.1
Cohort H	Grade 5	159	234.3	37.5	228.4	240.1
District 3						
Cohort A	Grade 5	68	269.4	37.8	260.4	278.4
	Grade 6	68	287.5	39.2	278.2	296.8
	Grade 7	68	309.9	42.2	299.8	319.9
Cohort F	Grade 5	24	265.0	43.9	247.4	282.6
	Grade 6	24	278.5	47.3	259.6	297.5
Cohort H	Grade 5	28	267.7	50.4	249.0	286.3

[a]Many study students were lost due to transition from elementary to middle schools and teacher withdrawal from participation in Year 1

Cohort F gained in performance on standardized tests. However, gains in performance on the common items of the External Assessment System were evident in number, and performance on the rest of the items was lower than Cohort A.

Cohorts B, G, and I In recognition that MiC might be used only in middle schools, Cohorts B, G, and I began the study in sixth grade. Beginning in 1997–

1998, Cohort B was in the study for three years, Cohort G was in the study only in sixth and seventh grades, and Cohort I was only in the study in sixth grade. The performance of Cohort B was statistically significant from the first year to the second year, but only showed a small increase in the third year (see Table 6). In contrast, the performance of Cohort G was statistically greater than Cohort B in both years. Cohort I performed significantly higher and nearly significantly higher than grades 6 and 8 in Cohort B, respectively, at the end of the first year. At the end of the third year, half the students in Cohort B solved contextualized problems in which they used simple calculations, while the other half applied routine procedures to familiar kinds of problems. The performance of Cohort G was higher than Cohort B in the same grade levels. At the end of two years, nearly half of the students solved contextualized problems in which they used simple calculations, and more students were able to translate a contextualized or non-contextualized, generally non-routine problem into mathematical terms by applying a formula or relationship or specific mathematical knowledge than Cohort B. In comparison, fewer students in Cohort H were able to translate a contextualized or non-contextualized, generally non-routine problem into mathematical terms by applying a formula or relationship than Cohort B and fewer students completed assessment items at the lowest level than Cohort B at the end of the first year. No data was available for District 3 due to a misunderstanding by eighth-grade teachers in Year 3. In the other districts, growth in CA was found for Cohorts B and G, although a greater increase was evident in District 1. This is an important finding because these students did not study the MiC fifth-grade instructional units.

Results of other analyses provided additional insight into the performance of Cohort B. In Cohort B, both girls and boys showed gains in CA over the three years, with boys scoring a little higher than girls. Gains were also apparent in CA by content strands, with the exception of a slight decrease in geometry in the third year. On the standardized tests administered in each district, Cohort B showed a loss from sixth to seventh grade, but a gain from seventh to eighth grade. This contrasts with substantial gain in CA from Year 1 to Year 2 and slight gain in CA from Year 2 to Year 3. Gains from year to year were also evident in performance on over half of the common items on the External Assessment System across the grade levels. The performance of Cohort B on 35 % of the common items was comparable to or greater than the original eighth-grade samples on national and international assessments, especially in the number and statistics content strands. In Cohort G girls and boys showed gains in CA over the two years, and growth was evident in all four content strands. On the common items on the External Assessment System, Cohort G showed large gains in performance on nearly all items. The performance of Cohort G on 55 % of the common items was comparable to or greater than the original eighth-grade samples on national and international assessments, especially in number, geometry, and statistics. CA performance for Cohort I was higher in sixth grade than Cohort B, but lower than Cohort G.

Cohorts C and J In recognition that MiC might be used in seventh and eighth grades without implementation in sixth grade, Cohorts C and J started the study in

Table 6 Classroom achievement for MiC cohorts B, G, and I, overall and by district

		(N)	Mean	SD	95 % Confidence Interval	
					Lower	Upper
Overall						
Cohort B	Grade 6	50	215.1	44.8	202.7	227.5
	Grade 7	50	247.8	41.8	236.2	259.4
	Grade 8	50	252.4	39.2	241.5	263.3
Cohort G	Grade 6	111	259.5	50.7	250.1	268.9
	Grade 7	111	273.4	53.1	263.5	283.3
Cohort I	Grade 6	246	236.1	46.2	230.3	241.9
District 1						
Cohort B	Grade 6	23	203.2	45.5	184.7	221.8
	Grade 7	23	257.5	38.1	242.0	273.1
	Grade 8	23	263.1	39.2	247.3	279.3
Cohort G	Grade 6	13	210.5	42.6	187.3	233.6
	Grade 7	13	244.7	53.3	215.7	273.6
Cohort I	Grade 6	51	216.1	46.1	203.4	228.7
District 2						
Cohort B	Grade 6	13	232.6	52.9	203.8	261.3
	Grade 7	13	238.6	57.8	207.2	270.0
	Grade 8	13	239.7	38.5	218.8	260.6
Cohort G	Grade 6	11	207.6	43.4	182.0	233.3
	Grade 7	11	216.8	31.8	198.0	235.6
Cohort I	Grade 6	130	236.3	40.8	229.3	243.3
District 3						
Cohort B	Grade 6	0[a]				
	Grade 7	0				
	Grade 8	0				
Cohort G	Grade 6	64	290.6	33.2	282.5	298.8
	Grade 7	64	299.5	43.2	288.9	310.1
Cohort I	Grade 6	32	286.1	34.6	274.2	298.1
District 4						
Cohort B	Grade 6	14	218.5	30.1	202.7	234.3
	Grade 7	14	240.4	27.0	226.3	254.5
	Grade 8	14	246.3	37.6	226.6	265.9
Cohort G	Grade 6	23	225.3	32.2	212.1	238.5
	Grade 7	23	244.2	42.2	227.0	261.5
Cohort I	Grade 6	33	217.6	40.5	203.7	231.4

[a]In District 3, CA could not be calculated over three years because both assessments were not completed in Year 3

Table 7 Classroom achievement for MiC cohorts C and J, overall and by district

		(*N*)	Mean	*SD*	95 % Confidence Interval	
					Lower	Upper
Overall						
Cohort C	Grade 7	148	251.3	41.1	244.6	257.9
	Grade 8	148	263.8	44.6	256.6	271.0
Cohort J	Grade 7	320	255.0	51.6	249.4	260.7
District 1						
Cohort C	Grade 7	29	247.3	36.8	233.9	260.7
	Grade 8	29	244.4	41.4	229.3	259.5
District 2						
Cohort C	Grade 7	38	243.1	32.7	232.7	253.5
	Grade 8	38	258.4	26.4	250.0	266.8
District 3						
Cohort C	Grade 7	50	276.2	31.7	267.4	285.0
	Grade 8	50	302.2	30.6	293.7	310.7
District 4						
Cohort C	Grade 7	31	224.8	47.0	208.2	241.3
	Grade 8	31	226.6	38.6	213.0	240.2

seventh grade. Beginning in 1997–1998, Cohort C was in the study for two years, and Cohort J was in the study for one year. The performance of Cohort C was nearly statistically significant from one year to another (see Table 7). The performance of District 3 was significantly higher than the other districts, and the performance of District 4 was lower that other districts. The performance of Cohort J was similar to the first year CA performance of Cohort C. At the end of eighth grade, more students in Cohort C solved contextualized problems in which they used simple calculations, and more students were able to translate a contextualized or non-contextualized, generally non-routine problem into mathematical terms by applying a formula or relationship or specific mathematical knowledge. Both girls and boys showed gains in CA over the two years, with girls scoring a little higher than boys. Gains were also apparent in CA by content strands, particularly in number and statistics. On the standardized tests administered in each district, Cohort C's increase in performance was consistent with gains in CA. On the External Assessment System common items, Cohort C showed increases in performance on nearly all items. The performance of Cohort C on 60 % of the common items was comparable to or greater than the original eighth-grade samples on national and international assessments, especially in number and geometry. The finding in the number strand is interesting because there are only a few MiC instructional units devoted to number in seventh and eighth grades.

In summary, the longitudinal studies examined implementation of MiC in three situations: from fifth grade in elementary schools through sixth and seventh grades in middle schools; from sixth through eighth grade; and from seventh grade to eighth grade. Even though the number of students in the cohorts was small due to factors noted above, there were various examples of increased performance for students who studied MiC. Increases in CA were statistically significant for students who studied MiC over three years beginning with the fifth-grade instructional units, and many of these students solved problems that involved translation of a contextualized or non-contextualized, generally non-routine problem into mathematical terms by applying a formula or relationship or specific mathematical knowledge. Increases in CA were also noted for students who began their study of MiC in Grade 6. However, the statistically significant gain in performance was achieved at the end of the second year, with a modest increase in the third year. Increases in CA were also evident for students who studied MiC over two years beginning in Grade 7. These results are interesting in that students did not have the benefit of studying fifth- and sixth-grade MiC units.

Answer to the Research Question

The results of these analyses suggest that the MiC instructional approach did have a positive impact on students' mathematical achievement. The grade-level-by-year studies pointed out differences among teacher/student groups, varying from homogeneous grouping to differences in instructional practices and opportunity to learn with understanding. The cross-sectional comparisons suggested that student performance increases over grade levels, and, as teachers and students became more familiar with the MiC units and instructional approach, student performance increased. In longitudinal comparisons, even though the samples were small, the performance of cohorts of individual students showed that MiC had a substantial impact on student performance over two or three years.

Conclusion

Conducting research in schools is complex. Variation in the ways the curriculum is implemented is expected, especially when a new and different standards-based curriculum is implemented. Attempts to capture patterns in instructional practices in the daily interactions mathematics classrooms are not easy, and the importance of teachers completing requested data collection and students completing assessments with intellectual curiosity is difficult to communicate. However, in this summative evaluation of *Mathematics in Context*, rich observation data were collected, interactions that occurred in study classrooms were documented in multiple ways, and students were followed longitudinally.

In this research, students' prior achievement had an important impact on classroom achievement. However, the ways in which curricular materials were implemented also influenced differences in student achievement over time. Some MiC teachers implemented the curriculum well, with instructional practices aligned with teaching mathematics for understanding and teaching multiple instructional units in various content strands with few supplementary conventional materials. Other teachers either taught MiC with conventional pedagogy or heavily supplemented MiC with conventional materials. This variation in implementation led to differences in student achievement. Regardless of other differences in the teacher/student groups or student cohorts, when MiC was implemented well, students' performance increased. Students expanded their knowledge of mathematics, reasoned about mathematical ideas at deeper levels, and applied mathematical skills in number and other content strands.

References

Carpenter, T. P., & Lehrer, R. (1999). Teaching and learning mathematics with understanding. In E. Fennema & T. A. Romberg (Eds.), *Classrooms that promote mathematical understanding* (pp. 19–32). Mahwah: Erlbaum.

Clements, D. H. (2007). Curriculum research: toward a framework for "research-based" curricula. *Journal for Research in Mathematics Education, 28*(1), 35–70.

Cohen, D. K., McLaughlin, M. W., & Talbert, J. E. (Eds.) (1993). *Teaching for understanding: challenges for policy and practice* (pp. 167–206). San Francisco: Jossey-Bass.

Dekker, T., Querelle, N., van Reeuwijk, M., Wijers, M., Fejis, E., de Lange, J., Shafer, M. C., Davis, J., Wagner, L., & Webb, D. (1997–1998). *Problem solving assessment system.* Madison: University of Wisconsin.

Fennema, E., & Romberg, T. A. (Eds.) (1999). *Classrooms that promote mathematical understanding* (pp. 19–32). Mahwah: Erlbaum.

Freudenthal, H. (1983). *Didactical phenomenology of mathematical structures.* Dordrecht: D. Reidel.

Gravemeijer, K. (1994). Educational development and developmental research in mathematics education. *Journal for Research in Mathematics Education, 25*(5), 443–471.

Hiebert, J. (1999). Relationships between research and the NCTM standards. *Journal for Research in Mathematics Education, 30*(1), 3–19.

Hiebert, J., Carpenter, T. P., Fennema, E., Fuson, K. C., Wearne, D., Murray, H., Olivier, A., & Human, P. (1997). *Making sense: teaching and learning mathematics with understanding.* Portsmouth: Heinemann.

International Association for the Evaluation of Educational Achievement (1996). *TIMSS mathematics items: released set for population 2 (seventh and eighth grades).* The Hague: Author.

National Center for Education Statistics (1990). *National assessment of educational progress: grade 8 mathematics assessment.* Washington: Author.

National Center for Education Statistics (1992). *National assessment of educational progress: grade 8 mathematics assessment.* Washington: Author.

National Center for Research in Mathematical Sciences Education & Freudenthal Institute (Eds.) (1997–1998). *Mathematics in context.* Chicago: Encyclopaedia Britannica.

National Council of Teachers of Mathematics (1989). *Curriculum and evaluation standards for school mathematics.* Reston: Author.

National Council of Teachers of Mathematics (1991). *Professional standards for teaching mathematics.* Reston: Author.

National Council of Teachers of Mathematics (1995). *Assessment standards for school mathematics.* Reston: Author.

Organisation for Economic Co-operation and Development (1999). *Measuring student knowledge and skills: a new framework for assessment.* Paris: OECD Publications.

Romberg, T. A. (2001). *Designing middle-school mathematics materials using problems set in context to help students progress from informal to formal mathematical reasoning.* Madison: Wisconsin Center for Education Research.

Romberg, T. A., & Shafer, M. C. (2008). *The impact of reform mathematics instruction on student achievement: an example of standards-based curriculum research.* New York: Routledge.

Romberg, T. A., & Webb, D. C. (1997–1998). *External assessment system.* Madison: University of Wisconsin.

Romberg, T. A., Shafer, M. C., Webb, D. C., & Folgert, L. (Eds.) (2005). *The impact of MiC on student achievement. Longitudinal/cross-sectional study of the impact of teaching mathematics using mathematics in context on student achievement: monograph 5.* Madison: University of Wisconsin-Madison.

Shafer, M. C. (2004). Conduct of the study. In T. A. Romberg & M. C. Shafer (Eds.), *Purpose, plans, goals, and conduct of the study. Longitudinal/cross-sectional study of the impact of teaching mathematics using mathematics in context on student achievement: monograph 1* (pp. 51–93). Madison: University of Wisconsin-Madison.

Shafer, M. C. (2005). *Instruction, opportunity to learn with understanding, and school capacity. Longitudinal/cross-sectional study of the impact of teaching mathematics using mathematics in context on student achievement: monograph 3.* Madison: University of Wisconsin-Madison.

Stigler, J. W., & Hiebert, J. (1999). *The teaching gap: best ideas from the world's teachers for improving education in the classroom.* New York: The Free Press.

Strauss, A. L. (1987). *Qualitative analysis for social scientists.* Cambridge: Cambridge University Press.

Turner, R., & O'Connor, G. (2005). The development of a single scale for mapping progress in mathematical competence. In T. A. Romberg, D. C. Webb, M. C. Shafer, & L. Folgert (Eds.), *Measures of student performance. Longitudinal/cross-sectional study of the impact of teaching mathematics using mathematics in context on student achievement: monograph 4* (pp. 27–66). Madison: University of Wisconsin-Madison.

Curriculum and Achievement in Algebra 2: Influences of Textbooks and Teachers on Students' Learning about Functions

Sharon L. Senk, Denisse R. Thompson, and Jamie L.W. Wernet

Abstract Textbooks are a major factor in creating opportunities for learning in high school mathematics. However, teachers sometimes skip or modify lessons in the textbook. Thus, the *enacted curriculum* can be quite different from the *intended curriculum* of the textbook. This chapter describes a study of the intended, enacted, and attained curriculum conducted in ten matched pairs of Algebra 2 classes in five high schools in the United States. In particular, because functions are a major content strand of high school mathematics across the world, we discuss relationships between students' achievement on items testing their knowledge of functions and the opportunities to learn provided by their textbooks and teachers.

Keywords Achieved curriculum · Algebra 2 · Enacted curriculum · Intended curriculum · High school · Functions · Textbook influence

For almost four decades, curriculum materials have been seen as a major factor in creating opportunities for learning in high school mathematics. Begle (1973) found that the content of the textbook "seems, at present to be the only variable that on the one hand we can manipulate and on the other hand does affect student learning" (p. 209). Recent research confirms a strong positive relationship between secondary students' achievement and the opportunities provided by the textbook curriculum (Harwell et al. 2009; Romberg and Shafer 2008; Schoen et al. 2010; Senk and Thompson 2003; Schmidt et al. 2001; Tarr et al. 2008a, 2008b; Valverde et al. 2002).

Recent studies have also documented that teachers use textbooks in many ways (Remillard 2005; Remillard et al. 2009). In secondary schools, mathematics teachers

The original evaluation study from which the research in this report is drawn was funded by the University of Chicago School Mathematics Project.

S.L. Senk (✉) · J.L.W. Wernet
Michigan State University, East Lansing, USA
e-mail: senk@msu.edu

D.R. Thompson
University of South Florida, Tampa, USA

Y. Li, G. Lappan (eds.), *Mathematics Curriculum in School Education*,
Advances in Mathematics Education, DOI 10.1007/978-94-007-7560-2_24,
© Springer Science+Business Media Dordrecht 2014

often skip lessons or entire chapters in textbooks (Thompson and Senk 2010). They also modify the cognitive demand of tasks in a textbook (Henningsen and Stein 1997; Tarr et al. 2008a, 2008b). Even if the classroom teaching is consistent with the intent of a textbook, the teacher may assign problems for students to complete at home that are not consistent with the authors' intent (Thompson and Senk 2010). Thus, the *enacted curriculum* can be quite different from the *intended curriculum* in textbooks; and the actual *achieved* curriculum may be different than either the intended or enacted curriculum (Valverde et al. 2002).

Achievement in school subjects has also been found to be positively associated with students' *opportunity to learn* [OTL] (Floden 2002; Törnroos 2005). OTL research has been prominent in international comparison studies under the assumption that opportunities students had to learn the content being assessed must be taken into consideration to interpret achievement results in cross-national comparisons. However, OTL has also been used in domestic studies focusing on the intended curriculum, the enacted curriculum, or both (Floden 2002), using teacher logs, teacher surveys, and classroom observations. Specific information collected about OTL ranges from the number of instructional hours in a year, to how much of the textbook is covered, to how much time is spent in class on relevant tasks.

In this chapter, we report results from a secondary analysis of data about the intended, enacted, and achieved curriculum in 20 Algebra 2 classes in the United States.[1] Data come from the evaluation study of a textbook developed by the University of Chicago School Mathematics Project [UCSMP] (Thompson and Senk, in preparation).[2] Specifically, we report on students' opportunities to learn about functions, and how their knowledge of functions is related to the opportunities to learn provided by their textbooks and teachers.

Literature Review

The Role of Functions in School Mathematics

Ever since the National Committee on Mathematical Requirements (1923) proposed that

> the function concept should serve as a unifying element running through the instruction in the mathematics of the secondary school (in Bidwell and Clason 1970, p. 389),

---

[1] In about 90 % of U.S. high schools, the mainstream curriculum consists of a sequence of three full-year courses, Algebra 1-Geometry-Algebra 2 or Algebra 1-Algebra 2-Geometry, which students begin in either Grade 8, 9, or 10 (Dossey et al. 2008). Other high schools use some version of integrated curricula combining topics from algebra, geometry, and other mathematical subjects.

[2] The UCSMP is a curriculum research and development project for Grades K-12 that was established in the United States in 1983. With funding from both private and public foundations, it is one of the longest lasting curriculum projects in the history of the United States (Usiskin 2003).

functional thinking—that is, thinking in terms of and about relationships between variable quantities—has been proposed for the school mathematics curriculum in the United States. However, as pointed out by Buck (1970) and Kilpatrick and Izsák (2008), it was not until the 1960s that functions began to appear regularly in the school mathematics curriculum. Presently, functions are considered "crucial for students to learn but challenging for teachers to teach" (Cooney et al. 2010, p. 7). Although some U.S. curricula introduce aspects of functional thinking in the upper elementary or middle grades, a formal study of functions generally begins after students have acquired some skill in operating with expressions.

In recent decades, competing views on the role of functions in the school algebra curriculum have emerged (Kieran 2007). In the United States, traditional algebra curricula typically have a strong symbolic orientation, focusing on simplifying expressions, factoring polynomials, and solving equations or inequalities. In such curricula, functions are a topic, but they are not central; rather, recognizing mathematical forms is a central goal. In contrast, contemporary nontraditional "reform" algebra curricula take a *functional perspective* (Kieran, p. 709) in which functions form the basis for teaching algebra. This perspective can be traced to the 1980s when some educators suggested that graphical and symbolic features of computing technology could have substantial effects on the mathematics curriculum (Fey 1984; Heid 1988). Courses taught from a functional perspective typically emphasize multiple representations, real-world problems, and modeling.

For example, Chazan (2008) notes that the equation $3x + 2 = 7$ traditionally has been conceptualized as a question about numbers and solution sets. That is, the solution to the equation is the number that can be substituted for x to get a true sentence, and the solution set is $\{5/3\}$. However, in another curriculum, $3x + 2 = 7$ might be thought of as asking a question about a function, that is, "For what input(s) will the function $f(x) = 3x + 2$ produce an output of 7?" Alternately, a curriculum might teach students to think of $3x + 2 = 7$ as derived from a comparison of two functions of one variable where the function determined by $f(x) = 3x + 2$ is compared to the constant function $g(x) = 7$, with the intent of finding the value of x where the two functions have the same value.

Two recent documents have focused on the importance of functions in contemporary school mathematics. The *Common Core State Standards for Mathematics* [CCSSM] were developed from a desire to achieve a "more focused and coherent" mathematics curriculum (Common Core State Standards Initiative 2010, p. 3).[3] These standards are intended to highlight the mathematics that all students at a grade level should study during the school year. The standards for high school specify the mathematics that "all students should study in order to be college or career ready;" they are grouped into six conceptual categories, including separate sets of standards for algebra and functions (p. 57). For each of these two conceptual categories, four domains of standards are identified, as shown in Table 1.

Within each domain, clusters of standards provide details and examples of the mathematics intended to be studied. There is also a brief description of the link be-

---

[3]As of March 2012, 45 of the 50 states and several U.S. territories had adopted these standards.

Table 1 Domains of standards for algebra and functions in the Common Core State Standards for Mathematics

Algebra	Functions
• Seeing structure in expressions	• Interpreting functions
• Arithmetic with polynomials and rational expressions	• Building functions
• Creating equations	• Linear, quadratic, and exponential models
• Reasoning with equations and inequalities	• Trigonometric functions

tween algebra and functions; for example, determining an output value of a function involves evaluating an expression, and solutions to an equation can be visualized by determining when two functions have the same output (CCSSM 2010, pp. 63–71).

In *Essential Understandings of Functions: Grades 9–12*, Cooney et al. (2010) describe five big ideas about "overarching concepts that are central to [functions] and link numerous smaller mathematical ideas into coherent wholes" (p. viii):

- The function concept, including the classical definition of function and the idea that domain and range of a function do not have to be sets of numbers;
- Co-variation and rate of change, including how one variable changes with respect to another and how rates of change determine what kind of real world phenomenon a function can model;
- Families of functions, specifically highlighting linear, exponential, quadratic, and trigonometric functions;
- Combining and transforming functions through composition, finding inverses, and arithmetic operations; and
- Multiple representations of functions, including equations, graphs, tables, and verbal descriptions. (pp. 8–11)

The function topics recommended by the CCSSM and Cooney and his colleagues are consistent with recommendations in other mathematics education literature. For instance, one habit of mind explicated by Driscoll (1999) was *building rules to represent functions*. He specifically posited that moving between multiple representations of functions leads to a more integrated understanding of functions. Also, Leinhardt et al. (1990) conceptualized function tasks as requiring two key actions—interpretation and construction. These are not mutually exclusive and center around what a student is doing with representations of functions. Again, this conceptualization aligns with the recent core recommendations.

Learning and Teaching of Functions

Cooney et al. (2010) report that students often gain only a narrow view of functions limited to equations and rules rather than a complex understanding allowing for flexible thinking about quantitative relations. In addition, students often acquire misconceptions about functions. Misconceptions tend to fall into three broad categories: desire for regularity (e.g., students do not consider irregular graphs such as piecewise graphs to be functions); a point-wise focus (e.g., difficulty translating from graphs to equations, difficulty with the slope concept); and difficulty with abstractions of the graphical world (e.g., thinking of the graph as a picture) (Leinhardt et al. 1990, pp. 44–45).

Large-scale assessments also provide information about students' performance on function tasks. The National Assessment of Educational Progress [NAEP], for example, assesses samples of students in the United States at grades 4, 8, and 12 (ages 9, 13, and 17, respectively). The 12th grade tests explicitly address linear, exponential, power, quadratic, and trigonometric functions as well as algebraic representations, including written descriptions, equations, and graphs. According to results on individual NAEP tasks, functions are a difficult topic for 12th-grade students. From the 17 function tasks used since 1990,[4] only two questions were rated easy, meaning more than 60 % of students nationwide solved them correctly. Both questions were multiple-choice items on interpreting and connecting representations. Two of the tasks were rated medium (40–60 % of students answered correctly) and 13 were rated hard (less that 40 % answered correctly), including the five function questions on the most recent exam in 2009.

The Trends in International Mathematics and Science Study (TIMSS) Advanced assessment was administered in 1995 and 2008 to students in their final year of secondary school to compare knowledge of advanced mathematics and physics in participating countries. The U.S. participated in 1995, but not in 2008. The mathematics content includes algebra, calculus, and geometry; functions comprise a part of the algebra domain and are identified to be "an important unifying idea in mathematics" (Garden et al. 2006, p. 13). Specifically, assessment items require students to generate and interpret multiple representations of functions, identify key characteristics of functions, and compose functions. As reported by Mullis et al. (2009), average scores on the algebra portion of the exam varied from a low of 24 % in the Philippines to a high of 62 % in the Russian Federation (p. 83). Great variation was also evident in student performance on specific tasks. For example, on a task requiring students to generate a quadratic function given the x- and y-intercepts, the percent of students who answered correctly ranged from 8 % (Sweden) to 64 % (Lebanon). These results suggest differences in curricular emphases on algebra and functions among countries.

Teaching students about functions demands strong knowledge of graphing and functions as well as knowledge about how students think about functions (Kieran 2007; Leinhardt et al. 1990). Some authors have offered suggestions for how to address misconceptions and provide entry into the function concept. Leinhardt et al. (1990) suggested focusing on the following points in order to address common student misconceptions: functions establish relationships between changing quantities,

---

[4]The items are available through the NAEP Questions Tool v4.0, downloaded from http://nces.ed. gov/nationsreportcard/itmrlsx/search.aspx?subject=mathematics on February 17, 2012.

slope and the link between algebraic and graphical representations, and directionality in the Cartesian system. They also emphasized drawing on students' intuitions of functions as an entry point into teaching functions. Specific recommended entry points include investigating and generalizing patterns, qualitatively interpreting graphs, and using graphs as the basis for topics such as function transformations (Driscoll 1999; Kieran 2007; Leinhardt et al. 1990).

Many scholars report links between the use of graphing calculators or other related technologies and students' achievement. Calculators afford students opportunities to "experiment with properties of... functions and their graphs and build computational models of functions" (CCSSM 2010, p. 67), transform functions and analyze the effects of changing parameters when learning about the characteristics of families of functions (NCTM 2000), and work with multiple representations—particularly symbolic and graphical representations—in a manageable way (Kieran 2007; Leinhardt et al. 1990). Kieran (2007) cited several studies showing that using graphing calculators leads to increased student understanding of functions, particularly modeling, interpreting, translating, and working with multiple representations of functions. Zbiek and Heid (2008) give examples that show how graphing calculators and Computer Algebra Systems "can help students understand that functions are not merely symbolic rules; thinking about functions requires acknowledging input variables and domains" (p. 258).

Research Questions

As noted earlier, this chapter addresses questions about relations between the intended, enacted, and attained curriculum related to functions. In this chapter we report on a secondary analysis of data from a UCSMP evaluation study of the differences in teachers' enactment and students' achievement in Algebra 2, in order to address the following questions.[5]

1. What opportunities to learn functions are provided by teachers using the Third Edition, Field-Trial Version of UCSMP *Advanced Algebra* (Flanders et al. 2006) and comparison Algebra 2 textbooks?
2. At the end of the school year, how does the knowledge of functions of students in classes using UCSMP *Advanced Algebra* (Flanders et al. 2006) compare to that of students using the comparison curriculum?
3. At the end of the school year, how is students' knowledge of functions related to the curriculum materials (textbooks) used, and opportunities their teachers provide for learning from their textbooks?

---

[5] In addition to the five schools described in this chapter, five additional schools that either did not have comparison classes or had comparisons between the second and third editions of UCSMP *Advanced Algebra* were involved in the evaluation study. In this chapter, we include only those schools in which comparison classes used a non-UCSMP textbook.

Methods

Design

Schools for the evaluation study were recruited by posting a Call for Study Schools on the UCSMP website, in UCSMP publications, and through mathematics education list serves. Researchers requested schools with at least four classes of Algebra 2 students with students identified neither as gifted nor having special needs. From the schools that applied, participating schools were selected to provide as much diversity as possible in the sample; the five schools whose data are included in this paper are from four different states. In each school, two or three classes taught by one teacher were assigned the *UCSMP Advanced Algebra* textbook (Flanders et al. 2006); two other classes taught by a different teacher were assigned the textbook regularly used in that school. Four of the textbooks used in the comparison classes were typical of Algebra 2 books in use across the U.S. at the time the study was conducted (Dossey et al. 2008). The *Intermediate Algebra* (Lial and Hornsby 2000) was designed for use in college mathematics courses, but is sometimes used in high schools. (See Appendix for the list of textbooks used by comparison classes.)

A pretest-posttest matched pair design was used. To ensure comparability of prerequisite knowledge among students using different curricula, classes within each school were matched on the basis of two pretests administered at the beginning of the school year. The two best-matched pairs were selected for the final sample. (For further details about pretest scores and matching procedures, see Thompson and Senk in preparation.) Throughout the year, both UCSMP and comparison teachers provided information about the lessons taught, questions assigned, and other comments about each chapter they used. Near the end of the school year mathematics achievement was measured by three posttests.

Samples

Schools and Teachers   All five schools are publicly funded with enrollments ranging from 675 to 4200 students. The two smallest schools are in rural areas, one in the South, one in the Northern Midwest. Two schools are located in suburbs of a large city in the Midwest and one is on the urban fringe of a city in the East. Four schools have Grades 9–12, but one (School 25) enrolls only students in Grades 10–12. Four of the schools enrolled more than 90 % white students, but School 37 had more than one-third minority students.

All teachers were certified in their states to teach secondary school mathematics. The UCSMP teachers had on average 8.8 years teaching experience before entering this study, and the comparison teachers had 9.2. Eight of the ten teachers had taught Algebra 2 before, but no teacher had ever taught from the first or second editions of the UCSMP *Advanced Algebra* textbook (Flanders et al. 2006).

Table 2 Grade and gender of students in final sample

Grade	UCSMP *Advanced Algebra*					Non-UCSMP Comparison				
	10	11	12	na	Total	10	11	12	na	Total
M	28	49	12	3	92	36	52	10	1	99
F	28	53	2	2	85	30	71	7	1	109
na		1		1	2	1	3		1	5
Total	56	103	14	6	179	67	126	17	3	213

Note: na indicates either gender or grade was not available

Students Only students who took both pretests, all three posttests, and did not change teachers or class sections are included in the final sample for this study. Overall, data were collected from 392 students in 20 classes taught by 10 teachers. In each of the UCSMP and comparison groups, almost 60 % of the students were in Grade 11, with the next largest group in Grade 10. Table 2 describes the distribution of students by grade and gender.

Instruments

The regular classroom teacher administered all pretests and posttests during normal class periods. Although students were told to try their best, their scores did not influence their final grade in the course.

Pretest 1 was the TerraNova *Algebra I* (McGraw Hill 2005), a 32 item standardized test focused on knowledge of first-year algebra (Cronbach alpha = 0.621).[6] Students had 40 minutes to answer the items.

Pretest 2 consists of 25 multiple-choice items and 3 constructed response items. Many of the items on this pretest and on the posttest described below had been used on previous UCSMP studies or were released items from NAEP or TIMSS. (Cronbach alpha for the multiple choice items = 0.564.)

Advanced Algebra Posttest 1 is a 35 item multiple-choice posttest that assesses mathematics important to a second year of algebra, regardless of curriculum used; topics tested include operating with real numbers and matrices, solving linear and non-linear equations and inequalities, and developing, graphing, and analyzing functions. Students were given 40 minutes to complete the test. Calculators were not permitted. The test has a Cronbach alpha of 0.70.

Advanced Algebra Posttest 2 is a 20 item multiple-choice posttest designed to assess content of algebra and functions on which technology might be helpful. Students were given 30 minutes to complete the test and were permitted to use calcula-

---

[6]The Cronbach alpha measures reported here were obtained using test results only from the students in this sample.

tors, including graphing calculators with or without computer algebra systems. The Cronbach alpha for this test is 0.55.

Advanced Algebra Problem Solving and Understanding (PSU) *Test* is a 12-item constructed response test about algebra and functions, with students expected to show their work or explain their thinking for each item. Students were given 40 minutes to complete the test and were permitted to use calculators, including those with computer algebra systems. Items were scored using rubrics and procedures developed in previous UCSMP studies (Thompson and Senk 1993, 1998). The Cronbach alpha for this test is 0.70.

In this chapter, we report performance on subtests of each posttest consisting of only those items that address function concepts. All three authors worked independently to identify posttest items classified as addressing functions using the descriptors in the CCSSM. All discrepancies were resolved by consensus. These procedures generated three subtests on functions: 17 of the 35 items on Posttest 1 ($\alpha = 0.46$), 11 of the 20 items on Posttest 2 ($\alpha = 0.38$); and 9 of the 12 items on the PSU Test ($\alpha = 0.64$).[7] Thus, the three function subtests contain a total of 55 % (37 of the 67 items) of the items on the original posttests.

Table 3 shows how the items on the three function subtests map to the function clusters in the CCSSM. Notice that, although the data for this study were collected a few years before the release of the CCSSM, the items used to assess knowledge of functions are well distributed across the clusters of the Common Core. Sample items from the function subtests are shown in Table 4.

Chapter Coverage Forms were completed by each teacher for every chapter of his or her textbook. The teacher indicated whether or not each lesson was taught, how many days were spent on the lesson, and which questions from the lesson were assigned. These forms provide a glimpse into the extent to which each teacher enacted the mathematics in the textbook. Data derived from analyzing the Chapter Coverage Forms are used as one measure of opportunity to learn about functions.

Opportunity-to-Learn Mathematics on Posttests Forms were completed by each teacher for all three posttests using questions similar to those on international comparative tests (Schmidt et al. 1992). For each posttest item, teachers responded to the following question:

> During this school year, did you teach or review the mathematics needed for your students to answer this item correctly?

a. Yes, it is part of the text I used.
b. Yes, although it is not part of the text I used.
c. No, because it is not part of the text I used.
d. No, although it is part of the text I used.

Teachers' responses to this question provide a glimpse into the connection between the enacted and assessed curriculum and provide a second measure of opportunity to learn about functions.

---

[7] Cronbach alpha reliability measures were run again for only those items comprising each subtest.

Table 3 Correspondence between functions in the Common Core State Standards and posttest items

CCSSM Function Clusters	Posttest 1 Items	Posttest 2 Items	PSU Test Items
Interpreting functions			
Understand the concept of a function and use function notation	1, 13, 19, 21, 31	43, 47	5, 7
Interpret functions that arise in terms of the context		53	
Analyze functions using different representations	3, 14, 16, 20, 28, 29	49	4, 9, 10
Building functions			
Build a function that models a relationship between two quantities	10	40, 46	
Build new functions from existing functions	26, 34	37, 44	6
Linear, Quadratic, and Exponential Models			
Construct and compare linear, quadratic, and exponential models and solve problems	15, 25	52, 54	2, 12
Interpret expressions for functions in terms of the situation they model			8
Trigonometric Functions			
Extend the domain of trigonometric functions using the unit circle		39	
Model periodic phenomena with trigonometric functions	32		
Prove and apply trigonometric identities			

Functions in the Intended Curriculum

All textbooks used in the study treat linear, quadratic, exponential, logarithmic, polynomial, and rational functions, although the treatment and emphasis vary across topics. All textbooks except the one by Lial and Hornsby, which was designed for a college course, address all the CCSSM clusters of standards for functions identified in Table 3. The book by Lial and Hornsby addresses everything but the standards related to trigonometry. However, the placement of the introduction to the functions section varies, as does the extent to which the word *function* is used in titles of lessons. The UCSMP *Advanced Algebra* (Flanders et al. 2006) introduces functions the earliest (Lesson 1-2); the book by Lial and Hornsby (2000) introduces functions the latest (Lesson 3-5). The percent of lessons with the word *function* in the title ranges from 9 % ([UCSMP] Flanders et al. 2006; Lial and Hornsby 2000) to 19 % (Larson et al. 2001).

However, even when a lesson does not have the word *function* in the title, the concept of function may play a central role. In theory, after the concept of function is defined and function notation is introduced, authors are free to use these concepts whenever appropriate. For instance, none of the nine lessons in Chap. 2 of

Table 4 Sample function items from each posttest

Instrument	Item No.	Item Stem
Posttest 1	1	If $f(x) = x^3$, find $f(-4)$.
Posttest 1	3	Which parabola is the graph of the set of all points satisfying $y = x^2 - 1$? (options are graphs).
Posttest 1	16	(Graphs of the lines $\overleftrightarrow{AC}$ and $\overleftrightarrow{BC}$ are shown on a grid.) An equation for $\overleftrightarrow{AC}$ is $y = \frac{1}{3}x + 4$. An equation for $\overleftrightarrow{BC}$ is $y = -5x + 18$. What is the solution to the system $y = \frac{1}{3}x + 4$ and $y = -5x + 18$? (Options are coordinates of specific points identified on the grid.)
Posttest 2	40	A rectangular piece of metal 17 cm by 28 cm is to be made into a box by cutting squares x cm by x cm from the corners and folding up the edges. Which of the following is a formula for the volume of this box?
Posttest 2	43	In 43 and 44, refer to the graphs of functions f and g at right. What is the value of $g(1)$?
Posttest 2	44	What is the value of $f(g(1))$? (Using the above diagram.)
Posttest 2	53	What is the y-intercept of the equation for the line through the point $(-4, 5)$ with slope 6?
PSU	2	Consider the values in the table at the right. Find an equation that relates x and y.
PSU	5a	What is meant in mathematics by the word *function*?
PSU	5b	Give a real life example to illustrate your definition above.

Questions 43 and 44 are released items from NAEP

the *UCSMP Advanced Algebra* (Flanders et al. 2006) has *functions* in the title. The chapter does, however, introduce direct and inverse variation—important concepts

Table 5 Number and percent of textbook lessons potentially related to functions

Textbook	School(s) using the textbook	Total number of textbook lessons	Lessons potentially related to functions	
			Number	% of total no. of lessons
Bellman et al. (2004)	25	98	53	54
Flanders et al. (2006)	all	116	78	67
Larson et al. (2001)	37	97	56	58
Lial and Hornsby (2000)	38	64	49	77
Schultz et al. (2001)	28, 36	93	42	45

related to co-variation and rate of change that are part of the *Essential Understandings* (Cooney et al. 2010) and CCSSM (2010). Furthermore, in that chapter students investigate graphs, tables, and equations of linear and quadratic functions and connections between the representations.

Thus, for our final count of a textbook's lessons which *potentially* provide opportunities to learn about functions, we first counted the number of lessons between the first lesson in each textbook that introduced functions and the last lesson of the book. Second, we excluded lessons about trigonometry, combinatorics, probability, statistics, and matrices (because these topics were not covered in all textbooks) and did not count lessons on conic sections (because circles, ellipses, hyperbolas, and some parabolas are not functions). The result was the number of lessons potentially related to functions.[8] Table 5 compares the number of lessons that potentially relate to functions to the total number of lessons in each book.

Because the *UCSMP Advanced Algebra* (Flanders et al. 2006) introduces functions earlier than the other books, it has more lessons potentially related to functions than the others. In contrast, the Lial and Hornsby textbook has the greatest percent of lessons devoted to this topic.

UCSMP classes were provided graphing calculators with computer algebra systems on loan for use throughout the year in sufficient quantities to assign to students for use in school and at home. Most comparison classes had some access to graphing calculators, but usually without computer algebra systems. On the PSU Test, students reported access to technology for the test. About 97 % of students overall had calculator access, with 87 % of UCSMP and 74 % of comparison students having a calculator that could graph functions; 89 % of UCSMP and 8 % of comparison students had calculators that could simplify algebraic expressions.

---

[8]We acknowledge that this method potentially overcounts the number of lessons related to functions in some textbooks. However, a detailed look at every lesson in each textbook to determine whether function concepts were explicitly addressed was beyond the scope of this secondary analysis.

School	UCSMP Teacher Coverage (%)	Comparison Teacher Coverage (%)
25	80	68
28	72	31
36	73	69
37	80	86
38	76	84

Table 6 Function Lesson Coverage by school and teacher

Results

Opportunity to Learn

Two measures of Opportunity to Learn are reported here: Function Lesson Coverage and Posttest Opportunity to Learn Functions.

Function Lesson Coverage   Overall, UCSMP teachers taught from 58 % (Schools 28 and 37) to 63 % (School 25) of the lessons in their textbook. In contrast, comparison teachers taught from 29 % (School 28) to 86 % (School 38) of their textbook lessons. Function Lesson Coverage is defined to be the percent of the number of lessons potentially related to functions (see Table 5) that were taught by the teacher. Table 6 reports the Function Lesson Coverage for each school and teacher.

The range of Function Lesson Coverage was greater among comparison teachers than among UCSMP teachers. Chi-squared tests of differences indicate that the UCSMP and comparison teachers taught approximately equal percentages of the lessons related to functions in four schools; but in School 28, the percent of lesson coverage was significantly different at the 0.05 level. Throughout the year the comparison teacher in School 28 taught many lessons using materials she had created in lieu of working with the textbook assigned by the school.[9]

Posttest Opportunity to Learn Functions   Figure 1 gives three displays illustrating teachers' responses to the question about whether or not they taught the mathematics necessary to solve the items on the three function subtests.

Figure 1 suggests that students had differing opportunities to learn about functions in these 20 classes. For Posttest 1, the teachers covered only two items in common: item 1 on evaluating a function; and item 16 on the relation between the solution to a system of linear equations and the coordinates of points on a graph. On Posttest 2, the teachers again indicated that they had all taught the mathematics

---

[9]During the year the comparison teacher in School 28 taught linear relations and functions, linear systems including linear programming, polynomials including quadratics and factoring, arithmetic and geometric sequences and series. The teacher did not teach exponential, logarithmic, rational or radical functions.

for only two of the items: item 43 about evaluating a function from a graph; and item 53 about finding the y-intercept of a line with a given slope passing through a particular point. On the PSU test, there was only one item for which all teachers reported teaching the necessary mathematics: item 5 asking students to tell what is meant by the word *function* in mathematics, and to give a real life example of a function. Overall, there were only 5 of the 37 functions items (13.5 %) across these three tests that were common opportunities for all students. These items were all in the CCSSM Interpreting Functions cluster.

Data from UCSMP teachers show that 19 of the 37 items (51 %) were taught by 4 of the 5 teachers, with 12 in the cluster on Interpreting Functions, 3 in Building Functions, and 4 in Linear, Quadratic, and Exponential Functions. Data from comparison teachers show that 15 of the 37 items (40 %) were taught by 4 of the 5 teachers, with 11 items in the cluster on Interpreting Functions, 1 in Building Functions, and 3 in Linear, Quadratic, and Exponential Functions. The major focus was on the basic aspects of Interpreting Functions for both groups.

Achievement on the Functions Subtests

Tables 7, 8, and 9 report the achievement results on the three function subtests, and the Posttest Opportunity to Learn Functions. As noted in Table 7, in four of the ten matched pairs, the UCSMP students outperformed the comparison students, and in the other six pairs, there was no significant difference in mean performance. Overall, using a dependent measures t-test, the UCSMP classes outperformed the comparison classes by about 6 % on the functions items on Posttest 1, a difference that is statistically significant. (See footnote *b* to Table 7.)[10] This difference corresponds to an effect size greater than one, indicating that the mean score on this posttest of a typical UCSMP class is more than one standard deviation greater than the mean score of a typical comparison class.[11]

As noted in Table 8, on the function items from Posttest 2, UCSMP students outperformed comparison students in four of the ten matched pairs and comparison students outperformed UCSMP students in one pair. Overall, although the mean of the difference between scores of UCSMP and comparison classes was about 5 %, this difference was not statistically significant. The achievement difference corresponds to an effect size of slightly more than half a standard deviation favoring the UCSMP classes.

As the results in Table 9 indicate, on the constructed-response items on the Problem Solving and Understanding Test, UCSMP students outperformed comparison

---

[10] A dependent measures t-test on the mean of the differences of the class means provides a method to test the overall effect of the two curricula (Gravetter and Wallnau 1985, p. 373).

[11] Effect size was determined using measures appropriate for matched groups. The effect size is $d = t_c \cdot \sqrt{\frac{2(1-r)}{n}}$, where d = effect size, t_c is based on the difference of the pair means, r is the correlation between the pair means, and n is the number of matched pairs (Dunlap et al. 1996).

		Posttest 1 Items															
School	Teacher	1	3	10	13	14	15	16	19	20	21	25	26	28	29	31	32	34
25	U																	
25	C																	
28	U																	
28	C																	
36	U																	
36	C																	
37	U																	
37	C																	
38	U																	
38	C																	

		Posttest 2 Items										
School	Teacher	37	39	40	43	44	46	47	49	52	53	54
25	U											
25	C											
28	U											
28	C											
36	U											
36	C											
37	U											
37	C											
38	U											
38	C											

		PSU Test Items								
School	Teacher	2	4	5	6	7	8	9	10	12
25	U									
25	C									
28	U									
28	C									
36	U									
36	C									
37	U									
37	C									
38	U									
38	C									

Fig. 1 Items on functions subtests for which content was reported as taught by UCSMP and comparison teachers, indicated as U and C, respectively (A *gray box* indicates that the teacher reported teaching the mathematics needed to answer the item)

students in six of the ten matched pairs of classes; in five of the six cases, the UCSMP class mean was more than 10 % greater than the comparison mean. Overall, the mean of the differences between scores of UCSMP and comparison classes was about 8 %, a difference that is statistically significant, with an effect size of over one standard deviation.

To provide insight into performance on specific items, Table 10 reports the overall percent correct for UCSMP and comparison students for the items shown in Table 4. Items about functions were of varying difficulty for this sample, even when all teachers report teaching the content necessary for an item. For example, defining a function (PSU 5a) was more difficult for both UCSMP and comparison students than giving an example of a function (PSU 5b), and giving an example was much more difficult than using function notation (item 1). On items 3 (identifying a graph of a parabola) and 40 (a symbolic representation for volume of a box), the UCSMP students performed considerably better than their comparison peers.

Functions Achievement Related to Opportunity to Learn

Research indicates that one of the strongest predictors of future performance is prior achievement (Begle 1973; Bloom 1976) and that opportunities to learn are also related to students' performance. So, we used multiple regression to test if curriculum and our two OTL measures would predict function achievement when prerequisite knowledge, as measured by the pretests, was controlled. Assumptions of normality of function achievement were tested, with skewness and kurtosis within acceptable ranges.

Recall that the three function subtests were administered under different conditions (e.g., calculator/no calculator, multiple-choice/constructed-response), so we did not believe it appropriate to combine the results into a single function measure. Rather, we ran three separate regressions using SPSS 20. For each functions subtest, we examined five predictor variables: Pretest 1, the *Terra Nova Algebra* Test; Pretest 2, a UCSMP designed test; Function Lesson Coverage (see Table 6); Posttest OTL for that subtest (see Fig. 1 and Tables 7–9); and curriculum (UCSMP or comparison). The independent variable, achievement on a functions subtest, and the first four predictor variables are each reported as a percent; curriculum is a dummy variable with the UCSMP curriculum coded as 1 and the comparison curriculum coded as 0. Table 11 reports the coefficients of the predictor variables and their significance for all three regressions; the Variance Independence Factor for each regression indicates low multi-collinearity.

For Posttest 1, all five predictor variables are significant, and together they account for slightly more than a quarter of the variance. Four of the variables correlate positively with achievement, but Function Lesson Coverage was negatively correlated, suggesting that the greater the percent of lessons that were taught about functions, the lower the achievement. Curriculum is the strongest predictor of achievement on the functions subtest of Posttest 1, with students studying from the UCSMP *Advanced Algebra* textbook having about a 5 % advantage over the students study-

Table 7 Mean percent correct on 17 function items from posttest 1 and posttest opportunity to learn functions

School	UCSMP Third Edition					non-UCSMP Comparison					SE	t	df	p
	Class	n	mean	sd	OTL %	Class	n	mean	sd	OTL %				
25	160	17	40.48	14.54	88	163	23	29.41	9.87	82	3.86	2.870	38	0.007[a]
	162	17	38.41	14.72	88	164	20	34.71	13.89	82	4.71	0.786	35	0.437
28	165	15	46.27	13.13	59	168	26	38.91	14.89	47	4.63	1.590	39	0.120
	167	15	49.41	15.21	59	169	23	35.29	10.79	47	4.21	3.352	36	0.002[a]
36	181	16	31.62	9.08	59	179	12	34.31	9.98	76	3.62	-0.745	26	0.463
	182	19	32.51	12.91	59	180	13	33.03	14.52	76	4.89	-0.107	30	0.915
37	183	22	44.65	12.27	82	185	21	38.66	13.36	76	3.91	1.534	41	0.133
	184	20	43.53	13.55	82	186	24	43.87	18.19	76	4.92	-0.070	42	0.945
38	187	22	36.63	13.21	82	190	24	23.28	10.62	41	3.52	3.792	44	<0.001[a]
	188	16	36.76	9.24	82	189	27	23.31	12.90	41	3.69	3.647	41	0.001[a]
Overall[b]	3rd	179	39.93	13.75		non	213	33.28	14.62					

Note:

[a]Indicates significant difference between the classes at the pair level

[b]Using a dependent measures t-test, the mean of the pair differences (UCSMP – comparison) is significant: $\bar{x} = 6.549$, $s_{\bar{x}} = 6.355$, $t = 3.259$, $p = 0.010$. Effect size = 1.042

Table 8 Mean percent correct on 11 function items from posttest 2 and posttest opportunity to learn functions

School	UCSMP Third Edition					non-UCSMP Comparison					SE	t	df	p
	Class	n	mean	sd	OTL %	Class	n	mean	sd	OTL %				
25	160	17	41.71	17.03	91	163	23	25.30	12.55	45	4.67	3.515	38	0.001[a]
	162	17	43.85	16.77	91	164	20	30.00	12.55	45	4.83	2.869	35	0.007[a]
28	165	15	42.42	14.85	64	168	26	32.52	13.89	45	4.62	2.146	39	0.038[a]
	167	15	37.58	15.70	64	169	23	30.04	11.45	45	4.40	1.712	36	0.095
36	181	16	26.14	12.80	36	179	12	25.76	13.33	73	4.98	0.076	26	0.940
	182	19	22.49	12.99	36	180	13	37.06	15.51	73	5.06	−2.882	30	0.007[a]
37	183	22	44.63	18.38	73	185	21	41.99	16.88	64	5.39	0.489	41	0.628
	184	20	45.00	18.76	73	186	24	42.80	15.04	64	5.09	0.431	42	0.669
38	187	22	32.23	16.53	64	190	24	22.73	12.57	36	4.31	2.206	44	0.033[a]
	188	16	25.00	16.76	64	189	27	21.55	14.95	36	4.93	0.700	41	0.488
Overall[b]	3rd	179	36.26	18.00		non	213	30.73	15.50					

Note:

[a]Indicates significant difference between the classes at the pair level

[b]Using a dependent measures t-test, the mean of the pair differences (UCSMP − comparison) is not significant: $\bar{x} = 5.13$, $s_{\bar{x}} = 8.687$, $t = 1.867$, $p = 0.095$. Effect size $= 0.618$

Table 9 Mean percent on 9 function items from the problem solving and understanding test and posttest opportunity to learn functions

School	UCSMP Third Edition					non-UCSMP Comparison					SE	t	df	p
	Class	n	mean	sd	OTL %	Class	n	mean	sd	OTL %				
25	160	17	34.95	13.15	89	163	23	14.19	9.62	78	3.60	5.772	38	<0.001[a]
	162	17	29.24	21.55	89	164	20	17.21	10.72	78	5.47	2.201	35	0.034[a]
28	165	15	38.43	18.48	89	168	26	18.33	10.82	44	4.56	4.410	39	<0.001[a]
	167	15	26.67	10.63	89	169	23	15.09	11.77	44	3.76	3.075	36	0.004[a]
36	181	16	13.79	7.87	44	179	12	19.61	9.66	100	3.31	-1.757	26	0.091
	182	19	12.07	5.45	44	180	13	15.84	8.45	100	2.45	-1.535	30	0.135
37	183	22	28.34	12.43	78	185	21	23.39	11.67	67	3.68	1.345	41	0.186
	184	20	31.76	14.24	78	186	24	29.78	11.29	67	3.85	0.516	42	0.609
38	187	22	24.06	14.08	89	190	24	8.21	6.66	67	3.20	4.948	44	<0.001[a]
	188	16	18.20	9.86	89	189	27	10.57	7.31	67	2.63	2.904	41	0.006[a]
Overall[b]	3rd	179	25.68	15.45		non	213	17.01	11.55					

Note:

[a]Indicates significant difference between the classes at the pair level

[b]Using a dependent measures t-test, the mean of the pair differences (UCSMP − comparison) is not significant: $\bar{x} = 8.53$, $s_{\bar{x}} = 9.264$, $t = 2.912$, $p = 0.017$. Effect size = 1.113

Table 10 Percent correct on function items shown in Table 4 and percent of teachers who reported having provided posttest opportunity to learn for that item

Item number	CCSSM Function Cluster	UCSMP		Non-UCSMP	
		% correct[a]	% of teachers	% correct[b]	% of teachers
1	Interpreting	83	100	77	100
3	Interpreting	65	80	46	80
16	Interpreting	46	100	42	100
40	Building	53	100	32	40
43	Interpreting	68	100	60	100
44	Building	30	60	25	60
53	Interpreting	39	100	27	100
PSU 2	Linear Models	24	80	12	100
PSU5a	Interpreting	5	100	2	100
PSU 5b	Interpreting	49	100	36	100

Note: On the PSU items, the percent correct is based on the percent of students who received a rubric score that was considered successful, i.e., a score of 3 or 4 (out of 4) on PSU 2, and a score of 2 (out of 2) on each of PSU 5a and 5b

[a] $n = 179$ for UCSMP

[b] $n = 213$ for comparison

ing from a comparison textbook when their pretest scores and the OTL provided by their teachers are the same.

For Posttest 2, although both pretests and the Posttest OTL were significant, neither curriculum nor Function Lesson Coverage was significant. The three significant predictors account for about 20 % of the variance on the functions subtest of Posttest 2.

For the functions subtest of the PSU test, all five variables were significant predictors, with Function Lesson Coverage having a small negative effect, and curriculum having the largest positive effect. Overall, the five predictors determined more than a third of the variance on the PSU subtest. Students studying from the UCSMP *Advanced Algebra* textbook had about a 6 % advantage over the students studying from a comparison textbook on the PSU, when their pretest scores and the OTL provided by their teachers are controlled.

Discussion

Generally, the results of this study support claims that teachers enact the curriculum in different ways. The teachers covered varying numbers of functions lessons and reported providing different opportunities for students to learn functions, which influenced student achievement.

Table 11 Unstandardized regression coefficients and significance for models predicting posttest achievement from pretest knowledge, posttest opportunity to learn functions, and function lesson coverage[a]

Predictor Variable	Posttest 1[b]			Posttest 2[c]			PSU Test[d]		
	β	t	p	β	t	p	β	t	p
Constant	14.057	3.664	<0.001*	0.600	0.135	0.893	−13.740	−3.878	<0.001*
Pretest 1	0.293	4.943	<0.001*	0.207	2.925	0.004*	0.272	5.099	<0.001*
Pretest 2	0.267	4.595	<0.001*	0.187	2.695	0.007*	0.308	5.768	<0.000*
Posttest OTL Functions	0.118	2.639	0.009*	0.344	6.529	<0.001*	0.207	5.311	<0.000*
Function Lesson Coverage	−0.160	−3.742	<0.001*	−0.045	−0.903	0.367	−0.098	−2.344	0.020*
Curriculum	5.000	3.573	<0.001*	−0.566	−0.325	0.746	5.841	4.691	<0.001*

Note: For curriculum, UCSMP was coded 1 and non-UCSMP was coded 0

[a]Collinearity was tested for the predictor variables and was not an issue

[b]$F(5, 386) = 28.515$, $p < 0.001$, $R^2 = 27.0\%$

[c]$F(5, 386) = 21.634$, $p < 0.001$, $R^2 = 21.9\%$

[d]$F(5, 386) = 39.890$, $p < 0.001$, $R^2 = 34.1\%$

Opportunity to Learn Functions—The Intended and Enacted Curriculum

Teachers using both the UCSMP and comparison curricula reported considerable variation in the percent of textbook lessons taught and in the percent of items on the posttests for which they reported teaching the needed mathematics. Thus, it is clear that students in the 20 classrooms studied received widely different opportunities to learn functions both within and across schools.

These differences are not particularly surprising to people familiar with education in the United States. The U.S. Constitution gives the right to regulate education to individual states; in many states this right is then granted to local education agencies. So, looking across schools we often see great variation in topics covered in comparable courses. The results presented here indicate this is true for Algebra 2, and for function topics in particular. These differences are noteworthy for several reasons.

First, many Algebra 2 students continue into a pre-calculus course where the curriculum builds on the work with functions begun in Algebra 2; so, opportunities to learn functions in Algebra 2 are important for students' future success. The differences in OTL in this study suggest students are entering pre-calculus courses with significantly different prior experiences.

Second, functions are included in the CCSSM (2010) as topics that all students should learn to be ready for college and future careers. Hence, the lack of common focus related to functions within and across schools is particularly problematic. It remains to be seen whether adoption of CCSSM will lead to more uniformity of content covered in Algebra 2 courses. Large-scale assessments based on the CCSSM are being developed in the U.S. to measure college and career readiness; without greater consistency in the enacted curriculum, some students will have significant advantage over others.

Curriculum developers should consider how functions are presented in Algebra 2 textbooks. Our analysis of the Posttest OTL related to functions suggests that the functions topics emphasized by teachers, particularly among comparison classes, focus mainly on interpreting functions, which includes basic information about functions as well as using multiple representations. Teachers generally paid less attention to building functions. On the one hand, this supports the claim that students have only a narrow perspective on functions, including facts and rules (Cooney et al. 2010). On the other hand, the emphasis on multiple representations is promising, as that is required for a holistic understanding of functional relationships (Cooney et al. 2010; Driscoll 1999; Leinhardt et al. 1990).

Knowledge of Functions—The Achieved Curriculum

Without accounting for differences in OTL, the students in classes using the UCSMP curriculum performed significantly better than comparison students on Posttest 1 and the PSU, with differences in mean scores greater than one standard deviation on both. This implies that the curriculum matters for those posttests. Though UCSMP students also outperformed comparison students by an average of about 5 % on Posttest 2, the difference was not statistically significant. The somewhat low reliability of the subtest (Cronbach's $\alpha = 0.38$) may contribute to this result. Another possible explanation is that the calculator leveled the playing field on this multiple choice test. This result supports the idea that calculator use enhances students' understanding of functions (Kieran 2007; NCTM 2000; Zbiek and Heid 2008), but also suggests that this support is limited to situations where the calculator is actually used on assessments.

Because UCSMP personnel developed the posttests, some may question their fairness. Recall, however, that only posttest items that could be mapped directly to the CCSSM functions standards were included in this secondary analysis so that the adoption of CCSSM standards will mean that all students should learn the concepts covered by items such as these. Furthermore, UCSMP students still outperformed comparison students on the items for which all teachers reported covering the material required.

The students in classes using the UCSMP textbook performed better than the comparison students on a range of function topics, but the widest gaps were mainly on interpreting functions questions. Most of these questions involved interpreting or connecting multiple representations. This may reflect the emphasis that the UCSMP curriculum places on analyzing functions using multiple representations throughout the text.

Overall, student performance on many functions items was fairly low across curricula. Again, this reflects previous findings that students struggle with function concepts, especially when it comes to flexible thinking about covariation (Cooney et al. 2010; Leinhardt et al. 1990). The difficulty students have with functions on large scale assessments such as NAEP and TIMSS Advanced also suggests that this is not just a local concern.

Curriculum and OTL Measures as Related to Achievement—The Intended, Enacted, and Achieved Curriculum

When prior achievement (measured by two pretest scores), two OTL measures (Function Lesson OTL and Posttest OTL Functions), and the curriculum type are used to predict end-of-course achievement on the functions subtests, all five variables are significant on the subtests of Posttest 1 and the Problem Solving and Understanding Test. In both cases, curriculum type favors the UCSMP curriculum. Students studying from the UCSMP textbook scored between 5 % and 6 % higher than those using the comparison textbooks, even when the other predictors are controlled.

Although Function Lesson Coverage has a significant effect on achievement on these two functions subtests, the magnitude of the effect is negative. That is, the greater percent of lessons taught, the lower the achievement of the students in either curriculum. It is not clear what explains this apparent anomaly. It could be that teachers in the study felt pressure from either the researchers or from their school district to cover certain topics; that is, they sacrificed quality of teaching for quantity of lessons taught. Or it could be, as noted earlier, that this measure overestimates the attention given to functions in the textbook lessons counted, and hence is not a valid measure of emphasis on functions.

In contrast, the regression analysis using the same five predictor variables for the functions subtest of Posttest 2 found that only the two pretests and Posttest Opportunity to Learn Functions were significant. Neither Function Lesson Coverage nor curriculum was significant. As mentioned earlier, having access to a graphing calculator on a multiple-choice test may negate the curricular effect noted on the other two functions tests. However, it is important to note that graphing calculators were also permitted on the PSU, and on the functions subtest of the PSU, curriculum is significant. The differential effect of calculators on the two subtests may be due to differences in item format. The UCSMP curriculum provides numerous opportunities for students to write about mathematics, and perhaps this experience provided students with sufficient background to do better on free response items on which they needed to explain their thinking.

Summary

We observed considerable variation in the intended, enacted, and achieved curriculum of Algebra 2 related to functions. The textbook used by UCSMP students was a significant predictor of their end of course achievement, whether or not prior achievement and OTL measures were taken into account. Performance on function-related items was consistent with similar national assessments such as NAEP.

These findings have implications for textbook development, classroom instruction, and large-scale assessments. The results also suggest that much more research is needed to understand the connections among intended, enacted, and assessed curricula, particularly as the nation moves towards more testing with high stakes for both students and teachers. The measures used here to understand opportunity to learn at the classroom level potentially provide a means to study these connections at scale.

References

Begle, E. G. (1973). Lessons learned from SMSG. *Mathematics Teacher, 66,* 207–214.

Bidwell, J. K., & Clason, R. G. (1970). *Readings in the history of mathematics education.* Washington: National Council of Teachers of Mathematics.

Bloom, B. (1976). *Human characteristics and school learning.* New York: McGraw-Hill.

Buck, R. C. (1970). Functions. In E. G. Begle & H. G. Richey (Eds.), *Mathematics education, sixty-ninth yearbook of the national society for the study of education, part I* (pp. 236–259). Chicago: University of Chicago Press.

Chazan, D. (2008). The shifting landscape of school algebra in the United States. In C. E. Greenes & R. Rubenstein (Eds.), *Algebra and algebraic thinking in school mathematics* (pp. 19–23). Reston: National Council of Teachers of Mathematics.

Common Core State Standards for Mathematics (2010). Retrieved November 10, 2010 from http://www.corestandards.org/assets/CCSSI_Math%20Standards.pdf.

Cooney, T. J., Beckmann, S., Lloyd, G. M., Wilson, P. S., & Zbiek, R. M. (2010). *Developing essential understanding of functions for teaching mathematics in grades 9-12.* Reston: National Council of Teachers of Mathematics.

Dossey, J., Halvorsen, K., & McCrone, S. (2008). *Mathematics education in the United States 2008: a capsule summary fact book.* Reston: National Council of Teachers of Mathematics.

Driscoll, M. (1999). *Fostering algebraic thinking.* Portsmouth: Heinemann.

Dunlap, W. P., Cortina, J. M., Vaslow, J. B., & Burke, M. J. (1996). Meta-analysis of experiments with matched groups or repeated measures designs. *Psychological Methods, 1*(2), 170–177.

Fey, J. T. (1984). *Computing and mathematics: the impact on secondary school curricula.* Reston: National Council of Teachers of Mathematics.

Floden, R. E. (2002). The measurement of opportunity to learn. In A. C. Porter & A. Gamoran (Eds.), *Methodological advances in cross-national achievement* (pp. 231–266). Washington: National Academies Press.

Garden, R. A., Lie, S., Robitaille, D. R., Angell, C., Martin, M. O., Mullis, I. V. S., Foy, P., & Arora, A. (2006). *TIMSS advanced 2008 assessment frameworks.* Boston: TIMSS & PIRLS International Study Center, Boston College.

Gravetter, F. J., & Wallnau, L. B. (1985). *Statistics for the behavioral sciences.* St. Paul: West Publishing Company.

Harwell, M., Post, T., Cutler, A., Maeda, Y., Anderson, E., Norman, K., & Medhamie, A. (2009). The preparation of students from national science foundation–funded and commercially developed high school mathematics curricula for their first university mathematics course. *American Educational Research Journal*, 46, 203–231.

Heid, M. K. (1988). Resequencing skills and concepts in applied calculus using the computer as a tool. *Journal for Research in Mathematics Education*, 19, 3–25.

Henningsen, M., & Stein, M. K. (1997). Mathematical tasks and student cognition: classroom-based factors that support and inhibit high-level mathematical thinking and reasoning. *Journal for Research in Mathematics Education*, 28(5), 524–549.

Kieran, C. (2007). Learning and teaching of algebra at the middle school through college levels: building meaning for symbols and their manipulation. In F. K. Lester (Ed.), *Second handbook of research on mathematics teaching and learning* (pp. 707–762). Charlotte: Information Age Publishing.

Kilpatrick, J., & Izsák, A. (2008). A history of algebra in the school curriculum. In C. E. Greenes & R. Rubenstein (Eds.), *Algebra and algebraic thinking in school mathematics* (pp. 1–18). Reston: National Council of Teachers of Mathematics.

Leinhardt, G., Zaslavsky, O., & Stein, M. K. (1990). Functions, graphs, and graphing: tasks, learning, and teaching. *Review of Educational Research*, 60(1), 1–64.

McGraw-Hill (2005). *TerraNova algebra I*. Monterrey: Author.

Mullis, I. V. S., Martin, M. O., Robitaille, D. F., & Foy, P. (2009). *TIMSS advanced 2008 international report: findings from IEA's study of achievement in advanced mathematics and physics in the final year of secondary school*. Chestnut Hill: TIMSS & PIRLS International Study Center, Boston College.

National Committee on Mathematical Requirements (1923). *The reorganization of mathematics in secondary education*. Washington: Mathematical Association of America.

National Council of Teachers of Mathematics (2000). *Principles and standards for school mathematics*. Reston: Author.

Remillard, J. T. (2005). Examining key concepts in research on teachers' use of curricula. *Review of Educational Research*, 75(2), 211–246.

Remillard, J., Herbal-Eisenmann, B., & Lloyd, G. (Eds.) (2009). *Mathematics teachers at work: connecting curriculum materials and classroom instruction*. New York: Routledge.

Romberg, T. A., & Shafer, M. C. (2008). *The impact of reform instruction on student mathematics achievement: an example of a summative evaluation of a standards based curriculum*. New York: Routledge.

Schoen, H. L., Ziebarth, S. W., Hirsch, C. R., & BrckaLorenz, A. (2010). *A five-year study of the first edition of the core-plus mathematics curriculum*. Charlotte: Information Age.

Schmidt, W. H., McKnight, C., Houang, R. T., Wang, H. C., Wiley, D. E., Cogan, L. S., & Wolfe, R. G. (2001). *Why schools matter: a cross-national comparison of curriculum and learning*. San Francisco: Jossey-Bass.

Schmidt, W. H., Wolfe, R. G., & Kifer, E. (1992). The identification and description of student growth in mathematics achievement. In L. Burstein (Ed.), *The IEA study of mathematics III: student growth and classroom processes* (pp. 59–99). Oxford: Pergamon.

Senk, S. L., & Thompson, D. R. (Eds.) (2003). *Standards-based school mathematics curricula: what are they? What do students learn?* Mahwah: Erlbaum.

Tarr, J. E., Chávez, Ó., Reys, R. E., & Reys, B. J. (2008a). From the written to the enacted curricula: the intermediary role of middle school mathematics teachers in shaping students' opportunity to learn. *School Science and Mathematics*, 106(4), 191–201.

Tarr, J. E., Reys, R. E., Reys, B. J., Chávez, Ó., Shih, J., & Osterlind, S. J. (2008b). The impact of middle-grades mathematics curricula and the classroom learning environment on student achievement. *Journal for Research in Mathematics Education*, 39(3), 247–280.

Thompson, D. R., & Senk, S. L. (1993). Assessing reasoning and proof in high school. In N. Webb & A. Coxford (Eds.), *Assessment in the mathematics classroom* (pp. 167–176). Reston: National Council of Teachers of Mathematics.

Thompson, D. R., & Senk, S. L. (1998). Using rubrics in high school mathematics courses. *The Mathematics Teacher, 91*, 786–793.

Thompson, D. R., & Senk, S. L. (2010). Myths about curriculum implementation. In B. Reys, R. Reys, & R. Rubenstein (Eds.), *Mathematics curriculum: issues, trends, and future directions* (pp. 249–263). Reston: National Council of Teachers of Mathematics.

Thompson, D. R., & Senk, S. L. (in preparation). *An evaluation of the third edition of UCSMP advanced algebra*. Chicago: University of Chicago School Mathematics Project.

Törnroos, J. (2005). Mathematics textbooks, opportunity to learn and student achievement. *Studies in Educational Evaluation, 31*, 315–327.

Usiskin, Z. (2003). A personal history of the UCSMP secondary school curriculum, 1960-1999. In G. M. A. Stanic & J. Kilpatrick (Eds.), *A history of school mathematics* (pp. 673–736). Reston: National Council of Teachers of Mathematics.

Valverde, G. A., Bianchi, L. J., Wolfe, R. G., Schmidt, W. H., & Houang, R. T. (2002). *According to the book: using TIMSS to investigate the translation of policy into practice through the world of textbooks*. Dordrecht: Kluwer Academic Publisher.

Zbiek, R. M., & Heid, M. K. (2008). Digging deeply into intermediate algebra: using symbols to reason and technology to connect symbols and graphs. In C. E. Greenes & R. Rubenstein (Eds.), *Algebra and algebraic thinking in school mathematics* (pp. 247–259). Reston: National Council of Teachers of Mathematics.

Appendix: Textbooks Used in the Study

Bellman, A. E., Bragg, S. C., Charles, R. I., Handlin, W. G. Sr., & Kennedy, D. (2004). *Algebra 2*. Needham: Prentice Hall.

Flanders, J., Karafiol, P. J., Lassak, M., McMullin, L., Sech, J. B., Weisman, N., & Usiskin, Z. (2006). *Advanced algebra (Third edition, field trial version)*. Chicago: The University of Chicago School Mathematics Project.

Larson, R., Boswell, L., Kanold, T. D., & Stiff, L. (2001). *Algebra 2*. Evanston: McDougal Littell.

Lial, M. L., & Hornsby, J. (2000). *Intermediate algebra* (8th ed.). Reading: Addison Wesley Longman.

Schultz, J. E., Ellis, W. Jr., Hollowell, K., & Kennedy, P. A. (2001). *Algebra 2*. Austin: Holt, Rinehart and Winston.

Learning Paths and Learning Supports for Conceptual Addition and Subtraction in the US Common Core State Standards and in the Chinese Standards

Karen C. Fuson and Yeping Li

Abstract The results of the Fuson and Li (ZDM Math. Educ. 41:793–808, 2009) analysis of the major early numerical aspects and learning supports for single-digit and multi-digit adding and subtracting in a representative Chinese textbook series and a US textbook series (*Math Expressions*) are related to the Chinese standards and to the US Common Core State Standards for these topics. Similar learning paths and visual-quantitative supports for mathematical thinking were identified in the textbooks from both countries, the US standards, and the experimental Chinese standards (2001). The new Chinese standards (2011) were less specific about learning paths and supports, though these appeared in examples. Criteria for judging the best variations of the multi-digit adding and subtracting variations were proposed and used. This analysis identified the best variations as the "New Groups Below" for adding and the "Ungroup First" for subtracting. The somewhat different levels in the adding and subtracting learning paths for East Asia and the US are summarized.

Keywords Addition · Subtraction · Language effects · Learning supports · Cross-cultural textbook analysis · Standards

Introduction

Several studies document ways in which East Asian mathematics textbooks support conceptual understanding by students (Cai 2008; Li 2007, 2008; Li et al. 2009a,b,c; Murata 2004, 2008; Murata and Fuson 2006; Watanabe 2006). Some of these studies also describe ways in which mathematics textbooks from the US fail to support conceptual understanding in these ways. One exception (Fuson and Li 2009) is the support for single-digit and multi-digit addition and subtraction in the most-used Chinese text and in a US second-generation NSF math textbook *Math Expressions*

K.C. Fuson (✉)
Northwestern University, Evanston, IL, US
e-mail: karenfuson@mac.com

Y. Li
Texas A&M University, College Station, TX, US

Y. Li, G. Lappan (eds.), *Mathematics Curriculum in School Education*,
Advances in Mathematics Education, DOI 10.1007/978-94-007-7560-2_25,
© Springer Science+Business Media Dordrecht 2014

(Fuson 2006/2009). In that study, Fuson and Li reported extensive linguistic, visual-quantitative, and written-numeric supports for mathematical thinking in the Chinese textbooks and for the US textbook for the grades analyzed (Grades 1, 2, and 3 in both countries and Kindergarten for *Math Expressions*).

The diverse results from textbook analyses across countries suggest the need to examine and understand possible influences from curriculum standards that help guide the development of textbooks and possible learning paths embedded in textbooks. In many countries textbooks are a commonly used teaching resource that embodies the mandated curriculum. Therefore, it is also important to analyze the curriculum documents themselves as they are the primary source on which teachers and textbook writers draw in creating learning resources and planning learning experiences. Thus a major objective of this chapter is to analyze the extent to which curriculum standards in China and the US provide a coherent learning path that supports conceptual understanding of addition and subtraction.

China has a centralized education system, where curriculum standards are developed and used to provide overall guidelines for school education across the nation (Liu and Li 2010). While textbooks are developed as aligned with the curriculum standards, instructional activities and planning also follow information provided and highlighted in the curriculum standards including curricular goals, content, and their specifications at different grade levels. Before 2001, mathematics curriculum standards were called national mathematics teaching syllabus. The current version of the Chinese Mathematics Curriculum Standards (CMCS, Ministry of Education 2011) was revised from an experimental version that was published in 2001 (Ministry of Education 2001).

The United States has an education system with goals set by each of the 50 states, and districts within each state may also set goals. In the past, this has led to standards that vary extremely across states, resulting in a "mile wide and inch deep" curriculum (Schmidt et al. 1997). In the last decade, however, governors of many states organized a process to produce a set of standards that would be the same across all states that chose to participate. Standards were written by an appointed committee with advisors. The standards were then revised to accommodate the many comments elicited from across the nation. The final standards are now called the Common Core State Standards (CCSS) for the United States (National Governors Association Center for Best Practices, Council of Chief State School Officers 2010). Almost all states agreed to use these standards; states that did not agree have standards that are similar to the CCSS.

If our analysis indicates that the new US CCSS standards require conceptual supports, then all mathematics books in the United States will need to include such supports, as the US textbook *Math Expressions* did in the Fuson and Li analysis (2009). This would be a significant step forward given that other analyses have not found such supports in many US textbooks. For China, the related question is whether the conceptual supports in textbooks exist because they are mandated in the mathematics curriculum standards or for other reasons. If they are not mandated, it seems that there is widespread cultural agreement that such supports facilitate learning and thus there is no need to mandate these in the mathematics standards.

In the following sections, the major results of the Fuson and Li (2009) analysis will first be summarized. Then features of the CCSS and Mathematics Curriculum Standards for China for the target mathematics domains will be presented and compared to the analysis of the textbooks. Then criteria for mathematically-desirable and accessible multi-digit methods that support conceptual learning and fluency will be summarized and applied to the variations of methods found in Fuson and Li (2009). Finally, the somewhat different learning paths for multi-digit adding and subtracting in the US and East Asia will be summarized.

A Coherent Learning Path of Meaning-Making Supports in Textbooks

An important framework for the Fuson and Li (2009) analysis was the Fuson and Murata (2007) Class Learning Path Model that integrated teaching principles from two US National Research Council reports (Donovan and Bransford 2005; Fuson et al. 2005; Kilpatrick et al. 2001), the NCTM process standards (National Council of Teachers of Mathematics 2000), and from teaching in Japanese classrooms. This model discusses the importance of a coherent learning path that supports student movement from primitive to more advanced methods that are mathematically desirable. Mathematically-desirable methods show important mathematical features, generalize across numbers and situations, and are efficient in computation. Fuson and Murata also discuss how it is possible to teach mathematically-desirable methods so that students can understand them. These accessible but mathematically-desirable methods have the numerals organized and written to support place value. These methods also do not have misleading written-numeric features that interfere with understanding or stimulate errors.

Consistent with the previous study (Fuson and Li 2009), written-numeric supports in this paper refer to the extent to which the written numerical method is presented with notated intermediate steps that make the written method more accessible to students and easier to carry out. Visual-quantitative supports refer to those clarifying text illustrations to show visually important quantitative aspects of the concepts involved. Linguistic supports mean how clearly a language expresses mathematical ideas. For example, Chinese language often expresses ideas more clearly than English, especially in the initial learning of numerical concepts.

Single-Digit Adding and Subtracting

For single-digit adding and subtracting, Fuson and Li (2009) found that both the East Asian and US textbooks took a coherent learning path consisting of methods that moved through the three levels identified in extensive international research (e.g., see research in Fuson 1992):

- Level 1: Count all and take-away
- Level 2: Count on keeping track of the second addend
- Level 3: Recompose the addends to make a new problem.

The mathematically-desirable recomposing method is make-a-ten, because it can be used for all single-digit sums over ten. For example, one can recompose the 6 in $8 + 6$ to become $10 + 4 : 8 + 6 = 8 + 2 + 4 = 10 + 4 = 14$. In both textbooks, children's methods are elicited and discussed, and then support is provided to move through the entire learning path to an accessible and mathematically-desirable method.

There are three conceptual prerequisites for the make-a-ten methods (see also Murata 2004, and Murata and Fuson 2006, for a discussion of how these are taught in a Japanese classroom). The prerequisites are easier to discuss if we introduce terminology used in the US *Math Expressions* program. Two addends that compose a number are called *partners* (e.g., in the make-a-ten method above for $8 + 6$, 8 and 2 are partners of 10, and 2 and 4 are partners of 6). To carry out the addition or subtraction make-a-ten methods, children must

(a) know the partners to ten for the numbers 9, 8, 7, and 6 to do the first step,
(b) know all of the partners of a given number to find the second step, and
(c) know the total $10 + n$ composed to be written as $1n$ (or know that $1n$ decomposes to be $10 + n$).

Step (c) is the step that is very easy if you say the written teen number using ten as in many East Asian languages (e.g., 12 is said as *ten two*). This step is more difficult in English where there are no verbal cues that 12 is equal to ten plus two. Both textbooks helped children learn the prerequisites for the make-a-ten method. The extensive work involved in finding two partners of a number for prerequisites (a) and (b) also supports children during the embedded addend thinking required for Level 2 of "counting on to add or to subtract" (e.g., $14 - 8$ is thought of as $8 + ? = 14$).

Details of how the Chinese books provide a coherent sequence of visual-quantitative supports (illustrations and drawings in the book) are given in Fuson and Li (2009) including seeing numbers 6 to 10 as 5-groups, which facilitates adding and subtracting and the make-a-ten method. Various linguistic supports in the math words in Chinese are then summarized including the easier teen numbers with the ten said explicitly and the more meaningful words for the parts of an addition and of a subtraction equation. Written-numeric supports that show the make-a-ten method are also displayed beginning with break-apart addend (partner) drawings (an upside down V with the total at the top and addends at each leg).

Details of how the *Math Expressions* books provide a coherent sequence of visual-quantity supports (illustrations and drawings in the book) are also given in Fuson and Li (2009). Because the Level 3 make-a-ten method is more difficult in English than in Chinese, mastery of Level 2 counting on methods was facilitated and emphasized early in Grade 1. These counting on methods are the accessible and mathematically-desirable methods for adding and subtracting that can become very fluent and then merge for many children into the make-a-ten methods or directly into known sums. Emphasizing subtracting as finding an unknown addend and counting on to find an unknown addend eliminated the many common errors made by US children counting down to subtract. The visual-quantitative supports for moving to these Level 2 methods and for the prerequisites for the Level 3 methods were described, e.g., 5-group patterns as in East Asia shown on a Number Parade and on student pages and penny strips showing ten pennies on one side and a dime on the back used to make teen numbers with an obvious group of ten. Written-numeric supports such as the addend drawings (developed independently and called Math Mountains) were also described. Various linguistic and visual-quantitative supports needed to compensate for various difficulties in English were also described, e.g., using tens-in-teens words as well as English words: one ten four ones for 14; secret-code cards in which a unit card, for example a 4, is placed on top of the 0 in the 10 card to make 14 so children could imagine the 0 hiding under the 4 and be supported to think of 14 as ten and 4 (10 and 4) even though their word for fourteen obfuscates this composition from a ten and 4 ones.

Multi-digit Adding and Subtracting

For multi-digit adding and subtracting, Fuson and Li (2009) found in both textbooks a coherent learning path of methods that moved rapidly to accessible and mathematically-desirable methods. Again, students' methods are initially elicited and discussed, but then support was provided to learn one or more accessible and mathematically-desirable methods. The irregularities in the English words for 11 through 99 required special learning supports relating drawings of tens and ones (later: hundreds, tens, and ones and larger quantities) to secret-code cards that showed the numbers in expanded notation with all zeroes but could be layered to show just the place value numbers (e.g., 379). Students used English number words and place-value number words to describe all of the quantities *three hundreds seven tens nine ones.*

East Asian books showed the meanings of multi-digit adding and subtracting with pictures of quantities such as bundled sticks or base-ten blocks. The feature that differs from many US texts that show similar pictures is that each step is shown so that students can relate what happens with the quantities to what happens in the written numeric method. In *Math Expressions* math drawings that showed hundreds, tens, and ones were built up and used so that students could make math drawings that would relate to their written numeric method as they explained and related steps in the drawing and the written method.

For multi-digit adding, all methods found in both textbooks, and in the Japanese and Korean books examined, used the same core approaches based on place-value: Two multi-digit numbers were added by adding like multi-units (numbers in like places) and making new larger unit(s) as needed (grouping/carrying). There were variations in the written-numeric supports for this core approach (i.e., how much a method showed the place value meanings) and in the order in which steps were carried out (e.g., adding hundreds or ones first). Numbers for the steps were written in different places and in different ways. Different variations existed in the books for the same country. These variations also varied in how clear and easy the method was to carry out.

For multi-digit subtracting, all methods used the same core approaches: Like multi-units were subtracted and ten more next-smaller units were made from one larger multi-unit as needed (ungrouping/borrowing) in order to do these subtractions. There were variations in the written methods including methods that showed only part of the step of getting ten next-smaller units when needed. Most methods involved alternating between the two aspects of the core approach (ungrouping then subtracting one place), but one method did all of the ungrouping first and then all of the subtracting.

Are There Coherent Learning Paths and Meaning-Making Supports in the US CCSS and Mathematics Curriculum Standards for China?

Core attributes of the US Common Core State Standards (CCSS) for single-digit and multi-digit adding and subtracting are given in Table 1. Table 1 indicates that most of the central aspects of the examined textbooks are specified in the CCSS. Coherent learning paths that begin with understanding and move to fluency are identified for single-digit and multi-digit addition and subtraction. These learning paths initially use visual-quantitative supports and then move to fluency without such supports. The answer for Chinese Mathematics Curriculum Standards (CMCS) standards is more complex and is given separately below for single-digit and multi-digit numbers where the contents of the US standards are also discussed in more detail.

Single-Digit Adding and Subtracting in Curriculum Standards

US The three levels of the CCSS single-digit learning path begins in Kindergarten with Level 1 and moves to Levels 2 and 3 in Grade 1 (see Table 1). Students continue with these levels in Grade 2. Students are to use visual-quantitative supports such as objects or drawings for this learning path. Fluency is specified for particular numbers at each grade level. Inclusion of these levels of student thinking is an important step forward because Fuson and Li (2009) explained that the learning path in many US textbooks at the time of the development of the *Math Expressions* program was to move from Level 1 directly to recall of memorized facts. In the US, there was, and still is, the idea that these "facts" can and should be learned as separate rote bits of information rather than as a set of interrelated triads that have many relationships accessible to reasoning and that go through the well-established research-based learning path of three levels.

The CCSS Operations and Algebraic Thinking (OA) Progression (The Common Core Writing Team 2011a) that explicates the OA standards makes it clear that math

Table 1 Core attributes of the US common core standards for single-digit and multi-digit addition and subtraction

Overall attributes

1. Research-based learning paths and the use of learning supports are specified.
2. Understanding and fluency are both crucial foci and mentioned specifically, and the standards are focused and coherent across grades so there is time to focus on understanding and on fluency.

Single-digit addition and subtraction

The standards specify a learning path of three levels of single-digit addition/subtraction strategies from Kindergarten through grade 2: (1) direct model counting all, (2) count on, (3) make a ten and other methods that recompose the addends.

Kindergarten children add and subtract within 10 using Level 1 methods (K.OA.1, 2), and they learn prerequisites for Level 2 and Level 3 methods (K.OA.3, 4; NBT.1). Children use visual-quantitative supports such as objects or drawings.
Grade 1 children add and subtract within 20 using Level 2 and 3 strategies (1.OA.6). Visual-quantitative supports are not mentioned explicitly, but are implicit because they are described in the OA Progression (2011a) and are used in the many studies about these strategies.
Grade 2 children fluently add and subtract within 20 using Level 2 and 3 strategies (2.OA.2) as outlined in 1.OA.6.

The standards specify fluency for adding and subtracting to specific totals by grade level: K.OA.5: totals ≤ 5; 1.OA.6: totals ≤ 10; 2.OA.2: totals ≤ 20 including by end of Grade 2, know from memory all sums of two one-digit numbers.

Multi-digit addition and subtraction

For multi-digit computation, the standards specify a learning path in which students first develop, discuss, and use concrete models or drawings and strategies based on place value and properties of operations, and they relate the strategy to a written method and explain the reasoning used (explanations may be supported by drawings or objects). They use the visual-quantitative supports for adding within 100 in Grade 1 (1.NBT.4) and for adding and subtracting within 1,000 in Grade 2 (2.NBT.7, 9). Grade 1 specifies "understand that in adding two-digit numbers, one adds tens and tens, ones and ones; and sometimes it is necessary to compose a ten."
Students then move to fluency to specific totals by grade level:

In Grade 2 they fluently add and subtract within 100 using strategies based on place value, properties of operations, and/or the relationship between addition and subtraction (2.NBT.5).
In Grade 3 they fluently add and subtract within 1000 using strategies and algorithms based on place value, properties of operations, and/or the relationship between addition and subtraction (3.NBT.2).
In Grade 4 they fluently add and subtract using the standard algorithm for totals through 1,000,000 (4.NBT.4).

Note: There are place value standards that support these computation standards

textbooks and teachers are to support this learning path of student reasoning and use of strategies and not just move immediately to fact fluency: "The word *fluent* is used in the Standards to mean "fast and accurate." Fluency in each grade involves a mixture of just knowing some answers, knowing some answers from patterns (e.g., "adding 0 yields the same number"), and knowing some answers from the use of strategies. It is important to push sensitively and encouragingly toward fluency of the designated numbers at each grade level, recognizing that fluency will be a mixture of these kinds of thinking that may differ among students. The extensive work relating addition and subtraction means that subtraction can frequently be solved by thinking of the related addition, especially for smaller numbers. It is also important that these patterns, strategies and decompositions still be available in Grade 3 for use in multiplying and dividing and in distinguishing adding and subtracting from multiplying and dividing. So the important press toward fluency should also allow students to fall back on earlier strategies when needed. By the end of the K-2 grade span, students have sufficient experience with addition and subtraction to know single-digit sums from memory (2.OA.2). As should be clear from the foregoing this is not a matter of instilling facts divorced from their meanings, but rather as an outcome of a multi-year process that heavily involves the interplay of practice and reasoning (pp. 18–19)."

The extended East Asian experience in supporting students through this meaningful learning path suggests a further clarification of what "known from memory" means. Murata (2004) reported that many Japanese students interviewed about their use of the make-a-ten method did not clearly distinguish between using the strategy and "just knowing" the total. These seemed to merge into such a rapid use of the strategy that it was not externally, and even sometimes internally, distinguishable from "just knowing." Therefore, "known from memory" might be a strategy that is done so quickly that others cannot tell whether the answer is obtained by just knowing or by rapid use of a strategy. These "known from memory" sums for the US CCSS can be seen as the culmination of a three-year process in which patterns (e.g., for adding 0 or adding 1), strategies, and remembered results merge to become sums "known from memory" but in ways that might differ across students. What fluency actually entails may differ between East Asian and at least some US students because the general make-a-ten method is more difficult in English, and thus fewer students use this Level 3 method.

No specific linguistic supports are described in the US CCSS, but the need for additional supports for the irregular English number words from 11 to 99 is identified and discussed in the Numbers Base Ten (NBT) Progression (2011b). In addition to these English-Chinese number word differences, Fuson and Li (2009) found that Chinese words for the parts of addition and subtraction equations were more meaningful than those in English. The auditory confusion between *sum* and *some* led to the use in *Math Expressions* of *total* instead of *sum* in the early grades. The difficult words for subtraction (*subtrahend, minuend*) led to the use of *addend* in subtraction as well as addition, providing the further benefit of relating addition and subtraction in the context of equation forms. Further analyses of other linguistic differences reported in Fuson and Li (2009) for these or other topics might be helpful (see also Song and Ginsburg 1987).

China An examination of the Chinese Mathematics Curriculum Standards (CMCS, Ministry of Education 2011) indicates that these standards emphasize the development of students' understanding of numerical concepts (up to 10,000 from grades 1–3) and computations (adding/subtracting of two-digit and three-digit numbers, and multiplying 1-digit times 3-digit and 2-digit times 2-digit numbers, dividing two-digit or three-digit numbers by a 1-digit number). In classroom instruction, CMCS requires teachers to use real world contexts to develop students' number concepts through observations, hands-on work, and problem solving. It emphasizes oral computations, estimations, and students' sharing of different computation methods. Further suggestions are also provided for teaching, assessment, and textbook development. For instance, CMCS in its experimental version (Ministry of Education 2001) included six general suggestions for textbook development, including (1) selecting and using problems and tasks that are engaging and closely related to students' daily lives; (2) providing students with opportunities for active thinking, collaborations, and discussions; (3) using multiple forms and representations to present materials; (4) introducing important mathematics concepts and ideas step by step; (5) leaving some flexibilities in content design; and (6) introducing related background information of selected mathematics concepts. These suggestions provide general guidelines for textbook writers to develop and include written-numeric, visual-quantitative, and linguistic supports in textbooks. Its current version (Ministry of Education 2011) still contains six general suggestions for textbook development, with similar but more comprehensive intentions. These suggestions include (1) textbook writing should emphasize scientific quality, (2) textbook writing should emphasize coherence and structure, (3) textbook content should show its development process, (4) textbook content should connect with students' reality, (5) textbook content design should leave some flexibilities, and (6) textbook should be readable and user friendly. In contrast to the US CCSS, the Chinese CMCS do not provide many specifics except some examples. Fluency is not specified for particular grade levels. The Chinese CMCS uses sample problems and solutions to illustrate its general suggestions rather than the detailed descriptions in the US CCSS. And the CMCS does not specify the single-digit learning progression from Levels 1–3 in Kindergarten to Grade 1 even though Fuson and Li (2009) found these levels in the textbook. However, this learning progression has been used for many years in China, so perhaps it is less necessary that it be specified.

Multi-digit Adding and Subtracting in Curriculum Standards

US The CCSS coherent learning path that begins with understanding and moves to fluency for multi-digit addition and subtraction starts with methods that use place value and properties of operations. These methods are initially grounded in visual-quantitative supports (concrete models or drawings) and related to a written method and explained (see Table 1). This is the approach reported by Fuson and Li (2009) for the Chinese (and other East Asian) and *Math Expressions* textbooks. In the US CCSS, fluency without the use of visual-quantitative supports is at Grade 2 within 100 and at Grade 3 within 1000. In the US CCSS and in

Math Expressions students generalize the standard algorithm through 1,000,000 in Grade 4.

China   An examination of the Chinese Mathematics Curriculum Standards (CMCS) and textbooks indicates that sharing and discussing different ways of doing multi-digit computations is part of the approach. Computations with numbers larger than three digits are not emphasized in Grades 1–3, but estimation may involve simple 4-digit numbers. Numbering in Chinese uses different names for larger numbers through the first 5 places that students need to learn by Grade 3 (i.e., 个 — ones, 十 —tens, 百 —hundreds, 千 —thousands, 万 —ten thousands). The use of distinct names with the meaning of different place values likely helps students to extend their computation skills to larger numbers when needed.

Many Methods or One in Curriculum Standards?

Fuson and Li (2009) reported variation in how multi-digit adding and subtracting methods were written even within the same country. The standards of both countries explicitly or implicitly allow different methods to be used. But the US CCSS calls the early methods that are used with drawings *strategies*, the later methods *algorithms*, and specifies that students are eventually to use the standard algorithm. The differences in these terms are discussed in Fuson and Beckmann (2012). These terms are not differentiated or even used in China, so the differences are not important for this paper. We will call all of these *methods*. But it is important for this paper to convey that "the standard algorithm" does not mean one single algorithm, but rather a collection of variations of written methods that use the same mathematical approach. The term "standard algorithm" is not defined in the CCSS, but in the NBT progression (The Common Core Writing Team 2011b) and in Fuson and Beckmann (2012), standard algorithms implement and are characterized by this mathematical approach:

- they decompose numbers into base-ten units and then carry out single-digit computations with those units using the place values to direct the place value of the resulting number; and
- they clearly use the one-to-ten uniformity of the base ten structure as they generalize to large whole numbers and to decimals.

All of the methods identified in Fuson and Li (2009) use this mathematical approach. This approach was classified by Fuson et al. (1997) as *decompose-tens-and-ones* methods rather than as *begin-with-one-number* methods that add or count on from one addend. Fuson and Beckmann analyze both of these kinds of methods and conclude that only the *decompose-tens-and-ones* methods (more generally, *decompose-place-values* methods) qualify as a standard algorithm.

Criteria for Mathematically-Desirable and Accessible Algorithms for Multi-digit Adding and Subtracting

Given the variation between methods reported in Fuson and Li (2009) and supported in the standards for both countries explicitly or implicitly, an important educational question is: Are there variations that are more supportive of understanding and explaining and also easier to carry out than other variations? To address this question, we first identify aspects of multi-digit adding and subtracting in Table 2 that vary in how methods are written. These issues arise from mathematical aspects of multi-digit adding/subtracting or from the research literature about typical errors or preferences of children.

In Table 3 we show the major methods from Fuson and Li (2009) and then answer the questions from Table 2 to identify which methods clarified more conceptual issues or were easier to carry out. Because, as discussed above, all of the methods used in Fuson and Li (2009) benefited from visual-quantitative supports, these supports are shown in Table 3. The Secret-Code Cards show the 0 in the tens numbers hiding under the ones, and thus enable students to move from the first Expanded

Table 2 Conceptual issues for multi-digit adding and subtracting

Adding

(a) Add like quantities
   Is adding like quantities made easier by using vertical form and aligning like places (units)?
(b) Group (carry) 10 units to make 1 new next-larger unit (ten, hundred, etc.) if needed

   (B1) Is it easy to see the total that includes the new grouped unit (e.g., 14 ones or 14 tens)?
   (B2) Do you write that teen total in the usual order (1 ten then the ones)?
   (B3) Is it easy to see where to write the new unit?
   (B4) Is it easy to add units that include that new unit?

(c) MDN + MDN = MDN
   Are the two addends and the total kept separate? If not, the problem is changed.
(d) Can you go from left to right?
   Many English-speaking students prefer to do math in the same direction as they read. So this preference would vary by language.

Answers of yes in Table 3 mean that the written method addresses that conceptual issue.

Subtracting

Issues a (Subtracting like quantities), c, and d are the same as those described above for Adding.

(b) Ungroup (borrow) 1 to make 10 new next-smaller units if needed

   (B1) Is it easy to see the total that includes 10 of the new ungrouped unit (e.g., 14 ones or 14 tens)?
   (B2) Do you write that teen total in the usual order (1 ten then the ones)?
   (B3) Is it easy to see and/or to see where to write the new ungrouped unit?
   (B4) Is it easy to subtract from the units that include that new ungrouped unit?

(e) Does the method avoid the common subtracting error of subtracting top from bottom?
(f) Does the method do all of one kind of step first and then all of the other kind of step?

Table 3 The support of multidigital addition methods for the conceptual issues in Table 2

A. Expanded Notation Methods

	A2. $L \to Rt$	A3. $Rt \to L$	a) Yes all
A1.			b1) Yes all
$58 = 50 + 8$	58	58	b2) Yes all
$+\ 36 = 30 + 6$	$+\ 36$	$+\ 36$	b3) Yes all
$80 + 14$	80	14	b4) Yes 2 & 3
$= 94$	14	80	c) Yes all
	94	94	d) Yes 2

Secret-Code Cards

A. New Groups Below Method

a) Yes
b1) Yes
b2) Yes
b3) Yes
b4) Yes
c) Yes
d) No

A. New Groups Above Method

a) Yes
b1) No
b2) No
b3) No
b4) No
c) No
d) No

Notation Method (A1) to the two forms that do not write out the expanded forms for the addends but do for the sums (A2 and A3). The quantity drawings that show tens and ones help students see how to align the numbers vertically (especially for cases where the number of digits differs such as 8 and 65) and why one adds the numbers in like places (because they are like quantities tens and ten or ones and ones that can be readily distinguished in the math drawings). Each of these visual-quantity supports is helpful because they address different conceptual issues. The drawings for tens and ones in the Chinese books serve the same functions as the drawings in Table 3. The quantity drawings can support any method.

One of the Expanded Notation methods (the right to left A3 method) and the New Groups Below method (method B) address all of the mathematical issues a, b, and c from Table 2. The first and second Expanded Notation methods read from left to right (and are yes for d), so they are easier for some students. The New Groups Above method C does not support any conceptual issues except that it aligns like places (a). The problems with this method are:

- b1: The total is separated in space so that it is difficult to see as a total 14.

- b2: Usually students are to write down the 4 and carry/group the 1, so they must write 14 opposite to their usual order of writing 1 then 4.
- b3: Writing the new 1 ten above the left-most place instead of the next-left place is a well-documented error; it arises more with problems of 3-digits or more.
- b4: To add the column with the new unit above, students must add the 1 to one of the numbers in that place, remember that number and ignore the number they just used, and add the mental number to the other number they see. Or they add the two numbers there originally but then often forget to add the 1 on the top.

The Expanded Notation methods are useful for initial understanding, and the second and third such methods (A2 and A3) easily generalize to 3 or even 4 places. But these methods get complex for numbers as large as 1,000,000, so they cannot be considered totally general methods. Therefore, two approaches seem sensible. In the initial Chinese Mathematics Curriculum Standards (Ministry of Education 2001), the sharing of different computation methods is specifically emphasized, including the Expanded Notation method, for example, $58 + 36 = (50 + 30) + (8 + 6) = 80 + 14 = 94$. Methods adding on from the first number were also described (e.g., $58 + 36 = 58 + 30 + 6 = 88 + 6 = 94$; $58 + 36 = 58 + 2 + 34 = 60 + 34 = 94$) as was the method of New Groups Below. However, in the current new version of the Chinese Mathematics Curriculum Standards (Ministry of Education 2011) these examples do not appear, implying that students are to generate different methods but that teachers do not necessarily teach all different methods. In *Math Expressions* the Expanded Notation methods are used through Grade 3 because some English-speaking children benefit from working with the expanded forms for a longer time because of the irregular decade words in English. However, New Groups Below is introduced in Grade 1 and continued in all subsequent grades because of its conceptual advantages and because it generalizes. New Groups Above is introduced by the teacher in *Math Expressions* as a method used by some people if a student does not bring it into the class because it is considered by some people to be "the standard algorithm." All methods in Table 3 can be related to each other.

Results of the related analysis of Table 2 issues for the multi-digit subtracting methods reported in Fuson and Li (2009) are shown in Table 4. Conceptual issues a, b, c, and d for subtraction were similar to those for addition. Two new issues arise for subtracting. The use of the vertical form for adding like places suggests an extremely common subtraction error: Subtract the top from bottom number instead of ungrouping to get more (e.g., for 94–36, get 62). This error is increased in the US partly by the common practice of introducing problems with no ungrouping (e.g., 78–43) in Grade 1 and only moving to ungrouping problems a year later in Grade 2. The US CCSS will hopefully prevent this common textbook practice because no general 2-digit subtractions are in the US Grade 1 standards. In the East Asian textbooks examined, problems with no ungrouping are introduced first but the textbooks move immediately to problems requiring ungrouping, so Chinese students do not experience this difficulty.

Visual-quantitative supports of models or drawings that show hundreds, tens, and ones were used in all textbooks in the Fuson and Li (2009) analysis for subtracting. These might not have been needed so much for knowing issue (a) *subtracting like*

Table 4 The support of multidigital substraction methods for the conceptual issues in Table 2

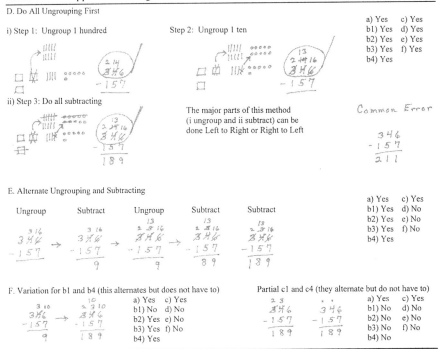

D. Do All Ungrouping First

i) Step 1: Ungroup 1 hundred   Step 2: Ungroup 1 ten

a) Yes c) Yes
b1) Yes d) Yes
b2) Yes e) Yes
b3) Yes f) Yes
b4) Yes

ii) Step 3: Do all subtracting

The major parts of this method (i ungroup and ii subtract) can be done Left to Right or Right to Left

Common Error

E. Alternate Ungrouping and Subtracting

Ungroup   Subtract   Ungroup   Subtract   Subtract

a) Yes c) Yes
b1) Yes d) No
b2) Yes e) No
b3) Yes f) No
b4) Yes

F. Variation for b1 and b4 (this alternates but does not have to)

a) Yes c) Yes
b1) No d) No
b2) Yes e) No
b3) Yes f) No
b4) Yes

Partial c1 and c4 (they alternate but do not have to)

a) Yes c) Yes
b1) No d) No
b2) No e) No
b3) No f) No
b4) No

quantities because of the previous work on multi-digit adding. These models illustrate directly the ungrouping (borrowing) needed to get more units in a top number in order to be able to subtract from it. *Math Expressions* also used a special visual-quantitative support—the magnifying glass (see Table 4)—to interfere with the common subtracting error and to help with conceptual issue c: seeing the three multi-digit numbers involved in the subtracting rather than only seeing the vertical frame for (a) subtracting like quantities. Students draw a *magnifying glass* (an ellipse) around the top number that is big enough to hold all of the ungrouping, with a little stick at the top right for the handle. The *magnifying glass* is introduced as something that reminds us to *look inside the top number* to check in each column to see if there is enough to subtract. This support serves to inhibit the subtract-smaller-from-larger number error that is often made before students even think about ungrouping. The *magnifying glass* also makes a visual grouping that emphasizes the top multi-digit number as a whole and thus facilitates a discussion about whether the value of the top number is changed when it is ungrouped. Because many US students view multi-digit subtraction as successive vertical operations on columns of single digits, many think that ungrouping does change the value of the top number (e.g., see literature reviewed in Fuson 1990). Students enjoy the metaphor of the looking glass, but they drop this step when they no longer need it.

Table 4 shows the two major subtracting methods Fuson and Li (2009) found in the textbooks. These methods are the same for 2-digit numbers but differ for numbers of 3 or more digits. The common top from bottom error is shown at the right of the second row. In the third row is an alternating method of subtracting in which a student can ungroup to make more ones if needed and then subtracts the ones, ungroups to make more tens if needed and then subtracts tens, etc. This method increases the common error even for students who know they should ungroup. For example, in the second step students see a 3 on the top and a 5 below and they have just subtracted the ones, so they are in subtracting mode. *Two* pops into their mind as the difference of 3 and 5, and they write 2 in the tens column instead of ungrouping to get more tens on the top. In the bottom row are variations of this method found in East Asian books. In Method F the ungrouped 10 of the new unit may be written above that place to make it easier to subtract by using make-a-ten. In the first method G only the new, reduced, larger unit resulting from the ungrouping is written. This method was also invented in *Math Expressions* classes by Grade 4 students who said they did not need to write the 1 for the tens because they knew it was there. The second method G is an even more abbreviated ungrouping recording: Neither the reduced larger unit or the increased smaller unit is shown; a dot shows a column that has been decreased by 1 to ungroup.

The top two rows show the *Math Expressions* Do All Ungrouping First method (D). Doing all ungrouping first eliminates top from bottom errors. Answers to the conceptual issues for subtraction in Table 3 show that this Do All Ungrouping First method (D) is the most conceptually supportive. It has the further advantage that either major step (ungrouping or subtracting) can be done left-to-right, which many students like. Both major steps can also be done right-to-left, for students who prefer this. Deep mathematical discussions ensue when students explain why they can go in either direction and why they get the same answer both ways. Any of the East Asian methods shown in Table 4 could be done as a non-alternating method by doing all ungrouping first.

Somewhat Different Learning Paths in China and the US

Ma (1999) identified three steps in multi-digit adding and subtracting that Fuson and Li (2009) verified in other East Asian books. Ma called these levels, but we use the term "steps" to differentiate these from the three levels used in single-digit adding/subtracting. In Ma's Step 1, the make-a-ten methods for teen addition and subtraction were developed, each in a separate unit. In Step 2, multiple methods were given for 2-digit problems. In Step 3 for problems with 3-digit and larger numbers, the books focused on one generalizable mathematically-desirable method, with the variations as discussed above.

Our analysis of the US CCSS indicates a related but somewhat different sequence for students in the United States, partly because of the limitations of English number words that cause difficulty with the make-a-ten methods for children speaking English (or other European languages with irregular tens). The East Asian Steps 1 and 2 become mixed in the US. Make-a-ten methods can be introduced and discussed in Grades 1 and 2. But because these methods are more difficult in English than in Chinese, many students stick to Level 2 counting on methods. The Level 3 make-a-ten methods may begin to be used by more students when they are grouping and ungrouping in multi-digit adding and subtracting because the group of ten is salient and important then. Limited use of the make-a-ten methods is also due to limited teaching of the make-a-ten methods and their prerequisites in the US. Multi-digit expanded notation methods as well as the New Groups Below method are conceptually important to introduce early on. Students may invent other methods especially for totals within 100. The US Step 1 is formed by this mixture of single-digit and multi-digit methods and occurs in Grades 1 and 2. Step 2 occurs with numbers greater than 100 but less than 1000, where it is important for more children to move to New Groups Below although some may continue to use Expanded Notation methods or adding on methods especially in Grade 2. The Do All Ungrouping First method is now important for subtraction involving 3 digits (this method D and the alternating variation E are not distinguishable for 2-digit subtraction). In Step 3 all students focus as in East Asia on a generalizable mathematically-desirable method in Grade 3 within 1000 and go on in Grade 4 to larger problems within 1,000,000.

Conclusions

The analysis of the US and Chinese standards indicated differences between these countries' standards. The US CCSS have explicit learning paths and supports as can be seen in Chinese and the US *Math Expressions* textbooks in Fuson and Li (2009). Therefore, all US programs in the future should have such supports as mandated in the standards even though such supports have not appeared consistently before. This is an important step forward for students and teachers in the US. The Chinese standards were less explicit about learning paths and supports, but the presence of these learning paths and supports in textbooks suggest that there is cultural knowledge that may make it less necessary to be explicit in the standards. Hopefully this cultural knowledge will be sufficient to maintain such learning paths and supports in future textbooks.

Our analysis identified methods that show variations of written steps that can support conceptual issues in multi-digit adding and subtracting, reduce errors, and make steps easier to carry out. These New Groups Below and Do All Ungrouping First methods are as efficient and succinct as related variations that are viewed by some in the US as the standard algorithm (New Groups Above C and the Alternating Subtraction Method E), and these superior methods do not have the disadvantages of these inferior variations. Thus, the best variations are the New Groups Below method (B) for addition and the Do All Ungrouping First method (D) for subtraction. Hopefully the use of these superior variations will become widespread in both the US and China.

Finally, we summarized the somewhat different organization of steps in Ma's learning path for China and the US. These differences were primarily the results of linguistic limitations of English teen (11 to 19) words compared to Chinese words, but they also are due to limited teaching of the make-a-ten methods and their prerequisites in the US. The final Step 3 in Ma's book (1999) is similar in China and the US and could become even more similar if both countries moved to using the multi-digit variations we identified as superior.

Acknowledgements   The first author wishes to thank all of the teachers and students with whom she has worked in the classroom research underlying this paper. That classroom research was partially funded by National Science Foundation Grant Numbers ESI-9816320, RED-935373, and REC-9806020. Any opinions, findings, and conclusions or recommendations expressed in this paper are those of the author and do not necessarily reflect the view of the National Science Foundation. We would also like to thank reviewers for their thoughtful comments on a prior version of this article.

References

Cai, J. (2008). Some highlights of the similarities and differences in intended, planned/ implemented, and achieved curricula between China and the United States. In Z. Usiskin & E. Willmore (Eds.), *Mathematics curriculum in Pacific Rim countries: China, Japan, Korea, and Singapore* (pp. 157–181). Charlotte: Information Age Publishing.

Donovan, M. S. & Bransford, J. D. (Eds.) (2005). *How students learn: mathematics in the classroom* (pp. 217–256). Washington: National Academy Press.

Fuson, K. C. (1990). Conceptual structures for multiunit numbers: implications for learning and teaching multi-digit addition, subtraction, and place value. *Cognition and Instruction, 7,* 343–403.

Fuson, K. C. (1992). Research on whole number addition and subtraction. In D. Grouws (Ed.), *Handbook of research on mathematics teaching and learning* (pp. 243–275). New York: Macmillan.

Fuson, K. C. (2006/2009). *Math expressions, grades K, 1, 2, 3, 4, 5.* Boston: Houghton Mifflin Harcourt Publishers.

Fuson, K. C., & Beckmann, S. (2012). Standard algorithms in the common core state standards. *National Council of Supervisors of Mathematics Journal of Mathematics Education Leadership, 14*(2), 3–19.

Fuson, K. C., & Li, Y. (2009). Cross-cultural issues in linguistic, visual-quantitative, and written-numeric supports for mathematical thinking. *ZDM Mathematics Education, 41,* 793–808.

Fuson, K., & Murata, A. (2007). Integrating NRC principles and the NCTM process standards to form a class learning path model that individualizes within whole-class activities. *National Council of Supervisors of Mathematics Journal of Mathematics Education Leadership, 10*(1), 72–91.

Fuson, K. C., Wearne, D., Hiebert, J., Human, P., Murray, H., Olivier, A., Carpenter, T., & Fennema, E. (1997). Children's conceptual structures for multi-digit numbers at work in addition and subtraction. *Journal for Research in Mathematics Education, 28,* 130–162.

Fuson, K. C., Kalchman, M., & Bransford, J. D. (2005). Mathematical understanding: an introduction. In M. S. Donovan & J. D. Bransford (Eds.), *How students learn: history, math, and science in the classroom* (pp. 217–256). Washington: National Academy Press.

Kilpatrick, J., Swafford, J., & Findell, B. (Eds.) (2001). *Adding it up: helping children learn mathematics.* Washington: National Academy Press.

Li, Y. (2007). Curriculum and culture: an exploratory examination of mathematics curriculum materials in their system and cultural contexts. *The Mathematics Educator, 10*(1), 21–38.

Li, Y. (2008). What do students need to learn about division of fractions? *Mathematics Teaching in the Middle School, 13,* 546–552.

Li, Y., Chen, X., & An, S. (2009a). Conceptualizing and organizing content for teaching and learning in selected Chinese, Japanese, and US mathematics textbooks: the case of fraction division. *ZDM Mathematics Education, 41*, 809–826.

Li, Y., Chen, X., & Kulm, G. (2009b). Mathematics teachers' practices and thinking in lesson plan development: a case of teaching fraction division. *ZDM Mathematics Education, 41*, 717–731.

Li, Y., Zhang, J., & Ma, T. (2009c). Approaches and practices in developing school mathematics textbooks in China. *ZDM Mathematics Education, 41*, 733–738.

Liu, J., & Li, Y. (2010). Mathematics curriculum reform in the Chinese mainland: changes and challenges. In F. K. S. Leung & Y. Li (Eds.), *Reforms and issues in school mathematics in East Asia—sharing and understanding mathematics education policies and practices* (pp. 9–31). Rotterdam: Sense.

Ma, L. (1999). *Knowing and teaching elementary mathematics: teachers' understanding of fundamental mathematics in China and the United States.* Mahwah: Lawrence Erlbaum.

Ministry of Education, P. R. China (2001). *Mathematics curriculum standard for compulsory education (experimental version).* Beijing: Beijing Normal University Press.

Ministry of Education, P. R. China (2011). *Mathematics curriculum standards for compulsory education.* Beijing: Beijing Normal University Press.

Murata, A. (2004). Paths to learning ten-structured understanding of teen sums: addition solution methods of Japanese grade 1 students. *Cognition and Instruction, 22*, 185–218.

Murata, A. (2008). Mathematics teaching and learning as a mediating process: the case of tape diagrams. *Mathematical Thinking and Learning, 10*, 374–406.

Murata, A., & Fuson, K. (2006). Teaching as assisting individual constructive paths within an interdependent class learning zone: Japanese first graders learning to add using ten. *Journal for Research in Mathematics Education, 37*, 421–456.

National Council of Teachers of Mathematics (2000). *Principles and standards for school mathematics.* Reston, VA: Author.

National Governors Association Center for Best Practices, Council of Chief State School Officers (2010). The common core state standards math. Washington, DC: Author.

Schmidt, W. H., McKnight, C. C., & Raizen, S. A. (1997). *A splintered vision: an investigation of US science and mathematics education.* Dordrecht: Kluwer.

Song, M.-J., & Ginsburg, H. P. (1987). The development of informal and formal mathematical thinking in Korean and US children. *Child Development, 58*, 1286–1296.

The Common Core Writing Team (2011a). The OA progression for the common core state standards. commoncoretools.wordpress.com.

The Common Core Writing Team (2011b). The NBT progression for the common core state standards. commoncoretools.wordpress.com.

Watanabe, T. (2006). The teaching and learning of fractions: a Japanese perspective. *Teaching Children Mathematics, 12*, 368–374.

The Virtual Curriculum: New Ontologies for a Mobile Mathematics

Nathalie Sinclair and Elizabeth de Freitas

Abstract This chapter draws on new ideas in the philosophy of mathematics to explore alternative ways of designing curriculum. Our main aim is to trouble common assumptions about the nature of mathematics that controls the scope and sequence of the mathematics curriculum in the US. We argue that mathematical concepts are characteristically *virtual* rather than ideal abstractions, and we show how this new approach to concepts could form the basis for a very different curricular unfolding. We then argue that certain digital technologies can play an important role in promoting mathematics learners' encounters with the virtual.

Keywords Virtual · Concept · Mobility · Digital technology · Dynamic geometry

Introduction

One of the underlying tenets of the mathematics curriculum is the gradual movement of mathematical ideas from the concrete to the progressively more abstract. Pedagogical theories vary widely, of course, in terms of *how* these mathematical ideas should be taught. And these theories rely, in turn, on a range of philosophical assumptions about the nature of knowledge as well as the nature of mathematics itself. For example, the curriculum one endorses if one assumes that mathematical objects are the result of historically and socially-situated human construction will differ from the curriculum that assumes mathematical objects are Platonic ideals that exist independent of human activity. In the former, there might be more emphasis on various ways of interpreting mathematical objects and the relations between them, while in the latter the emphasis will be on achieving *the correct* understanding of the object. Despite the enormous changes over the past few decades regarding the nature of knowledge (and of learning) as well as the nature of mathematics (and its

N. Sinclair (✉)
Simon Fraser University, Burnaby, Canada
e-mail: nathsinc@sfu.ca

E. de Freitas
Adelphi University, Garden City, USA

Y. Li, G. Lappan (eds.), *Mathematics Curriculum in School Education*,
Advances in Mathematics Education, DOI 10.1007/978-94-007-7560-2_26,
© Springer Science+Business Media Dordrecht 2014

continued development), and the ensuing shifts in the priority of curriculum-style documents, we see a prevailing inertness regarding the overall scope and sequence of the mathematics curriculum.

In this chapter, we propose to draw on some new ideas in the philosophy of mathematics to explore their possible ramifications on the design of curriculum. Our main contention will be that the 'natural' and long taken-for-granted assumption about the abstract nature of mathematics—and the trajectory toward it by which the concrete is left behind—can and should be questioned. We believe that the concrete-abstract binary imposes a straightjacket on mathematics and misrepresents the actual activity of doing mathematics. By conceptualizing mathematics as being characteristically *virtual*, that is, as bridging the concrete and the abstract, we will show that it is possible to rethink basic assumptions about the way mathematical ideas should be sequenced in a curriculum and about the framing of the curriculum in terms of topics.

We begin by providing a brief overview of some main conceptualizations of curriculum in mathematics education research—we will use these to illustrate the scope of our own argument. We then outline a mathematical philosophy of the virtual, which we contrast to current prevalent philosophical positions, drawing principally on the work of Gilles Châtelet. We then investigate how the notion of the virtual could change our understanding of mathematical concepts, which often become the topics through which the curricular path or trajectory is defined. We offer a richer, double-functioning notion of concept and show how it could form the basis of a very different curricular unfolding. We then focus in on particular concepts of the curriculum and explore how Châtelet's idea of virtuality might offer alternatives both in terms of the order in which concepts are usually taught, and in terms of the underlying goals behind the teaching of these concepts. Finally, while Châtelet's use of the construct *virtual* is not tied to digital technologies, we will argue that such technologies can play an important role in promoting mathematics learners' encounters with the virtual.

Conceptualizations of the Mathematics Curriculum

The notion of scope and sequence pervades discussions about mathematics curriculum. Scope and sequence involve an ordered list of topics, often containing little attention to the ways certain units relate to others or to the temporal dimension of curriculum construction (Ball and Cohen 1996). This can make it hard to inquire into whether and how sequencing might change and what affect such a change might have on scope. As a structure for curriculum, it suggests that there is a natural order of concepts that must be followed (and "acquired") before moving on. Beyond the basic scope and sequence construct, Dietiker (2012) writes that the mathematics education literature offers three additional conceptualizations of curriculum: *curriculum map, learning trajectory* and *story*. The former was used by Dewey (1902) to distinguish between the "logical" organization of content as opposed to the everyday "psychological" experiences of the learner. This conceptualization encompasses more than scope and sequence in the sense that it invites reflection on the way in which the parts of the terrain relate to each other.

A related conceptualization of curriculum is that of the *learning trajectory* (Brey-fogle et al. 2010), which focuses on the path taken by the intended curriculum, and the critical moments along that path that mark progress toward a future goal. From this, a related student-oriented construct of *hypothetical learning trajectory* (Clements and Sarama 2004; Confrey et al. 2009) emerged, which describes the increasing levels of sophistication students demonstrate as they learn a concept during clinical interviews and teaching experiments. Such an approach focuses on the developmental progression of children. While Confrey et al. (2009) acknowledge that there is not only one trajectory through the "conceptual corridor," the metaphor of trajectory itself evokes imagery of a single, vectored direction. A powerful alternative approach to the role of concepts in mathematical activity is found in the fallibilism articulated by Imre Lakatos in the 1960s. According to Lakatos, mathematical activity is primarily concerned with concept formation and deformation. We are always working with ill-defined or ambiguous concepts, and as we try to prove things about them, we stretch them in new directions. Ernest (1991, 1998) has suggested that fallibilist philosophies might be useful in rethinking school mathematics, since fallibilism honors the creative or inventive nature of mathematics without prescribing an overly confining trajectory.

The mathematician Paul Lockhart (2008) uses the metaphor of story to help explain the importance of context and motivation in relation to any given "content":

> Mathematical structures, useful or not, are invented and developed within a problem context, and derive their meaning from that context. Sometimes we want one plus one to equal zero (as in so-called 'mod 2' arithmetic) and on the surface of a sphere the angles of a triangle add up to more than 180 degrees. There are no "facts" per se; everything is relative and relational. It is the story that matters, not just the ending. (p. 17)

As Dietiker (2012) argues, the metaphor of story attends much more to the ongoing temporal unfolding of mathematical development rather than the culminating mathematical goals, facts or content. Further, the conceptualization of story suggests that there would be a different story if the sequence were changed, and that changing one part of the story would have an effect on the rest. Not only are there different paths from A to B (as with hypothetical learning trajectories), but there are ways of getting to B that do not begin at A and, as such, it becomes even more important to focus on the problems that gave rise to A in the first place and the reciprocal relations between A and B. In line with this approach, the mathematical problem or question focuses less on which path to take to move through a given sequence of predetermined concepts, and more on which stories are worth telling regarding mathematical events and characters.

In the next section, we develop the notion of virtuality, which will lead to a rethinking of the mathematical concept. We will use this to argue that certain stories are in fact more significant than others and that some of these stories may upset the assumed sequence or trajectory of school mathematics.

Mathematics and Virtuality

Châtelet's (1993/2000) interest in the virtual originates in his dissatisfaction with
Aristotle's solution to the paradox that emerges when the mathematical and the
physical are considered ontologically distinct. In other words, the paradox concerns
the impossibility of a *causal* relationship between the mathematical (as that which
pertains to eternal truths) and the physical (as that which pertains to the contingent
and the real). Aristotle's solution was to infer the existence of some superior being
that can ensure cohesion between the two natures.[1] Châtelet proposes an alternative solution, claiming that the *virtual*—a state of being that is both physical and
mathematical—is the necessary link between the two realms; in so doing, he will
challenge the Aristotelian embargo against motion in mathematics. In other words,
he will reconceive mathematical entities as being material objects on and with which
mathematicians perform thought experiments. These thought experiments are not
the disembodied mental ruminations with which we typically associate mathematical thinking but, rather, gestural choreographies and exploratory diagramming. As
Châtelet (2000) suggests, "One could even say that the radical thought experiment
is an experiment where Nature and the Understanding switch places" (p. 12). One
consequence of this new ontology of mathematics is the ensuing challenge to the
dominant epistemology in which the mathematical is 'abstract' and the physical
'concrete.'

Châtelet credits Leibniz with properly recognizing the dynamics of virtuality.
Leibniz was critical of the Cartesians of his time for whom geometry involved abstract things like points and curves fixed in a rigid grid-like space. Bertrand Russell
(1903) nicely evokes this Cartesianism in his assertion that "a point of space is a
position, and can no more change its position than a leopard can change its spots.
The motion of a point of space is a phantom directly contrary to the law of identity [...]" (p. 405).) For Leibniz, space is much more flexible, positioning is relative, and points have weight; points are creators of new things (like circles, lines,
intersections)—they are "explosive forces." Instead of seeing points as things to be
designated—since, according to Châtelet, "designation assassinates the virtual"—
Leibniz sees points as forces of motion. Working with points as forces of motion
enables a kind of "experimental provocation" (p. 15) that, according to Châtelet,
leads to encounters with the virtual. When points are seen as mobile material entities, the mathematician can direct them to new places; instead of requiring that
they obey the physical laws of position in a two-dimensional plane, these points can
move along curves, for example, and encounter other curves that do not intersect
in the Cartesian plane. For Châtelet, such mobile, material thought experiments entailed new discoveries in the history of mathematics, such as the complex plane in
which two non-intersecting curves can in fact meet. The space in which these non-
intersecting curves meet is a virtual space that was carved out by mathematicians

---

[1]As Châtelet writes, Aristotle later sketched out another solution to the problem, which Leibniz
studied and eventually developed along the lines described in this chapter.

such as Abel. This virtual space is not abstract, claims Châtelet, because it retains the mobility and temporal quality that was forged by the mathematician.

Châtelet's approach to mathematics is distinguished from both Platonic and Aristotelian traditions because of how he leverages the two couplets: the virtual/actual and the possible/real. Mathematical activity, according to Châtelet, involves both *actualizing the virtual* and *realizing the possible*. Both realization and actualization bring forth something new into the situation (the possible and the virtual), but realization plays by the rules of logic while actualization involves a different kind of determination, one that generates something ontologically new (like the meeting place of two non-intersecting curves). The virtual marks that which is latent in an entity; but it is not the Platonic ideal of the entity for the crucial reason that Châtelet's virtuality is arrived at through mobile inventiveness. This is what makes the virtual more concrete. On the other hand, the possible is that which structures and limits the appearance of the entity according to current rules of inference and perceptual habits. The virtual (or potential) pertains to the indeterminacy at the source of all actions, whereas the possible pertains to the compliance of our actions with logical constraints. Thus novelty, genesis and creativity (rather than conditions of possibility) are fundamental concepts in a theory of actualization. Actualizing the virtual involves "an intrinsic genesis, not an extrinsic conditioning" (Deleuze 1994, p. 154).

It's essential that we resist the tendency to imagine the virtual as the *form* that is somehow buried in matter and waiting to be conjured or evoked. If the virtual is simply the articulating or actualizing of an *a priori* invisible form, then we are heading back to Platonism and the premise that ideal mathematical entities find their inaccurate and fuzzy realizations in the real world. The virtual is not a realm of forms to be mirrored in the physical world. The virtual does not resemble the actual. This lack of resemblance is crucial in appreciating the power of the virtual to disrupt common Platonist epistemologies about mathematics.[2] Moreover, since the virtual partakes of the physical, the paradox of causality that confounded Plato and Aristotle is circumvented. The virtual in sensible matter becomes intelligible, not by a reductionist abstraction or a "subtraction of determinations" (Aristotle's approach to abstraction), but by the actions (diagrams and gestures) that awaken the virtual or potential multiplicities that are implicit in any surface. Indeed, Châtelet's study of creative moments in the history of mathematics shows exactly how, in each case, the virtual is evoked, often through diagramming experiments whose sources Châtelet can trace to mobile gestural acts.

In this chapter, we are probing the possibility of privileging virtual encounters in the curriculum. Naturally, we do not expect learners to create mathematical spaces that are new to the discipline. But we can investigate whether they can create mathematical spaces that are new to them. Our line of questioning requires that we first re-examine familiar mathematical ideas in terms of their latent virtualities. Is the

---

[2] It is for this reason that Châtelet eschews the use of the word 'representation' to talk about the mobile, temporal inscriptions (gestures and diagrams) that actualize the virtual. Speaking in terms of representation implies that the inscriptions are meant to resemble—rather than *be*—a mathematical entity.

virtual evoked only rarely, in major turning points of the discipline? Or is the virtual woven through the fabric of mathematics? In the latter case, how might we recover the virtuality of ideas that have slowly become inert? Consider the triangle. In an advanced geometry course, we are taught to think of the triangle as an abstract geometric shape determined by its definition. Much earlier on in the curriculum, however, we are told to think of it as a concrete shape, perhaps in the form of a plastic tile or a pencil drawing. In between these extremes, we might see the emergence of other triangles of varying ontology, each partaking of the physical to some degree, each carrying with it some trace of the virtual motion by which it emerged. How would the curriculum change if we rethink the triangles generated through transformations, stretched into differing shapes and sizes, in terms of this virtual mobility?

Thinking in terms of mobility is instrumental in recovering the virtual. Instead of seeing the triangle as a rigid figure or as a sign perched in space, what happens if we think of it as a mobility? A triangle exists in motion, depleting itself into the infinitely small or exploding into linearity or bending along non-planar surfaces. It is not in the realm of the possible to have an infinitely small or uni-dimensional triangle. But with a sweep of the hand (perhaps one dragging the vertex of a dynamic triangle), the triangle can collapse, disappear, burst and morph. The virtual triangle is the one that is always moving, defined more by behavior—especially behavior at extremes—than by propositional sentences about static entities. The gestural orchestration or use of an "allusive device" is always an act of movement whereby the virtual is actualized. It is important to keep in mind that the virtual somehow retains the trace of this movement rather than abandoning the gesture that brought it into being. Aristotelian abstraction, on the other hand, is contemptuous of the hand and the movement by which the possible was determined. Abstraction strips mathematical entities of their physical emergence and pretends that they have no experiential history. Although many scholars assume that it is this act of stripping that makes mathematics so effective in science, Châtelet's entire historical project is to contest this assumption and show how inventions in mathematics prove effective precisely because they retained a trace of the gestures that brought them forth. More often than not it is in the diagrams created by the mathematicians where we see these gestures continue. Mathematics must be made to quiver "with the virtualities that inhabit it" and students invited to "reactivate a productivity" that congeals and stiffens too quickly after its articulation (Châtelet 2000, p. 103).

What consequences might our attempt to excavate the virtuality of mathematical ideas have on the shape of the mathematics curriculum? Might we simply be encouraged to rethink pedagogical choices (the tools and tasks that are used) or might there also be changes in terms of curricular choices, that is, choices about whether, when and why learners are asked to work with it? In the next section, we focus on the way in which an idea like the triangle comes to be framed as a curricular entity—an element in the sequence—and investigate how the notion of virtuality might disturb the current topic-driven curriculum.

Mobilizing Mathematics Concepts

Debates about mathematics curriculum often pivot around the distinction between procedural and conceptual knowledge. Educators and researchers use this distinction in order to argue for a particular focus in the curriculum, advocating for the importance of mathematical concepts such as function, prime number, infinitesimal, etc. Despite this ongoing attention to conceptual knowledge, there is little discussion about what actually constitutes a concept more generally, and how a concept might be different from a topic. *What is a mathematical concept?* Concepts are often considered abstract universals detached from the particularities of their concrete instances. They are typically treated as immaterial logical constraints on a given situation (Tall 2011). Our aim is to question this approach to concepts. What might it mean for a concept to be deeply material and operate on an ontological level? How does a mathematical concept remain vibrant and creative, without being reduced to a topic with a set of prescriptive procedures that relate to it? Might it be the case that our weak formulation of concepts is exactly what leads to an over-emphasis on procedural skill in mathematics classrooms?

If we compare our curriculum to the way that the Russian mathematical circles are designed, we can see radically different approaches to what constitutes a concept. Rather than focusing on a topic like multiplication or triangles, Russian mathematical circles are organized around multi-purpose devices that help one map the structure of mathematical relationships and invent new mathematical objects. The idea of a sequence of concepts is thus downplayed in favor of a collection of actions, thus coming closer to curriculum as story in the sense that the focus is on *what can be done* rather than *what is*. In part, this is due to the fact that the curriculum is based on rich problem solving, but we focus here on the fact that this approach seems to use the notion of a concept *as a device*, one that works both logically and ontologically. We use the term ontological to refer to the ways in which mathematics is a creative and material activity that literally invents new kinds of entities, as outlined in the section above. For both novices and experts, mathematics involves both realizing the possible (logical) and actualizing the virtual (ontological). For a concept to function in both these ways, it must sustain a certain vibrancy and vitality. In other words, a concept of this kind must be a *multi-purpose device* that resists reification while carving out new mathematical entities. Châtelet (2000) refers to these as "allusive devices" that give rise to thought experiments "that penetrate closer to the heart of relation and operativitivity" by being deliberately productive of ambiguity (p. 12). The concept is worked as though it were a kind of material media (clay, oil, ink) that lends itself to particular kinds of activity and rendering.

For instance, even/odd parity is a concept that helps render the structural relationship between numbers and helps the student map the terrain in which numbers live, but also functions importantly as a concept that engenders new kinds of mathematical objects. Parity is precisely the kind of concept that simultaneously works on both the logical level and the ontological level.[3] Parity marshals logical constraints

---

[3]The simultaneous functioning we are describing here might evoke for readers a comparison with the process/content distinction made in the *NCTM Standards*. An important difference, however,

and mathematical entities. For instance, the Ancient Greek proof of the irrationality of radical 2 relies extensively on even/odd parity. Parity is exploited in this famous proof to unleash and make actual the virtual (the irrational number) *while* operating according to the laws of legitimate inference. Parity is a working concept; that is, a concept that quite literally performs a sculpting or creative activity that brings the new number into being. And yet simultaneously parity operates as a logical instrument by which the possible is realized. The sculpting tool of parity works both the realm of the possible and the realm of the virtual.

Other concepts that are used in Russian circles (Fomin et al. 1996) are divisibility, invariants, the pigeon-hole principle, the triangle inequality and graphs (networks). The dilemma, as always, is that any list of concepts can be denigrated to a set of topics once they are taken up in practice. How does one resist that and *honor the concept as creative force*? How do we ensure that the concept is put to work in engendering new mathematical entities? How do we invite students to grasp the mobility and potentiality of the concept? Perhaps the way to ensure that the concept remains operative and mobile and creative rather than staid, is to focus on whether the work itself is creative, that is to say, work that continues to be committed to bringing the new into being (a process of becoming). In other words, work that unleashes the virtual. When the concept is used only as a logical tool, while the ontological aspect (actualizing the virtual) is abandoned, the activity reduces to adhering to logical constraints. In such cases, the ossified concept doesn't sustain the mobility from which it came forth.

One can easily see concepts in our current curriculum that have been emptied of their mobility and power, but might be resuscitated. For instance, the Pythagorean Theorem is often treated as no more than a tool for calculating lengths in triangles, rather than an assemblage of concepts and an inventive medium through which something new might emerge. In re-conceptualized the concepts at work in a Pythagorean relation, we could recast the derivation of the theorem as an activity that literally brought forth the squares on the sides of the triangle. These squares are actualized, not only out of logical necessity or inductive reasoning, but out of some material *potential* linked to the triangle. In honoring the ontological aspect we begin to think about the squares as invented objects. The aspect of necessity attached to the logical is then opened up with the aspect of contingency attached to the act of creation. We might then see how the squares might have been something else, like semicircles or trapezoids, materialized on the sides of the triangle. According to this approach, the Pythagorean theorem becomes an assemblage of concepts that actualizes various kinds of virtual shapes on the plane. And if we use it in 3-space, it becomes a concept for conjuring lines and other multi-dimensional objects. In this way, we can think of it as a concept that does more than measure, and more than adhere to the rules of logic—it actualizes virtual entities.

---

is that the same concept (parity, in this case) partakes of both the content and the process. Moreover, when functioning on the ontological level, parity has much greater precision and power than process strands such as representation, communication and visualization.

Can we rethink the curriculum and re-invest our concepts with ontological power? Can we recast our concepts in terms of the way they both realize the possible and actualize the virtual? And to what extent will this involve a shift from an emphasis on logical necessity towards an opening for contingency? In reflecting on these questions, we come to appreciate the way in which attention to ontological power can help loosen the grip of logical necessity that so strongly structures our current curricula. We are not denying the role of logical necessity in mathematics, but we believe that the relationship between the logical and the ontological needs to be re-examined, and that exciting new directions in mathematics curriculum might ensue if we questioned the ways (and the whys) in which the ontological is banished.

Since Piaget, the mathematics curriculum has been heavily influenced by what Lundin (2011) calls a "developmental ideology," namely, a rationale based on theories about the order and age at which children (can/should) develop knowledge of mathematical concepts. This ideology assumes that learning is a problem of construction, with its ensuing metaphor of starting from the ground up and making sure the foundations are solid. Within the ideology of development, the discipline stays fixed and immobile while the child moves slowly up, forming concepts along the way. Current theories of learning, inspired by a Vygotskian attention to sociocultural factors and, in particular, the mediating effects of language, also often subscribe to the development ideology. For example, the learning trajectory approach acknowledges the role played by tasks, tools and the teacher in children's mathematical learning, but there's still a sense in which the child is seen as scaling the edifice, acquiring knowledge of concepts along the way. The learning trajectory theorists allow for the possibility that there are multiple ways in which a learner might develop these prescribed concepts and that any description of the learning process must account for the broad environment in which the learning takes place, but the concepts themselves remain fixed.

We are interested in questioning this hidden assumption about concepts within the ideology of development. Châtelet's insistence on the fraudulence of the concrete/abstract dichotomy invites the possibility of moving very differently in and around the edifice of mathematics. In fact the edifice image reveals itself to be a poor metaphor for a mathematics that is about virtuality and mobility, unless we are prepared to adorn with suitable devices that permit alternative modes of access and movement. If we look closely at learning trajectories, they fail to take seriously the way in which the learner and the mathematics change as they engage in mathematical activity. Furthermore, while contemporary versions of the developmental ideology acknowledge the importance of tools in learning, these tools are often coerced into playing certain roles (along a hoped-for trajectory?) and then eventually discarded.

We contend that the developmental ideology draws on a particular philosophy of mathematics, one that acknowledges to some degree the contingent and socialcultural nature of knowledge, as well as the embodied nature of mathematical understanding, but continues to invest in an image of mathematics that denies the materiality of its concepts. This image of mathematics remains wedded to the logical—albeit broadened to embrace both the deductive and the inductive—but refuses the ontological aspect. Concepts are abstracted away from the physical situation, and the learner is granted only enough embodiment to perform that abstraction. Thus the ideology of development simply sustains Aristotle's philosophical paradox because it remains committed to an abstract/concrete binary which ultimately abandons mathematics to a realm of the inert and disembodied. Brian Rotman (2008) proposes a very different approach to the philosophy of mathematics that resonates strongly with Châtelet's technologies-driven historical studies (technologies of gestures and diagrams). Rather than focusing on the typical issue of how technology will change the role of logical necessity in mathematics, Rotman provocatively claims that the advent of digital technologies will lead to new kinds of gestural and diagrammatic inventions. He anticipates the slow disappearance of the alphabet— that sequential, disembodied and static mode of inscription that has dominated the western intellectual landscape- by other kinds of sensory modalities enabled by digital interfaces. For the mathematician, this would entail moving away from a world dominated by symbolic formal language (also sequential, disembodied and static) and toward one experienced "as much through touch as vision, through tactile, gestural, and haptic means" (Rotman, p. 8, citing de Kerckhove 2006, p. 8). Central to Rotman's argument is his assertion that mathematics has been, and will continue to be, involved in a two-way co-evolutionary relationship with machines. If in the past, mathematicians were able to deny any machinic agency through their discourse of detemporalisation, decontextualisation and depersonalisation, the increasing presence and power of current digital technologies will assert itself. In this sense, mathematical activity will be seen more clearly as something that co-involves the discipline, the seeing/touching/hearing/smelling mathematician and the material world. From Rotman, we thus find a materialist post-human philosophy of mathematics that invites us to look for curricular possibilities that are less driven by developmental assumptions. This frees us to pursue a curriculum of encounters with the virtual.

Making Mathematics Quiver

In the section Conceptualizations of the Mathematics Curriculum, we showed how mobility could virtualize the triangle, and in section Mathematics and Virtuality we showed how we might rekindle the ontological aspects of mathematical concepts like parity, and reconceive them as sculpting devices that bring forth the new. In this section, we elaborate on a more central set of concepts associated with the primary school mathematics curriculum related to number sense. Our goal will be to show how mobilizing these concepts can lead to important changes in terms of the sequencing of the curriculum. We begin with the topic of multiplication, which Châtelet discusses in his historical study of mathematical inventiveness. Châtelet cites a provocative statement by the early 19th century philosopher Franz von Baader: "It is a mistake of our mathematical manuals to begin with addition and subtraction, which are dead and devoid of concept, and not with living operations" (cited in Châtelet 2000, p. 123). Baader was critiquing those who thought of the world mechanically, in terms of the sum of its parts, suggesting instead that a much more dynamic and organic approach was needed: Baader saw multiplication as a "living operation" in the sense that it could penetrate and explore as do natural forces.

Why (and how) should multiplication precede addition? Châtelet argues that the notion of addition involves the banal idea of the juxtaposition of parts, and he chastises mathematicians who wrongly think of multiplication as repeated addition. Instead, he promotes Baader's sense of multiplication as a "reciprocal penetration of factors; it produces an interiorization, and intensification." According to Châtelet, it is precisely this device of "genuine multiplication, an operation productive of plurality" that the geometer Hermann Grassmann used in his theory of extensions (a foundational text in linear algebra, developing, in particular, the idea of linear space, linear independence, span and dimension). Indeed, while addition is "derived from the decomposition of an already established unit," Châtelet shows that Grassmann's notion of multiplication creates an entirely new space.

One of Grassmann's guiding motivations was to move beyond the arithmetical notion of multiplication, which distinguishes the multiplicand and the multiplier— always privileging one over the other (two jumps of three or three jumps of three?), despite its commutativity. Grassmann begins with an entirely different notion of multiplication, inspired by his father. In the following, we see that this notion isn't simply the geometric conception with which we are familiar through the so-called area model:

> The rectangle itself is the *true geometrical product* [...]. If the concept of multiplication is taken in its purest and mot general sense, then one comes to view a construction as something constructed from elements already constructed [...]. In geometry, the point is the original "producing" elements; from it through construction the line emerges [...]. Just as the line came from the point, so the rectangle comes from the line. (cited in Crowe 1985, p. 59)

In this view of multiplication, we have more than the static rectangle: we start with the point as the first unit, and by making it travel in a direction we obtain a line segment; then, we make that segment play the same role as the original point and move it in another direction; a surface is now *produced*. The rectangle, in this case, is not simply the thing that supports intuition, as we see in many textbooks—it's a mobile unit. Moreover, the rectangle treats base and height on the same footing, with each being able to act on the other. For Châtelet, it's the gestures that give rise to this new idea of multiplication, and it's the virtuality at the source of the concept that gives rise to the gestures. Move your index finger up a certain extent until you've produced a line segment, then push that segment over a certain extent to obtain your rectangle. These gestures permit the construction of the figure and in this way it's not the geometric diagram of the rectangle itself that matters, but its underlying mobility.

According to Châtelet, it is this conceptualisation of multiplication that enables Grassmann to develop the notion of the product of vectors and their orientation. But for our present purposes, the mobile production of the rectangle suffices. It provides an example of a way of thinking about multiplication that engages the virtual. Instead of being an extension of addition (a way of thinking that eventually breaks down when working with rational numbers), whose main focus is numerical, the dynamic arithmetic of Grassmann's multiplication produces a new space not predetermined through logical possibility but actualized through ontological potentiality. From our perspective, not only does this notion of multiplication necessarily involve the new, it does so in a way that is *entirely accessible to the young learner*, even the one who hasn't mastered addition. In other words, it dismantles the hierarchy of operations that pervades the school mathematics curriculum. Interestingly, based on McCrink and Spelke's (2010) findings that young children (before they enter primary school) have a sense of multiplication as scaling that precedes any use of repeated addition, one wonders just how "natural" the existing order is.

Confrey et al. (2009) have also questioned the usual order of operations in curriculum (addition, subtraction, multiplication and division) and argued that division should precede multiplication. Their arguments are based on the conceptualization of division as fair sharing, and draw on the fact that children have extensive experience with this process in their everyday lives, thus making it more accessible to them in the classroom. Our virtual curriculum approach has a different motivation in that it seeks to exploit the virtuality of mathematical ideas, catalyzing their mobility and indeterminacy and granting students a different kind of accessibility, one that has more to do with the virtuality of the concept itself and less to do with making its abstract content more concrete. Repeated addition is accessible, but it privileges the logical over the ontological. Similarly, we might ask: does division as fair sharing mobilize the virtuality at the source of the division/multiplication device?

The use of digital technologies can support encounters with the virtual in several key ways, the most important of them being that of mobility. As can be seen in a variety of dynamic mathematics software environments, mathematical entities are frequently put in motion and dynamic transformation. In fact, Grassmann's description of the multiplication rectangle may seem quite natural to modern ears familiar with dynamic geometry environments (DGEs). A given point can drag out a line segment and that line segment can drag out a rectangular area. Not only can this rectangle be produced in full mobility, but so can many others, quickly and precisely so that the imagery evoked by Grassmann can become a physico-mathematical experiment for learners.

Another feature of digital technologies that enables encounters with the virtual relates to what we call their *numerical nonchalance*. The computer doesn't care what kind of number the learner wants to use: whole numbers are interchangeable with irrational ones; they can dissolve into the background while material configurations take centre stage. Again using the example of a DGE, any length of line segment can be used (up to a certain level of precision), not just nice, neat whole numbers. Moreover, the value assigned to the area of the rectangle is foregrounded by the shape and size of that rectangle, which learners can slide, stack or rotate. We will return to this numerical nonchalance shortly, but here we want to focus on the way it shifts the meaning of multiplication for the learner from a result to be computed with certain values in a certain way, to a transformation of two numbers into a new entity that grows and shrinks in accordance with the changing value of the given numbers.

The numerical nonchalance of digital technologies also invites a re-thinking of the whole number obsession of the primary school curriculum. Many curricula require a progression of whole number learning, starting with 1–10, then 11–20, then extending to 100 and perhaps even 1000. This upward extension reveals the inductively-generated possibility of numbers. There are no new mathematical ideas involved in learning about, say, 30 or 642. But these small whole numbers are convenient because they can be used to introduce addition, which is also a staple of primary school curriculum and which also—as argued above—offers little in terms of virtual encounters.

The history of mathematics points to several encounters with the virtual that the small set of counting numbers could entail: the concept of zero and its bringing into existence of nothing; the flight into integers; the excavation into rational numbers. A curriculum that was less concerned with operations and more with creativity might delay the upward extension of the counting numbers and the early practicing of addition-as-grouping in favour of providing opportunities for children to engage with the new virtual spaces created by the concepts mentioned above. But Châtelet's notion of the virtual would promote this engagement by refusing to domesticate these concepts into the possible or the real. This is a key pedagogical issue in the sense that when we introduce learners to new ideas, our attraction to so-called real world connections or metaphors can betray that part of the real that is virtual.

We argue that mathematics is shot through with the virtual, a phrase that resonates with Gattegno's mantra that mathematics is shot through with infinity. (For Gattegno, finding the infinite in a concept or relation was equivalent to finding its deeper animating idea.) So, taking a concept like 0, for example, we can ask: what's the underlying virtuality? How does it get deadened? In some textbooks, 0 is introduced by recursive subtracting of 1 or by counting down. So students are invited to imagine 5 objects, then 4, then 3, then 2, then 1, then. . . In this stepwise descent, 0 is squarely placed in the real terrain of taking away the last remaining object, and we can hear the teacher saying "it's like eating the last cookie or using the last tissue." Since humans were presumably engaged in such activities before the number 0 was invented, we should suspect that these activities weren't enough to warrant the creation of a new construct, which must strike many children as suspect.

Instead of being the nothing that is arrived at after subtraction, it can be the fundamental starting point out of which motion arises. This carving out of the starting point with mobile aspirations casts 0 in a very different light, one that invites the placing of the index finger or the pencil tip on the paper: 'here is zero.' The point doesn't merely represent zero, it is the starting point out of which motion will produce magnitude and eventually roll over the counting numbers. But more, as Châtelet argues, the 0 thus conceptualized marks out not just one path, but a symmetry of choices toward the positive or negative magnitudes. In this sense, zero is "produced by a *thought experiment*, by a compensation devise capable of enveloping a Two with minimal means" (p. 82, *emphasis in original*). More, it can be "understood as a 'middle,' as the product of the neutralization of $+A$ by $-A$, which also makes it possible to open zero out into two branches, and it is just this allusion to opening that permits the conquest of the clichés associated with iteration" (p. 82).

Fig. 1 The numberline

$$\leftarrow\!\!\!+\!\!\!+\!\!\!+\!\!\!+\!\!\!+\!\!\!+\!\!\!+\!\!\!+\!\!\!+\!\!\!+\!\!\!+\!\!\!\rightarrow$$

-5 -4 -3 -2 -1   0   1   2   3   4   5

Fig. 2 Accentuating the role
of 0

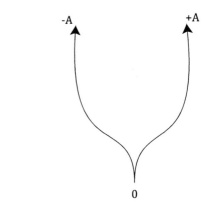

(In referring to "iteration," Châtelet means the kind of mechanical repeated juxtaposition of numbers that characterizes addition and subtraction (and some conceptions of multiplication).) This 0 is the crotch of two fingers, the fulcrum of the teeter-totter. It is not the clichéd taking away of the last cookie because it requires the carving out of a new space that, once created, generates new mathematical objects (negative cookies!).

The concept of 0 that we are proposing to offer to your learners here resonates to a certain extent with the numberline model that many mathematics educators have been advocating (see Saxe et al. 2007), which actualizes the arithmetic-is-motion-along-a-path metaphor identified by Lakoff and Núñez (2000). We see the numberline as a powerful diagram for evoking the concept of zero we have been discussing, especially when used in its potential form (*not* as the marked segment from 1 to 10 that can be found on the desks and the walls of many primary school classrooms, but as the one that evokes the infinite direction and density of the mathematical number line).

One runs the risk of taming the mobility of zero by failing to acknowledge its generative power, which isn't just in the middle, as in the number-line (Fig. 1), but is also in the singular fulcrum that originates motion as in the diagram below (Fig. 2, taken from Châtelet 2000, p. 83, based on Argand's work). What is intriguing about Argand's diagram is the way that zero evokes new and as yet unscripted directions, new branches of mobility that might invent alternative symmetries of choice.

In a computer-based environment, the virtuality can be further promoted without having to proceed through the usual development of number sense from natural to whole to rational numbers and then integers. The mobility and numerical nonchalance of a DGE, for example, enables the learner to move in any direction (positive or negative)—and usually that learner loves going as far as possible into those exuberating, large numbers. Addition can be done on the numberline without worrying about sticking faithfully to discrete positions along the line. What matters in addition is less the value obtained but the invariances that erupt: when one addend is at 0, the other addend moves along with the sum; as one addend moves, the other follows the sum on a rigid leash, no matter what the values of the numbers involved. Mobility and numerical nonchalance invite the learner to move into the virtual space of the negative numbers as well as virtual space of the reals.

Virtuality can be thought of as a kind of intensity or potential energy that is embedded in that which is actualized in physical extension. The number line offers a wonderful example to explore this idea of the virtual, because the line exemplifies the very idea of extension. According to Descartes, extension is the one defining quality of matter to which all other qualities, including motion, are derivative. Disrupting this Cartesian image of matter involves rethinking extension as somehow made muscular through the mobility of the virtual. Châtelet contrasts the lateral stretch of extension with the cutting and folding of new virtual dimensions through "intension".[4] The virtual is a kind of intensity that operates through intension. The virtual invites in(ter)vention because it is precisely what makes extension plastic and elastic through its intensity. The virtual is the "indeterminate dimension" in matter and quite literally destabilizes the rigidity of extension (p. 20). He describes these elastic folds in terms of transversal and vertical impulses that push through the apparent rigidity of extension. In rethinking curriculum, we might want to recast the number line as an elastic, so that students can carve out the virtual real numbers embedded between whole numbers by grabbing and dragging the digital number line so that it stretches and brings forth an infinitude of numbers that were imperceptible a moment earlier. New numbers will be displayed that have never been seen by the learner before. Students can then explore the density of the number line through this interaction, an interaction made all the more embodied when we imagine our gestures as creative acts cutting up matter in new ways. The number line is the quintessential form of extension, and thus it is crucial to see how this example helps us rethink extension (and the related concept of dimension) as a quivering space of potential rather than an interval contained between two fixed points. Through the eruptions of the virtual, the concept of extension is "charged with tensions and reveals itself as the positive condition for the birth of structure" (p. 105). We can see in this example the power of digital dynamic diagrams in affording the students this kind of opportunity.

Related Ideas about the Virtual

Shaffer and Kaput (1999) use the word 'virtual' to describe the computer-based culture we now inhabit. The distinctive feature of this culture is the externalisation of symbolic *processing*. Drawing on Merlin Donald's evolutionary perspective,

---

[4] In this he follows the scholastic tradition of contrasting extension—that being the interval actually travelled and its duration in time—with intension—that being its quickness, slowness or "lateness" (Châtelet 2000, p. 38). As odd as this distinction might seem to modern readers, it is used by Châtelet to disrupt the privileging of position over motion, and to try and imagine motion as the ontogenetic force by which position (or extension) comes into being.

Shaffer & Kaput show how the forms of representation now available have enabled human cognition to move beyond the theoretic culture previously inhabited, one in which involved the creation of external symbolic systems. They then argue that "mathematics education in a virtual culture should strive to give students generative fluency to learn varieties of representational systems, provide opportunities to create and modify representational forms, develop skill in making and exploring virtual environments, and emphasize mathematics as a fundamental way of making sense of the world, reserving most exact computation and formal proof for those who will need those specialized skills" (p. 97). We find this argument compelling, especially in terms of its focus on the possibilities learners should have to create and modify mathematical forms. Our approach differs in situating the changes—and the new opportunities—more squarely within new mathematical ontology, one in which mobility and materiality help identify where these opportunities might be and how they might affect the sequence and shape of the curriculum.

The concept of the virtual has also been taken up in media studies. Burbules' (2006), for instance, describes the virtual as that which creates the "feeling of immersion" that we have all experienced, in some context or another. For Burbules, this feeling involves an extension or elaboration of what is present in experience. There is a sense that the virtual pertains to what is *potentially* present, but isn't actually present: "Actively going beyond the given is part of what engages us deeply in it" (Burbules 2006, p. 41). While such experiences can be had in many contexts, Burbules argues that digital technologies have particular characteristics that make them uniquely capable of engendering them. He identifies five such features: mobility, inhabitance, action at a distance, haptic sensitivity, and performative identities.

All of these features point to the potential/virtual in terms of transformations to space and time: mobility is about being able to really move things (lines, points, ourselves) in new spaces (not the ones that necessarily satisfy our normal physical laws); inhabitation is about the extension or transformation of space and time (time travel or instant motion, exact replication of previous experiences); action at a distance is about our ability to transform the temporal dimension of our participation; haptic sensitivity is about the way in which our bodies are firmly implicated in the virtual spaces we explore—enabling a rapprochement of body and machine—and how sight, touch and feel create "as if" experiences; and, finally, performative identities is about the extension and transformation of our identities in cyberspaces.

As we have argued already, mobility takes on a particularly poignant role in mathematics, in part because of the ongoing program of detemporalisation that *is* formal mathematics and in part because of the status of mathematical objects as being more or less inaccessible to actually being moved. While mobility emerges as the central feature in our Châtelet-inspired take on the virtual, we note in passing that the features of inhabitation and action at a distance, are already readily available in a variety of digital technologies for mathematics education. While some of these features may seem familiar and even banal (one could fast-forward and replay old tape recorders, after all, as well as control them at a distance), the relevance to mathematics should not be overlooked for the simple reason that they contribute to the experience of mobility. As Sinclair and Jackiw (2011) write, digital "technologies newly permit the literal reinscription, reproduction, and transformation of time-based phenomena. They are thus literally, as well as metaphorically, dynamic."

While digital technologies have first and foremost enabled human interaction with mathematics through sight, the haptic sensitivity that Burbules identifies relates to all the human senses. Again, mobility comes into play most centrally. Papert recognized this in his attention to the body syntonicity that the Turtle Geometry microworld enabled. By controlling and watching the turtle move on the screen, the child became the turtle, turning right or moving forward along with it. The motion of the turtle invited the body into the machine. Similarly, we have noticed the frequency with which learners dragging objects on the screen *become* those objects and use first person narratives to describe how they are moving, where they are going, and what they hope to find there. With the recent advent of touch-base technologies, this haptic sensitivity will become even more intense. Instead of being once-removed from the point you are dragging on the screen, you can now literally touch that point directly, as you would touch any other concrete object. The material presence is unavoidable.

Burbules' notion of performative identities, which emerges from his considera-tion of technologies such as social networks and virtual realities, seems at first much less relevant in our examples. However, we follow Rotman (2008) in asserting the way in which mathematical activity co-involves the discipline, the person and the material world—and that this co-involvement means that mathematical activity does not just produce more mathematics (or more learning), but also produces a new per-son in a new material world. Although we don't have space here to explore this, we are fascinated by the question of how curriculum might foster occasions for learners to perform new identities as they move in new ways in the classroom.

We have used Burbules' five features as a way to point to the role digital tech-nologies might play in occasioning virtual encounters, in the sense of Châtelet. As mentioned above, Châtelet's (2000) "allusive devices" can be thought of as tech-niques or technologies of excavation and invention by which the new comes into being. Continuing his historical study of mathematics and applying it to contempo-rary contexts would mean looking at the role of digital technologies in mathematics. Although some of the work in media and technology studies uses the term virtual to designate the *not real*, we note that Burbules aims to avoid that association and in-stead study the virtual in terms of spatio-temporal experiences. Although this has the advantage of embedding the virtual *in* the real, we underline the fact that Burbules' construct of the virtual might lend itself to merely a psychological theory about indi-vidual experiences and thereby lose sight of the complex ontology involved in such experiences.

Conclusion

In this chapter, we have used Châtelet's idea of virtuality to re-think questions and assumptions about the school mathematics curriculum. We first examined the very idea of a mathematical concept, and the way in which concepts are turned into a sequence of topics in the course of curriculum-making. Following the ontological shift of Châtelet's materialist perspective, and inspired by the Russian mathematics circles, we proposed arranging curricula in a more story-like structure, in terms of concepts that have both logical and ontological import. Such concepts would refuse to be subverted, supplanted and replaced by intermediary symbols, acting as "signposts to the next world, placed in this one" (Pimm 2006, p. 181, citing Graham-Dixon 1996). In such a curriculum, there would be an intrinsic flexibility (no need to always have parity, for example—one could easily substitute something like symmetry) since far fewer assumptions about either sequentiality or concrete/abstract would be required.

While this first finding pertains to the curriculum as a whole, our second focuses more specifically on local curricular concerns. By imitating Châtelet's refusal to fall into the concrete versus abstract distinction, we showed how the ideas of multiplication and of zero could be encountered by learners in all their virtuality, as opposed to mere logical derivatives of addition. We also argued that multiplication could even be encountered *before* addition in a curriculum sequence. Within the context of our first finding, multiplication might be enveloped by devices such as dilation or dimension.

Finally, we argued that virtual encounters could be occasioned through the use of digital technologies, based on the two characteristic features of mobility and numerical nonchalance. Mobility relates directly to Châtelet's notion of the virtual. Numerical nonchalance works in part to free the mathematics teacher and curriculum from the shackles of the numerical operations. However, it also plays into Rotman's call for haptic, machinic mathematical activity, which escapes the dominant symbolic approach privileging the written calculation. Burbules' work on the virtual provided stimulus to consider the use of digital technologies in the context of promoting virtual encounters. In addition to his compatibility with Châtelet on the centrality of mobility, Burbules also provokes us to consider the crucial role of identity or performative identity in our thinking about curriculum. Such aperformative identity—be it the learner-with-dynamic-numberline or some other assemblage—demands a curriculum responsive to her human and machinic capacity *for* and desiring *of* the virtual.

References

Ball, D. L., & Cohen, D. K. (1996). Reform by the book: what is—or might be—the role of curriculum materials in teacher learning and instructional reform? *Educational Researcher, 25,* 6–8, 14.

Breyfogle, M. L., Roth McDuffie, A., & Wohlhuter, K. A. (2010). Developing curricular reasoning for grades pre-K-12 mathematics instruction. In B. Reys, R. E. Reys, & R. Rubenstein (Eds.), *Mathematics curriculum: issues, trends, and future directions, 72nd yearbook.* Reston: National Council of Teachers of Mathematics.

Burbules (2006). Rethinking the virtual. In J. Weiss et al. (Eds.), *The international handbook of virtual learning environments* (pp. 37–58). Dordrecht: Springer.

Châtelet, G. (1993). *Les enjeux du mobile*. Paris: Seuil [English translation by R. Shore & M. Zagha, *Figuring space: philosophy, mathematics and physics*. Dordrecht: Kluwer, 2000].

Clements, D. H. & Sarama, J. (Eds.) (2004). Hypothetical learning trajectories. *Mathematical Thinking and Learning*, 6(2), 81–89.

Confrey, J., Maloney, A., Nguyen, K., Mojica, G., & Myers, M. (2009). Equipartitioning/splitting as a foundation of rational number reasoning. In M. Tzekaki, M. Kaldrimidou&, & C. Sakonidis (Eds.), *Proceedings of the 33rd conference of the international group for the psychology of mathematics education* (Vol. 1). Thessaloniki: PME.

Crowe, M. (1985). *A history of vector analysis: the evolution of the idea of a vectorial system*. New York: Dover Publications.

de Freitas, E., & Sinclair, N. (2012). Diagram, gesture, agency: theorizing embodiment in the mathematics classroom. *Educational Studies in Mathematics*, 80, 133–152.

Deleuze, G. (1994). *Difference and repetition*. New York: Columbia University Press (English translation by P. Patton).

Dewey, J. (1902). The child and the curriculum. In L. A. Hickman & T. M. Alexander (Eds.), *The essential Dewey* (Vol. 1, pp. 236–245). Chicago: Indiana University Press.

Dietiker, L. (2012). *The mathematics textbook as story: a literary approach to interrogating mathematics curriculum*. Unpublished PhD dissertation, East Lansing, MI: Michigan State University.

Ernest, P. (1991). *The philosophy of mathematics education*. London: Routledge Falmer.

Ernest, P. (1998). *Social constructivism as a philosophy of mathematics*. Albany: State University of New York Press.

Fomin, D., Genkin, S., & Itenberg, I. (1996). *Mathematical circles (Russian experience)*. Providence: American Mathematical Society.

Lakatos, I. (1978). *Mathematics, science and epistemology: philosophical papers* (Vol. 2). Cambridge: Cambridge University Press. J. Worral & G. Currie (Eds.).

Lakoff, G., & Núñez, R. (2000). *Where mathematics comes from: How the embodied mind brings mathematics into being*. New York: Basic Books.

Lockhart, P. (2008). A mathematician's lament. Retrieved from http://www.maa.org/devlin/devlin_03_08.html.

Lundin, S. (2011). Hating school, loving mathematics. *Educational studies in mathematics* (Preprint in November 2011).

McCrink, K., & Spelke, E. S. (2010). Core multiplication in childhood. *Cognition*, 116(2), 204–216.

Pimm, D. (2006). Drawing on the image in mathematics and art. In N. Sinclair, D. Pimm, & W. Higginson (Eds.), *Mathematics and the aesthetic: new approaches to an ancient affinity* (pp. 160–189). New York: Springer.

Rotman, B. (2008). *Becoming beside ourselves: the alphabet, ghosts, and distributed human beings*. Durham: Duke University Press.

Russell, B. (1903). *The principles of mathematics*. Cambridge: Cambridge University Press.

Saxe, G. B., Shaughnessy, M. M., Shannon, A., Langer-Osuna, J. M., Chinn, R., & Gearhart, M. (2007). Learning about fractions as points on the number line. In *The learning of mathematics, 69th yearbook of the National Council of Teachers of Mathematics* (pp. 221–236). Reston: NCTM.

Shaffer, D. W., & Kaput, J. (1999). Mathematics and virtual culture: a cognitive evolutionary perspective on technology and mathematics education. *Educational Studies in Mathematics*, 37(2), 97–119.

Sinclair, N., & Jackiw, N. (2011). On the origins of dynamic number in the breakdown of structural, metaphori, and historic conceptions of human mathematics. In P. Liljedahl, S. Oesterle, & D. Allan (Eds.), *Proceedings/actes 2010 annual meeting/rencontreannuelle 2010* (pp. 137–146). Burnaby: CMESG/GCEDM.

Tall, D. (2011). Crystalline concepts in long-term mathematical invention and discovery. *For the Learning of Mathematics*, 31(1), 3–8.

Part VI
Cross-national Comparison and Commentary

Forty-Eight Years of International Comparisons in Mathematics Education from a United States Perspective: What Have We Learned?

Zalman Usiskin

Abstract In 1963-64, the International Evaluation Association undertook the first international study of school mathematics performance. The mean score of United States students at grades 8 and 12 was at or near the bottom of all participating nations. On the second and third international studies undertaken in the 1980s and 1990s, U.S. students seem to have fared relatively better than before, a trend that seems to have continued into the TIMSS and PISA assessments over the past decade. Nevertheless, with few exceptions, at each announcement of results it is typical to point out how poorly U.S. students fare. In all these eras, results have been used by some to encourage reform in mathematics classrooms and by others to push back reform. This chapter displays and examines summary results from the IEA, TIMSS, and PISA studies to glean conclusions about performance of students in the United States over time and about the operation and interpretation of international comparisons in mathematics education in general.

Keywords IEA · PISA · TIMSS · International assessment · Comparative mathematics education

Studies of the relative standing of the performance of United States students compared to students in other nations are among the few research studies in mathematics education that receive press coverage and that are also known in the general education community. There is ample reason for this beyond the attractiveness of the question; these studies are large and tend to be done using the latest research techniques. However, results in the press tend to be oversimplified, and these oversimplifications are often accepted by policy makers without questioning them and without considering all of the information that has been gathered by researchers and other observers that might explain the results. It is also rare that one finds any placement of results in a historical context or even a present-day social context.

From a policy perspective, this lack of context is perilous, because the Common Core Standards for school mathematics in grades K-12, which almost every state in

Z. Usiskin (✉)
The University of Chicago, Chicago, USA
e-mail: z-usiskin@uchicago.edu

Y. Li, G. Lappan (eds.), *Mathematics Curriculum in School Education*,
Advances in Mathematics Education, DOI 10.1007/978-94-007-7560-2_27,
© Springer Science+Business Media Dordrecht 2014

the United States has adopted, and on which students will be tested beginning in the school year 2014-15, are very much based on conclusions from these studies.

Nagy (1996) has detailed the following difficulties that occur when interpreting results of international comparisons:

difficulties in test construction and design
difficulties with (overall) test content
difficulties in measuring opportunity to learn
difficulties in the choice of (item) content for international tests
difficulties caused by different social conditions in participating countries
difficulties in the language of test items
difficulties in school enrolment patterns
difficulties caused by sampling and participation rates
difficulties in test and score accuracy.

Each of the studies discussed in this paper has been reported in volumes that demonstrate its complexity. Thus this paper also oversimplifies the results and does not discuss all of the difficulties in mounting these studies and cautions to bear in mind.

Two of the difficulties identified by Nagy concern curriculum, the choice of overall test content and the choice of item content. Consider the following scenario. Suppose 75 % of country A's content in a given year is taught in country B, and 80 % of country B's content in a given year is taught in country A. From this information it can be calculated that, if a test is given evenly covering all the content in either country, then 40 % of the test will consist of items unfamiliar to one of the two countries.[1] If the test is over the common curriculum, then the test will cover only 60 % of the topics taught in one or the other of the countries. In international comparisons there are not two countries, but ten or twenty. It is easy see that a test that is fair to one country could easily be quite unfair to another. We find that situation even when we are comparing performance between two different textbooks in the U.S., or between an honors class and a regular class using the same textbook in the same school. Consequently, it is essentially impossible to compare two different curricula using the same test, and any test that is over only common elements to the curricula will, by that very property, not include those things that are new, or that might make one of the curricula better than anything else in the world. By their very nature, fair comparison tests are conservative.[2]

With international tests, there is a little less conservatism because countries will opt out if they think the test does not cover their curriculum. Still, there has never been an international test that allows the latest in technology. For instance, in 2007, calculators were allowed on only 1 of the 14 booklets of TIMMS tests administered at the 8th grade level.

---

[1] Let x be the amount of content in country A. Then $.75x$ is taught in country B and $.80(.75)x$, or $.60x$ is taught in both countries A and B.

[2] When the Department of Education under President George W. Bush initiated the What Works Clearinghouse that required a particular kind of comparison study of any curriculum in order to certify that it was promising, nothing unique to a new curriculum could be tested and be fair to both groups, so essentially nothing new could be tested.

Table 1 IEA Study of Mathematics (First International Mathematics Study). Mean scores of the grade most containing 13-year-olds[a]

Country	n	Mean score (70 items)
Israel	3,232	32.3
Japan	2,050	31.2
Belgium	2,645	30.4
Finland	841	26.4
West Germany	4,475	25.4
England	3,089	23.8
Scotland	5,718	22.3
Netherlands	1,443	21.4
France	3,449	21.0
Australia	3,078	18.9
U.S.	6,544	17.8
Sweden	2,828	15.3

[a]Sample-selection data is not generally available. It is likely that samples in a number of countries would not meet today's National Center for Education Statistics guidelines for non-participation and exclusion

Source: Husen (1967), II, p. 23

IEA Study of Mathematics (FIMS)

The first international comparison test was conducted during the 1963-64 school year. In virtually all the countries in which this study was conducted, this was the first time for their overall student performance to be compared with student performance in other countries. It is now called FIMS, but at that time it was the IEA study. It was state-of-the-art for its time.

Testing was done with four populations: 13-year-olds, students in the grade most containing 13-year-olds, students in the last year of high school who were in non-technical tracks, and students in the last year of high school who were in technical tracks. Results of the study were published in two volumes (Husen 1967).

A summary of the data from the 13-year-olds (Table 1) reflects that the mean U.S. score was significantly lower than 9 of the other 11 countries and higher only than one, Sweden. One reason for these low means may have been that the selection of the samples was not uniform in the countries. The U.S. and Sweden seem to have used randomized samples whereas the sample in some countries is known to have been selected from the best students, as in the case of Israel, and may have not adequately sampled from poorer students, as in the case of some of the European countries. Nevertheless, FIMS was the best comparison available at the time.

At the level of the last year of high school, the situation is more complicated. Some advanced students take mathematics while others don't, and countries differ in the typical ages of students in that year. So the FIMS study designers tested two non-intersecting samples of students. Table 2 shows the results for students who were *not* enrolled in advanced mathematics courses.

The difference in ages makes it difficult to compare performance in the various countries. For instance, German and Swedish students were 2 years older than U.S. students, on average. Still, the results show U.S. students extraordinarily behind all

Table 2 IEA Study of Mathematics (First International Mathematics Study).[a] Mean scores of non-mathematics students in their last year of secondary school

[a]Sample-selection data is not generally available. It is likely that samples in a number of countries would not meet today's National Center for Education Statistics guidelines for non-participation and exclusion

Source: Husen (1967), II, p. 25

Country	n	Mean age	Mean score (58 items)
West Germany	643	19 y 9	27.7
Japan	4,372	17 y 8	25.3
Belgium	1,004	18 y 0	24.2
Finland	399	19 y 2	22.5
England	1,782	17 y 11	21.4
Scotland	2,123	17 y 1	20.7
Sweden	222	19 y 7	12.6
U.S.	2,042	17 y 10	8.3
Not enough data to compare means			
France	192	18 y 9	26.2
Netherlands	50	18 y 7	24.7

their international counterparts except Sweden, even being behind countries where students were about the same age.

When mean scores are so different, one has to wonder not just whether the samples were comparable, or the ages comparable, or whether the test was a fair test for both groups. Here the mean scores are so different because of the structure of schooling in the various countries. In some countries, by this time, mathematics and other students who will have technical majors have been separated out from other students. In the U.S. this separation had not yet occurred. Thus the U.S. sample of *non-mathematics* students excluded all of those students who were taking precalculus or calculus courses and by so doing the sample excluded virtually all of the best students regardless of their major interest. On the other hand, the non-mathematics sample from other countries included fine students who were not majoring in mathematics because they were already involved in concentrations that did not include mathematics.

Table 3 shows mean scores of those students who were taking mathematics in the last year of high school. Again the U.S. mean score was lower by a good amount that any other country. At this time, about 18 % of U.S. students took precalculus or calculus as seniors in high school. In other countries, as we have noted, the population was more select because 45 years ago, by the age of 15 or 16, their students were already specializing and taking a great deal more mathematics than just a single course.

Because of the non-equability of the samples, particularly at the 12th grade, it is impossible to know how the U.S. would have fared with some matched sample. This did not keep the press from making conclusions. Two reports of the study (Hutchinger 1967a, 1967b) appeared in the *New York Times*, 5 days apart. The first report, "U.S. Ranked Low in Math Teaching" (Hutchinger 1967a), was on the front page. Its subtitle is "Japan does the best job in subject". The second report (Hutchinger 1967b), "The U.S. Gets Low Marks in Math", is far back in the news-

Table 3 IEA Study of Mathematics (First International Mathematics Study).[a] Mean scores of mathematics students in their last year of secondary school

Country	n	Mean age	Mean score (69 items)
Israel	146	18 y 2	36.4
England	967	17 y 11	35.2
Belgium	519	18 y 1	34.6
France	222	18 y 7	33.4
Netherlands	462	18 y 2	31.9
Japan	818	17 y 8	31.4
West Germany	649	19 y 10	28.8
Sweden	776	19 y 7	27.3
Scotland	1,422	17 y 6	25.5
Finland	369	19 y 1	25.3
Australia	1,089	17 y 2	21.6
U.S.	1,660	17 y 9	13.8

[a]Sample-selection data is not generally available. It is likely that samples in a number of countries would not meet today's National Center for Education Statistics guidelines for non-participation and exclusion

Source: Husen (1967), II, p. 24

paper. There is a response from the U.S. Department of Education pointing out that U.S. students scored lower at the 12th grade because the U.S. keeps more students in school. The newspaper reporter is skeptical about that explanation.

Data were collected about the students, about their schools, and about the curriculum. Both *New York Times* articles point out that students who studied from the new math, which was then at about its peak usage in high schools, scored higher than other students perhaps because of the conceptual nature of the new math.

The FIMS researchers explained some of the differences by coining a new phrase: "opportunity to learn" (OTL). OTL was felt to explain many of the differences among countries. It was clear that any future study would need to take OTL into account.

Second International Mathematics Study (SIMS)

Eighteen years later, in 1981-82, the second international mathematics study (SIMS) took place. The U.S. national report was under the direction of Ken Travers of the University of Illinois. The first results came out in 1983 but the main report for the U.S., "The Underachieving Curriculum", did not appear until four years later (McKnight et al. 1987). This report summarized the results and also showed analyses to debunk some of the simple explanations often given for differences in the performances of nations, such as time in school classrooms, class size, or amount of teacher preparation.

Again 13-year-olds were studied but, as a result of the importance of content and OTL, no single mean score was provided for a country. Instead, five subscores on what have become rather standard areas of mathematical content in the elementary

Table 4 Second International Mathematics Study. Mean percent of core items correct, 13-year-olds

Country	Arithmetic	Algebra	Geometry	Measurement	Statistics
Japan	60.3	60.3	57.6	68.6	70.9
Netherlands	59.3	51.3	52.0	61.9	65.9
Hungary	56.8	50.4	53.4	62.1	60.4
Belgium (Flem.)	58.0	52.9	42.5	58.2	58.2
France	57.7	55.0	38.0	59.5	57.4
Canada (B.C.)	58.0	47.9	42.3	51.9	61.3
Belgium (Fr.)	57.0	49.1	42.8	56.8	52.0
Hong Kong	55.1	43.2	42.5	52.6	55.9
Canada (Ont.)	54.5	42.0	43.2	50.8	57.0
Scotland	50.2	42.9	45.5	48.4	59.3
England & Wales	48.2	40.1	44.8	48.6	60.2
Finland	45.5	43.6	43.2	51.3	57.6
New Zealand	45.6	39.4	44.8	45.1	57.3
U.S.	51.4	42.1	37.8	40.8	57.7
Israel	49.9	44.0	35.9	46.4	51.9
Sweden	40.6	32.3	39.4	48.7	56.3
Thailand	43.1	37.7	39.3	48.3	45.3
Luxembourg	45.4	31.2	25.3	50.1	37.3
Nigeria	40.8	32.4	26.2	30.7	37.0
Swaziland	32.3	25.1	31.1	35.2	36.0

Source: Medrich and Griffith (1992), pp. 70–74

school were used (Table 4). The 20 countries are ordered by the mean of the subscore means for the five areas.

As a whole, the U.S. did somewhat better on SIMS than in FIMS, but still ranked below many countries.[3]

It is instructive to look at the subscores. In Arithmetic and Algebra, the U.S. mean was at about the middle of all countries. In Geometry, it was significantly below 9 countries and significantly above only 3 countries. The situation was even worse with measurement, where the U.S. mean was significantly below all but 2 countries, both African developing nations. I believe that U.S. students were at a disadvantage because all measurements in this international study were in metric, which led to poorer performance on measurement items and resulted in U.S. students having less time for items in other areas. This reflected not just a lack of OTL in school, but a

---

[3]In Canada, the curriculum of Ontario was considered so different from the curriculum of British Columbia, and other provinces did not participate, so it was decided that it would be better to analyze the two provinces as if they were separate countries.

Table 5 Second International Mathematics Study. Mean percent of core items correct, 17-year-olds "who are still engaged in the serious study of mathematics"

Country	Number	Algebra	Geometry	Functions/Calculus	Yield
Hong Kong	78	78	65	71	N.A.
Japan	68	78	60	66	12
England & Wales	59	66	51	58	6
Finland	57	69	48	55	15
Sweden	62	61	49	51	12
New Zealand	51	57	43	48	11
Canada (Ont.)	47	57	42	46	10
Belgium (Flem.)	48	55	42	46	10
Israel	46	60	35	45	6
Belgium (Fr.)	44	55	38	43	N.A.
Scotland	39	48	42	32	18
U.S.	40	43	31	29	13
Canada (B.C.)	43	47	30	21	30
Hungary	28	45	30	26	50
Thailand	33	38	28	26	N.A.

Source: Medrich and Griffith, pp. 75–78

lack of opportunity to see the mathematics outside of school. It seemed that when U.S. students had the opportunity to learn, the students did rather well. For instance, in the statistics strand U.S. students were outscored in only two countries. This may be explained by the fact that U.S. students saw statistics not only in mathematics but also in social studies and, if they were interested in sports or politics, by reading newspapers. This result strongly suggests that OTL *outside of school* may be a significant variable in mathematics performance.

Learning from the first international study, SIMS did not look at students in their last year of secondary school because of the age differences. Instead, it looked at 17-year-olds from 15 countries. Table 5 shows mean scores on four mathematics areas for these countries. Again, learning from the first study, SIMS took note of the percent of the age group in the population, calling it *yield*. The U.S. yield of 13 % at this time means that, of 17-year-olds in the United States, about 13 % were taking precalculus or higher mathematics courses. In contrast, in Ontario 19 %, and in British Columbia 30 % were taking courses at this level, and in England and Wales and Israel only 6 % of students.

U.S. 17-year-olds were significantly outscored in all four areas of mathematics by a majority of the countries in every area. The only countries that fared worse on average were British Columbia and Hungary, each of which with a far larger portion of their student bodies still engaged in mathematics, and Thailand, a developing country.

Ten years after SIMS, researchers from the National Center for Education Statistics analyzed both FIMS and SIMS and in mathematics and science and came up with seven systematic patterns (Medrich and Griffith 1992, pp. 30–35).

1. Opportunity to learn is a significant variable in performance internationally.
2. The amount of tracking is not a significant variable in performance. Although tracking in the U.S. was felt to hamper performance, tracking in some countries helps performance.
3. Schooling affects learning more in some subjects than others. In particular, it affects learning more in those subjects that are not encountered outside of school.
4. Family background is a significant variable in performance.
5. Except for Japan, the more students that are retained in the study of a subject, the poorer the performance. That is, yield is negatively related to performance.
6. Generally, the "best students" in the United States do less well on the international achievement surveys when compared with the "best students" from other countries.
7. Students from less developed countries do less well on tests of achievement than students from more developed countries.

The Situation in the U.S.: 1963-64 to 1981-82

Because the FIMS and SIMS tests were not matched, to help understand U.S. performance on external comparisons between the 1960s and the 1980s, it is useful to examine performance of U.S. students on internal comparisons. NAEP (the National Assessment of Educational Progress) did not start collecting data on mathematics until 1973, so there are no randomly-selected samples dating back all the way to 1963-64. The best data come from the College Board SAT tests administered by the Educational Testing Service (ETS).

Figure 1 shows 58 years of mean scores of students on the SAT-Math and SAT-Verbal, from 1952 to 2009, scaled to represent the original SAT scores. The highest mean score was in 1963, in the new math era. Later scores in the 1960s went down from that peak, but in 1977 a blue-ribbon commission of ETS determined that the reason for the decline was the increase in numbers of students taking the test (Wirtz et al. 1977). In the 1970s, however, the decline in performance is real as percents of students taking the SAT remained reasonably constant. The 1970s was very much a back-to-basics era, in which individual paper-and-pencil skills were identified and emphasized as the goals of school mathematics and resulted in the lowest scores ever just at the time that SIMS was undertaken.

It seems that problem-solving movement of the 1980s, a reaction to back-to-basics, started a significant increase in SAT math scores that continued through the Standards movement of the 1990s, resulting in an unprecedented increase in SAT scores that has begun to lapse in recent years perhaps because in 2006 the SAT added a third test for students to take. The mean scores on the Verbal test, renamed Critical Reasoning in 2006, have shown a far worse long-term trend.

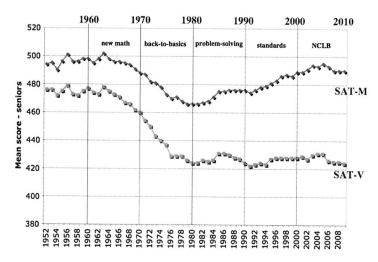

Fig. 1 Mean scores of high school seniors on the SAT-Mathematics and SAT-Verbal Tests, 1952–2010.
SAT scores were recalibrated in 1996. These scores have been adjusted to place them on the original scale. The decade identifiers "new math", "back-to-basics", are additions by this author. Source: For 1952–1975, Wirtz et al., p. 6; for 1975 on, College Board (2012), p. iii

Table 6 Percentage of public and private high school graduates taking selected mathematics courses in high school, selected years, 1982–2009

Course	1982	1990	2000	2009
Any mathematics (≥1 yr)	98.5	99.9	99.8	100.0
Algebra I (≥1 yr)	55.2	63.7	61.7	68.5
Geometry (≥1 yr)	47.1	63.2	78.3	88.3
Algebra II (≥0.5 yr)	39.9	52.9	67.8	75.5
Trigonometry (≥0.5 yr)	8.1	9.6	7.5	6.1
Analysis/precalculus (≥0.5 yr)	6.2	13.3	26.7	35.3
Statistics/probability (≥0.5 yr)	1.0	1.0	5.7	10.8
Calculus (all) (≥1 yr)	5.0	6.5	11.6	15.9
Calculus (Advanced Placement)	1.6	4.1	7.9	11.0

Source: National Center for Education Statistics (2012), p. 232

Overall, it can be argued that today's large population of college-intending students knows as much mathematics as yesteryear's much more select population, and the reason for this is probably that they have taken as much mathematics as that earlier select population did. Supporting that notion are data from the National Center for Education Statistics (Table 6), obtained from a random sample of high school transcripts.

Fig. 2 Trend in NAEP mathematics average scores for 9-, 13-, and 17-year-old students

In 1982, over 55 % of high school students graduated with no more than algebra or geometry on their transcripts, but by 2009, that percent was less than 12 %. In the same time period, the percent of high school graduates with a second year of algebra or more increased from 40 % to 75 %, and calculus enrolments tripled. We can impute that the kinds of students who used to finish their high school mathematics with algebra or geometry are now all taking a second year of algebra and many of them even more mathematics. These data explain why high school teachers who have been teaching for many years often state that their students today are not the same as they were ten or twenty years ago. This is true: half or more of the students are not from the same population.

NAEP

The first National Assessment of Educational Progress (NAEP) study of mathematics was administered in 1973, responding to a call for reliable national data about performance in many subjects and more specifically to questions about the effectiveness of the new math curricula. Data from unreleased items were used to initiate what is now known as the long-term longitudinal study of NAEP. The items used for the long-term study have not changed since 1978; for the most part, they test basic skills.

Mean scores for students in this study from 1973 through 2008 are shown in Fig. 2. Scores from 1973 to 1982 mirror the SAT in that the mean scores of 17-year-olds decline. In this period, the mean scores of 13-year-olds climbed a little and the scores of 9-year-olds were stagnant. But, as the graph shows, during the

1980s, there was a great increase in the mean scores of 9-year-olds on NAEP and there were smaller increases among 13-year-olds and 17-year-olds. These increases continued through the 1990s and 2000s for the latter populations while the mean score of 17-year-olds has remained stagnant.

TIMSS

In 1994-95, the first administration of the Third International Mathematics and Science Study (TIMSS) was conducted. Because of the striking differences in countries in SIMS at the 8th grade level, it was decided to test also at the 4th grade level. Perhaps the existence of tests at the 4th grade in NAEP in the U.S. had something to do with this; certainly it told nations that testing at this age was possible. Surprisingly, there is no mention of SIMS or of FIMS in the U.S. national report of TIMSS. And so we lost a major opportunity for research to build on itself and for longitudinal data back to 1981-82, years which on national measures were a low point for the U.S. This was such a blatant weakness that a few years later TIMSS changed what the acronym represents to "*The* International Mathematics and Science Study". Later, the acronym TIMSS was changed again to stand for "Trends in International Mathematics and Science Study", but the trends begin only in the 1990s and not in the 1960s.

Testing in the first round of TIMSS took place at 4th, 8th, and 12th grade. The first results to be published were from the 8th grade (Table 7). The United States scored at 500, significantly below the international average of 513 and the average of 527 for all countries that met the sampling specifications. Singapore was highest at 643, with Korea and Japan also scoring above 600. No country of the G8 economic front that met the sampling criteria scored lower than the U.S.[4]

TIMSS allowed samples that were not taken from the population of all students in a country. In particular, smaller groups within the U.S. were allowed to participate as countries. One of these groups consisted of the public schools in three townships (Glenbrook, New Trier, and Niles) in the north suburbs of Chicago. These suburbs range from middle class to affluent and are not unlike similar affluent suburbs around virtually every large city in the U.S. These school districts wanted to be tested against the best in the world, and so they called themselves the "First In the World" Consortium. The consortium's 8th graders scored at 587, even with Hong Kong and not statistically significantly different from Korea and Japan. Only Singapore's mean was significantly higher. The implication was that students in more affluent suburbs of the U.S. were getting an education second-to-none—well, second only to Singapore.

TIMSS also analyzed results of the 8th grade test by strands, though not identical to those in SIMS (Table 8). The U.S. score is statistically equal to the international mean in all strands except for geometry and measurement. U.S. students performed

---

[4]England and Germany did not meet sampling criteria.

Table 7 Mean scores of 8th grade students on TIMSS 1994-95 from all countries that met sampling specifications

Country	Mean score	Country	Mean score
Singapore	643	Ireland	527
Korea	607	Canada	527
Japan	605	Sweden	519
Hong Kong	588	New Zealand	508
Consortium	587	Norway	503
Belgium-Flemish	565	United States	500
Czech Republic	564	Spain	487
Slovak Republic	547	Iceland	487
Switzerland	545	Lithuania	477
France	538	Cyprus	474
Hungary	537	Portugal	454
Russian Federation	535	Iran	428

Source: Beaton et al. (1996), p. 22

above the international average in data and probability, below average in proportionality, and statistically equal to the international average in algebra, in fractions and in number sense. These data are certainly not what one would expect from efforts in recent years at the national level that have been motivated by the scores on international assessments, e.g., the charge to the 2008 National Mathematics Advisory Panel to look at algebra and the view represented in the Common Core State Standards that fractions and algebra are where the most increased attention is needed. It might have been more reasonable to conclude that the best way for the U.S. to improve its performance on international tests is to go metric, spend more time on geometry, and teach proportionality while doing so.

In 1998, the 4th grade TIMSS results were released. For the first time in these international comparisons, U.S. students scored above an international average. Only Singapore, Korea, Japan, Hong Kong, the Netherlands, the Czech Republic, and Austria scored higher. Canada, Hungary, Australia, Ireland, Slovenia, and Israel scored statistically equal, and Norway, England, Scotland, and many other countries scored lower. U.S. 4th-graders did even better in science than in mathematics.

For once, positive news received strong play. Newspapers and even President Clinton were elated (Bennet 1997). The results were announced in a White House ceremony. Clinton called the results "a road map to higher performance", and urged states to embrace his voluntary testing against national standards in reading for 4th graders and in math for 8th graders. He also remarked, "This report proves that we don't have to settle for second-class expectations or second-class goals." But, remembering the 8th grade results, he said we are doing a very good job in the early grades but have got a lot more work to do in the later grades.

Table 8 Average percent correct by 8th graders by mathematics content area on TIMSS 1994-95 from all countries that met sampling specifications

Country	Fractions & Number Sense	Geometry	Algebra	Data Representation, Analysis & Probability	Measurement	Proportionality
Singapore	84	76	76	79	77	75
Japan	75	80	72	78	67	61
Korea	74	75	69	78	66	62
Hong Kong	72	73	70	72	65	62
Belgium (Fl)[a]	71	64	63	73	60	53
Czech Rep.	69	66	65	68	62	52
Slovak Rep.	66	63	62	62	60	49
Switzerland	67	60	53	72	61	52
Hungary	65	60	63	66	56	47
France	64	66	54	71	57	49
Russian Fed.	62	63	63	60	56	48
Canada	64	58	54	69	51	48
Ireland	65	51	53	69	53	51
Sweden	62	48	44	70	56	44
New Zealand	57	54	49	66	48	42
Norway	58	51	45	66	51	40
England[a]	54	54	49	66	50	41
U.S.[a]	59	48	51	65	40	42
Latvia[a]	53	57	51	56	47	39
Spain	52	49	54	60	44	40
Iceland	54	51	40	63	45	38
Lithuania[a]	51	53	47	52	43	35
Cyprus	50	47	48	53	44	40
Portugal	44	44	40	54	39	32
Iran	39	43	37	41	29	36
Intl. Average	**58**	**56**	**52**	**62**	**51**	**45**

[a]The national desired population did not cover all of the international desired population

Source: Beaton et al. (1996), p. 41

When the 12th grade results came out a few months later, it seemed that we had a lot more work to do in the high school as well. Three different tests were given to three different samples. In the mathematics test given to all students, U.S. students were statistically even with the international average but below all others in that category, and only Cyprus and South Africa scored lower. In the advanced mathematics test, given to precalculus and calculus students (mirroring the situation in

Table 9 Distribution of advanced mathematics items by content category, TIMSS 1995

Category	Percent of items[a]	Number of points
Numbers & Equations	26	22
Calculus	23	19
Geometry	35	29
Probability & Statistics	11	8
Validation & Structure	5	4
Totals	**100**	**82**

[a]There were a total of 65 items

Source: TIMSS (undated), p. vi

FIMS), U.S. students scored significantly lower than the international average. The only ray of hope was that Advanced Placement calculus students scored slightly higher than the international average of advanced mathematics students. Now President Clinton remarked, "There is something wrong with the system and it is our generation's responsibility to fix it." (quoted in Bronner 1998)

An article in *The New York Times* (Bronner 1998) notes that 23 countries participated but only 16 countries participated in the Advanced Mathematics category. Furthermore, only six countries (France, Switzerland, Greece, Sweden, Canada, and the Czech Republic) met the sampling guidelines; the U.S. did not. All but the Czech Republic still had mean scores significantly above the U.S. The Russian Federation, which had the second highest mean score among all the countries, only tested 3 % of its students. So, just as in FIMS 30 years before, results were reported by the media with little regard for the sample.[5]

Another aspect of all these studies that was almost completely ignored is the substance of the test. What was being tested? It was assumed by the media and virtually all who commented on these tests that the items reflected what the country wants students to know. Yet Table 9 shows the distribution of items on the 12th grade TIMSS advanced mathematics test and shows that the distribution of items does not reflect the time devoted to various topics in the U.S. curriculum. Well over half of the precalculus curriculum in the U.S. is devoted to algebra and functions, but only 26 % of items were in that category. In the U.S., from algebra through calculus one of five years is spent on geometry, about 20 % of the time, but on the test 35 % of the items covered geometry.[6] For U.S. precalculus students to take a test in which 23 % of the items were on calculus doomed them to poor performance. In all, 58 %

---

[5]From the countries that met the sampling guidelines, the mean scores were: France (557), Switzerland (533), Greece (513), Sweden (512), Canada (509), and Czech Republic (469). For the countries that did not meat the guidelines, the mean scores were: Russian Federation (542), Australia (525), Denmark (522), Cyprus (518), Lithuania (516), Slovenia (475), Italy (474), Germany (465), United States (442), and Austria (436).

[6]A reviewer of this paper pointed out that some of the released TIMSS items classified as geometry and calculus would normally be taught in algebra or precalculus courses in the U.S., so that the match between topic and course is not as strong as I have indicated. Since not all items were released and we do not know the performance of students on them, the public cannot further test the claim that the distribution of items does not reflect the U.S. curriculum.

of the items on the advanced mathematics portion of TIMSS were on geometry or calculus, and only 26 % were on arithmetic or algebra.

Rather than looking at the possible mismatch between the curriculum and the test, the U.S. curriculum was called "a mile wide and an inch deep" (Schmidt et al. 1996, p. 34) and much of the blame for the poor performance was placed on textbooks. Repeating this theme, the National Mathematics Advisory Panel of 2008 exhorted publishers to produce shorter and more focused textbooks, and it is one of the reasons many people want common standards for the nation.

The "mile wide, inch deep" characterization does not fit well the U.S. high school curriculum. At the high school level, the U.S. curriculum is most often focused into algebra one year, geometry the next, algebra and functions the next, and functions the 4th year. This curriculum is often criticized because geometry is taught in a single year and algebra in two separate years rather than spreading them out over all years.

Indeed, the view of TIMSS researchers and others that the U.S. relative standing internationally has anything to do with the length or focus of U.S. textbooks has not been backed up by any research. One could just as easily argue that the high performance of U.S. students at 4th grade or the high performance in places like the schools in the First in the World Consortium was due to the very same textbooks.

TIMSS-R

In 1999, TIMSS was repeated and 13 of the 50 U.S. states participated as countries. These states did not include those that have traditionally had the highest or lowest performing students but the state results still showed wide variance, from quite a bit above international means to quite a bit below. This verified what previous studies had shown, that U.S. national mean scores mask performance that ranges from top-of-the-world in various parts of the country to the equal of third-world countries in other parts.

This was the picture as the U.S. entered the 21st century. With the exception of the 4th grade scores in the 1990s, the picture painted by U.S. scores in an international context was bleak. U.S. 8th graders rarely scored above the international mean and, except for the best students, on most tests 12th graders were uniformly poor. However, I have offered reasons why the picture may not be as bad as it was portrayed either by researchers or by the media.

This picture is quite different from a quote that began the National Mathematics Advisory Panel (2008) and is also in its summary. "During most of the 20th century, the United States possessed peerless mathematical prowess—not just as measured by the depth and number of the mathematical specialists who practiced here but also by the scale and quality of its engineering, science, and financial leadership, and *even by the extent of mathematical education in its broad population*." (Summary p. xi; Report, p. 1, emphasis mine)

That panel would have us believe that mathematics in schools was in good health through most of the 20th century, but that during the last part of the century, things

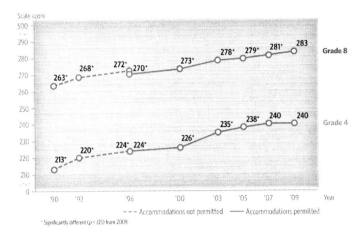

Fig. 3 Trends in 4th grade and 8th grade NAEP mathematics average scores 1990–2009.
Source: National Center for Education Statistics (2009), pp. 8, 23

went sour. The unwritten implication here is that things were fine until the *NCTM Standards* (1989), but the Standards were a failure. Now, due to that failure, dramatic action was needed. This was the main belief that led to the panel and later led to the Common Core Standards.

Not only is this belief not supported by data, but the data suggest that quite the opposite was true. Figure 2 showed that on the NAEP long-term longitudinal study, for both 9-year-olds and 13-year-olds, there were small improvements during the 1990s. Figures 3a and 3b show means on the standard NAEP assessment at 4th and 8th grade, for which a short-term longitudinal study was started in 1990. There was a steady and significant improvement on NAEP during the 1990s that has extended to the most recent NAEP tests.

TIMSS 2003 and 2007

TIMSS was given in 2003 and 2007 at the 4th and 8th grades. In 2003, at 4th grade, the U.S. now performed worse than it had relative to other countries in 1994-95 (Table 10a). Though the mean score in the U.S. had increased from 1994-95, the means of other countries increased more. At 8th grade, the U.S. mean was in the top half of all countries for the first time (Table 10b), but that result is deceptive, since many developing nations with low scores participated.

In 2007, over 40 countries participated at each grade level. Tables 11a and 11b show the means of all participating countries. The U.S. mean was more towards the top at each grade level than in early administrations of TIMSS. Furthermore, three of the countries with higher means at grade 4 did not test a representative sample, so their mean scores are not trustworthy. In short, the U.S. mean was higher internationally in 2007 than ever before.

Table 10a Average mathematics scale scores of 4th-grade students by country, TIMSS, 2003

Country	Average score	Country	Average score
International Average	495	Cyprus	510
Singapore	594	Moldova	504
Hong Kong SAR	575	Italy	503
Japan	565	Australia	499
Chinese Taipei	564	New Zealand	493
Belgium (Fl)	551	Scotland	490
Netherlands	540	Slovenia	479
Latvia	536	Armenia	456
Lithuania	534	Norway	451
Russian Federation	532	Iran	389
England	531	Philippines	356
Hungary	529	Morocco	347
United States	518	Tunisia	339

Source: Mullis et al. (2004), pp. 34–5

In the light of these national and international data, it is difficult to defend the view that U.S. students performed well before the NCTM Standards but their performance declined after that. Indeed, the truth is just the opposite. U.S. students languished until the problem-solving era of the 1980s and, on every measure of performance, both nationally and internationally, scores of U.S. students significantly improved after the NCTM Standards appeared in 1989.

PISA 2003, 2006, 2009

PISA, the Program for International Student Assessment, created under the auspices of the Organization for Economic and Cultural Development (OECD), is now the comparative international study involving the largest number of countries. Because PISA tests the ability of 15-year-old students to apply school knowledge to tasks one might see outside of school, it is quite different from TIMSS, which is far more dedicated to school mathematics. PISA is given to 15-year-olds because that is an age at which virtually all young people in almost all countries are in school. PISA occurs each 3 years, with testing in a given year focused on reading, mathematics, or science. 2003 was a mathematics year for PISA, 2006 was a science year, and 2009 was a math year, so there are more data for math from 2003 than from 2006 or 2009.

There are two parts to the PISA mathematics assessment: mathematics literacy and problem-solving. In 2003, Mathematical Literacy was defined as "an individual's capacity to identify and understand the role that mathematics plays in the world, to make well-founded judgments and to use and engage with mathematics in

Table 10b Average mathematics scale scores of 8th-grade students by country, TIMSS, 2003

Country	Average score	Country	Average score
International Average	467	Armenia	478
Singapore	605	Serbia[b]	477
Republic of Korea	589	Bulgaria	476
Hong Kong SAR	586	Romania	475
Chinese Taipei	585	Norway	461
Japan	570	Moldova	460
Belgium (Fl)	537	Cyprus	459
Netherlands	536	Macedonia[a]	435
Estonia	531	Lebanon	433
Hungary	529	Jordan	424
Malaysia	508	Iran	411
Latvia	508	Indonesia[b]	411
Russian Federation	508	Tunisia	410
Slovak Republic	508	Egypt	406
Australia	505	Bahrain	401
United States[a]	504	Palestinian Authority	390
Lithuania[b]	502	Chile	387
Sweden	499	Morocco[a]	387
Scotland	498	Philippines	378
Israel[a]	496	Botswana	366
New Zealand	494	Saudi Arabia	332
Slovenia	493	Ghana	276
Italy	484	South Africa	264

[a]The country did not meet international sampling or other guidelines

[b]The national desired population did not cover all of the international desired population

Source: Mullis et al. (2004), pp. 34–5

ways that meet the needs of that individual's life as a constructive, concerned and reflective citizen." (OECD 2003, p. 15).[7] Problem solving in PISA is interdisciplinary, defined as "an individual's capacity to use cognitive processes to confront and resolve real, cross-disciplinary situations where the solution path is not immediately

---

[7]For the 2012 administration of PISA, the definition of mathematical literacy was modified to "an individual's capacity to formulate, employ, and interpret mathematics in a variety of contexts. It includes reasoning mathematically and using mathematical concepts, procedures, facts, and tools to describe, explain, and predict phenomena. It assists individuals to recognise the role that mathematics plays in the world and to make the well-founded judgments and decisions needed by constructive, engaged and reflective citizens." (OECD 2010a, p. 4).

Table 11a Average mathematics scale scores of 4th-grade students by country, TIMSS, 2007

Country	Average score	Country	Average score
International Average	500	Slovenia	502
Hong Kong SAR	607	Armenia	500
Singapore	599	Slovak Republic	496
Chinese Taipei	576	Scotland	494
Japan	568	New Zealand	492
Kazakhstan[b]	549	Czech Republic	486
Russian Federation	544	Norway	473
England	541	Ukraine	469
Latvia	537	Georgia[b]	438
Netherlands[a]	535	Iran	402
Lithuania[b]	530	Algeria	378
United States[b]	529	Columbia	355
Germany	525	Morocco	341
Denmark	523	El Salvador	330
Australia	516	Tunisia	327
Hungary	510	Kuwait	316
Italy	507	Qatar	296
Austria	505	Yemen	224
Sweden	503		

[a]The country came close but did not meet international sampling or other guidelines

[b]The national target population did not cover all of the international target population

Source: Gonzales et al. (2008), p. 7

obvious and where the literacy domains or curricular areas that might be applicable are not within a single domain of mathematics, science or reading." (Ibid., p. 15)

On mathematical literacy in 2003, the mean score of students in most OECD countries was well above the U.S. mean and only a few Mediterranean countries and Mexico were below, as seen in Table 12. The results on problem solving mirrored those for mathematical literacy.

When student performance in each country was adjusted for the GDP of the country per capita, the U.S. adjusted mean was the second lowest of all OECD countries, higher only than Mexico. Finland and the Czech Republic were highest (OECD 2004, p. 358). This extraordinarily poor performance is reminiscent of U.S. performance on FIMS.

In PISA 2006 only mathematical literacy was tested. The results in 2006 mirrored those for 2003. The surprise to many people was that in both 2003 and 2006 Finland scored highest of OECD countries, only a little under Hong Kong in 2003, and Finland maintained the highest OECD score in 2006, just a little under Taiwan.

Table 11b Average mathematics scale scores of 8th-grade students by country, TIMSS, 2007

Country	Average score	Country	Average score
International Average	500	Ukraine	462
Chinese Taipei	598	Romania	461
Korea	597	Bosnia and Herzegovina	456
Singapore	593	Lebanon	449
Hong Kong	572	Thailand	441
Japan	570	Turkey	432
Hungary	517	Jordan	427
England	513	Tunisia	420
Russia	512	Georgia[b]	410
United States	508	Iran	403
Lithuania[b]	506	Bahrain	398
Czech Republic	504	Indonesia	397
Slovenia	501	Syria	395
Armenia	499	Egypt	391
Australia	496	Algeria	387
Sweden	491	Colombia	380
Malta	488	Oman	372
Scotland	487	Palestinian Authority	367
Serbia[b]	486	Botswana	364
Italy	480	Kuwait	354
Malaysia	474	El Salvador	340
Norway	469	Saudi Arabia	329
Cyprus	465	Ghana	309
Bulgaria	464	Qatar	307
Israel[a]	463		

[a]The country came close but did not meet international sampling or other guidelines

[b]The national target population did not cover all of the international target population

Source: Gonzales et al. (2008), p. 7

In 2009 again only mathematical literacy was tested. The results for the U.S. were consistent with 2003 and 2006 in that the U.S. mean of 487 was significantly below the OECD mean of 496 (Table 13). The U.S. had gained somewhat over time, having been 17 points below the OECD mean in 2003 and just 9 points below the mean in 2009. But U.S. students still scored poorly compared to students in most other countries.

A not atypical media response was that of Ada Kasparian.

The disparaging news coverage on the public school system in United States is more justi-fied than ever, especially after a new study by the Program for International Student Assess-

Table 12 Mean student score in mathematical literacy, PISA, 2003, by country

Country	Average score	Country	Average score	Country	Average score
OECD Average	500	Austria	506	Non-OECD Countries	
Finland	544	Germany	503	Hong Kong	550
Korea	542	Ireland	503	Liechtenstein	536
Netherlands	538	Slovak Republic	498	Macao-China	527
Japan	534	Norway	495	Latvia	483
Canada	532	Luxembourg	493	Russia	468
Belgium	529	Poland	490	Serbia and Montenegro	437
Switzerland	527	Hungary	490	Uruguay	422
Australia	524	Spain	485	Thailand	417
New Zealand	523	United States	483	Indonesia	360
Czech Republic	516	Portugal	466	Tunisia	359
Iceland	515	Italy	466		
Denmark	514	Greece	445		
France	511	Turkey	423		
Sweden	509	Mexico	385		

Source: OECD (2004), p. 356

ment (PISA) indicated that students in the U.S. lagged far behind the Chinese in academic performance. In fact, 15-year-old Chinese students in Shanghai out-performed all students internationally in all three categories, including math, science, and reading. According to Time Magazine, this is the first time China participated in a PISA study, and the results are stunning because researchers did not expect the country to do as well as it did (Kasparian 2010).

This reaction ignores the fact that Shanghai is not representative of China. Historically, it was the most western-oriented of all of China and in a most affluent part of the country. For this reason, from even before the current economic growth of China, it has had its own curriculum different from the rest of the country. Second, because the area is known to have top schools, if a child from another province is a very good student, his or her parents may send that child to Shanghai to afford the best chance of attending the best universities in the country. This practice is quite similar to that of parents in the U.S. who move to high-performing suburbs or send their children to private schools in order to increase their chances of getting into an elite college. People would never consider the highest-performing suburban schools and private schools as a barometer of how the entire U.S. performs, but some media were quick to do just that in the case of Shanghai.

However, the misreading of Shanghai as all of China still does not explain why Japan, Singapore, Hong Kong, and Korea consistently score among the highest of all countries. It is natural to ask what these countries (and also Shanghai!) are doing and

Table 13 Mean student score in mathematical literacy, PISA, 2009, by country

Country	Average score	Country	Average score	Country	Average score
OECD Average	496	Hungary	490	Croatia	460
Korea	546	Luxembourg	489	Dubai	453
Finland	541	United States	487	Serbia	442
Switzerland	534	Ireland	487	Azerbaijan	431
Japan	529	Portugal	487	Bulgaria	428
Canada	527	Spain	483	Romania	427
Netherlands	526	Italy	483	Uruguay	427
New Zealand	519	Greece	466	Thailand	419
Belgium	515	Israel	447	Trinidad & Tobago	414
Australia	514	Turkey	445	Kazakhstan	405
Germany	513	Chile	421	Montenegro	403
Estonia	512	Mexico	419	Argentina	388
Iceland	507	Non-OECD Countries		Jordan	387
Denmark	503	Shanghai-China	600	Brazil	386
Slovenia	501	Singapore	562	Colombia	381
Norway	498	Hong Kong	555	Albania	377
France	497	Chinese Taipei	543	Tunisia	371
Slovak Republic	497	Liechtenstein	536	Indonesia	371
Austria	496	Macao-China	525	Qatar	368
Poland	495	Latvia	482	Peru	365
Sweden	494	Lithuania	477	Panama	360
Czech Republic	493	Russia	468	Kyrgystan	331
United Kingdom	492				

Source: OECD (2010b), p. 134

emulate them. And, if curriculum is the key variable, why not take their curricula? However, it is as just important to remember the cautions of Nagy.

Nagy's difficulties that apply to Japan, Korea, and Finland deal with opportunity to learn, different social conditions in the countries, and different school enrolment patterns. In Japan and Korea, a huge amount of instruction in mathematics takes place outside of school. In Korea, more money is spent on education by parents than is spent on education by the government. It is reported that half of all Japanese children attend academic jukus. The education ministries in both Korea and Japan have been embarrassed by this lack of faith in what students learn in school and has tried to do something about it by downplaying the exams that are critical in determining what secondary schools and what colleges a person can attend, but the juku schools are so ingrained in the culture that the government's actions have had no effect. It is not atypical for a student to go to school during the day and then every day to juku until well into the night (Watanabe 2007).

It is more difficult to identify why students in Finland score so highly on PISA. My understanding is that Finnish researchers have not been able to identify any school variable or curricular reasons for their students' performance. Some feel that it is the competence of, respect for, and independence given to teachers in Finland. One Finnish mathematics educator presented me with a different theory more related to mathematics. Finland has one of the highest levels of home computer usage per capita in the world. Children are using information technology all of the time, and in that usage they are developing problem-solving skills, organizational skills, and literacy that goes well beyond what is taught in school.[8] Their experiences outside of school are unable to be measured accurately or are even ignored by researchers whose expertise is with in-school variables, but he feels they account for the difference. These same explanations of high performance apply to the First In the World consortium mentioned above and can explain many of the differences in performance of various groups within the U.S. This suggests that s student performance could be improved by policies that encourage high-performing students to go into teaching and that give attention to what children do outside of school.

An additional social situation is at work in Singapore and Hong Kong. Singapore, with a population of about 4.5 million, is not comparable to the U.S. nor perhaps to any other country except when Hong Kong is considered as a country. Singapore sits next to Malaysia and Hong Kong to mainland China in the same way that U.S. affluent suburbs are not far from inner cities. In 2000, 28 % of the labor force in Singapore consisted of foreign workers and large numbers of workers in both places come from outside that territory[9] (Yeoh and Lin 2012). The vast majority are in jobs that Singaporeans consider too low-level. Many workers in Singapore commute from Malaysia across the bridge each morning and go back each evening, so their children do not go to school in Singapore. In Singapore in 2005, 18 % of the population were nonresidents who either were not allowed to have their children with them or whose children were not tested. It is as if U.S. students in affluent suburbs were tested but not students in the cities. The same is true to a lesser degree in Hong Kong with workers from the mainland of China. In 2000, 217,000 of the territory's 3,200,000 workers were domestics who come in from the mainland.

The view of these international tests is not the same in many other countries as it is in the U.S. They have always had national curricula, so do not attribute recent performance to that—in fact, many countries with national curricula score well below the U.S. These countries generally ascribe their standing to a carefully designed curriculum that is taken in a high-pressure society in which students need to work hard to succeed, and so spend a great deal of time on schoolwork outside of

---

[8]For an independent supporting argument, see Keith Devlin, *Mathematics Education for a New Era: Video Games as a Medium for Learning* (A.K. Peters/CRC Press, 2011).

[9]In 2010, over a third of the labor force in Singapore was foreign (Yeoh and Lin 2012).

school.[10] They look to other countries for guidance on future directions in curriculum, including the U.S., knowing that more curriculum research is done here than anywhere else in the world and that some of the best curriculum materials in the world are created in North America! This is particularly true when it comes to the use of technology, which is increasing in all of these countries. For instance, since 2007 about half of the grade 6 national test in Singapore allows calculators.

Summary

In sum, what have we learned?

1. Comparing mathematics performance among countries is very difficult. Tests cannot be fair to countries in which curricula differ.
2. Many results of international comparisons are reported without enough regard for the differences in sample selection or content tested. Giving the mean as designating the performance of all students in the United States masks the enormous differences in public schools in different locations.
3. Opportunity-to-learn, not only in school but also out of school, is probably the most significant determiner of mathematics performance.
4. Of all age groups, U.S. 12th-graders have performed worst internationally compared to students in other countries, but some of the differences are due to the fact that a majority of the highest-performing 12th-graders in mathematics in the U.S. do not specialize in mathematics but are simultaneously still studying a broad curriculum.
5. On internal assessments at all grade levels, U.S. students in recent years have substantially higher scores than their peers of a generation ago.
6. The scores of students in the U.S. are related to socio-economics of their individual families, but the economic well-being of the U.S. has not been related to its mean performance on international assessments, for mean scores of U.S. have never been near the top compared to other countries on international assessments.

References

Beaton, A. E., Mullis, I. V. S., Martin, M. O., Gonzales, E. J., Kelly, D. L., & Smith, T. A. (1996). *Mathematics achievement in the middle school years: IEA's third international mathematics and science study.* Boston: Boston College, Center for the Study of Testing, Evaluation, and Educational Policy.

---

[10]At a meeting of about 200 mathematics educators of Chinese ancestry at the International Congress of Mathematical Education in Seoul Korea in August, 2012, one speaker attributed the high performance of Chinese students on international tests to a cultural tradition dating back to Confucius in which individuals are expected to work hard to perform well on tests.

Bennet, J. (1997). Fourth graders successful, study shows. *The New York Times*, 11 Jun 1997, available at http://www.nytimes.com/1997/06/11/us/fourth-graders-successful-study-shows. html?pagewanted=all&src=pm, accessed 9 Nov 2011.

Bronner, E. (1998). U.S. trails the world in math and science. *The New York Times*, 25 Feb 1998, available at http://www.nytimes.com/1998/02/25/us/us-trails-the-world-in-math-and-science. html?pagewanted=all&src=pm, accessed 9 Nov 2011.

College Board (2012). *2012 college-bound seniors total group profile report*. New York: Author.

Gonzales, P., et al. (2008). *Highlights from TIMSS 2007: mathematics and science achievement of U. S. fourth- and eighth-grade students in an international context (NCES 2009-001)*. Washington: U.S. Department of Education, Institute of Education Sciences, National Center for Education Statistics.

Husen, T. (Ed.) (1967). *International study of achievement in mathematics: a comparison of twelve countries* (Vols. I and II). Stockholm: Almqvist & Wiksell.

Hutchinger, F. M. (1967a). U.S. ranked low in math teaching. *New York Times* 7 Mar 1967, p. 1.

Hutchinger, F. M. (1967b). The U.S. gets low marks in math. *New York Times* 12 Mar 1967, p. 205.

Kasparian, A. (2010). China beats the U.S. in education. http://www.examiner.com 15 Dec 2010, accessed 11 Nov 2011.

McKnight, C. C., Crosswhite, F. J., Dossey, J. A., Kifer, E., Swafford, J. O., Travers, K. J., & Cooney, T. J. (1987). *The underachieving curriculum*. Champaign: Stipes Publishing Co.

Medrich, E. A., & Griffith, J. E. (1992). *International mathematics and science assessments: what have we learned?* Washington: National Center for Education Statistics.

Mullis, I. V. S., Martin, M. O., Gonzales, E. J., & Chrostowski, S. J. (2004). *TIMSS 2003 international mathematics report: findings from IEA's trends in international mathematics and science study at the fourth and eighth grades*. Boston: Boston College, Lynch School of Education, TIMSS & PIRLS International Study Center.

Nagy, P. (1996). International comparisons of student achievement in mathematics and science: a Canadian perspective. *Canadian Journal of Education*, 21(4), 396–413, downloadable from http://www.csse.ca/CJE/Articles/FullText/CJE21-4.htm, accessed 3 Nov 2011.

National Mathematics Advisory Panel (2008). *Foundations for success*. Washington: U.S. Department of Education.

National Center for Education Statistics (2009). *The nation's report card: mathematics 2009 (NCES 2010-451)*. Washington: U.S. Department of Education, Institute of Education Sciences.

National Center for Education Statistics (2012). *Digest of education statistics 2011 (NCES 2012-001)*. Washington: U.S. Department of Education, Institute of Education Sciences.

National Council of Teachers of Mathematics (1989). *Curriculum and evaluation standards for school mathematics*. Reston: The Council.

OECD (2003). *The PISA 2003 assessment framework—mathematics, reading, science and problem solving knowledge and skills*. Paris: Organization for Economic Co-operation and Development.

OECD (2004). *Learning for tomorrow's world: first results from PISA 2003*. Paris: Organization for Economic Co-operation and Development.

OECD (2010a). *The PISA 2012 mathematics framework*. Paris: Organization for Economic Co-operation and Development.

OECD (2010b). *PISA 2009 results: what students know and can do: student performance in reading, mathematics and science* (Vol. I). Paris: Organization for Economic Co-operation and Development.

Schmidt, W. H., McKnight, C. C., & Raizen, S. A. (1996). *A splintered vision: an investigation of U.S. science and mathematics education*. Dordrecht: Kluwer.

TIMSS (undated). *TIMSS: IEA's third international mathematics and science study. Released item set for the final year of secondary school: mathematics and science literacy, advanced mathematics, and physics*. Boston: Boston College, Lynch School of Education, TIMSS & PIRLS International Study Center.

Watanabe, R. (2007). The juku system: the other face of Japan's education system. www.education-in-japan.info/sub109.html, accessed 9 Dec 2012.

Wirtz, W., et al. (1977). *On further examination. Report of the advisory panel on the scholastic aptitude test score decline.* New York: College Entrance Examination Board.

Yeoh, B. S. A., & Lin, W. (2012). Rapid growth in Singapore's immigrant population brings policy changes. www.migrationinformation.org/Profiles/display.cfm?ID=570, accessed 9 Dec 2012.

(Mathematics) Curriculum, Teaching and Learning

Ngai-Ying Wong, Qiaoping Zhang, and Xiaoqing Li

Abstract As mathematics curricula around the world have undergone significant reform in recent years, it is time to re-think the role of the curriculum for mathematics learning and teaching. What shape would such a curriculum have (the final product) if it does undergo this kind of reform? Who are the 'end-users' of the curriculum and what are the inter-relationships among the curriculum, the teachers, and the students? This chapter attempts to summarize and comment on the various chapters in this book and to initiate further reflection and discussion on these issues.

Keywords Mathematics curriculum · Mathematics teaching · Mathematics curriculum reform

Prologue

Mathematics curricula around the world have been undergoing reform for more than a decade, so it is now time to re-think the role of the curriculum in the learning and teaching of mathematics. The chapters in this book contribute to our understanding of the role and purpose of a mathematics curriculum, as well as of mathematics teaching and learning in the context of reform in the various educational regions.[1] Rather than setting out a firm position on various issues, the authors have chosen to raise a number of questions on various related aspects, in the hope that these questions would act as fuel to drive further reflection and professional discourse.

---

[1] The term 'region' is used throughout this chapter for consistency. Some regions (e.g., Japan) are countries, while others (e.g., Hong Kong) are not.

The word 'mathematics' is in parentheses since we believe that many of the issues in this chapter are not confined to mathematics.

N.-Y. Wong (✉) · Q. Zhang
Department of Curriculum and Instruction, The Chinese University of Hong Kong, New Territories, Hong Kong
e-mail: nywong@cuhk.edu.hk

X. Li
Department of Psychology, Shenzhen University, Shenzhen, China

Y. Li, G. Lappan (eds.), *Mathematics Curriculum in School Education*,
Advances in Mathematics Education, DOI 10.1007/978-94-007-7560-2_28,
© Springer Science+Business Media Dordrecht 2014

607

Standardization in the Current Reform of the Mathematics Curriculum

In the West, prior to the modern mathematics movement of the 1960s, there had been virtually no change in the mathematics curriculum and textbooks for a very long time. There was little difference between the pre-second-world-war and post-second-world-war traditional textbooks because both were based on what has since been called the pre-1800 model (Cooper 1985). Following the modern mathematics movement, there were widespread reforms of the mathematics curriculum around the world at the turn of the millennium (Wong et al. 2004). Among other factors, these changes were triggered by several large-scale international comparisons, such as the Second IEA Mathematics Study (SIMS), the 1992 International Assessment of Education Progress (IAEP) mathematics study, and the Third International Mathematics and Science Study (TIMSS).[2] Though Hirabayashi did state that "having a high achievement in international mathematics studies is not the only criterion" for a good curriculum (as quoted in Curriculum and Textbook Workgroup 2002, p. 6; see also Wong et al. 2004), it appears that improving the position of one's country/region in the 'international league table' is still a major goal in the current trend towards mathematics curriculum reform (Anderson 2014; Pang 2014; Stephens 2014).

To avoid falling behind, and to maintain standards, the first thing to do is to establish what the standards are (Reys 2014). Thus, the idea of standardization quietly crept into the mathematics curriculum and teaching. Besides the need to keep up the standard, there is an interest in standardizing (unifying) the mathematics curriculum across the regions and having it benchmarked against the ones used in other countries or regions. Setting up a national curriculum became a trend in Australia, Brazil, Israel, Japan, Korea, Singapore, the UK, the USA (though the US mathematics standard was prepared by a non-governmental body, the National Council of Teachers of Mathematics), and the Chinese regions (Anderson 2014; Even and Olsher 2014; Garnica 2014; Pang 2014; Reys 2014; Stephens 2014; Tam et al. 2014; Wong et al. 2014). All of these cases involved conformation to a single curriculum standard. The first matter to consider is whether such a move is desirable and viable.

It is interesting to note that, although educational autonomy and decentralization were always stressed in the West (van Zanten and van den Heuvel-Panhuizen 2014), there is a long history of a centralized curriculum in the East. Inevitably, if there is too much emphasis on curricular autonomy, there is a possibility that the resulting curriculum will be too laissez-faire. However, too much centralized control has its drawbacks as well. This is particularly an issue in educational regions in the East where there is already a long tradition of a centralized curriculum. The question is whether pushing for strict standardization would further tighten the existing centralized control, which would run counter to the call for school-based curriculum development (Wong and Tang 2012).

There are two more issues to be considered. Firstly, as the notion of the 'curriculum' has expanded to encompass a large number of components, such as attainment

---

[2]This was later renamed 'Trends in International Mathematics and Science Study.'

targets, teaching approaches, and learning activities, would it still be possible for the central curriculum designers to really know what is happening in each district, each school, and each classroom (even with each student), in order to be able to design an ideal curriculum? Secondly, the above issue will become even more salient when processing abilities, including the so-called generic skills or higher-order thinking skills (e.g., problem solving, creativity and communication), are given greater emphasis in the current reform of the mathematics curriculum. This is particularly true if an attempt is made to use attainment indicators as inputs into the standard mathematics curriculum. How can the mastery of these generic skills be turned into measurable outcomes? In practice, can these generic skills be acquired step by step in line with the progress towards the attainment standards? Or can they only be nurtured holistically? All of these questions deserve reflection on the part of those who care about the mathematics curriculum (Wong et al. 2004).

Curriculum, Textbook and Instruction

After the curriculum is reformed, it needs to be implemented. The model of 'intended, implemented, and attained curricula' has been used since SIMS to analyze the mathematics curriculum (Travers and Westbury 1989). Similar frameworks were also proposed by scholars such as Goodlad (1979) and Marsh and Willis (2007). This type of framework for curriculum analysis is also used in various chapters in this book (for example Reys 2014; Senk et al. 2014). However, the 'intended, implemented, and attained curricula' model might give the impression that action would be taken only in that order. Indeed, it is often emphasized that the word *curriculum* originates in the Latin *currere*, which means 'to race.' In simplistic terms, curriculum designers would set the course (racecourse) for students to follow, leading them to their destination. The first step in this process is to design an intended curriculum. The next step is to guide teachers on how to implement the curriculum. This involves providing them with a set of well-designed curriculum documents, textbooks, and other 'accessories,' as well as a good methodology for instruction. The final step is to cross-check whether the expected curriculum targets have been achieved (e.g., Anderson 2002; Martone and Sireci 2009).

At the present time, the concept of the curriculum can be very broad (see further discussion in later sections). School documents, newspaper articles, committee reports, and many academic textbooks refer to any or all of the subjects offered or prescribed as 'the curriculum of the school' (Marsh 2004, p. 3). Nevertheless, the textbook is still the means most frequently used to actualize the curriculum. In this book, a series of chapters focus on the textbook (Even and Olsher 2014; Li et al. 2014; Senk et al. 2014). Thus textbooks can be seen as a further manifestation of the intended curriculum. Undoubtedly, the design of both the curriculum and the related documents is crucial for effective teaching, especially for novice teachers, giving them confidence that if they follow the curriculum design, they will achieve the desired learning outcomes.

Along with the above line of thought, after the curriculum is designed, the next step could be to design the instruction components, which is the focus of a number of chapters in this book (Huang et al. 2014; Reys 2014; Shafer 2014; Wong et al. 2014). With a carefully designed curriculum and the relevant curriculum documents at hand to guide the teachers on effective instructional methods, it is very likely that the curriculum goals would be achieved, unless there is 'infidelity' in the process, that is, the curriculum is not being implemented strictly in line with its original design (Achinstein and Ogawa 2006; Fullan 2007; Kimpston 1985; O'Donnell 2008; Synder et al. 1992; see also van Zanten and van den Heuvel-Panhuizen 2014).

Once the curriculum standard is laid down, the next step is to design the curriculum material (textbooks included), and then to equip the teachers with the various skills needed to implement the instructional design. If this process is respected, the teachers would then deliver their teaching as prescribed, and arrive at the expected students' learning outcomes. This logic will be considered again towards the end of this chapter. In the following section, one factor—the teacher—that might affect the implementation of the curriculum is examined.

The Curriculum and the Teacher

After the curriculum is finalized, it is the teacher who has to deliver it. So one source of curriculum infidelity is the teacher. Teachers should be professional enough to implement the curriculum as designed, and benefit from the assistance of the underlying instructional design of the curriculum documents. Both the beliefs and knowledge of the teachers (of all kinds, including subject knowledge, pedagogical content knowledge, curriculum knowledge, and knowledge about the students: Bromme 1994; Shulman 1987; Sullivan and Wood 2008) are seen to be of the utmost importance in guaranteeing that the intended curriculum is successfully implemented, and thus yields the expected attainments. However, such an approach still reflects the linear mentality (Fig. 1).

The advocate of a 'teacher-proof curriculum' (Apple 1993; Priestley 2002), at the peak of behaviorism, further reinforces this line of thought. The curriculum (together with the textbooks) is a 'script' for the teachers to play their parts (Wong 2009). Yet in recent years, teacher ownership (of the curriculum), teacher autonomy, and the community of learning (Cochran-Smith and Lytle 1999; Kirk and MacDonald 2001) among the teachers have been emphasized, which opens up another option for the role of the curriculum (Even and Olsher 2014). Stein et al. (2014) point out that we could guarantee a high-quality instruction even though we use the curricular in a congruent manner. Indeed, in reality, a teacher cannot and should not be only a faithful executor of the intended curriculum (including the textbooks). The roles and inter-relationships among the curriculum, the textbook, and the teacher (not to mention the students, who will be discussed later in this chapter) need to be re-thought (Cohen et al. 2003; Li 2011; McCaffrey et al. 2001).

Fig. 1 The curriculum,
teacher, and teaching

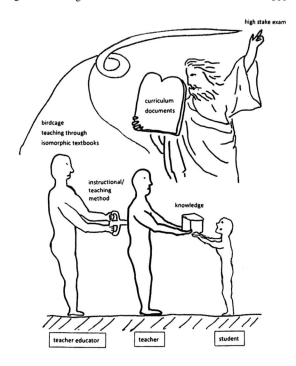

A number of chapters in this book touch upon the inter-relationships among the curriculum, the teachers, and the teaching process. Some of them focus on the connectedness among the three, while others focus on how curriculum change can facilitate teacher professionalism (Brown and Hodgen 2014; Cai et al. 2014; Takahashi 2014). The notion of teacher ownership of the curriculum is not new, while the concept of the teacher as a reflective practitioner was discussed previously in the 1980s (Schön 1983). From this perspective, the teacher should own the curriculum, and evolve to become an educational researcher, an assessment expert (assessment not just *of* but *for* learning) and a curriculum designer (Clandinin and Connelly 1992). The teaching of each lesson would involve an element of curriculum design and not just the blind respect of a pre-designed instructional practice.

There is yet another aspect of teacher ownership, namely, involving teachers in the curriculum development process. Even and Olsher (2014) describe how teachers became more genuine participants in the process of textbook development, which made them more active participants in curriculum development. Their needs, wishes, and aspirations were also fed back to the professional curriculum developers and the policy makers. Wong et al. (2014) contains an extensive discussion of this idea. Superficial 'town hall' consultations may alienate the teachers and adversely affect the way that they view the curriculum. That chapter then considers the need for curriculum reformers to carefully listen to and to synthesize the views of the various stakeholders holistically (see also Lam et al. in press).

Curriculum, Teaching and Learning

Most, if not all, curriculum design is done out of goodwill and in the hope that it will help students to learn more effectively. In other words, the purpose of all of these efforts is not just to promote teaching but also to facilitate learning. In that sense, the student is the end-user for the curriculum, yet the student voice is often under-represented in curriculum design (Geiger et al. 2014). Most curriculum design is based on a 'hypothetical learning trajectory' (Fuson and Li 2014; Simon 1995), which is essentially an adult perspective (and in particular that of the curriculum designers) rather than a delineation of actual student learning. Furthermore, such a 'hypothetical learning trajectory' often describes the 'shortest learning path.' However, in reality, it is quite natural for students to loop in their learning process. There is a need for students to 'hatch' as they loop around too. Therefore, it seems that the students' opinions, such as their appraisal and/or diagnosis of their learning process, should play a role in curriculum design (Geiger et al. 2014). In the holistic review of the mathematics curriculum in Hong Kong, the opinions of the various stakeholders, including university professors, employers, parents, and students, were solicited. In particular, a questionnaire survey was conducted among 10,000 students (as well as 60 interviews) (Tam et al. 2014). The conclusion was that the student should have a role in the whole curriculum design process.

It should also be noted that there is a subtle difference between teaching and learning in curriculum design. In the specific context of mathematics, the mathematics curriculum should help students develop their understandings of mathematical **concepts**, in order to **solve** mathematics **problems**, but the words in bold deserve deeper reflection. There is a vast number of meanings of both 'learning' and 'having learned.' Should we allow/encourage students to develop their own concepts (as advocated by constructivism)? Should we impart to them a set of mathematical concepts? Or should we take both of these aspects into account in the design and implementation of a curriculum? Aside from 'ethical' considerations, is it really possible to stop students from conceptualizing their own mathematical experience? In addition, do we have a set of prescribed concepts (conceptual frameworks) for each particular mathematical object? Take division as an example. Is it the inverse of multiplication, the solution to '$bx = a$,' sharing, grouping, dividing a pizza pictorially, or dividing a rectangle pictorially? Can we say that division is any of the above, or that all of them together comprise the notion of division? Is the above list exhaustive, and can these representations help students **understand** division and **solve** problems? What are the grounds for not accepting that students have their own (internal) representations and self-invented problem-solving strategies? And if we value the ability of students to 're-invent' mathematics (Freudenthal 1991; van den Heuvel-Panhuizen 2001), how can we make that re-invention happen, rather than let students just imitate the standard problem-solving strategies (even though these standard strategies are often the 'best and most efficient' ones). All of these questions deserve deeper investigation when we seek to develop a curriculum that enhances **student** learning (Carpenter et al. 1998; Clarke 1997; Fuson et al. 1997; Huang et al. 2014; Threlfall 2000; Tsang 2005).

Attained Curriculum: Student Performance and Problem Solving

Once the curriculum is designed and implemented, it is of undoubted interest to examine whether the desired learning outcomes are attained (Shafer 2014). But first it has to be established what criteria of student performance could be used for this. As mentioned above, there are different facets of 'having learned.' Could these be finding the correct answer, mastering the 'right' procedure to solve problems, stating the definition, drawing a few standard pictorial representations, or all of these? Should attention also be paid to 'deep procedural knowledge,' which is characterized by connectedness and a flexible use of procedures (Star and Rittle-Johnson 2008)? Howe (2014) describes the three pillars of mathematics, namely, conceptual understanding, computational skills, and coordination (which might be closely related to connectedness as mentioned above). This listing suggests that there may be a variety of expected learning outcomes (the attained curriculum), which are at the same time the curriculum objectives. It can also be asked whether or not students' non-cognitive achievements are significant, such as their interest in learning, their self-efficacy, and other affective factors and beliefs. These notions are all emphasized in the current curriculum reform, yet care has to be taken that they do not become parts of the formal, high-stake assessments process (Wong et al. 2004). All of these points provide food for reflection after reading the various chapters in this book.

When considering learning outcomes in mathematics, inevitably, problem solving emerges as a central issue. However, what is the relationship between a generic ability for problem solving and a problem-solving ability in mathematics? This issue is not new and was raised at the beginning of the famous report by Cockcroft:

> It is often suggested that mathematics should be studied in order to develop powers of logical thinking, accuracy and spatial awareness. The study of mathematics can certainly contribute to these ends, but the extent to which it does so depends on the way in which mathematics is taught. Nor is its contribution unique; many other activities and the study of a number of other subjects can develop these powers as well. We therefore believe that the need to develop these powers does not in itself constitute a sufficient reason for studying mathematics rather than other things. (Cockcroft 1982, p. 1)

As students go on to different walks of life after they finish school, and do not restrict themselves to the fields of mathematics or science, it is essential for them to nurture their general (and not mathematics-specific) problem-solving abilities. However, in the context of mathematics learning, this nurturing is done through tackling mathematics problems. How to bridge the gap between these two forms of problem solving, the mathematical and the generic, becomes a task for everyone. It is not confined to learning objectives but also extends to how learning outcomes are assessed.

What Is the Curriculum, in Real Terms?

From the above discussions, it is apparent that the term 'curriculum,' mathematics curriculum included, could have very different meanings in different regions. This point should be borne in mind when reading the chapters in this book (and other related articles). In some regions (e.g., China and the UK), the curriculum is mandatory and by law has to be followed. In other countries (e.g., the USA), its use is only recommended. In still other places (e.g., Hong Kong), it is used as a 'trade off' to justify a government subsidy, because a school has to conform to the official curriculum if it wants to obtain government funding.

How detailed the curriculum is depends on the level of curriculum control. In some countries, the curriculum document is just a (loose) framework within which different authorities develop their own curriculum. In other countries, where the three (or four) column approach has become popular, not only are the learning targets and contents laid down, but the teaching activities and assessment methods are also suggested (Wong et al. 2004). Thus curriculum documents play different roles and take different forms in different countries and regions.

There are also differences in the end-users of the curriculum. Theoretically, the main audience is the teachers. However, in many cases, when the textbooks are closely aligned to the curriculum, the teachers do not necessarily refer to the curriculum since they believe it is enough to follow the textbooks. In such cases, when drafting a curriculum document, should the textbook developers also be a major target audience? The students are another end-user group. If the students have chosen to study independently (whether they are home-school students, foreign students, or adult students), should the curriculum document also cater to their needs? For instance, could the curriculum be so detailed that it could be followed fully even without a teacher? This question is even more salient for textbooks. Should text books be written with the teachers in mind, to guide them in their teaching; or for the students, making it possible to study fully by following them?

Returning to the previous discussion on the 'intended—implemented—attained' linear mentality of the curriculum, the curriculum documents are often taken as a starting point for the engineering of a prospective educational reform. In other words, a curriculum document is released to initiate the process of changing the curriculum in subsequent years. However, there are other possibilities too, including the suggestions by Tam et al. (2014). These authors reviewed the historical development of the Hong Kong primary mathematics curriculum in the period 1960–1980. They showed that the curriculum (document) can be seen as a summary and consolidation of a long-term experiment in teaching. It is an 'end'-product of curriculum reform rather than a starting point. Genuine curriculum reform often originates in day-to-day classroom teaching (Fullan 1999; Stigler and Hiebert 1999). Such teaching experiments could include providing students with more learning opportunities (Anderson 2014) rather than adding specific contents. Again, Geiger et al. (2014) show that offering challenging learning activities and genuine opportunities to students helped them to develop a positive view of mathematics learning and see the connectedness of their learning both within and outside mathematics.

What Mathematics Are We Looking at?

Some of the issues discussed above are general rather than mathematical. When it is boiled down to mathematics, naturally, the aim is for the students to learn some mathematics by following the mathematics curriculum. However, mathematics may be 'just' one means of nurturing a responsible citizen and an 'educated person.' For some time, the school mathematics curriculum has been criticized as being 'de-mathematized' (Zhang 2005). Can this criticism be answered by putting more mathematics back into the school curriculum, or would it be better to explore the *path* of mathematization (Freudenthal 1991; NCTM 1989)?

To this end, students need to be helped to undergo an ontological shift (Chi 1992) from the concrete to the abstract, from the particular to the general, from their own real-life experience to entities in the mathematical world, and from realistic to esoteric mathematics (Cooper and Dunne 1998). For instance, Sinclair and de Freitas (2014) suggest that conceptualizing mathematics as being characteristically *virtual* can bridge the space between the concrete and the abstract. Huang et al. (2014) point out that this shift can occur at several points. The shift occurring at several points is echoed by previous discussions on the design of the *bianshi* curriculum (Wong et al. 2009, 2012a, 2012b). An additional issue is whether or not the ultimate goal of the mathematization process is to achieve a unified, universal form of mathematics. A great deal of discussion has taken place on the subtle differences that might exist between formal/symbolic mathematics, hands-on mathematics, real-life mathematics, mathematics in the ICT environment, etc. (Artigue 2001; Lopez-Real and Leung 2006). When we say that our mathematics curriculum builds a path of mathematization for the students, we need to understand what type of mathematics that path leads to.

Concluding Remarks

As was said at the beginning of this introduction, it is time to re-think the mathematics curriculum, and the learning and teaching of mathematics, as well as to re-think the textbooks, teachers, and students. A number of questions arise from the above discussion. Could and should the curriculum encompass all the aspects of teaching and learning? Should the curriculum be a guideline for teaching or a means to enhance the professionalism of teachers? What is the primary concern or goal of curriculum reform, for example a means to improve the position in the 'international league table,' or a contribution to the whole-person development? Some of these questions have already been raised in articles such as Wong et al. (2004) (though it was published a decade ago), but the authors hope that these questions can continue to provide food for further reflections and investigation as the chapters of this book are read.

As Albert Einstein (1879–1955) said, "Education is that which remains, if one has forgotten everything he learned in school" (Einstein 1950, p. 36). A well-designed curriculum, together with effective delivery, is a necessity and lays the foundation for the emergence of wisdom. However, this may be just the first half of the 'story' (Wong et al. 2012a, 2012b). One has to 'transcend'[3] the *way* after 'entering,' and going along with the *way* (Wong 2006). As a conclusion, two little Chan stories can illustrate this point:

There was a group of learned monks visiting Master Big Pearl (a great Chan master in the Tang dynasty). One of them asked, "Can Master take a question?" Master replied, "Just like a big pond reflecting the moon, feel free to search on it (implying that one can only touch the shadow rather than the moon!)." A monk asked, "Who is the Buddha?" Master answered, "Sitting on the other side of the pond (i.e. Master Big Pearl himself), other than the Buddha, who can it be?" Everyone was stunned. After a while, another monk asked, "What teaching method do you use to enlighten the others?" Master said, "I did not use any method." The monk murmured, "This is the style of Chan masters." Master asked back, "Then, what method do you use?" The monk replied, "I teach the *Diamond sutra*." Master asked, "How many times have you taught?" The monk replied, "More than 20." Master asked, "Who spoke the *sutra*?" The monk responded in a loud voice, "Are you kidding, isn't it spoken by the Buddha?" Master said, "[But isn't it precisely said in the *sutra* that], if someone said the Buddha has anything to teach, it is a blasphemy, and that person doesn't understand the meaning. But if someone said the *sutra* is not spoken by the Buddha, it is blasphemy against the *sutra* itself. What do you think then?" ... The monk said, "I am getting confused here." Master said, "You never had understood, so how can you say you get confused ... You taught the *sutra* over 20 times, but you have not yet attained Buddhahood (the essence of the teaching)."

One day a company of several monks came to visit Zhauzhou (778–897) (another great Chan master in the Tang Dynasty). The first one asked, "I am just a beginner, Master, please reveal to me the teaching." Zhauzhou asked, "Have you taken breakfast today?" The monk responded "Yes sir." Master spoke with a loud voice, "Why then are you stand idling there, go now and wash the bowl!" The monk attained realization upon hearing this. The second monk asked, "I am also a novice, could Master please teach me?" Zhauzhou asked, "When did you arrive?" Reply, "Just today." Question, "Have you drunk the tea?" Reply, "Yes sir." Master then said, "You should then report to the reception immediately!" Again, this monk attained realization. At this moment, a third monk who had been studying in the monastery for a long time said, "Sir, I have been here for more than 10 years and never heard your teachings. I wish to take leave from here and learn from others." Zhauzhou was very angry upon hearing this, "Young man, why have you wrongly accused me? Starting from the first day you arrived, whenever you presented me with tea, I drank for you! You presented me with rice, I ate for you. When you

---

[3]In Wong (2006), originally the word 'exiting' was used, but 'transcending' is a more appropriate term.

bowed, I lowered my eyebrows, and when you prostrated yourself, I nodded my head. I have been teaching you in each of these instances!"

References

Achinstein, B., & Ogawa, R. T. (2006). (In)fidelity: what the resistance of new teachers reveals about professional principles and prescriptive educational policies. *Harvard Educational Review, 76*(1), 30–63.

Anderson, J. (2014). Forging new opportunities for problem solving in Australian mathematics classrooms through the first national mathematics curriculum. In Y. Li & G. Lappan (Eds.), *Mathematics curriculum in school education*. Dordrecht: Springer.

Anderson, L. W. (2002). Curricular alignment: a re-examination. *Theory Into Practice, 41*(4), 255–260.

Apple, M. W. (1993). *Official knowledge: democratic education in a conservative age*. London: Routledge.

Artigue, M. (2001). *Learning mathematics in a CAS environment: the genesis of a reflection about instrumentation and the dialectics between technical and conceptual work*. Paper presented at the CAME meeting, Utrecht, July 2001.

Bromme, R. (1994). Beyond subject matter: a psychological topology of teachers' professional knowledge. In R. Biehler, R. W. Scholz, R. Stässer, & B. Winkelmann (Eds.), *Didactics of mathematics as a scientific discipline* (pp. 73–78). Dordrecht: Kluwer.

Brown, M., & Hodgen, J. (2014). Curriculum, teachers and teaching: experiences from systemic and local curriculum change in England. In Y. Li & G. Lappan (Eds.), *Mathematics curriculum in school education*. Dordrecht: Springer.

Cai, J., Nie, B., Moyer, J. C., & Wang, N. (2014). Teaching mathematics using standards-based and traditional curricula: a case of variable ideas. In Y. Li & G. Lappan (Eds.), *Mathematics curriculum in school education*. Dordrecht: Springer.

Carpenter, T. P., Franke, M. L., Jacobs, V., & Fennema, E. (1998). A longitudinal study of invention and understanding in children's multidigit addition and subtraction. *Journal for Research in Mathematics Education, 29*, 3–20.

Chi, M. T. H. (1992). Conceptual change within and across ontological categories: examples from learning and discovery of science. In R. N. Giere (Ed.), *Minnesota studies in the philosophy of science: Vol. 15. Cognitive models of science* (pp. 129–186). Minneapolis: University of Minnesota Press.

Clandinin, D. J. M., & Connelly, F. (1992). Teacher as curriculum maker. In P. W. Jackson (Ed.), *Handbook of research on curriculum* (pp. 363–401). New York: Macmillan.

Clarke, S. (1997). Going mental—part 2: talking about mathematical thinking. *Primary Maths and Science*, 6–8.

Cochran-Smith, M., & Lytle, S. L. (1999). Relationships of knowledge and practice: teacher learning in communities. In A. Iran-Nejar & P. D. Pearson (Eds.), *Review of research in education* (pp. 249–305). Washington: AERA.

Cockcroft, W. H. (Chairperson) (1982). *Mathematics counts (Report of the committee of inquiry into the teaching of mathematics in schools)*. London: HMSO.

Cohen, D. K., Raudenbush, S. W., & Ball, D. L. (2003). Resource, instruction, and research. *Educational Evaluation and Policy Analysis, 25*(2), 119–142.

Cooper, B. (1985). *Renegotiating secondary school mathematics: a study of curriculum change and stability*. London: Falmer Press.

Cooper, B., & Dunne, M. (1998). Anyone for tennis? Social class differences in children's responses to national curriculum mathematics testing. *The Sociological Review, 46*(1), 115–148.

Curriculum and Textbook Workgroup (2002). *Draft report, ICMI comparative study*. Hong Kong: The University of Hong Kong.

Einstein, A. (1950). *Out of my later years*. New York: Philosophical Library.

Even, R., & Olsher, S. (2014). Teachers as participants in textbook development: the integrated mathematics wiki-book project. In Y. Li & G. Lappan (Eds.), *Mathematics curriculum in school education*. Dordrecht: Springer.

Freudenthal, H. (1991). *Revisiting mathematics education (China lectures)*. Dordrecht: Kluwer.

Fullan, M. (1999). *Change forces: the sequel*. London: The Falmer Press.

Fullan, M. (2007). *The meaning of educational change* (4th ed.). New York: Teachers College Press.

Fuson, K. C., & Li, Y. (2014). Learning paths and learning supports for conceptual addition and subtraction in the US common core state standards and in the Chinese standards. In Y. Li & G. Lappan (Eds.), *Mathematics curriculum in school education*. Dordrecht: Springer.

Fuson, K. C., Wearne, D., Hiebert, J., Human, P., Murray, H., Olivier, A., Carpenter, T. P., & Fennema, E. (1997). Children's conceptual structures for multi-digit numbers and methods of multi-digit addition and subtraction. *Journal for Research in Mathematics Education, 28*, 130–162.

Garnica, A. V. M. (2014). Brief considerations on educational directives and public policies in Brazil regarding mathematics education. In Y. Li & G. Lappan (Eds.), *Mathematics curriculum in school education*. Dordrecht: Springer.

Geiger, V., Goos, M., & Dole, S. (2014). Curriculum intent, teacher professional development and student learning in numeracy. In Y. Li & G. Lappan (Eds.), *Mathematics curriculum in school education*. Dordrecht: Springer.

Goodlad, J. I. (1979). *Curriculum inquiry: the study of curriculum practice*. New York: McGraw-Hill.

Howe, R. (2014). Three pillars of first grade mathematics and beyond. In Y. Li & G. Lappan (Eds.), *Mathematics curriculum in school education*. Dordrecht: Springer.

Huang, R., Ozel, Z. E. Y., Li, Y., & Osborne, R. V. (2014). Does classroom instruction stick to textbooks? A case study of fraction division. In Y. Li & G. Lappan (Eds.), *Mathematics curriculum in school education*. Dordrecht: Springer.

Kimpston, R. D. (1985). Curriculum fidelity and the implementation tasks employed by teachers: a research study. *Journal of Curriculum Studies, 17*(2), 185–195.

Kirk, D., & MacDonald, D. (2001). Teacher voice and ownership of curriculum change. *Journal of Curriculum Studies, 33*(5), 551–567.

Lam, C. C., Wong, N. Y., Ding, R., Li, S. P. T., & Ma, Y. (in press). Basic education mathematics curriculum reform in the greater Chinese region—trends and lessons learned. In B. Sriraman, J. Cai, K. Lee, L. Fan, Y. Shimuzu, L. C. Sam, & K. Subramanium (Eds.), *The first sourcebook on Asian research in mathematics education: China, Korea, Singapore, Japan, Malaysia, & India*. Charlotte: Information Age.

Li, X. (2011). *Quality of instructional explanation and its relation to student learning in primary mathematics*. Unpublished doctoral dissertation. Hong Kong: The Chinese University of Hong Kong.

Li, Y., Zhang, J., & Ma, T. (2014). School mathematics textbook design and development practices in China. In Y. Li & G. Lappan (Eds.), *Mathematics curriculum in school education*. Dordrecht: Springer.

Lopez-Real, F., & Leung, A. (2006). Dragging as a conceptual tool in dynamic geometry environments. *International Journal of Mathematics in Science and Technology, 37*(6), 665–679.

Marsh, C. J., & Willis, G. (2007). *Curriculum: alternative approaches, ongoing issues* (4th ed.). Upper Saddle River: Merrill Prentice Hall.

Marsh, J. (2004). *Key concepts for understanding curriculum* (3rd ed.). London: Routledge Falmer.

Martone, A., & Sireci, S. G. (2009). Evaluating alignment between curriculum, assessment, and instruction. *Review of Educational Research, 79*(4), 1332–1361.

McCaffrey, D. F., Hamilton, L. S., Stecher, B. M., Klein, S. P., Bugliari, D., & Robyn, A. (2001). Interactions among instructional practices, curriculum, and student achievement: the case of standards-based high school mathematics. *Journal for Research in Mathematics Education, 32*(5), 493–517.

National Council of Teachers of Mathematics (NCTM) (1989). *Curriculum and evaluation standards for school mathematics*. Reston: Author.

O'Donnell, C. L. (2008). Defining, conceptualizing and measuring fidelity of implementation and its relationship to outcomes in K-12 curriculum intervention research. *Review of Educational Research, 78*(1), 33–84.

Pang, J. S. (2014). Changes to the Korean mathematics curriculum: expectations and challenges. In Y. Li & G. Lappan (Eds.), *Mathematics curriculum in school education*. Dordrecht: Springer.

Priestley, M. (2002). Global discourses and national reconstruction: the impact of globalization on curriculum policy. *The Curriculum Journal, 13*(1), 121–138.

Reys, B. J. (2014). Mathematics curriculum policies and practices in the U.S.: the common core state standards initiative. In Y. Li & G. Lappan (Eds.), *Mathematics curriculum in school education*. Dordrecht: Springer.

Schön, D. A. (1983). *The reflective practitioner: how professionals think in action*. London: Temple Smith.

Senk, S. L., Thompson, D. R., & Wernet, J. (2014). Curriculum and achievement in algebra 2: influences of textbooks and teachers on students' learning about functions. In Y. Li & G. Lappan (Eds.), *Mathematics curriculum in school education*. Dordrecht: Springer.

Shafer, M. C. (2014). The impact of a standards-based mathematics curriculum on classroom instruction and student performance: the case of mathematics in context. In Y. Li & G. Lappan (Eds.), *Mathematics curriculum in school education*. Dordrecht: Springer.

Shulman, L. (1987). Knowledge and teaching: foundations of new reform. *Harvard Educational Review, 57*, 1–22.

Simon, M. (1995). Reconstructing mathematics pedagogy from a constructivist perspective. *Journal for Research in Mathematics Education, 26*(2), 114–145.

Sinclair, N., & de Freitas, E. (2014). The virtual curriculum: new ontologies for a mobile mathematics. In Y. Li & G. Lappan (Eds.), *Mathematics curriculum in school education*. Dordrecht: Springer.

Star, J. R., & Rittle-Johnson, B. (2008). Flexibility in problem solving: the case of equation solving. *Learning and Instruction, 18*, 565–579.

Stein, M. K., Kaufman, J., & Kisa, M. T. (2014). Mathematics teacher development in the context of district managed curriculum. In Y. Li & G. Lappan (Eds.), *Mathematics curriculum in school education*. Dordrecht: Springer.

Stephens, M. (2014). The Australian curriculum: mathematics—how did it come about? What challenges does it present for teachers and for the teaching of mathematics? In Y. Li & G. Lappan (Eds.), *Mathematics curriculum in school education*. Dordrecht: Springer.

Stigler, J. W., & Hiebert, J. (1999). *The teaching gap: best ideas from the world's teachers for improving education in the classroom*. New York: Free Press.

Sullivan, P. & Wood, T. (Eds.) (2008). *International handbook of mathematics teacher education: Volume 1. knowledge and beliefs in mathematics teaching and teaching development*. Rotterdam: Sense Publishers.

Synder, J., Bolin, F., & Zumwalt, K. (1992). Curriculum implementation. In P. W. Jackson (Ed.), *Handbook of research on curriculum* (pp. 402–435). New York: Macmillan.

Takahashi, A. (2014). Supporting the effective implementation of a new mathematics curriculum: a case study of school-based lesson study at a Japanese public elementary school. In Y. Li & G. Lappan (Eds.), *Mathematics curriculum in school education*. Dordrecht: Springer.

Tam, H. P., Wong, N.-Y., Lam, C.-C., Ma, Y., Lu, L., & Lu, Y.-J. (2014). Decision making in the mathematics curricula among the Chinese mainland, Hong Kong, and Taiwan. In Y. Li & G. Lappan (Eds.), *Mathematics curriculum in school education*. Dordrecht: Springer.

Threlfall, J. (2000). Mental calculation strategies. In T. Rowland & C. Morgan (Eds.), *Research in mathematics education* (Vol. 2, pp. 77–90). London: British Society for Research into Learning Mathematics.

Travers, K. J. & Westbury, I. (Eds.) (1989). *The IEA study of mathematics I: analysis of mathematics curricula*. Oxford: Pergamon.

Tsang, K. W. F. (2005). Invented strategies versus standard algorithms, creativity versus formality. In N. Y. Wong (Ed.), *Revisiting mathematics education in Hong Kong for the new millennium* (pp. 141–155). Hong Kong: Hong Kong Association for Mathematics Education.

van den Heuvel-Panhuizen, M. (2001). Realistic mathematics education in the Netherlands. In J. Anghileri (Ed.), *Principles and practices in arithmetic teaching: innovative approaches for the primary classroom* (pp. 49–63). Buckingham: Open University Press.

van Zanten, M., & van den Heuvel-Panhuizen, M. (2014). Freedom of design: the multiple faces of subtraction in Dutch primary school textbooks. In Y. Li & G. Lappan (Eds.), *Mathematics curriculum in school education*. Dordrecht: Springer.

Wong, K. Y., Koyama, M., & Lee, K.-H. (2014). Mathematics curriculum policies: a framework with case studies from Japan, Korea, and Singapore. In Y. Li & G. Lappan (Eds.), *Mathematics curriculum in school education*. Dordrecht: Springer.

Wong, N. Y. (2006). From "Entering the way" to "Exiting the way": in search of a bridge to span "Basic skills" and "Process abilities". In F. K. S. Leung, K.-D. Graf, & F. J. Lopez-Real (Eds.), *Mathematics education in different cultural traditions: a comparative study of East Asia and the West* (pp. 111–128). New York: Springer.

Wong, N. Y. (2009). Exemplary mathematics lessons: what lessons we can learn from them? *ZDM—The International Journal on Mathematics Education, 41,* 379–384.

Wong, N. Y., & Tang, K. C. (2012). Mathematics education in Hong Kong under colonial rule. *BSHM Bulletin: Journal of the British Society for the History of Mathematics, 27,* 1–8.

Wong, N. Y., Han, J. W., & Lee, P. Y. (2004). The mathematics curriculum: towards globalisation or westernisation? In L. Fan, N. Y. Wong, J. Cai, & S. Li (Eds.), *How Chinese learn mathematics: perspectives from insiders* (pp. 27–70). Singapore: World Scientific Press.

Wong, N. Y., Lam, C. C., Sun, X., & Chan, A. M. Y. (2009). From "exploring the middle zone" to "constructing a bridge": experimenting the spiral bianshi mathematics curriculum. *International Journal of Science and Mathematical Education, 7*(2), 363–382.

Wong, N. Y., Lam, C. C., & Chan, A. M. Y. (2012a). Teaching with variation. In Y. Li & R. Huang (Eds.), *How Chinese teach mathematics and improve teaching* (pp. 105–119). New York: Routledge.

Wong, N. Y., Wong, W. Y., & Wong, E. W. Y. (2012b). What do the Chinese value in (mathematics) education? *ZDM—The International Journal on Mathematics Education, 44*(1), 9–19.

Zhang, D. (2005). Educational mathematics: the educational state of mathematics. *Journal of Mathematics Education, 14*(3), 1–4 [in Chinese].

Improving the Alignment Between Values, Principles and Classroom Realities

Malcolm Swan

Abstract The curricular reforms described in this book are wide-ranging and are driven by many external factors and value systems. They usually begin with a vision of 'how things should be', but as we have seen, their implementation is often a travesty of their aims. In this chapter I begin with a synthesis of the values exhibited in curricula across the world, then go on to analyse the kinds of classroom activity that are implied when these are taken seriously. This process will be illustrated through a specific case—a national consultation in England that attempted to elicit, prioritise and exemplify apparently competing values held by mathematics educators. I argue that the misalignment of the intended and enacted curriculum is at least partly due to the almost universal lack of vivid exemplification in curriculum specifications and consequent reductive interpretations of them by their users. An argument is thus made for a serious systematic design-research effort into the production of beautiful examples that illustrate and effectively communicate our core values to the key educational stakeholders.

Keywords Alignment · Classroom reality · Curriculum reform · Principle · Value

Introduction

Across the world politicians are demanding that more citizens should study mathematics to a higher level than ever before. The reforms described in this book appear primarily to arise from a desire for change in:

- *Economic competitiveness.* Most nations view the quality of mathematics education in schools as an indicator of their economic prospects in the 21st century. International comparisons of standards are rife, and the uses and abuses made of TIMSS and PISA studies in arguing for reform are reported in many chapters.
- *Student participation and dispositions towards mathematics.* There is a great concern in many countries that students cease to study mathematics at the earliest

M. Swan (✉)
University of Nottingham, Nottingham, UK
e-mail: malcolm.swan@nottingham.ac.uk

Y. Li, G. Lappan (eds.), *Mathematics Curriculum in School Education*,
Advances in Mathematics Education, DOI 10.1007/978-94-007-7560-2_29,
© Springer Science+Business Media Dordrecht 2014

possible opportunity and that even those who are most successful have such negative dispositions towards the subject that they avoid scientific careers. The negative correlation between attitude and performance in TIMSS is striking. This is attributed in many cases to the way the subject is taught and is evidenced by attempts to reduce the amount of content (such as in the 2011 changes in Korea) and increase the emphasis on inquiry-based learning, such as those currently being promoted across the EU (Rocard 2007).

- *Control and coherence.* In countries with a history of state autonomy, such as the USA and Australia, new curricula have been introduced in an attempt to centralise and regain control of the curriculum. This is usually seen as a necessary precursor to further major reform (e.g. Reys, Anderson, this volume).

For these reasons, curriculum documents are created to specify those aspects of Mathematics that are to be valued and taught. There are, almost universally, major mismatches between the intended curriculum described in policy documents, the tested curriculum embodied in examinations, and the implemented curriculum taught in most classrooms. Burkhardt (this volume) notes the main causes: "underestimating the challenge; misalignment and mixed messages; unrealistic pace of change; pressure with inadequate support; inadequate evaluation in depth; and inadequate design and 'engineering'". A recent statement by a Dutch politician on the release of a new curriculum specification illustrates the problem rather vividly: "The hard work has been done now all you have to do is implement it" (van den Akker 2012). Other authors in this volume describe how centralised, 'top down' reforms have mostly resulted in only superficial implementations (Brown, Cavanah), whereas the more successful cases have been mostly local, and underpinned with sustained professional development and aligned assessment and curriculum materials (e.g. Hoe, Brown, Ma).

In this chapter, I focus on the challenges that influencing and implementing policy reform offers to curriculum and assessment designers. I look again at the values that are commonly emphasised in policy documents and consider the implications that these pose for the design of classroom activities. For me, the greatest research needs lay at the interface of policy and implementation, in particular the almost universal lack of quality exemplification in policy documents. Such documents begin by conveying 'worthy values', with which most agree, including processes (or 'practices') that students should learn to perform, and the hierarchical content domain that students should 'master' ('scope and sequence'). Unfortunately, it is usually only the latter that is assessed in most high stakes examinations and little attention is paid to the design challenges of drawing connections between values, principles, practices and content in curriculum implementation. In addition, for reforms to have impact, there should be some succinct attempt to articulate the research-based principles that underlie effective teaching of the various curriculum elements.

The Nature of Values

Values may be characterized as those preferences, principles, and convictions that act to guide our actions and the standards by which we judge particular actions to be desirable. (Halstead and Taylor 2000, p. 2). They are what we consider 'ought to be the case', and as such have an almost moral dimension. They may be held to different degrees, from simple preferences, reflecting tastes or sentiments, to more complex organised states of commitment and prioritization (Atweh 2008; Krathwohl et al. 1964). Attitudes become values as they are thoughtfully chosen, prized, cherished, affirmed and acted on repeatedly (Raths et al. 1987, p. 199). This is not a straightforward process, particularly when values conflict. A teacher may simultaneously value opportunities to develop a deep understanding of mathematics, to broaden students' awareness of its applications, of its cultural and historical evolution, of the need to cover content and to develop the fluency and speed needed for examination success. Prioritizing these, particularly in a results-oriented culture can lead to painful and difficult decisions and inconsistencies between values and actions (Bishop et al. 2003).

Values may be both individually and culturally based. Education systems are often determined by tacit cultural values that cannot be ignored when, for example, making international comparisons. In a recent review of mathematics teaching in higher attaining countries, it was argued that high attainment was more closely linked to cultural values than to specific mathematics teaching practices (Askew et al. 2010).

While the pedagogical practices clearly vary considerably between nations (Schoenfeld, this volume), the aspirations exhibited in Mathematics curricula reform documents are often strikingly similar (Askew et al. 2010; Stigler et al. 1999; Stigler and Hiebert 1999). They typically emphasise the societal, personal and intrinsic value of studying mathematics.

In the current English national curriculum: Mathematics is deemed essential for 'national prosperity', 'public decision-making' and 'participation in the knowledge economy'; It equips pupils with 'uniquely powerful ways to describe, analyse and change the world' and can 'stimulate moments of pleasure and wonder'; and it provides an 'international language' that transcends cultural boundaries and is therefore worth studying 'as a means for solving problems' and 'for its own sake' (QCA 2007). Mathematics is even seen to offer opportunities for spiritual, moral, social, and cultural development (DfEE/QCA 1999). The current national documents then go on to describe the importance of developing key 'concepts' (competence, creativity, applications and implications, critical understanding) and 'processes' (representing, analyzing, interpreting and evaluating, communicating and reflecting), before listing the content to be covered. This list is extensive and, currently, the only one taken seriously in assessment. As I write this, however, the national curriculum is being rewritten under political direction that it is to be focused on only 'core knowledge', with a stronger emphasis on 'fluency in arithmetic' (DfE 2013). 'Key concepts' and 'key processes' are being replaced with more general statements requiring reasoning and problem solving.

In the US, The NCTM Standards have aspirations similar to the current English national curriculum. It emphasises that mathematics is important for 'one's personal life,' as part of our 'cultural heritage', for 'the workplace', and for 'the scientific and technical community' and then details the processes of problem solving, communicating, reasoning, making connections, concepts, procedures and dispositions (NCTM 1989, 2000). The recent Common Core State Standards for Mathematics (NGA and CCSSO 2010) emphasises the importance of both technical procedures and understanding, along with the development of eight 'mathematical practices' that include making sense, reasoning, constructing arguments, modelling, choosing and using appropriate tools, attending to precision, making use of structure and regularity in repeated reasoning.

The high performing countries along the Pacific Rim have values that resonate with these. In Singapore, for example, the current curriculum has mathematical problem solving at its heart, and is summarized by the five inter-related components of concepts, skills, processes, attitudes, and metacognition (Soh 2008). The concepts and skills aspects are subdivided into mathematical content areas (e.g. numerical, algebraic); the processes into reasoning, communication, connections, applications, modelling; meta-cognition into monitoring of one's own thinking and self-regulation; and attitudes into beliefs, interest, appreciation, confidence and perseverance. In reaction to the transmission styles of the past, the Chinese national curriculum reform stresses the importance of students becoming active and creative students. "'Exploration', 'co-operation', 'interaction', and 'participation' are central leitmotifs of its theory of student learning (Halpin 2010, p. 259). Citing the general secretary (2004), Guan and Meng (2007, p. 595) state that:

> The form of instructions should no longer follow the "teacher-talk, student-listen" model, rather, there should be dynamic interactivity, an engaged cooperation between teachers and students. Instructions should focus on a student's comprehensive development instead of exam-oriented education.

Lew (2008) summarises the 'ultimate goal' of the Korean curriculum as to cultivate students with creative and autonomous minds by achieving three aims: (i) to understand basic mathematical concepts and principles through concrete and everyday experiences; (ii) to foster mathematical modelling abilities through the solving of various problems posed with and without mathematics, and (iii) to keep a positive attitude about mathematics and mathematics learning by emphasizing a connection between mathematics and the real world.

A Synthesis of Values

From these and other documents, it is possible to synthesise five distinct aspects of learning mathematics: (i) developing fluency when recalling facts and performing skills; (ii) interpreting concepts and representations; (iii) developing strategies for investigation and problem solving; (iv) awareness of the nature and values of the educational system and (v) an appreciation of the power of mathematics in society.

The table below (Swan 2006; Swan and Lacey 2008b) expands and develops these categories in order to explore appropriate types of classroom activity that might result. Mathematics teaching will look very different depending on the relative value that is ascribed to these purposes.

The rows in this table resonate with complementary theories/metaphors of learning. The first row is the focus of 'behaviourists', who emphasise the value of terminology and fluency in the performance of 'skills'. This trend is evident in learning activities that break 'mathematics' up into 'subskills' and 'key facts' that are taught until fluency is attained. Complex skills are then built by learning sequences of subskills. The process of learning is generally conducted by clear exposition, followed by consolidation and practice. The second and third rows reflect the focus of 'constructivists' who recognise the value of encouraging students to construct concepts and strategies through exploration or creativity and discussion. Also reflected is the emphasis on metacognitive aspects in monitoring decisions in the course of problem solving. The fourth and final rows reflect the current focus of 'social constructivists' who emphasise that students should appreciate the way mathematics has evolved historically, how it is used by the world, and how they may use their mathematics to gain power over their own environment. This also includes students reflecting on their own role as a student in an educational environment and combines elements of metacognition, in which a student develops an awareness of effective personal strategies for learning, with an awareness of the social values and discourses of education. The intention is also that students become aware of the nature of the assessment system and how they may portray their own abilities to their best advantage when presenting themselves to the world. On the right of Table 1, I have begun to list a few of the activities implied by these outcomes. It is immediately clear that most textbooks (at least in England) do not embody the full range of activity types.

The inclusion of learning objectives is usually non contentious in general curriculum descriptions. We want students to be able to perform in all of these aspects. As they become elaborated and incorporated into implemented curricula, however, the time and emphasis each is given becomes an issue. There are also potential tensions and incompatibilities in the teaching methods that need to be employed.

What Types of Classroom Activity Are Implied by These Values?

Teaching methods for developing factual knowledge and procedural fluency and for developing conceptual understanding are quite different.[1] By facts we mean items of information that are unconnected or arbitrary, including notational conventions (Cockcroft 1982). By fluency we mean the ability to carry out a mathematical procedure quickly and efficiently without effortful thought. In both cases, individual

---

[1] In England, the current draft national curriculum states that 'varied and frequent' practice for fluency *will lead* to improved conceptual understanding. This paragraph explains why this may not be the case.

Table 1 Values in learning mathematics and implications for classroom activities

Outcomes	Examples of types of mathematical learning activity implied
Fluency in recalling facts and performing skills	Memorising names and notations
	Practising algorithms and procedures for fluency and 'mastery'
Conceptual understanding and interpretations for representations	Discriminating between examples and non-examples of concepts
	Generating representations of concepts
	Constructing networks of relationships between concepts
	Interpreting and translating between representations of concepts
Strategies for investigation, problem solving and modelling	Formulating situations and problems for investigation
	Constructing, sharing, refining, and comparing strategies for exploration and solution
	Monitoring one's own progress during problem solving and investigation
	Interpreting, evaluating solutions and communicating results
Awareness of the nature and values of the educational system	Recognising different purposes of learning mathematics
	Developing appropriate strategies for learning/reviewing mathematics
	Appreciating aspects of performance valued by the examination system
Appreciation of the power of mathematics in society	Appreciating mathematics as human creativity (+ historical aspects)
	Creating and critiquing 'mathematical models' of situations
	Appreciating uses/abuses of mathematics in social contexts
	Using mathematics to gain power over problems in one's own life

work on exercises in which the facts and procedures are used repeatedly with immediate feedback are undoubtedly helpful, though one might argue that all such practice should be set within the context of meaningful, substantial problems. The development of conceptual structures, (which of course should underpin procedural knowledge) requires the careful negotiation of meaning in which objects are compared and classified, definitions are built, and representations are created, shared, interpreted and compared. These are essentially social, collaborative activities. There is considerable research evidence to show, for example, the superiority of conflict discussion over guided discovery methods for concept development. (Bell 1993; Swan 2006). The creation of a *network* of connections between concepts requires non-linear exploratory work—difficult to design and embody in hierarchical curricula specifications.

The fundamental differences between teaching for concept development and for problem solving strategies are less well understood. In a current project for which we are developing formative assessment lessons to support the Common Core State Standards in the US, we are discriminating carefully between these two types of lessons (Swan et al. 2012). A concept-focused lesson concerns interpreting and representing a predetermined 'big idea', such as place value or proportion. Where applications or 'word problems' are used in such a lesson, they are purely illustrative. In a problem-solving lesson, however, students are offered a substantial problem to tackle for which no solution method is obviously apparent. The purpose of the lesson is for students to develop the ability to *select*, *apply* and *compare* appropriate mathematical methods. In a true problem-solving lesson the teacher therefore cannot predict which methods the students will choose. We do know, however, that students are unlikely to choose methods that they have only just acquired. There is often a several year gap between being introduced to a method and being able to select and use it autonomously. We also know that students usually prefer more 'tangible' numerical or graphical approaches to algebraic ones. This presents the teacher with a dilemma—how does one reveal the power of an algebraic approach without 'forcing' students to use it, in which case the lesson is no longer a true problem-solving lesson, but a mere exercise in algebra? One possible solution is to follow up students' own attempts to solve a problem with a critiquing activity. We offer students a range of pre-prepared alternative attempts at solving the problem, all of which are imperfect, and invite students to try and improve and complete these. As different approaches are then contrasted and compared in whole class discussions (akin to the Japanese practice of 'neriage'), ideas are combined and refined into collaborative solutions.

Currently, we are also elaborating a limited number of different task *genres* that seem essential for concept development. All involve collaborative work in which students create a shared product, for example, posters describing their ideas. Research is needed to elicit the design principles for their effective construction. Examples are:

- *Classifying and defining.* Students are presented with a collection of mathematical objects (numbers, expressions, graphs etc), and are asked to create /or apply classifications devised by others. They discriminate, recognise properties and develop mathematical language and definitions.
- *Interpreting and translating between multiple representations.* Students are given a collection of cards that show different representations of mathematical objects—words, diagrams, algebraic symbols, tables, graphs. They share interpretations, compare and group the cards in ways that made connections between underlying concepts. They show how one may be transformed into another by linking cards. The discussion of common 'misconceptions' is encouraged by the inclusion of distracters.
- *Creating and solving variants of mathematical problems.* Students devise new problems or variants of existing problems, prepare solutions then challenge other students to solve them. They offer support when the solver becomes stuck. This promotes awareness of the structures underlying problems, and focuses attention on the doing and undoing processes in mathematics.

- *Analyzing and challenging generalizations.* Students are given statements or assertions that typically embody general principles or common 'misconceptions'. (Such as "The shape with the greater area has a greater perimeter", "the more digits in the number the greater is its value"). Their task is to challenge these and define domains for their validity.

Teaching for 'awareness' is a further distinctive curriculum goal. This includes cultivating students' awareness of how mathematics fits together as a discipline, how best students may learn something new and how they may best communicate their ideas to others, for example in a high stakes examination. It also includes those 'metacognitive aspects of learning, such as 'monitoring one's own thinking' while solving a problem (as referred to in, for example, the Singaporean National Curriculum). It is widely recognised that when students remain unaware of the purpose of an activity, they often pay undue attention to unimportant or superficial aspects of it. They may, for example, focus more on the appearance of their work or the coverage of material rather than the quality and depth of reasoning employed. Twenty years ago, we conducted a curriculum research project to develop a range of reflective experiences in real classroom settings through which students might acquire such awareness (Bell et al. 1993). These usually required students to change their classroom roles, from consumers of learning to task designers, assessors, textbook authors, and so on. Examples of effective curriculum activities included:

- Preparing summary materials from which other, younger, students could learn.
- Conducting student-student interviews on what has been learned.
- Construct tests of other students' understanding (and mark schemes).
- Planning and teaching a topic to students from another class.
- Planning an outline for a new textbook; deciding which concepts are important and describing how these link together.
- Observing other students working and decide how their problem solving approaches might be improved.
- Conducting 'mini debates' on general learning issues such as: "Do we learn more from working on a few hard problems or from working on many short exercises?"
- Assessing their own progress against given criteria.

Finally, few would dispute that developing an appreciation of the evolution, importance and power of mathematics in society is a laudable goal for the mathematics curriculum. Across the world, however, this only occupies a small part of a teacher's normal agenda. In Science teaching in the UK, there has been a lively debate about the relative emphases that should be on students appreciating the significance and impact of scientific ideas (such as pollution and climate change) and students doing their own science. A similar debate has not been evident in Mathematics. Notably, there is almost no teaching of the cultural history of Mathematics in English schools. Over the years, however, there have been a number of projects across the world to introduce real world modelling and simulation into the curriculum. Recently, for example, we designed a lesson sequence in which students are invited to role play a town planning situation in which their task is to spend a given budget on reducing the number of road accidents in the town (Swan and Pead 2008). They are supplied with a computer database showing the locations and police records of the accidents and their task is to present a convincing case to the town council by analysing these. The activity, which is designed to take about 5 hours, models how planners have actually used mathematics to reduce road accidents by 25 % in one English city. It is interesting to note that this particular activity is now being taken up and used in Japan to plug a perceived gap in the curriculum.

The Perceived Mismatch Between Ideal and Implemented Values in England

In England, there is a clear mismatch between the values and principles held by the educational community and those implemented in classrooms. A few years ago, I chaired a national consultation, commissioned by the National Centre for Excellence in Teaching Mathematics (NCETM), to review and describe the values and practices considered to be most important and effective by the community (Swan and Lacey 2008a).[2] This consultation involved 150 mathematics educators, with representation drawn mostly from secondary teachers, adult education teachers and teacher educators. An initial conference was held to stimulate debate by: (i) identifying, confirming and agreeing values and principles that underpin the effective teaching and learning of mathematics; (ii) illustrating, through examples, how practice may reflect and interpret these values and principles, and (iii) exploring the factors that inhibit or modify their implementation. This was followed by a series of six one-day regional colloquia that were designed to test levels of agreement with the values and principles articulated at the initial conference, and to amend and refine them as appropriate, as well as to begin to build a collection of lesson accounts that illustrate what the values and principles may look like in practice. These days began with the participants writing descriptions of the most inspirational mathematics lesson they had ever experienced. Later these were discussed in relation to the values they revealed.

In both the initial conference and subsequent colloquia, there was broad agreement as to the type of learning outcomes valued and the different types of classroom activity that these outcomes might imply, as summarized in Table 1 above. Participants were asked to compare their "vision for an ideal mathematics curriculum" with the values that are implied by the "curriculum that is currently implemented in most schools and other settings". In Table 2, I have separated out the teachers' responses from those obtained from university educators and other participants. The results show a remarkable consistency: both sets of participants consider that fluency in recalling facts and performing skills currently dominates the curriculum while in fact it should be the least valued of the five outcomes. Both sets of participants also agree that conceptual understanding and strategies for investigation and problem solving should take up the most curriculum time.

---

[2]Although the report of the project was 2008, the analysis presented here is new and previously unpublished.

Table 2 The values of teachers compared with the values of university and other educators. Mean ratings showing how frequently mathematics respondents felt that lessons should *ideally* include each learning outcome and also how frequently mathematics lessons, *actually do* reflect each learning outcome (1 = hardly ever, 4 = almost every lesson). Standard deviations are in brackets. The final column shows the proportion of lesson accounts that participants allocated to each category

Purposes	Mean ratings (S.D.) Teachers in schools and colleges (n = 45)		Mean ratings (S.D.) University and other educators (n = 89)		% of lesson descriptions in each category
	Ideal	Actual	Ideal	Actual	
A. Fluency in recalling facts and performing skills	2.58 (0.75)	3.61 (0.54)	2.60 (0.78)	3.81 (0.5)	33 %
B. Conceptual understanding and interpretations for representations	3.56 (0.59)	2.29 (0.59)	3.49 (0.55)	1.99 (0.66)	60 %
C. Strategies for investigation and problem solving	3.69 (0.63)	2.18 (0.76)	3.71 (0.48)	2.00 (0.70)	61 %
D. Awareness of the nature and values of the educational system	3.13 (0.76)	1.70 (0.85)	3.02 (0.71)	1.59 (0.86)	11 %
E. Appreciation of the power of mathematics in society	3.13 (0.79)	1.34 (0.68)	3.05 (0.71)	1.28 (0.57)	23 %

Each colloquium day started with an invitation to each participant to write an account of a memorable, inspirational mathematics lesson, either taught or observed. Over seventy rich lesson descriptions emerged. These offer an alternative perspective on participants' values. As may be seen from the final column in Table 2, most of the lessons were related to conceptual understanding and strategies for investigation and problem solving. Each lesson description was coded and analyzed. In almost all of the lessons reported, students were clearly actively engaged in constructing their own mathematical meanings and methods using the types of activities reported earlier. Below I briefly describe the categories and offer one or two examples of each. (Numbers in brackets refer to the number of examples of each type generated).

- *Students creating definitions* (5). E.g. Students were asked to bring a selection of reading books to school and they then discussed different ways of defining and measuring 'readability'.
- *Students comparing representations and solution methods* (15). E.g. Students sorted cards that contained different representations such as travel graphs and written descriptions of journeys.
- *Students generating their own examples and problems* (10). E.g. Students devising their own financial problems, equations, probability tasks, geometry questions and 'magic tricks'. Other students then had to try to solve or explain these. When

solvers became stuck or were unable to understand the problems, they asked the originators for help or clarification.

- *Students justifying and proving conjectures* (15). E.g. Students set out to find the number of factors of $n!$ (factorial n). After an initial conjecture that the answer was $2n - 1$ (this works when $n = 1, 2, 3, 4, 5$), students found that this failed for $n = 6$. This was resolved in discussion by relating the number of factors to the prime factorization.
- *Students tackling ill-defined problems* (2). E.g. Students were given incomplete problems and were asked what additional information they needed to know. They estimated the missing data and then attempted to solve them.
- *Students learning through practical work* (23). Examples included the use of measuring and weighing devices to check estimations; plastic strips to explore properties of triangles; plastic cubes for constructing geometric solids; paper folding for exploring properties of polygons; and even a 'washing line' to help order statements written on cards. Five participants also emphasised the use of students' own bodies to represent mathematical objects and/or as sources for data. One example involved students standing outside on a grid to represent data points on a graph. Students positioned themselves according to their shoe sizes and hand spans. The resulting human scatterplot was filmed from above and played back afterwards for analysis.
- *Students working with electronic resources* (12). E.g. Students began by imagining and mentally manipulating sets of parallel lines, and then subsequently constructed their own geometric computer animations. This was linked to the Hungarian mathematician, Bolyai's excitement at his discovery of hyperbolic geometry.

In reporting this brief summary of the lesson descriptions, I hope to have captured some of the richness and excitement that was conveyed by participants. Throughout, the overriding theme that emerged was one of students' active involvement and enthusiasm in constructing their own mathematics. What seemed to be missing from the lessons reported by participants, yet was clearly valued, was the power of mathematics in society. Perhaps, as noted earlier, this was simply due to the fact that this aspect is almost entirely missing from mathematics classrooms in England.

It should also be noted that the disconnection between the values endorsed by participants through these lesson accounts and the reality in most classrooms was universally recognised. Participants identified four related obstacles to change: the narrow set of values implied by the nature and content of national tests and examinations; the poor quality of textbooks and other resources (many produced by examiners that work for awarding bodies); the social acceptance that it is 'OK' to be mathematically incompetent; and teachers' own lack of confidence in their subject knowledge and fear of stepping 'out of line' with local interpretations of national inspection criteria.

Principles for Teaching and Learning

Unlike the values listed above, where arguments over relative worth are subjective, principles for learning have been established on the basis of more solid research. These are not normally included in curriculum documents as it is declared that the specified curriculum should only specify *what* is taught, not *how* it should be taught. This argument, however, dodges our responsibility to help teachers apply the wisdom of research to daily practice. Without such principles, we find external pressures (such as those from senior managers in schools) compel teachers to aim for short term, superficial goals, such as 'curriculum coverage' rather than deeper learning.

In the national consultation, participants were also asked to develop a set of research-based generic principles that they believed would improve the quality of lessons in mathematics. In preparation for this, the list of principles in Table 3, drawn from our previous research (Swan 2006), were offered as a starting point. Participants were asked to critique this list and add their own modifications. 64 % (46/72) of participants totally agreed with the initial version of the principles presented, 32 % mainly agreed, expressing reservations whilst 4 % expressed particular concerns. Of those who expressed concern, 35 % (9/26) related to the use of technology and 23 % cited concerns about the confusion that may be caused when exposing and discussing common misconceptions. The principles were subsequently revised, based on suggestions from participants. These revisions are also shown in the table.

Space does not permit me to describe the many research foundations for this list here, but they are considerable (for example Askew 2001). The choices of principles, however, were made deliberately in order to challenge common practices that undermine effective practices. For example the final statement is an attempt to counteract the common request from senior school managers for teachers to list the objectives on the board in front of the class at the start of each lesson. As such it is a political tool to assist teachers in counteracting such pressures. In a mischievous mood, we asked participants to list the most *unhelpful* principles that they have heard articulated. These usually contain just enough validity to undermine our best efforts to reform school practices. Here is their list (without comment):

- Learn how to do it first—understanding can always come later.
- Practice makes perfect, mnemonics and short cuts are helpful.
- Reinforcement/consolidation tasks improve understanding.
- There is a correct way to teach, an optimal sequence to learn.
- Learning must be preceded by instruction.
- Share lesson objectives with students beforehand. Lessons should be in 3-parts.
- Cover the syllabus (at all costs).
- Presentation and neatness are very important.
- There is a right way to solve problems.
- Knowing the answer is important.
- Keep learners busy. Learners go off-task if they talk.
- Don't confuse learners by showing them incorrect methods.
- Use technology wherever possible.

Table 3 Principles for the effective teaching of mathematics. Final changes or additions made after consultation with participants are shown in italics

Teaching is more effective when it...

builds on the knowledge learners already have	This means developing formative assessment techniques and adapting our teaching to accommodate individual learning needs.
exposes and discusses common misconceptions *and other surprising phenomena*	Learning activities should expose current thinking, create 'tensions' by confronting learners with inconsistencies and surprises, and allow opportunities for resolution through discussion.
uses higher-order questions	Questioning is more effective when it promotes explanation, application and synthesis rather than mere recall.
makes appropriate use of *whole class interactive teaching, individual work and* cooperative small group work	*Collaborative group work is more effective after learners have been given an opportunity for individual reflection.* Activities are more effective when they encourage critical, constructive discussion, rather than argumentation or uncritical acceptance. Shared goals and group accountability are important.
creates connections between topics *both within and beyond mathematics and with the real world*	Learners often find it difficult to generalise and transfer their learning to other topics and contexts. Related concepts (such as division, fraction and ratio) remain unconnected. Effective teachers build bridges between ideas.
encourages reasoning rather than 'answer getting'	Often, learners are more concerned with what they have 'done' than with what they have learned. It is better to aim for depth than for superficial 'coverage'.
uses rich, collaborative tasks	The tasks we use should be accessible, extendable, encourage decision-making, promote discussion, encourage creativity, encourage 'what if' and 'what if not?' questions.
uses *resources, including* technology, in *creative and* appropriate ways	*ICT offers new ways to engage with mathematics. At its best it is dynamic and visual: relationships become more tangible. ICT can provide feedback on actions and enhance interactivity and learner autonomy. Through its connectivity, ICT offers the means to access and share resources and—even more powerfully—the means by which learners can share their ideas within and across classrooms.*
confronts difficulties rather than seeks to avoid or pre-empt them	*Effective teaching challenges learners and has high expectations of them. It does not seek to 'smooth the path' but creates realistic obstacles to be overcome. Confidence, persistence and learning are not attained through repeating successes, but by struggling with difficulties.*
develops mathematical language through communicative activities	*Mathematics is a language that enables us to describe and model situations, think logically, frame and sustain arguments and communicate ideas with precision. Learners do not know mathematics until they can 'speak' it. Effective teaching therefore focuses on the communicative aspects of mathematics by developing oral and written mathematical language.*
recognises both what has been learned and also how it has been learned	*What is to be learned cannot always be stated prior to the learning experience. After a learning event, however, it is important to reflect on the learning that has taken place, making this as explicit and memorable as possible. Effective teachers will also reflect on the ways in which learning has taken place, so that learners develop their own capacity to learn.*

Implications for Research

The values, principles and sample lesson activities articulated within the consultation seem to go to the heart of what it means to be mathematical. Most curricula specifications are sterile artefacts that, whatever the aspirations of the 'worthy words' in their introductions, continue to be interpreted by politicians, assessors and teachers in conservative, reductive ways. The descriptive language we use changes, but the reality in classrooms does not.

We need to develop a clearer vision of how the values, principles and content relate and the direct implications this has for the tasks we offer to students. Detailed exemplification is essential and this must be designed in a careful, systematic, research-based way. Here is not the place here to review research methodologies, but it seems clear to me that more serious effort needs to be devoted to *Design Research* approaches to curriculum development. Design research seeks the *transformation* of educational practices in typical classrooms, reducing the credibility gap between educational research and classroom practice through interventionist, iterative, theory-driven studies of designs in action (Burkhardt and Schoenfeld 2003; Kelly 2003; van den Akker et al. 2006). The main research question (in education) is 'How is this design (curriculum specification) interpreted and enacted by its intended audience (typical teachers and students), and how can it be redesigned and supported in ways that more fully realise our values?' Currently we are undertaking such an exercise in order to support the implementation of the Common Core State Standards in the US by the careful design of exemplary lessons (Swan et al. 2012). This is a slow process requiring much more time and funding than educational publishers are usually willing to provide. In engaging in this process, however, we are slowly developing and sharing a *professional vision* (Schoenfeld 2009) for designing learning experiences (not just 'tasks') that are not only engaging, but also take account of the teachers' role in facilitating learning.

In this chapter I have attempted to illustrate the importance of explicitly reconciling our theories, values, principles and curricular aspirations with the design of lessons for real children, and the importance of exemplification. We need exemplary design, not only for teachers and classrooms, but also to communicate our core values to politicians, examination bodies and other key educational stakeholders.

Although I cannot pretend to have done justice to the wonderful range of contributions that others have made within this book, I hope to have drawn out some common themes and provided a provocation for future research.

References

Askew, M. (2001). British research into pedagogy. In M. Askew & M. Brown (Eds.), *Teaching and learning primary numeracy: policy, practice and effectiveness: a review of British research for the British educational research association in conjunction with the British society for research into learning mathematics*. Southwell: BERA.

Askew, M., Hodgen, J., Hossain, S., & Bretscher (2010). *Values and variables: mathematics education in high-performing countries*. London: Nuffield Foundation.

Atweh, B., & Seah, W. T. (2008). *Theorising values and their study in mathematics education*. Paper presented at the AARE 2007 International Educational Research Conference. From http://www.aare.edu.au/07pap/atw07578.pdf.

Bell, A. (1993). Some experiments in diagnostic teaching. *Educational Studies in Mathematics, 24*(1).

Bell, A., Swan, M., Crust, R., & Shannon, A. (1993). *Awareness of Learning, reflection and transfer in school mathematics* (Report of ESRC Project R000-23-2329), Shell Centre for Mathematical Education, University of Nottingham.

Bishop, A. J., Seah, W. T., & Chin, C. (2003). *Values in mathematics teaching: the hidden persuaders?* (2nd ed.). Dordrecht: Kluwer.

Burkhardt, H., & Schoenfeld, A. (2003). Improving educational research: toward a more useful, more influential and better-funded enterprise. *Educational Researcher, 32*(9), 3–14.

Cockcroft, W. H. (1982). *Mathematics counts*. London: HMSO.

DfE (2013). Draft programmes of study for KS4 English, maths and science. Available from http://www.education.gov.uk/schools/teachingandlearning/curriculum/nationalcurriculum2014/.

DfEE/QCA (1999). *Mathematics, the national curriculum for England*. London: Department for Education and Employment Qualifications and Curriculum Authority.

Guan, Q., & Meng, W. (2007). China's new national curriculum reform: innovation, challenges and strategies. *Frontiers of Education in China, 2*(4), 579–604.

Halpin (2010). National curriculum reform in China and England: origins, character and comparison. *Frontiers of Education in China, 5*(2), 258–269.

Halstead, J., & Taylor, M. (2000). Learning and teaching about values: a review of recent research. *Cambridge Journal of Education, 30*(2), 169–202.

Kelly, A. (2003). Theme issue: the role of design in educational research. *Educational Researcher, 32*(1), 3–4.

Krathwohl, D. R., Bloom, B. S., & Masia, B. B. (1964). *Taxonomy of educational objectives, book 2: affective domain*. New York: Longman.

Lew, H. C. (2008). Some characteristics in the Korean National Curriculum and its revising process. In Z. Usiskin & E. Willmore (Eds.), *Mathematics curriculum in Pacific Rim countries: China, Japan, Korea, Singapore*. Charlotte: Information Age Publishing.

NCTM (1989). *Curriculum and evaluation standards for school mathematics*. Reston: National Council of Teachers of Mathematics.

NCTM (2000). *Principles and standards for school mathematics*. Reston: National Council of Teachers of Mathematics.

NGA & CCSSO (2010). *Common core state standards for mathematics*. National Governers Association, Council of Chief State School Officers.

QCA (2007). Mathematics: programmes of study for key stage 3 & 4 and attainment targets. In Q. a. C. Authority (Eds.).

Raths, L. E., Harmin, M., & Simon, S. B. (1987). Selections from 'values and teaching'. In J. P. F. Carbone (Ed.), *Value theory and education* (pp. 198–214). Malabar: Robert E Krieger.

Rocard, M. (2007). *EUR22845—science education now: a renewed pedagogy for the future of Europe*.

Schoenfeld, A. (2009). Bridging the cultures of educational research and design. *Educational Designer, 1*(2). Retrieved from http://www.educationaldesigner.org/ed/volume1/issue2/article5/.

Soh, C. K. (2008). An overview of mathematics education in Singapore. In Z. Usiskin & E. Willmore (Eds.), *Mathematics curriculum in Pacific Rim countries* (pp. 23–36). Charlotte: Information Age Publishing.

Stigler, J. W., & Hiebert, J. (1999). *The teaching gap* (2nd ed.). New York: The Free Press.

Stigler, J. W., Gonzales, P., Kawanaka, T., Knoll, S., & Serrano, A. (1999). *The TIMSS videotape classroom study: methods and findings from an exploratory research project on eighth-grade mathematics instruction in Germany, Japan, and the United States (NCES 1999-074)*. Washington: National Center for Education Statistics.

Swan, M. (2006). *Collaborative learning in mathematics: a challenge to our beliefs and practices*. London: National Institute for Advanced and Continuing Education (NIACE) for the National Research and Development Centre for Adult Literacy and Numeracy (NRDC).

Swan, M., & Lacey, P. (2008a). *Mathematics matters*. National Centre for Excellence in Teaching Mathematics.

Swan, M., & Lacey, P. (2008b). *Mathematics matters—an executive summary*. National Centre for Excellence in Teaching Mathematics.

Swan, M., & Pead, D. (2008). *Reducing road accidents: case study*.

Swan, M., Clarke, N., Dawson, C., Evans, S., Jobert, M., & Foster, C. (2012). Mathematics assessment project, http://map.mathshell.org/materials/pd.php. Available from http://map.mathshell.org/materials/index.php.

van den Akker, J. (2012). *How can design research support curriculum development?* International Society for Design and Development in Education Conference, Utrecht.

van den Akker, J., Graveemeijer, K., McKenney, S., & Nieveen, N. (Eds.) (2006). *Educational design research*. London: Routledge.

Index

Y. Li, G. Lappan (eds.), *Mathematics Curriculum in School Education*, Advances in Mathematics Education, DOI 10.1007/978-94-007-7560-2, © Springer Science+Business Media Dordrecht 2014

Author Index

Y. Li, G. Lappan (eds.), *Mathematics Curriculum in School Education*,
Advances in Mathematics Education, DOI 10.1007/978-94-007-7560-2,
© Springer Science+Business Media Dordrecht 2014

Author Biographies

Judy Anderson is Associate Professor of Mathematics Education and Associate Dean of Learning and Teaching of the Faculty of Education and Social Work at the University of Sydney, Australia. Her research has encompassed middle years engagement and motivation, teachers' problem-solving beliefs and practices, and teachers' use of national testing and other assessment data to plan, program and support student learning. With a background in secondary mathematics teaching and school mathematics curriculum development, Judy remains committed to supporting teachers in classrooms. In her role as president of the Australian Association of Mathematics Teachers (2008–2009), she advocated for the development of a high quality national mathematics curriculum for all Australian students.

Margaret Brown is an Emeritus Professor of Mathematics Education at King's College London. She previously taught in primary and secondary schools and trained teachers. She has directed or co-directed more than 25 research projects in the learning, teaching and assessment of mathematics at all phases, from early years to higher and adult education. She has contributed to development of curriculum and assessment at the national level since 1987 through membership of several government committees, and has been chair of the Joint Mathematical Council of the United Kingdom and of the Education Panel in the 2008 UK Research Assessment Exercise, president of the Mathematical Association and of the British Educational Research Association. She has been awarded honorary degrees at two universities and has recently been awarded the Kavli medal of the Royal Society for her contribution to research in Mathematics Education.

Hugh Burkhardt spent the first half of his academic career working in theoretical elementary particle physics and applied mathematics. During this period in the 1960s, reforms in mathematics education led him to experiment in the teaching of mathematical modeling of practical everyday life problems, initially to undergraduates and high school teachers. His 1976 appointment as Director of the Shell Centre for Mathematical Education at Nottingham shifted the balance of his work towards K-12 mathematics, still with real world problem solving a key learning goal and technology a useful tool. He became concerned at the mismatch of official goals and classroom practice, observing that high-stakes examinations largely determine what is taught—and that they are badly aligned with official learning goals. This has made him acutely aware of the challenges of system change.

Jinfa Cai is a Professor of Mathematics and Education. He is interested in how students learn mathematics and solve problems, and how teachers can provide and create conducive learning environments so that students can make sense of mathematics. He has received a number of awards, including a National Academy of Education Spencer Fellowship, an American Council on Education Fellowship, an International Research Award, and a Teaching Excellence Award. He has been serving on the Editorial Boards for several international journals, such as the Journal for Research in Mathematics Education. He was a visiting professor in various institutions, including Harvard University. He has just completed a term as a Program Director at the U.S. National Science Foundation and a co-chair of American Educational Research Association's Special Interest Group on Research in Mathematics Education (AERA's SIG-RME).

Shelley Dole is an Associate Professor in the School of Education at The University of Queensland, where she co-ordinates Mathematics Curriculum Studies for prospective primary and middle school teachers in the pre-service Bachelor of Education program. Over the 20 years she has worked in education, she has taught in primary, secondary and tertiary teaching institutions throughout Australia. Her research interests include mathematics curriculum change and innovation; learning difficulties, misconceptions and conceptual change associated with learning mathematics; and particularly rational number topics of ratio and percent and the development of proportional reasoning and multiplicative structures. She has lead two major Australian Research Council projects focusing on numeracy across the curriculum and the development of proportional reasoning, with teachers and schools in Queensland and South Australia. In 2009, she won a University of Queensland Award for Teaching Excellence, and in 2010 was the recipient of an Australian Award for University Teaching.

Ruhama Even is Full Professor at the Weizmann Institute of Science, holds the Rudy Bruner Chair of Science Teaching, and is head of the Mathematics Group in the Department of Science Teaching. Her main research interests include education and professional development for math teachers and teacher educators, comparative analysis of textbooks, and the interactions among math curriculum, teachers, and classrooms. She is section editor of the Encyclopedia of Mathematics Education, has been member of the International Committee of PME and co-chair of ICMI Study 15 on the professional education and development of teachers of mathematics. Ruhama Even earned her Ph.D. in Mathematics Education from Michigan State University in 1989.

James Fey is Professor Emeritus in the Department of Mathematics and the Department of Teaching and Learning, Policy and Leadership at the University of Maryland. The focus of his professional scholarship has been a series of projects that have designed, developed, and tested innovative curricula and instructional materials for middle and high school mathematics, with special concentration on problem based learning of algebra.

Elizabeth de Freitas is an Associate Professor at Adelphi University in New York. Her research interests include philosophical and socio-cultural approaches to mathematics and mathematics education. Her current research projects center around diagramming practices and spatial sense. Among her publications are articles in Educational Studies in Mathematics, Qualitative Inquiry, Mathematics Teacher Education, Teaching Education, and The Canadian Journal of Science, Mathematics and Technology Education. She is also co-editor of the book *Opening the research text: Critical insights and in(ter)ventions into mathematics education*, published by Springer Verlag.

Karen C. Fuson is Professor Emerita of Learning Sciences, School of Education and Social Policy, and of the Department of Psychology, Northwestern University. She has published over eighty research articles on mathematics teaching and learning. She was a member of the National Research Council's Mathematics Learning Study Committee that wrote *Adding It Up* and the Committee on Early Childhood Math that wrote *Mathematics Learning in Early Childhood: Paths Toward Excellence and Equity*. She wrote the chapter on whole numbers for the NCTM Research Companion to the 2000 Standards and wrote the introductory chapter for the National Research Council's *How Students Learn: Mathematics in the Classroom*. She is a co-author on five of the NCTM grade-level books for teachers about the focal points (PK, K, G1, G2, G5). She worked on the Common Core Math Standards and on the learning progressions for these standards. Professor Fuson is the author of a K-6 math program *Math Expressions* published by Houghton Mifflin Harcourt.

Antonio Vicente Marafioti Garnica is professor of the Mathematics Department, School of Sciences, São Paulo State University (UNESP), Bauru Campus, and of the Graduate Program in Mathematics Education, UNESP, Rio Claro Campus. Editor of BOLEMA (Mathematics Education Bulletin, created in 1985—the oldest journal in this field in Brazil), his Master Dissertation focuses on the possibilities of a hermeneutical exam for mathematical texts, and his Doctoral Thesis discusses the role of formal proofs in undergraduate courses for Math teachers' formation. His main research themes are the History of Mathematics Education in Brazil and the development of Math teachers. The research project "Mapping of mathematics teacher education and practice in Brazil", developed under his coordination, is conducted by a group of researchers with the objective of understanding how policies related to teacher education are effectively implemented in different regions of the country. The methodological framework of this project is given by Oral History. Conceived as a new qualitative approach that still needs a philosophical foundation in Mathematics Education, the methodology of Oral History is also being studied by Garnica since 2002.

Vince Geiger is an Associate Professor of Education at the Australian Catholic University in Queensland Australia. He is the Deputy Director of the Australian Catholic University's Mathematics Teaching and Learning Research Centre and the Deputy Head of School for Research in the Faculty of Education, Queensland campus. He is a Former President of the Australian Association of Mathematics Teachers and is an Associate Editor of the Mathematics Education Research Journal. His work in undergraduate pre-service teacher education programs has been recognized by an Australian award for university teaching and he is actively involved in programs related to the professional learning of teachers. His research interests include creative and innovative approaches to the teaching and learning of mathematics, teachers' pedagogy associated with effective numeracy practice, the use of digital tools in enhancing mathematics teaching and learning, mathematical modeling as a vehicle for the effective teaching and learning of mathematics, the professional learning of primary and secondary teachers, and the development of tertiary mathematics educators as researchers.

Merrilyn Goos is a Professor of Education at The University of Queensland, Australia, where she has worked for 20 years as a mathematics teacher educator and mathematics education researcher. For the last five years she served as Director of the university's Teaching and Educational Development Institute, working with all Faculties and disciplines to improve the quality of teaching and learning in the university. Her work as a university teacher has been recognized through a national teaching excellence award and a national teaching fellowship aimed at building the capacity for assessment leadership in university course coordinators. Her research interests include mathematics teacher education, the professional formation of mathematics teacher educators, numeracy education in school and non-school contexts, school reform, and teaching and learning in higher education. She is currently President of the Mathematics Education Research Group of Australia and an Associate Editor of *Educational Studies in Mathematics*.

Marja van den Heuvel-Panhuizen is Professor of Mathematics Education at the Freudenthal Institute for Mathematics and Science Education (FIsme) at the Science Faculty and the Faculty of Social and Behavioral Sciences of Utrecht University, the Netherlands. She is a Board Member of FIsme and Chair of their Research Program. From 2005 to 2010 she was a visiting professor at IQB of Humboldt University Berlin, where she was involved in a national project on the evaluation and implementation of the standards for primary school mathematics in Germany. In 2012 she received the Svend Pedersen Lecture Award from the Department of Mathematics and Science Education of Stockholm University. Her research interests lie with instruction theory for mathematics education and the further development of the didactics of mathematics as a scientific discipline. Her special interest is assessment. Her focus is on mathematics education in primary school, special education, and early childhood. She is involved in research projects on picture books, ICT in mathematics education, students' early algebraic thinking, identifying special education students' mathematical potential, disclosing student's difficulties in solving context problems, improving classroom assessment, revealing children's talent in understanding phenomena in science and technology, and textbook analysis.

Jeremy Hodgen is a Professor of Mathematics Education at King's College London. He has recently led the ESRC-funded project, Increasing Competence and Confidence in Algebraic and Multiplicative Structure (ICCAMS), which includes a comparison of current Key Stage 3 students' mathematical understandings with those of 30 years ago. His comparative research has shown the UK to have an unusually low participation rate in upper secondary mathematics. He is a member of the team coordinating the Targeted Initiative in Science and Mathematics Education in the UK. He has published widely on the teaching, learning and assessment of mathematics and on mathematics teacher education. Previously, he taught mathematics in both primary and secondary schools.

Roger Howe has been teaching and doing research in the Mathematics Department at Yale University for over 35 years. His mathematical research investigates symmetry and its applications. He has held visiting positions at many universities and research institutes in the U.S., Europe and Asia. He is a member of the American Academy of Arts and Sciences and the U.S. National Academy of Sciences.

Dr. Howe also devotes substantial time to issues of mathematics education. He has served on a multitude of committees, including those for several of the major reports on U.S. math education. He has served as a member and as Chair of the Committee on Education of the American Mathematical Society. He served on the Steering Committee of the Park City/IAS Mathematics Institute, and has helped to organize a series of meetings devoted to increasing the contribution of mathematicians to mathematics education, especially to refining understanding of the mathematical issues in K-12 mathematics curricula. He is currently a member of the U.S. National Commission on Mathematics Instruction, and a member of the Executive Committee of the International Commission on Mathematics Instruction. In 2006, he received the Award for Distinguished Public Service from the American Mathematical Society.

Rongjin Huang is an associate professor of mathematics education at the Middle Tennessee State University. He is one of the Chinese team leaders for the Learner's Perspective Study. His research interests include mathematics classroom research, mathematics teacher education, and comparative mathematics education. He has conducted several research projects and had extensive publications of his scholarly work. He is co-editor of three Chinese books and three English books, including *How Chinese Teach Mathematics and Improve Teaching* (2012, Routledge). He is also a guest editor of *ZDM-International Journal on Mathematics Education*, and has actively involved in the organization of activities at various national and international conferences such as AERA, NCTM and ICME.

Julia Kaufman is a Research Associate at University of Pittsburgh and a RAND Adjunct. Her research focuses on how instructional policies and programs can support high-quality teaching and learning. She is also interested in the development of measures that can yield the best evidence about the quality of teachers' instruction. Her expertise includes applying rigorous mixed methods designs in order to understand the factors influencing teacher instruction and student performance in school. She recently completed an IES-funded Carnegie Mellon and RAND Traineeship (*CMART*) in interdisciplinary education research.

Miray Tekkumru Kisa is a doctoral student in the Learning Sciences and Policy Ph.D. Program at the University of Pittsburgh and works at the Learning Research and Development Center as a graduate student researcher. Miray previously attended the Bogazici University (Istanbul, Turkey) where she received her bachelor's degree in science education and a master's degree in secondary school science and mathematics education. She has project and work experiences in improving science and mathematics teaching and learning in-and out-of-school settings. Her research focuses on designing tools and environments to support teachers' learning and studying their effectiveness, teacher cognition and teacher thinking, and implementation of cognitively demanding tasks in science classrooms.

Masataka Koyama has been a professor of mathematics education at Hiroshima University in Japan since 2007, and Vice-dean of Graduate School and Faculty of Education since 2009. He obtained his B.Ed., M.Ed., and Ph.D. from Hiroshima University. He began his career as an assistant professor of mathematics education at Hyogo University of Teacher Education in 1986 and moved back to Hiroshima University as a lecturer of mathematics education in 1991. His research includes students' mathematical understanding, an international comparative study on students' mathematical attainments, mathematics teachers' professional development, and school mathematics curricula and textbooks for primary and secondary schools. He teaches prospective secondary school mathematics teachers in the undergraduate and Master programs and prospective university educators/researchers of mathematics education in the Ph.D. program at Hiroshima University. He is also actively involved in the international and national activities for society of mathematics education and the teachers' professional development through lesson study of mathematics in primary and secondary schools.

Chi Chung Lam is a professor in the Department of Curriculum and Instruction, The Chinese University of Hong Kong. His research interests include curriculum change and implementation, teacher beliefs, and curriculum evaluation.

Glenda Lappan is University Distinguished Professor, Department of Mathematics and Division of Science and Mathematics Education, Michigan State University, USA. She is currently a Director of the Connected Mathematics Project and

Co-PI for the NSF-funded Center for the Study of Mathematic Curriculum. From 1989–91 she served as a Program Director at the National Science Foundation. From 1997–2001 she was President of the National Council of Teachers of Mathematics. She served as the Chair of the grades 5–8 writing group for the National Council of Teachers of Mathematics' (NCTM) *Curriculum and Evaluation Standards for School Mathematics* (1989), and as Chair of the Commission that developed the NCTM *Professional Standards for Teaching Mathematics* (1991). She served as President of NCTM during the development and release of the 2000 *NCTM Principles and Standards for School Mathematics*. She is past Chair of the Conference Board of the Mathematical Sciences and Vice Chair of the US National Commission on Mathematics Instruction. From 1997–1999 she served on the Advisory Board for Education and Human Resources at the National Science Foundation. She was appointed by the Secretary of Education to serve on the National Education Research Policy and Priorities Board for the Department of Education from 1996 to 2003. Her research and development interests are in the connected areas of students' learning of mathematics and mathematics teacher professional growth and change at the middle and secondary levels.

Kyeong-Hwa Lee has been a professor of mathematics education at Seoul National University in Korea since 2011, and Vice-dean of College of Education since 2012. She obtained her B.Ed., M.Ed., and Ph.D. from Seoul National University. Her research interests include mathematics curriculum and textbook analysis, mathematical reasoning and creativity development, gender issues in mathematics, and mathematics teachers' professional development. She has been involved in mathematics curriculum revision and mathematics textbook development in primary and secondary level since 1998. Also, she has been involved for many years in designing and implementing educational programs for mathematically talented students. She has studied gender differences in mathematics achievement and affective domain and has identified and nurtured female students who have potential in mathematics.

Ngan Hoe Lee is an Assistant Professor at the National Institute of Education (NIE), Nanyang Technological University, Singapore. He holds a Bachelor of Science (First Class Honors in Pure Mathematics) from Monash University, Australia, a Diploma in Education (Distinction) from the Institute of Education, Singapore, a Master of Science in Education (Curriculum and Instruction—Mathematics Education) from Southern Illinois University at Carbondale, USA, and a Doctor of Philosophy in Education from the Psychological Studies and Mathematics & Mathematics Education Academic Groups in NIE, Nanyang Technological University, Singapore. He taught Mathematics and Physics in a secondary school before becoming a Gifted Education Specialist at the Ministry of Education. At NIE, he teaches pre- and in-service courses in mathematics education and supervises postgraduate students pursuing Masters and PhD degrees. His involvement in research projects includes international comparative studies, such as the Teacher Education Study in Mathematics (TEDS-M) and the International Comparative Research to Identify Unique and Promising practices in Mathematics and Science Teacher Preparation for APEC Economies. He has been invited to work with academics, curriculum planners, teachers, students, social workers and parents in both Singapore and overseas, such as Bhutan, Chile, Hong Kong, Indonesia, Macau, Shanghai, Thailand, United Kingdom and the United States. His publication and research interests include the teaching and learning of mathematics at both primary and secondary levels, covering areas such as mathematics curriculum development, metacognition and mathematical problem solving/modeling, technology and mathematics education, textbooks and mathematics education. He is a co-author of the two primary mathematics packages *Shaping Maths* and *Maths Works* used in Singapore schools.

Xiaoqing Li is currently working as an assistant professor in the Department of Psychology at Shenzhen University in Mainland China. She holds a Ph.D. degree from The Chinese University of Hong Kong, specializing in educational psychology. She gained her Masters degree at the Institute of Developmental Psychology at the Beijing Normal University. Her research interests and publications are in the areas of classroom processes, curriculum and instruction, educational assessment, and teacher education.

Yeping Li is a Professor of Mathematics Education, holder of the Claude H. Everett, Jr. Endowed Chair in Education, and Head of the Department of Teaching, Learning and Culture at Texas A&M University. His research interests focus on issues related to mathematics curriculum and teacher education in various education systems and understanding how factors related to mathematics curriculum and teachers may come together to shape effective classroom instruction. He is the editor-in-chief of the *International Journal of STEM Education* published by Springer, and also the editor of a monograph series *Mathematics Teaching and Learning* published by Sense Publishers. In addition to co-editing several books and special issues of journals, he has published over 100 articles that focus on three related topic areas of study (i.e., mathematics curriculum and textbook studies, teachers and teacher education, and classroom instruction). He has also organized and chaired many group sessions at various national and international professional conferences, such as ICME-10 in 2004, ICME-11 in 2008, and ICME-12 in 2012. He received his Ph.D. in Cognitive Studies in Education from the University of Pittsburgh, USA.

Lije Lu is a professor in the Department of Curriculum and Instruction, the Faculty of Education, Northeast Normal University, China. Her research interests include curriculum policy, teacher learning, and student teacher practice.

Yu-Jen Lu is a PhD candidate of the Graduate Institute of Science Education at the National Taiwan Normal University. He has served for many years as a mathematics teacher leader for the Yilan County Teacher Training Center in Taiwan. Currently, he is the Dean for General Affairs of an elementary school in Yilan. He is interested in the development of assessment report systems and in issues related to mathematics teacher leadership and mathematics teacher education.

Tingting Ma is a research scientist for the National Science Foundation funded project, Knowledge for Algebra Teaching for Equity (KATE). She earned her Ph.D. in Mathematics Education from Texas A&M University, USA.

Yunpeng Ma is a professor in the Department of Curriculum and Instruction, the Faculty of Education, Northeast Normal University, China. He is a deputy director in the Curriculum Section of the China Education Association, and deputy director in the Elementary Mathematics Section of the China Education Association. His research interests include curriculum implementation and evaluation, mathematics curriculum, and instruction.

John (Jack) Moyer is a professor of mathematics specializing in mathematics education in the Department of Mathematics, Statistics and Computer Science at Marquette University. He received his M.S. in mathematics in 1969, and his Ph.D. in mathematics education in 1974, both from Northwestern University. Since 1980 he has been an investigator or director of more than 70 private- and government-funded projects. The majority of the projects have been conducted in formal collaboration with the Milwaukee Public Schools to further the professional development of Milwaukee-area middle school teachers and the mathematics development of their students.

Bikai Nie is a research associate and a part-time student in the Statistics Program for a Master's degree at the University of Delaware. Previously, he taught at the School of Mathematics and Statistics in Central China Normal University. He has ten years of experience teaching mathematics in both middle school and high school. He received his Ph.D. in Mathematics Education from East China Normal University.

Shai Olsher is a PhD student in the Department of Science Teaching at the Weizmann Institute of Science. His research interests are interactions between teachers and textbooks, and technology for mathematics teachers' work. He wrote a television series on preparation for the Israeli matriculation exam for the Israeli Educational Television, and was involved in integrating technologies into different teaching settings in the private sector. Holds an MA degree in Exact Sciences Education from Tel-Aviv University, 2009.

Rebecca V. Osborne graduated from Texas A&M University with Master's degree in Education. She currently resides in the United States.

Zeynep Ebrar Yetkiner Özel is an assistant professor of the Faculty of Education at Fatih University, Istanbul, Turkey. Her research interests include mathematics teacher education, mathematics curriculum studies, comparative mathematics education, and quantitative research methods. She has published several articles in national and international research journals and presented papers in various conferences and workshops at national and international levels.

JeongSuk Pang is an Associate Professor of Mathematics Education at the Korea National University of Education (KNUE), South Korea. Pang received her Ph.D. in Curriculum and Instruction from Louisiana State University in 2000. She worked as a post-doctoral researcher at the University of Pennsylvania and a senior researcher at Korea Education and Research Information Service. While her publications have extensively covered various aspects of elementary mathematics education, Pang is particularly interested in the analysis of mathematics classroom culture and professional development, for both pre-service and in-service teachers. She has been actively involved in developing new mathematics curriculum and its concomitant textbook series. She received the best professor award at KNUE and she has been serving as an international director of the Korea Society of Educational Studies in Mathematics. Pang also served as a member of the International Committee of the International Group for the Psychology of Mathematics Education (2008–2012).

Barbara Reys is a Curator's Professor and the Lois Knowles Faculty Fellow in Mathematics Education at the University of Missouri-Columbia. She also directs the Center for the Study of Mathematics Curriculum, funded by NSF. Dr. Reys served as a writing group leader for the National Council of Teachers of Mathematics (NCTM) *Principles and Standards for School Mathematics* (2000), on the NCTM Board of Directors, and as President of the Association of Mathematics Teacher Educators. She recently served as a member of the Mathematics Work Team for the development of the *Common Core State Standards Initiative* and on the Conference Board of the Mathematical Sciences Writing Team that developed the new guidelines for the preparation of K-12 teachers of mathematics. Her current research focuses on the role and influence of official curriculum documents, including national standard, state-level curriculum frameworks, and district-adopted mathematics textbooks.

Alan Schoenfeld is the Elizabeth and Edward Conner Professor of Education and Affiliated Professor of Mathematics at the University of California at Berkeley. He is a Fellow of the American Association for the Advancement of Science and of the American Educational Research Association, and a Laureate of the education honor society Kappa Delta Pi. Schoenfeld has served as President of the American Educational Research Association and Vice President of the National Academy of Education. In 2011 he was awarded the International Commission on Mathematics Instruction's Klein Medal, the highest international distinction in mathematics education.

A mathematician by training, Schoenfeld became a mathematics educator in order to understand and share the pleasures and power of mathematical thinking. His work has focused on problem solving, assessment, teachers' decision-making, and issues of equity and diversity. His current work focuses on understanding teaching practices in powerful mathematics classrooms. Schoenfeld has written, edited, or co-edited more than two hundred pieces on thinking and learning, including twenty-two books. His most recent book, *How we Think*, provides detailed models of human decision making in complex situations such as teaching.

Sharon L. Senk is a Professor at Michigan State University with appointments in the Program of Mathematics Education and the Department of Mathematics. She has also taught mathematics at Newton North High School in Massachusetts and at Syracuse University. Dr. Senk served as Co-Director of the Secondary Component of the University of Chicago School Mathematics Project (UCSMP) during the development of the first and second editions of the UCSMP curriculum materials, and as a consultant on evaluation for the third edition materials. Her research involves curriculum evaluation and analysis, the learning and teaching of secondary school mathematics, and the preparation of elementary and secondary mathematics teachers both in the U.S. and abroad.

Mary C. Shafer is an Associate Professor of Mathematics Education in the Department of Mathematical Sciences at Northern Illinois University. She co-authored a book with Thomas Romberg entitled *The Impact of Reform Mathematics Instruction on Student Achievement: An Example of Standards-Based Curriculum Research*, which was published in 2008. Her other publications have focused on classroom assessment that promotes understanding in mathematics, teachers' developing formative assessment in mathematics as they use standards-based curricula, and linking the results of formal assessments to teaching practices. She is currently studying the impact of a new graduate degree specialization in middle school mathematics education funded through a U.S. Department of Education, Mathematics and Science Partnership grant. The focus of the research is on teachers' changes in knowledge of mathematics and teaching practices, teachers' transformative professional growth, and the impact of these changes on their students' mathematics achievement and mathematical dispositions.

Nathalie Sinclair is an Associate Professor at Simon Fraser University in the Faculty of Education and a Canada Research Chair in Tangible Mathematics Learning. Her research interests focus on the use of expressive technologies in mathematics learning, with growing attention to the primary school years, and on the role of aesthetics in mathematical thinking and learning. She has also developed technology-enhanced tasks involving the use of The Geometer's Sketchpad to accompany the Connected Mathematics Project middle school textbooks. Recent books include; Essential Understandings of Geometry (Grades 6-8 as well as 9-12), published by the NCTM and Mathematics and Beauty: Aesthetic approaches to teaching children, published by Teachers College Press.

Mary Kay Stein holds a joint appointment at the University of Pittsburgh as Professor of Learning Sciences and Policy and Senior Scientist at the Learning Research and Development Center. Her research focuses on mathematics teaching and learning in classrooms and the ways in which policy and organizational conditions shape teachers' practice. Stein's most recent research examines how curricula can serve as a learning tool for teachers in large-scale improvement efforts. She is the lead author of a widely used casebook for mathematics professional development, *Implementing Standards-Based Mathematics Instruction.*

Max Stephens is a senior research fellow in the Graduate School of Education at The University of Melbourne with a long-standing interest in curriculum and assessment at the university and government levels. He has recently undertaken several major projects for the Australian Government, for example in the interpretation of international assessments in Mathematics, and for the Victorian State government on curriculum leadership in mathematics. He has strong international interests in curriculum development in Asia, most notably in the Peoples Republic of China, Japan and Thailand.

Malcolm Swan is Professor of Mathematics Education at the University of Nottingham, UK. He leads the design team of the Center for Research in Mathematics Education, playing the principal role in the design and development of many of its products. His research is mainly into the theory, development and evaluation of teaching situations and professional development in mathematics education. This includes: the design of situations which foster reflection, discussion and metacognitive activity; the design of situations in which children construct mathematical concepts and develop problem solving strategies; and the design of formative and evaluative assessment. Malcolm was awarded the International Society for Design and Development in Education Prize for design for *the Language of Functions and Graphs.* Funded by the UK government, he led the design of *Improving Learning in Mathematics,* curriculum and professional development resources were sent to all mathematics teachers in secondary and further education in England. Malcolm is currently leading the development of 'Classroom Challenges', a series of formative assessment lessons supporting the *Common Core State Standards for Mathematics* in the US, funded by the Gates foundation.

Akihiko Takahashi is an Associate Professor of mathematics education at DePaul University in the United States. He teaches mathematics teaching and learning, and mathematics for prospective teachers. He also provides workshops and seminars for practicing teachers using ideas from the U.S. and Asian countries. He was an elementary teacher in Japan before becoming an educator of mathematics teachers. During his elementary teaching career, he was nationally active in mathematics lesson study and mentored 200 pre-service teachers. He received his Ph.D. from the University of Illinois at Urbana-Champaign; his dissertation research focused on internet use in mathematics education.

Hak Ping Tam currently an Associate Professor of the Graduate Institute of Science Education at the National Taiwan Normal University. He recently completed a three year term as the chairperson of his institute. He is interested in research issues related to mathematics curriculum, mathematics assessment, automatic Chinese essay

scoring, problem solving, and applied statistics. He has participated in various local and international large-scale assessment programs, of both low- and high-stakes
status. His current research project focuses on designing a statistics curriculum with
a unified theme from primary to senior high school that facilitates application to the
science curriculum.

Denisse R. Thompson is a Professor of Mathematics Education at the University
of South Florida, where she teaches mathematics education courses at the undergraduate, graduate, and doctoral levels. She previously taught at the high school and
community college levels. She served for 10 years on the Board of Directors for
the Florida Council of Teachers of Mathematics (FCTM) and served as President
of the organization from 2008-2009. She was honored by FCTM as the Kenneth
Kidd Mathematics Educator of the Year in 2004 and by the Florida Association of
Mathematics Teacher Educators as the 2010 Mathematics Teacher Educator of the
Year. She has authored or co-authored over 15 books, 25 book chapters, and 50
journal articles. Her major research interests include mathematical literacy, the use
of literature and media in the teaching of mathematics, and curriculum evaluation,
having served as the Director of Evaluation for the third edition secondary materials
developed by the University of Chicago School Mathematics Project.

Zalman Usiskin is a professor emeritus of education at the University of Chicago
and the overall director of the University of Chicago School Mathematics Project
(UCSMP), a position he has held since 1987. He is also a co-Principal Investigator
of the Center for the Study of Mathematics Curriculum. His research has focused
on the teaching and learning of arithmetic, algebra, and geometry, with particular
attention to the applications of mathematics at all levels and the use of transformations and related concepts in geometry, algebra, and statistics. He is the author or
co-author of over 150 articles and other papers on mathematics and mathematics
education, dozens of books and book-length research monographs, including textbooks for each of grades 6 through 12. His interests in mathematics education are
broad, including matters related to curriculum, instruction, and testing; international
mathematics education; the history of mathematics education; and educational policy. He has served on the Mathematical Sciences Education Board of the National
Research Council, the Board of Directors of the National Council of Teachers of
Mathematics, the test-development committee of the National Assessment of Educational Progress, and the United States National Commission on Mathematics
Instruction, which he chaired from 1998 to 2001.

Ning Wang received her Ph.D. in Educational Measurement and Statistics from the
University of Pittsburgh. She also received a master's degree in Research Methodology and another master's degree in mathematics education. Currently, she is an
Associate Professor at the Center for Education, Widener University, and teaching
research methodology courses at the Master's and Doctoral level. Dr. Wang has extensive experience in the validation of assessment instruments in various settings,
scaling using Item Research Theory (IRT), and conducting statistical data analysis

using Hierarchical Linear Modeling and Structural Equation Modeling. In particular, she is interested in the applications of educational measurement, statistics, and research design techniques in the exploration of the issues in the teaching and learning of mathematics.

Jamie Wernet is a doctoral student in the Program of Mathematics Education at Michigan State University where she studies K-12 mathematics teaching and learning. Her research focuses on algebra learning and instruction in secondary classrooms, particularly around the use of contextual tasks and student engagement. Previously, she worked as a high school mathematics teacher, tutor, and curriculum coordinator in Michigan.

Dylan Wiliam is an Emeritus Professor of Educational Assessment at the Institute of Education, University of London where, from 2006 to 2010 he was its Deputy Director. In a varied career, he has taught in urban public schools, directed a large-scale testing program, served a number of roles in university administration, including Dean of a School of Education, and pursued a research programme focused on supporting teachers in developing their use of assessment to support learning (sometimes called formative assessment). He was the co-author, with Paul Black of a major review of the research evidence on formative assessment published in 1998 and has subsequently worked with many groups of teachers, in both the UK and the USA, on developing formative assessment practices.

Khoon Yoong Wong, BSc (Hons), Dip Ed (Tasmania), PhD (Queensland), is an associate professor at the National Institute of Education, Singapore. Over a period of about four decades, he has worked as a mathematics educator in Australia, Brunei Darussalam, Malaysia, and Singapore, and conducted research in several aspects of mathematics learning, problem solving, assessment, and teacher education in these countries. He was a member of several separate national committees established to review the national mathematics curriculum in Brunei Darussalam, Malaysia, and Singapore. He also consults for education institutes in Chile, Hong Kong, the Philippines, and the US. His main teaching areas are in secondary mathematics pedagogy and research methodology. Most recently his research includes the Teacher Education and Development Study in Mathematics (TEDS-M) under the International Association for the Evaluation of Educational Achievement (IEA), Quality of Teacher Preparation in Secondary Mathematics and Science among seven APEC countries, and the Singapore Mathematics Assessment and Pedagogy Project. He is the chief editor of *The Mathematics Educator*, published by the Association of Mathematics Educators, Singapore.

Ngai-Ying Wong is a professor in the Department of Curriculum and Instruction, the Faculty of Education, The Chinese University of Hong Kong, where he is the Chair of the Board of Undergraduate Studies and the program director of the Master of Science in Mathematics Education. He is the founding President of the Hong Kong Association for Mathematics Education. His research interests include classroom environment, mathematics curriculum reform, beliefs about mathematics, *bianshi* teaching, Confucian Cultural Heritage learner's phenomena and student activities.

Hung-Hsi Wu is a professor emeritus of mathematics, Department of Mathematics, University of California, Berkeley, CA, USA.

Marc van Zanten, Msc, is a PhD student at the Freudenthal Institute for Mathematics and Science Education (FIsme) in the Science Faculty of Utrecht University, the Netherlands. He is a former primary school teacher, currently working as a teacher educator at Saxion University of Applied Sciences, specializing in primary school mathematics education. In addition, he is a researcher at FIsme. In 2008, he was a member of the National Committee that established the Reference Standards for mathematics, and in 2009 he was Chair of the Committee that developed the Dutch Knowledge Base on Mathematics for primary school teachers. Since 2007, he has served as Chair of the Dutch Panama-conference, an annual conference on mathematics education for educators and researchers. In his PhD-research, he investigates textbooks for primary school mathematics education, focusing on the learning opportunities textbooks offer to students, and the guidance textbooks provide for teachers and teacher-trainees in developing and carrying out their mathematics teaching.

Jianyue Zhang is a senior editor at People's Education Press and also a research fellow at the Curriculum and Teaching Material Research Institute, Beijing, China. He earned his doctoral degree in Psychology from Beijing Normal University, China.

Qiaoping Zhang is a lecturer in the Department of Curriculum and Instruction, The Chinese University of Hong Kong. After receiving a B.Sc. degree in mathematics and a Master of Philosophy in education, he taught courses in mathematics and mathematics education in Hubei University. After earning his Ph.D. degree at the Chinese University of Hong Kong, he taught mathematics for foreign students and mathematics teaching methods for pre-service teachers in Shanghai, China. Currently he is teaching courses in mathematics education at both the graduate and undergraduate levels at the Chinese University of Hong Kong. His research interests include affects in mathematics education, beliefs about mathematics, and the knowledge of mathematics teacher and mathematics curriculum reform.

CPSIA information can be obtained at www.ICGtesting.com
Printed in the USA
LVOW10*1207080414

380795LV00001B/1/P